A Framework for Human Resource Management

SIXTH EDITION

Gary Dessler

Florida International University

Prentice Hall

Boston   Columbus   Indianapolis   New York   San Francisco   Upper Saddle River
Amsterdam   Cape Town   Dubai   London   Madrid   Milan Munich   Paris   Montreal   Toronto
Delhi   Mexico City   Sao Paulo   Sydney   Hong Kong   Seoul   Singapore   Taipei   Tokyo

Acquisitions Editor: Jennifer M. Collins
Editorial Director: Sally Yagan
Editor in Chief: Eric Svendsen
Director of Editorial Services: Ashley Santora
Editorial Project Manager: Meg O'Rourke
Marketing Manager: Nikki Jones
Marketing Assistant: Ian Gold
Production Project Manager: Clara Bartunek
Creative Director: Jayne Conte
Cover Designer: Bruce Kenselaar

Cover Illustration: Getty Images
**Manager, Cover Visual Research &
    Permissions:** Karen Sanatar
Composition: Integra Software Services,
    Pvt. Ltd.
Full-Service Project Management: Shiny Rajesh
Printer/Binder: STP Courier Westford
Cover Printer: STP Moore Langen
Typeface: 10/12 Palatino

Credits and acknowledgments borrowed from other sources and reproduced, with permission, in this textbook appear on appropriate pages within text.

Library of Congress Cataloging-in-Publication Data

Dessler, Gary
    A framework for human resource management / Gary Dessler.—6th ed.
        p. cm.
    Includes bibliographical references and index.
    ISBN-13: 978-0-13-255637-8 (alk. paper)
    ISBN-10: 0-13-255637-5 (alk. paper)
    1. Personnel management.   I. Title.
    HF5549.D43788 2011
    658.3—dc22

                                                        2010016617

10 9 8 7 6 5 4

Prentice Hall
is an imprint of

www.pearsonhighered.com

ISBN-13: 978-0-13-255637-8
ISBN-10:   0-13-255637-5

To my mother

BRIEF CONTENTS

CONTENTS

SECTION 2   TRAINING, DEVELOPMENT, AND COMPENSATION

SECTION 3 MANAGING EMPLOYEE RELATIONS

PREFACE

A Framework for Human Resource Management provides students and practicing managers with a concise but thorough review of essential human resource management concepts and techniques in a highly readable and understandable form. Most of the books in this market (including my *Human Resource Management*, 12th edition, and *Fundamentals of Human Resource Management*, 2nd edition) contain 14 to 18 chapters and 450 to 800 large-trim-size pages. At about 430 small-trim pages and 10 chapters plus Module A, *Framework* distills the essential HR material large books typically contain, but without repetition, extensive reviews of research findings, or in-depth discussions.

Adopters use this book in various ways. Many adopt it as the basic textbook for the human resource management course, perhaps supplementing it with extra cases or with applied human resource management exercises. Others adopt it with complementary textbooks in courses that blend several topics (such as HR and organizational behavior) or in specialized courses (such as "HR for Entrepreneurial Companies"). Because *Framework* contains a practical and up-to-date review of essential human resource management concepts and techniques, practicing human resource and line managers find it useful for updating their HR skills.

NEW TO THE 6TH EDITION

Given its gratifying acceptance and the reviewers' comments, *Framework 6's* themes, approach, and outline are basically the same as edition 5's. All managers have personnel responsibilities, so I again aimed this book at all students of management, not just those who are or will be human resource managers. The book's basic idea—to provide a concise but thorough review of HR concepts and techniques—is the same. I kept the same table of contents and basically the same topic coverage. Each chapter again touches on, with examples, how managers use strategic human resource management and technology. Adopters can again order a Human Resource Certification Institute guide. In addition to the end-of-chapter case incidents, there are *five comprehensive cases* at the end of the book.

However, I have made several important changes. I of course *updated* the HR practices, methods, topics, data, examples, figures/tables, relevant legal and HR findings, and notes in all chapters. In addition, I made the following changes and additions:

1. *New Managing HR in Challenging Times Features.* The economic challenges the United States and world faced starting around 2008 prompted most employers to re-think the costs and benefits of how they delivered their human resource

services. New *Managing HR in Challenging Times* features in most chapters illustrate the skills managers need to manage human resources in challenging times.

2. ***Updates and Features.*** You'll find dozens of *new examples and research references and topics,* including, for example, onboarding and mobile learning. I also updated for this edition many of the book's *figures and tables.*

3. ***Expanded Diversity Coverage.*** I expanded the coverage of diversity and diversity management significantly in Chapter 2, to include, for instance, topics such as today's diverse workforce, diversity's potential pros and cons, and multicultural consciousness, and added new *Managing the New Workforce* features in some chapters.

4. ***Reviewer-Suggested Changes.*** I made dozens of changes in response to reviewers' suggestions, including, for instance, expanding the book's diversity topics coverage, expanded occupational hazards coverage in Chapter 10, providing more detail on wage curves in Chapter 7, and expanding the discussion of the influence of motivation and motivation theories on compensation.

5. *New Design.* We redesigned the text, to make it easier to read and more visually appealing.

INSTRUCTOR'S RESOURCE CENTER

At www.pearsonhighered.com, instructors can access a variety of print, digital, and presentation resources available with this text in downloadable format. Registration is simple and gives you immediate access to new titles and new editions. As a registered faculty member, you can download resource files and receive immediate access and instructions for installing course management content on your campus server.

The following supplements are available for download to adopting instructors:

- **Instructor's Manual with Test Item File**—ISBN: 0-13-255642-1.
- **TestGen Test Generating Software**—ISBN: 0-13-139332-4.
- **Power Points**—ISBN: 0-13-139333-2.
- **Videos on DVD**—ISBN: 0-13-139334-0.

ACKNOWLEDGMENTS

No book ever reaches the light of day without the dedicated efforts of many people, and *Framework* is no exception. I am grateful to past and present reviewers:

Mark Barnard, Edgewood College
Kathleen Barnes, East Stroudsburg University
Gerald Baumgardner, Penn College
Jerry Bennett, Western Kentucky University
Stephen Betts, William Paterson University
Genie Black, Arkansas Tech University
David Lawrence Blum, Moraine Park Technical College
Michael Bochenek, Elmhurst College
Henry Bohleke, Owens Community College

Richard Brocato, Mount Saint Mary's University
Patricia Buhler, Goldey-Beacom College
Jackie Bull, Immaculata University
Melissa Cardon, Pace University
Martin Carrigan, The University of Findlay
Yvonne Chandler, Seattle Community Colleges
Charlie Cook, University of West Alabama
Roger Dean, Washington and Lee University
Karen Dielmann, Lebanon Valley College and Elizabethtown College
Michael Dutch, Greensboro College
William Ferris, Western New England College
John Fielding, Mount Wachusett Community College
Michael Frew, Oklahoma City University
Eugene Garaventa, College of Staten Island, CUNY
Alyce Giltner, Shawnee Community College
Armand Giroux, Mitchell College
Caren Goldberg, American University
John Gronholt, Modesto Junior College
Janet Henquinet, Metropolitan State University, St. Paul, MN
William Hodson, Indiana University
Peter Hughes, Cambridge College, Lawrence, MA
John Kachurick, College Misericordia
Dennis Kimble, Central Michigan University
Jacqueline Landau, Salem State College
Cheryl Macon, Butler County Community College
Patricia Morrow, Middlesex Community College
Arlene Nicholas, Salve Regina University
Kay Nicols, Texas State University-San Marcos
Jacquelyn Palmer, Wright State University
Rich Patterson, Western Kentucky University
Diana Peaks, Jacksonville University
Jane Philbrick, Savannah State University
Larry Phillips, Indiana University South Bend
Tracy Porter, Cleveland State University
Chris Osuanah, J. Sargeant Reynolds Community College and University
    of Phoenix
David Radosevich, Montclair State University
Carlton R. Raines, Lehigh Carbon Community College
Dr. Michael J. Renahan, College of Saint Elizabeth
Fritz Scherz, Morrisville State College
Biagio Sciacca, Penn State University
Dan Scotti, Providence College
Robert W. (Bill) Service, Samford University
John Shaw, Mississippi State University
Walter Siganga, Southern Illinois University Edwardsville
Marjorie Smith, Mountain State University
Chester Spell, Rutgers University

Jerry Stevens, Texas Tech University
Susan Stewart, University of Puget Sound
Michele Summers, Purdue University
Vicki Talor, Shippensburg University
Jeff Walls, Indiana Institute of Technology
Carol Williams, Pearl River Community College
Angela Willson, Yuba College
Jenell Wittmer, University of Toledo

I am grateful to the professors, students, managers, and Prentice Hall sales associates who have helped make this a top-selling book, not only in English but also in several languages, including Chinese.

At Pearson, I appreciate the efforts of all the professionals on the sixth edition team, including Eric Svendsen, editor in chief; Jennifer M. Collins, acquisitions editor; Judy Leale, senior managing editor; Clara Bartunek, production editor; and Susie Abraham, editorial project manager.

At home, I appreciate all my wife Claudia's support, and my son Derek's support, assistance, and practical suggestions.

Web sites to which we refer in the text sometimes change or are discontinued because companies change names, are bought or sold, merge, or fail. They were accurate when the book went into production. If you have a problem connecting, please try to identify the new site. We apologize in advance for any inconvenience.

Chapter 1

Managing Human Resources Today

- What Is Human Resource Management?
- Trends Influencing Human Resource Management
- The Human Resource Manager Today
- Strategic Planning and Strategic Human Resource Management
- The Plan of This Book

When you finish studying this chapter, you should be able to:

- Answer *the question "What is human resource management?"*
- Discuss *the components of the changing environment of human resource management.*
- Describe *the nature of strategic planning.*
- Give *examples of human resource management's role as a strategic partner.*

INTRODUCTION

Most L.L.Bean customers find its staff knowledgeable, helpful, and understanding. What's not so obvious is that a staff like that is no accident. It's the product of a well-thought-out human resource plan for recruiting, selecting, training, and rewarding employees. For example, L.L.Bean candidates should be "Friendly, Dependable, Helpful & Authentic"; "Trustworthy & Honest"; and "Outdoor Oriented & Environmentally Aware."[1] In return, L.L.Bean offers competitive pay and a full range of benefits including a cash performance bonus, multiple medical and insurance plans, a pension program, and an advanced management program.[2] It also offers something more. When L.L.Bean's Web sales first exceeded its phone sales, it closed four local call centers but arranged for the 220 employees to work from their homes. And instead of sending jobs abroad, it keeps its jobs close to the town where L.L.Bean started 100 years ago.[3] Like many employers today, L.L.Bean uses effective human resource practices to stay ahead of competitors.

WHAT IS HUMAN RESOURCE MANAGEMENT?

Human resource management refers to the practices and policies you need to carry out the personnel aspects of your management job, specifically, acquiring, training, appraising, rewarding, and providing a safe, ethical, and fair environment for your company's employees. These practices and policies include, for instance:

> Conducting job analyses (determining the nature of each employee's job)
> Planning labor needs and recruiting job candidates
> Selecting job candidates
> Orienting and training employees
> Appraising performance
> Managing wages and salaries (how to compensate employees)
> Providing incentives and benefits
> Communicating (interviewing, counseling, disciplining)

And what a manager should know about:

> Equal opportunity, ethics, and affirmative action
> Employee health, safety, and ethical treatment
> Grievances and labor relations

Why Is HR Management Important to All Managers?

Why are these concepts and techniques important to all managers? Perhaps it's easier to answer this by listing some of the personnel mistakes you don't want to make while managing. For example, you don't want

> To have your employees not performing at peak capacity
> To hire the wrong person for the job
> To experience high turnover
> To find employees not doing their best
> To have your company taken to court because of your discriminatory actions
> To have your company cited under federal occupational safety laws for unsafe practices
> To allow a lack of training to undermine your department's effectiveness
> To commit any unfair labor practices

Why Study This Book?   Carefully studying this book can help you avoid mistakes like these. More important, it can help ensure that you get results—through people. Remember that you could do everything else right as a manager—lay brilliant plans, draw clear organization charts, set up modern assembly lines, and use sophisticated accounting controls—but still fail, for instance, by hiring the wrong people.

On the other hand, many managers—from presidents to supervisors—have been successful even without adequate plans, organizations, or controls. They were successful because they had the knack for hiring the right people for the right jobs and motivating, appraising, and developing them. Remember as you read this book that getting results is the bottom line of managing and that, as a manager, you will have to get these results through people. That fact hasn't changed from the dawn of management. As one company president summed it up,

> For many years it has been said that capital is the bottleneck for a
> developing industry. I don't think this any longer holds true. I think it's
> the workforce and the company's inability to recruit and maintain a good
> workforce that does constitute the bottleneck for production. I don't know
> of any major project backed by good ideas, vigor, and enthusiasm that has
> been stopped by a shortage of cash. I do know of industries whose growth
> has been partly stopped or hampered because they can't maintain an
> efficient and enthusiastic labor force, and I think this will hold true even
> more in the future.[4]

HR for Entrepreneurs   And here is another reason to study this book. You may well end up as your own human resource manager. More than half the people working in the United States work for small firms. Therefore, most people graduating in the next few years will either work for small businesses or create new small businesses of their own. Especially if you are managing your own small firm, you'll have to be skilled at human resource management.[5]

Line and Staff Aspects of HRM

All managers are, in a sense, human resource managers because they all get involved in activities such as recruiting, interviewing, selecting, and training. Yet most firms also have a human resource department with its own human resource manager. How do the duties of this departmental HR manager and his or her staff relate to line managers' human resource duties? Let's answer this question by starting with short definitions of line versus staff authority.

Line Versus Staff Authority

Authority is the right to make decisions, to direct the work of others, and to give orders. Managers usually distinguish between line authority and staff authority. **Line managers** are authorized to give orders. **Staff managers** are authorized to assist and advise line managers in accomplishing their goals.

In popular usage, managers associate line managers with managing functions (like sales or production) that the company needs to exist. Staff managers generally run departments that are advisory or supportive, like purchasing, human resource management, and quality control. This distinction makes sense as long as the "staff" department is, in fact, advisory. However, strictly speaking, it's not the department's name that determines if the manager is line or staff. It is the nature of the manager's authority. The line manager can issue orders. The staff manager can advise.

Human resource managers are staff managers. They assist and advise line managers in areas like recruiting, hiring, and compensation. However, we'll see that line managers still have human resource duties.

From Line to Staff   Managers may move from line to staff positions (and back) during their careers. For example, line managers in production and sales may well make career stopovers as staff human resource managers (another good reason for all managers to know something about HR). One survey found that about a fourth of large U.S. businesses appointed managers with no human resources experience as their top human resource executives. Their employers assumed they may find it easier to integrate the firm's human resource management efforts with the rest of the business.[6]

Line-Staff HR Cooperation   HR and line managers share responsibility for most human resource activities. For example, human resource and line managers in about two thirds of the firms in one survey shared responsibility for skills training.[7] (Thus the supervisor might describe what training the new employee needs, HR might design the training, and the supervisor might then do the actual training.)

Line Managers' Human Resource Management Responsibilities

In any case, all supervisors spend much of their time on HR-type tasks. Indeed, the direct handling of people always has been part of every line manager's responsibility, from president to first-line supervisor.

For example, one company outlines its line supervisors' responsibilities for effective human resource management under the following general headings:

1. Placing the right person in the right job
2. Starting new employees in the organization (orientation)
3. Training employees for jobs that are new to them
4. Improving the job performance of each person
5. Gaining cooperation and developing smooth working relationships
6. Interpreting the company's policies and procedures
7. Controlling labor costs
8. Developing the abilities of each person
9. Creating and maintaining departmental morale
10. Protecting employees' health and physical conditions

In small organizations, line managers may carry out all these personnel duties unassisted. But as the organization grows, line managers need the assistance, specialized knowledge, and advice of a separate human resource staff.

Organizing the Human Resource Department's Responsibilities

The human resource department provides this specialized assistance. Figure 1.1 shows typical human resource management jobs. These include compensation and benefits manager, employment and recruiting supervisor, and employee relations executive. Examples of job duties include:

Recruiters: Maintain contact within the community and publicize openings to search for qualified job applicants.[8]

Equal employment opportunity (EEO) representatives or affirmative action coordinators: Investigate and resolve EEO grievances, examine organizational practices for potential violations, and compile and submit EEO reports.

Job analysts: Collect and examine detailed information about job duties to prepare job descriptions.

Compensation managers: Develop compensation plans and handle the employee benefits program.

Training specialists: Plan, organize, and direct training activities.

HR in Small Businesses   Employers usually have about one HR professional per 100 employees. Small firms (say, with less than 100 employees) generally can't afford a full-time human resource manager. Their human resource management therefore tends to be "ad hoc and informal." For example, concludes one survey, small firms tend to use "unimaginative" recruiting practices like relying on newspaper ads and to do little formal training.[9] However, that certainly does not need to be the case. Techniques like those in this book can boost the small business owner's "HR IQ."

The New Human Resources Organization   Employers are also experimenting with offering human resource services in new ways. For example, some employers now organize their HR services in the following groups:[10]

- The *transactional HR* group focuses on using centralized call centers and vendors (such as benefits advisors) to provide specialized support in day-to-day transactional HR activities (such as changing benefits plans) to the company's employees.
- The *corporate HR* group focuses on assisting top management in "top-level" issues such as developing the company's long-term strategic plan.
- The *embedded HR* group assigns HR generalists (also known as "relationship managers" or "HR business partners") to departments like sales and production, to provide the assistance the departments need.
- The *centers of expertise* groups are like specialized HR consulting firms within the company, for instance providing specialized assistance in areas such as organizational change.

Figure 1.1 Human Resource Department Organization Chart

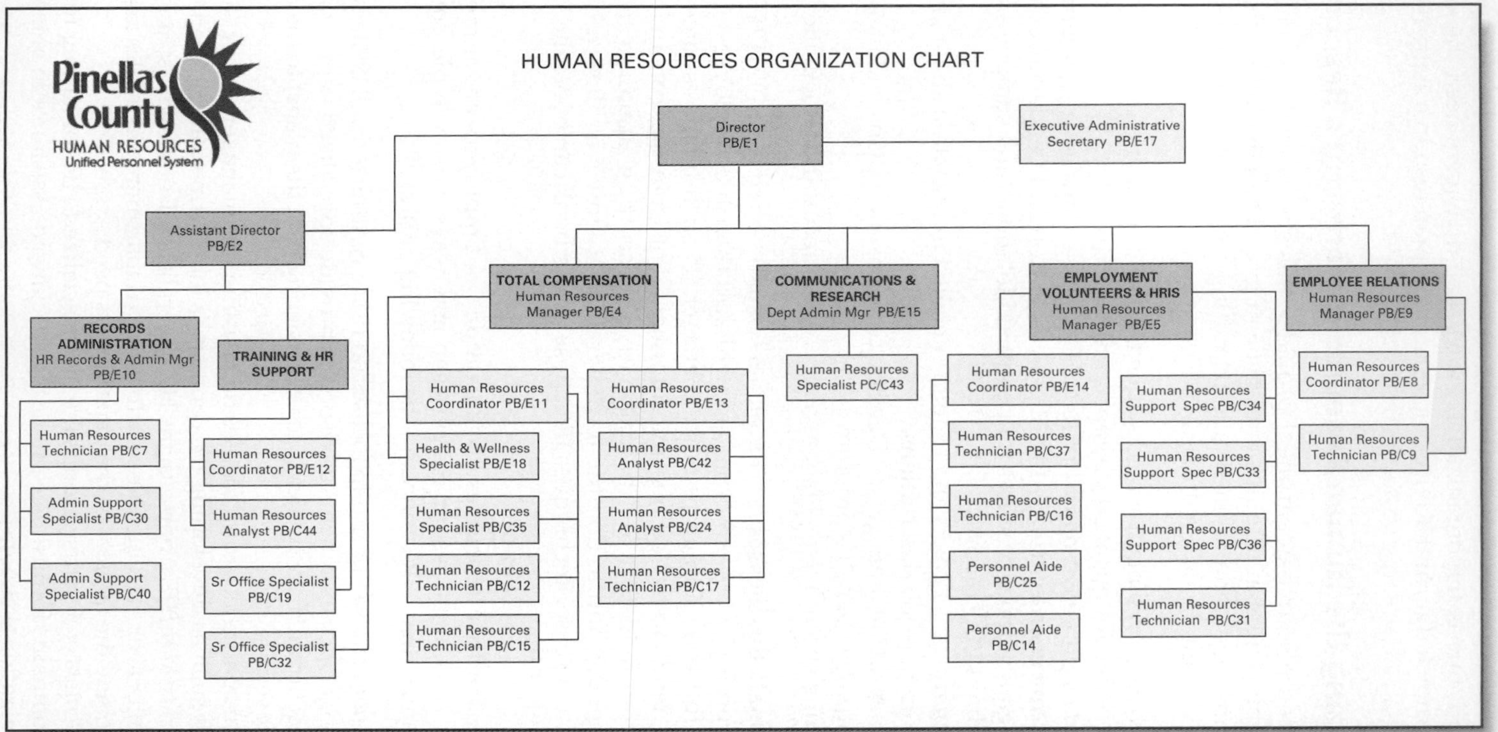

HUMAN RESOURCES ORGANIZATION CHART

Source: http://www.co.pinellas.fl.us/persnl/pdf/orgchart.pdf, accessed April 1, 2009.

IBM Example   Randy MacDonald, IBM's head of human resources, says the traditional human resource organization improperly isolates HR functions into "silos" such as recruitment, training, and employee relations. He says this silo approach means there's no one team of human resource specialists focusing on the needs of specific groups of employees. MacDonald therefore reorganized IBM's human resources function. He segmented IBM's 330,000 employees into executive and technical employees, managers, and rank and file. Separate human resource management teams (consisting of recruitment, training, and compensation specialists, for instance) now focus on each employee segment. These specialized teams help the employees in each segment get precisely the talent, learning, and compensation they require.[11]

TRENDS INFLUENCING HUMAN RESOURCE MANAGEMENT

IBM's new approach reflects the fact that employers' human resource priorities have evolved. In the early 1900s, "personnel" first took over hiring and firing from supervisors, ran the payroll department, and administered benefit plans. As technology in employee testing emerged, personnel began playing expanded roles in employee selection, training, and promotion.[12]

Union legislation in the 1930s meant more emphasis on protecting the firm in its interaction with unions. The discrimination legislation of the 1960s and 1970s meant large potential lawsuits and penalties, and thus an expansion of HR's "protector" role.[13]

Today, employers increasingly rely on their employees' motivation and performance to provide them with a competitive edge. In today's business environment, highly trained and committed employees, not machines, are often a firm's main competitive advantage. That requires a new kind of human resource manager. The transformation of *personnel* into *human resource management* reflects this. Let's sum up the trends that are influencing how employers manage their human resource functions.[14]

Globalization

Globalization refers to the tendency of firms to extend their sales, ownership, and/or manufacturing to new markets abroad. Thus Mercedes produces its M-class cars in Tuscaloosa, Alabama, while Dell produces PCs in China. Free trade areas—agreements that reduce tariffs and barriers among trading partners—further encourage international trade. NAFTA (the North American Free Trade Agreement) and the EU (European Union) are examples. Globalization has boomed. For example, the total sum of U.S. imports and exports rose from $47 billion in 1960, to $562 billion in 1980, to about $4.3 *trillion* recently.[15] More globalization means more competition, and more competition means more pressure to be "world class"—to lower costs, to make employees more productive, and to do things better and less expensively.

This pressures employers and their HR teams to institute practices that get the best from their employees.

Technological Advances

Technology is changing the nature of almost everything businesses do. For example, the Spanish retailer Zara doesn't need the expensive inventories that burden competitors like The Gap.[16] Zara operates its own Internet-based worldwide distribution network, linked to the checkout registers around the world. When its headquarters in Spain sees a garment "flying" out of a store, Zara's computerized manufacturing system dyes the required fabric, cuts and manufactures the item, and speeds it to that store in days.

The Nature of Work

Technology is also changing the nature of work. Skilled machinist Chad Toulouse illustrates the modern blue-collar worker. After an 18-week training course, this former college student now works as a team leader in a plant where about 40% of the machines are automated. In older plants, machinists would manually control machines that cut chunks of metal into engine parts. Today, Chad and his team spend their time typing commands into computerized machines that create precision parts for products like water pumps.[17] That's why human resource managers recently listed "critical thinking/problem solving" and "information technology application" as the two skills most likely to increase in importance over the next 5 years.[18]

Service Jobs

Technology is not the only trend driving this change from "brawn to brains." Today over two thirds of the U.S. workforce is employed in producing and delivering services, not products. Between 2004 and 2014, almost all the new 19 million new jobs added in the United States will be in services, not in goods-producing industries.[19]

Human Capital

For employers, this all means a growing need for "knowledge workers" and human capital. *Human capital* refers to the knowledge, education, training, skills, and expertise of a firm's workers.[20] Said one management guru, "the center of gravity in employment is moving fast from manual and clerical workers to knowledge workers, who resist the command-and-control model that business took from the military 100 years ago."[21] This places a big premium on having effective human resource practices.

Example   Here's an example. A bank installed special software that made it easier for customer service representatives to handle customers' inquiries. Seeking to capitalize on the new software, the bank upgraded the customer service representatives' jobs. The bank gave them new training, taught them how to sell more services, gave them more authority to make decisions, and raised their wages. Here, the new computer system dramatically improved profitability.

A second bank installed a similar system but did not change the workers' jobs. Here, the system helped the service reps handle a few more calls. But this bank saw none of the big performance gains the first bank got by turning its reps into sales-people.[22] The moral is that today's employers need more effective human resource management selection, training, pay, and other practices than did their predecessors, to capitalize on new technology.[23]

Offshoring

The search for greater efficiencies is prompting employers to export more jobs abroad. For example, Bank of America's Merrill Lynch has some of its security analysis work done in India. Figure 1.2 summarizes the situation. It shows that between 2005 and 2015, about 3 million U.S. jobs, ranging from office support and computer jobs to management, sales, and even legal jobs, will likely move offshore.[24]

Demographic Trends

The U.S. workforce is also fast becoming older and more multiethnic.[25] Table 1.1 provides a bird's-eye view. For example, between 1996 and 2016, the percent of the workforce classified as "white, non-Hispanic" will drop from 75.3% to 64.6%. Those of Hispanic origin will rise from 9.5% to 16.4%. The percentages of younger workers will fall, while those over 55 years of age will leap from 11.9% of the workforce in 1996 to 22% in 2016.

At the same time, demographic trends will make hiring more challenging.[26] In the United States, experts expect an estimated shortfall of about 14 million college-educated workers by 2020.[27] One study of 35 large global companies' senior human resource managers said "talent management"—the acquisition, development, and retention of talent to fill employment needs—was their top concern.[28]

Figure 1.2 Employment Exodus: Projected Loss of Jobs and Wages

Source: Michael Shroeder, "States Fight Exodus of Jobs," *Wall Street Journal*, June 3, 2003, p. 84. Copyright © 2003 Dow Jones & Co., Inc. Reprinted by permission of Dow Jones & Co., Inc. via Copyright Clearance Center.

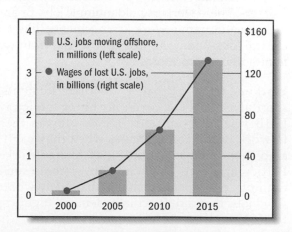

Table 1.1 Demographic Groups as a Percent of the Workforce, 1986–2016

AGE, RACE, ETHNICITY	1986	1996	2006	2016
Age: 16–24	19.8%	15.8	14.8	12.7
25–54	67.5	72.3	68.4	64.6
55 +	12.6	11.9	16.8	22.7
White, non-Hispanic	79.8	75.3	69.1	64.6
Black	10.7	11.3	11.4	12.3
Asian	2.9	4.3	4.4	5.3
Hispanic origin	6.9	9.5	13.7	16.4

Source: Adapted from www.bls.gov/emp/emplabor01.pdf, accessed October 20, 2008.

"Generation Y"   Furthermore, some experts contend that many younger workers may have different work values than did their parents.[29] One study found older employees more likely to be work-centric (to focus more on work than on family regarding career decisions). Younger workers tend to be more family-centric or dual-centric (balancing family and work life).[30] *Fortune* magazine says that today's "Millennial" or "Generation Y" employees bring challenges and strengths. It says they may be "the most high maintenance workforce in the history of the world."[31] Employers such as Lands End and Bank of America therefore teach their managers to give these new employees quick feedback and recognition.[32] But growing up using computers and e-mail will also make them the most high performing.[33]

Retirees   Many call "the aging workforce" the biggest demographic threat affecting employers. The basic problem is that there aren't enough younger workers to replace the baby boom era older workers retiring.[34] One survey found that 41% of surveyed employers are bringing retirees back into the workforce.[35]

Nontraditional Workers   At the same time, there has been a shift to nontraditional workers. These workers hold multiple jobs, or are "contingent" or part-time workers, or have alternative work arrangements (like a mother and daughter sharing one clerical job). Today, almost 10% of American workers—13 million people—fit this nontraditional workforce category.

Workers from Abroad   With retirements triggering projected workforce shortfalls, many employers are hiring foreign workers for U.S. jobs. The country's H-1B visa program lets U.S. employers recruit skilled foreign professionals to work in the United States when they can't find qualified U.S. workers. U.S. employers bring in about 181,000 foreign workers per year under these programs. Particularly with high unemployment, such programs face opposition. For example, one study concluded that many workers brought in under the programs filled jobs that didn't actually demand highly specialized skills, many paying less than $15 an hour.[36]

Economic Challenges and Trends

All these trends are occurring within the context of economic upheaval. Deregulation was one reason. Around the world, the rules that prevented commercial banks from expanding into new businesses such as stock brokering were relaxed. Giant multinational "financial supermarkets" such as Citibank quickly emerged. As economies boomed, more businesses and consumers went deeply into debt. Homebuyers bought homes, often with little money down. Banks freely lent money to developers to build more homes. For almost 20 years, U.S. consumers actually spent more than they earned. On a grander scale, the United States itself became a debtor. Its balance of payments (exports minus imports) went from a healthy positive $3.5 billion in 1960, to a not-so-healthy *minus* $19.4 billion in 1980 (imports exceeded exports), to a huge $378 billion deficit in 2009.[37] The only way the country could keep buying more from abroad than it sold was by borrowing money. So much of the boom was built on debt.

As you can see in Figure 1.3, gross national product (GNP)—a measure of U.S. total output—boomed between 2001 and 2007. During this period, home prices leaped as much as 20% per year. Unemployment remained docile at about 4.7%.[38] Then, a few years ago, all these measures fell off a cliff. GNP fell. Home prices dropped by 20% or more (depending on city). Unemployment nationwide rose to more than 10%.

Why did all this happen? That is a complicated question, but all those years of accumulating debt seems to have run their course. Banks and other financial institutions (such as hedge funds) had trillions of dollars of worthless loans on their books.

Figure 1.3 Changes in Gross National Product (GNP)

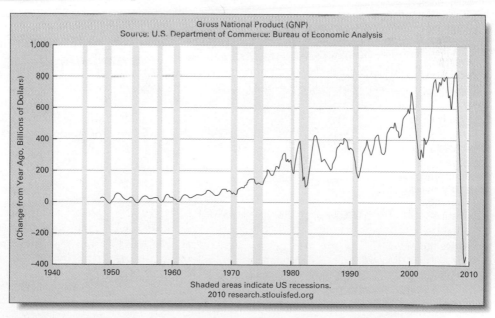

Source: http://research.stlouisfed.org/fred2/fredgraph?chart_type=line&s[1][id]=GNP&s[1]
[transformation]=ch1, accessed April 18, 2009.

Governments stepped in to try to prevent their collapse. Lending dried up. Many businesses and consumers stopped buying. The economy tanked.

Economic trends will turn positive again, perhaps as you read these pages. However, after what the world went through the past few years, it's doubtful that the deregulation, leveraging, and globalization that drove economic growth will continue unabated. That may mean slower growth for many countries, perhaps for years. The challenging times mean that employers will have to be more frugal and creative in managing their human resources.[39] We'll use boxed "Managing HR in Challenging Times" features in most chapters to illustrate how HR managers manage in challenging times. Note below the changes from October 2008 to December 2008 as the economy worsened.

Managing HR in Challenging Times: Adjusting HR Policies to Challenging Times

As you can see in the following table, as the United States slipped into recession, employers began adjusting their HR policies to adapt them to the new economic realities. Given the recent events in the economy and financial markets, what changes have you made or do you expect to make in HR policies?

	Already made change (December)	Already made change (October)	Expect to make change in next 12 months (December)	Expect to make change in next 12 months (October)	No change expected (December)	No change expected (October)
Add/increase restrictions to company travel policy	48%	34%	16%	21%	36%	45%
Hiring freeze	47%	30%	18%	25%	35%	45%
Layoffs/ reduction in force	39%	19%	23%	26%	38%	55%
Downgrade or cancel company holiday party	35%	19%	8%	18%	57%	64%
Increase communication to employees about their benefits	32%	35%	35%	35%	33%	31%
Eliminate or reduce the hiring of seasonal workers	28%	17%	16%	18%	56%	65%

(Continued)

	Already made change (December)	Already made change (October)	Expect to make change in next 12 months (December)	Expect to make change in next 12 months (October)	No change expected (December)	No change expected (October)
Organization-wide restructuring	23%	14%	21%	23%	57%	64%
Eliminate or reduce training	23%	10%	18%	18%	59%	72%
Raise employee contribution to health care premiums	20%	21%	17%	25%	63%	54%
Increase communication to employees about their pay	16%	18%	43%	37%	41%	45%
HR function restructuring	14%	15%	21%	19%	66%	66%
Salary freeze	13%	4%	19%	12%	67%	84%
Mandatory holiday shutdown	13%	6%	5%	2%	83%	92%
Reduce or eliminate other employee programs	12%	8%	12%	11%	75%	81%
Salary reductions	5%	2%	6%	4%	89%	94%
Early retirement window	3%	4%	6%	5%	92%	91%
Reduce employer 401(k)/403(b) match	3%	2%	7%	4%	90%	94%
Reduced workweek	2%	4%	6%	4%	93%	92%

Source: Watson Wyatt, *Effect of Economic Crisis on HR Programs.* Update, December 2008, p. 5. http://www.watsonwyatt.com/news/pdfs/2008-WT-0065.pdf, accessed April 4, 2010.

THE HUMAN RESOURCE MANAGER TODAY

Trends like globalization and economic upheaval confront employers with new challenges. They therefore expect that their human resource managers exhibit the skills required to help the company address these new challenges. In practice, this boils down to several implications for human resource managers.

They Focus More on Big Picture Issues

First, human resource managers are *more involved in strategic, "big picture" issues.* Here's a quick example. Several years ago, Wisconsin-based Signicast Corp.'s president, Terry Lutz, and his board decided to build a new, computerized plant. Signicast produces metal parts from a casting process. To compete, it needed the new automated plant. Mr. Lutz and his team understood that "in the real world, new automation technology requires a new kind of employee." They knew the computerized plant was useless without employees who could work in self-managing teams and run the plant's computerized equipment.

Lutz and his management team worked closely with and relied on their human resource management team to select and train the tech-friendly people the new plant required.[40] By formulating and executing the hiring and other personnel practices that Signicast needed to make the plant a success, the HR team was supporting Signicast's new strategy.

The point is that human resource managers *need to be strategic.* They don't just do transactional things like signing onboard new employees. Employers want them to be the firms' *internal consultants*, making changes that help employees contribute to the company's success.[41]

They Find New Ways to Provide Transactional Services

But then, who does the day-to-day transactional things like recruiting and testing employees, and managing their benefits?[42] The answer is that today's human resource managers also must *offer those traditional transactional HR services in new ways.* For example, they *outsource* more of these services (such as benefits administration) to outside vendors.[43] They use *technology* (such as intranet-based Web sites) to enable employees to self-administer benefits plans. Table 1.2 lists important ways employers use technology to support their human resource management activities.[44]

Improving HR Productivity Through Technology   For example, when Dell had to add about 15,000 employees in 51 countries, its talent acquisition group asked, "How could technology help us better manage this task?" Dell installed a Web-based applicant tracking system. This automated the process of recruiting employees and of managing their progress through the hiring process. The vendor then worked with Dell to develop customized recruiting metrics, such as managers' evaluations of the new hires. Dell can now correlate (1) new hires' work performance with (2) the various recruitment sources. That enables them to

Table 1.2 Some Ways HR Managers Use Technology

TECHNOLOGY	HOW USED BY HR
Application Service Providers (ASPs)	ASPs host and manage service (such as for processing employment applications), for the employer from their own remote computers
Web portals	Employers use these, for instance, to enable employees to manage their own benefits and update their personal information
Streaming PC video	Used, for instance, to facilitate distance training
Personal digital assistants	For example, some firms provide incoming managers with preloaded personal digital assistants. These contain information the new managers need to better adjust to their new jobs, such as key contact information and digital images of the manager's new employees
Monitoring software	Used to track employees' Internet and e-mail activities or performance
Integrated human resource information systems (HRIS)	Used to integrate the employer's separate HR systems, for instance, by automatically updating employee's qualifications list when he or she completes a training program.
Electronic signatures	Employers can use these legally valid e-signatures to expeditiously obtain applicant and employee signatures
The Web	Managers make extensive use of the Web, as for doing salary surveys

Source: Adapted from Samuel Greengard, "10 HR Technology Trends for 2001," *Workforce, HR Trends and Tools for Business Results* 80, no. 1 (January 2001): 20–22; Jim Meade, "Analytical Tools Give Meaning to Data," *HR Magazine* 46, no. 11 (November 2001): 97 ff. Connie Winkler, "Quality Check," *HR Magazine* (May 2007): 93–98 and Bill Roberts, "Using a Road Map for HR Technology," *HR Magazine* 55, no. 1 (January 2010): 49–52.

focus their recruiting dollars on the more effective recruitment sources.[45] Internet-based applications like these ("e-HR") lead to lower HR function costs.[46]

They Manage Ethics

Ethics refers to the standards someone uses to decide what his or her conduct should be. Ethical decisions always involve *morality*, matters of serious consequence to society's well-being, such as murder, lying, or stealing (as via financial Ponzi schemes).

One survey found that six of the ten most serious ethical issues—workplace safety, security of employee records, employee theft, affirmative action, comparable work, and employee privacy rights—were human resource management related.[47] We will explain ethics in human resource management more fully in Chapter 8.

They Build High-Performance Work Systems

Today's competitive and economic challenges are forcing managers to focus more on *productivity and performance* improvement.

Human resource management practices are invaluable in that effort. For example, we'll see in this book that well-trained employees perform better than untrained ones, and safe workplaces produce fewer lost-time accidents and costs than do unsafe ones. In one recent study, employee selection and training in a large fast-food chain improved customer service.[48] Offering employees training opportunities is also associated with higher levels of employee commitment and reduced voluntary early retirement.[49]

A *high-performance work system* is a set of human resource management policies and practices that together produce superior employee performance. For example, in one study, the high-performance plants paid more (median wages of $16 per hour compared with $13 per hour for all plants); trained more (83% offered more than 20 hours of training per year, compared with 32% for all plants); used more sophisticated recruitment and hiring practices (tests and validated interviews, for instance); and used more self-managing work teams. These plants also had the best overall performance, in terms of higher profits, lower operating costs, and lower turnover.[50]

They Understand Evidence-Based Human Resource Management

Saying you have a "high-performance" organization assumes that you can measure how you're doing.[51] For example, "How much will that new testing program save us in reduced employee turnover?" [52]

Providing evidence such as this is the heart of *evidence-based human resource management.* This is the use of data, facts, analytics, scientific rigor, critical evaluation, and critically evaluated research/case studies to support human resource management proposals, decisions, practices, and conclusions.[53] Put simply, evidence-based human resource management means using the best available evidence in making decisions about the human resource management practices you are focusing on.[54] The evidence may come from *actual measurements* you make (such as, how did the trainees like this program?). It may come from *existing data* (such as, what happened to company profits after we installed this training program?). Or it may come from published *research studies* (for instance, median HR expenses as a proportion of companies' total operating costs average about 0.8%[55]).

Examples   One insurance firm was thinking about cutting costs by buying out highly paid senior underwriters. But after looking at the data, the human resources manager discovered that these underwriters accounted for a disproportionate share of the company's revenue. Eliminating them could be disastrous! Instead, the firm decided to replace call center employees with less expensive employees. As another example, BASF Corp. analyzed data showing the relationship among its employees' stress and productivity, and discovered that stress-reduction programs would more than pay for themselves in increased productivity.[56]

They Can Measure HR Performance

In today's performance-based environment, employers expect their human resource managers to be able to measure their effectiveness. For example, IBM's Randall MacDonald needed $100 million from IBM to reorganize its HR operations. He told top management, "I'm going to deliver talent to you that's skilled and on time and ready to be deployed. I will be able to measure the skills, tell you what skills we have, what [skills] we don't have [and] then show you how to fill the gaps or enhance our training."[57]

Sample Metrics   To make claims like these, human resource managers need performance measures (or "metrics"). For example, HR expenses as a proportion of companies' total operating costs average about 0.8%. There tends to be between 0.9 and 1.0 human resource staff persons per 100 employees.[58] Employers can request benchmark comparisons from services such as the Society for Human Resource Management's Human Capital Benchmarking Service and its database of over 1,500 organizations.[59]

The HR Scorecard   Managers often use an *HR Scorecard* process to help measure the human resource function's effectiveness. The *HR Scorecard* is a concise measurement system, often presented in a desktop display that summarizes at a glance HR-related measures in graphs and charts. It shows the quantitative standards, or "metrics," the firm uses to measure each HR activity (such as training), the employee behaviors resulting from these activities (such as performance), and the organizational outcomes of those employee behaviors (such as profits).

They Have New Proficiencies[60]

In turn, activities such as measuring and dealing with technology demand *new human resource management proficiencies.* Human resource managers still need skills in areas such as employee selection and training. But now they also require broader *business knowledge and competencies.* For example, to assist top management in formulating strategic plans, the human resource manager needs to understand strategic planning, marketing, production, and finance.[61] He or she must also be able to "speak the CFO's language," by explaining human resource activities in financially measurable terms.[62]

Studies show that top managers recognize the crucial role human resource managers can play in achieving a company's strategic goals.[63] Partly as a result, human resource executives are increasingly well paid. For example, in 2009, the head of human resources and labor relations at Delta Air Lines earned about $5 million in total compensation, and the head of human resources at eBay earned over $4 million.[64]

HR Certification

With managing human resources becoming more complex, HR managers are turning to certification to illustrate their mastery of modern practices. Three levels of exams from the Society for Human Resource Management test the professional's knowledge of all aspects of human resource management, including management practices, staffing, development, compensation, labor relations, and health and safety. Those who successfully complete all requirements earn the SPHR (senior professional in HR), PHR (professional in HR) certificate, or GHR (Global HR). The Human Resource Certification Institute also offers state certification testing for California's human resource professionals.[65] Managers can take an online HRCI assessment exam at www.HRCI.org (or by calling 866-898-HRCI).

STRATEGIC PLANNING AND STRATEGIC HUMAN RESOURCE MANAGEMENT

A human resource manager's main responsibility is to institute policies and practices that produce the employee competencies and behaviors the company needs to achieve its strategic goals. Human resource managers therefore need to understand strategic planning. A **strategy** is the company's plan for how it will match its internal strengths and weaknesses with external opportunities and threats in order to maintain a competitive advantage. Let's look at an example.

Strategy and HR Example

Like many firms, Albertson's Markets faced cost pressures from Walmart. Albertson's relied on its human resource managers to help it achieve its strategic goals of improving service while reducing costs. Reducing personnel-related costs and improving Albertson's performance meant hiring employees who were customer focused, as well as reducing turnover, improving retention, and eliminating time-consuming manual HR processes for store managers.

Albertson's human resource management team chose a computer system from Unicru (www.unicru.com) to help them accomplish this. The system collects and analyzes the information entered by applicants online. It ranks applicants based on the extent to which they exhibit the customer-focused traits that predict success in retail jobs. It also helps track candidates throughout the screening process and tracks reasons for departure. Human resource managers were able to present a compelling business argument to illustrate the new system's return on investment. Working as a partner in Albertson's strategy design and implementation process, the HR team thus helped Albertson's achieve its strategic goals.[66]

Basics of Strategic Planning

Managers engage in three levels of strategic planning (see Figure 1.4).[67]

Corporate Strategy   At the top, company-wide level, many firms consist of several businesses. For instance, PepsiCo includes Frito-Lay North America, PepsiCo Beverages North America, PepsiCo International, and Quaker Oats North America.

Figure 1.4

Three Levels of Strategies in Multiple-Business Firms

Source: Gary Dessler, Ph.D.

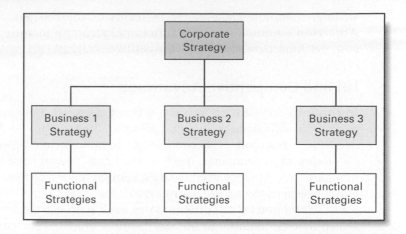

PepsiCo therefore needs a *corporate-level strategy.* A company's **corporate-level strategy** identifies the portfolio of businesses that, in total, comprise the company and the ways in which these businesses relate to each other. For example, a *diversification* strategy implies that the firm will expand by adding new products. A *vertical integration* strategy means the firm expands by, perhaps, producing its own raw materials or selling its products directly. *Consolidation*—reducing the company's size—and *geographic expansion*—for instance, taking the business abroad—are some other corporate strategy possibilities.

Competitive Strategy   At the next level down, each of these businesses (such as Quaker Oats) needs a *business-level/competitive strategy.* A **competitive strategy** identifies how to build and strengthen the business's long-term competitive position in the marketplace. It identifies, for instance, how Pizza Hut will compete with Papa John's. Companies try to achieve competitive advantages for each of their businesses. We can define **competitive advantage** as any factors that allow an organization to differentiate its product or service from those of its competitors to increase market share.[68]

Managers use several competitive strategies to achieve competitive advantage. One, *cost leadership*, means the company aims to become the low-cost leader in an industry. Walmart is a typical industry cost leader: It maintains its competitive advantage in part through its satellite-based distribution system.

In a *differentiation* competitive strategy, a business seeks to be unique in its industry in ways valued by buyers.[69] Thus Volvo stresses safety, and Papa John's Pizza stresses fresh ingredients. Like Mercedes-Benz, firms can usually charge a premium price if they successfully differentiate their products. Still other firms choose to compete as *focusers.* They carve out a market niche (as for Rolls-Royce cars) and compete by providing something their customers can get in no other way.

Functional Strategy   Finally, each individual business has departments, such as manufacturing, sales, and human resource management. **Functional strategies** identify the basic courses of action that each of the business's departments will pursue in order to help the business attain its competitive goals. These functional strategies should make sense in terms of the business/competitive strategy. Albertson's human resource functional strategy included using technology to support Albertson's low-cost competitive strategy.

HR and Competitive Advantage

In order to compete effectively, a business must have one or more *competitive advantages*, which are factors that allow an organization to differentiate its product or service from those of its competitors to increase market share.

Today, most companies (such as Ford and Nissan) have access to the same technologies, so technology itself is rarely enough to set a company apart. It's usually the employees and the management system that make the difference. For example, the Ritz-Carlton hotel chain differentiates itself with extraordinary customer service—which it achieves through human resource practices such as careful screening and extensive training.

Strategic Human Resource Management

With intense global competition, human resource management plays a bigger role in planning and achieving a firm's success than it has in the past, so top managers expect their human resource managers to help develop and execute the firm's strategic plan. **Strategic human resource management** means formulating and executing HR policies and practices that produce the employee competencies and behaviors the company needs to achieve its strategic aims.[70] The term *HR strategies* refers to the specific human resource function courses of action the company pursues to achieve its aims. Albertson's strategic goals include lowering costs. One human resource strategy thus includes using a new, more efficient Web-based system to hire customer-focused employees. Figure 1.5 summarizes the relationship between HR strategy and the company's strategic plans and results. The human resource manager has roles in both formulating and executing the company's strategic plan.

HR's Role in Formulating Strategy   Formulating a strategic plan requires identifying, analyzing, and balancing the firm's *external opportunities and threats* and its *internal strengths and weaknesses*. The resulting strategic plan should exploit the firm's strengths and opportunities and minimize or neutralize its threats and weaknesses.

The human resource team plays several roles here. For example, it's in a good position to supply competitive intelligence, such as details regarding competitors' incentive plans and information about pending labor laws. It is also in the best position to give advice about the company's internal human strengths and weaknesses. For example, farm equipment manufacturer John Deere developed a workforce that was exceptionally talented in factory automation. This led Deere to establish a new-technology division to offer automation services to other companies.

HR's Role in Executing Strategy   As at Albertson's, human resource managers also help their firms execute their strategies. For example, studies show that mergers or acquisitions in which the human resource teams were involved (for instance, in helping plan and lead the integration of the compensation and benefits plans) were more likely to succeed.[71]

Figure 1.5 Linking Corporate and HR Strategies

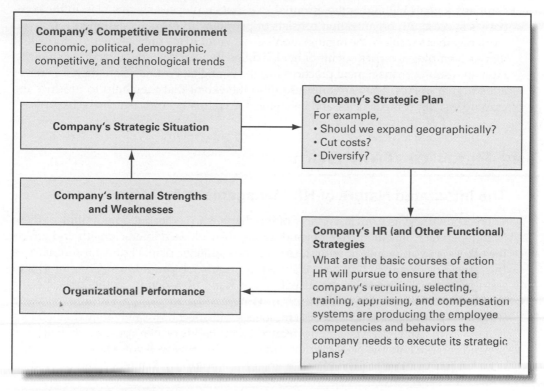

Source: © 2010 Gary Dessler, Ph.D.

Strategy and HR   For example, to improve the performance of one recently acquired Ritz-Carlton Hotel (the Portman Ritz-Carlton, in Shanghai), new general manager Mark DeCocinis introduced the Ritz-Carlton company's human resource system. He knew its practices would produce the high-quality service behaviors the Portman required. For example, DeCocinis and his managers personally interviewed each job candidate. They delved deeply into each candidate's values, selecting only employees who cared for and respected others: "our selection focuses on talent and personal values because these are things that can't be taught. . . ." Their efforts paid off. In the past few years, the Portman Ritz-Carlton was named the "best employer in Asia" and "overall best business hotel in Asia." Profits soared. Effective human resource management helped the Portman Ritz-Carlton achieve its strategic aims.

The Employee's Role in Executing the Company's Strategic Plan   Managerial planning follows the chain of command. Top management sets a goal (or goals) for the company as a whole. Then top management's plans and goals become the targets for which lower-level departments design derivative pslans. The vice president produces a plan for her department. Then her own department heads produce plans for their departments, and so on down to individual employees' goals. In this way, the planning process produces a hierarchy of plans and goals.

The idea that each employee's goals should support the department's and company's goals highlights the essential role that employees always play in the company's success. An organization consists of people with formally assigned roles who work together to achieve the organization's goals. A company only succeeds to the extent that each employee carries out his or her job diligently, competently, and conscientiously. Human resource management practices like the Shanghai Portman's are therefore never ends in themselves. They are only useful to the extent that they help to produce the employee skills, competencies, and behaviors the company needs to achieve its goals.

THE PLAN OF THIS BOOK

The Integrated Nature of HR Management Activities

This section presents a brief overview of the chapters to come; but do not think of these as independent unrelated chapters and topics. Instead, each interacts with and affects the others, and all should fit with the employer's strategic plan. Figure 1.6 summarizes this idea. For example, how you test and interview job candidates (Chapter 4) and train and appraise job incumbents (Chapters 5 and 6) depends on the job's specific duties and responsibilities (Chapter 3). How good a job you are doing selecting (Chapter 4) and training (Chapter 5) employees will affect how safely they do their jobs (Chapter 10). An employee's performance and thus his or her appraisal (Chapter 6) depends on not only the person's motivation but also how well you identified the job's duties (Chapter 3) and screened and trained the employee (Chapters 4 and 5). And, as

Figure 1.6 Strategy and the Basic HR Process

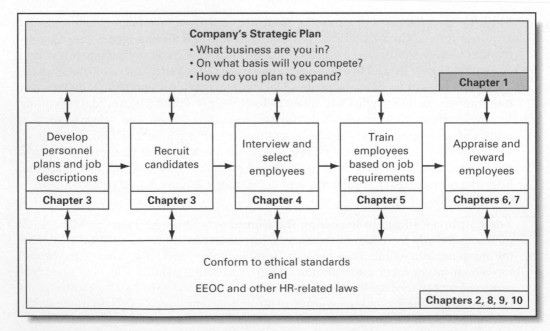

we've seen, each of your HR policies in each area—for instance, how you recruit and compensate employees—should make sense in terms of the company's strategic plan. The following is an outline of the chapters to come:

Chapter 2: Managing Equal Opportunity and Diversity What you'll need to know about equal opportunity laws as they relate to human resource management activities such as interviewing and selecting employees and managing diversity

Part I: Recruiting and Placing Employees

Chapter 3: Personnel Planning and Recruiting How to analyze a job to determine the job's specific duties and responsibilities, as well as what sorts of people to hire

Chapter 4: Testing and Selecting Employees Techniques such as testing that you can use to ensure that you're hiring the right people

Chapter 5: Training and Developing Employees Providing the training and development necessary to ensure that your employees have the knowledge and skills required to accomplish their tasks

Part II: Appraising and Compensating Employees

Chapter 6: Performance Management and Appraisal Techniques for managing and appraising performance and managing careers

Chapter 7: Compensating Employees How to develop equitable pay plans, including incentives and benefits

Part III: Employee Rights and Safety

Chapter 8: Ethics and Fair Treatment in Human Resource Management Ensuring ethical and fair treatment through discipline and grievance management

Chapter 9: Managing Labor Relations and Collective Bargaining Concepts and techniques concerning the relations between unions and management, including the union-organizing campaign, and negotiating a collective bargaining agreement

Chapter 10: Protecting Safety and Health The causes of accidents, how to make the workplace safe, and laws governing your responsibilities in regard to employee safety and health

Module A: Managing HR Globally Applying human resource management policies and practices in a global environment

REVIEW

Summary

1. Staffing, personnel management, or human resource management includes activities such as recruiting, selecting, training, compensating, appraising, and developing employees.

2. HR management is a part of every line manager's responsibilities. It includes placing the right person in the right job and then orienting, training, and compensating the person to improve his or her job performance.

3. The human resource manager and his or her department provide various staff services to line management; for example, the HR manager or department assists in the hiring, training, evaluating, rewarding, promoting, and disciplining of employees at all levels.

4. Changes in the environment of human resource management are requiring HR to play a strategic role in organizations. These changes include growing workforce diversity, rapid technological change, globalization, and changes in the nature of work, such as the movement toward a service society and a growing emphasis on education and human capital.

5. One consequence of changes in the work environment is that HR management must be involved in both the formulation and the implementation of a company's strategies, given the need for the firm to use its employees as a competitive advantage.

6. We defined strategic human resource management as "formulating and executing HR systems—HR policies and practices—that produce the employee competencies and behaviors the company needs to achieve its strategic aims." HR is a strategic partner in that it works with other top managers to formulate the company's strategy as well as to execute it.

KEY TERMS

- human resource management
- authority
- line manager
- staff manager
- ethics
- strategy
- corporate-level strategy
- competitive strategy
- competitive advantage
- functional strategy
- strategic human resource management

DISCUSSION QUESTIONS

1. Explain what HR management is and how it relates to line management.
2. Give several examples of how HR management concepts and techniques can be of use to all managers.
3. Compare the work of line and staff managers. Give examples of each.
4. Why is it important for a company to make its human resources into a competitive advantage? How can HR contribute to doing so?
5. What is strategic human resource management, and what is HR's role in the strategic planning process?

INDIVIDUAL AND GROUP ACTIVITIES

1. Working individually or in groups, contact the HR manager of a local bank. Ask the person how he or she is working as a strategic partner to manage human resources, given the bank's strategic goals and objectives. Back in class discuss the responses of the different HR managers.
2. Working individually or in groups, interview an HR manager. Based on

that interview, write a short presentation regarding HR's role today in building competitive organizations.

3. Working individually or in groups, bring several business publications such as *BusinessWeek* and the *Wall Street Journal* to class. Based on their contents, compile a list entitled "What HR Managers and Departments Do Today."

4. Based on your personal experiences, list 10 examples showing how you did use (or could have used) human resource management techniques at work or school.

5. Laurie Siegel, senior vice president of human resources for Tyco International, took over her job just after numerous charges forced the company's previous executives to leave the firm. Hired by new CEO Edward Breen, Siegel had to tackle difficult problems. For example, she had to help hire a new management team. She had to do something about what the outside world viewed as questionable ethics at her company. And she had to revamp the company's top management compensation plan, which many felt contributed to the allegations by some that some former company

officers had used the company as a sort of private ATM.

Working individually or in groups, conduct an Internet search and library research to answer the following questions: What human resource management–related steps did Siegel take to help get Tyco back on the right track? Do you think she took the appropriate steps? Why or why not? What, if anything, do you suggest she do now?

6. Working individually or in groups, develop a list showing how trends such as workforce diversity, technological trends, globalization, and changes in the nature of work have affected the college or university you are now attending or the organization for which you work.

7. Working individually or in groups, develop several examples showing how the new HR management practices mentioned in this chapter (using technology, for instance) have or have not been implemented to some extent in the college or university you are now attending or in the organization for which you work.

APPLICATION EXERCISES

Case Incident   Jack Nelson's Problem

As a new member of the board of directors for a local bank, Jack Nelson was being introduced to all the employees in the home office. When he was introduced to Ruth Johnson, he was curious about her work and asked her what her machine did. Johnson replied that she really did not know what the machine was called or what it did. She explained that she had been working there for only 2 months. She did, however, know precisely how to operate the machine. According to her supervisor, she was an excellent employee.

At one of the branch offices, the supervisor in charge spoke to Nelson confidentially, telling him that "something was wrong," but she didn't know what. For one thing, she explained, employee turnover was too high, and no sooner had one employee been put on the job than another one resigned. With customers to see and loans to be made, she explained, she had little time to work with the new employees.

All branch supervisors hired their own employees without communication with the home office or other branches. When an opening developed, the supervisor tried to find a suitable employee to replace the worker.

After touring the 22 branches and finding similar problems in many of them, Nelson wondered what the home office should do or what action he should take. The banking firm was generally regarded as a well-run institution that had grown from 27 to 191 employees during the past 8 years. The more he thought about the matter, the more puzzled Nelson became. He couldn't put his finger on the problem, and he didn't know whether to report his findings to the president. ■

QUESTIONS

1. What do you think is causing some of the problems in the bank's home office and branches?
2. Do you think setting up an HR unit in the main office would help?
3. What specific functions should an HR unit carry out? What HR functions would then be carried out by supervisors and other line managers?

Source: From *Supervision in Action,* 4/e, by Claude S. George © 1985. Adapted by permission of Prentice Hall Inc., Upper Saddle River, NJ.

Continuing Case

LearnInMotion.com: Introduction

A main theme of this book is that HR management—activities like recruiting, selecting, training, and rewarding employees—are not just the job of some central HR group, but rather one in which every manager must engage. Perhaps nowhere is this more apparent than in the typical small service business. Here the owner-manager usually has no personnel staff. However, the success of his or her enterprise often depends largely on the effectiveness with which workers are recruited, hired, trained, evaluated, and rewarded.

To help illustrate and emphasize the front-line manager's HR role, we will use a continuing ("running") case, based on an actual small business in the northeastern United States. Each segment will illustrate how the case's main players—owner-managers Jennifer Mendez and Mel Hudson—confront and solve personnel problems each day by applying the concepts and techniques presented in that particular chapter. The names of the company and principals have been changed, as have some details, but the company, people, and HR and other problems are otherwise real. Here's some background information you'll need to answer questions that arise in subsequent chapters.

LEARNINMOTION.COM: A PROFILE

Jennifer and Mel graduated from State University as business majors in June 2004 and thought up LearnInMotion.com as a result of a project they worked on together in their entrepreneurship class. The professor had divided the students into two- or three-person teams and given them the assignment "create a business plan for a dot-com company."

The idea the two came up with was LearnInMotion.com. The basic idea of the Web site was to list a vast array of Web-based, DVD-based, or textbook-based business-related continuing-education-type courses for working people who wanted to take a course in business from the comfort of their own homes. The idea was that users could come to the Web site to find and then take a course in one of several ways. Some courses could be completed interactively on the Web via the site; others were in a form that was downloadable directly to the user's computer; others (which were either textbook or DVD based) could be ordered and delivered (in selected cities) by independent contractor delivery people using bicycles or motorized scooters. Their business mission was "to provide work-related learning when, where, and how you need it."

Based on their research, they knew the market for work-related learning like this was booming. The $63 billion U.S. corporate training market is growing at 10% annually, for instance, with no firm controlling more than 2%. In 2004, when they created their plan, 76 million adult U.S. learners participated in at least one education activity. Over 100,000 U.S. training and consulting firms offered seminars, courses, and other training. They estimated that worldwide markets were at least two or three times the U.S. market.

At the same time, professional development activities like these were increasingly Internet based. Thirteen percent of training was delivered via the Internet when they did their class project, and projections were for the e-learning/distance learning market to grow over 90% annually for the following 3 years. Tens of thousands of on- and offline training firms, universities, associations, and other content providers were trying to reach their target customers via the Internet. Jennifer and Mel thought they were in the right place at the right time. And perhaps they were.

Their business plan contained about 25 pages, including financial projection, and covered the usual array of topics: company summary, management, market trends and opportunities, competition, marketing plan, and financial plan. The one-page executive summary contained a synopsis of the plan and covered "the business," "the market," "strategies," "competition," "value proposition," "the revenue drivers," "the management," and "financials and funding." Revenue drivers referred to how the company would generate revenues (in this case, online banner ads and sponsorships, content providers' listing fees, and fees for courses actually taken). Financials and funding included basic financial projections as well as likely "exit strategies," which in this case included the possibility of a public offering, or sale of the site, perhaps to one of the super portals that were aggregating specialized sites as part of their strategies. They got an A for the business plan, an A for the course, and a standing ovation from the businesspeople the professor had invited to help evaluate the presentations.

When the two graduated in June 2004, it looked like the Internet boom would go on. Even then, it was not unusual for entrepreneurs still in their teens to create and sell Web sites for literally hundreds of millions of dollars. Jennifer's father had some unused loft space in the SoHo area of New York, so with about $45,000 of accumulated savings, Jennifer and Mel incorporated and were in business. They retained the services of an independent contractor programmer and hired two people—a Web designer to create the graphics for the site (which would then be programmed by the programmer) and a content manager whose job was basically to keypunch information onto the site as it came in from content providers. By the end of 2004, they also completed upgrading their business plan into a form they could show to prospective venture capitalists. They sent the first version to three New York area venture capitalists. Then they waited.

And then they waited some more. They never heard back from the first three venture capitalists, so they sent their plan to five more. By now it was March 2005, and a dramatic event occurred: The values of most Internet and Internet-related sites dropped on the stock market. In some cases, entrepreneurs who had been worth $1 billion in February 2004 were worth $20 million or less by April. "Well, $20 million isn't bad," Mel said, so they pressed on. By day they called customers to get people to place ads on their site, to get content providers to list their available courses, and to get someone—anyone—to deliver textbook- and CD-ROM-based courses, as needed, in the New York area.

By May 2005, they had about 300 content providers offering courses and content through LearnInMotion.com. In the summer, they got their first serious nibble from a venture capital firm. They negotiated with this company through much of the summer, came to terms in the early fall, and closed the deal—getting just over $1 million in venture funding—in November 2005.

After a stunning total of $75,000 in legal fees (they had to pay both their firm's and the venture capital firm's lawyers to navigate the voluminous disclosure documents and agreements), they had just over $900,000 to spend. The funding, according to the business plan, was to go toward accomplishing four main goals: redesigning and expanding the Web site, hiring about seven more employees, moving to larger office space, and driving up sales. LearnInMotion.com was off and running. ■

QUESTIONS AND ASSIGNMENTS

1. Would a company like this with just a few employees and independent contractors have any HR tasks to address? What do you think those might be?
2. Based on your review of the online catalogs of firms such as OfficeMax, Staples, and HRNext.com, what basic HR systems would you recommend to Jennifer and Mel?

Experiential Exercise
Helping "The Donald"

Purpose: The purpose of this exercise is to provide practice in identifying and applying the basic concepts of human resource management by illustrating how managers use these techniques in their day-to-day jobs.

Required Understanding: Be thoroughly familiar with the material in this chapter, and with at least several episodes of *The Apprentice*, the TV show in which developer Donald Trump starred.

How to Set Up the Exercise/Instructions:

1. Divide the class into teams of three to four students.
2. Read this: As you know by watching "The Donald" as he organizes his business teams for *The Celebrity Apprentice*, human resource management plays an important role in what Donald Trump and the participants on his separate teams need to do to be successful. For example, Donald Trump needs to be able to appraise each of the participants. And, for their part, the leaders of each of his teams need to be able to staff his or her teams with the right participants and then provide the sorts of training, incentives, and evaluations that help their companies succeed and that therefore make the participants themselves (and especially the team leaders) look like "winners" to Mr. Trump.
3. Watch several of these shows (or reruns of the shows), and then meet with your team and answer the following questions:
   a. What specific HR functions (recruiting, interviewing, and so on) can you identify Donald Trump using on this show? Make sure to give specific examples based on the show.
   b. What specific HR functions (recruiting, selecting, training, and so on) can you identify one or more of the team leaders using to help manage their teams on the show? Again, please give specific answers.
   c. Provide a specific example of how HR functions (such as recruiting, selecting, interviewing, compensating, appraising, and so on) contributed to one of the participants coming across as particularly successful to Mr. Trump. Can you provide examples of how one or more of these functions contributed to Mr. Trump telling a participant "You're fired"?
   d. Present your team's conclusions to the class. ∎

Chapter 2

Managing Equal Opportunity and Diversity

- Selected Equal Employment Opportunity Laws
- Defenses against Discrimination Allegations
- Illustrative Discriminatory Employment Practices
- The EEOC Enforcement Process
- Diversity Management and Affirmative Action Programs

When you finish studying this chapter, you should be able to:

- Summarize *the basic equal employment opportunity laws regarding age, race, sex, national origin, religion, and handicap discrimination.*

- Explain *the basic defenses against discrimination allegations.*

- Present *a summary of what employers can and cannot do with respect to illegal recruitment, selection, and promotion and layoff practices.*

- Explain *the Equal Employment Opportunity Commission enforcement process.*

INTRODUCTION

As if it didn't face enough challenges with the subprime meltdown, Citigroup also faced a possible $1 billion class-action discrimination lawsuit. Several female former employees alleged that the banking giant discriminated against women when it cut jobs in the economic turndown.

SELECTED EQUAL EMPLOYMENT OPPORTUNITY LAWS

Hardly a day goes by without reports of equal opportunity–related lawsuits at work. One survey of corporate general counsels found that employment lawsuits were their biggest litigation fears.[1] Hiring or transferring employees without understanding equal employment law is fraught with peril.

Background

Legislation barring discrimination against minorities in the United States is nothing new.[2] For example, the Fifth Amendment to the U.S. Constitution (ratified in 1791) states, "no person shall . . . be deprived of life, liberty, or property, without due process of the law."[3] Other laws made discrimination against minorities illegal by the early 1900s, at least in theory.[4] But as a practical matter, Congress and various presidents were reluctant to take dramatic action on equal employment until the early 1960s. At that point, "they were finally prompted to act primarily as a result of civil unrest among the minorities and women" who eventually became protected by the new equal rights legislation.[5]

Equal Pay Act of 1963

The **Equal Pay Act of 1963** (amended in 1972) was one of the first new laws passed. It made it unlawful to discriminate in pay on the basis of sex when jobs involve equal work—equivalent skills, effort, and responsibility—and are performed under similar working conditions. However, differences in pay do not violate the act if the difference is based on a seniority system, a merit system, a system that measures earnings by quantity or quality of production, or a differential based on any factor other than sex.

Title VII of the 1964 Civil Rights Act

What the Law Says   **Title VII of the 1964 Civil Rights Act** was another of these new laws. Title VII (amended by the 1972 Equal Employment Opportunity Act) says an employer cannot discriminate based on race, color, religion, sex, or national origin. Specifically, it states that it shall be an unlawful employment practice for an employer:[6]

1. *To fail or refuse to hire or to discharge an individual or otherwise to discriminate against any individual* with respect to his or her compensation, terms, conditions, or privileges of employment, because of such individual's race, color, religion, sex, or national origin.
2. *To limit, segregate, or classify his or her employees or applicants for employment* in any way that would deprive or tend to deprive any individual of employment opportunities or otherwise adversely affect his or her status as an employee, because of such individual's race, color, religion, sex, or national origin.

The **Equal Employment Opportunity Commission (EEOC)** was instituted by Title VII. It consists of five members, appointed by the president with the advice and consent of the Senate. Each member of the EEOC serves 5 years. The EEOC has a staff of thousands to assist it in administering the civil rights law.

The EEOC receives and investigates job discrimination complaints. When it finds reasonable cause that the charges are justified, it attempts to reach an agreement. If this fails, the EEOC can go directly to court to enforce the law. Discrimination charges may be filed by the EEOC on behalf of an aggrieved individual, as well as by the individuals themselves. We explain this procedure later in this chapter.

Executive Orders

Under executive orders that U.S. presidents issued years ago, most employers who do business with the U.S. government have an obligation beyond that imposed by Title VII. Executive Orders 11246 and 11375 don't just ban discrimination; they require that contractors take **affirmative action** to ensure equal employment opportunity (we also explain affirmative action later in this chapter). These orders also established the **Office of Federal Contract Compliance Programs (OFCCP)** within the Labor Department. It is responsible for ensuring the compliance of federal contracts.[7] President Obama recently directed more funds and staffing to the OFCCP.[8]

Age Discrimination in Employment Act of 1967

The **Age Discrimination in Employment Act (ADEA) of 1967,** as amended, makes it unlawful to discriminate against employees or applicants for employment who are 40 years of age or older, effectively ending most mandatory retirement.[9]

Vocational Rehabilitation Act of 1973

The **Vocational Rehabilitation Act of 1973** requires employers with federal contracts over $2,500 to take affirmative action for the employment of handicapped persons. The act does not require hiring an unqualified person. It does require that an employer take steps to accommodate a handicapped worker unless doing so imposes an undue hardship on the employer.

Pregnancy Discrimination Act of 1978

Congress passed the **Pregnancy Discrimination Act (PDA)** in 1978 as an amendment to Title VII. The act broadened the definition of sex discrimination to encompass pregnancy, childbirth, or related medical conditions. It prohibits using these for discrimination in hiring, promotion, suspension or discharge, or any other term or condition of employment. For example, if an employer offers its employees disability coverage, then the employer must treat pregnancy and childbirth like any other disability.[10]

Progressive human resource thinking notwithstanding, several years ago an auto dealership fired an employee after she told them she was pregnant. The reason?

Allegedly, "in case I ended up throwing up or cramping in one of their vehicles. They said pregnant women do that sometimes, and I could cause an accident."[11]

Federal Agency Guidelines

The federal agencies charged with ensuring compliance with these laws and executive orders issue their own implementing guidelines. The overall purpose of these **federal agency guidelines** is to specify the procedures these agencies recommend employers follow in complying with the equal opportunity laws.

Uniform Guidelines on Employee Selection Procedures   The EEOC, Civil Service Commission, Department of Labor, and Department of Justice have approved uniform guidelines for employers.[12] They set forth "highly recommended" guidelines regarding matters such as record keeping, preemployment inquiries, and affirmative action. The OFCCP has its own *Manual of Guidelines.* The American Psychological Association published its own (nonlegally binding) *Standards for Educational and Psychological Testing.*

Historically, all these guidelines have fleshed out the procedures to use in complying with equal employment laws. For example, they lay out acceptable procedures for validating—determining the accuracy and usefulness of—selection tools such as tests.[13]

Selected Court Decisions Regarding Equal Employment Opportunity (EEO)

Several early (pre-1980s) court decisions helped to form the interpretive foundation for EEO laws such as those involving sexual harassment. We summarize some important decisions in this section.

Griggs v. Duke Power Company   *Griggs v. Duke Power Company* (1971) was a landmark case because the Supreme Court used it to define unfair discrimination. In this case, a suit was brought against the Duke Power Company on behalf of Willie Griggs, an applicant for a job as a coal handler. The company required its coal handlers to be high school graduates. Griggs claimed that this requirement was illegally discriminatory because it wasn't related to success on the job and because it resulted in more blacks than whites being rejected.

Griggs won the case. The decision of the Court was unanimous, and in his written opinion, Chief Justice Burger laid out three guidelines affecting equal employment legislation. First, the court ruled that discrimination on the part of the employer *need not be overt*; in other words, the employer does not have to be shown to have intentionally discriminated against the employee or applicant—it need only be shown that discrimination took place. Second, the court held that an employment practice (in this case requiring the high school diploma) must be shown to be *job related* if it has an unequal impact on members of a **protected class.** In the words of Justice Burger,

> The act proscribes not only overt discrimination but also practices that are fair in form, but discriminatory in operation. The touchstone is business necessity. If an employment practice which operates to exclude Negroes cannot be shown to be related to job performance the practice is prohibited.[14]

Third, Burger's opinion placed the burden of proof on the employer to show that the hiring practice is job related. Thus the *employer* must show that the employment practice (in this case, requiring a high school diploma) is needed to perform the job satisfactorily if it has a disparate impact on (unintentionally discriminates against) members of a protected class.

Albemarle Paper Company v. Moody   In the *Griggs* case, the Supreme Court decided that a screening tool (such as a test) had to be job related or valid—that is, performance on the test must relate to performance on the job. The 1975 *Albemarle Paper Company v. Moody* case is important because it helped to clarify what the employer must do to prove that the test or other screening tool is related to performance on the job. For example, the Court said that before using a test to screen job candidates, the performance standards for the job in question should be clear and unambiguous. That way, the employer can identify which employees were performing better than others were (and thus whether the tests were effective). The Court here also cited the EEOC guidelines concerning acceptable selection procedures, and made these guidelines the "law of the land."[15]

The Civil Rights Act of 1991

Subsequent Supreme Court rulings in the 1980s had the effect of limiting the protection of women and minority groups under equal employment laws (for instance, by placing more burden for showing discrimination on the employee); this prompted Congress to pass a new Civil Rights Act. The first President George Bush signed the **Civil Rights Act of 1991 (CRA 1991)** into law in November 1991.

First, CRA 1991 addressed the issue of *burden of proof.* We'll discuss filing and responding to a discrimination charge later in this chapter, but assume for a moment that the plaintiff (say, a rejected applicant) demonstrates that an employment practice (such as a test) has a disparate (or "adverse") impact on a particular group.[16] Requiring a college degree for a job would have an adverse impact on some minority groups, for instance.[17]

Then, once the plaintiff shows such disparate impact, the *employer* now has the *burden of proving* that the challenged practice is job related for the position in question. For example, the employer has to show that lifting 100 pounds is actually required for the position in question—that it is a business necessity.

CRA 1991 also makes it easier to sue for *money damages.* It provides that an employee who is claiming *intentional discrimination* (which is called **disparate treatment**) can ask for both compensatory damages and punitive damages, if he or she can show the employer engaged in discrimination "with malice or reckless indifference to the federally protected rights of an aggrieved individual." (See also the *Global Issues in HR* box.)

Finally, under CRA 1991, an employer generally can't avoid liability by proving it would have taken the same action—such as terminating someone—even without the discriminatory motive. If there is any such motive, the practice may be unlawful.[18]

Sexual Harassment

Sexual harassment is a violation of Title VII when such conduct has the purpose or effect of substantially interfering with a person's work performance or creating an

Global Issues in HR: Applying Equal Employment Law in a Global Setting

Globalization complicates the task of complying with equal employment laws. For example, Dell announced big additions to its workforce in India. Are U.S. citizens working for Dell abroad covered by U.S. equal opportunity laws? Are non-U.S. citizens covered? In practice, the answers depend on U.S. laws, international treaties, and the laws of the countries in which the U.S. firms are doing business. For example, the Civil Rights Act of 1991 specifically covers U.S. employees of U.S. firms working abroad. But in practice, the laws of the country in which the U.S. citizen is working may take precedence.[19] Table 2.1 provides guidelines for when U.S. equal employment law applies.[20]

Table 2.1 Guidelines For When U.S. Employment Discrimination Laws (Title VII, ADEA, ADA) Apply to International Employers

No.	GUIDELINES
1.	U.S. employment discrimination laws apply to jobs located inside the United States when the employer is a U.S. entity and the employee is authorized to work in the United States.
2.	U.S. employment discrimination laws *do not* apply to jobs located inside the United States when the employer is a foreign entity exempted by a treaty, even though the employee is authorized to work in the United States.
3.	U.S. employment discrimination laws apply to jobs located inside the United States when the employer is a foreign entity *not* exempted by a treaty and the employee is authorized to work in the United States.
4.	U.S. employment discrimination laws *do not* apply to jobs located outside the United States when the employer is a foreign entity, even though the employee is a U.S. citizen.
5.	U.S. employment discrimination laws *do not* apply to jobs located outside the United States even if the employer is a U.S. entity, if the employees are foreign citizens.
6.	U.S. employment discrimination laws apply to jobs located outside the United States when the employer is a U.S. entity and the employee is a U.S. citizen, if compliance with U.S. laws would *not* violate foreign laws.

Source: Richard Posthuma et al., "Applying U.S. Employment Discrimination Laws to International Employees: Advice for Scientists and Practitioners," *Personnel Psychology*, 2006 (59) p. 710. Reprinted by permission of Wiley-Blackwell.

intimidating, hostile, or offensive work environment. The EEOC guidelines further assert that employers have a duty to maintain workplaces free of sexual harassment and intimidation. The Civil Rights Act of 1991 added teeth to this by permitting victims of intentional discrimination, including sexual harassment, to have jury trials and to collect compensatory damages in cases in which the employer acted with "malice or reckless indifference" to the individual's rights.[21]

The EEOC guidelines define **sexual harassment** as unwelcome sexual advances, requests for sexual favors, and other verbal or physical conduct of a sexual nature that takes place under any of the following conditions:

1. Submission is explicitly or implicitly a term or condition of an individual's employment.

2. Submission to or rejection of such conduct is the basis for employment decisions affecting such individual.
3. Such conduct has the purpose or effect of unreasonably interfering with an individual's work performance or creating an intimidating, hostile, or offensive work environment.

Sexual harassment laws also cover occasions when women harass men and when there is same-sex harassment.[22] In one recent year, the EEOC received 13,867 sexual harassment charges, 15.9% of which were filed by males.[23]

Proving Sexual Harassment

An employee can prove sexual harassment in three main ways:

Quid Pro Quo   The most direct is to prove that rejecting a supervisor's advances adversely affected a "tangible employment action" such as hiring, firing, promoting, or compensating. Thus in one case the employee showed that continued job success and advancement were dependent on her agreeing to her supervisor's sexual demands.

Hostile Environment Created by Supervisors   One need not show that the harassment had tangible consequences such as a demotion. For example, in one case, the court found that a male supervisor's sexual harassment had substantially affected a female employee's emotional and psychological ability to the point that she felt she had to quit her job. Even though no direct threats or promises were made in exchange for sexual advances, the fact that the advances interfered with the woman's performance and created an offensive work environment were enough to prove that sexual harassment had occurred. However, U.S. Supreme Court Justice Antonin Scalia has said courts must carefully distinguish between "simple teasing" and truly abusive behavior.[24]

Hostile Environment Created by Coworkers or Nonemployees   An employee's coworkers or customers can also cause the employer to be held responsible for sexual harassment. In one case, the court held that a sexually provocative server's uniform that the employer required led to lewd customer comments. When she complained she was fired. Because the employer could not show a job-related necessity for requiring such a uniform, the court ruled that the employer, in effect, was responsible for the sexually harassing behavior. Such abhorrent client behavior is more likely when the clients are in positions of power, and when they have less reason to think they'll be penalized.[25]

Sexual Harassment Court Decisions

The U.S. Supreme Court used the *Meritor Savings Bank, FSB* v. *Vinson* case to endorse the EEOC's guidelines on sexual harassment. Then two other U.S. Supreme Court decisions further clarified the law on sexual harassment.

In the first, *Burlington Industries* v. *Ellerth*, the employee accused her supervisor of *quid pro quo* harassment. She said her boss propositioned and threatened her with demotion if she did not respond. The threats were not carried out, and she was in fact promoted. In the second case, *Faragher* v. *City of Boca Raton,* the employee accused the employer of condoning a hostile work environment: She said she quit her lifeguard job after repeated taunts from other lifeguards. The Court ruled for the employees in both cases.

The Court's decisions in these cases have several important implications for employers.

First, the decisions make it clear that in a *quid pro quo* case it is *not* necessary for the employee to have suffered tangible job action (such as being demoted) to win the case.

Second, the decisions spell out an important defense against harassment suits. The Court said that an employer could defend itself by showing two things. First, "that the employer exercised care to prevent and correct promptly any sexually harassing behavior."[26] Second, that the plaintiff "unreasonably failed to take advantage of any preventive or corrective opportunities provided by the employer." The Supreme Court said that the employee's failing to use formal organizational reporting systems would satisfy the second component.

Sensible employers promptly promulgated strong harassment policies, trained managers and employees regarding their responsibilities, instituted reporting processes, investigated charges promptly, and then took corrective actions promptly, as required.[27]

Sexual Harassment Causes

Sexual harassment is more likely to occur under certain circumstances. The most important factor is a permissive social climate, one where employees conclude there's a risk to victims for complaining, that complaints won't be taken seriously, and that there's a lack of sanctions against offenders.[28] Minority women are particularly at risk.[29]

People also differ in what they view as offensive. In one study, about 58% of employees reported experiencing at least some potentially harassment-type behaviors at work. Of these, about 25% found it fun and flattering and about half viewed it as benign. But on closer examination, about four times as many men as women found the behavior flattering or benign.[30] "Women perceive a broader range of socio-sexual behaviors as harassing."[31]

Most people assume that sexual motives drive sexual harassment, but that's not always so. **Gender harassment** is "a form of hostile environment harassment that appears to be motivated by hostility toward individuals who violate gender ideals." Thus in one case, her bosses told a high-performing female accountant to "walk more femininely [and] dress more femininely."[32]

Adding to the causes is the unfortunate fact that most victims don't sue or complain. "The few women who do formally complain do so only after encountering frequent, severe sexual harassment; at that point, considerable damage may have already occurred."[33] The harassers themselves sometimes don't even realize that their abominable behavior is offending others.[34]

What the Manager/Employer Should Do

Given this, employers should do two things: They should take steps (such as issuing a strong policy statement) to ensure harassment does not take place. Second, once apprised of such a situation, they should take immediate corrective action, even if the offending party is a nonemployee.[35] (See the *HR in Practice* box for specific steps.)

HR in Practice: What Employers Should Do to Minimize Liability in Sexual Harassment Claims

1. Take all harassment complaints seriously.

2. Issue a strong policy statement condemning harassment. EEOC standards state that such a policy should contain several things, including,
   - A clear explanation of the prohibited conduct;
   - Assurance of protection against retaliation;
   - A clear and confidential complaint process;
   - Prompt, thorough, and impartial investigations; and
   - An assurance that the employer will take immediate and appropriate corrective action.[36]

3. Inform all employees about the policy prohibiting sexual harassment and of their rights.

4. Develop and implement a complaint procedure.

5. Establish a management response system that includes an immediate reaction and investigation by senior management.[37]

6. Commence management training sessions with supervisors and managers, to increase their awareness of the issues.[38]

7. Discipline managers and employees involved in sexual harassment.

8. Keep thorough records of complaints, investigations, and actions taken.

9. Conduct exit interviews that uncover any complaints and that acknowledge by signature the reasons for leaving.

10. Republish the sexual harassment policy periodically (see Figure 2.1).

11. Encourage upward communication to discover any evidence of sexual harassment.[39]

Figure 2.1 What to Cover in a Sexual Harassment Policy

The EEOC says the antiharassment policy should contain a clear explanation of the prohibited conduct; assurance of protection against retaliation for employees who make complaints or provide information related to such complaints; a clearly described complaint process that provides confidentiality and accessible avenues of complaint as well as prompt, thorough, and impartial investigations; and clear assurance that the employer will take immediate and appropriate corrective action where harassment has occurred.

Source: http://www.eeoc.gov/policy/docs/currentissues.html, accessed May 18, 2010.

Unfortunately, taking what courts call "reasonable" steps to prevent harassment may not be enough. In one study, researchers surveyed about 6,000 U.S. military employees. Their findings showed that reporting incidents of harassment often triggered retaliation. Under such conditions, it's no wonder that for many of these employees, the most "reasonable" thing to do was to avoid reporting. Managers therefore must ensure that the organization's climate (including management's real willingness to eradicate harassment) supports employees who feel harassed.[40]

What the Employee Can Do

Employees should understand how courts define sexual harassment. For example, "hostile environment" sexual harassment generally means that the discriminatory intimidation was sufficiently severe to alter the conditions of employment. Courts in these cases look at whether the discriminatory conduct is frequent or severe; whether it is physically threatening or humiliating or a mere offensive utterance; and whether it unreasonably interferes with an employee's work performance. They also look at whether an employee welcomed the conduct, or instead immediately made it clear that the conduct was unwelcome. The steps an employee can take include:

1. Be aware of and follow the employer's harassment procedure.
2. File a verbal contemporaneous complaint with the harasser and the harasser's boss stating that the unwanted overtures are unwelcome and should cease.
3. Write and deliver to the accused a polite low-key letter that does three things: provides a detailed statement of the facts, describes his or her feelings and what damage the writer thinks the behavior caused, and states that he or she would like the relationship be on a purely professional basis.
4. If the unwelcome conduct does not cease, file verbal and written reports with the harasser's manager and/or the human resource director.
5. If the letters and appeals to the employer do not suffice, the accuser should turn to the local office of the EEOC to file the necessary claim.
6. If the harassment is of a serious nature, the employee can also consult an attorney about suing the harasser for assault and battery and intentional infliction of emotional distress and to recover compensatory and punitive damages.

The Americans with Disabilities Act

What Is the ADA?   The **Americans with Disabilities Act (ADA)** of 1990 prohibits employment discrimination against qualified disabled individuals.[41] It also requires that employers make "reasonable accommodations" for physical or mental limitations, unless doing so imposes an "undue hardship" on the business.

Under the ADA, "impairment" includes any physiological disorder or condition, cosmetic disfigurement, or anatomical loss affecting one or more of several body systems, or any mental or psychological disorder.[42] However, the act doesn't list specific disabilities. Instead, the EEOC's regulations provide that an individual is disabled if he or she has a physical or mental impairment that substantially limits one or more major life activities. The act does set forth certain conditions that it does not regard as disabilities, including homosexuality, voyeurism, compulsive gambling, pyromania, and certain disorders resulting from the person's currently using illegal drugs.[43]

Simply being disabled does not qualify someone for a job, of course. Instead, the act prohibits discrimination against qualified individuals—those who, with (or without) a reasonable accommodation, can carry out the essential functions of the job. This means that the individual must have the requisite skills, educational background, and experience to do the job's essential functions. A job function is essential when it is the reason the position exists, or because the function is so specialized, the employer hires the person doing the job for his or her expertise or ability to perform that particular function.[44]

Reasonable Accommodation   If the individual can't perform the job as currently structured, the employer is required to make a reasonable accommodation, unless doing so would present an undue hardship. *Reasonable accommodation* might include redesigning the job, modifying work schedules, or modifying or acquiring equipment (such as adding curb ramps and widening door openings).[45]

Court cases illustrate what "reasonable accommodation" means. For example, a Walmart door greeter was treated for back problems. When she returned to work, she asked to sit on a stool while on duty. The employer rejected her request, contending that standing was an essential part of the greeter's job. She sued, but the federal court agreed with the employer that door greeters must act in an "aggressively hospitable manner," which can't be done sitting.[46]

The ADA in Practice   By most measures, workplace disabilities are on the rise, and employers need to accommodate increasing numbers of disabled employees and ADA complaints.[47]

However, employers usually prevailed. A main reason is that employees failed to show that they were disabled and qualified to do the job.[48] Doing so is more complicated than proving that one is of a particular age, race, or gender.

A U.S. Supreme Court decision typifies what plaintiffs faced. An assembly-line worker sued Toyota, arguing that carpal tunnel syndrome and tendonitis prevented her from doing her job (*Toyota Motor Manufacturing of Kentucky, Inc.* v. *Williams*). The Court ruled that the ADA covers carpal tunnel syndrome and tendonitis if her impairments affect not only her job performance but her daily living activities too. Here, the employee admitted that she could perform personal tasks and chores such as washing her face and doing laundry. The court said the disability must be central to the employee's daily living (not just job) to qualify under the ADA.[49]

Many other judgments similarly denied the plaintiff's claim.[50] A federal judge held that Home Depot did not violate the ADA by barring a deaf worker from training to operate a forklift. The firm's policies prohibit those who can't hear store associates' warnings from holding such positions.[51] On the other hand, one U.S. Circuit Court of Appeals held that punctuality was not an essential job function for a laboratory assistant who was habitually tardy. (The court decided he could perform the job's $7^1/2$ hours of data entry even if he arrived late.[52])

The types of disabilities alleged in ADA charges have been surprising. Mental disabilities account for the greatest number of ADA claims.[53] The ADA does protect employees with certain intellectual disabilities, including those with IQs below 70 to 75.[54] However, employers need not accommodate all mental disabilities. In one case, a social worker threatened to throw her coworker out a window and to "kick her [butt]." After transfer to another job, a doctor diagnosed her as paranoid. After repeatedly telling her supervisor she was "ready to kill her," she was fired. She sued under ADA. The court dismissed her case because, although she had a debilitating mental illness, ADA does not require retention of employees who make threats.[55]

The "New" ADA   The era in which employers prevail in most ADA claims probably ended January 1, 2009. On that day, the ADA Amendments Act (ADAAA) of 2008 became effective. The EEOC had been interpreting what "substantially limits" means very narrowly. The new ADAAA's basic effect will be to make it much easier for employees to show that their disability is influencing one of their "major life activities." It does this by adding examples like reading, concentrating, thinking, sleeping, and communicating to the list of ADA major life activities. Employers will henceforth have to redouble their efforts to ensure they're complying with the ADA.[56]

Legal Obligations   There are at least three practical ADA legal obligations for employers:

- Employers may not make preemployment inquiries about a person's disability, but they may ask questions about the person's ability to perform specific job functions.
- The timing of any offer is important. The central issue is this: In the event the hiring employer rescinds an offer after the medical exam, the applicant must be able to identify the specific reason for the rejection. For example, in one case, the courts found that American Airlines had violated the ADA by not making a "real" offer to three candidates before requiring them to take their medical exams because American still hadn't checked their background references. In this case, the medical exams showed the candidates had HIV and American rescinded their offers, thus violating the ADA.[57]
- Employers must make a reasonable accommodation, unless doing so would result in undue hardship.

Other Implications for Employers and Managers   The ADA does give managers and employers leeway in what they can do or ask.[58]

First, employers may require that the employee provide documentation of the disorder and assess what effect that disorder has on the employee's job performance. Employers may also ask questions like these: Does the employee have a disability that substantially limits a major life activity? Is the employee qualified to do the job? Can the employee perform the essential functions of the job? Can you provide a reasonable accommodation?[59]

Second, employers generally "do not need to allow *misconduct or erratic performance* (including absences and tardiness), even if that behavior is linked to the disability."[60]

Third, the employer does not have to *create a new job* for the disabled worker or reassign that person to a light-duty position for an indefinite period, unless such a position exists.[61]

Fourth, one expert advises, *"don't treat employees* as if they are disabled." If they can control their conditions (for instance, through medication), they usually won't be considered disabled. However, if they are treated as disabled (for instance, with respect to the jobs they're assigned), they'll normally be "regarded as" disabled and protected under the ADA.[62]

Many employers simply take a progressive approach. Common employer concerns about people with disabilities (for instance, that they have more accidents) are generally baseless.[63] So, for example, Walgreens has a goal of filling at least one third of the jobs at its two large distribution centers with people with disabilities.[64]

Improving Productivity Through HRIS: Accommodating Disabled Employees
Technology makes it easier for employers to accommodate disabled employees. For example, the National Federation of the Blind estimates that about 70% of working-age blind adults are unemployed or underemployed, although they have the requisite education. Yet numerous technologies would enable most of these people to work successfully. For example, a screen-reading program called JAWS converts text from computer screen into Braille while speaking it.[65] Employees with mobility impairments benefit from voice recognition software that allows them to input information into their computers and interactively communicate (for instance, via e-mail) without touching a keyboard. Real-time translation captioning enables employees with hearing and/or speech impairments to participate in lectures and meetings. Arizona had IBM Global Services create a disability-friendly Web site, "Arizona@YourService," to help link prospective employees and others to various agencies.[66]

Genetic Information Non-Discrimination Act of 2008 (GINA)

GINA prohibits discrimination by health insurers and employers based on people's genetic information. Specifically, it prohibits the use of genetic information in employment, prohibits the intentional acquisition of genetic information about applicants and employees, and imposes strict confidentiality requirements.[67]

The Federal Employment Non-Discrimination Act (ENDA)

ENDA would prohibit workplace discrimination based on sexual orientation and gender identity if Congress passes it.[68] Many states bar discrimination at work based on sexual orientation.[69]

State and Local Equal Employment Opportunity Laws

In addition to the federal laws, all states and many local governments also prohibit employment discrimination.

Most state and local laws cover employers not covered by federal legislation (such as those with fewer than 15 employees). For example, one State of Florida statute prohibits wage rate discrimination based on sex in employer and labor organizations not subject to the federal Fair Labor Standards Act.[70]

State and local equal employment opportunity agencies (often called *human resources commissions,* or *fair employment commissions*) also play a role in the equal employment compliance process. When the EEOC receives a discrimination charge, it usually defers it for a time to the relevant state and local agencies. If these agencies don't achieve satisfactory remedies, the charges are referred back to the EEOC for resolution.

Summary Table 2.2 summarizes selected equal employment opportunity legislation, executive orders, and agency guidelines.

Table 2.2 Summary of Important Equal Employment Opportunity Actions

ACTION	WHAT IT DOES
Title VII of 1964 Civil Rights Act, as amended	Bars discrimination because of race, color, religion, sex, or national origin; instituted EEOC
Executive orders	Prohibit employment discrimination by employers with federal contracts of more than $10,000 (and their subcontractors); require affirmative action programs
Federal agency guidelines	Indicate policy covering discrimination based on sex, national origin, and religion, as well as on employee selection procedures; for example, require validation of tests
Supreme Court decisions: *Griggs* v. *Duke Power Company, Albemarle Paper Company v. Moody*	Ruled that job requirements must be related to job success; that discrimination need not be overt to be proved; that the burden of proof is on the employer to prove the qualification is valid
Equal Pay Act of 1963	Requires equal pay for men and women for performing similar work
Age Discrimination in Employment Act of 1967	Prohibits discriminating against a person aged 40 or over in any area of employment because of age
State and local laws	Often cover organizations too small to be covered by federal laws
Vocational Rehabilitation Act of 1973	Requires affirmative action to employ and promote qualified handicapped persons and prohibits discrimination against handicapped persons
Pregnancy Discrimination Act of 1978	Prohibits discrimination in employment against pregnant women, or related conditions
Vietnam Era Veterans' Readjustment Assistance Act of 1974	Requires affirmative action in employment for veterans of the Vietnam War era
Wards Cove v. *Atonio,* and *Patterson* v. *McLean Credit Union*	Made it more difficult to prove a case of unlawful discrimination against an employer
Americans with Disabilities Act of 1990	Requires most employers to make reasonable accommodations for disabled employees at work; prohibits discrimination
Civil Rights Act of 1991	Places burden of proof back on employer and permits compensatory and punitive money damages for discrimination
Genetic Information Non-Discrimination Act of 2008 (GINA)	Prohibits discrimination by health insurers and employers based on people's genetic information

DEFENSES AGAINST DISCRIMINATION ALLEGATIONS

What Is Adverse Impact?

To understand how employers defend themselves against employment discrimination claims, we should first briefly review some basic legal concepts.

Adverse impact plays a central role in discriminatory practice allegations. Under the Civil Rights Act of 1991, a person who believes he or she has been unintentionally discriminated against need only establish a prima facie case of discrimination; this means showing that the employer's selection procedures had an adverse impact on a protected minority group. *Adverse impact* "refers to the total employment process that results in a significantly higher percentage of a protected group in the candidate population being rejected for employment, placement, or promotion."[71] "Employers may not institute an employment practice that causes a disparate [adverse] impact on a particular class of people unless they can show that the practice is job related and necessary."[72]

What does this mean? If a minority or other protected group applicant for the job feels he or she has been discriminated against, the applicant need only show that the selection procedures resulted in an adverse impact on his or her minority group. (There are several ways to do this. One is by showing, say, that 80% of the white applicants passed the test, but only 20% of the black applicants passed; if this is the case, a black applicant has a prima facie case proving adverse impact.) Then, it becomes the employer's burden to prove that its test, application blank, interview, or the like is a valid predictor of performance on the job and that it was applied fairly and equitably to both minorities and nonminorities.[73]

Discrimination law distinguishes between disparate *treatment* and disparate *impact*. Disparate treatment means intentional discrimination. It "requires no more than a finding that women (or protected minority group members) were intentionally treated differently . . . because of their gender (or minority status)." *Disparate impact* claims do not require proof of discriminatory intent. Instead, the plaintiff must show that there is a significant disparity between the proportion of (say) women in the available labor pool and the proportion hired and that there's an apparently neutral employment practice (such as word-of-mouth advertising) causing the disparity.[74] Proving that there was a business necessity for the practice is usually the defense for disparate impact claims.

Bringing a Case of Discrimination: Summary   Assume that an employer rejects someone for a job based on a test score (or some other employment practice, such as interview questions or application blank responses). Further, assume that the person believes that he or she was discriminated against due to being in a protected class and decides to sue the employer.

All he or she has to do is show (to the court's satisfaction) that the employer's test had an adverse impact on members of his or her minority group. Then, the burden of proof shifts to the employer, which then has the burden of defending itself against the charges of discrimination.

The employer can then use two defenses. These are the **bona fide occupational qualification (BFOQ)** defense and the business necessity defense. Either can justify an employment practice that has been shown to have an adverse impact on the members of a minority group. (A third defense is that the decision was made on the basis of legitimate nondiscriminatory reasons, such as poor performance, having nothing to do with the alleged prohibited discrimination.)

Bona Fide Occupational Qualification

One approach an employer can use is to claim that the employment practice is a bona fide occupational qualification for performing the job. Specifically, Title VII provides that

> it should not be an unlawful employment practice for an employer to hire an employee . . . on the basis of religion, sex, or national origin in those certain instances where religion, sex, or national origin is a bona fide occupational qualification reasonably necessary to the normal operation of that particular business or enterprise.

For example, an employer can use age as a BFOQ to defend itself against a disparate treatment (intentional discrimination) charge when federal requirements impose a compulsory age limit, such as a ceiling of age 65 for pilots.[75] Actors required for youthful or elderly roles suggest other instances when age may be a BFOQ, although the courts set the bar high: The reason for the discrimination must go to the essence of the business. The BFOQ defense is not explicitly allowed for race or color.

A Texas man recently filed a complaint against Hooters of America, alleging that one of its franchisees would not hire him as a waiter because it "merely wishes to exploit female sexuality as a marketing tool to attract customers and insure profitability" and so was limiting hiring to females.[76] Hooters argued a BFOQ defense before reaching a confidential settlement with him.

Business Necessity

The **business necessity** defense requires showing that there is an overriding business purpose for the discriminatory practice and that the practice is therefore acceptable.

It's not easy to prove that a practice is a business necessity. The Supreme Court has made it clear that business necessity does not encompass such matters as avoiding inconvenience. One Court of Appeals held that *business necessity* means an "irresistible demand" and that to be retained the practice "must not only directly foster safety and efficiency" but be essential to these goals.[77]

Thus it is not easy to prove that a practice is required for business necessity. For example, an employer cannot generally discharge employees whose wages have been garnished merely because garnishment (requiring the employer to divert part of the person's wages to pay his or her debts) creates an inconvenience. On the other hand, many employers have used this defense successfully. Thus, in *Spurlock* v. *United Airlines*, a minority candidate sued United Airlines, stating that its requirements that a pilot candidate have 500 flight hours and a college degree were unfairly discriminatory. The Court agreed that these requirements did have an adverse impact on members of the person's minority group. However, the Court held that in light of the cost of the training program and the tremendous human and economic risks involved in hiring unqualified candidates, the selection standards were a business necessity.[78]

Attempts by employers to show that their selection tests or other screening practices are valid are an example of the business necessity defense. Where such validity can be established, the courts have often supported the use of the test or other practice as a business necessity. Used in this context, the word *validity* means the degree to which the test or other employment practice is related to or predicts performance on the job. We discuss validation in Chapter 4.

ILLUSTRATIVE DISCRIMINATORY EMPLOYMENT PRACTICES

A Note on What You Can and Cannot Do

In this section, we present several illustrations of what managers can and cannot do under equal employment laws. But before proceeding, keep in mind that most federal laws, such as Title VII, do not expressly ban preemployment questions about an applicant's race, color, religion, sex, age, or national origin. Similarly:

> With the exception of personnel policies calling for outright discrimination against the members of some protected group, it is not really the intrinsic nature of an employer's personnel policies or practices that the courts object to. Instead, it is the result of applying a policy or practice in a particular way or in a particular context that leads to an adverse impact on some protected group.[79]

For example, it's not illegal to ask a job candidate about her marital status. You can ask such a question as long as you can show either that you do not discriminate or that you can defend the practice as a BFOQ or business necessity.

In other words, illustrative inquiries and practices such as those summarized on the next few pages are not illegal per se. But, in practice, there are two reasons to avoid such questionable practices. First, although federal law may not bar such questions, many state and local laws do. Second, the EEOC has said that it disapproves of such practices as asking women their marital status. Employers who use such practices thus increase their chances of having to defend themselves.

Recruitment

Word of Mouth   You cannot rely on word-of-mouth dissemination of information about job opportunities when your workforce is substantially all white or all members of some other class such as all female or all Hispanic. Doing so might reduce the likelihood that others will become aware of the jobs.

Misleading Information   It is unlawful to give false or misleading information to members of any group or to fail to advise them of work opportunities and the procedures for obtaining them.

Help Wanted Ads   "Help wanted—male" and "Help wanted—female" advertising classifieds are violations of laws forbidding sex discrimination in employment unless sex is a BFOQ for the job advertised.[80] Also, you cannot advertise in any way that suggests that the employer discriminates against applicants based on age (as in "young" man or woman).

Selection Standards

Educational Requirements   An educational requirement (like a high school degree) may be held illegal when (1) it can be shown that minority groups are less likely to possess the educational qualification, and (2) such qualifications are also not job related.[81]

Tests   According to former Chief Justice Burger, "Nothing in the [Title VII] act precludes the use of testing or measuring procedures; obviously they are useful. What Congress has forbidden is giving these devices and mechanisms controlling force unless they are demonstrating a *reasonable measure of job performance*." But remember that the fact that it screens out a disproportionate number of minorities or women is not *by itself* sufficient to prove that the test *unfairly* discriminates. One must also show that the test results are not job related.

Preference to Relatives   You cannot give preference to relatives of your current employees with respect to employment opportunities if your current employees are substantially nonminority.

Height, Weight, and Physical Characteristics   Few applicants or employees can demonstrate weight-based disability (in other words that they are 100% above their ideal weight and there is a physiological or psychological cause for their obesity). Few are thus entitled to reasonable accommodations under the ADA. However, some minority groups have a higher incidence of obesity, so employers must ensure that their weight rules aren't adversely impacting those groups.

Managers still must be vigilant against stigmatizing obese people. Studies leave little doubt that obese individuals are less likely to be hired, less likely to receive promotions, more likely to get less-desirable sales assignments, and more likely to receive poor customer service as customers.[82]

Health Questions   Under the ADA, "Employers are generally prohibited from asking questions about applicants' medical history or requiring pre-employment physical examinations." However, one can use such questions and exams once the job offer has been extended to determine that the applicant can safely perform the job.[83]

Arrest Records   You cannot ask about or use a person's arrest record to disqualify him or her for a position because there is always a presumption of innocence until proof of guilt.[84] In addition, arrest records in general have not been valid for predicting job performance, and a higher percentage of minorities than nonminorities have arrest records.

Application Forms   Employment applications generally shouldn't contain questions pertaining, for instance, to applicants' disabilities, workers' compensation history, age, arrest record, marital status, or U.S. citizenship. Personal information required for legitimate reasons (such as who to contact in case of emergency) are best collected after you've hired the person.[85]

Sample Discriminatory Promotion, Transfer, and Layoff Procedures

Any employment practices regarding pay, promotion, termination, discipline, or benefits that (1) the employer applies differently to different classes of persons, (2) have the effect of adversely affecting members of a protected group, and (3) cannot be shown to be required as a BFOQ or business necessity may be illegally discriminatory.[86] For example, employers may not discriminate against employees in connection with their benefits plans.[87]

Uniforms   When it comes to discriminatory uniforms and suggestive attire, courts frequently side with the employee. For example, requiring waitresses to wear sexually suggestive attire as a condition of employment has been ruled as violating Title VII in many cases.[88]

THE EEOC ENFORCEMENT PROCESS

Processing a Charge

File Claim   The EEOC enforcement process begins with someone filing a claim.[89] Under CRA 1991, the discrimination claim must be filed within 300 days (when there is a similar state law) or 180 days (where there is no similar state law) after the alleged incident took place (two years for the Equal Pay Act).[90] The filing must be in writing and under oath, by (or on behalf of) the aggrieved person or by a member of the EEOC who has reasonable cause to believe that a violation occurred. In practice, the EEOC typically defers a person's charge to the relevant state or local regulatory agency; if the latter waives jurisdiction or cannot obtain a satisfactory solution to the charge, they refer it back to the EEOC. The number of private-sector discrimination charges filed with the EEOC was about 93,277 in one recent year.[91]

After a charge is filed (or the state or local deferral period has ended), the EEOC has 10 days to serve notice of the charge on the employer. The EEOC then investigates the charge to determine whether there is reasonable cause to believe it is true; it is supposed to make this determination within 120 days. If it finds no reasonable cause, the EEOC must dismiss the charge, in which case the person who filed the charge has 90 days to file a suit on his or her own behalf. If it does find reasonable cause, the EEOC must attempt to conciliate. If this conciliation is not satisfactory, the EEOC may bring a civil suit in a federal district court or issue a notice of right to sue to the person who filed the charge. Figure 2.2 summarizes important questions an employer should ask upon receiving notice from the EEOC of a bias complaint.

Figure 2.2 Questions to Ask When an Employer Receives Notice that EEOC Has Filed a Bias Claim

1. Exactly what is the charge and is your company covered by the relevant statutes? (For example, Title VII and the American with Disabilities Act generally apply only to employers with 15 or more employees; the Age Discrimination in Employment Act applies to employers with 20 or more employees; but the Equal Pay Act applies to virtually all employers with one or more employees.) Did the employee file his or her charge on time, and was it processed in a timely manner by the EEOC?

2. What protected group does the employee belong to? Is the EEOC claiming disparate impact or disparate treatment?

3. Are there any obvious bases upon which you can challenge and/or rebut the claim? For example, would the employer have taken the action if the person did not belong to a protected group? Does the person's personnel file support the action taken by the employer?

4. If it is a sexual harassment claim, are there offensive comments, calendars, posters, screensavers, and so on on display in the company?

5. In terms of the practicality of defending your company against this claim, who are the supervisors who actually took the allegedly discriminatory actions and how effective will they be as potential witnesses? Have you received an opinion from legal counsel regarding the chances of prevailing? Even if you do prevail, what do you estimate will be the out-of-pocket costs of taking the charge through the judicial process? Would you be better off settling the case, and what are the prospects of doing so in a way that will satisfy all parties?

Sources: Fair Employment Practices Summary of Latest Developments, January 7, 1983, p. 3, Bureau of National Affairs, Inc. (800-372-1033); Kenneth Sovereign, *Personnel Law* (Upper Saddle River, NJ: Prentice Hall, 1999), pp. 36–37; "EEOC Investigations—What an Employer Should Know," Equal Employment Opportunity Commission (http://www.eeoc.gov/policy/docs/medfin5.pdf), accessed May 18, 2010.

Voluntary Mediation   The EEOC refers about 10% of its charges to a voluntary mediation mechanism. If the plaintiff agrees to mediation, the employer is asked to participate. A mediation session usually lasts up to 4 hours. If no agreement is reached or one of the parties rejects participation, the charge is then processed through the EEOC's usual mechanisms.

Faced with an offer to mediate, three responses are generally possible: agree to mediate, make a settlement offer without participating in mediation, or prepare a "position statement" for the EEOC. If the employer does not mediate or make an offer, the position statement is required. It should include information relating to the company's business and the charging party's position, a description of any rules or policies and procedures that are applicable, and the chronology of the offense that led to the adverse action.[92]

The EEOC is expanding its mediation program. For example, it signed more than 18 nationwide agreements and 300 local agreements for mediation with participating employers. Under this program, the EEOC refers all eligible discrimination charges filed against these employers to the commission's mediation unit, rather than to the usual charge processing system.[93]

How to Respond to Employment Discrimination Charges

There are several things to keep in mind when confronted by a charge of illegal employment discrimination. We can summarize important points as follows:

1. *Be methodical.* Is the charge signed, dated, and notarized by the person who filed it? Did he or she file it within the time allowed? Does the charge name the proper employer? Is the employer subject to federal antidiscrimination statutes (for instance, only companies with 15 or more employees are subject to Title VII)?[94]

2. Remember that *EEOC investigators are not judges* and are not empowered to act as courts. They cannot make findings of discrimination on their own but can merely make recommendations. Its only recourse is to file a suit or issue a notice of right to sue to the person.

3. Some *experts advise meeting with the employee* who made the complaint to determine all relevant issues. For example, ask, *What happened? Who was involved? Was the employee's ability to work affected? Were there any witnesses?* Then prepare a written statement summarizing the complaints and facts involved and request that the employee sign and date this.[95]

4. *Give the EEOC a position statement* based on your own investigation of the matter. Say something like, "Our company has a policy against discrimination and we would not discriminate in the manner outlined in the complaint." Support your case with some statistical analysis of the workforce, copies of any documents that support your position, and an explanation of any legitimate business justification for the actions you took.

5. Ensure that there is information in the EEOC file demonstrating *lack of merit* of the charge. Often the best way to do that is not by answering the EEOC questionnaire but by providing a detailed statement (as in no. 4).

6. *Limit the information supplied* as narrowly as possible to only those issues raised in the charge itself. For example, if the charge only alleges sex discrimination, do not invite further scrutiny by responding to the EEOC's request for a breakdown of employees by age.

7. *Seek as much information as possible* about the charging party's claim in order to ensure that you understand the claim and its ramifications.

8. Prepare for the EEOC's *fact-finding conferences.* The EEOC's emphasis here is often on settlement. Therefore, thoroughly prepare witnesses who are going to testify, especially supervisors.

9. Finally, keep in mind that *preventing such claims is usually better than having to deal with them.* For example, where there's a climate that seems to support racism, there is a higher likelihood of racial discrimination.[96]

DIVERSITY MANAGEMENT AND AFFIRMATIVE ACTION PROGRAMS

To some extent, demographic trends are rendering moot the original goals driving equal employment legislation. Employers now have little choice but to willingly push for diversity.

Today's Diverse Workforce

For example, between 1996 and 2016, the percent of the workforce the Bureau of Labor Statistics classifies as "white, non-Hispanic" will drop from 75.3% to 64.6%.[97] The percentage that is of Hispanic origin will rise from 9.5% to 16.4%. The percentages of younger workers will fall while those over 55 will leap from 11.9% in 1996 to 22% in 2016. Women already constitute just over half the workforce.

The bottom line is that companies today are striving for racial, ethnic, and sexual workforce balance, "not because of legal imperatives, but as a matter of enlightened economic self-interest."[98] The result is **diversity,** which means being diverse or varied, and at work means *having a workforce comprised of two or more groups of employees with various racial, ethnic, gender, cultural, national origin, handicap, age, and religious backgrounds.*[99]

Diversity's Potential Pros and Cons

The resulting workforce diversity produces both benefits and threats for employers.

Some Downsides   Demographic differences can produce behavioral barriers that undermine collegiality and cooperation. Potential problems include these:

- **Stereotyping** is a process in which someone ascribes specific behavioral traits to individuals based on their apparent membership in a group.[100] For example, "older people can't work hard." *Prejudice* means a bias toward prejudging someone based on that person's traits. For example, "we won't hire him because he's old."
- **Discrimination** means taking specific actions toward or against the person based on the person's group.[101]

  In the United States and many countries, we've seen that it's generally illegal to discriminate at work based on a person's age, race, gender, disability, or country of national origin. But in practice, discrimination is often subtle. For example, many argue that a "glass ceiling," enforced by an "old boys' network" (friendships built in places like exclusive clubs), effectively prevents women from reaching top management. Equal opportunity laws aim to prohibit and eliminate discrimination.
- **Tokenism** occurs when a company appoints a small group of women or minorities to high-profile positions, rather than more aggressively seeking full representation for that group. Tokenism is a diversity barrier when it slows the process of hiring or promoting more members of the minority group.[102]
- **Ethnocentrism** is the tendency to view members of other social groups less favorably than one's own. For example, one study found that managers attributed the performance of some minorities less to their abilities and effort and more to help they received from others.[103]
- Discrimination against women goes beyond glass ceilings. Working women also confront **gender-role stereotypes,** the tendency to associate women with certain (frequently nonmanagerial) jobs. In one study, attractiveness was advantageous for female interviewees when the job was nonmanagerial. When the job was managerial, there was a tendency for a woman's attractiveness to reduce her chances of being hired.[104]

Some Diversity Benefits   The key is properly managing these potential threats. In one study, researchers examined the diversity climate in 654 stores of a large U.S. retail chain. They defined diversity climate as the extent to which employees in the stores reported believing that the firm promotes equal opportunity and inclusion. They found the greatest sales growth in stores with the highest pro-diversity climate, and the lowest in stores that reported less-hospitable diversity climates.[105] The following Strategy and HR feature provides another example.

Strategy and HR   Workforce diversity makes strategic sense. IBM created several minority task forces focusing on groups such as women and Native Americans. One effect of these teams has been internal: In the 10 or so years since forming them, IBM has boosted the number of U.S.-born ethnic minority executives by almost $2^{1}/_{2}$ times.[106]

However, the firm's diversity program also had big effects on IBM's strategy of expanding its markets and business results. For example, one task force focused on expanding IBM's market among multicultural and women-owned businesses. They did this in part by providing "much-needed sales and service support to small and midsize businesses, a niche well populated with minority and female buyers."[107] As a direct result, this market grew from $10 million to more than $300 million in revenue in just 3 years.

Managing Diversity

Managing diversity means maximizing diversity's potential advantages while minimizing the potential barriers—such as prejudices and bias—that can undermine the functioning of a diverse workforce. In practice, diversity management involves both compulsory (legal) and voluntary actions. We've seen there are many compulsory legal actions employers must take to minimize discrimination.

However, compulsory actions won't guarantee a close-knit and thriving community. *Diversity management* therefore also relies on taking steps to encourage all employees to work together productively.[108]

Top–Down Programs   This starts at the top. The employer institutes a diversity management program. One aim here is to make employees more sensitive to and better able to adapt to individual cultural differences. One diversity expert concluded that five sets of voluntary organizational activities are at the heart of the typical company-wide diversity management program. We can summarize these as follows:

   Provide strong leadership.   Companies with exemplary reputations in
      managing diversity have CEOs who champion diversity. Leadership
      means, for instance, becoming a role model for the behaviors required
      for the change.
   Assess the situation.   Common tools for measuring a company's
      diversity include equal employment hiring and retention metrics,
      employee attitude surveys, management and employee evaluations,
      and focus groups.[109]

Provide diversity training and education. The most common starting point for a diversity management effort is usually an employee education program.

Change culture and management systems. Combine education programs with other concrete steps aimed at changing the organization's culture. For example, appraise supervisors based partly on their success in reducing intergroup conflicts.

Evaluate the diversity management program. For example, do employee attitude surveys indicate any improvement in employees' attitudes toward diversity?

Multicultural Consciousness In July 2009, after a heated exchange on his doorstep, Cambridge, Massachusetts, police arrested Professor Henry Louis Gates Jr., a nationally known African American Harvard professor, for disorderly conduct. Professor Gates initially accused the police of racially profiling him. The arresting officer (who his department had appointed as a trainer to show fellow officers how to avoid racial profiling) denied any racial motives. President Obama, at a news conference, accused the Cambridge police of using less than good judgment. Whatever else one can say about the episode, it seems that three people who should know quite a bit about multicultural consciousness differed dramatically about how culturally sensitive the other person had been.

One moral to this story is that being "sensitive to and adapting to individual cultural differences" is easier said than done. People tend to view the world through the prism of their own experiences. Sometimes it's not easy for even the most well-meaning person to appreciate how people who are different from us may be feeling. This suggests that it's useful to take steps to personally develop a diversity consciousness. Figure 2.3 summarizes the steps one expert suggests.[110]

Boosting Workforce Diversity

Employers use various means to increase workforce diversity. Many companies, such as Baxter Healthcare Corporation, start by adopting *strong company policies* advocating the benefits of a culturally, racially, and sexually diverse workforce: "Baxter

Figure 2.3 Steps in Developing Diversity Consciousness

1. **Take an active role in educating yourself.** For example, read articles that can help give you a better perspective on where people from other cultures are "coming from."

2. **Put yourself in a learning mode in any multicultural setting.** For example, suspend judgment and view the person you're dealing with just in terms of the experiences you've actually had with him or her.

3. **Move beyond your personal comfort zone.** For example, put yourself in more situations where you are an "outsider."

4. **Don't be too hard on yourself if misunderstandings arise.** As this expert says, "The important thing is to acknowledge our mistakes and learn from them."[111]

5. **Realize that you are not alone.** Remember that there are other people, including colleagues, friends, and mentors at work, who you can turn to for advice on diversity issues.

International believes that a multi-cultural employee population is essential to the company's leadership in healthcare around the world." Baxter then *publicizes* this philosophy throughout the company.

Next, Baxter takes *concrete steps* to foster diversity at work. These include recruiting minority members to the board of directors, interacting with representative minority groups, and diversity training. The latter aims at sensitizing all employees about the need to value differences, build self-esteem, and generally create a more hospitable environment for the firm's diverse workforce.

Equal Employment Opportunity versus Affirmative Action

Equal employment opportunity aims to ensure that anyone, regardless of race, color, disability, sex, religion, national origin, or age, has an equal chance for a job based on his or her qualifications. *Affirmative action* goes beyond equal employment opportunity by requiring the employer to make an extra effort to hire and promote those in a protected group. Affirmative action thus includes specific actions (in recruitment, hiring, promotions, and compensation) to eliminate the present effects of past discrimination.

Steps in an Affirmative Action Program

According to the EEOC, the employer ideally takes eight steps in an affirmative action program:

1. Issues a written equal employment policy indicating that it is an equal employment opportunity/affirmative action employer.
2. Appoints a top official with responsibility and authority to direct and implement the program.
3. Publicizes the equal employment/affirmative action commitment.
4. Surveys present minority and female employment to determine locations where affirmative action programs are especially desirable.[112]
5. Develops goals and timetables to improve utilization of minorities, males, and females.
6. Develops and implements specific programs to achieve these goals. Here, review the entire human resource management system (including recruitment, selection, promotion, compensation, and disciplining) to identify barriers to equal employment opportunity.
7. Establishes an internal audit and reporting system to monitor and evaluate progress.
8. Develops support for the affirmative action program, both inside the company (among supervisors, for instance) and in the outside community.[113]

Affirmative Action Today   Affirmative action is still a significant workplace issue today. The incidence of major court-mandated programs is down. However, many employers still engage in voluntary programs. Executive Order 11246 (issued in 1965) requires federal contractors to take affirmative action to improve employment opportunities for women and racial minorities. It covers about 26 million workers—about 22% of the U.S. workforce.

Voluntary Programs   In implementing voluntary affirmative action programs, the employer should ensure that its program does not conflict with the Civil Rights Act of 1991, which two experts say may "bar employers from giving any consideration whatsoever to an individual's status as a racial or ethnic minority or as a woman when making an employment decision."[114] Employers should emphasize the external recruitment and internal development of better-qualified minority and female employees "while basing employment decisions on legitimate criteria."[115]

Avoiding an employee backlash to affirmative action programs is important. Nonminorities may object to what they see as "reverse discrimination" if the employer seems to favor minorities. Current employees need to see that the program is fair. *Transparent selection procedures* help in this regard. *Communication* is also crucial. Make clear that the program doesn't involve preferential selection standards. Provide details on the qualifications of all new hires (both minority and nonminority). *Justifications* for the program should emphasize redressing past discrimination and the practical value of diversity, not underrepresentation.[116]

As noted, affirmative action is still very much a workplace issue today. For example, in 2009, the U.S. Supreme Court decided an important "reverse discrimination" suit brought by Connecticut firefighters. In *Ricci* v. *DeStefano*, 19 white firefighters and one Hispanic firefighter said the city of New Haven should have promoted them based on their successful scores. The city argued that certifying the tests would have left them vulnerable to lawsuits by minorities for violating Title VII.[117] The Court decided in favor of the white firefighters.

Improving Productivity Through HRIS   The HR manager who wants to assess the efficiency and effectiveness of his or her company's EEOC and diversity efforts has numerous measures or metrics from which to choose. These might include, for example, the number of EEOC claims per year, the cost of HR-related litigation, and various measures for analyzing the survival and loss rate among new diverse employee groups.

Even for a company with just several hundred employees, keeping track of metrics like these is expensive. The HR manager may therefore want to rely on various computerized solutions. One package, called *Measuring Diversity Results*, provides several diversity-related software options. This vendor's packages let the manager more easily calculate the cost-per-diversity hire, a workforce profile index, and the numeric impact of voluntary turnover among diverse employee groups.

REVIEW

Summary

1. Legislation barring discrimination is not new. For example, the Fifth Amendment to the U.S. Constitution (ratified in 1791) states that no person shall be deprived of life, liberty, or property without due process of law.

2. Legislation barring employment discrimination includes Title VII of the 1964 Civil Rights Act (as amended), which bars discrimination because of race, color, religion, sex, or national origin; various executive orders; federal guidelines (covering procedures for

validating employee selection tools, etc.); the Equal Pay Act of 1963; and the Age Discrimination in Employment Act of 1967. In addition, various Court decisions (such as *Griggs* v. *Duke Power Company*) and state and local laws bar various aspects of discrimination.

3. Title VII of the Civil Rights Act created the EEOC. It has the power to go directly to court to enforce the law.

4. The Civil Rights Act of 1991 placed the burden of proof back on employers and held that a nondiscriminatory reason was insufficient to let an employer avoid liability for an action that also had a discriminatory motive.

5. The Americans with Disabilities Act prohibits employment discrimination against the disabled. Specifically, the firm cannot discriminate against qualified persons if the firm can make reasonable accommodations without undue hardship to the business.

6. A person who believes he or she has been discriminated against must prove either that he or she was subjected to unlawful disparate treatment (intentional discrimination) or that the procedure in question has a disparate impact (unintentional discrimination) on members of his or her protected class. Once a prima facie case of disparate treatment is established, an employer must produce evidence that its decision was based on legitimate reasons (such as BFOQ).

7. An employer should avoid various specific discriminatory human resource management practices. For example:

   a. *In recruitment.* An employer usually should not rely on word-of-mouth advertising or give false or misleading information to minority-group members.

   b. *In selection.* An employer should avoid using any educational or other requirements where (1) it can be shown that minority-group members

are less likely to possess the qualification and (2) such requirement is also not job related.

8. In practice, a person's charge to the EEOC is often first referred to a local agency. When the EEOC finds reasonable cause to believe that discrimination occurred, it has 30 days to try to conciliate. Important points for the employer to remember include (1) EEOC investigators can only make recommendations, (2) you cannot be compelled to submit documents without a court order, and (3) limit the information you do submit. Also, make sure you clearly document your position (as the employer).

9. An employer can use three basic defenses in the event of a discriminatory practice allegation. One is *business necessity.* Attempts to show that tests or other selection standards are valid are one example of this defense. *Bona fide occupational qualification* applies when, for example, religion, national origin, or sex is a bona fide requirement of the job (such as for actors or actresses). A third is that the decision was made on the basis of legitimate nondiscriminatory reasons (such as poor performance) having nothing to do with the prohibited discrimination alleged.

10. There are eight steps in an affirmative action program, based on suggestions from the EEOC. These are (1) issue a written equal employment policy, (2) appoint a top official, (3) publicize the policy, (4) survey present minority and female employment, (5) develop goals and timetables, (6) develop and implement specific programs to achieve goals, (7) establish an internal audit and reporting system, and (8) develop support of in-house and community programs.

11. Recruitment is one of the first activities to which EEOC laws and procedures are applied. We turn to this in Chapter 3.

KEY TERMS

- Equal Pay Act of 1963
- Title VII of the 1964 Civil Rights Act
- Equal Employment Opportunity Commission (EEOC)
- affirmative action
- Office of Federal Contract Compliance Programs (OFCCP)
- Age Discrimination in Employment Act (ADEA) of 1967
- Vocational Rehabilitation Act of 1973
- Pregnancy Discrimination Act (PDA)
- federal agency guidelines
- *Griggs* v. *Duke Power Company*
- protected class
- *Albemarle Paper Company* v. *Moody*
- Civil Rights Act of 1991 (CRA 1991)
- disparate impact
- disparate treatment
- sexual harassment
- gender harassment
- Americans with Disabilities Act (ADA)
- adverse impact
- bona fide occupational qualification (BFOQ)
- business necessity
- diversity
- stereotyping
- discrimination
- tokenism
- ethnocentrism
- gender-role stereotypes

DISCUSSION QUESTIONS

1. What is Title VII? What does it state?
2. What important precedents were set by the *Griggs* v. *Duke Power Company* case? The *Albemarle* v. *Moody* case?
3. What is adverse impact? How can it be proven?
4. Assume that you are a supervisor on an assembly line; you are responsible for hiring subordinates, supervising them, and recommending them for promotion. Compile a list of discriminatory management practices that you should avoid.
5. Explain the defenses and exceptions to discriminatory practice allegations.
6. What is the difference between affirmative action and equal employment opportunity?
7. Explain how you would set up an affirmative action program.

INDIVIDUAL AND GROUP ACTIVITIES

1. Working individually or in groups, respond to these three scenarios based on what you learned in this chapter. Under what conditions (if any) do you think the following constitute sexual harassment? (a) A female manager fires a male employee because he refuses her requests for sexual favors. (b) A male manager refers to female employees as "sweetie" or "baby." (c) A female employee overhears two male employees exchanging sexually oriented jokes.
2. Working individually or in groups, discuss how you would set up an affirmative action program.
3. Compare and contrast the issues presented in recent court rulings on affirmative action. Working individually or in groups, discuss the current direction of affirmative action.

4. Working individually or in groups, write a paper entitled "What the Manager Should Know about How the EEOC Handles a Person's Discrimination Charge."

5. Explain the difference between affirmative action and equal employment opportunity.

6. Assume you are the manager in a small restaurant; you are responsible for hiring employees, supervising them, and recommending them for promotion. Working individually or in groups, compile a list of potentially discriminatory management practices you should avoid.

APPLICATION EXERCISES

Case Incident   A Case of Racial Discrimination?

John Peters was a 44-year-old cardiologist on the staff of a teaching hospital in a large city in the southeastern United States. Happily married with two teenage children, he had served with distinction for many years at this same hospital.

Alana Anderson was an African American registered nurse on the staff at the same hospital with Peters. Unmarried and without children, she lived in a hospital-owned apartment on the hospital grounds and devoted almost all her time to her work at the hospital or to taking additional coursework to further improve her already excellent nursing skills.

The hospital's chief administrator, Gary Chapman, took enormous pride in what he called the extraordinary professionalism of the doctors, nurses, and other staff members at his hospital. Although he took a number of rudimentary steps to guard against blatant violations of equal employment opportunity laws, he believed that most of the professionals on his staff were so highly trained and committed to the highest professional standards that "they would always do the right thing," as he put it.

Chapman was therefore upset to receive a phone call from Peters, informing him that Anderson had (in Peters's eyes) "developed an unwholesome personal attraction" to him and was bombarding the doctor with Valentine's Day cards, affectionate personal notes, and phone calls—often to the doctor's home. Concerned about hospital decorum and the possibility that Peters was being sexually

harassed, Chapman met privately with Anderson, explained that Peters was very uncomfortable with the personal attention she was showing to him, and asked that she please not continue to exhibit her show of affection for the doctor.

Chapman assumed that the matter was over. Several weeks later, when Anderson resigned her position at the hospital, Chapman didn't think much of it. He was therefore shocked and dismayed to receive a registered letter from a local attorney, informing him that both the hospital and Peters and Chapman personally were being sued by Anderson for racial discrimination. Her claim was that Chapman, in their private meeting, had told her, "We don't think it's right for people of different races to pursue each other romantically at this hospital." According to the lawyer, his preliminary research had unearthed several other alleged incidents at the hospital that apparently supported the idea that racial discrimination at the hospital was widespread. ∎

QUESTIONS

1. What do you think of the way Chapman handled the accusations from Peters and his conversation with Anderson? How would you have handled them?
2. Do you think Peters had the basis for a sexual harassment claim against Anderson? Why or why not?
3. What would you do now if you were Chapman to avoid further incidents of this type?

Continuing Case

LearnInMotion.com: A Question of Discrimination

One of the problems LearnInMotion's Jennifer and Mel faced concerned the inadequacies of the firm's current personnel management practices and procedures. The previous year had been a swirl of activity—creating and testing the business model, launching the site, writing and rewriting the business plan, and finally getting venture funding. And, it would be accurate to say that in all that time, they put absolutely no time into employee manuals, personnel policies, or HR-related matters.

Almost from the beginning, it was apparent to both of them that they were "out of our depth" (as Mel put it) when it came to the letter and spirit of equal employment opportunity laws. Having both been through business school, they were familiar with the general requirements, such as not asking applicants their ages. However, those general guidelines weren't always easy to translate into practice during the actual applicant interviews. Two incidents particularly concerned them. One of the applicants for a sales position was in his 50s, which made him about twice as old as any other applicant. While Mel didn't mean to be discriminatory, he found himself asking this candidate questions that he did not ask of other, younger candidates, questions such as "Do you think you'll be able to get up to speed selling an Internet product?" and "You know, we'll be working very long hours here; are you up to that?" There was also a problem with a candidate for the other position (content manager). This person had been incarcerated for a substance abuse problem several years before. Mel asked him several questions about this, as well as whether he was now "clean" or "under any sort of treatment." Jennifer thought questions like these were probably OK, but she wasn't sure.

There was also a disturbing incident in the office. There were already two content management employees, Ruth and Dan, whose job was to place the courses and other educational content on the Web site. Dan, along with Alex the Web surfer, occasionally used vulgarity—for instance, when referring to the problems the firm was having getting the computer supplier to come to the office and repair a chronic problem with the firm's server. Mel's attitude was that "boys will be boys." However, Jennifer saw Ruth cringe several times when "the boys" were having one of these exchanges, and felt strongly that this behavior had to stop. However, she was not sure language like this constituted "a hostile environment" under the law, although she did feel that at a minimum it was uncivil. The two owners decided it was time to implement some HR policies. They hoped these would ensure that their company and its employees adhere to the letter and the spirit of the equal employment opportunity laws. Now they want you, their management consultants, to help them actually do it. Here's what they want you to do for them. ∎

QUESTIONS AND ASSIGNMENTS

1. Our company is in New York City. We now have only about five employees and are only planning on hiring about three or four more. Is our company covered by equal rights legislation? (Hint: Does the government's Web site provide any clues?)
2. Were we within our legal rights to ask the possibly age-related and substance abuse–related questions? Why or why not?
3. Did Dan and Alex create a hostile environment for Ruth? Why or why not? How should we have handled this matter?
4. What have we been doing wrong up to now with respect to EEO-related matters, and how do you suggest we rectify the situation in the future?

Experiential Exercise
Too Informal?

Dan Jones had run his textile plant in a midsize southern town for many years without a whiff of trouble with the EEOC. In fact, a professor from a local college had once told him to be more careful about how applicants were recruited and screened and employees were treated. However, Jones's philosophy was "If it ain't broke, don't fix it," and because he'd never had any complaints, he assumed that his screening process wasn't "broke."

For many years Jones had no problems. If he needed a new employee, he simply asked his current employees (most of whom were Hispanic) if they had any friends. Sometimes, he would also ask the local state employment office to list the open jobs and send over some candidates. He then had his sewing supervisor and plant manager (both also Hispanic) interview the applicants. No tests or other background checks were carried out, in part, said Jones, because "most of these applicants are friends and relatives of my current employees, and they wouldn't send me any lemons."

Now Jones is being served with a formal notice from the county's Equal Rights Commission. It seems that of the 20 or so non-Hispanic applicants sent to Jones's firm last year from the state employment office, none had received a job offer. In fact, Jones's supervisor had not even returned the follow-up card to the employment office to verify that each applicant had shown up and been interviewed. Jones was starting to wonder if his HR process was too informal.

Purpose: The purpose of this exercise is to provide practice in analyzing and applying knowledge of equal opportunity legislation to a realistic problem.

Required Understanding: Be thoroughly familiar with the material presented in this chapter. In addition, read "Too Informal?" the case on which this experiential exercise is based.

How to Set Up the Exercise/Instructions:

1. Divide the class into groups of four or five students.
2. Each group should develop answers to the following:
   a. How could the EEOC prove *adverse impact?*
   b. Cite specific discriminatory personnel practices at Dan Jones's company.
   c. How could Jones's company defend itself against the allegations of discriminatory practice?
3. If time permits, a spokesperson from each group can present his or her group's findings. Would it make sense for this company to try to defend itself against the discrimination allegations? ∎

Chapter 3

Personnel Planning and Recruiting

- What Is Job Analysis?
- The Recruitment and Selection Process
- Workforce Planning and Forecasting
- Recruiting Job Candidates
- Developing and Using Application Forms

When you finish studying this chapter, you should be able to:

- Describe *the basic methods of collecting job analysis information.*
- Conduct *a job analysis.*
- Explain *the process of forecasting personnel requirements.*
- Compare *eight methods for recruiting job candidates.*
- Explain *how to use application forms to predict job performance.*

INTRODUCTION

With more than 110 restaurants, and growing fast, The Cheesecake Factory must attract and hire 24,000 people per year. For Cheesecake's head of human resources, that means casting a wide recruiting net—"You don't find all the people you need from one source," he says. So having the right recruiting sources is crucial to The Cheesecake Factory's success.[1]

WHAT IS JOB ANALYSIS?

Job Analysis Defined

Organizations consist of jobs that have to be staffed. **Job analysis** is the procedure through which you determine the duties of these jobs and the characteristics of the people to hire for them. The analysis produces information on the job's activities (such as cleaning, selling, or teaching) and human requirements (such as education and skills). You can then use this information for developing **job descriptions** (what the job entails) and **job specifications** (what kind of people to hire for the job).[2] A supervisor or HR specialist normally does the job analysis, perhaps using a questionnaire like the one on pages 100–101 (Figure A3.2).

Job analysis information is crucial for several human resource management activities.[3] For example, you'll use information regarding the job's duties to decide what sort of people to recruit and hire, and to validate tests for selecting workers for the job.

Methods of Collecting Job Analysis Information

In practice, employers usually collect job analysis data from several job incumbents, using questionnaires and interviews. They then average data from different departments to determine how much time a typical employee (say, a sales assistant) spends on each task (such as interviewing).[4] Job analysis data reported by job incumbents display the lowest reliability, while those collected by job analysts are usually more reliable.[5]

Traditionally, job analysts might take several days to interview five or six sample employees and their managers. A faster but still adequate process might take just 3 or 4 hours.[6] The steps include:

1. Greet participants;
2. Briefly explain the job analysis process and reason, and the participants' roles in this process;
3. Spend about 15 minutes getting agreement on the job's basic summary;
4. Identify the job's broad functional areas, such as "administrative" and "supervisory";
5. Identify tasks within each functional area; and, finally
6. Print the task list and get the group to sign it.

Managers use various techniques to do a job analysis (to collect information on the job's duties, responsibilities, and activities). Popular techniques are as follows.

Interviews   Job analysis interviews involve interviewing job incumbents or one or more supervisors who know the job. Typical questions include "What is the job being performed?" "What are the major duties?" and "What exactly do you do?"

Interviews are advantageous. Most important, interviewing is simple and lets workers report activities that might not otherwise surface. For example, the interview could unearth important activities that occur only occasionally, or informal communication (between, say, a production supervisor and sales manager).

Interviewing's major problem is distortion of information. Employers often use job analysis as a prelude to changing a job's pay rate. Employees, therefore, sometimes view them as efficiency evaluations, and so exaggerate some responsibilities and minimize others. [7] In one study researchers listed duties either as tasks ("record phone messages") or as abilities ("ability to record phone messages").[8] Respondents were more likely to include the ability versions, perhaps because they thought abilities impressed others.[9]

Questionnaires   Employees can also complete questionnaires to describe their duties and responsibilities.

Some questionnaires are structured checklists. Each lists perhaps hundreds of specific duties or tasks (such as "change and splice wire"). Each employee must indicate whether he or she performs each task and, if so, how much time is spent on each. Alternatively, the questionnaire may simply ask the employee to "describe the major duties of your job."

As in Figure A3.2 (pages 100–101), a typical questionnaire might combine several open-ended questions (such as "Is the incumbent performing duties he/she considers unnecessary?") with structured questions (concerning, for instance, previous experience required).

Observation   Direct observation is useful when jobs consist of observable activity. Jobs such as janitor and accounting clerk are examples. On the other hand, observation is usually not appropriate when the job entails mental activity (lawyer, design engineer). Nor is it useful if the employee engages in important activities that might occur only occasionally, such as a nurse who handles emergencies.

Participant Diary/Logs   Another approach is to ask workers to keep a diary/log or list of what they do during the day (along with the time). This can produce a very complete picture of the job. Some employees may try to exaggerate some activities and underplay others. However, the detailed, chronological nature of the log tends to mediate against this. Some employees compile their logs by periodically dictating what they're doing into a handheld dictating machine.

Using Internet-Based Data Collection   Most of these job analysis methods suffer from problems. For example, face-to-face interviews and observations can be time consuming. Collecting any information from internationally dispersed employees is challenging.[10]

Internet-based job analysis is one solution.[11] The human resource department distributes standardized job analysis questionnaires to dispersed employees via their company intranets, with instructions to complete and return the forms.

Other Job Analysis Methods   You may encounter several other job analysis methods, most notably those in this chapter's appendix.

Writing Job Descriptions

The job analysis should provide the basis for writing a job description. A job description is a written statement of *what* the jobholder does, *how* he or she does it, and under *what conditions* the job is performed. The manager in turn uses this information to write a job specification that lists the knowledge, abilities, and skills needed to perform the job. Figure 3.1 presents a typical job description. As is usual, it contains several types of information.

Job Identification As in Figure 3.1, the job identification section contains the job title, such as marketing manager or inventory control clerk.

Job Summary The job summary should describe the general nature of the job, listing only its major functions or activities.

Figure 3.1 Sample Job Description, Pearson Education

JOB TITLE: Telesales Representative		**JOB CODE:** 100001	
RECOMMENDED SALARY GRADE:		**EXEMPT/NONEXEMPT STATUS:** Nonexempt	
JOB FAMILY: Sales		**EEOC:** Sales Workers	
DIVISION: Higher Education		**REPORTS TO:** District Sales Manager	
DEPARTMENT: In-House Sales		**LOCATION:** Boston	
		DATE: April 2010	

SUMMARY (Write a brief summary of job.)

The person in this position is responsible for selling college textbooks, software, and multimedia products to professors, via incoming and outgoing telephone calls, and to carry out selling strategies to meet sales goals in assigned territories of smaller colleges and universities. In addition, the individual in this position will be responsible for generating a designated amount of editorial leads and communicating to the publishing groups product feedback and market trends observed in the assigned territory.

SCOPE AND IMPACT OF JOB

Dollar responsibilities (budget and/or revenue)

The person in this position is responsible for generating approximately $2 million in revenue, for meeting operating expense budget of approximately $4000, and a sampling budget of approximately 10,000 units.

Supervisory responsibilities (direct and indirect)

None

Other

REQUIRED KNOWLEDGE AND EXPERIENCE (Knowledge and experience necessary to do job)

Related work experience

Prior sales or publishing experience preferred. One year of company experience in a customer service or marketing function with broad knowledge of company products and services is desirable.

Formal education or equivalent

Bachelor's degree with strong academic performance or work equivalent experience.

Skills

Must have strong organizational and persuasive skills. Must have excellent verbal and written communications skills and must be PC proficient.

Other

Limited travel required (approx 5%)

(Continued)

PRIMARY RESPONSIBILITIES (List in order of importance and list amount of time spent on task.)

Driving Sales (60%)

- Achieve quantitative sales goal for assigned territory of smaller colleges and universities.
- Determine sales priorities and strategies for territory and develop a plan for implementing those strategies.
- Conduct 15-20 professor interviews per day during the academic sales year that accomplishes those priorities.
- Conduct product presentations (including texts, software, and Web site); effectively articulate author's central vision of key titles; conduct sales interviews using the PSS model; conduct walk-through of books and technology.
- Employ telephone selling techniques and strategies.
- Sample products to appropriate faculty, making strategic use of assigned sampling budgets.
- Close class test adoptions for first edition products.
- Negotiate custom publishing and special packaging agreements within company guidelines.
- Initiate and conduct in-person faculty presentations and selling trips as appropriate to maximize sales with the strategic use of travel budget. Also use internal resources to support the territory sales goals.
- Plan and execute in-territory special selling events and book-fairs.
- Develop and implement in-territory promotional campaigns and targeted e-mail campaigns.

Publishing (editorial/marketing) 25%

- Report, track, and sign editorial projects.
- Gather and communicate significant market feedback and information to publishing groups.

Territory Management 15%

- Track and report all pending and closed business in assigned database.
- Maintain records of customer sales interviews and adoption situations in assigned database.
- Manage operating budget strategically.
- Submit territory itineraries, sales plans, and sales forecasts as assigned.
- Provide superior customer service and maintain professional bookstore relations in assigned territory.

Decision-Making Responsibilities for This Position:

Determine the strategic use of assigned sampling budget to most effectively generate sales revenue to exceed sales goals.
Determine the priority of customer and account contacts to achieve maximum sales potential.
Determine where in-person presentations and special selling events would be most effective to generate most sales.

Submitted By: Jim Smith, District Sales Manager	Date: April 10, 2007
Approval:	Date:
Human Resources:	Date:
Corporate Compensation:	Date:

Source: Courtesy of HR Department, Pearson Education.

Relationships   A relationships statement may show the jobholder's relationships with others inside and outside the organization and might look like this for a human resource manager:

Reports to: Vice president of employee relations
Supervises: Human resource clerk, test administrator, labor relations director, and one secretary
Works with: All department managers and executive management
Outside the company: Employment agencies, executive recruiting firms, union representatives, state and federal employment offices, and various vendors

Responsibilities and Duties This is the heart of the job description. Here, list and describe in several sentences each of the job's major duties. For instance, supplement the duty "selects, trains, and develops subordinate personnel" with "develops spirit of cooperation and understanding."

Human resource managers formerly used the Department of Labor's *Dictionary of Occupational Titles* to find and itemize a job's duties and responsibilities. As an example of the information managers could glean from it, the *Dictionary of Occupational Titles* lists a human resource manager's specific duties and responsibilities as "plans and carries out policies relating to all phases of personnel activity," "recruits, interviews, and selects employees to fill vacant positions," and "conducts wage survey within labor market to determine competitive wage rate." Today, the U.S. Department of Labor's *Occupational Information Network*, or O*NET (and its Standard Occupational Classification, as in Figure 3.2), has largely replaced the *Dictionary of Occupational Titles.* The O*NET site (http://online.onetcenter.org/) enables users to see the most important characteristics of an occupation, as well as the training, experience, and education it requires.[12] O*NET also lists the occupation's skills, including *basic skills* such as reading, *process skills* such as critical thinking, and *transferable skills* such as persuasion.[13]

During 2010, the Department of Labor conducted a once-per-decade update of its standard occupational classification system, updating job descriptions for more than 800 occupations (about 20% of the total).[14]

Authority This section defines the limits of the jobholder's authority. For example, the jobholder might have authority to approve purchase requests up to $5,000, discipline department personnel, and recommend salary increases.[15]

Figure 3.2 Marketing Manager Description from Standard Occupational Classification

Source: http://www.bls.gov/soc/2000/soc_a2c1.htm, accessed May 18, 2010

Standards of Performance   Some job descriptions contain a standards-of-performance section. This lists standards the employee is expected to achieve in each of the job's main duties and responsibilities.

Working Conditions and Physical Environment   The job description also lists the job's general working conditions, such as noise level, hazardous conditions, and heat.

Internet-Based Job Descriptions   More employers are turning to the Internet to write their job descriptions. One site, www.jobdescription.com, illustrates why. Search by alphabetical title, keyword, category, or industry to find the desired job title. This leads you to a generic job description for that title—say, "Computers & EDP systems sales representative." You can then use the wizard to customize the generic description for this position. For example, you can add specific information about your organization, such as job title, job codes, department, and preparation date. And you can indicate whether the job has supervisory abilities, and choose from a list of possible desirable competencies.[16] Others use O*NET (see the chapter appendix) to create job descriptions.

Writing Job Descriptions That Comply with the ADA   As explained in Chapter 2, the Americans with Disabilities Act (ADA) does not require job descriptions. However, most ADA lawsuits revolve around the question: What are the essential functions of the job? (Essential job functions are those duties that employees must be able to perform, with or without reasonable accommodation.)[17] Without a job description listing these functions as "essential," it's difficult to prove that the functions are essential.[18]

Writing Job Specifications

The job specification starts with the job description and then answers the question: What human traits and experience are required to do this job well? It shows what kind of person to recruit and for what qualities to test that person. It may be a separate section on the job description (as at the end of the first page of Figure 3.1) or a separate document.

Writing job specifications for trained employees is straightforward. For example, suppose you want to fill a position for a trained bookkeeper. Here, your job specifications might focus mostly on traits such as length of previous service, or relevant training. Thus it's usually not too difficult to determine the human requirements for placing already trained people on a job.

It's more complicated when you're filling jobs with untrained people. Here you must specify qualities such as physical traits, personality, or sensory skills that imply some potential for performing the job or for being trainable. For example, suppose the job requires detailed manipulation on a circuit board. You might want to ensure that the person scores high on a test of finger dexterity. Your goal, in other words, is to identify those personal traits—or human requirements—that predict which candidate would do well on the job. Employers identify the job's required human traits using either a judgmental approach or statistical analysis.

Common sense is required when compiling a list of the job's human requirements. Certainly job-specific human traits such as manual dexterity and education are important. However, it's important not to ignore work behaviors (such as conscientiousness) that apply to most jobs but might not normally be unearthed through a job analysis.[19]

Job Analysis in a "Jobless" World

A job is a set of closely related activities carried out for pay, but over the past few years, job descriptions have tended to become less detailed and restrictive.

This drift away from more detailed job descriptions reflects the fact that most workplaces need to be more flexible today. Global competition means more pressure for performance. Firms are therefore instituting high-performance workplace policies and practices. These include management systems (such as "just-in-time production methods") based on flexible, multiskilled job assignments. In turn, flexible jobs and teamwork assume that job assignments may change frequently. Changes like these have blurred the meaning of *job* as a set of clearly delineated responsibilities. Employers want and need employees to define their jobs more broadly. The bottom line is that there's a trend toward new ways to analyze and describe jobs. One of these is competency-based job analysis.

Competency-Based Job Analysis

What Are Competencies? We can define *competencies* as demonstrable characteristics of the person that enable performance (we'll look at examples in a moment). We can say that *competency-based job analysis* means describing the job in terms of measurable, observable, behavioral competencies (knowledge, skills, and/or behaviors) that an employee doing that job must exhibit to do the job well. This contrasts with the traditional way of describing the job in terms of job duties and responsibilities (splice wires, answer phones).[20]

Traditional job analysis focuses on "what" a job is in terms of job duties and responsibilities. *Competency analysis* focuses on the competencies or skills the worker must exhibit to actually accomplish the work.[21] Traditional job analysis is job focused. Competency-based analysis is worker focused—specifically, what must he or she be competent to do?

An Example In practice, competency-based analysis often comes down to identifying the skills an employee needs to do the job.[22] For example, at British Petroleum's (BP's) exploration division, senior managers wanted a faster-acting, flatter organization and empowered employees. To facilitate this they sought to shift employees' attention from a job description "that's-not-my-job" mentality to one that would motivate them to learn the new skills they needed to accomplish broader flexible responsibilities.

The solution was replacing job descriptions with a skills matrix (Figure 3.3). They created skills matrices for various jobs within two groups of employees: those on a management track and those whose aims lay elsewhere (such as to stay in engineering). HR prepared a matrix for each job (such as drilling managers). As in Figure 3.3, the matrix listed (1) the basic skills needed for that job (such as technical

Figure 3.3 The Skills Matrix for One Job at BP

H	H	H	H	H	H	H
G	G	G	G	G	G	G
F	F	F	F	F	F	F
E	E	E	**E**	E	E	E
D	D	D	D	**D**	**D**	D
C	**C**	C	C	C	C	**C**
B	B	**B**	B	B	B	B
A	A	A	A	A	A	A
Technical Expertise	Business Awareness	Communication and Interpersonal	Decision Making and Initiative	Leadership and Guidance	Planning and Organizational Ability	Problem Solving

Note: The shaded boxes (D, C, B, E, D, D, C) indicate the minimum level of skill required for the job.

expertise), and (2) the minimum level of each skill required for that job. The emphasis is no longer on specific job duties. Instead, the focus is on motivating employees to develop the skills needed for their broader responsibilities.

The skills matrix method prompted other HR changes in this division. For example, it instituted a new skills-based pay plan that awards raises based on skills improvement.

THE RECRUITMENT AND SELECTION PROCESS

Employers use job analysis and job descriptions for several things—for example, to develop training programs. But the most familiar use for job descriptions is for deciding what types of people to recruit and select for the company's jobs.

This *recruiting and selecting process* is a series of steps, as follows:

1. Do workforce planning and forecasting to determine the positions to fill.
2. Build a pool of candidates for these jobs by recruiting internal or external candidates.
3. Have the applicants fill out application forms and perhaps undergo an initial interview.

4. Utilize various selection techniques such as tests, background investigations, and physical exams to choose job candidates.
5. Send one or more job candidates to the supervisor responsible for the job.
6. Have the candidate(s) go through one or more selection interviews with the supervisor and other relevant parties, and determine to which candidate(s) to make an offer.

Workforce planning and recruiting (steps 1 through 3) are the subjects of the remainder of this chapter. Chapter 4 then focuses on employee selection techniques including tests (steps 4 through 6).

WORKFORCE PLANNING AND FORECASTING

When Dan Hilbert became staffing manager at Valero Energy Corp., the company was doing no employment planning. After studying Valero's demographic and turnover data, he found that Valero would soon be facing employment gaps that were much higher than they could fill with their present recruitment procedures. The question was, what should they do about it?[23]

Workforce (or personnel, or employment) **planning** is the process of formulating plans to fill all the employer's future openings, based on (1) projecting open positions and (2) deciding whether to fill these with inside or outside candidates. Most firms use the term *succession planning* to refer to planning how to fill the company's most important top executive positions.

Workforce planning relates to talent management. *Talent management* involves identifying, recruiting, hiring, and developing high-potential employees. One survey of CEOs of large companies said they typically spent between 20% and 40% of their time on talent management.[24]

Strategy and Workforce Planning   Personnel planning is (or should be) an integral part of a firm's strategic planning processes. For example, when JDS Uniphase decided to expand its Melbourne, Florida, operations, it expanded its employment there from 140 people to almost 750. The firm needed to make specific plans showing how many of what sorts of people to hire and where these new employees should come from.

Workforce planning cannot be unduly mechanical. The heart of personnel planning involves predicting the skills and competencies the employer will need to execute its strategy. Personnel planning therefore can't just involve extrapolating the past. Instead, it must be a collaborative process. At IBM and Hewlett-Packard, for instance, human resource executives routinely discuss with their firm's finance and other executives the personnel ramifications of their company's strategic plans, for instance in terms of the employee capabilities the firms will need to achieve their goals.[25]

Inside or Outside Candidates?   One big question is always whether to fill projected openings with current employees or by recruiting from outside.

Each option produces its own set of HR plans. Current employees may require training, development, and coaching before they're ready to fill new jobs. Going outside requires deciding what recruiting sources to use and what the availability will be.

How does the manager decide how many employees he or she needs over the next few years? In planning employment requirements, you'll need to forecast three things: personnel needs, the supply of inside candidates, and the supply of outside candidates. We'll start with personnel needs.

How to Forecast Personnel Needs

Traditional personnel planning involves using simple tools like *ratio analysis* or *trend analysis* to estimate staffing needs based on sales projections and on historical sales to personnel relationships. Knowing your product's or service's anticipated demand is paramount. The usual process is therefore to forecast revenues first. Then estimate the size of the staff required to achieve this volume, for instance, by using historical ratios. In addition to expected demand, staffing needs may reflect:

1. Projected turnover (as a result of resignations or terminations)
2. Quality and skills of your employees (in relation to your company's changing needs)
3. Strategic decisions to upgrade the quality of products or services or enter into new markets
4. Technological and other changes resulting in increased productivity
5. The financial resources available

Larger employers computerize the workforce planning process. *Computerized forecasts* enable the manager to build more variables into his or her personnel projections.[26] For example, newer workforce planning systems enable managers to factor in specific goals, such as reducing inventory on hand.[27]

Trend Analysis   Computerized planning aside, there are several simple ways to estimate future personnel needs. **Trend analysis** involves studying your firm's employment levels over the past 5 years or so to predict future needs. Thus, you might compute the number of employees in your firm at the end of each of the past 5 years, or perhaps the number in each subgroup (such as salespeople, engineers, and administrative) at the end of each of those years. The purpose is to identify employment trends you think might continue into the future.

Ratio Analysis   Another approach, **ratio analysis,** means making forecasts based on the ratio between some causal factor (such as sales volume) and the number of employees required (for instance, number of salespeople). For example, suppose you find that a salesperson traditionally generates $500,000 in sales. Then, if the sales revenue-to-salespeople ratio remains the same, you would require six new salespeople next year (6 times $500,000 in sales) to produce, say, the desired extra $3 million in sales.

Scatter Plots   The **scatter plot** is another method. It shows graphically how two variables (such as a measure of business activity and your firms' staffing levels) are related. If they are, then if you can forecast the level of business activity, you should also be able to estimate your personnel requirements.

For example, assume a 500-bed hospital expects to expand to 1,200 beds over the next 5 years. The director of nursing and the human resource director want to forecast the requirement for registered nurses. The human resource director decides to determine the relationship between size of hospital (in terms of number of beds) and number of nurses required. She calls several hospitals of various sizes and gets the following figures:

Size of Hospital (Number of Beds)	Number of Registered Nurses
200	240
300	260
400	470
500	500
600	620
700	660
800	820
900	860

Figure 3.4 shows the hospital size (in beds) on the horizontal axis. The number of nurses is on the vertical axis. If the two factors are related, then the points will tend to fall along a straight line, as they do here. If you carefully draw in a line to minimize the distances between the line and each one of the plotted points, you will be able to estimate (forecast) the number of nurses needed for each given hospital size. Thus, for a 1,200 bed hospital, the human resource director would assume she needs about 1,210 nurses.[28]

Managerial judgment always plays a role in employment planning. It's rare that any historical trend will continue unchanged. Important factors that may influence your forecast include decisions to upgrade product quality or enter into new markets, financial resources, and technological changes resulting in increased productivity. Periods of depressed economic activity generally prompt employers to cut staffing levels as a way to maintain productivity.

Figure 3.4
Determining the Relationship Between Hospital Size and Number of Nurses

Note: After fitting the line, you can extrapolate—project— how many employees you'll need, given your projected volume.

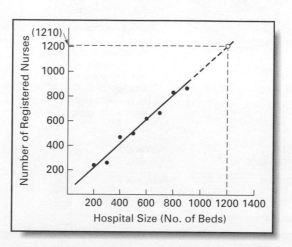

Forecasting the Supply of Inside Candidates

The preceding forecast provides only half the staffing equation, by answering the question: How many employees will we need? Next, the manager must try to assess the projected *supply* of both internal and external candidates.

A qualifications inventory can facilitate forecasting the supply of internal candidates. **Qualifications inventories** contain summary data, such as each of your current employee's performance record, educational background, and promotability, compiled manually or in a computerized system. **Personnel replacement charts** (Figure 3.5) show the present performance and promotability for each potential replacement for important positions. As an alternative, you can develop a *position replacement card* for each position, showing possible replacements as well as present performance, promotion potential, and training required by each possible candidate.

Computerized Information Systems   Employers can't maintain qualifications inventories on hundreds or thousands of employees manually. Many firms computerize this information, and there are a number of packaged systems available for accomplishing this task.

Typically, employees fill out a Web-based survey in which they describe their background and experience. The system also maintains records of performance appraisals and training. When a manager needs a qualified person, he or she describes the

Figure 3.5 Management Replacement Chart Showing Development Needs of Potential Future Divisional Vice Presidents

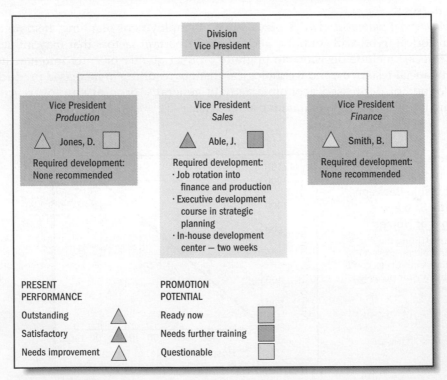

position (for instance, in terms of the education and skills it entails) and then enters this information. After scanning its bank of possible candidates, the program presents the manager with a list of qualified candidates.

The employer should secure all its employee data.[29] Much of the data are personal (such as Social Security numbers and illnesses). And legislation, including the Federal Privacy Act of 1974 (which applies to federal workers), the New York Personal Privacy Act of 1985, and the Health Insurance Portability and Accountability Act (HIPAA) (which regulates medical records), gives legal rights regarding who has access. A growing problem is that peer-to-peer file sharing applications jump firewalls. Pfizer Inc. lost personal data on about 17,000 current and former employees this way.[30]

Succession Planning   Forecasting the availability of inside candidates is particularly important in succession planning. In brief, *succession planning* means the plans a company makes to fill its most important executive positions. In practice, the process involves an integrated series of steps. For example, potential successors for top management might be routed through the top jobs at several key divisions as well as overseas, and might then go through the Harvard Business School's Advanced Management Program. As a result, a more comprehensive definition of *succession planning* is "the process of ensuring a suitable supply of successors for current and future key jobs arising from business strategy, so that the careers of individuals can be planned and managed to optimize the organization's needs and the individuals' aspirations."[31] Succession planning includes these activities:

- Analysis of the future demand for managers and professionals by company level, function, and skill
- Audit of existing executives and projection of likely future supply from internal and external sources
- Planning of individual career paths based on objective estimates and assessments of potential and career interests
- Training and development to prepare individuals for future expected roles
- Accelerated promotions
- Planned strategic recruitment, to fill short-term needs and to provide people to develop to meet future needs[32]

Improving Productivity Through HRIS: Succession Planning Systems   When Larry Kern became president of Dole Food Co. Inc. several years ago, each of its separate operating companies handled most of their own HR activities and succession planning. Kern's strategy involved improving financial performance by reducing redundancies and centralizing certain activities, including succession planning.[33] Technology helped Dole do this. Dole decided to use special software from Pilat NAI. Pilat NAI runs the succession planning software and keeps all the data on its own servers for a monthly fee.

The Pilat succession planning system is easy to use. Managers get access to the program via the Web using a password. They fill out online résumés for themselves, including career interests, and note special considerations such as geographic restrictions. They also assess themselves on four competencies. When the manager completes his or her succession planning input, the program automatically notifies the manager's boss. The latter then assesses his or her subordinate and indicates his or her overall potential and whether the person should be promoted. This assessment, plus the online résumés, then goes automatically to the division head and the divisional HR director. Dole's senior vice president for HR for North America then uses the information to create a career development plan for each manager.[34]

Forecasting the Supply of Outside Candidates

If there are not enough qualified inside candidates to fill anticipated openings, employers turn to projecting supplies of outside candidates—those not currently employed by your organization. This may require forecasting general economic conditions, local market conditions, and occupational market conditions. For example, unemployment rates of almost 10% in the United States in 2010 signaled to HR managers that finding good candidates would be easier.[35]

The first step is to forecast general economic conditions and, for instance, the expected prevailing rate of unemployment. Usually, the lower the rate of unemployment, the more difficult it is to recruit personnel. Look for economic projections online, for example, from the U.S. Congressional Budget Office (CBO), www.cbo. gov/showdoc.cfm?index=1824&sequence=0; the Bureau of Labor Statistics (BLS), www.bls.gov/news.release/ecpro.toc.htm; and from private sources such as economists and the Bank of America, www.bankofamerica.com/newsroom/press/press. cfm?PressID=press.20040312.02.htm.

Local labor market conditions are also important. For example, the growth of computer and semiconductor firms recently prompted lower unemployment in cities like Seattle, quite aside from general economic conditions in the country.

Finally, you may want to forecast the availability of potential job candidates in specific occupations. For example, information technology–related jobs, such as for network systems and data communications analysts, are among the most in-demand occupations for the period 2006–2016.[36] Sources such as *Occupational Outlook Quarterly* from the U.S. Labor Department can be useful here.

RECRUITING JOB CANDIDATES

Once authorized to fill a position, the next step is to develop an applicant pool, either from internal or external sources. Recruiting is important because the more applicants you have, the more selective you can be in your hiring. With baby boomers now retiring and fewer teenagers entering the labor pool, recruitment will be a challenge in the years ahead. By several estimates, the shortage of workers will grow from almost nothing today to about 20 million workers by 2020. At that point, the U.S. labor force may only be able to fill about 90% of the available jobs.[37] Effective recruitment is more important than most managers realize. The more qualified applicants you have, the more selective you can be in whom you hire.

The Complex Job of Recruiting Employees   Recruiting does not just involve placing ads or calling employment agencies. For one thing, we just saw that your recruitment efforts should make sense in terms of your company's strategic plans. As with JDS Uniphase, filling a large number of anticipated openings implies that you've carefully thought through when and how you will do your recruiting—the sources you will use, for instance.

Second, we'll see that some recruiting methods are superior to others, depending on who you're recruiting and what your resources are.

Third, the success you have with your recruiting depends on nonrecruitment issues and policies. For example, deciding to pay a 10% higher salary than most firms in your locale should, other things equal, help you build a bigger applicant pool faster.[38] Similarly, employers who send effective recruiters to campus and build relationships with opinion leaders such as career counselors and professors have better recruiting results.[39]

Then there are the numerous legal considerations. For example, the EEOC compliance manual makes it clear that with a nondiverse workforce, the EEOC may view relying on word-of-mouth referrals as a barrier to equal employment opportunity.[40] A combination of factors is also making it more difficult to hire workers from abroad. Security concerns and rising resistance from Congress is making it more difficult to obtain the coveted work visas permitting work in the United States.[41] The *HR in Practice* box provides another factor to consider.

Recruiting Effectiveness   Given all this, it's also important to assess how effectively the employer is spending its recruiting dollars. Should we advertise for clerical applicants on the Web or in Sunday's paper? Should we use this employment agency or that one? One survey found that only about 44% of the 279 firms surveyed make formal attempts to evaluate the outcomes of their recruitment efforts.[42] This inattention flies in the face of common sense.

Internal Sources of Candidates

Although recruiting may bring to mind job boards and classified ads, filling open jobs with current employees (internal recruiting) is often an employer's best bet. To be effective, this approach requires using job posting, and personnel records.[43] **Job posting** means "posting the open job—on company bulletin boards and/or Intranet—and listing its attributes, such as qualifications, supervisor, working schedule, and pay scale" (as in Figure 3.6). Some union contracts require such postings to ensure that union members get first choice. Yet posting is also good practice in nonunion firms, as

HR in Practice: The Hiring Manager's Obligations

The recruiting manager should be careful not to interfere with the applicant's obligations to his or her current employer. In general, even without a written contract, courts hold that employees have a duty of loyalty to their current employers during their employment.[44] For example, they are generally expected to maintain the confidentiality of confidential information such as customer lists. In general, the hiring manager has both an ethical and legal obligation to respect the prospective employee's duty of loyalty. To the extent that the hiring manager participates in any breach of that loyalty—for instance, inquiring about customers' buying patterns or about new products—the hiring manager may share in the liability for the breach. One way to handle this problem is to make it clear at the outset that you expect applicants to honor their duty of loyalty to their current employers.[45]

Figure 3.6 Job Posting Form for Hard Copy or Web Submissions

JOB POSTING FORM

Please complete all applicable areas and return via e-mail (JobForm@bigCo.com) or
FAX (123-456-7890)

Date Posted _____

Reply no later than _____

Type of Employment   Summer _____   Part-Time _____   Full-Time _____

Job Title of Open Position _____

Employer _____ Department _____

Location Address _____

Web Site _____

Pay Scale _____ Shifts/Hours _____ # of Vacancies _____

Brief Job Description _____
_____
_____
_____
_____
_____
_____

Qualifications: Required Skills and Abilities _____
_____
_____
_____
_____
_____

Desired Skills and Abilities _____
_____
_____
_____
_____
_____
_____

How to Apply: By FAX or e-mail as above, no later than _____ . Please ensure
HR has updated copy of your résumé. Selections will be made by _____ .

it facilitates the promotion of qualified inside candidates. Personnel records are also useful here. An examination of personnel records (including qualifications inventories) may reveal individuals who have potential for further training or who already have the background for the open job.

Recruiting via the Internet

You may not be able to fill your recruiting needs with internal candidates. In that case, one turns to outside sources, often starting with the Internet.[46]

Many firms use their company Web sites. For example, GE's home page (www.ge.com) includes a link to www.gepowercareers.com. GE's site also includes numerous job-seeker aids, like a button for "military officer." Others, of course, post positions on Internet job boards such as Careerbuilder.com and Monster.com, on the sites of professional associations (such as the American Institute of Chemical Engineers), or the sites of their local newspapers. Other employers simply screen through job boards' résumé listings.[47]

Whether using one's own site or a job board, it's important to capitalize on the Web's advertising strengths. For example, the Cheesecake Factory doesn't just post short help wanted ads on the Web. Instead, it usually includes the whole job description.[48] Ideally, you should also include a way (such as a checklist of the job's human requirements) for potential applicants to gauge the extent to which the job is a good fit.[49] As for all advertised ads, more information is usually better than less. Job applicants view ads with more specific job information as more attractive and more credible.[50] Studies suggest that employers should probably include employee testimonials on their recruitment Web sites. Testimonials in the form of video and audio have the most impact.[51]

Accountants Deloitte & Touche Tohmatsu created a global recruitment site, thus eliminating its 35 local recruiting Web sites.[52] Challenging times are prompting employers to reevaluate how they use Web recruiting, as the accompanying *Managing HR in Challenging Times* feature illustrates.

New sites capitalize on social networking. Users supply their name, location, and the kind of work they do on sites like LinkIn.com. These sites facilitate developing

Managing HR in Challenging Times: Reducing Recruitment Costs

Challenging economic times prompt employers to cut recruiting costs. One expert says employers should ask for deals with recruitment sites. For example, get a 1-year discount on a shorter contract. Employers are also turning to free (or almost free) recruitment options. Free or low-cost recruitment resources include Craigslist and Jobbing.com. More employers are also using their states' one-stop career centers, not for just nonexempt employees, but for professional and administrative employees as well.[53] Others use text messaging. For example, at one diversity-oriented conference, Hewitt Associates displayed posters asking attendees to text message *hewdiversity* to a specific five-digit number. Each person texting in then periodically received text messages about Hewitt openings.[54]

personal relationships for networking, hiring, and employee referrals.[55] (If you're an applicant, note that U.S. laws generally *do not* prohibit job boards from sharing your data with other sources. One reportedly had personal information on over a million subscribers stolen.)[56] Some top online recruiting job sites include yahoohotjobs, jobcentral, collegerecruiter, careerbuilder, monster, and job.com.

Job boards account for about 12.3% of recent hires. Other major sources include company Web site (20.1%), referrals (27.3%), plus others such as temp to hire, rehires, and employment agencies.

Recruiters may be moving away from major job boards such as careerbuilder.com. Instead, they're seeking passive candidates (people not actively looking for jobs) through employee referrals and by using social networking sites such as LinkedIn.[57] One Massachusetts staffing firm uses its Facebook and LinkedIn pages to announce openings. Other firms use Twitter to announce job openings to job seekers who subscribe to their Twitter feeds.[58] ResumePal, from the career site Jobfox, is a recruiting innovation. ResumePal is an online standard job application. Jobseekers submit it to participating employers, who can then use the standardized application's keywords to identify viable candidates (http://www.resumepal.com/Site/Default.aspx).[59]

User-Friendly Employer Sites   Some estimate employers have only about 4 minutes "before online applicants will turn their attention elsewhere."[60] For example, make it easy to get from the home page to the career section in just one or two clicks; allow job seekers to apply online and via fax or e-mail, and include a tool that lets visitors register and receive e-mail notices about new jobs.[61]

Advantages and Disadvantages   Internet ("e-") recruiting's wide use reflects its advantages—it is quick, cheap, and effective. Job boards tend to cost less than print ads and allow employers to post more information. Internet recruiting responses also come in almost at once.

However, that's a double-edged sword. The ease of responding encourages unqualified job seekers to apply. Overall, though, more applicants are usually better than fewer, and more companies are digitizing and processing applicants electronically.[62] E-recruiting also has potential legal pitfalls. For example, fewer minorities use the Internet, so employers may inadvertently exclude minority applicants.[63]

Applicant Tracking Services   More firms today install applicant-tracking systems to support their on- and offline recruiting efforts. Well-known applicant tracking systems (such as recruitsoft.com and Itrack-IT solutions) help employers manage large numbers of applicants, by screening, categorizing, keeping track of applicants, and matching them to jobs. Systems like these also help employers compile reports, such as "applicants by reject reason."[64] Many employers outsource this tracking work to application service providers (ASPs). These process the applicants who go to your site, using their own systems. Other employers let job boards post their open jobs and process the online applications.[65] Major suppliers of e-recruiting tracking (and other) services include Automatic Data Processing (ADP.com), HRSmart (hrsmart.com), Silkroad Technology (silkroad.com), and Monster (monster.com).[66]

Advertising as a Source of Candidates

Placing a help wanted print ad begins with deciding where to place the ad. The best medium (such as your local paper, the Web, the *Wall Street Journal,* or a technical journal) depends on the job. The local newspaper or the Web is usually the best source of blue-collar help, clerical employees, and lower-level administrative employees. For professionals, you can advertise on the Web or in trade and professional journals such as the *American Psychologist, Sales Management, Chemical Engineering,* and *American Banker.* Help wanted ads in papers such as the *Wall Street Journal* are good sources of middle- or senior-management personnel. One drawback to print advertising is that there may be a week or more between insertion of the ad and publication.

Employment Agencies as a Source of Candidates

There are three types of employment agencies: (1) those operated by federal, state, or local governments; (2) those associated with nonprofit organizations; and (3) privately owned agencies.

Public state employment agencies exist in every state, aided and coordinated by the U.S. Department of Labor. The latter also maintains a nationwide computerized job bank to which state employment offices connect. Public agencies are a major source of blue-collar and often white-collar workers.

These agencies' usefulness is rising. Beyond just filling jobs, counselors will visit an employer's work site, review the employer's job requirements, and even assist the employer in writing job descriptions. And most states have turned their local state employment service agencies into "one-stop" shops. Under a single roof, employers and job seekers can access an array of services such as recruitment services, employee training programs, and local and national labor market information.

Other employment agencies are associated with *nonprofit organizations*. For example, most professional and technical societies have units that help their members find jobs. Many public welfare agencies try to place people who are in special categories, such as those who are disabled.

Private employment agencies are important sources of clerical, white-collar, and managerial personnel. Their fees are usually set by state law and are posted in their offices. Most often, the employer pays the fees.

Some reasons you might want to turn to an agency include the following:

- Your firm does not have its own human resource department.
- Your firm has found it difficult to generate a pool of qualified applicants.
- You must fill an opening quickly.
- There is a perceived need to attract a greater number of minority or female applicants.
- The recruitment effort aims to reach employed individuals who might feel more comfortable dealing with employment agencies than with competing companies.

On the other hand, employment agencies are no panacea. For example, the employment agency's screening may let unqualified applicants go directly to the supervisors doing the hiring, who then naively hire the unscreened candidates.

Temporary Workers Many employers supplement their permanent employee base by hiring contingent or temporary workers, often through temporary help agencies. Also called *part-time* or *just-in-time* workers, the *contingent workforce* is big, growing, and not limited to clerical or maintenance staff. Each year upward of 100,000 people find temporary work in engineering, science, or management support occupations.

Employers can hire such workers either directly or through temporary staff agencies. The employer usually pays direct-hire temps directly, as it does all its employees. However, it classifies them separately from regular employees, usually as casual, seasonal, or temporary employees.[67] Temporary employees typically receive few if any benefits (such as pensions).

If you hire temps through agencies, the agency usually pays the employees' salaries and (any) benefits. For instance, Nike Inc. signed a multimillion-dollar deal with Kelly Services to manage Nike's temporary hires.[68]

Using such agencies requires care. Several years ago, federal agents rounded up illegal "contract" workers in 60 Walmart stores. The case underscores the need for employers to understand the source of the contract employees who work on their premises handling activities such as, in Walmart's case, after-hours store cleaning, under the auspices of contingent staffing firms.[69]

Alternative Staffing Temporary employees are examples of alternative staffing—basically, the use of nontraditional recruitment sources. Other alternative staffing arrangements include "contract technical employees" (highly skilled workers like engineers, who are supplied for long-term projects under contract from an outside technical services firm). The use of alternative staffing sources is widespread and growing. About 1 of 10 U.S. employees is employed in some type of alternative work arrangement.

Executive Recruiters as a Source of Candidates

Executive recruiters (also called *headhunters*) are special employment agencies that employers retain to seek out top-management talent. They fill jobs in the $80,000 and up category, although $120,000 is often the lower limit. The percentage of your firm's positions filled by these services might be small. However, these jobs include the most crucial executive and technical positions. For top executive positions, headhunters may be your only source. The employer pays their fees.[70]

Many (but not all) of these firms are specialized, a fact that facilitates quickly finding candidates when, for instance, an academic recruiter is asked to fill a university president's spot. But even specialists will need to advertise for candidates. And most of these firms are also adept at using Internet-linked databases to create a list of potential candidates.

Pros and Cons Headhunters have many contacts and are especially adroit at contacting qualified employed candidates who are not actively seeking jobs. They can also keep your firm's name confidential until late in the search process. The recruiter can save top management time by doing the preliminary work of advertising for and screening applicants. The recruiter's fee might actually be insignificant compared to the cost of the executive time saved.

But there are drawbacks. As an employer, you must carefully explain the sort of candidate you require and why. Some recruiters may be more interested in persuading you to hire a candidate than in finding one who will do the best job. Sometimes, what clients say or think they want isn't really what they need. Therefore, be prepared for some in-depth dissecting of your request.[71] Also, meet the person who will actually be handling your search, and nail down the exact charges. Make sure the recruiter checks candidates' references, but double-check the final candidate's references yourself.[72]

Candidates' Caveats   As a job candidate, keep several things in mind when dealing with executive search firms. Some of these firms may present an unpromising candidate to a client just to make their other candidates look better. Some eager clients may also jump the gun, undermining your present position prematurely. Finally, do not confuse executive search firms with the many executive assistance or coaching firms that help out-of-work executives find jobs. The latter charge the job seekers handsome fees to assist with things like résumé preparation and interview skills. They rarely actually reach out to prospective employers to find their clients jobs.

Also, know that recruiters are usually coy about revealing the full amount they're willing to pay. For example, one researcher found that 9 out of 10 recruiters say they do not reveal, during hiring interviews, the full amount they're willing to pay for the job. There's often more flexibility than applicants realize.[73]

College Recruiting and Interns as Sources of Candidates

College recruiting is an important source of management trainees and of professional and technical employees.

Campus recruiting has two main problems. First, it's expensive. Schedules must be set well in advance, company brochures printed, and much recruiting time spent on campus. Second, even more than usual, the recruiter needs to be personable and effective.[74] Students complain that some recruiters are unprepared, show little interest, act superior, and don't know what to ask.

Campus recruiters should have two goals. The main goal is determining whether a candidate is worthy of further consideration. Exactly which traits you look for depends on your specific recruiting needs. However, the checklist in Figure 3.7 is typical. Traits to assess include motivation, communication skills, education, appearance, and attitude.

The second aim is to attract ("recruit") good candidates to your firm. A sincere and informal attitude, respect for the applicant, and prompt follow-up letters can help here.

Internships   Many college students get their jobs through college internships, a recruiting approach that has grown dramatically.

Internships can be win-win situations. For students, an internship may mean being able to hone business skills, check out potential employers, and learn more about their career likes (and dislikes). Employers can use the interns to make useful contributions while evaluating them as possible full-time employees. One survey found that employers offer jobs to over 70% of their interns.[75]

Collaborating with a college or university's career center facilitates on-campus recruiting.[76] The Shell Group of companies reduced the schools its recruiters visit

Figure 3.7 Candidate Evaluation Form for On/Off Campus Use

Candidate Evaluation Form

Interviewer _____   Date _____

Candidate
Name _____   Position _____

Scoring

Candidate evaluation forms are to be completed by the interviewer to rank the candidate's overall qualifications for the position to which they have applied. Under each heading the interviewer should give the candidate a numerical rating and write specific job-related comments in the space provided. The numerical rating system is based on the following.

5 - Exceptional	4 - Above Average	3 - Average	2 - Satisfactory	1 - Unsatisfactory

Educational Background - Does the candidate have the appropriate educational qualifications or training for this position?

Rating: 1 2 3 4 5

Comments:

Prior Work Experience - Has the candidate acquired similar skills or qualifications through past work experiences?

Rating: 1 2 3 4 5

Comments:

Technical Qualifications/Experience - Does the candidate have the technical skills necessary for this position?

Rating: 1 2 3 4 5

Comments:

Verbal Communication - How were the candidate's communication skills during the interview (i.e. body language, answers to questions)?

Rating: 1 2 3 4 5

Comments:

Candidate Enthusiasm - How much interest did the candidate show in the position and the company?

Rating: 1 2 3 4 5

Comments:

Knowledge of Company - Did the candidate research the company prior to the interview?

Rating: 1 2 3 4 5

Comments:

(Continued)

Teambuilding/Interpersonal Skills - Did the candidate demonstrate, through their answers, good teambuilding/interpersonal skills?

Rating: 1 2 3 4 5

Comments:

Initiative - Did the candidate demonstrate, through their answers, a high degree of initiative?

Rating: 1 2 3 4 5

Comments:

Time Management - Did the candidate demonstrate, through their answers, good time management skills?

Rating: 1 2 3 4 5

Comments:

Customer Service - Did the candidate demonstrate, through their answers, a high level of customer service skills/abilities?

Rating: 1 2 3 4 5

Comments:

Salary Expectations - What were the candidate's salary expectations? Were they within the range for the position?

Rating: 1 2 3 4 5

Comments:

Overall Impression and Recommendation - Final comments and recommendations for proceeding with the candidate.

Rating: 1 2 3 4 5

Comments:

Source: Society for Human Resource Management (SHRM). www.shrm.org/hrtools/forms_published/ 2CMS_002131.asp, accessed August 9, 2007.

to 26, based on things like academic program quality, number of students enrolled, and student body diversity.[77] The recent recession reduced the number of firms recruiting on college campuses. Between 2008 and 2009, about 52% of employers surveyed said they decreased such activities.[78]

Outsourcing and Offshoring

Rather than bringing people in to do the company's jobs, outsourcing and offshoring send the jobs out. *Outsourcing* means having outside vendors supply services (such as benefits management) that the company's own employees previously did in-house. *Offshoring* is a narrower term. It means having outside vendors *abroad* supply services that the company's own employees previously did in-house.

Outsourcing and offshoring are contentious. Particularly in challenging economic times, employees, unions, legislators, and even many business owners feel that "shipping jobs out" (particularly overseas) is ill-advised. That notwithstanding, employers are sending more jobs out, and not just blue-collar jobs. As explained in Chapter 1, current projections show that about 3 million white-collar jobs moved abroad in the past few years. But rising overseas wages (call-center hourly wages in India rose from $2 an hour in 1998 to $6 in 2008, for instance), higher oil prices, and quality issues are prompting more U.S. employers to bring their jobs home.[79]

Referrals and Walk-Ins as a Source of Candidates

With *employee referrals* campaigns, the firm posts announcements of openings and requests for referrals on its Intranet and bulletin boards. It may offer prizes for referrals that culminate in hiring.

Employee referral programs have pros and cons. The biggest advantage is that referrals tend to generate "more applicants, more hires, and a higher yield ratio [hires/applicants]."[80] Current employees usually do provide accurate information about the applicants they refer, and those hired through referrals subsequently tend to be among the lower turnover employees.[81] The new employees may also come with a more realistic picture of the employer after speaking with friends who work there. Referral programs may also result in higher-quality candidates, insofar as employees are reluctant to refer less-qualified candidates. But the success of the campaign depends on your employees' morale. And the campaign can backfire if an employee's referral is rejected and the employee becomes dissatisfied. Using referrals exclusively may also be discriminatory if most of your current employees (and their referrals) are, say, white.

Employee referral programs are popular. They have been the source of almost half of all hires at AmeriCredit since the firm kicked off its "you've got friends, we want to meet them" employee referral program. Employees making a referral receive $1,000 awards, with the payments spread over a year. As the head of recruiting says, "Quality people know quality people."[82]

Walk-Ins   Particularly for hourly workers, *walk-ins*—direct applications made at your office—are a major source of applicants, and you can even encourage them by posting "for hire" signs on your property. Treat all walk-ins courteously and diplomatically, for the sake of both common decency and your firm's reputation. Many employers thus give every walk-in a brief interview, even if it is only to get information in case a position should open in the future. If possible, all applicants should also receive a response, and preferably, a personalized one.[83]

Don't underestimate the importance of employee referrals. One review of recruitment sources concluded, for instance, "Referrals by current personnel, in-house job postings, and the rehiring of former employees are the most effective [recruiting] sources. Walk-ins have been slightly less effective, and the least effective sources are newspaper ads, school placement services, and employment agencies (government/private)."[84]

Customers as Candidates   The Container Store uses a successful variant of the employee referrals campaign. They train their employees to recruit new employees from among the firm's customers. For example, if an employee sees that a customer seems interested in the Container Store, the employee might say, "If you love shopping here, you'd love working here."[85]

Telecommuters   Hiring "telecommuters" is another option. For example, JetBlue Airways uses at-home agents who are JetBlue employees to handle its reservation needs. These "crew members" all live in the Salt Lake City area, and work from their homes. They use JetBlue-assigned computers and technology, and receive JetBlue training.[86]

Strategy and HR   To support its fast-growth strategy, The Cheesecake Factory uses four recruiting sources: employee referrals, promotions of current employees, search firms, and online job postings. The firm's head of HR says the Web has become "our No. 1 source of recruitment, with between 30% and 35% of our new managers coming through it." For most jobs, it posts the entire job description. This helps provide potential applicants with a realistic picture of the job. The server's CareerBuilder.com description includes a 765-word list of duties, for instance.[87]

Military Personnel

Returning and discharged U.S. military personnel provide an excellent source of trained recruits. Several military branches have programs to facilitate soldiers finding jobs. For example, the U.S. Army's Partnership for Youth Success enables someone entering the army to select a post-army corporate partner for an employment interview, as a way to help soldiers find jobs after leaving the army.[88]

Recruiting a More Diverse Workforce

As noted earlier, the composition of the U.S. workforce is changing. More employees will be older, minorities, and women. This means taking special steps to recruit older workers, minorities, and women.

Many factors contribute to successful diversity recruiting. For example, flexible hours make it easier to attract and keep single parents. Overall, the important thing is to take steps that say, "This is a good place for diverse employees to work." This might include using diverse ads, emphasizing inclusiveness in policy statements, and using minority and female recruiters.[89]

Employers can boost the numbers of qualified minority applicants. The basic aim is to unearth applicants with the desired qualities (such as cognitive ability and conscientiousness). So, for example, seek out candidates based on academic achievement information such as dean's lists. Google posted math puzzles on large signs in subway stations in major cities. When people who solved the puzzles followed a Web link, Google encouraged them to submit résumés.[90]

Older Workers as a Source of Candidates   Employers are looking to older workers as a source of recruits, for several reasons. Because of recessions, buyouts, and early retirements, many workers who retired early want to reenter the job market. Furthermore, the number of retirees is rising as the baby boom generation retires, and employers are having trouble replacing them with younger workers. For wary employers, a survey by the American Association of Retired Persons (AARP) and the Society for Human Resource Management (SHRM) concluded that older workers actually tend to have lower absenteeism and more reliability than younger workers do.[91]

Recruiting and attracting older workers involve any or all of the sources described earlier (advertising, employment agencies, and so forth), but with one big difference, since older workers have some special preferences.[92] The most effective ads here emphasize schedule flexibility.[93] For example:

- *Develop flexible work options.* At Wrigley Company, workers over age 65 can progressively shorten their work schedules; another company uses "mini-shifts" to accommodate those interested in working less than full time.
- *Offer flexible benefit plans.* Older employees often put more emphasis on longer vacations or on continued accrual of pension credits than do younger workers. Include full benefits for part-timers.[94]

Recruiting Single Parents   About two thirds of all single parents are in the workforce, so they represent an important source of candidates.

Formulating an effective program for attracting single parents should begin with understanding the problems that they face in balancing work and family life. In one survey, working single parents (most are single mothers) described as a no-win situation the challenge of having to both do a good job at work and be a good parent. However, most were hesitant to dwell on their single-parent status at work for fear that such disclosures would jeopardize their jobs.[95] Given such concerns, the first step in attracting (and keeping) single parents is to make the workplace as user-friendly for single parents as practical. Many firms institute *flextime* programs to provide employees some flexibility (such as 1-hour windows at the beginning or end of the day) but they "may not be sufficient to really make a difference."[96] Accountants Deloitte and Touche instituted a "Career Customization Program." Employees periodically complete short surveys indicating whether they want to "maintain," "dial up," or "dial down" their hours and responsibilities. They then work with their managers to reformulate their responsibilities.[97]

Supervisor training is especially important: "Very often, the relationships which the single mother has with her supervisor and co-workers is a significant factor influencing whether the single-parent employee perceives the work environment to be supportive."[98]

Recruiting Minorities and Women   The same prescriptions apply to recruiting minorities and women. In other words, employers have to formulate plans for attracting minorities and women, including reevaluating personnel policies and developing flexible work options.

To the extent that many minority applicants may not meet the educational or experience standards for a job, many companies (such as Aetna Life & Casualty) offer remedial training in arithmetic and writing. Recruiting via online diversity data banks or minority-focused recruiting publications are other options. Checking with your own minority employees can also be useful. The *Global Issues* box provides an additional perspective.

Sometimes the easiest way to recruit women and minorities is to make sure that they don't quit in the first place. For example, the accounting firm KPMG works to make sure female employees on maternity leave want to return. It sends expectant mothers a basket containing a description of its parental leave benefits as well as a baby bottle, a rattle, and a tiny "My mom works at KPMG" T-shirt.[103]

Welfare-to-Work Employers are also implementing various "welfare-to-work" programs for attracting and assimilating as new employees former welfare recipients.

The key to such programs' success is the employer's pretraining assimilation program. During these, participants receive counseling and basic skills training spread over several weeks.[104] For example, Marriott hired 600 welfare recipients under its Pathways to Independence program. The heart of the program was a 6-week preemployment training program. This taught work and life skills and was designed to rebuild workers' self-esteem and instill positive attitudes about work.[105]

The Disabled The EEOC estimates that nearly 70% of the disabled are jobless, but it certainly doesn't have to be that way.[106] Thousands of employers in the United States and elsewhere have found that disabled employees provide an excellent and largely untapped source of competent, productive labor for jobs ranging from information technology to creative advertising to receptionist.

DEVELOPING AND USING APPLICATION FORMS

Purpose of Application Forms

Once you have a pool of applicants, the selection process can begin, and for most employers the application form is the first step in this process. (Some firms first require a brief, prescreening interview.) The **application form** is a quick way to collect verifiable (and therefore reasonably accurate) historical data (education, prior work history, and so on) from the candidate.

A filled-in form provides five types of information. First are data on *substantive matters*, such as, does the applicant have the required education? Second, you can draw some conclusions about the applicant's *career progress*. Third, you can draw tentative conclusions regarding the applicant's *employment stability*. (However, with recent recessions and downsizings, this is a less accurate gauge.) Fourth, it provides information to *check references* and to assess the veracity of the applicant's answers.

Finally, employers use application information ("bio data") to *predict* employee tenure and performance. Thus in one study, researchers found that applicants who had longer tenure with previous employers were less likely to quit and had higher performance six months after hire.[107]

Most employers need several application forms. For technical and managerial personnel, the form may require detailed answers concerning such areas as education. The form for hourly factory workers might focus on tools and equipment the applicant used.

Equal Opportunity and Application Forms

Employers should carefully review their application forms to ensure they comply with equal employment laws. Questions concerning race, religion, age, sex, or national origin aren't necessarily illegal under federal laws, but are illegal under some state laws. However, the EEOC views them with disfavor. And if the applicant shows that the questions screen out a disproportionate number of protected group applicants, the employer will have to prove that the potentially discriminatory items are related to success on the job and not unfairly discriminatory.

Perhaps due to their proliferation, online application forms may be particularly susceptible to illegal or inadvisable questions. One survey of 41 Internet-based applications found that over 97% contained at least one inadvisable question. Questions regarding the applicant's age and driver's license information led the list.[108]

Figure 3.8 presents the approach the FBI uses to collect applicant information. The Employment History section requests information on each prior employer, including job title, duties, and supervisor. Also, note that in signing the application, good practice dictates that the applicant certifies several things. For example, that falsified statements may be cause for dismissal; that investigation of credit, employment, and driving records is authorized; that a medical examination may be required; that drug screening tests may be required; and that employment is for no definite period of time.

Mandatory Dispute Resolution   Although the EEOC is generally opposed, more employers are requiring applicants to sign mandatory alternative dispute resolution forms as part of the application process. These generally require applicants to agree to arbitrate certain legal disputes related to their application for employment or employment with the company.

Courts, federal agencies, and even arbitrators are concerned that binding arbitration strips away too many employees' rights (*voluntary* arbitration is not under

Figure 3.8 Employment Application

FEDERAL BUREAU OF INVESTIGATION

**Preliminary Application for
Special Agent Position
(Please Type or Print in Black Ink)**

Date: _____

I. PERSONAL HISTORY

Name in Full (Last, First, Middle)	List College Degree(s) Already Received or Pursuing, Major, School, and Month/Year:

Marital Status: ☐ Single ☐ Engaged ☐ Married ☐ Separated ☐ Legally Separated ☐ Widowed ☐ Divorced

Birth Date (Month, Day, Year) Birth Place:	Social Security Number: (Optional)	Do you understand FBI employment requires availability for assignment anywhere in the U.S.?

Current Address

Street _____ Apt. No. _____

Home Phone _____
Area Code _____ Number _____

City _____ State _____ Zip Code _____

Work Phone _____
Area Code _____ Number _____

Are you: CPA ☐ Yes ☐ No   Licensed Driver ☐ Yes ☐ No   U. S. Citizen ☐ Yes ☐ No

Have you served on active duty in the U. S. Military? ☐ Yes ☐ No If yes, indicate branch of service and dates (month/year) of active duty. Include military school attendance (month/year):

How did you learn or become interested in FBI employment as a Special Agent?	Have you previously applied for FBI employment? ☐ Yes ☐ No If yes, location and date:

Do you have a foreign language background? ☐ Yes ☐ No   List proficiency for each language on reverse side.

Have you ever been arrested for any crime (include major traffic violations such as Driving Under the Influence or While Intoxicated, etc.)? ☐ Yes ☐ No If so, list all such matters on a continuation sheet, even if not formally charged, or no court appearance or found not guilty, or matter settled by payment of fine or forfeiture of collateral. Include date, place, charge, disposition, details, and police agency on reverse side.

II. EMPLOYMENT HISTORY

Identify your most recent three years FULL-TIME work experience, after high school (excluding summer, part-time and temporary employment).

From Month/Year	To Month/Year	Title of Position and Description of Work	# of hrs. Per week	Name/Location of Employer

III. PERSONAL DECLARATIONS

Persons with a disability who require an accommodation to complete the application process are required to notify the FBI of their need for the accommodation.

Have you used marijuana during the last three years or more than 15 times? ☐ Yes ☐ No

Have you used any illegal drug(s) or combination of illegal drugs, other than marijuana, more than 5 times or during the last 10 years? ☐ Yes ☐ No

All information provided by applicants concerning their drug history will be subject to verification by a preemployment polygraph examination.

Do you understand all prospective FBI employees will be required to submit to an urinalysis for drug abuse prior to employment? ☐ Yes ☐ No

Please do not write below this line.

I am aware that willfully withholding information or making false statements on this application constitutes a violation of Section 1001. Title 18, U.S. Code and if appointed, will be the basis for dismissal from the Federal Bureau of Investigation. I agree to these conditions and I hereby certify that all statements made by me on this application are true and complete, to the best of my knowledge.

Signature of applicant as usually written (**Do Not Use Nickname**)

attack).[109] In one study, making employment arbitration mandatory had a significantly negative impact on the attractiveness to the subjects of the company as a place to work.[110]

After You Receive the Application

After you receive the application, screening the applicants begins, and we turn to selection and screening in Chapter 4. Here you'll review the applicant's résumé and application, as well as any other information you've gleaned during the screening process.

Video Résumés More candidates are submitting video résumés, a practice replete with benefits and threats. About half of responding employers in one survey thought video résumés might give employers a better feel for the candidate's professional demeanor and presentation skills. The problem is that a video résumé makes it more likely rejected candidates may claim discrimination.[111] Extra EEO-related diligence is required.

Courtesy Some employers develop expensive recruiting programs and then drop the ball by treating candidates discourteously. A Monster.com survey illustrates this. What interviewer behaviors most annoyed job seekers? Seventy percent of job seekers listed, "Acting as if there is no time to talk to me." About half listed "turning interview into cross-examination" and "showing up late."[112]

REVIEW

Summary

1. Developing an organization structure results in jobs that have to be staffed. Job analysis is the procedure through which you find out (1) what the job entails and (2) what kinds of people should be hired for the job. It involves six steps: (1) Determine the use of the job analysis information, (2) collect background information, (3) select the positions to be analyzed, (4) collect job analysis data, (5) review information with participants, and (6) develop a job description and job specification.

2. Always ask yourself: Will the new employee understand the job if he or she reads the job description?

3. The job specification supplements the job description to answer the question: What human traits and experience are necessary to do this job well? It tells

what kind of person to recruit and for what qualities that person should be tested. Job specifications are based on the educated guesses of managers or on statistical analysis.

4. Increasingly, firms don't want employees to feel limited by a specific set of responsibilities such as those listed in a job description. As a result, more employers are deemphasizing detailed job descriptions, often substituting summaries of the competencies or skills required for the position.

5. Developing personnel plans requires three forecasts: one for personnel requirements, one for the supply of outside candidates, and one for the supply of inside candidates. To predict the need for personnel, first project the demand for the product or service. Next relate personnel needs to these estimates.

6. Once personnel needs are projected, the next step is to build a pool of qualified applicants. We discussed several sources of candidates, including internal sources, the Web, advertising, employment agencies, executive recruiters, college recruiting, and referrals and walk-ins. It is unlawful to discriminate against any individual with respect to employment because of race, color, religion, sex, national origin, or age (unless these are bona fide occupational qualifications).

7. Once you have a pool of applicants, the work of selecting the best can begin. We turn to employee selection in the Chapter 4.

KEY TERMS

- job analysis
- job description
- job specification
- workforce planning
- trend analysis
- ratio analysis
- scatter plot
- qualifications inventories
- personnel replacement charts
- job posting
- application form

DISCUSSION QUESTIONS

1. What items are typically included in a job description? What items are not shown?
2. What is job analysis? How can you make use of the information it provides?
3. We discussed several methods for collecting job analysis data. Compare these methods, explain what each is useful for, and list the pros and cons of each.
4. Explain how you would conduct a job analysis.
5. Compare five sources of job candidates.
6. What types of information can an application form provide?

INDIVIDUAL AND GROUP ACTIVITIES

1. Bring to class several classified and display ads from the Sunday help wanted ads. Analyze the effectiveness of these ads.
2. Working individually or in groups, develop a five-year forecast of occupational market conditions for an occupation such as accountant or nurse.
3. Working individually or in groups, visit the local office of your state employment agency. Come back to class prepared to discuss the following questions: What types of jobs seem to be available through this agency, predominantly? To what extent do you think this agency would be a good source of professional and/or managerial applicants? What sorts of paperwork are applicants to the state agency required to complete before their applications are processed? What other services does the office provide?
4. Working individually or in groups, interview a manager between the ages of 25 and 35 at a local business

who manages employees age 40 or older. Ask the manager to describe three or four of his or her most challenging experiences managing older employees.

5. Working individually or in groups, review help wanted ads placed over the past few Sundays by local employment agencies. Do some employment agencies seem to specialize in some types of jobs? If you were an HR manager, which local agencies would you turn to first, based on their help wanted ad history, for these jobs: engineers, secretaries, accountants, and factory workers?

6. Working individually or in groups, obtain copies of job descriptions for clerical positions at the college or university you attend or the firm where you work. How would you improve the descriptions?

APPLICATION EXERCISES

Case Incident Finding People Who Are Passionate about What They Do

Trilogy Enterprises Inc. provides software solutions to giant global firms for improving sales and performance. It prides itself on its unique and unorthodox culture.

There is no dress code and employees make their own hours, often very long. They tend to socialize together (the average age is 26), both in the office's well-stocked kitchen and on company-sponsored events and trips to places like local dance clubs and retreats in Hawaii. An in-house jargon has developed, and the shared history of the firm has taken on the status of legend. Responsibility is heavy and comes early, with a "just do it now" attitude that dispenses with long apprenticeships. New recruits are given a few weeks of intensive training, known as Trilogy University and described by participants as "more like boot camp than business school." Information is delivered as if with "a fire hose," and new employees are expected to commit their expertise and vitality to everything they do. Jeff Daniel, director of college recruiting, admits the intense and unconventional firm is not for everybody. "But it's definitely an environment where people who are passionate about what they do can thrive."

The firm employs about 700 such passionate people. Trilogy's managers know the rapid growth they seek depends on having a staff of the best people they can find, quickly trained and given broad responsibility and freedom as soon as possible. CEO Joe Liemandt says, "At a software company, people are everything. You can't build the next great software company, which is what we're trying to do here, unless you're totally committed to that. Of course, the leaders at every company say, 'People are everything.' But they don't act on it."

Trilogy makes finding the right people (it calls them "great people") a company-wide mission. Recruiters actively pursue the freshest people in the job market, scouring college career fairs and computer science departments for talented overachievers with ambition and entrepreneurial instincts. Top managers conduct the first rounds of interviews, letting prospects know they will be pushed to achieve but will be well rewarded. Employees take top recruits and their significant others out on the town when they come to Austin for the three-day preliminary visit. A typical day might begin with grueling interviews but end with mountain biking or laser tag. Executives have been known to fly out to meet and woo hot prospects.

One year, Trilogy reviewed 15,000 résumés, conducted 4,000 on-campus interviews, flew 850 prospects in for interviews, and hired 262 college graduates, who account for over a third of its current employees. The cost per hire was $13,000; Jeff Daniel believes it was worth every penny. ∎

QUESTIONS

1. Identify some of the established recruiting techniques that underlie Trilogy's unconventional approach to attracting talent.
2. What particular elements of Trilogy's culture most likely appeal to the kind of employees it seeks? How does it convey those elements to job prospects?

Source: Chuck Salter, "Insanity, Inc.," *Fast Company*, January 1999, pp. 101–108; and http://www.trilogy.com/careers.php, Accessed May 18, 2010/

Continuing Case

LearnInMotion.com: Who Do We Have to Hire?

As the excitement surrounding the move into their new offices wound down, the two principal owners of LearnInMotion.com, Mel and Jennifer, turned to the task of hiring new employees. In their business plan they'd specified several basic aims for the venture capital funds they'd just received, and hiring a team topped the list. They knew their other goals—boosting sales and expanding the Web site, for instance—would be unreachable without the right team.

They were just about to place their ads when Mel asked a question that brought them to a stop: "What kind of people do we want to hire?" It seemed they hadn't really considered this. They knew the answer in general terms, of course. For example, they knew they needed at least two salespeople, plus a programmer, a Web designer, and several content management people to transform the incoming material into content they could post on their site. But it was obvious that job titles alone really didn't provide enough guidance. For example, how could they decide what sorts of experiences and skills they had to look for in their candidates if they didn't know exactly what these candidates would have to do? They wouldn't even know what questions to ask.

And that wasn't all. For example, there were obviously other tasks to do, and these weren't necessarily included in the sorts of things that salespeople, programmers, Web designers, or content management people typically do. Who was going to answer the phones? (Jennifer and Mel had

originally assumed they'd put in an automated call directory and voice-mail system until they found out it would cost close to $10,000.) Who was going to keep track of the monthly expenses and compile them for the accountants, who'd then produce monthly reports for the venture capitalist? Would the salespeople generate their own leads? Or would LearnInMotion.com have to hire Web surfers to search and find the names of people for the sales staff to call or e-mail? What would happen when the company had to purchase supplies, such as fax paper or computer disks? Would the owners have to do it themselves, or should they have someone in-house do it for them? The list went on and on.

It was obvious, in other words, that the owners had to get their managerial act together and draw up the sorts of documents they'd read about as business majors—job descriptions, job specifications, and so forth. The trouble is, it all seemed a lot easier when they read the textbook. Now they want you, their management consultants, to help them actually do it. Here's what they want you to do for them. ∎

QUESTIONS AND ASSIGNMENTS

1. Draw up a set of job descriptions for each of the positions in the case: salesperson, Web designer, programmer, and content manager. You may use whatever sources you want, but preferably search relevant

Web sites, since you want job descriptions and lists of duties that apply specifically to dot-com firms.

2. Next, using sources similar to those in Question 1 (and whatever other sources you can think of), draw up specifications for each of these jobs, including things such as desirable work habits, skills, and experience.

3. Next, keeping in mind that this company is on a tight budget, write a short proposal explaining how it should accomplish the other activities it needs done, specifically answering the phones, compiling sales leads, producing monthly reports, and purchasing supplies.

Experiential Exercise
The Nursing Shortage

As of March 2009, the U.S. economy was improving in many respects, but unemployment was still high, and employers were still holding back on their hiring. However, while many people were unemployed, that was not the case with nurses. Virtually every hospital was aggressively recruiting nurses. Many were turning to foreign trained nurses, for example, by recruiting nurses in the Philippines. Experts expected nurses to be in very short supply for years to come.

Purpose: The purpose of this exercise is to give you experience creating a recruitment program.

Required Understanding: You should be thoroughly familiar with the contents of this chapter, and with the nurse recruitment program of a hospital such as Lenox Hill Hospital in New York (see www.lenoxhillhospital.org/nursing/index.jsp) accessed may 18, 2010.

How to Set Up the Exercise/Instructions: Set up groups of four to five students for this exercise. The groups should work separately and should not converse with each other. Each group should address the following tasks:

1. Based on information available on the hospital's Web site, create a hard-copy ad for the hospital to place in the Sunday edition of the *New York Times*. Which (geographic) editions of the *Times* would you use and why?
2. Analyze and critique the hospital's current online nurses' ad. How would you improve on it?
3. Prepare in outline form a complete nurses' recruiting program for this hospital, including all recruiting sources your group would use. ■

Enrichment Topics in Job Analysis

Additional Job Analysis Methods

Job Analysis Record Sheet   You may encounter several other job analysis methods. Thus the U.S. Civil Service Commission has a standardized procedure for comparing and classifying jobs. Information is compiled on a *job analysis record sheet*. Identifying information (such as job title) and a brief summary of the job are listed first. Next list the job's tasks in order of importance. Then, for each task, specify such things as the knowledge required (for example, the principles the worker must be acquainted with to do his or her job), skills required (for example, the skills needed to operate machines), and abilities required (for example, mathematical, reasoning or interpersonal abilities).

Position Analysis Questionnaire   The *position analysis questionnaire* (PAQ) is a very structured job analysis questionnaire.[1] The PAQ is filled in by a job analyst, who should be acquainted with the job to be analyzed. The PAQ contains 194 items, each of which (such as "written materials") represents a basic element that may play a role in the job. The job analyst decides whether each item plays a role and, if so, to what extent. In Figure A3.1, for example, "Written materials" might receive a rating of 4, indicating that written materials (such as books, reports, office notes) play a considerable role in this job.

The PAQ's advantage is that it provides a quantitative score for any job in terms of how that job rates on five basic job traits such as "having decision-making/communications/social responsibilities." The PAQ lets you assign a single quantitative score or value to each job. You can therefore use the PAQ results to compare jobs relative to one another; you can then use this information to assign pay levels for each job.

U.S. Department of Labor Procedure   The *U.S. Department of Labor (DOL) procedure* also aims to provide a standardized method for quantitatively comparing different jobs. The heart of this analysis is a rating of each job in terms of *data, people,* and *things*. As illustrated in Table A3.1, a set of basic activities called *worker functions* describes what a worker can do with respect to data, people, and things. With respect to *data*, for instance, the basic functions include synthesizing, coordinating, and copying. Note also that each worker function has been assigned an importance level. Thus "coordinating" is 1, and "copying" is 5. If you were analyzing the job of a receptionist/clerk, for example, you might label the job 5, 6, 7, which would represent copying data, speaking/signaling people, and handling things.

A Practical Job Analysis Method

Without their own job analysts or (in many cases) HR managers, many small-business owners and managers face two hurdles when doing job analyses and job descriptions. First, they often need a more streamlined approach than those provided by questionnaires like the one shown in Figure A3.2. Second, there is always the reasonable fear that in writing their job descriptions, they will overlook duties that subordinates should be assigned. What they need is a source listing positions they might encounter, including a listing of the duties normally assigned to these positions.

Help is at hand: The small-business owner has at least two options. Web sites like www.jobdescription.com   provide   customizable

Figure A3.1 Portions of a Completed Page from the Position Analysis Questionnaire

A. Information Input

A1. Visual Sources of Job Information

Using the response scale at the left, rate each of the following items on the basis of the extent to which it is used by the worker as a source of information in performing the job.

Extent of Use

0 Does not apply
1 Nominal/very infrequent
2 Occasional
3 Moderate
4 Considerable
5 Very substantial

1. Written materials
E.g., books, reports, office notes, articles, job instructions, or signs

2. Quantitative materials
Materials that deal with quantities or amounts, e.g., graphs, accounts, specifications, or tables of numbers

3. Pictorial materials
Pictures or picture-like materials used as sources of information, e.g., drawings, blueprints, diagrams, maps, tracings, photographic films, x-ray films, or TV pictures

4. Patterns or related devices
E.g., templates, stencils, or patterns used as sources of information when observed during use (Do not include materials described in Item 3.)

5. Visual displays
E.g., dials, gauges, signal lights, radarscopes, speedometers, or clocks

6. Measuring devices
E.g., rules, calipers, tire pressure gauges, scales, thickness gauges, pipettes, thermometers, or protractors used to obtain visual information about physical measurements (Do not include devices described in item 5.)

7. Mechanical devices
E.g., tools, equipment, or machinery that are sources of information when observed during use or operation

Source: Reprinted by permission of PAQ Services, Inc.

Table A3.1 Basic U.S. Department of Labor (DOL) procedure Worker Functions

	DATA	PEOPLE	THINGS
	0 Synthesizing	0 Mentoring	0 Setting up
	1 Coordinating	1 Negotiating	1 Precision working
	2 Analyzing	2 Instructing	2 Operating/controlling
	3 Compiling	3 Supervising	3 Driving/operating
Basic Activities	4 Computing	4 Diverting	4 Manipulating
	5 Copying	5 Persuading	5 Tending
	6 Comparing	6 Speaking/signaling	6 Feeding/offbearing
		7 Serving	7 Handling
		8 Taking instructions/helping	

Note: Determine employee's job "score" on data, people, and things by observing his or her job and determining, for each of the three categories, which of the basic functions illustrates the person's job. "0" is high; "6," "8," and "7" are lows in each column.

Figure A3.2 Job Analysis Questionnaire for Developing Job Descriptions. *Use a questionnaire like this to interview job incumbents, or have them fill it out.*

Job Analysis Information Sheet

Job Title_____ Date _____

Job Code_____ Dept. _____

Superior's Title _____

Hours worked _____ AM to _____ PM

Job Analyst's Name _____

    1. **What is the job's overall purpose?**

_____

    2. **If the incumbent supervises others**, list them by job title; if there is more than one employee with the same title, put the number in parentheses following.

_____

_____

_____

    3. **Check those activities** that are part of the incumbent's supervisory duties.

        ☐ Training

        ☐ Performance appraisal

        ☐ Inspecting work

        ☐ Budgeting

        ☐ Coaching and/or counseling

        ☐ Others (please specify) _____

    4. **Describe the type and extent of supervision** received by the incumbent.

_____

    5. **JOB DUTIES:** Describe briefly WHAT the incumbent does and, if possible, HOW he/she does it. Include duties in the following categories:

        a. daily duties (those performed on a regular basis every day or almost every day)

_____

        b. periodic duties (those performed weekly, monthly, quarterly, or at other regular intervals)

_____

        c. duties performed at irregular intervals

    6. Is the incumbent performing duties he/she considers unnecessary? If so, describe.

_____

    7. Is the incumbent performing duties not presently included in the job description? If so, describe.

_____

    8. **EDUCATION:** Check the box that indicates the educational requirements for the job (*not* the educational background of the incumbent).

        ☐ No formal education required   ☐ Eighth grade education

        ☐ High school diploma (or equivalent)   ☐ 2-year college degree (or equivalent)

        ☐ 4-year college degree (or equivalent)   ☐ graduate work or advanced degree (specify:)

        ☐ professional license (specify:)

(Continued)

9. **EXPERIENCE**: Check the amount of experience needed to perform the job.

☐ None	☐ Less than one month
☐ One to six months	☐ Six months to one year
☐ One to three years	☐ Three to five years
☐ Five to ten years	☐ More than ten years

10. **LOCATION:** Check location of job and, if necessary or appropriate, describe briefly.

☐ Outdoor	☐ Indoor
☐ Underground	☐ Pit
☐ Scaffold	☐ Other (specify)

11. **ENVIRONMENTAL CONDITIONS:** Check any objectionable conditions found on the job and note afterward how frequently each is encountered (rarely, occasionally, constantly, etc.)

☐ Dirt	☐ Dust
☐ Heat	☐ Cold
☐ Noise	☐ Fumes
☐ Odors	☐ Wetness/humidity
☐ Vibration	☐ Sudden temperature changes
☐ Darkness or poor lighting	☐ Other (specify)

12. **HEALTH AND SAFETY**: Check any undesirable health and safety conditions under which the incumbent must perform and note how often they are encountered.

☐ Elevated workplace	☐ Mechanical hazards
☐ Explosives	☐ Electrical hazards
☐ Fire hazards	☐ Radiation
☐ Other (specify)	

13. **MACHINES, TOOLS, EQUIPMENT, AND WORK AIDS**: Describe briefly what machines, tools, equipment, or work aids the incumbent works with on a regular basis:

14. Have concrete work standards been established (errors allowed, time taken for a particular task, etc.)? If so, what are they?

15. Are there any personal attributes (special aptitudes, physical characteristics, personality traits, etc.) required by the job?

16. Are there any exceptional problems the incumbent might be expected to encounter in performing the job under normal conditions? If so, describe.

17. Describe the successful completion and/or end results of the job.

18. What is the seriousness of error on this job? Who or what is affected by errors the incumbent makes?

19. To what job would a successful incumbent expect to be promoted?

[*Note*: This form is obviously slanted toward a manufacturing environment. But it can be adapted quite easily to fit a number of different types of jobs.]

Source: Reprinted from http://www.hrnext.com/, July 28, 2001 with permission of the publisher. Copyright © 2001 Business and Legal Reports, Inc., 141 Mill Rock Road East, Old Saybrook, CT 06475.

Figure A3.3 Job Description Questionnaire

**Background Data
for Job Description**

Job Title _____   Department _____

Job Number _____   Written By _____

Today´s Date _____   Applicable Codes _____

   I. **Applicable Job Titles from O*NET:**

  II. **Job Summary:**
      (List the more important or regularly performed tasks)

 III. **Reports To:**

 IV. **Supervises:** _____

  V. **Job Duties:** _____
      (Briefly describe, for each duty, what *employee does and, if possible,* how
      *employee does it. Show in parentheses at end of each duty the approximate
      percentage of time devoted to duty.)*

     A. Daily Duties:

     B. Periodic Duties:
        (Indicate whether weekly, monthly, quarterly, etc.)

     C. Duties Performed at Irregular Intervals:

---

descriptions by title and industry. The Department of Labor's O*NET is second alternative. We focus here on using O*NET for creating job descriptions.

Step 1. Decide on a Plan

Start by developing at least the outline of a corporate plan. What do you expect your sales revenue to be next year and in the next few years? What products do you intend to emphasize? What areas or departments in your company do you think will have to be expanded, reduced, or consolidated, given where you plan to go with your firm over the next few years? What kinds of new positions do you think you'll need to accomplish your goals?

Step 2. Develop an Organization Chart

Next, develop a company organization chart.[2] Show who reports to each of the managers and supervisors in the firm. Start by drawing up the organization chart as it is now. Then, produce a chart showing how you'd like your chart to look in the immediate future (say, in 2 months) and perhaps other charts showing how you'd like your organization to evolve over the next 2 or 3 years.

You can use several tools here. For example, Microsoft (MS) Word includes an organization charting function: On the Insert menu, click Object, then Create New. In the Object type box, click MS Organization Chart. Software packages such as OrgPublisher from TimeVision of Irving, Texas, are another option.[3]

Step 3. Use a Job Analysis/Description Questionnaire

Next, use a job analysis questionnaire to determine what each job entails. You can use one of the more comprehensive questionnaires (see Figure A3.2); however, the job description questionnaire in Figure A3.3 (page 102) is a simpler and often satisfactory alternative. Fill in the required information, and then ask the supervisors and/or employees to list the job's duties (on the bottom of the page), breaking them into daily duties, periodic duties, and duties performed at irregular intervals. You can distribute a sample of one of these duties (Figure A3.4) to facilitate the process.

Step 4. Obtain Lists of Job Duties from O*NET.

The list of job duties you uncovered in the previous step may or may not be complete. We'll therefore use O*NET to compile a more comprehensive list. (Refer to Figure A3.5 for a visual example as you read along.) Start by going to http://online.onetcenter.org (top). Click on Find Occupations. Assume you want to create job descriptions for retail salespeople. Type in Retail Sales for the occupational titles drop-down box. This brings you to the Find Occupations Search Result (middle). Clicking on Retail Salespersons—snapshots—produces the job summary and specific occupational duties for retail salespersons (bottom). For a small company or department, you might want to combine the duties of the retail salesperson with those of first-line supervisors/managers of retail salespeople.

Figure A3.4 Background Data for Examples

Example of Job Title: Customer Service Clerk

Example of Job Summary: Answers inquiries and gives directions to customers, authorizes cashing of customers' checks, records and returns lost charge cards, sorts and reviews new credit applications, works at customer-service desk in department store.

Example of One Job Duty: Authorizes cashing of checks: authorizes cashing of personal or payroll checks (up to a specified amount) by customers desiring to make payment by check. Requests identification, such as driver's license, from customers and examines check to verify date, amount, signature, and endorsement. Initials check and sends customer to cashier.

Figure A3.5

Shown in these Three Screen Captures, O*NET Easily Allows the User to Develop Job Descriptions.

Source: Reprinted by permission of O*NET OnLine.

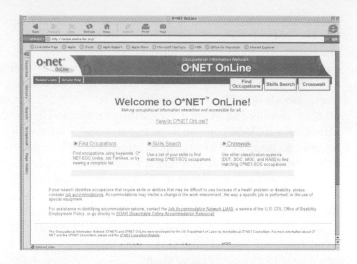

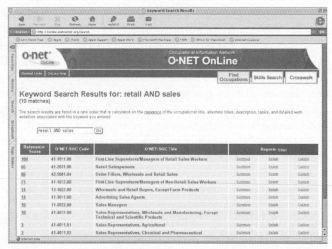

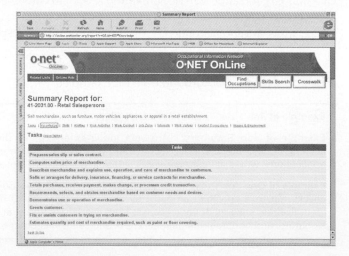

Step 5. Compile the Job's Specification from O*NET

Next, return to the Snapshot for Retail Salesperson (bottom). Instead of choosing occupation-specific information, choose, for example, Worker Experiences, Occupational Requirements, and Worker Characteristics. You can use this information to develop a job specification for the job.

Step 6. Complete Your Job Description

Finally, using Figure A3.3, write a job summary for the job. Then use the information obtained in steps 4 and 5 to create a complete listing of the tasks, duties, and human requirements of each of job you must fill.

Chapter 4

Testing and Selecting Employees

- The Basics of Testing and Selecting Employees
- Using Tests at Work
- Interviewing Prospective Employees
- Using Other Selection Techniques

When you finish studying this chapter, you should be able to:

- Define *basic testing concepts, including validity and reliability.*

- Discuss *at least four basic types of personnel tests.*

- Explain *the pros and cons of background investigations, reference checks, and preemployment information services.*

- Explain *the factors and problems that can undermine an interview's usefulness, and techniques for eliminating them.*

INTRODUCTION

 oogle job candidates used to have a dozen or more grueling interviews. Then, the firm would routinely reject candidates with years of work experience if they had just average college grades. But, Google's new HR head says, "Everything works if you're trying to hire 500 people a year, or 1000." Once it was hiring thousands of people per year, the slow hiring process bogged it down. Google therefore reduced the interview load (to about five) and no longer puts so much weight on GPA.[1]

The Basics of Testing and Selecting Employees

With a pool of applicants, your next step is to select the best person for the job. This usually means whittling down the applicant pool by using the screening tools in this chapter, including tests, background checks, and interviews.

Why Careful Selection Is Important

Selecting the right employees is important for several reasons. First, your own performance always depends on your subordinates. Employees with the right skills and attributes will do a better job for you and the company. Employees without these skills or who are obstructionist won't perform effectively, and your own performance and the firm's will suffer.

Second, you want to screen out undesirables. By some estimates, almost 25% of employees say they've had knowledge of illicit drug use among coworkers, and 7% reported being victims of coworkers' physical threats.[2] The time to screen out undesirables is before they are in the door, not after.

Third, screening is important because you don't want to waste money. Hiring and training even a clerk can cost $5,000 or more in fees and supervisory time. The total cost of hiring a manager could easily be 10 times as high, including search fees, interviewing time, reference checks, and moving expenses.

Legal Implications and Negligent Hiring   Finally, selection is important because of the legal implications of incompetent hiring. For one thing (as we saw in Chapter 2), EEO legislation requires that you avoid unfairly discriminating against any protected group.[3]

Furthermore, courts will find employers liable when employees with criminal records or other problems use their access to customers' homes or similar opportunities to commit crimes. Hiring workers with such backgrounds without proper safeguards is *negligent hiring*. For example, lawyers sued Walmart alleging that several employees with criminal convictions had assaulted young girls. Walmart then instituted a program of criminal background checks.[4]

Avoiding negligent hiring claims requires taking "reasonable" action to investigate the candidate's background. For example, employers "must make a systematic effort to gain relevant information about the applicant, verify documentation, follow up on missing records or gaps in employment, and keep a detailed log of all attempts to obtain information."[5]

Reliability

Effective screening is therefore important and depends, to a large degree, on the basic testing concepts of validity and reliability. **Reliability** refers to the test's consistency. It is "the consistency of scores obtained by the same person when retested with the identical tests or with an equivalent form of a test."[6] Test reliability is essential: If a person scored 90 on an intelligence test on Monday and 130 when retested on Tuesday, you probably wouldn't trust the test.

There are several ways to estimate a test's consistency or reliability. You could administer the same test to the same people at two different points in time, comparing their test scores at Time 2 with their scores at Time 1; this would be a *retest estimate*. Or you could administer a test and then administer an equivalent test at a later date; this would be an *equivalent-form estimate*. The Scholastic Aptitude Test is an example of the latter.

A test's internal consistency is another measure of its reliability. For example, assume you have 10 items on a test of vocational interest. These items are each supposed to measure the person's interest in working outdoors. You administer the test and then statistically analyze the degree to which responses to these items vary together. This would provide a measure of the internal reliability of the test; experts call this an *internal comparison estimate*. Internal consistency is one reason you often find apparently repetitive questions on tests.

Validity

Any test is a sample of a person's behavior, but some tests more clearly reflect the behavior being sampled. A typing test, for instance, clearly corresponds to an on-the-job behavior—typing. At the other extreme, there may be no apparent relationship between the items on the test and the behavior. For example, in the Rorschach test illustrated in Figure 4.1, the person is asked to explain how he or she interprets the blurred picture. The person's interpretation (what he or she "reads into" the picture) is then used to draw conclusions about the person's personality. In such personality tests, it is harder to "prove" that the tests are measuring what they are purported to measure—that they are *valid*.

Test validity answers the question; does this test measure what it's supposed to measure? Stated differently, "validity refers to the confidence one has in the meaning attached to the scores."[7] With respect to employee selection tests, the term *validity* often refers to evidence that the test is job related, in other words, that performance on the test is a *valid predictor* of subsequent performance on the job. A selection test must be valid because, without proof of its validity, there is no logical or legally permissible reason to continue using it.

In employment testing, there are two main ways to demonstrate a test's validity: **criterion validity** and **content validity.** Demonstrating criterion validity means demonstrating that those who do well on the test also do well on the job, and that those who do poorly on the test do poorly on the job. In psychological measurement, a *predictor* is the measurement (in this case, the test score) that you are trying to relate to a *criterion*, such as performance on the job. In criterion validity, the two should be closely related. The term *criterion validity* comes from that terminology.

The employer demonstrates the content validity of a test by showing that the test constitutes a fair sample of the content of a job. For example, if the content of a typing test is a representative sample of the typist's job, then the test is probably content valid.

Figure 4.1 A Slide from the Rorschach Test

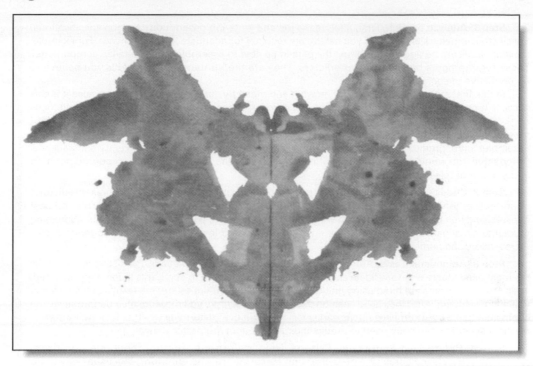

Source: http://en.wikipedia.org/wiki/File:Rorschach1.jpg, accessed July 27, 2009.

How to Validate a Test

What makes a test such as the Graduate Record Examination (GRE) useful for college admissions directors?

The answer is usually that people's scores on the test have been shown to be predictive of how people perform. Thus, other things equal, students who score high on the GRE also do better in graduate school.

Strictly speaking, an employer should be sure that scores on the test are related in a predictable way to performance on the job before using that test to screen employees. In other words, it is important that you validate the test before using it. You generally do this by ensuring that test scores are a good predictor of some criterion such as job performance. In other words, you should demonstrate the test's *criterion validity.*

At best, invalid tests (tests not related to employee performance) are a waste of time. At worst, they may be discriminatory (if they screen out larger proportions of minority candidates). Tests you buy "off the shelf" should include information on their validity. The Society for Industrial and Organizational Psychology says that "Experienced and knowledgeable test publishers have (and are happy to provide) information on the validity of their testing products."[8] But ideally, employers should revalidate the tests for the job(s) at hand. This validation process (see Figure 4.2) usually requires the expertise of an industrial psychologist.

Figure 4.2 How to Validate a Test

Step 1: Analyze the Job. First, analyze the job and write job descriptions and job specifications. Specify the human traits and skills you believe are required for adequate job performance. For example, must an applicant be aggressive? Must the person be able to assemble small, detailed components? These requirements become your predictors. They are the human traits and skills you believe to be predictive of success on the job.

In this first step, you must also define what you mean by "success on the job" because it is this success for which you want predictors. The standards of success are called *criteria*. You could focus on production-related criteria (quantity, quality, and so on), personnel data (absenteeism, length of service, and so on), or judgments (of worker performance by persons such as supervisors). For an assembler's job, predictors for which to test applicants might include manual dexterity and patience. Criteria that you would hope to predict with your test might then include quantity produced per hour and number of rejects produced per hour.

Step 2: Choose the Tests. Next, choose tests that you think measure the attributes (predictors) important for job success. This choice is usually based on experience, previous research, and best guesses, and you usually won't start off with just one test. Instead, you choose several tests, combining them into a test battery aimed at measuring a variety of possible predictors, such as aggressiveness, extroversion, and numeric ability.

Step 3: Administer Tests. Administer the selected test(s) to employees. Predictive validation is the most dependable way to validate a test. The test is administered to applicants before they are hired. Then these applicants are hired using only existing selection techniques, not the results of the new test you are developing. After they have been on the job for some time, you measure their performance and compare it to their performance on the earlier test. You can then determine whether their performance on the test could have been used to predict their subsequent job performance.

Step 4: Relate Test Scores and Criteria. Next, determine whether there is a significant relationship between scores (the predictor) and performance (the criterion). The usual way to do this is to determine the statistical relationship between scores on the test and performance through correlation analysis, which shows the degree of statistical relationship.

Step 5: Cross-Validate and Revalidate. Before putting the test into use, you may want to check it by cross-validating, by again performing steps 3 and 4 on a new sample of employees. At a minimum, an expert should validate the test periodically.

Ethical and Legal Questions in Testing

Equal Employment Opportunity Aspects of Testing   We've seen that various federal and state laws bar discrimination on the basis of race, color, age, religion, sex, disability, and national origin. With respect to testing, these laws boil down to two things: (1) You must be able to prove that your tests are related to success or failure on the job, and (2) you must prove that your tests don't unfairly discriminate against either minority or nonminority subgroups. If confronted by a legitimate discrimination charge, the burden of proof rests with you. Once the plaintiff shows that one of your selection procedures has an adverse impact on his or her protected class, you must demonstrate the validity and selection fairness of the allegedly discriminatory test or item. *Adverse impact* means there is a significant discrepancy between rates of rejection of members of the protected groups and others. For example, a federal court ruled that Dial Corp. discriminated against female job applicants at a meatpacking facility by requiring employees to take a preemployment strength test. The test had an adverse impact on women. Furthermore, there appeared to be no compelling need for strength on the job.[9]

You can't avoid EEO laws by not using tests. EEO laws apply to all screening or selection devices. In other words, the same burden of proving job relatedness falls on interviews and other techniques (including performance appraisals) that fall on tests.

Individual Rights of Test Takers and Test Security   Test takers have various privacy and information rights. Under the American Psychological Association's standard for educational and psychology tests (which guide professional psychologists but are not legally enforceable), they have the right to the confidentiality of the test results and the right to informed consent regarding the use of these results. They have the right to expect that only people qualified to interpret the scores will have access to them or that sufficient information will accompany the scores to ensure their appropriate interpretation. They have the right to expect that the test is secure; no person taking the test should have prior information concerning the questions or answers.

Using Tests as Supplements   Do not use tests as your only selection technique; instead, use them to supplement other techniques such as interviews and background checks. Tests are fallible. Even in the best cases, the test score usually accounts for only about 25% of the variation in the measure of performance. In addition, tests are often better at revealing which candidates will fail than which will succeed.

USING TESTS AT WORK

Tests can be effective. For example, researchers administered an aggression questionnaire to high school hockey players prior to the season. Preseason aggressiveness as measured by the questionnaire predicted the amount of minutes they subsequently spent in the penalty box for penalties like fighting and slashing.[10]

Tests are also widely used by employers. For example, about 41% of companies the American Management Association surveyed tested applicants for *basic skills* (defined as the ability to read instructions, write reports, and perform common workplace arithmetic tasks).[11]

Try the short test in Figure 4.3 to see how prone you might be to on-the-job accidents.

Types of Tests Used at Work

Employers use tests to measure a wide range of candidate attributes, including cognitive (mental) abilities, physical abilities, personality and interests, and achievement. Many firms have applicants take online or offline computerized tests—sometimes online, and sometimes by phone, using the keypad—to prescreen applicants prior to in-depth interviews.[12] Employers don't just use tests for lower-level workers. For example, Barclays Capital gave recent graduates aptitude tests instead of first-round interviews.[13] Employers also don't use tests just to find good

Figure 4.3 Sample Selection Test

CHECK YES OR NO	YES	NO
1. You like a lot of excitement in your life.		
2. An employee who takes it easy at work is cheating on the employer.		
3. You are a cautious person.		
4. In the past three years you have found yourself in a shouting match at school or work.		
5. You like to drive fast just for fun.		

Analysis: According to John Kamp, an industrial psychologist, applicants who answered no, yes, yes, no, no to questions 1, 2, 3, 4, and 5 are statistically likely to be absent less often, to have fewer on-the-job injuries, and, if the job involves driving, to have fewer on-the-job driving accidents. Actual scores on the test are based on answers to 130 questions.

Source: Courtesy of *The New York Times.*

employees, but also to screen out bad ones. By one account, about 30% of all employees say they've stolen from their employers; about 41% are managers.[14] In retail, employers apprehended about 1 out of every 28 workers for stealing.[15]

Example Outback Steakhouse (which now has 45,000 employees) has used preemployment testing since 1991, just 2 years after the company started. Outback is looking for employees who are highly social, meticulous, sympathetic, and adaptable. They use a special personality assessment test as part of their selection process. Applicants take the test, and the company then compares the candidate's results to the ideal Outback Steakhouse employee profile. Those who score low on certain traits (like compassion) don't move to the next step. Two managers interview those who do move on. The managers ask "behavioral" questions, such as, *What would you do if* a customer asked for a side dish we don't have on the menu?[16]

The basic types of tests are as follows.

Tests of Cognitive Abilities Employers often want to assess cognitive or mental abilities. For example, you may be interested in determining whether a supervisory candidate has the intelligence to do the paperwork required of the job or a book-keeper candidate has numeric aptitude.

Intelligence tests, such as IQ tests, are tests of general intellectual abilities. They measure not a single intelligence trait, but rather a basket of abilities, including memory, vocabulary, verbal fluency, and numeric ability. Today, psychologists often measure intelligence with individually administered tests such as the Stanford-Binet or the Wechsler test. Employers use other IQ tests such as the Wonderlic to provide quick measures of IQ for both individuals and groups of people.

There are also measures of specific mental abilities. Tests in this category are often called *aptitude tests* because they aim to measure the applicant's aptitudes for the job. For example, the Test of Mechanical Comprehension illustrated in Figure 4.4 tests the applicant's understanding of basic mechanical principles. It may therefore reflect a person's aptitude for jobs—such as engineer—that require mechanical comprehension.

Tests of Motor and Physical Abilities   There are many motor or physical abilities you might want to measure, such as finger dexterity, strength, manual dexterity, and reaction time (for instance, for police candidates). The Stromberg Dexterity Test is one example. It measures the speed and accuracy of simple judgment as well as the speed of finger, hand, and arm movements.

Figure 4.4   Two Problems from the Test of Mechanical Comprehension

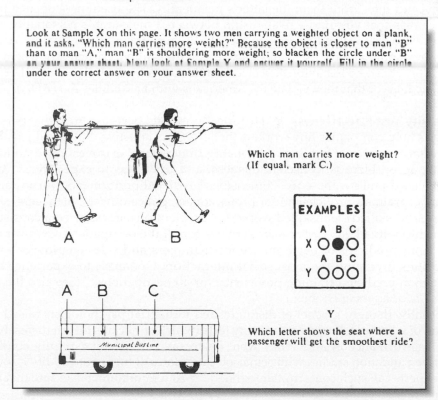

Look at Sample X on this page. It shows two men carrying a weighted object on a plank, and it asks, "Which man carries more weight?" Because the object is closer to man "B" than to man "A," man "B" is shouldering more weight; so blacken the circle under "B" on your answer sheet. Now look at Sample Y and answer it yourself. Fill in the circle under the correct answer on your answer sheet.

X
Which man carries more weight? (If equal, mark C.)

A   B

A   B   C

EXAMPLES
A B C
X ○ ● ○
A B C
Y ○ ○ ○

Municipal Bus Line

Y
Which letter shows the seat where a passenger will get the smoothest ride?

Measuring Personality   A person's mental and physical abilities alone seldom explain his or her job performance. As one consultant put it, most people are hired based on qualifications, but most are fired for nonperformance. And *nonperformance* (or *performance*) "is usually the result of personal characteristics, such as attitude, motivation, and especially, temperament."[17] Employers use personality and interests inventories for measuring and predicting such intangibles. (Similarly, online dating services like eHarmony.com have prospective members take online personality tests, and reject those whom its software judges are unmatchable.) Employers such as Acxiom Corp. use tests like the Birkman Method® (http://www.birkman.com/) personality assessment to help new employees better understand the tasks at which they're best.[18]

Personality tests measure basic aspects of an applicant's personality, such as introversion, stability, and motivation. Many of these tests are projective, meaning that the person taking the test must interpret or react to an ambiguous stimulus such as an inkblot or clouded picture. Because the pictures are ambiguous, the person supposedly projects into the picture his or her own attitudes about life. Thus a security-oriented person might describe the image in Figure 4.1 (page 109) as "A giant bug coming to get me."

Personality tests—particularly the projective type—are the most difficult to evaluate and use. An expert must analyze the test taker's interpretations and reactions and infer from them the latter's personality. The usefulness of such tests then assumes that you find a relationship between a measurable personality trait (such as extroversion) and success on the job. Because they are personal in nature, employers should always use personality tests with caution, particularly where the focus is on aberrant behavior. Rejected candidates may (validly) claim that the results are false or that they violate the Americans with Disabilities Act (ADA).

Personality Test Effectiveness   Historically, most experts assumed that personality tests help companies hire workers that are more effective. Industrial psychologists often study the "big five" personality dimensions: extroversion, emotional stability, agreeableness, conscientiousness, and openness to experience.[19] One study focused on how these five dimensions predicted performance (for instance, in terms of training proficiency) for professionals, police officers, managers, sales workers, and skilled/semiskilled workers. Conscientiousness showed a consistent relationship with all job performance criteria for all the occupations. Extroversion was a valid predictor of performance for managers and sales employees—two occupations involving the most social interaction. Openness to experience and extroversion predicted training proficiency for all occupations.[20] (See also the following *Global Issues in HR* box.)

Recently, though, a panel of distinguished industrial psychologists raised the question of whether *self-report* personality tests (which applicants fill out themselves) predict performance at all.[21] They went on to say that if you carefully conduct predictive validation studies with actual job candidates, it turns out validity is low.[22] Other experts call such concerns "unfounded."[23] At a minimum, make sure that any personality tests you use actually do predict performance.[24]

Interest Inventories   *Interest inventories* compare one's interests with those of people in various occupations. Thus, if a person takes the Strong-Campbell Interest Inventory,

Global Issues in HR: Would Your Company Pick You to Be an International Executive?

With many firms going global, you may well apply for an assignment that involves time abroad. A great many overseas assignments fail, so employers are often anxious to screen out the high-risk candidates. Why do such assignments fail? *Personality* is one factor. For example, in a study of 143 expatriate employees, extroverted, agreeable, and emotionally stable individuals were less likely to want to leave early.[25] Another study focused on 838 lower-, middle-, and senior-level managers from 6 international firms and 21 countries. Here 14 personal characteristics successfully distinguished the managers identified by their companies as high potential from those identified as not high potential. These included such things as sensitive to cultural differences, courage to take a stand, seeks opportunities to learn, takes risks, is open to criticism, and is flexible.[26] The candidate's intentions are also important. For example, people who want expatriate careers try harder to adjust to such a life.[27]

It's not all about personality, of course. One study asked 338 international assignees from various countries and organizations to specify which traits were important for the success of managers on foreign assignment. The researchers identified five factors that contribute to success in such assignments: *job knowledge and motivation, relational skills, flexibility/adaptability, extracultural openness,* and *family situation* (spouse's positive opinion, willingness of spouse to live abroad, and so on). The five factors were not equally important in the foreign assignees' success, according to the assignees; "Family situation was generally found to be the most important factor, a finding consistent with other research on international assignments and transfers."[28]

These findings underscore a truism regarding international assignee selection: It's usually family and personal problems, not incompetence or personality, that are the culprits. For example, in one study, U.S. managers listed, in descending order of importance, the reasons for leaving early: inability of spouse to adjust, managers' inability to adjust, other family problems, managers' personal or emotional immaturity, and inability to cope with larger overseas responsibility.[29]

---

he or she receives a report comparing his or her interests to those of people already in occupations such as accounting, engineering, management, and medical technology.

Achievement Tests   An *achievement test* is, basically, a measure of what a person has learned. Most of the tests you take in school are achievement tests. They measure your knowledge in areas such as economics, marketing, or management. In addition to job knowledge, achievement tests can measure applicants' abilities; a typing test is one example.[30]

Computerized Testing   Computerized tests are increasingly replacing paper-and-pencil and manual tests. For example, one auto repair chain, City Garage, knew they couldn't implement their growth strategy without changing how they tested and hired employees.[31] Their old hiring process consisted of a paper-and-pencil application and one interview, immediately followed by a hire/don't hire decision. This was unsatisfactory. For one thing, local shop managers didn't have time to evaluate every applicant, so "if they had been shorthanded too long, we would hire pretty much anybody who had experience," said City's training director. Complicating the problem was that City Garage competitively differentiates itself by letting customers interact directly with technicians. Therefore, finding mechanics who react positively to customer inquiries is essential.

City Garage's solution was to purchase the Personality Profile Analysis (PPA) online test from Dallas-based Thomas International USA. Now, after a quick application and background check, likely candidates take the 10-minute, 24-question PPA. City Garage staff then enter the answers into the PPA software system and receive test results in less than 2 minutes. These show whether the applicant is high or low in four personality characteristics. It also produces follow-up questions about potential problem areas. For example, applicants might be asked how they've handled possible weaknesses such as lack of patience. If candidates answer those questions satisfactorily, they're asked back for all-day interviews, after which hiring decisions are made.

Web-Based Testing   Employers of course also use the Web to test and screen applicants. For example, the financial firm Capital One's online system eliminates the previous time-consuming paper-and-pencil test process.[32] Applicants for call center jobs complete an online application and online math and biodata tests. They also take an online role-playing call simulation. For this, they put on a headset, and the program plays seven different customer situations. Applicants (playing the role of operators) answer multiple-choice questions online regarding how they would respond.

Studies suggest that proctored Web-based and paper-and-pencil tests of applicants produce similar results, for instance, on personality and judgment tests.[33] However, a test may take longer for applicants on the Web, due to downloading time and the fact that there are fewer items presented on the viewable page. Similarly, there is "currently no way to completely prevent [online] test takers from cheating or copying items during testing."[34]

Work Samples and Simulations

With work sample-type tests, examinees respond to situations representative of the jobs for which they're applying.

Work Sampling   The **work sampling technique** tries to predict job performance by requiring job candidates to perform one or more actual samples of the job's tasks. (Thus for an auto mechanic's test, one task might include using a digital engine meter.) The basic procedure is to select a sample of several tasks crucial to performing the job and then to test applicants on them.[35] An observer monitors and assesses performance.

Realistic tests like work sampling measure actual job tasks, so it's harder to fake answers. The work sample content—being actual tasks the person must perform—is also not as likely to be unfair to minorities (as might a personnel test that possibly emphasized middle-class concepts and values).[36] Work sampling also does not delve into the applicant's personality, so there's less chance of applicants viewing it as an invasion of privacy.

Management Assessment Centers   In a **management assessment center,** management candidates come together, take tests, and make decisions in simulated but realistic situations, and observers score them on their performance.[37] The time at the assessment center is usually 2 or 3 days. It involves 10 to 12 management candidates performing realistic management tasks (such as making presentations) under the observation of expert assessors. The center may be a plain conference room, but often it is a room with a one-way mirror to facilitate unobtrusive observations. Examples of the simulated but realistic exercises included are as follows:

- *The in-basket.* Here the candidate confronts an accumulation of reports, memos, notes of incoming phone calls, letters, and other materials. The candidate takes appropriate action on each of these materials.
- *The leaderless group discussion.* A leaderless group receives a discussion question and must arrive at a group decision. The raters evaluate each group member's interpersonal skills, acceptance by the group, leadership ability, and influence.
- *Individual presentations.* Raters evaluate a participant's communication skills and persuasiveness by having the person make an oral presentation on an assigned topic.

Employers use assessment centers for selection, promotion, and development. Supervisor recommendations usually play a big role in choosing center participants. Line managers usually act as assessors and typically arrive at their ratings through consensus.[38] Centers are expensive to set up, but at least one study (of 40 police candidates) found they are well worth the cost.[39]

Situational Judgment Tests   Situational judgment tests "are designed to assess an applicant's judgment regarding a situation encountered in the workplace." As an example, "You are facing a project deadline and are concerned that you may not complete the project by the time it is due. It is very important to your supervisor that you complete a project by the deadline. It is not possible to get anyone to help you with the work. You would:[40]

A. Ask for an extension of the deadline.
B. Let the supervisor know that you may not meet the deadline.
C. Work as many hours as it takes to get the job done by the deadline.
D. Explore different ways to do the work so it can be completed by the deadline.
E. On the date that it is due, hand in what you have done so far.
F. Do the most critical parts of the project by the deadline and complete the remaining parts after the deadline.
G. Tell your supervisor that the deadline is unreasonable.
H. Give your supervisor an update and express your concern about your ability to complete the project by the deadline.
I. Quit your job.

Studies suggest that situational judgment tests are effective and widely used.[41]

Strategy and HR   Having to add thousands of new employees each year, Google's top managers revamped the firm's employee selection process. Google no longer requires most candidates to endure a dozen interviews over many months. They've streamlined the process, in part by testing all their current employees to see what makes them successful. Then Google tests candidates to see if they too have these traits.

INTERVIEWING PROSPECTIVE EMPLOYEES

Although not all companies use tests or assessment centers, it is very unusual for a manager not to interview a prospective employee; interviewing skills are thus indispensable. An **interview** is a procedure designed to solicit information from a person's oral responses to oral inquiries. A *selection interview* is "a selection procedure designed to predict future job performance on the basis of applicants' oral responses to oral inquiries."[42]

Types of Selection Interviews

As you probably know from your own experience, there are several types of selection interviews.

Structure   First, the interview may be *nonstructured* or *structured*. In the former, you ask questions as they come to mind, and there is generally no set format to follow. In a structured or directive interview, questions and perhaps even acceptable responses are specified in advance, and the responses may be rated for appropriateness of content (see Figure 4.5, pages 119–121). In practice, interviews vary in the degree to which the interviewer took steps to structure or standardize the interview process.[43]

Type of Questions   Second, the interviewer can use various types of questions. In *situational interviews*, questions focus on the candidate's ability to project what his or her behavior *would be* in a given situation.[44] For example, you might ask a candidate for a supervisor position how he or she would respond to a subordinate coming to work late three days in a row. A *behavioral interview* is another type of interview. Here you ask interviewees how they behaved in the past in some situation. Thus an interviewer might ask, "Did you ever have a situation in which a subordinate came in late? If so, how did you handle the situation?" Thus when Citizens Banking Corporation in Flint, Michigan, found that 31 of the 50 people in its call center quit in 1 year, Cynthia Wilson, the center's head, switched to behavioral interviews. Many of those who left did so because they didn't enjoy fielding questions from irate clients. So Wilson no longer tries to predict how candidates will act based on asking them if they want to work with angry clients. Instead, she asks behavioral questions like, "Tell me about a time you were speaking with an irate person and how you turned the situation around." Wilson says this makes it much harder to fool the interviewer; only four people left her center in the following year.[45] More employers today are using behavioral interviews.[46]

Figure 4.5 Structured Interview Guide

APPLICANT INTERVIEW GUIDE

To the interviewer: This Applicant Interview Guide is intended to assist in employee selection and placement. If it is used for all applicants for a position, it will help you to compare them, and it will provide more objective information than you will obtain from unstructured interviews.

Because this is a general guide, all of the items may not apply in every instance. Skip those that are not applicable and add questions appropriate to the specific position. Space for additional questions will be found at the end of the form.

Federal law prohibits discrimination in employment on the basis of sex, race, color, national origin, religion, disability, and, in most instances, age. The laws of most states also ban some or all of the above types of discrimination in employment as well as discrimination based on marital status or ancestry. Interviewers should take care to avoid any questions that suggest that an employment decision will be made on the basis of any such factors.

Job Interest

Name _____ Position applied for _____

What do you think the job (position) involves? _____

Why do you want the job (position)? _____

Why are you qualified for it? _____

What would your salary requirements be? _____

What do you know about our company? _____

Why do you want to work for us? _____

Current Work Status

Are you now employed? _____ Yes _____ No. If not, how long have you been unemployed? _____

Why are you unemployed? _____

If you are working, why are you applying for this position? _____

When would you be available to start work with us? _____

Work Experience

(Start with the applicant's current or last position and work back. All periods of time should be accounted for. Go back at least 12 years, depending upon the applicant's age. Military service should be treated as a job.)

Current or last
employer _____ Address _____

Dates of employment: from _____ to _____

Current or last job title _____

What are (were) your duties? _____

Have you held the same job throughout your employment with that company? _____ Yes _____ No. If not, describe the

various jobs you have had with that employer, how long you held each of them, and the main duties of each. _____

_____

What was your starting salary? _____ What are you earning now? _____ Comments _____

_____

Name of your last or current supervisor _____

What did you like most about that job? _____

What did you like least about it? _____

Why are you thinking of leaving? _____

Why are you leaving right now? _____

Interviewer's comments or observations _____

_____

(Continued)

What did you do before you took your last job? _____

Where were you employed? _____

Location _____ Job title _____

Duties _____

Did you hold the same job throughout your employment with that company? _____ Yes _____ No. If not,

describe the jobs you held, when you held them, and the duties of each._____

_____

What was your starting salary? _____ What was your final salary? _____

Name of your last supervisor _____

May we contact that company? _____ Yes _____ No

What did you like most about that job? _____

What did you like least about that job? _____

Why did you leave that job? _____

Would you consider working there again? _____

Interviewer: If there is any gap between the various periods of employment, the applicant should be asked about them. _____

_____

Interviewer's comments or observations _____

_____

What did you do prior to the job with that company? _____

What other jobs or experience have you had? Describe them briefly and explain the general duties of each. _____

_____

Have you been unemployed at any time in the last five years? _____ Yes _____ No. What efforts did you make to find work?

_____

What other experience or training do you have that would help qualify you for the job applied for? Explain how and where you

obtained this experience or training. _____

_____

Educational Background

What education or training do you have that would help you in the job for which you have applied? _____

_____

Describe any formal education you have had. (Interviewer may substitute technical training, if relevant.) _____

_____

Off-Job Activities

What do you do in your off-hours? _____ Part-time job _____ Athletics _____ Spectator sports _____ Clubs _____ Other

Please explain. _____

Interviewer's Specific Questions

Interviewer: Add any questions to the particular job for which you are interviewing, leaving space for brief answers.
(Be careful to avoid questions which may be viewed as discriminatory.)

_____

_____

_____

Personal

Would you be willing to relocate? _____

Are you willing to travel? _____ Yes _____ No

What is the maximum amount of time you would consider traveling? _____

_____

(Continued)

Are you able to work overtime? _____

What about working on weekends? _____

Self-Assessment

What do you feel are your strong points? _____

_____

What do you feel are your weak points? _____

_____

Interviewer: Compare the applicant's responses with the information furnished on the application for employment. Clear up any

discrepancies. _____

_____

Before the applicant leaves, the interviewer should provide basic information about the organization and the job opening, if this has not already been done. The applicant should be given information on the work location, work hours, the wage or salary, type of remuneration (salary or salary plus bonus, etc.), and other factors that may affect the applicant's interest in the job.

Interviewer's Impressions

Rate each characteristic from 1 to 4, with 1 being the highest rating and 4 being the lowest.

Personal Characteristics	1	2	3	4	Comments
Personal appearance					
Poise, manner					
Speech					
Cooperation with interviewer					
Job-Related Characteristics					
Experience for this job					
Knowledge of job					
Interpersonal relationships					
Effectiveness					

Overall Rating for Job

1	2	3	4	5
_____ Superior	_____ Above average	_____ Average	_____ Marginal	_____ Unsatisfactory
	(well qualified)	(qualified)	(barely qualified)	

Comments or remarks _____

_____

_____

Interviewer _____ Date _____

Source: Adapted from The Dartnell Corporation, © 1992.

How Administered   We can also classify interviews based on how we administer them. For example, most interviews are *one-on-one:* Two people meet alone, and one interviews the other by seeking oral responses to oral inquiries. Most selection processes are also sequential. In a *sequential interview,* several people interview the applicant in sequence before making a hiring decision. In a *panel interview* the candidate is interviewed simultaneously by a group (or panel) of interviewers, rather than sequentially.

Managers conduct some interviews by *phone*. Somewhat counterintuitively, such interviews can actually be more accurate than face-to-face ones. This is because the telephone interviews may let both parties focus more on substantive answers, rather than on things like handshake firmness or smiles. (Or perhaps candidates—somewhat surprised by unexpected calls from recruiters—simply give answers that are more spontaneous.)[47] In a typical study, interviewers tended to evaluate applicants more favorably in telephone versus face-to-face interviews, particularly where the interviewees were less physically attractive. The interviewers came to about the same conclusions regarding the interviewees whether the interview was face to face or by videoconference. Applicants themselves preferred face-to-face interviews.[48]

For better or worse, some employers are using a speed dating approach to interviewing applicants. One employer sent e-mails to all applicants for an advertised position. Four hundred (of 800) showed up. Over the next few hours, applicants first mingled with employees, and then (in a so-called speed dating area) had one-on-one contacts with employees for a few minutes. Based on this, the recruiting team chose 68 candidates for follow-up interviews.[49]

How Useful Are Interviews?

While virtually all employers use interviews, the statistical evidence regarding their validity is mixed. Much of the early research gave selection interviews low marks for reliability and validity.[50] However, today studies confirm that the "validity of the interview is greater than previously believed."[51] The key is that the interview's usefulness depends on how you administer it. Specifically, we can make the following generalizations:

- With respect to predicting job performance, *situational interviews* yield a higher mean (average) validity than do behavioral interviews.
- *Structured interviews* are more valid than unstructured interviews for predicting job performance. They are more valid partly because they are more reliable—for example, the same interviewer administers the interview more consistently from candidate to candidate.[52]
- Both when they are structured and when they are unstructured, *individual interviews* tend to be more valid than are panel interviews, in which multiple interviewers provide ratings in one setting.[53]

In summary, structured situational interviews (in which you ask the candidates what they would do in a particular situation) conducted one on one seem to be the most useful for predicting job performance. But in practice, effective interviewing also depends on avoiding common interviewing mistakes, a subject to which we now turn.

How to Avoid Common Interviewing Mistakes

Several common interviewing mistakes can undermine an interview's usefulness. We'll explain some of these common mistakes—and suggestions for avoiding them—in this section.

Snap Judgments   Perhaps the most consistent finding is that interviewers tend to jump to conclusions—make snap judgments—about candidates during the first few minutes of the interview. This often occurs even before the interview begins, based on test scores or résumé data.[54] One London-based psychologist interviewed the chief executives of 80 top companies. She came to this conclusion about snap judgments:

> Really, to make a good impression, you don't even get time to open your mouth. . . . An interviewer's response to you will generally be preverbal— how you walk through the door, what your posture is like, whether you smile, whether you have a captivating aura, whether you have a firm, confident handshake. You've got about half a minute to make an impact and after that all you are doing is building on a good or bad first impression. . . . It's a very emotional response.[55]

For interviewees, such findings underscore why it's important to start right with the interviewer. For interviewers, the findings underscore the importance of keeping an open mind until the interview is over.

Negative Emphasis   Jumping to conclusions is especially troublesome, given the fact that interviewers also tend to be more influenced by unfavorable than favorable information. Furthermore, their impressions are much more likely to change from favorable to unfavorable than from unfavorable to favorable. Often, in fact, interviews are mostly searches for negative information.

What are the implications? As an interviewer, remember to keep an open mind and work against being preoccupied with negative impressions. As an interviewee, remember the old saying that "You only have one chance to make a good first impression."

Not Knowing the Job   Interviewers who don't know what the job entails and what sort of candidate is best suited for it usually make decisions based on incorrect stereotypes about what makes a good applicant. They then erroneously match interviewees against these incorrect stereotypes. Interviewers should therefore know as much as possible about the position for which they're interviewing and about its required skills.[56]

Pressure to Hire   Being under pressure to hire undermines an interview's usefulness. In one study, several managers were told to assume that they were behind in their recruiting quota. A second group was told that they were ahead of their quota. Those behind evaluated the same recruits much more highly than did those ahead.[57]

Candidate Order (Contrast) Error   Candidate order (or contrast) error means that the order in which you see applicants affects how you rate them. In one study, researchers asked managers to evaluate a candidate who was "just average" after first evaluating several "unfavorable" candidates. The managers evaluated the average candidate more favorably than he might otherwise have been, because in contrast to the unfavorable candidates the average one looked better than he actually was.[58]

Influence of Nonverbal Behavior   It's not just what the candidate says but how he or she looks and behaves that determines the interview rating. For example, studies show that interviewers rate applicants who demonstrate more eye contact, head moving, smiling, and similar nonverbal behaviors higher.[59] In another study, vocal cues (such as the interviewee's pitch, speech rates, and pauses) and visual cues (such as physical attractiveness and smile) correlated with the evaluator's judgments of whether the interviewees could be trusted.[60] In one study of 99 graduating college seniors, the interviewee's apparent level of extroversion influenced whether he or she received job offers.[61] Extroverted applicants seem particularly prone to self-promotion, and self-promotion strongly affects the interviewer's perceptions of candidate job fit.[62]

Attractiveness[63]   In general, studies of attractiveness find that individuals ascribe more favorable traits and life outcomes to attractive people.[64] In another study, men were perceived to be more suitable for hire and more likely to advance to the next executive level than were equally qualified women, and more attractive candidates, especially men, were preferred over less attractive ones.[65] These stereotypes are changing. However, women still account for only about 16% of corporate officers at Fortune 500 companies.[66]

Race   Race also plays a role. One study examined racial differences in ratings when the interviewees appeared before three interview panels: panels in which the racial composition was primarily black, racially balanced, and primarily white.[67] On the primarily black panels, black and white raters judged black and white candidates similarly. On the other hand, in the primarily white and the balanced panels, white interviewers rated white candidates higher, and black interviewers rated black candidates higher.

Ingratiation   Interviewees boost their chances for job offers through self-promotion and ingratiation. *Ingratiation* involves, for example, agreeing with the recruiter's opinions. *Self-promotion* means promoting one's own skills and abilities to create the impression of competence.[68]

Implications   Evidence like this suggests two implications. With respect to nonverbal behavior (such as eye contact), it seems apparent that otherwise inferior candidates who are trained to "act right" in interviews are often appraised more highly than are more competent applicants who lack nonverbal skills. Interviewers should thus endeavor to look beyond the behavior to what the person is saying.

Similarly, because physical attributes are generally irrelevant to job performance, interviewers should guard against letting them influence their ratings. The accompanying *Managing the New Workforce* feature further illustrates this.

Applicant Disability and the Employment Interview   Researchers studied what disabled people who use assistive technology (such as voice recognition software) expect and prefer from interviewers.[69]

The basic finding was that interviewers tend to avoid addressing the disability, and therefore make their decisions without all the facts. What the disabled people

Would you hire someone's mother? As silly as that question seems, managers should be aware of a sad fact: Employers tend to view working mothers negatively.[70]

Here's an example. Researchers gave 100 working MBA students (34% female) copies of a job description summary for assistant vice president of financial affairs. The MBA students also got a "promotion applicant information form" to evaluate for each fictitious "applicant." The forms included researcher-created information such as marital status and supervisor comments. Some "applicants" were mothers.

The student evaluators viewed the mothers as less competent and were less likely to recommend them for the job. As the researchers say, "These data are consistent with mounting evidence that women suffer disadvantages in the workplace when they are mothers."[71]

prefer is an open discussion, one that allows the employer to reach a knowledgeable conclusion. Among the questions disabled persons said they would like interviewers to ask were these:

- Is there any kind of setting or special equipment that will facilitate the interview process for you?
- Is there any specific technology that you currently use or have used in previous jobs that assists the way you work?

Guidelines for Conducting an Interview

You can generally conduct the interview more effectively if you follow the guidelines outlined in this section.

Plan the Interview   Begin by reviewing the candidate's application and résumé, and note any areas that are vague or that may indicate strengths or weaknesses. Review the job specification to start the interview with a clear picture of the traits of an ideal candidate.

Structure the Interview   Take steps to structure or standardize the interview. There are several ways to do this.[72] They include:[73]

1. Study the job description and *base questions on actual job duties.*
2. Use *job knowledge, situational or behavioral questions*, and *objective criteria* to evaluate the interviewee's responses. Questions that ask for opinions and attitudes, goals and aspirations, and self-descriptions encourage self-promotion and allow candidates to avoid revealing weaknesses. Examples of structured questions include:
   - Situational questions like "Suppose you were giving a sales presentation and a difficult technical question arose that you could not answer. What would you do?"
   - Past behavior questions like "Can you provide an example of a specific instance where you developed a sales presentation that was highly effective?"

- Background questions like "What work experiences, training, or other qualifications do you have for working in a teamwork environment?"
- Job knowledge questions like "What factors should you consider when developing a TV advertising campaign?"

3. *Train interviewers* to avoid irrelevant or potentially discriminatory questions.[74]
4. Use the *same questions* with all candidates. This can improve consistency and reduce bias by giving all the candidates the same opportunity.
5. Use *rating scales* to rate answers. For each question, provide a range of sample ideal answers and a quantitative score for each. Then rate each candidate's answers against this scale.
6. Use *multiple interviewers.* Doing so can reduce bias by diminishing the importance of one interviewer's idiosyncratic opinions and by bringing in more points of view.
7. If possible, use a *structured interview form.* Interviews based on structured guides, like the one in Figure 4.5 (page 119), usually result in superior interviews.[75] At the very least, list your questions before the interview.
8. *Take brief notes* during the interview. Doing so may help to overcome "the recency effect" (in other words, putting too much weight on the last few minutes of the interview). It may also help the interviewer keep an open mind rather than making a snap judgment based on inadequate early information.[76]

The interview should take place in a private room where telephone calls are not accepted and you can minimize interruptions.

Establish Rapport　　The reason for the interview is to find out about the applicant. To do this, start by putting the person at ease, perhaps with a noncontroversial question, such as about the weather.

Ask Questions　　Try to follow a structured interview guide or the questions you wrote out ahead of time. You'll find a menu of additional questions to choose from in Figure 4.6.

One way to get answers that are more candid is to state you're going to conduct reference checks. Ask, "If I were to ask your boss, what's your best guess as to what he or she would say are your strengths, weaker points, and overall performance?"[77]

The *HR in Practice* box nearby summarizes some do's and don'ts for asking questions.

What *Not* to Ask.　　As a rule, avoid questions based on age, race, gender, national origin, handicap, or other prohibited criteria. Can you pick out the inappropriate questions in the following list?[78]

- What kinds of things do you look for in a job?
- What types of interests or hobbies are you involved in?
- Do you have any handicaps?
- What university subjects do you like the most?
- What qualities should a successful manager possess?
- Do you have any plans for marriage and children?
- What do you think you have to offer a company like ours?

Figure 4.6 Suggested Supplementary Questions for Interviewing Applicants

1. How did you choose this line of work?
2. What did you enjoy most about your last job?
3. What did you like least about your last job?
4. What has been your greatest frustration or disappointment on your present job? Why?
5. What are some of the pluses and minuses of your last job?
6. What were the circumstances surrounding your leaving your last job?
7. Did you give notice?
8. Why should we be hiring you?
9. What do you expect from this employer?
10. What are three things you will not do in your next job?
11. What would your last supervisor say your three weaknesses are?
12. What are your major strengths?
13. How can your supervisor best help you obtain your goals?
14. How did your supervisor rate your job performance?
15. In what ways would you change your last supervisor?
16. What are your career goals during the next 1–3 years? 5–10 years?
17. How will working for this company help you reach those goals?
18. What did you do the last time you received instructions with which you disagreed?
19. What are some of the things about which you and your supervisor disagreed? What did you do?
20. Which do you prefer, working alone or working with groups?
21. What motivated you to do better at your last job?
22. Do you consider your progress on that job representative of your ability? Why?
23. Do you have any questions about the duties of the job for which you have applied?
24. Can you perform the essential functions of the job for which you have applied?

Source: Reprinted from http://hr.blr.com with permission of the publisher Business and Legal Resources, Inc. 141 Mill Rock Road East, Old Saybrook, CT © 2004. BLR© (Business and Legal Resources, Inc.).

- What is your date of birth?
- What is the nature of your previous work experience?
- What kinds of things do you look for in a job?
- Have you ever been arrested for a crime?
- What do you consider your greatest strengths?

HR in Practice: Do's and Don'ts of Asking Interview Questions

- **Don't** ask questions that can be answered yes or no.
- **Don't** put words in the applicant's mouth or telegraph the desired answer, for instance, by nodding.
- **Don't** interrogate the applicant, or be patronizing, sarcastic, or inattentive.
- **Don't** monopolize the interview or let the applicant dominate the interview so you can't ask all your questions.

- **Do** ask open-ended questions.
- **Do** listen to the candidate.
- **Do** draw out the applicant's opinions and feelings by repeating the person's last comment as a question (e.g., "You didn't like your last job?").
- **Do** ask for examples.[79] For instance, if the candidate lists specific strengths, follow up with, "What are specific examples that demonstrate each of your strengths?"

With employers cutting their recruitment budgets, more are conducting initial interviews over the Internet. Webcam prices are now well below $100, and new recruitment sites (such as Inovahire.com) post free Webcam conferencing. And increasingly, with free applications like Skype widely used, there's no reason for not doing the initial interviews via Skype.

Having a Skype job interview probably doesn't require too many special preparations for the employer. However, Career FAQs (www.careerfaqs.com) says there are things that interviewees should keep in mind:[80]

- Look presentable. You might feel silly at home wearing a suit, but it will make a difference.

- Clean up the room. Whether from your own home or a busy office, don't have the interviewer see you sitting in front of junk.
- Test first. As Career FAQs says, "Five minutes before the video interview is not a good time to realize that your Internet is down."
- Do a dry run. Try recording yourself before the interview, answering some possible questions.
- Relax. The golden rule with an online interview is to treat it like any face to-face meeting. There is a real person on the other end of the call, so treat them like one. Smile, look confident and enthusiastic, make eye contact, and don't shout, but do speak clearly.

Close the Interview   Toward the close of the interview, leave time to answer any questions the candidate may have and, if appropriate, to advocate your firm to the candidate.

Try to end all interviews on a positive note. Tell the applicant whether there is an interest and, if so, what the next step will be. Similarly, make rejections diplomatically (for instance, "Although your background is impressive, there are other candidates whose experiences are closer to our requirements"). As one recruiter says, "An interview experience should leave a lasting, positive impression of the company, whether the candidate receives and accepts an offer or not."[81]

Review the Interview   After the candidate leaves, review your interview notes, and complete any structured interview guide. In challenging times, employers are saving money by using Skype-type interviews; the feature above elaborates on this.

USING OTHER SELECTION TECHNIQUES

Background Investigations and Reference Checks

About 82% of HR managers report checking applicants' backgrounds; 80% do criminal convictions searches, and 35% do credit history reports.[82]

There are two key reasons for checking backgrounds. One is to verify the facts provided by the applicant (for example, a survey found that 23% of 7,000 executive résumés contained exaggerated or false information).[83] The other reason is to uncover damaging background information such as criminal records. In Chicago, for instance, a pharmaceutical firm hired gang members in mail delivery and computer repair. The gang members were stealing almost a million dollars a year in computer parts and using the mail department to ship them to a nearby computer store they owned.[84]

What to Verify   The most commonly verified background areas are generally legal eligibility for employment (to comply with immigration laws), dates of prior employment, military service (including discharge status), education, and identification (including date of birth and address). Other items should include county criminal records (current residence, last residence), motor vehicle record, credit, licensing verification, Social Security number, and reference checks.[85] With diploma mills proliferating, you should check academic backgrounds.[86] Most employers at least try to verify an applicant's current position, salary, and employment dates with his or her current employer by phone (assuming that the candidate cleared doing so).[87] Others call the applicant's current and previous supervisors to try to discover more about the person's motivation, technical competence, and ability to work with others. Some employers check executive candidates' civil litigation records, with the candidate's prior approval.[88]

The position determines how deeply you search. For example, a credit and education check is more important for an accountant than a groundskeeper. Also periodically check, say, the credit ratings of current employees with easy access to company assets.

Checking Social Networking Sites   One employer went to Facebook.com and found that a top candidate described his interests as smoking marijuana and shooting people. The student may have been kidding but did not get the offer.[89] After conducting such online reviews, recruiters found that 31% of applicants lied about their qualifications and 19% posted information about their drinking or drug use, according to Careerbuilder.com.[90] However, while Googling is probably safe enough, checking social networking sites raises legal issues. For example, while the Fair Credit Reporting Act refers more to getting official reports, it's still probably best to get the candidate's prior approval for social networking searches.[91] And of course do not use a pretext or fabricate an identity.[92]

Using Preemployment Information Services   Online databases make it easy to check candidates' background information. Numerous employment-screening services access dozens of databases, by county, to compile background information for employers quickly.[93]

Although they are valuable, the employer should ensure the screening service doesn't ensnare it by taking any actions that conflict with Equal Employment Opportunity (EEO) laws. For example, under the ADA, employers should avoid preemployment inquiries into the existence or severity of a disability. In choosing a screening service, ensure it requires an applicant-signed release authorizing the background check, complies with relevant laws such as the Fair Credit Reporting Act, and uses only legal data sources. Major employment screening providers include ADP (www.ADP.com), employment background investigations (www.ADPII.andsay.com), and hireright/USIS commercial services (www.hireright.com).[94] A basic criminal check might cost $25; while a comprehensive background check costs about $200.[95]

Reference Check Effectiveness   Handled correctly, background checks are an inexpensive and straightforward way of verifying facts (such as current and previous job titles). However, reference checking has its limits. Most importantly, it's not always easy for references to prove that the bad reference they gave was warranted. The rejected applicant thus has various legal remedies, including suing for defamation.[96] In one case, a man was awarded $56,000 after being turned down for a job because, among other things, a former employer called him a "character."

It is not just the fear of lawsuits. Many supervisors don't want to diminish a former employee's chances for a job. Others give incompetents good reviews just to get rid of them. The bottom line is that you must ask the right questions and be vigilant for evasiveness.

Making Reference Checks More Productive   You can do several things to make your reference checking more productive.

First, use a structured form as in Figure 4.7. This helps ensure that you don't miss important questions.

Second, use the references offered by the applicant as merely a source for other references. For example, ask each reference, "Could you please give me the name of another person who might be familiar with the applicant's performance?" In that way, you begin getting information from references that may be more objective. Perhaps contact two superiors, two peers, and two subordinates from each previous job.

Third, also ask open-ended questions, such as "How much direction does the applicant need in his or her work?" to get the references to talk more about the candidate.

Fourth, companies fielding requests for references should ensure that only authorized managers give them. There are companies (such as Allison & Taylor Reference Checking Inc. (http://www.allisontaylor.com/)) that, for a fee, will call former employers on behalf of former employees who believe they're getting bad references. One supervisor, describing a former city employee, reportedly "said he was incompetent and said that he almost brought the city down on its knees."[97]

Finally, always get at least two forms of identification and obtain a job application. Always compare the application to the résumé (people are less creative on their application forms, where they must certify the information).[98]

Honesty Testing

Polygraph Tests   The *polygraph* (or *"lie detector"*) machine measures physiological changes such as perspiration. The assumption is that such changes reflect changes in the emotional stress that accompanies lying. The usual procedure is to attach the applicant or current employee to the machine with painless electronic probes. The polygraph expert then asks several true neutral questions (such as, Is your name Jane Smith?). After ascertaining the person's reactions to neutral questions, questions such as "Have you ever taken anything without paying for it?" are asked. In theory, the expert can determine whether the applicant is lying.

Doubts about the polygraph's accuracy culminated in the Employee Polygraph Protection Act of 1988. With few exceptions, it prohibits most employers from conducting polygraph exams of all applicants and most employees. Even

Figure 4.7 Reference Checking Form

(Verify that the applicant has provided permission before conducting reference checks.)

Candidate
Name _____

Reference
Name _____

Company
Name _____

Dates of Employment
From: _____ To: _____

Position(s)
Held _____

Salary
History _____

Reason for
Leaving _____

Explain the reason for your call and verify the above information with the supervisor (including the reason for leaving)
_____
_____

1. Please describe the type of work for which the candidate was responsible.
_____
_____

2. How would you describe the applicant's relationships with coworkers, subordinates (if applicable), and with superiors?
_____
_____

3. Did the candidate have a positive or negative work attitude? Please elaborate.
_____
_____

4. How would you describe the quantity and quality of output generated by the former employee?
_____
_____

5. What were his/her strengths on the job?
_____
_____

6. What were his/her weaknesses on the job?
_____
_____

7. What is your overall assessment of the candidate?
_____
_____

8. Would you recommend him/her for this position? Why or why not?
_____
_____

9. Would this individual be eligible for rehire? Why or why not?
_____
_____

Other comments?
_____
_____

Source: Society for Human Resource Management, © 2004. Reproduced with permission via Copyright Clearance Center.

Ask blunt questions. You can ask very direct questions. For example, there is probably nothing wrong with asking, "Have you ever stolen anything from an employer?" and "Is any information on your application misrepresented?"[99]

Ask for a credit check. Include a clause in your application form that gives you the right to certain background checks on the applicant, including credit checks and motor vehicle reports.

Check all references.

Consider using a test. Consider honesty tests and psychological tests as part of your honesty screening.

Test for drugs. Devise and institute a drug-testing program.

Conduct searches. Establish a search-and-seizure policy. This should state that all lockers, desks, and similar property remain the property of the company and may be inspected routinely.

Use caution. Rejection for dishonesty carries more stigma than does being rejected for, say, poor mechanical comprehension. Furthermore, some states, including Massachusetts and Rhode Island, limit the use of honesty tests. Therefore, protect your candidates and employees' privacy rights adhere to the law.

for ongoing investigations of theft, the employer's right to use polygraphs is limited.[100]

Honesty Tests   The virtual elimination of the polygraph as a screening device triggered a burgeoning market for other honesty testing devices. Paper-and-pencil or computerized honesty tests are psychological tests designed to predict job applicants' proneness to dishonesty. Most of these tests measure attitudes regarding things such as tolerance of others who steal and admission of theft-related activities.

Studies tend to support honesty tests' validity. One study focused on 111 employees hired by a major retail convenience store chain.[101] "Shrinkage" was estimated at 3% of sales, and internal theft was believed to account for much of this. The researchers found that scores on an honesty test successfully predicted theft, as measured by termination for theft.

In practice, detecting dishonest candidates involves not only tests but also a comprehensive procedure including reference checking and interviews. One expert suggests following the steps in the *HR in Practice* box above.

Graphology

Graphology (handwriting analysis) assumes that the writer's basic personality traits will be expressed in his or her handwriting. Handwriting analysis thus has some resemblance to projective personality tests.

Although some writers estimate that more than 1,000 U.S. companies use handwriting analysis, the validity of handwriting analysis is questionable. One reviewer says, "There is essentially no evidence of a direct link between handwriting analysis and various measures of job performance."[102]

Physical Exams

Physical examinations are often the next step in the selection process, and there are several reasons for requiring them. Such exams can confirm that the applicant qualifies for the physical requirements of the position and can unearth any medical limitations to take into account in placing the applicant. The examination can also detect communicable diseases. Under the ADA, a person with a disability can't be rejected for the job if he or she is otherwise qualified and if the person could perform the essential job functions with reasonable accommodation. A medical exam is permissible during the period between the job offer and the commencement of work, if one is standard practice for all applicants for that job category.[103]

Drug Screening

Most employers conduct drug tests. The most common practice is to test new applicants just before formally hiring them. Many firms also test current employees when there is reason to believe an employee has been using drugs, such as after a work accident or when there are behavioral symptoms like high absenteeism. Some firms administer drug tests on a random or periodic basis, while others do so only when transferring or promoting an employee.[104] Most employers conduct such tests by using urine sampling. Some use a test that analyzes small amounts of human hair.

Problems   Unfortunately, while roadside alcohol breathalyzers correlate closely with impairment levels, urine and blood tests for drugs only indicate whether drug residues are present.[105] They cannot measure impairment, habituation, or addiction.[106] Furthermore, "there is a swarm of products that promise to help employees beat drug tests."[107]

Drug testing therefore raises several issues. Some argue that drug testing violates citizens' rights to privacy and due process and are intrusive. Others argue that workplace drug testing might identify one's use of drugs during leisure hours but have little relevance to the job itself.[108]

In fact, one study concluded that other than alcohol, there is no clear evidence that drugs diminish safety or job performance.[109] Another study, in three hotels, concluded that preemployment drug testing seemed to have little or no effect on workplace accidents. However, a combination of preemployment and random ongoing testing was associated with a significant reduction in workplace accidents.[110]

Legal Issues   Several federal laws apply. Under the ADA, courts might well view a former drug user (one who no longer uses illegal drugs and successfully completed or is participating in a rehabilitation program) as a qualified applicant with a disability.[111] U.S. Department of Transportation regulations require firms with more than 50 eligible employees in transportation industries to conduct alcohol testing on workers with sensitive or safety-related jobs. These include mass-transit workers, air traffic controllers, and school-bus drivers.[112]

Particularly with safety-sensitive jobs, courts often side with employers. In one case, a U.S. Court of Appeals ruled that Exxon acted properly in firing a truck driver who failed a drug test. In this case, the employee drove a tractor-trailer carrying 12,000 gallons of flammable motor fuel and tested positive for cocaine. Exxon discharged him.[113]

Realistic Job Previews

A dose of realism makes a good screening tool. For example, Walmart found that many new associates quit within the first 90 days. After Walmart began explicitly explaining and asking about work schedules and work preferences, turnover improved.[114] In general, applicants who receive realistic job previews are more likely to turn down job offers but more likely to have lower turnover.[115]

Tapping Friends and Acquaintances

Testing and interviewing aside, don't ignore tapping the opinions of people you trust who have direct personal knowledge of the candidate. It may be an exaggeration, but as a CEO of Continental Airlines said, "the best possible interview is minuscule in value compared to somebody who's got even a couple of months of work experience with [the candidate]"[116]

Complying with the Immigration Law

Under the Immigration Reform and Control Act of 1986, people must prove that they are eligible for employment in the United States. A person does not have to be a U.S. citizen to be employed. However, employers should ask a candidate who is about to be hired whether he or she is a U.S. citizen or an alien lawfully authorized to work in the United States.

How to Comply There are two basic ways to show eligibility for employment. One is to show a document such as a U.S. passport or alien registration card with a photograph that proves both identity and employment eligibility.[117] The other is to show a document that proves the person's identity, along with a separate document showing the person's employment eligibility, such as a work permit. More employers are using the federal government's voluntary electronic employment verification program, E-Verify.[118] Federal contractors must use it.[119]

Employers can protect themselves against fraudulent documents in several ways. Systematic background checks are the most obvious. These should include employment verification, criminal record checks, drug screens, and reference checks. You can verify Social Security cards by calling the Social Security Administration. Employers can avoid accusations of discrimination by verifying the documents of all applicants, not just those they think are suspicious.[120]

Employers should not use the I-9 Employment Eligibility Verification form required to document eligibility to discriminate based on race or country of national origin.[121] The requirement to verify eligibility does not provide any basis to reject an applicant just because he or she is a foreigner, or not a U.S. citizen, or an alien residing in the United States, as long as that person can prove his or her identity and employment eligibility.

Making the Selection Decision

Once you've collected all your selection information, the question arises, how do you combine it all and make a selection decision? If you're only using one predictor (such as one test score) then the decision is straightforward. For example, hire the applicant with the highest score.

In practice, things are not so simple. For one thing, you'll probably not make your decision based on a single predictor (in this case, one test score). You'll also want to factor in the person's references, his or her interview and application information (such as school attended), and perhaps the results of other tests. In other words, you'll have not one but *multiple predictors* to juggle. Furthermore, you'll probably have more than one candidate.[122] Will you simply choose the one with the highest Wonderlic score? Probably not. So again, you'll need some way to weigh all the sources of information you have about each candidate and to make a choice.

How do you weigh all the input you have in reaching a selection decision? There are three basic approaches. You could use, *first*, a clinical (or "intuitive," or "judgmental") approach. This is one with which you're already probably familiar. Here you intuitively weigh all the evidence you have from the various sources about the candidate and make your decision. *Second*, you could take a statistical (or "mechanical") approach. In its purest sense, the mechanical approach involves quantifying all the information you collect about the candidate (including, for example, subjective information from references). You then combine all this quantified information to get an answer, perhaps using a formula that predicts the candidate's likely job success. And *third*, you could take a hybrid approach, one that fine-tunes the mechanical results you obtained from your formula with judgment. Strictly speaking, the mechanical/statistical approach is usually the most defensible.

A Practical Approach However, while it may be ideal to use such a mechanical approach, a more informal, subjective approach is still usually better than nothing. For example, suppose you have a job opening for an engineer.[123] You ask yourself what specific tasks this engineer will have to perform and the standards by which you'll measure that performance. Next, think of several activities you can ask your candidates to perform that would be similar to what you'd expect the person to do on the job. After identifying several of these activities, think about the weights you'd attach to each activity based on what you think is the relative importance of each activity. Then have each candidate perform each activity, and give each activity he or she performs a score using some simple rating system (such as 1 to 5, from low to high). Then multiply each candidate's score on each activity with weight for that activity and determine which candidate scores highest.

REVIEW

Summary

1. Test validity answers the question: What does this test measure? Criterion validity means demonstrating that those who do well on the test do well on the job. Content validity is demonstrated by showing that the test constitutes a fair sample of the content of the job.

2. As used by psychologists, the term *reliability* always means "consistency." One way to measure reliability is to administer the same (or equivalent) tests to the same people at two different points in time. Or you could focus on internal consistency, comparing the responses to roughly equivalent items on the same test.

3. There are many types of personnel tests in use, including intelligence tests, tests of physical skills, tests of achievement, aptitude tests, interest inventories, and personality tests.

4. Under equal opportunity legislation, an employer may have to prove that his or her tests are predictive of success or failure on the job. This usually requires a predictive validation study, although other means of validation are often acceptable.

5. Management assessment centers are screening devices that expose applicants to a series of real-life exercises. Examples of such real-life exercises include a simulated business game, an in-basket exercise, and group discussions.

6. Several factors and problems can undermine the usefulness of an interview: making premature decisions, letting unfavorable information predominate, not knowing the requirements of the job, being under pressure to hire, not allowing for the candidate order effect, and nonverbal behavior.

7. The steps in the interview include plan, establish rapport, structure, ask questions, close the interview, and review the data.

8. Other screening tools include reference checks, background checks, physical exams, and realistic previews.

9. Once you've selected and hired your new employees, they must be trained. We turn to training in Chapter 5.

KEY TERMS

- reliability
- test validity
- criterion validity
- content validity
- work sampling technique
- management assessment center
- interview

DISCUSSION QUESTIONS

1. Explain what is meant by *reliability* and *validity*. What is the difference between them? In what respects are they similar?

2. Write a short essay discussing some of the ethical and legal considerations in testing.

3. Give some examples of how interest inventories could be used to improve employee selection. In doing so, suggest several examples of occupational interests that you believe might predict success in various

occupations, including college professor, accountant, and computer programmer.

4. Why is it important to conduct preemployment background investigations? How would you go about doing so?

5. For what sorts of jobs do you think computerized interviews are most appropriate? Why?

6. Give a short presentation titled "How to Be Effective as an Interviewer."

7. Briefly discuss and give examples of at least five common interviewing mistakes. What recommendations would you give for avoiding these interviewing mistakes?

INDIVIDUAL AND GROUP ACTIVITIES

1. Working individually or in groups, develop a list of specific selection techniques that you would suggest your dean use to hire the next HR professor at your school. Explain why you chose each selection technique.

2. Working individually or in groups, access the publisher of a standardized test such as the Scholastic Assessment Test and obtain from it information regarding the test's validity and reliability. Present a short report in class discussing what the test is supposed to measure and the degree to which you think the test does what it is supposed to do, based on the reported validity and reliability scores.

APPLICATION EXERCISES

Case Incident   The Tough Screener

Everyone who knows Mark Rosen knows he is tough when it comes to screening applicants for jobs in his firm. His company, located in a large northeastern city, provides financial planning advice to wealthy clients, sells insurance, and sets up pension plans for individuals and businesses. His firm's clients range from professionals such as doctors and lawyers to business owners, who are sophisticated in financial matters and very busy people. They expect accurate advice provided in a clear and expeditious manner.

Rosen is always described as somewhat autocratic. The need to be very selective in whom he hires has led him to be extraordinarily careful about how he screens applicants. Some of his methods are probably beyond reproach. For example, he requires every applicant to provide a list of names and phone numbers of at least five people he or she worked with at each previous employer to use as references.

On the other hand, given legislation including the Civil Rights Act of 1991 and the ADA, some of his other "tough" screening methods could be problematic. For example, Rosen requires that all applicants take a purported honesty test, which he found in the catalog of an office supply store. He also believes it's extremely important to check every viable applicant's credit history and workers' compensation history. Unknown to his applicants, he runs a credit check on each of them, and retains the services of a firm that checks workers' compensation and driving violation histories. ■

QUESTIONS

1. What specific legal problems do you think Rosen might run into because of his firm's screening methods? How would you suggest he eliminate these problems?
2. Given what you know about Rosen's business, write a two-page proposal describing an employee testing and selection program that you would recommend. Say a few words about the sorts of tests, if any, you would recommend and the application form questions you would ask, as well as other methods, including drug screening and reference checking.

Continuing Case

LearnInMotion.com: Do You Have Sales Potential?

Of all the positions LearnInMotion had to fill, none were more pressing—or problematic—than those of the company's salespeople. The job was pressing because the clock was already ticking on the uses of the company's funds. The firm was already paying over $5,000 a month in rent and had signed obligations for a wide range of other expenses. These included monthly computer payments to Dell ($2,000 a month); a phone system ($800 a month); a burglar alarm ($200 a month); advertising ($4,000 a month); their own salaries ($10,000 a month); high-speed lines ($600 a month); phones ($400 a month); and the services of a consulting programmer ($4,000 a month). So, even "doing nothing" they were burning through almost $40,000 per month. They needed a sales force.

However, hiring good salespeople was becoming increasingly difficult. Hiring people like this should have been straightforward: LearnInMotion's salespeople have to sell to two basic types of customers. They have to try to get potential customers to purchase banner space or button space on LearnInMotion's various Web site pages. To make this easier, Jennifer and Mel had prepared an online media kit. It describes the Web site metrics—for instance, in terms of monthly page views, and in terms of typical user metrics such as reported age and income level. In addition to selling banner ads, salespeople also have to try to get the companies that actually produce and make available educational DVDs and courses to make those courses and programs available through LearnInMotion.com. None of these is "big-ticket" sales: Because the site is new and small, they can't really charge advertisers based on the number of users who click on their ads, so they simply charge a quarterly fee of $1,500 to list courses or to place ads. Content providers also have to agree to split any sales 50–50 with LearnInMotion. The Web surfer and office manager spend part of their time scouring the Web to identify potential customers. The salespeople then contact these people, "take them through" the Web site to show its functions, and answer the potential customer's questions.

This sales job, in other words, was typical, so it shouldn't have been so difficult to fill, but difficult it was. Perhaps it was because it was a dot-com, or perhaps they just weren't offering enough compensation; whatever it was, they were finding it extremely difficult to hire one, let alone two, good salespeople.

Perhaps the biggest problem was deciding which of the personable candidates who showed up actually had sales potential. Jennifer and Mel did learn a couple of interesting things about interviewing sales candidates. For example, when they asked the first what his average monthly sales had been in the past 6 months at his former employer, he answered, "Oh, I got the award for highest sales last month." That seemed great to Mel, until later Jennifer pointed out to him that that answer really didn't answer their question. Things got even "weirder"—to use Mel's term—when five out of six of the next sales candidates gave more or less the same answer: "I was the top producer"; "I was one of the top three producers"; "They sent me to Las Vegas for being the top sales producer"; and so on. Getting applicants to actually divulge, specifically, what their average monthly sales had been was, as they say, like pulling teeth. Given that fact, and the relatively few sales candidates they have had, it has become obvious to the owners that basing their hiring decision solely on the person's experience is not going to work. In other words, they have to have some way to ascertain whether the candidate has sales potential, and whether he or she has the cognitive aptitude to discuss LearnInMotion's services with customers. They want you, their management consultants, to help them. Here's what they want you to do for them. ■

QUESTIONS AND ASSIGNMENTS

1. What would be the advantages and disadvantages to our company of routinely administering a "sales potential" test to sales candidates? Which would you suggest?
2. Specifically, what other screening techniques should our company use to select high-potential sales candidates?
3. Tell us: What have we been doing wrong, and what should we do now?
4. Write a set of situational and behavioral questions you think we should ask candidates in our interviews with them.

Experiential Exercise

The Most Important Person You'll Ever Hire

Purpose: The purpose of this exercise is to give you practice using some of the interview techniques you learned from this chapter.

Required Understanding: You should be familiar with the information presented in this chapter, and read this: For parents, children are precious. It's therefore interesting that parents who hire "nannies" to take care of their children usually do little more than ask several interview questions and conduct what is often, at best, a perfunctory reference check. Given the often questionable validity of interviews, and the (often) relative inexperience of the father or mother doing the interviewing, it's not surprising that many of these arrangements end in disappointment. You know from this chapter that it is difficult to conduct a valid interview unless you know exactly what you're looking for and, preferably, structure the interview. Most parents simply aren't trained to do this.

How to Set Up the Exercise/Instructions:

1. Set up groups of five or six students. Two students will be the interviewees; the others will serve as panel interviewers. The interviewees will develop an interviewer assessment form, and the panel interviewers will develop a structured situational interview for a "nannie."
2. Instructions for the interviewees: The interviewees should leave the room for about 20 minutes. While out of the room, the interviewees should develop an "interviewer assessment form" based on the information presented in this chapter regarding factors that can undermine the usefulness of an interview. During the panel interview, the interviewees should assess the interviewers using the interviewer assessment form. After the panel interviewers have conducted the interview, the interviewees should leave the room to discuss their notes. Did the interviewers exhibit any of the factors that can undermine the usefulness of an interview? If so, which ones? What suggestions would you (the interviewees) make to the interviewers on how to improve the usefulness of the interview?
3. Instructions for the interviewers: While the interviewees are out of the room, the panel interviewers will have 20 minutes to develop a short structured situational interview form for a "nannie." The panel interview team will interview two candidates for the position. During the panel interview, each interviewer should be taking notes on a copy of the structured situational interview form. After the panel interview, the panel interviewers should discuss their notes. What were your first impressions of each interviewee? Were your impressions similar? Which candidate would you all select for the position and why?

Chapter 5

Training and Developing Employees

- Orienting Employees
- The Training Process
- Training Techniques
- Managerial Development and Training
- Managing Organizational Change Programs
- Evaluating the Training and Development Effort

When you finish studying this chapter, you should be able to:

- Describe *the basic training process.*
- Discuss *at least two techniques used for assessing training needs.*
- Explain *the pros and cons of at least five training techniques.*
- Explain *what management development is and why it is important.*
- Describe *the main development techniques.*

INTRODUCTION

At Stanford University, medical students rush to save a virtual patient. They use virtual reality headsets to control their on-screen avatars. The avatars are computerized simulations dressed in medical scrubs. Each avatar has a different role, such as nurse or emergency room technician. The students use their keypads to control their avatars in a virtual reality trauma center. One avatar props up the patient; another clears his airway. On the screen, the patient's vital signs react fittingly to the medical students' decisions. Then instructors replay the scenario, showing trainees what they did right and wrong.[1] Training, as we'll see, is increasingly high tech.[2]

ORIENTING EMPLOYEES

After screening and selecting new employees, management turns to the task of orienting and training them. **Employee orientation** (often called "onboarding" today) involves more than what most people realize.[3] It should at least provide new employees with the basic background information they need to perform their jobs, such as about company rules. But orientation should also contribute to socializing the employee into the employer's way of doing things. *Socialization* is the ongoing process of instilling in employees the attitudes, standards, values, and patterns of behavior that the organization expects.[4] Appreciating the company's culture and values distinguishes today's *onboarding* from traditional orientation.[5] For example, the Mayo Clinic's new "heritage and culture" program emphasizes core Mayo Clinic values such as teamwork, personal responsibility, and mutual respect.[6]

Types of Programs   Orientation programs range from brief introductions to lengthy formal programs. In either, new employees usually receive printed or Web-based handbooks covering things like working hours, performance reviews, getting on the payroll, and vacations, as well as a facilities tour. Other information might cover employee benefits, personnel policies, the employee's daily routine, company organization and operations, and safety regulations.[7] (Courts may find that your employee handbook's contents represent a contract with the employee, so make it clear that statements of company policies, benefits, and regulations do not constitute the terms and conditions of an employment contract.) In firms like Nissan, the onboarding takes up to a week. It may include videos, lectures by company officers, and exercises covering matters like company history, vision, and values.

Purposes   A successful orientation accomplishes four things. The new employee should feel welcome. He or she should understand the organization in a broad sense (its past, present, culture, and vision of the future). The employee should be clear about what the firm expects in terms of policies and procedures and work and behavior. And, hopefully, the person should begin becoming socialized into the firm's preferred ways of doing things.[8]

Technology   Technology improves orientation. For example, some firms provide new managers with preloaded personal digital assistants. These contain information such as key contact information, and even images of employees the new manager needs to know.[9] Some firms provide all new employees with URLs or disks containing discussions of corporate culture, videos of corporate facilities, and welcoming addresses from top managers. IBM uses virtual environments like Second Life to support orientation. The new employees choose virtual avatars, which then interact with other company avatars, for instance, to learn how to enroll for benefits.[10]

The HR specialist usually performs the first part of the orientation and explains matters like working hours and vacation. The employee's new supervisor continues the orientation by explaining the exact nature of the job, introducing the person to his or her new colleagues, and familiarizing the new employee with the workplace and the job.

THE TRAINING PROCESS

Training refers to the methods employers use to give new or present employees the skills they need to perform their jobs. Some training experts use the phrase "workplace learning and performance" in lieu of training, to underscore training's dual aims of employee learning and organizational performance.[11]

Companies spent about $826 per employee for training in one recent year and offered each about 28 hours of training.[12] Training has an impressive record of influencing organizational effectiveness, scoring higher than appraisal and just below goal setting in its effect on productivity.[13]

Training and Strategy

Training needs ideally flow from the employer's strategic plans. As one trainer says, "We don't just concentrate on the traditional training objectives anymore. . . . We sit down with management and help them identify strategic goals and objectives and the skills and knowledge needed to achieve them. Then we work together to identify whether our staff has the skills and knowledge, and when they don't, that's when we discuss training needs."[14] Thus when Signicast Corp. decided to transition to a new computerized production process, its human resource managers designed training programs that enabled the firm to implement its new high-tech strategy. One survey found that "establishing a linkage between learning and organizational performance" was the number-one pressing issue facing training professionals.[15]

The Training and Development Process

We can envision the training process as including four steps:

1. In the first, *needs analysis* step, you identify the specific knowledge and skills the job requires, and compare these with the prospective trainees' knowledge and skills.
2. In the second, *instructional design* step, you formulate specific training objectives, review possible training program content (including workbooks, exercises, and activities), and estimate a budget for the training program.[16]

3. The third step is to implement the program, by actually training the targeted employee group using methods such as online training.

4. Finally, is an evaluation step, in which you assess the program's success (or failures).

Training Needs Analysis   Assessing employees' training needs usually involves either *task analysis*—breaking the jobs into subtasks and teaching each to the new employee—or *performance analysis*—determining the nature of the performance problem. We'll look at each.

Employers use task analysis to determine *new* employees' training needs. With inexperienced personnel, your aim is to provide the skills and knowledge required for effective performance. How do you do this? **Task analysis** is a detailed study of the job to determine what specific skill—such as soldering (in the case of an assembly worker) or interviewing (in the case of a supervisor)—is required. The job description and job specification list the job's specific duties and skills and are the basic reference points for determining the training required. Figure 5.1 summarizes other methods for uncovering a job's training requirements.

For *current* employees, requests for training often start with line managers expressing concerns, such as "we're getting too many complaints from clients."[17] The first step here is therefore to determine what training, if any, is required. Some call this the "skills gapping" process. Ideally, employers determine the skills each job requires and the skills of the job's current or prospective employees. The employer then designs a training program to eliminate the skills gap.[18] The problem is that training may not be the solution. **Performance analysis** means verifying that there is a performance deficiency and determining whether that deficiency should be rectified through training or through some other means (such as transferring the employee or changing the compensation plan). Analytical tools here include:

- Supervisor, peer, self-, and 360-degree performance reviews
- Job-related performance data (such as productivity, absenteeism, accidents, waste, late deliveries, product quality, and customer complaints)
- Observation by supervisors or other specialists
- Interviews with the employee or his or her supervisor
- Tests of things like job knowledge, skills, and attendance
- Attitude surveys
- Assessment centers[19]

Performance analysis usually starts with appraising the employee's performance. Examples of specific performance deficiencies are:

"I expect each salesperson to make 10 new contracts per week, but John averages only six."
"Other plants our size average no more than two serious accidents per month; we're averaging five."

For current employees, distinguishing between "can't do" and "won't do" problems is the heart of performance analysis. First, determine whether it's a "can't do"

Figure 5.1 Tools for Uncovering a Job's Training Needs

Sources for Obtaining Job Data	*Training Need Information*
1. Job Descriptions	Outlines the job's typical duties and responsibilities but is not meant to be all-inclusive. Helps define performance discrepancies.
2. Job Specifications or Task Analysis	List specified tasks required for each job. More specific than job descriptions. Specifications may extend to judgments of knowledge and skills required of job incumbents.
3. Performance Standards	Objectives of the tasks of job, and standards by which they are judged. This may include baseline data as well.
4. Perform the Job	Most effective way of identifying a job's specific tasks, but has serious limitations in higher-level jobs because performance requirements typically have longer gaps between performance and resulting outcomes.
5. Observe Job—Work Sampling	Same as 4 above.

6. Review Literature Concerning the Job
    a. Research in other industries
    b. Professional journals
    c. Documents
    d. Government sources
    e. Ph.D. theses
	Possibly useful, but far removed from either unique aspects of the job within any specific organization or specific performance requirements.

7. Ask Questions About the Job
    a. Of the job holder
    b. Of the supervisor
    c. Of higher management
	Inputs from several viewpoints can often reveal training needs or training desires.

8. Training Committees or Conferences	Same as 7 above.

9. Analysis of Operating Problems
    a. Downtime reports
    b. Waste
    c. Repairs
    d. Late deliveries
    e. Quality control
	Indications of task interference, environmental factors, etc.

Source: Adapted from P. Nick Blanchard and James Thacker, *Effective Training Systems Strategies and Practices* (Upper Saddle River, NJ: Prentice Hall, 1999), pp. 138–39.

problem and, if so, its specific causes. For example, perhaps the employees don't know what to do or what your standards are, or there are obstacles such as lack of supplies. Perhaps job aids are needed, such as color-coded wires that show assemblers what wire goes where; or poor screening results in people who haven't the skills to do the job; or training is inadequate. On the other hand, it might be a "won't do" problem. Here, employees *could* do a good job if they wanted to. If this is the case, the manager may have to change the reward system, perhaps by implementing an incentive plan.

Competency Models   Training programs often aim to develop the competencies or skills the person needs to do his or her job. A **competency model** consolidates, usually in one diagram, an overview of the competencies (the knowledge, skills, and behaviors) someone would need to do a job well.

As an example, Figure 5.2 shows the competency model for a human resource manager. At the top of the pyramid, it shows four main roles the human resource manager needs to fill. Beneath that are the areas of expertise in which he or she must be expert, such as selection and training. At the base are the HR manager's essential "foundation" competencies, such as communicating effectively.

The model's aim is to identify and compile in one place the competencies that are crucial for executing the job. At Sharp Electronics, training managers first interview senior executives, to identify the firm's strategic objectives and to infer what competencies those objectives will require. Trainers also interview the job's top performers, to identify the competencies (such as "focuses on the customer") the latter believe comprise the job's core competencies. Subsequent training then aims, in part, to develop these competencies.[20]

Setting Training Objectives   After training needs have been uncovered, measurable training objectives should be set. Training or instructional objectives are "a description of a performance you want learners to be able to exhibit before you consider them competent."[21] For example:

> Given a tool kit and a service manual, the technician will be able to adjust the registration (black line along paper edges) on this Canon duplicator within 20 minutes according to the specifications.

Objectives specify what the trainee should be able to accomplish after successfully completing the training. They provide a focus for both the trainee's and the trainer's efforts and a benchmark for evaluating the success of the training program.

Training and Motivation   Training is futile if the trainee lacks the ability or motivation to benefit from it.[22] The employer can take steps to increase the trainee's motivation to learn. Providing opportunities for active practice improves motivation and learning.[23] Feedback—including periodic performance assessments and frequent verbal critiques—is also important.[24] The employer should also make the material meaningful. For example, provide an overview of the material and ensure that the program uses familiar examples to illustrate key points.[25]

Figure 5.2 Example of Competency Model for Human Resource Manager

Roles
Line Function
(Within HR)
Staff Function
(Advise, Assist)
Coordinative Function
(Monitor)
Strategic HR Function
(Formulate, Execute)

Areas of Expertise
HR Practices (Recruiting, Selection, Training, etc.)
Strategic Planning
Employment Law
Finance and Budgeting
General Management

Foundation Competencies

Interpersonal Competencies
- Communicate Effectively
- Exercise Leadership
- Negotiate Effectively
- Motivate Others
- Work Productively with Others

HR/Business/Management
- Institute Effective HR Systems
- Analyze Financial Statements
- Craft Strategies
- Manage Vendors

Personal Competencies
- Behave Ethically
- Exercise Good Judgment Based on Evidence
- Set and Achieve Goals
- Manage Tasks Effectively
- Develop Personally

ILLUSTRATIVE
HUMAN RESOURCE MANAGER
COMPETENCY MODEL

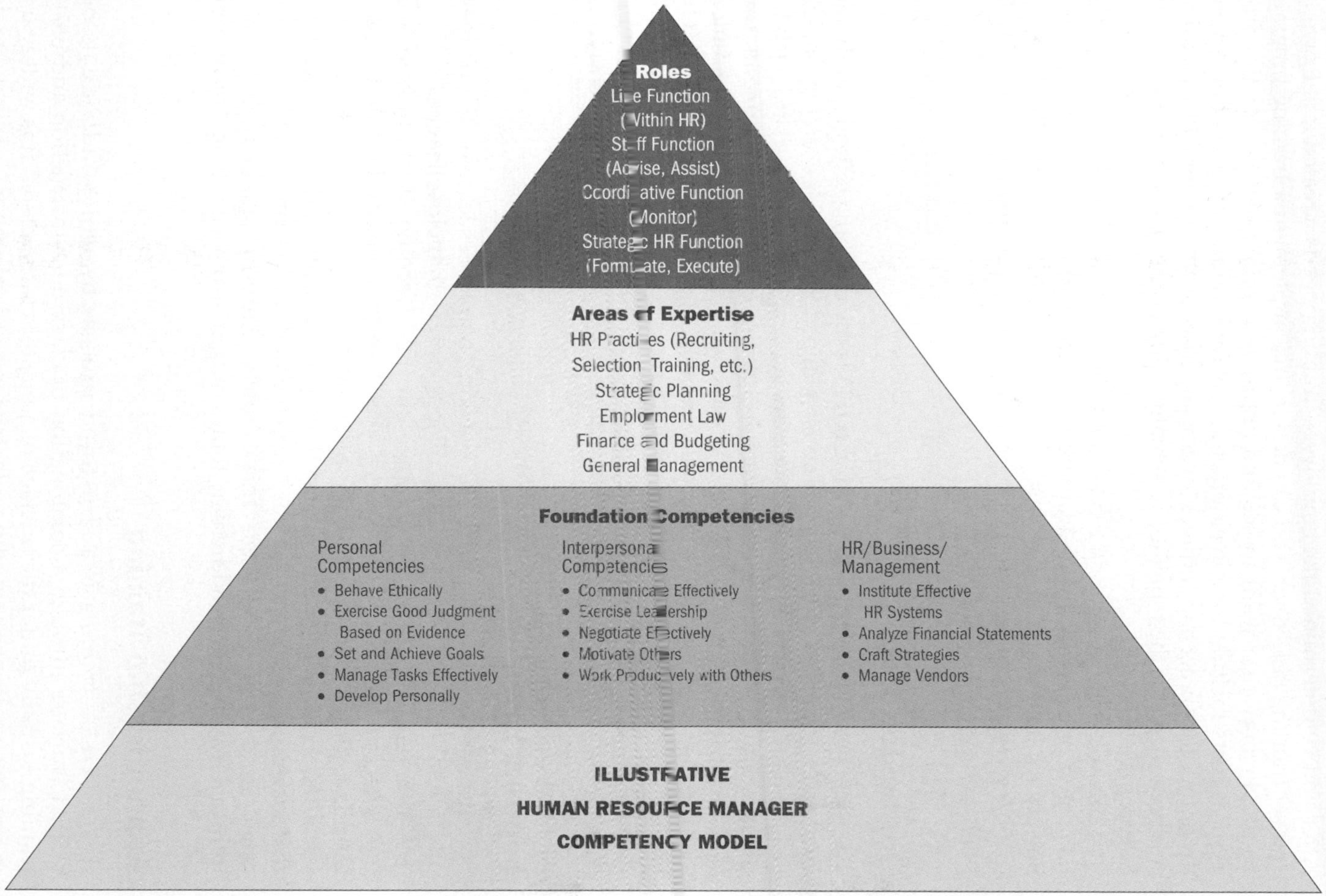

TRAINING TECHNIQUES

After you've determined the employees' training needs, created a perceived need, and set training objectives, you can design and implement a training program. The employer may first want to see and approve a *training budget* for the program. Typical costs include the development costs (of having, say, a vendor develop the program), the direct and indirect (overhead) costs of the trainers' time, participants' compensation (for the time they're actually being trained), and the cost of evaluating the program.

The budget will guide the program's design. Many employers simply choose packaged online and offline training programs from vendors like the American Society for Training and Development.[26] Many other vendors, including HRDQ (http://www.hrdqstore.com/), also provide turnkey training packages.[27] We look at popular training techniques next.

On-the-Job Training

The most familiar **on-the-job training (OJT)** is the coaching or understudy method. Here an experienced worker or supervisor trains the employee, on the job. Job rotation, in which an employee (usually a management trainee) moves from job to job at planned intervals, is another on-the-job technique. Special assignments similarly give lower-level executives firsthand experience in working on actual problems.

The Men's Wearhouse, with stores nationwide, uses on-the-job training. It has few full-time trainers. Instead, it has a formal process of "cascading" responsibility for training: Every manager is formally accountable for the development of his or her direct subordinates.[28] The challenging times feature shows other inexpensive options.

Informal Learning

Surveys estimate that as much as 80% of what employees learn on the job they learn through informal means, including collaboration with their colleagues.[29]

Although managers don't arrange informal learning, they can help to ensure that it occurs. For example, Siemens Power Transmission and Distribution, in North Carolina, places tools in cafeterias to capitalize on work-related discussions. Even installing white boards and keeping them stocked with markers can facilitate informal learning. Sun Microsystems implemented an informal online learning tool called Sun Learning eXchange. This is now a platform containing more than 5,000 informal learning items addressing topics ranging from sales to technical support.[30]

Apprenticeship Training

Apprenticeship training is a structured process by which individuals become skilled workers through a combination of classroom instruction and on-the-job training, usually under the tutelage of a master craftsperson. It is widely used for many occupations, including electrician and plumber.[31] When steelmaker Dofasco discovered that many of its employees would be retiring during the

Managing HR in Challenging Times: Free Training Alternatives

When the economy sours, training and development are often the first human resource management activities axed.[32] Recently, for instance, "morale and team building," "professional development," and "all staff training" were the three most likely cuts HR managers were going to make.

Managers can, however, turn to no-cost training alternatives. For example, some states have free training programs. In Pennsylvania, the Workforce and Economic Development Network of Pennsylvania (WEDnetPA) provides in-state employers with grants of up to $450 per employee for basic skills training (www.wednetpa.com). Web sites such as www.free-training.com are another option. The federal government's Small Business Administration (www.SBA.gov/training) provides a virtual campus that offers online courses, workshops, publications, and learning tools.[33]

Other employers turn to grants and other sources of support. For example, Titus, a heating and cooling manufacturer in Texas, received over $218,000 in grants from the Texas workforce commission to retrain employees. To find sources of training funds, check first with your local state unemployment agency. Many community colleges have workforce development or resource development officers who are familiar with funding sources.[34]

next 5 to 10 years, it revived its apprenticeship-training program. Applicants are prescreened; new recruits then spend about 32 months learning various jobs under the tutelage of experienced craftspersons.[35]

The U.S. Department of Labor's National Apprenticeship System promotes apprenticeship programs. Over 460,000 apprentices participate in 28,000 programs, and registered programs can receive federal and state contracts and other assistance.[36] Figure 5.3 lists popular recent apprenticeships.

Figure 5.3 Some Popular Apprenticeships

The U.S. Department of Labor's Registered Apprenticeship program offers access to 1,000 career areas, including the following top occupations:

- Able seaman
- Carpenter
- Chef
- Child care development specialist
- Construction craft laborer
- Dental assistant
- Electrician
- Elevator constructor
- Fire medic
- Law enforcement agent
- Over-the-road truck driver
- Pipefitter

Source: www.doleta.gov/oa, accessed June 15, 2010.

Behavior Modeling

Behavior modeling involves showing trainees the right (or model) way of doing something, letting each person practice the right way to do it, and providing feedback regarding performance. The basic behavior modeling procedure is as follows:

1. *Modeling.* First, trainees watch DVDs showing model persons behaving effectively in a problem situation.
2. *Role playing.* Next, the trainees are given roles to play in a simulated situation.
3. *Social reinforcement.* The trainer provides praise and constructive feedback based on how the trainee performs in the role play.
4. *Transfer of training.* Finally, trainees are encouraged to apply their new skills when they are back on their jobs.

Vestibule Training

Vestibule training is a technique in which trainees learn on the actual or simulated equipment they will use on the job but receive their training off the job. Such training is necessary when on-the-job training is too costly or dangerous. Putting new assembly-line workers right to work could slow production, for instance. As an example, UPS uses a realistic learning lab for a 46-hour, 5-day training program for drivers.[37] Vestibule training may just take place in a separate room with the equipment the trainees will actually use on the job (thus "vestibule" training). However, it often involves the use of equipment simulators, as in pilot training.

Audiovisual and Traditional Distance Learning Techniques

Audiovisual tools including DVDs, films, closed-circuit TV, and audiodiscs are widely used. Ford uses videos in its dealer training sessions to simulate sample reactions to customer complaints, for example. Firms, of course, also use various distance-learning methods for training. Distance learning includes traditional correspondence courses, as well as videoconferencing and Internet-based classes.[38] For example, the Macy's Satellite Network teletraining (television-based training) program supports training the firm's employees around the country.

Videoconference Distance Learning Videoconferencing is "a means of joining two or more distant groups using a combination of audio and visual equipment."[39] The communication often involves sending compressed audio and video signals over cable broadband lines, the Internet, or via satellite. Vendors such as Cisco offer videoconference products such as WebEx and TelePresence (http://www.cisco.com/en/US/products/ps10352/index.html). These make it easy to create Web-based videoconference training programs.

Computer-Based Training

In the Stanford University training room in this chapter's opening scenario, medical students wearing headsets use their keypads to control avatars in a virtual reality trauma center.[40]

In **computer-based training (CBT),** the trainee uses a computer-based system to increase his or her knowledge or skills interactively. Today this often means (as at Stanford) computerized simulations and multimedia.[41] But often, the computer-based training is less complex. For example, in one training program, recruitment trainees start with a computer screen that shows the "applicant's" employment application, as well as information about the job. The trainee then begins a simulated interview by typing in questions, which are answered by a videotaped model acting as the applicant and whose responses to a multitude of questions have been programmed into the computer. At the end of the session, the computer tells the trainee where he or she went wrong (perhaps in asking discriminatory questions, for instance) and offers further instructional material.

Strategy and HR: DVD-Based Training   To support its need for consistency, McDonald's has computer disk–based courses for its franchises' employees. The programs consist of graphics-supported lessons and require trainees to make choices to show their understanding.[42]

Simulated Learning   One survey asked training professionals what experiences qualified as "simulated learning." The percentages choosing each experience were:

- Virtual reality-type games, 19%
- Step-by-step animated guide, 8%
- Scenarios with questions and decision trees overlaying animation, 19%
- Online role play with photos and videos, 14%
- Software training including screenshots with interactive requests for responses, 35%
- Other, 6%[43]

As at Stanford, employers increasingly rely on computerized simulations to inject more realism into their training programs. For example, Orlando-based Environmental Tectonics Corporation created an Advanced Disaster Management simulation for emergency medical response trainees. One simulated scenario involves a passenger plane crashing into a runway. So realistic that it's "unsettling," trainees including firefighters respond to the simulated crash's sights and sounds via pointing devices and radios.[44]

Other employers capitalize on virtual environments such as Second Life for simulated learning. For example, British Petroleum (BP) uses it to train new gas station employees. The aim is to show new gas station employees how to use the safety features of gasoline storage tanks. BP built three-dimensional renderings of the tank systems in Second Life. Trainees could use these to "see underground" and observe the effects of the safety devices.[45]

Training via the Internet and Learning Portals

As in many colleges, employers also use Internet-based learning to deliver training. The training itself may simply include posting videos, written lectures, or PowerPoint slides, or sophisticated simulations.

Whether to use online "e-learning" often comes down to efficiency. Web learning doesn't necessarily teach faster or better. In one review of the evidence, Web-based instruction was a bit more effective than classroom instruction for teaching memory of facts and principles, and Web-based instruction and classroom instruction were equally effective for teaching information about how to perform a task.[46] But of course, the need to teach large numbers of students remotely, or to enable students to study at their leisure, often trumps the small differences in effectiveness.[47] Many firms simply let their employees take online courses offered by online providers such as Click2Learn.com. Others use their proprietary internal *intranets* to facilitate computer-based training.

Learning Portals   Companies increasingly convey their employee training through their internal intranet portals. They often contract with *applications service providers* such as SkillSoft (www.skillsoft.com) or, for health and safety training, PureSafety (www.puresafety.com) to deliver online training courses to the firms' employees.[48]

Learning Management Systems   Learning management systems (LMS) help employers identify training needs, and to schedule, deliver, and assess and manage the online training itself. For example, General Motors uses an LMS to help its dealers in Africa and the Middle East deliver training programs. The Internet-based LMS includes a course catalog, supervisor-approved self-enrollment, facilities and training schedule management, and assessment systems (including pre- and post-course tests). Dealers, supervisors, and employees review the list of courses on the LMS. They then choose courses based upon their needs, for instance in automobile transmissions or sales management. The system then automatically schedules the individual's training.[49]

In practice, many employers opt for "blended learning." Here the trainees use several delivery methods (such as manuals, in-class lectures, self-guided e-learning programs, and Web-based seminars, or "webinars") to learn the material.[50]

Mobile Learning

Mobile learning (or "on-demand learning") means delivering learning content on demand via mobile devices like cell phones, laptops, and iPhones, wherever and whenever the learner wants to access it.[51] For example, using dominKnow's (http://www.dominknow.com/) iPod touch and iPhone-optimized Touch Learning Center Portal, trainees can log in and take full online courses.[52]

Capital One Bank purchased 3,000 iPods for trainees who had enrolled in one of the instructor-led courses at its Capital One University.[53] The training department then had an Internet audio book provider create an audio learning site within Capital One's firewall. Employees used it to download the instructor-requested books and other materials to their iPods.[54] IBM uses mobile learning to deliver just-in-time information (for instance, about new product features) to its sales force. To increase accessibility, IBM's training department often breaks up, say, an hour program into 10-minute pieces.[55] J.P. Morgan encourages employees to use instant messaging (IM) as a quick learning device. Employers also use IM to supplement classroom training, for instance, by using IM for online office hours and for group chats. One training manager sends short personal development ideas each day for others to access via his Twitter account.[56]

The Virtual Classroom   Conventional Web-based learning tends to be limited to the sorts of online learning with which many college students are already familiar—reading PowerPoint slides, participating in instant message–type chat rooms, and taking online exams, for instance.

The virtual classroom takes online learning to a new level. A **virtual classroom** uses special collaboration software to enable multiple remote learners, using their PCs or laptops, to participate in live audio and visual discussions, communicate via written text, and learn via content such as PowerPoint slides.

The virtual classroom combines the best of Web-based learning offered by systems like Blackboard and WebCT, with live video and audio. For example, Elluminate Inc. makes one popular virtual classroom system, Elluminate live! (http://www.elluminate.com/demo/live_demo.jsp). It enables learners to communicate with clear two-way audio, build communities with user profiles and live video, collaborate with chat and shared whiteboards, and learn with shared applications such as PowerPoint slides.[57]

Training for Special Purposes

Training today does more than just prepare employees to perform their jobs. Training for special purposes—dealing with diversity, for instance—is required too. A sampling of special-purpose training programs follows.

Literacy Training Techniques   Functional illiteracy—the inability to do basic reading, writing, and arithmetic—is a serious problem at work. By one estimate, about 39 million people in the United States find it challenging to read, write, or do arithmetic.[58] A recent study called the American workforce "ill-prepared."[59]

Employers take various approaches to teaching basic skills. For example, at one Borg-Warner plant, managers chose employee participants and placed them in three classes of 15 students each based on test scores. There were two trainers from a local training company. Each session was to run a maximum of 200 hours. However, employees could leave when they reached a predetermined skill level, so some were in the program for only 40 hours and others stayed the whole course.[60] Classes were 5 days per week, 2 hours per day, with classes scheduled so that one hour was during the employee's personal time and the second was on company time. Employees could help each other (for instance, they paired someone good with decimals with someone who was not) and used timed exercises in math and reading.

Other employers turn to private firms like Education Management Corporation to design and provide the required education.[61] Another simple approach is to have supervisors teach basic skills. For example, if an employee needs to use a manual to find out how to change a part, teach that person how to use an index to locate the relevant section. Another approach is to bring in outside professionals (such as local high school teachers) to teach, say, remedial reading.

Diversity Training   With an increasingly diverse workforce, more firms have diversity training programs. *Diversity training* refers to "techniques for creating better cross-cultural sensitivity among supervisors and nonsupervisors with the aim of creating more harmonious working relationships among a firm's employees." For example, Adam's Mark Hotels & Resorts conducted a diversity training seminar for about 11,000 employees. It combined lectures, video, and employee role playing to foster sensitivity to race and religion.[62]

Diversity training is no panacea, and poorly conceived programs backfire. Potential negative outcomes include "the possibility of post-training participant discomfort, reinforcement of group stereotypes, perceived disenfranchisement or backlash by white males, and even lawsuits based on managers' exposure of stereotypical beliefs blurted out during 'awareness raising' sessions."[63]

There are many training programs aimed at counteracting potential problems associated with a diverse workforce. These include programs for improving interpersonal skills, understanding/valuing cultural differences, socializing into corporate culture, indoctrinating recent immigrants into the U.S. work ethic, and improving bilingual skills for English-speaking employees.

Training for Teamwork and Empowerment   You need to train most employees to be good team members. For instance, Toyota devotes many hours to training new employees to listen to each other and to cooperate. Its program uses short exercises to illustrate examples of good and bad teamwork.

Some firms use outdoor training such as Outward Bound to build teamwork. For example, the chief financial officer for Wells Fargo & Company helped organize a retreat for 73 of his firm's financial officers and accountants. While all his participants were already top performers, his goal was something more: "they are very individualistic in their approach to their work. . . . What I have been trying to do is get them to see the power of acting more like a team."[64]

Providing Employees with Lifelong Learning   Lifelong learning means providing employees with continuing learning experiences over their tenure with the firm, with the aims of ensuring they have the opportunity to learn the skills they need to do their jobs and to expand their horizons. With more emphasis today on employee empowerment and decision making, programs like these might range from training in English as a second language to computer literacy to college work. For example, one senior waiter at Rhapsody restaurant in Chicago received his undergraduate degree and began work toward a master of social work using the *lifelong learning account* (LiLA) program Rhapsody offers. Somewhat similar to 401(k) plans (but without the tax benefits), employers and employees contribute to LiLA plans, and the employee can use these funds to better him or herself.[65]

The following *Global Issues in HR* box discusses some special training needs abroad.

Global Issues in HR: Supervisory Training Abroad

Sometimes, supervisory training programs address special issues when implemented abroad. For example, Gap Inc. signed an agreement with a World Bank affiliate to provide supervisory training for line managers in the Cambodian garment factories of Gap's suppliers.[66] The firm's goal was to improve labor relations of their vendors abroad. Gap's supervisory training program therefore covers matters such as how to handle worker complaints, human resource management, personal productivity, and conflict resolution.

MANAGERIAL DEVELOPMENT AND TRAINING

Management development is any attempt to improve managerial performance by imparting knowledge, changing attitudes, or increasing skills. It thus includes in-house programs such as courses, coaching, and rotational assignments; professional programs such as management seminars; and university programs such as executive MBA programs.

The ultimate aim of such development programs, of course, is to enhance the future performance of the organization itself. For this reason, the overall management development process ideally consists of assessing the company's needs (for instance, to fill future executive openings, appraising the managers' performance, and then developing the managers themselves).[67]

The program should make sense in terms of the company's strategy and goals. This means involving top management in formulating the program's aims, and in specifying competencies and knowledge outcomes. Caterpillar Inc. created Caterpillar University to oversee its training and development programs. The university has a board of directors comprised of company executives. They set the university's policies and oversee "the alignment of the corporation's learning needs with the enterprises' business strategy."[68]

A survey listed the most popular management development methods. There is a trend toward supplementing traditional development methods (such as lectures and case discussions) with realistic methods like action learning, where trainees solve actual company problems.[69] The most popular development methods include classroom-based learning, executive coaching, action learning, 360-degree feedback, experiential learning, off-site retreats (where managers meet with colleagues for learning), mentoring, and job rotation.[70] We look at some of these. Figure 5.4 summarizes several principles for designing leader development programs (such as "use practical, concrete content").

Figure 5.4 Management and Leadership Development Guidelines

1. Design the program so that it flows from and makes sense in terms of the company's strategy and goals.
2. Involve the top management team in formulating the program's aims.
3. Make sure to design the program to improve manager's deficiencies and needs that you identify ahead of time.
4. Aim for practicality rather than just theory.
5. Specify concrete competencies and skills outcomes, not just knowledge and attitude changes, and use realistic learning methods like action learning projects, where trainees solve real company problems.
6. Aim for short, high-involvement, 3–4-day programs rather than longer immersion programs.

Sources: Adapted from P. Nick Blanchard and James Thacker, *Effective Training* (Upper Saddle River, NJ: Pearson, 2007), pp. 439–467; Jack Zenger, Dave Ulrich, and Norm Smallwood, "The New Leadership Development," *Training & Development* (March 2000): 22–27; W. David Patton and Connie Pratt, "Assessing the Training Needs of High Potential Managers," *Public Personnel Management* 31, no. 4 (Winter 2002): 465–474; and Ann Locke and Arlene Tarantino, "Strategic Leadership Development," *Training & Development* (December 2006): 53–55.

Managerial On-the-Job Training

On-the-job training isn't just for workers. It's also a popular manager development method. Important variants include **job rotation,** the **coaching/understudy method,** and **action learning.** *Job rotation* means moving management trainees from department to department to broaden their understanding of all parts of the business. The trainee—often a recent college grad—may spend several months in each department; this helps the trainee to not only broaden his or her experience but also discover the jobs he or she prefers. The trainee thus learns each department's business by actually doing it. With the *coaching/understudy* method, the new manager, of course, receives ongoing advice, often from the person he or she is to replace.

Action Learning

Action learning means letting managers work full time on real projects, analyzing and solving problems, usually in departments other than their own. The trainees meet periodically within a four- or five-person project group to discuss their findings. The groups then present their recommendations to the president and executive staff and the head of the division they've been studying.

The Case Study Method

The **case study method** presents a trainee with a written description of an organizational problem. The person analyzes the case, diagnoses the problem, and presents his or her findings and solutions in a discussion with other trainees.[71]

The case study method aims, first, to give trainees realistic experience in identifying and analyzing complex problems in an environment wherein their discussion leader can subtly guide their progress. Through the class discussion, trainees also learn that there are usually many ways to approach and solve organizational problems. They also learn that their own needs and values often influence the solutions they suggest.

Management Games

In computerized **management games,** trainees split into five- or six-person companies, each of which has to compete with the others in a simulated marketplace. Each company can make several decisions. For example, the group may decide what to spend on advertising, how much to hold in inventory, and how many of which product to produce. Usually, the game compresses a 2- or 3-year period into days, weeks, or months. As in the real world, each company usually can't see what decisions the other firms have made, although these decisions do affect their own sales. For example, if a competitor decides to increase its advertising expenditures, it may end up increasing its sales at others' expense.[72]

Improvisation is a recent variant. For example, Nike Corporation asked Second City Communications, the consulting arm of the improvisational group Second City, to help prepare Nike engineers to spend a month watching kids in playgrounds, to design new Nike shoes. Second City trainers used an improvisational game called "word ball." Here trainees pass a make-believe ball to one another, each time calling out one word. (Thus, the first person might pass the ball and call out "cat." Then the second catches and then passes on the make-believe ball and calls out "furry," and so on.) The aim was to get the Nike engineers "to instantly react without thinking, . . . to be unafraid to look foolish."[73]

Outside Programs and Seminars

Many vendors offer management development seminars and conferences. The American Management Association (AMA), for instance, provides thousands of courses in areas such as general management, human resources, and sales and marketing. Courses cover topics such as how to sharpen business writing skills, strategic planning, and assertiveness training.[74] Other vendors include AMR International, Inc., the Conference Board, and many universities.[75] The Society for Human Resource Management offers numerous courses for HR professionals.

Most of these programs offer continuing education units (CEUs) for course completion. CEUs generally can't be used to obtain degree credit, but do provide a record that the trainee completed the seminar.

University-Related Programs

Colleges and universities provide several types of management development activities. Many provide continuing education programs in leadership, supervision, and the like. As with the AMA, these range from 1- to 4-day programs to 1 to 4 months. Many also offer individual courses in areas such as business, management, and health-care administration. Managers can take these as matriculated or nonmatriculated students to fill skills gaps. Schools, of course, also offer degree programs such as the MBA.

Joint Programs   Some companies offer their employees in-house degree programs in cooperation with colleges and universities. Many also offer a variety of in-house lectures and seminars by university staff. For example, Technicon, a high-tech medical instruments company, had one university offer a program for its key managers.

University-based executive education is becoming more realistic, relying more on action learning, business simulations, and experiential learning.[76] Employers are also more sophisticated in managing university-related development programs. For example, Home Depot created a "preferred network" of university partners, and employees who take courses at in-network universities get discount course prices.[77]

Example   For example, when Hasbro Inc. needed to improve the creativity skills of its top executives, it turned to the Amos Tuck business school at Dartmouth University. It wanted "a custom approach . . . that would be built from the ground up to suit Hasbro's specific needs."[78]

Hasbro and Tuck's program directors designed a special version of Tuck's 1-week Global Leadership Development Program, with four elements. First, when participants first arrive, they receive sealed envelopes containing their "360-degree" performance assessment reports, carefully secured for confidentiality. Second, managers receive group and individual coaching from special "executive coaches." The aim here is to help Hasbro executives identify blind spots that may be hampering their performance and to develop plans to address them. Third, they participate in MBA-type courses, based on their and Hasbro's needs. Finally, the executives work in action-learning teams, under the guidance of Hasbro's in-house coaches.

In-House Development Centers

Many firms have **in-house development centers** or "universities." These usually combine classroom learning (lectures and seminars, for instance) with other techniques such as assessment centers and online learning to help develop employees and other managers. For example, at General Electric's (GE) Leadership Institute, courses range from entry-level programs in manufacturing and sales to a business course for English majors.

Learning Portals   For many firms, their online learning portals are becoming their virtual in-house development centers. Learning portals let even smaller firms have their own corporate universities, on the Web. Management consultants Bain & Company has a Web-based university for its employees. It conveniently coordinates all the company's training efforts and delivers Web-based modules covering topics from strategic management to mentoring.[79]

Executive Coaches   Many firms use executive coaches to develop their top managers' effectiveness. An *executive coach* is an outside consultant who questions the executive's boss, peers, subordinates, and (sometimes) family in order to identify the executive's strengths and weaknesses and to counsel the executive so he or she can capitalize on those strengths and reduce weaknesses.[80] Coaches come from a variety of backgrounds including teaching, counseling, and the mental health professions. Some employers encourage professional and management employees to coach each other.[81]

Executive coaching can be effective. Participants in one study included about 1,400 senior managers who had received "360-degree" performance feedback from bosses, peers, and subordinates. About 400 worked with an executive coach to review the feedback. Then, about a year later, these 400 managers and about 400 who did not receive coaching again received multisource feedback. Managers who received executive coaching were more likely to set more effective, specific goals for their subordinates and to have received improved ratings from subordinates and supervisors.[82] Because executive coaching can cost as much as $50,000 per executive, experts recommend using formal assessments prior to coaching, to uncover strengths and weaknesses and provide more focus for the coaching.[83]

Managing Organizational Change Programs

Today, intense international competition means companies have to change fast, perhaps changing their strategies to enter new businesses, or their organization charts, or their employees' attitudes and values.

Major organizational changes like these are never easy, but perhaps the hardest part of leading a change is overcoming the resistance to it. Individuals, groups, and even entire organizations may resist the change, perhaps because they're accustomed to the usual way of doing things or because of perceived threats to their power and influence.[84]

Lewin's Process for Overcoming Resistance

Psychologist Kurt Lewin formulated a model of change to summarize what he believed was the basic process for implementing a change with minimal resistance. To Lewin, all behavior in organizations was a product of two forces: those striving to maintain the status quo and those pushing for change. Implementing change meant either reducing the forces for the status quo or building up the forces for change. Lewin's process consisted of three steps:

1. *Unfreezing* means reducing the forces that are striving to maintain the status quo, usually by presenting a provocative problem or event to get people to recognize the need for change.
2. *Moving* means developing new behaviors, values, and attitudes, either by reorganizing the company or by using other management development techniques (such as team building).
3. *Refreezing* means building in the reinforcement to make sure the organization does not slide back into its former ways of doing things.

Of course, actually choosing the right methods that will help you accomplish each of those three steps and then applying them is the tricky part. You'll find a 10-step process for leading organizational change in the *HR in Practice* box.[85]

Organizational Development

There are many ways to reduce the resistance associated with organizational change. Among the suggestions are that managers impose rewards or sanctions to guide employee behaviors, explain why the change is needed, negotiate with employees, give inspirational speeches, or ask employees to help design the change.[86] Organizational development (OD) taps into the latter. **Organizational development** is a change process through which employees diagnose and formulate the change that's required and implement it, often with the assistance of trained consultants.

Action research is the foundation of most OD programs or interventions. It means gathering data about the organization and its operations and attitudes, with an eye toward solving a particular problem (for example, conflict between the sales and

HR in Practice: A 10-Step Process for Leading Organizational Change

1. *Establish a sense of urgency.* For instance, create a crisis by exposing managers to major weaknesses relative to competitors.

2. *Mobilize commitment to change through joint diagnosis of business problems.* Next, create one or more task forces to diagnose the business problems. Such teams can produce a shared understanding of what changes can and must be made, and thereby mobilize the commitment of those who must actually implement the changes.

3. *Create a guiding coalition.* No leader can accomplish any significant change alone. That's why most leaders create a guiding coalition of influential people who can be missionaries and implementers of change.

4. *Develop a shared vision.* Create a general statement of the organization's intended direction that evokes emotions in organization members.

5. *Communicate the vision.* Use multiple forums, repetition, and leading by example to foster support for the new vision.

6. *Remove barriers to the change.* Empower employees. Accomplishing the change usually requires the assistance of the employees themselves, but sometimes this requires empowering them— removing barriers that interfere with their being able to actually make the changes. For example, Sony's CEO removed his former studio executives and installed a new team when he set about fixing Sony's movie business. Former AlliedSignal CEO Lawrence Bossidy put all of his 80,000 employees through quality training within 2 years.

7. *Generate short-term wins.* Maintain employees' motivation by ensuring that they have short-term goals to achieve from which they receive positive feedback.

8. *Consolidate gains and produce more change.* As changes occur, the leader has to guard against renewed complacency. To do this, the leader and guiding coalition can use the increased credibility that comes from short-term wins to change all the systems, structures, and policies that don't fit well with the company's new vision.

9. *Anchor the new ways of doing things in the company's culture.* For example, if you want to emphasize more openness, camaraderie, and customer service, you as a leader must get the organization's employees to share those values. Do this by issuing a core value statement, by "walking the talk," and by using signs, symbols, rewards, and ceremonies to reinforce the values you want your employees to share.

10. *Monitor progress and adjust the vision as required.* For example, use regular surveys to monitor customer and employee attitudes.

production departments); feeding back these data to the employees involved; and then having them team-plan solutions to the problems.

Specific examples of OD efforts (or "interventions") include survey feedback, sensitivity training, and team building. **Survey feedback** uses questionnaires to survey employees' attitudes and to provide feedback. The aim here is usually to crystallize for managers that there is a problem to address. They then use the results to discuss and solve the problem.

Sensitivity training aims to increase participants' insights into their behavior and the behavior of others by encouraging an open expression of feelings in the trainer-guided "T-group laboratory" (the "T" is for training). Sensitivity training seeks to accomplish its aim of increasing interpersonal sensitivity by requiring frank, candid discussions of each other in the small off-site T-group, specifically discussions of participants' personal feelings, attitudes, and behavior. As a result, it is a controversial method surrounded by heated debate and is used much less today than in the past.

Finally, **team building** refers to OD techniques aimed at improving the effectiveness of teams at work. The typical team-building program begins with the consultant interviewing each of the group members prior to the group meeting. He or she asks what their problems are, how they think the group functions, and what obstacles are in the way of the group performing better.[87] The consultant usually categorizes the interview or attitude survey data into themes and presents the themes to the group at the beginning of the meeting. They might include, for example, "Not enough time to get my job done," or "I can't get any cooperation around here." The group then ranks the themes by importance. The most important ones form the agenda for the meeting. The group examines and discusses the issues, examines the underlying causes of the problem, and begins work on a solution to the problems.

Web-Based Tools   There are many Web-based tools you can use to facilitate organizational development programs. For example, there are Web-based surveys, including ones at surveymonkey.com, zoomerang.com, and brainbench.com. The manager will also find OD-related self-assessment tools at Web sites such as CPP.com.[88]

Building High-Performance Learning Organizations

In a fast-changing world, the last thing a company needs is for new information—about competitors' actions, customers' preferences, or technological improvements—to be ignored. Some firms, such as Microsoft and GE, are traditionally quick on their feet; others are not.

HR's Role in Building Learning Organizations   Firms such as GE have successfully transformed themselves into learning organizations. A **learning organization** "is an organization skilled at creating, acquiring, and transferring knowledge, and at modifying its behavior to reflect new knowledge and insights."[89]

Training is integral to developing such skills. Xerox, for instance, trains employees to analyze and display data on special simple statistical charts and to plan the actions they will take to solve the problem using special planning charts.

EVALUATING THE TRAINING AND DEVELOPMENT EFFORT

There are two basic issues to address when evaluating a training program. The first is how to design the evaluation study and, in particular, whether to use controlled experimentation. The second is what training effect to measure.

Controlled experimentation is the best method to use in evaluating a training program. A controlled experiment uses both a training group and a control group (the latter receives no training). Data (for instance, on quantity of production) are obtained both before and after the training effort in the group exposed to training and before and after a corresponding work period in the control group. In this way it is possible to determine the extent to which any change in performance in the training group resulted from the training itself rather than from some organization-wide change such as a raise in pay; we assume that the latter would have equally affected employees in both groups. This controlled approach is feasible.[90] In terms of current practices, however, few firms use it. Most simply measure trainees' reactions to the program; some also measure the trainees' job performance before and after training.

Training Effects to Measure

Employers can measure four basic categories of training outcomes:

1. *Reaction.* First, evaluate trainees' reactions to the program. Did they like the program? Did they think it worthwhile?
2. *Learning.* Second, test the trainees to determine whether they learned the principles, skills, and facts they were supposed to learn.
3. *Behavior.* Next, ask whether the trainees' behavior on the job changed because of the training program. For example, are employees in the store's complaint department more courteous toward disgruntled customers than previously?
4. *Results.* Finally, but probably most importantly, ask: What results were achieved in terms of the training objectives previously set? For example, Did the number of customer complaints drop? Did the reject rate improve?

Evaluation in Practice   In today's metrics-oriented industrial environment, employers increasingly demand quantified training evaluations, of reactions, learning, behavior, results, or some combination of these.[91] In one survey, most responding employers said they set formal response-rate goals (in terms of number of trainees responding) for end-of-training class evaluations. In general, the actual response rate depended on the method the employer used. The response rate of trainees was about 82% with paper-and-pencil end-of-class evaluation surveys, 59% with online surveys, and 53% with e-mail surveys. Response rates for delayed, follow-up surveys were only about 38%. About 90% of firms collecting end-of-class evaluation data use paper-and-pencil surveys.[92] McDonald's measures training effectiveness in several ways. They ask trainees to evaluate classes and test them on what they've learned. McDonald's also speaks with the employees' supervisors about how the trainees did before and after the training, to try to determine the extent to which the trainees changed their behavior.[93]

Computerization is facilitating the evaluation process. For example, Bovis Lend Lease offers its 625 employees numerous courses in construction and other subjects. The firm uses special learning management software to monitor which employees are taking which courses and the extent to which employees are improving their skills.[94]

Transfer of Training   Only about 10 to 35% of trainees transfer what they learned to their jobs. Managers can improve this. *Prior to training*, get trainee and supervisor input in designing the program, institute a training attendance policy, and encourage employees to participate. *During training*, provide trainees with training experiences (surroundings, equipment) that resemble the actual work environment. *After training* reinforce what trainees learned, for instance, by appraising and rewarding employees for using new skills, and by giving them the tools they need to use their new skills.[95] One training expert suggests asking the questions in the above *HR in Practice* box prior to designing and implementing the training event.[96]

REVIEW

Summary

1. The training process consists of four steps: needs analysis, instructional design, implementation, and evaluation.

2. Vestibule training, or simulated training, combines the advantages of on- and off-the-job training.

3. On-the-job training might take the form of the coaching/understudy method, job rotation, or special assignments and committees. Other training methods include audiovisual techniques, lectures, computer-aided instruction, apprenticeship training, simulated training, DVD/CD-ROM- and Internet-based training, learning portals, and special-purpose training.

4. Management development aims at preparing employees for future managerial jobs with the organization and at improving organizational effectiveness.

5. On-the-job experience is the most popular form of management development.

6. Managerial on-the-job training methods include job rotation, coaching, and action learning. Case studies, management games, outside seminars, university-related programs, behavior modeling, and in-house development centers are other methods.

7. Organizational development is an approach to instituting change in which employees themselves play a major role in the change process by providing data, by obtaining feedback on problems, and by team-planning solutions. There are several OD methods, including sensitivity training, team development, and survey feedback.

8. Overcoming employee resistance is a crucial aspect of implementing organizational change.

KEY TERMS

- employee orientation
- training
- task analysis
- performance analysis
- competency model
- on-the-job training (OJT)
- behavior modeling
- vestibule training
- computer-based training (CBT)
- virtual classroom
- lifelong learning
- management development
- job rotation
- coaching/understudy method
- action learning
- case study method
- management games
- improvisation
- in-house development centers
- organizational development (OD)
- survey feedback
- sensitivity training
- team building
- learning organization
- controlled experimentation

DISCUSSION QUESTIONS

1. Explain how you would go about developing a training program for teaching this course.
2. What do you think are some of the main drawbacks of relying on informal on-the-job training for helping new employees become accustomed to their jobs?
3. Experts argue that one reason for implementing special global training programs is the need to avoid lost business "due to cultural insensitivity." What sort of cultural insensitivity do you think this refers to, and how might that translate into lost business? What sort of training program would you recommend to avoid such cultural insensitivity?
4. Assume you have a professor who you believe is underperforming. How would you determine if training is the solution?

INDIVIDUAL AND GROUP ACTIVITIES

1. You're the supervisor of a group of employees whose task is to assemble disk drives that go into computers. You find that quality is not what it should be and that many of your group's devices come back for rework; your boss says, "You'd better start doing a better job of training your workers."
   a. What are some of the "staffing" factors that could be causing this problem?
   b. Explain how you would go about assessing whether it is in fact a training problem.
2. Pick out some task with which you are familiar—mowing the lawn, making a salad, or studying for a test—and develop a training program for it.
3. Working individually or in groups, develop a short training program on the subject "Guidelines for Giving a More Effective Lecture."
4. Find a provider of management development seminars. Obtain copies of its recent listings of seminar offerings. At what levels of managers are the offerings aimed? What seem to be the most popular types of development programs?
5. Working individually or in groups, develop several specific examples to illustrate how a professor teaching

human resource management could use at least four of the techniques described in this chapter in teaching his or her HR course.

6. Working individually or in groups, develop an orientation program for high school graduates entering your university.

7. A well-thought-out orientation program is especially important for employees (such as recent graduates) who have had little or no work experience. Explain why you agree or disagree with this statement.

8. John Santos is an undergraduate business student majoring in accounting. He just failed Accounting 101. Explain how you would use performance analysis to identify what, if any, are Santos's training needs.

APPLICATION EXERCISES

Case Incident — Reinventing the Wheel at Apex Door Company

Jim Delaney, president of Apex Door Company, has a problem. No matter how often he tells his employees how to do their jobs, they invariably "decide to do things their way," as he puts it, and arguments ensue between Delaney, the employee, and the employee's supervisor. One example is in the door-design department. The designers are expected to work with the architects to design doors that meet the specifications. Although it's not "rocket science," as Delaney puts it, the designers often make mistakes—such as designing in too much steel—a problem that can cost Apex tens of thousands of wasted dollars, especially considering the number of doors in, say, a 30-story office tower.

The order-processing department is another example. Although Jim has a specific, detailed way he wants each order written up, most of the order clerks don't understand how to use the multipage order form, and they improvise when it comes to a question such as whether to classify a customer as "industrial" or "commercial."

The current training process is as follows. None of the jobs have training manuals per se, although several have somewhat out-of-date job descriptions. The training for new employees is all on the job: Usually, the person leaving the company trains the new person during the 1- or 2-week overlap period, but if there's no overlap, the new person is trained as well as possible by other employees who have occasionally filled in on the job in the past. The training is basically the same for jobs throughout the company. ■

QUESTIONS

1. What do you think of Apex's training process? Why might it help to explain why employees "do things their way"?
2. What role do job descriptions play in training?
3. Explain in detail what you would do to improve the training process at Apex. Make sure to provide specific suggestions.

Continuing Case

LearnInMotion.com: The New Training Program

"I just don't understand it," said Mel. "No one here seems to follow instructions, and no matter how many times I've told them how to do things, they seem to do them their own way." At present, LearnInMotion.com has no formal orientation or training policies or procedures. Jennifer believes that is one reason why employees generally ignore the standards that she and Mel want employees to follow.

Several examples illustrate this. One of the jobs of the Web designer (her name is Maureen) is to take customers' copy for banner ads and adapt it for placement on LearnInMotion.com. She has been told several times not to tinker in any way with a customer's logo: Most companies put considerable thought and resources into logo design, and, as Mel has said, "whether or not Maureen thinks the logo is perfect, it's the customer's logo, and she's to leave it as it is." Yet just a week ago, they almost lost a big customer when Maureen, to "clarify" the customer's logo, modified its design before posting it on LearnInMotion.

That is just the tip of the iceberg. Jennifer and Mel feel it is the sales effort that is completely out of control. For one thing, even after several months on the job, it still seems as if the salespeople don't know what they're talking about. For example, LearnInMotion has several co-brand arrangements with Web sites like Yahoo! This means that if Yahoo! users are interested in ordering educational courses or CDs, other sites' users can easily click through to LearnInMotion. Jennifer has noticed that during conversations with customers, the two salespeople often have no idea which sites co-brand with LearnInMotion, or how to get to the LearnInMotion site from the partner Web site.

The salespeople also need to know more about the products themselves. For example, one salesperson was trying to sell someone who produces programs on managing call centers on the idea of listing its products under LearnInMotion's "communications" community. In fact, the "communications" community is for courses on topics such as "interpersonal communications" and "how to be a better listener." It has nothing to do with managing the sorts of call centers that, for instance, airlines use for handling customer inquiries. As another example, the Web surfer is supposed to get a specific e-mail address with a specific person's name for the salespeople to use; instead, he often just comes back with an "information@xyz"-type e-mail address of a Web site. The list goes on and on.

Jennifer feels the company has had other problems because of the lack of adequate orientation. For example, a question came up recently when employees found they weren't paid for the July 4 holiday: They assumed they'd be paid, but they were not. Similarly, when a salesperson left after barely a month on the job, there was debate about whether the person should receive severance pay and accumulated vacation pay. Other matters to cover during an orientation, says Jennifer, include company policy regarding lateness and absences, health and hospitalization benefits (there are none, other than workers' compensation), and matters like personal telephone calls and e-mail.

Jennifer believes that implementing orientation and training programs would help ensure that employees know how to do their jobs. She and Mel further believe that it is only when employees understand the right way to do their jobs that there is any hope those jobs will be carried out the way the owners want them to be. Now they want you, their management consultants, to help them. Here's what they want you to do for them. ■

QUESTIONS AND ASSIGNMENTS

1. Specifically, what should we cover in our new employee orientation program, and how should we convey this information?
2. In the HR course Jennifer took, the book suggested using task analysis to identify tasks performed by an employee. Should we use this for the salespeople? If so, what would be involved in the task analysis process if she used it (include some specific tasks)?
3. Which specific training techniques should we use to train our salespeople, Web designer, and Web surfer, and why?

Experiential Exercise
Flying the Friendlier Skies

Purpose: The purpose of this exercise is to give you practice in developing a training program for the job of airline reservation clerk for a major airline.

Required Understanding: You should be fully acquainted with the material in this chapter and should read the following description of an airline reservation clerk's duties:

Description: Customers contact our airlines reservation clerks to obtain flight schedules, prices, and itineraries. The reservation clerks look up the requested information on our airline's online flight schedule system, which are updated continuously. The reservation clerk must deal courteously and expeditiously with the customer and be able to find alternative flight arrangements quickly in order to provide the customer with the itinerary that fits his or her needs. Alternative flights and prices must be found quickly, so that the customer is not kept waiting and so that our reservations operations group maintains its efficiency standards. It is often necessary to look under various routings, since there may be a dozen or more alternative routes between the customer's starting point and destination.

You may assume that we just hired 30 new clerks, and that you must create a 3-day training program.

How to Set Up the Exercise/Instructions: Divide the class into teams of five or six students. Airline reservation clerks obviously need numerous skills to perform their jobs. This major airline has asked you to develop quickly the outline of a training program for its new reservation clerks. You may want to start by listing the job's main duties. In any case, please produce the requested outline, making sure to be very specific about what you want to teach the new clerks and what methods and aids you suggest using to train them. ∎

Chapter 6

Performance Management and Appraisal

- Basic Concepts in Performance Appraisal and Management
- Basic Appraisal Methods
- Some Practical Suggestions for More Effective Appraisals
- Coaching and Career Management
- Talent Management

When you finish studying this chapter, you should be able to:

■ Explain *the purpose of performance appraisal.*

■ Answer *the question, Who should do the appraising?*

■ Discuss *the pros and cons of at least eight performance appraisal methods.*

■ Explain *how to conduct an appraisal feedback interview.*

INTRODUCTION

With 39,000 employees worldwide, Seagate Technology needed a better way for managers to appraise each employee's performance.[1] With that many employees, it would hardly do to use the old time-consuming, paper-based forms. They needed a more modern approach.

Basic Concepts in Performance Appraisal and Management

Performance appraisal means evaluating an employee's current and/or past performance relative to his or her performance standards. You may equate appraisal forms like that in Figure 6.1 with performance appraisals, but appraisal involves more. Appraising performance also assumes that performance standards have been set, and that you give the employee feedback to help eliminate performance deficiencies or continue to perform above par. In this chapter we'll also address a modern approach to appraisal called *performance management,* which is the *continuous* process of identifying, measuring, and developing the performance of individuals and teams and *aligning* their performance with the organization's *goals.*

Why Appraise Performance?

Few things managers do are fraught with more peril than appraising subordinates' performance. Employees tend to be overly optimistic about what their ratings will be. And, they know that their raises, careers, and peace of mind may hinge on how you rate them. As if that's not enough, few appraisal processes are as fair and above-board as employers think they are. Hundreds of obvious and not-so-obvious problems (such as bias, and the tendency for managers to rate everyone "fair") undermine the process. However, the perils notwithstanding, performance appraisal is a crucial part of what managers do.[2]

There are actually three main reasons to appraise subordinates' performance. First, appraisals help the supervisor make *promotion and salary* raise decisions.[3] Second, the appraisal lets the boss and subordinate *develop a plan* for correcting any deficiencies. Third, appraisals facilitate *career planning,* by providing an opportunity to review the employee's career plans in light of his or her exhibited strengths and weaknesses.

Defining the Employee's Goals and Work Efforts

At the heart of performance appraisal and management is the idea that each employee's efforts should be goal directed.[4] The manager should appraise the employee based on the specific standards by which the employee expected to be measured. And the employee's goals should make sense in terms of the department's and the company's broader goals.

Thus, employees should always know ahead of time how and on what basis you're going to appraise them.[5] For a sales manager, for instance, set measurable goals for each expectation you have of him or her, such as for total sales and for maintaining sales force morale.

Setting Effective Goals

Setting goals is one thing; setting effective goals is another. One way to think of this is to remember that effective goals are "SMART." They are *specific*, and clearly

Figure 6.1   Classroom Teaching Appraisal by Students

Evaluating Faculty for Promotion and Tenure

Classroom Teaching Appraisal by Students

Teacher_____ Course _____

Term _____ Academic Year_____

Thoughtful student appraisal can help improve teaching effectiveness. This questionnaire is designed for that purpose, and your assistance is appreciated. Please do not sign your name.

Use the back of this form for any further comments you might want to express.

Directions: Rate your teacher on each item, giving the highest scores for exceptional performances and the lowest scores for very poor performances. Place in the blank space before each statement the rating that most closely expresses your view.

Exceptional			Moderately Good			Very Poor	Don't Know
7	6	5	4	3	2	1	X

_____ 1. How do you rate the agreement between course objectives and lesson assignments?

_____ 2. How do you rate the planning, organization, and use of class periods?

_____ 3. Are the teaching methods and techniques employed by the teacher appropriate and effective?

_____ 4. How do you rate the competence of the instructor in the subject?

_____ 5. How do you rate the interest of the teacher in the subject?

_____ 6. Does the teacher stimulate and challenge you to think and to question?

_____ 7. Does he or she welcome differing points of view?

_____ 8. Does the teacher have a personal interest in helping you in and out of class?

_____ 9. How would you rate the fairness and effectiveness of the grading policies and procedures of the teacher?

_____ 10. Considering all the above items, what is your overall rating of this teacher?

_____ 11. How would you rate this teacher in comparison with all others you have had in the college or university?

Source: Richard I. Miller, *Evaluating Faculty for Promotion and Tenure* (San Francisco: Jossey-Bass Publishers, 1987), pp. 164–165. © 1987, Jossey-Bass Inc., Publishers. All rights reserved. Reprinted with permission of John Wiley & Sons, Inc.

state the desired results. They are *measurable*, and answer the question, How much? They are *attainable*. They are *relevant*, and clearly derive from what the manager and company want to achieve. And, they are *timely*, and reflect deadlines and milestones.

Research provides useful insights into setting motivational goals. It suggests four things:

1. *Assign specific goals.* Employees who receive specific goals usually perform better than those who do not.
2. *Assign measurable goals.* Put goals in quantitative terms (such as "an average daily output of 300 units") and always include target dates or deadlines. If measurable results will not be available, then "satisfactory completion"—such as "satisfactorily completed his or her degree"—is the next best.
3. *Assign challenging but doable goals.* Goals should be challenging, but not so difficult that they appear unrealistic.
4. *Encourage participation.* Should you just tell your employees what their goals are, or should you let them participate with you in setting their goals? The evidence suggests that participatively set goals do *not* consistently result in higher performance. It is only when the participatively set goals are more difficult (are set higher) than the assigned ones that the participatively set goals produce higher performance. It does tend to be easier to set higher standards when your employees can participate in the process, so to that extent participation can facilitate performance.[6]

Who Should Do the Appraising?

Appraisals by the immediate supervisor are still the heart of most appraisals. The supervisor should be—and usually is—in the best position to observe and evaluate his or her subordinate's performance.

Yet relying solely on supervisors' ratings is not always advisable. For example, an employee's supervisor may not understand how customers and colleagues who depend on the employee rate the person's performance. Furthermore, it's conceivable that the supervisor may be biased. If so, there are several alternatives.

Peer Appraisals With more firms using self-managing teams, appraisal of an employee by his or her peers—**peer appraisal**—is more popular. At one firm, for example, an employee due for an annual appraisal chooses an appraisal chairperson. The latter then selects one supervisor and three peers to evaluate the employee's work.

One study found that peer appraisals had "an immediate positive impact on [improving] perception of open communication, task motivation, social loafing, group viability, cohesion, and satisfaction."[7] Peer appraisals are also good for predicting who will succeed in management.

Rating Committees Some companies use rating committees.[8] A rating committee is usually composed of the employee's immediate supervisor and three or four other supervisors.

Using multiple raters can be advantageous. It can help cancel out problems such as individual raters' bias, and provide a way to include in the appraisal the different facets of an employee's performance observed by different appraisers.[9]

Self-Ratings   The basic problem with self-ratings is that employees usually rate themselves higher than supervisors do.[10] One study found that, when asked to rate their own job performances, 40% of employees in jobs of all types placed themselves in the top 10%, and virtually all remaining employees rated themselves at least in the top 50%.[11] In another study, a person's self-ratings actually correlated negatively with the person's subsequent assessment center performance.[12]

Appraisal by Subordinates   Some firms let subordinates rate their supervisors' performance, a process some call **upward feedback**.[13] Such feedback can help top managers understand their subordinates' management styles, identify potential people problems, and take corrective action with individual managers, as required. For example, at FedEx, if a supervisor scores low on the item "I feel free to tell my manager what I think," FedEx supervisors are trained to ask their groups questions such as "What do I do that makes you feel that I'm not interested?"

Anonymity affects usefulness. Managers who get feedback from subordinates who identify themselves view the upward feedback more positively than do managers who get anonymous feedback. However, subordinates who must identify themselves tend to give inflated ratings.[14]

Research supports the usefulness of upward feedback. One study focused on 252 managers during five annual administrations of an upward feedback program. Managers who were initially "rated poor or moderate showed significant improvements in [their] upward feedback ratings over the five-year period." Furthermore, managers who met with their subordinates to discuss their upward feedback improved more than the managers who did not.[15]

360-Degree Feedback   With 360-degree feedback, the employer collects performance information from the employee's supervisors, subordinates, peers, and internal or external customers.[16] The usual process is to have the raters complete online appraisal surveys.[17] Computerized systems then compile all this feedback into individualized reports that go to the employee. The person may then meet with his or her supervisor to develop a self-improvement plan.

Results are mixed. Participants seem to prefer this approach, but one study concluded that multisource feedback led to "generally small" improvements on subsequent ratings. Improvement was most likely to occur when the recipients believed that change was necessary and had a positive view of the change process.[18] Such 360-degree appraisals are also more candid and helpful when it's clear they're for developmental rather than pay or promotion decisions.[19]

There are several ways to make such appraisals more useful.

- Anchor the 360-degree appraisal items (Excellent, Good, and so on) with behavioral descriptors (such as "effectively deals with conflicts").[20]
- Use a Web-based or a PC-based system such as EchoSpan 360 Appraisal (www.echospan.com).[21]

Even if you do not opt for a 360-degree approach, it still makes sense to have more than one supervisor who is familiar with the employee's work review the appraisal.[22] Multiple raters often do see different facets of an employee's performance.[23]

BASIC APPRAISAL METHODS

The manager usually conducts the appraisal using one or more of the methods described in this section.

Graphic Rating Scale Method

A **graphic rating scale** lists a number of traits and a range of performance for each. As in Figure 6.2, it lists traits (such as quality and reliability) and a range of performance values (in this case from unsatisfactory to outstanding) for each trait. The supervisor rates each subordinate by circling or checking the score that best describes the subordinate's performance for each trait and then totals the scores for all traits.

Alternation Ranking Method

Ranking employees from best to worst on a trait or traits is another popular method. Because it is usually easier to distinguish between the worst and best employees than to rank them, an **alternation ranking method** is useful. With this method a form like that in Figure 6.3 (page 177) is used to indicate the employee who is highest on the trait being measured and also the one who is the lowest, alternating between highest and lowest until you've addressed all employees to be rated.

Paired Comparison Method

With the **paired comparison method,** every subordinate to be rated is paired with and compared to every other subordinate on each trait.

For example, suppose there are five employees to be rated. With this method, a chart such as that in Figure 6.4 (page 178) shows all possible pairs of employees for each trait. Then for each trait, the supervisor indicates (with a plus or minus) who is the better employee of the pair. Next, the number of times an employee is rated better is added up. In Figure 6.4, employee Maria ranked highest (has the most plus marks) for "quality of work," and Art ranked highest for "creativity."

Forced Distribution Method

With the **forced distribution method,** the manager places predetermined percentages of subordinates in performance categories, as when professors "grade on a curve." About a fourth of Fortune 500 companies including Microsoft, Conoco, and Intel use forced distribution. GE popularized forced ranking, but now tells managers not to adhere to its famous 20/70/10 split.[24]

At one company, managers appraise employees in groups of about 30. There is a top 20%, a middle 70%, and a bottom 10%. The bottom 10% can either take an exit package or embark on a 90-day improvement plan. If they're still in the bottom

Figure 6.2 Sample Graphic Rating Form with Behavioral Examples

Sample Performance Rating Form

Employee's Name _____ Level: Entry-level employee

Manager's Name _____

Key Work Responsibilities	Results/Goals to be Achieved
1. _____	1. _____
2. _____	2. _____
3. _____	3. _____
4. _____	4. _____

Behavioral Assessment of Competencies

Communication

1	2	3	4	5

Below Expectations	Meets Expectations	Role Model
Even with guidance, fails to prepare straightforward communications, including forms, paperwork, and records, in a timely and accurate manner; products require minimal corrections. Even with guidance, fails to adapt style and materials to communicate straightforward information.	With guidance, prepares straightforward communications, including forms, paperwork, and records, in a timely and accurate manner; products require minimal corrections. With guidance, adapts style and materials to communicate straightforward information.	Independently prepares communications, such as forms, paperwork, and records, in a timely, clear, and accurate manner; products require few, if any, corrections. Independently adapts style and materials to communicate information.

Organizational Know-How

1	2	3	4	5

Below Expectations	Meets Expectations	Role Model
<performance standards appear here>	<performance standards appear here>	<performance standards appear here>

Personal Effectiveness

1	2	3	4	5

Below Expectations	Meets Expectations	Role Model
<performance standards appear here>	<performance standards appear here>	<performance standards appear here>

Teamwork

1	2	3	4	5

Below Expectations	Meets Expectations	Role Model
<performance standards appear here>	<performance standards appear here>	<performance standards appear here>

Achieving Business Results

1	2	3	4	5

Below Expectations	Meets Expectations	Role Model
<performance standards appear here>	<performance standards appear here>	<performance standards appear here>

(*Continued*)

Results Assessment

Accomplishment 1: _____

1	2	3	4	5
Low Impact		**Moderate Impact**		**High Impact**
The efficiency or effectiveness of operations remained the same or improved only minimally. The quality of products remained the same or improved only minimally.		The efficiency or effectiveness of operations improved quite a lot. The quality of products improved quite a lot.		The efficiency or effectiveness of operations improved tremendously. The quality of products improved tremendously.

Accomplishment 2: _____

1	2	3	4	5
Low Impact		**Moderate Impact**		**High Impact**
The efficiency or effectiveness of operations remained the same or improved only minimally. The quality of products remained the same or improved only minimally.		The efficiency or effectiveness of operations improved quite a lot. The quality of products improved quite a lot.		The efficiency or effectiveness of operations improved tremendously. The quality of products improved tremendously.

Narrative

_____

_____

_____

_____

_____

Areas to be Developed	Actions	Completion Date

Manager's Signature _____ Date _____

Employee's Signature _____ Date _____

The above employee signature indicates receipt of, but not necessarily concurrence with, the evaluation herein.

Source: "Sample Performance Rating Form" from Elaine D. Pulakos, *Performance Management: A Roadmap for Developing, Implementing and Evaluating Performance Management Systems* (SHRM Foundation, 2004), pp. 16–17.

Figure 6.3 Alternation Ranking Method

ALTERNATION RANKING SCALE

For the Trait: _____

For the trait you are measuring, list all the employees you want to rank. Put the highest-ranking employee's name on line 1. Put the lowest-ranking employee's name on line 20. Then list the next highest ranking on line 2, the next lowest ranking on line 19, and so on. Continue until all names are on the scale.

Highest-ranking employee

1. _____   11. _____
2. _____   12. _____
3. _____   13. _____
4. _____   14. _____
5. _____   15. _____
6. _____   16. _____
7. _____   17. _____
8. _____   18. _____
9. _____   19. _____
10. _____   20. _____

Lowest-ranking employee

10% in 90 days, they get a chance to resign and take severance pay. Some decide to stay, but "if it doesn't work out," the firm fires them without severance.[25]

While widely used, some balk at forced distribution appraisals. The biggest complaints: 44% said it damages morale, and 47% said it creates interdepartmental inequities, since "high-performing teams must cut 10% of their workers while low-performing teams are still allowed to retain 90% of theirs."[26] Some writers call them "Rank and Yank" appraisals.[27]

As most students know, with a forced distribution system, you're either in the top 5% or 10% (and thus get that "A"), or you're not. And, if you're in the bottom 5% or 10%, you get an "F," no questions asked. Your professor hasn't the wiggle room to give everyone As, Bs, and Cs. Given this, employers need to be doubly careful to protect forced rankings from managerial abuse.[28] Appoint a review committee to review any employee's low ranking. Train raters to be objective.

Critical Incident Method

The **critical incident method** entails keeping a record of uncommonly good or undesirable examples of an employee's work-related behavior and reviewing it with the employee periodically.

Figure 6.4 Paired Comparison Method

FOR THE TRAIT "QUALITY OF WORK"					
	Employee Rated:				
As Compared to:	A Art	B Maria	C Chuck	D Diane	E José
A Art		+	+		
B Maria	−		−	−	−
C Chuck	−	+		+	−
D Diane	+	+	−		+
E José	+	+	+	−	

Maria Ranks Highest Here (↑ under column B Maria)

FOR THE TRAIT "CREATIVITY"					
	Employee Rated:				
As Compared to:	A Art	B Maria	C Chuck	D Diane	E José
A Art					
B Maria	+		−	+	+
C Chuck	+	+		−	+
D Diane	+	−	+		−
E José	+	−	−	+	

Art Ranks Highest Here (↑ under column A Art)

Note: + means "better than," − means "worse than." For each chart, add up the number of +'s in each column to get the highest-ranked employee.

Employers often use critical incidents to supplement a rating or ranking method. Doing so forces the supervisor to monitor and think about the subordinate's appraisal all during the year. Keeping a running list of critical incidents should also provide concrete examples of what subordinates can do to eliminate performance deficiencies and opportunities for mid-year corrections.

Behaviorally Anchored Rating Scales

A behaviorally anchored rating scale (BARS) combines the benefits of both narrative critical incidents and quantitative ratings, by anchoring a quantified scale with specific narrative examples of good and poor performance.

Figure 6.5 is an example that shows the behaviorally anchored rating scale for the trait "salesmanship skills" used for armed forces recruiters. Note how the various performance levels are each anchored with specific behavioral examples such as "When a prospect states an objection to being in the Navy, the recruiter ends the conversation."

Appraisal Forms in Practice

Effective appraisal forms typically merge several approaches. For example, Figure 6.2 (pages 175–176) merges a graphic rating scale with critical examples. This form also illustrates an important fact regarding appraisals. Even if the company does not use a behaviorally anchored rating scale approach, anchoring the scale with illustrative examples, as here, usually improves the appraisal scale's reliability and validity.

Figure 6.5 Behaviorally Anchored Rating Scale

Salesmanship Skills

Skillfully persuading prospects to join the navy; using navy benefits and opportunities effectively to sell the navy; closing skills; adapting selling techniques appropriately to different prospects; effectively overcoming objections to joining the navy.

9 — A prospect stated he wanted the nuclear power program or he would not sign up. When he did not qualify, the recruiter did not give up; instead, he talked the young man into electronics by emphasizing the technical training he would
8 — receive.

The recruiter treats objections to joining the navy seriously; he works hard to counter the objections with relevant, positive arguments for a navy career.
7 —
When talking to a high school senior, the recruiter mentions names of other seniors from that school who have already enlisted.
6 —
When an applicant qualifies for only one program, the recruiter tries to convey to the applicant that it is a desirable program.
5 —
When a prospect is deciding on which service to enlist in, the recruiter tries to sell the navy by describing navy life at sea and adventures in port
4 —
During an interview, the recruiter said to the applicant, "I'll try to get you the school you want, but frankly it probably won't be open for another three months, so why don't you take your second choice and leave now."
3 —
The recruiter insisted on showing more brochures and films even though the applicant told him he wanted to sign up right now.
2 —
When a prospect states an objection to being in the navy, the recruiter ends the conversation because he thinks the prospect must not be interested.
1 —

Source: Berk, Ronald A. *Performance Assessment: Methods and Applications,* p. 103, Figure 3.2, "Salesmanship Skills." Copyright © 1986. Reproduced with permission of The Johns Hopkins University Press.

The Management by Objectives Method

The **management by objectives (MBO)** method requires the manager to set measurable goals with each employee and then periodically discuss the latter's progress toward these goals. The term *MBO* usually refers to an organization-wide goal setting and appraisal program that consists of six steps:

1. *Set the organization's goals.*   Establish an organization-wide plan for next year and set goals.
2. *Set departmental goals.*   Department heads and their superiors jointly set goals for their departments.
3. *Discuss departmental goals.*   Department heads discuss the department's goals with all subordinates in the department and ask them to develop their own individual goals. In other words, how can each employee contribute to the department attaining its goals?
4. *Define expected results (set individual goals).*   Department heads and their subordinates set short-term performance targets.
5. *Conduct performance reviews and measure the results.*   Department heads compare the actual performance of each employee with expected results.
6. *Provide feedback.*   Department heads hold periodic performance review meetings with subordinates to discuss and evaluate the subordinates' progress in achieving expected results.

Computerized and Web-Based Performance Appraisals

Appraisals today are most often Web or PC based. For example, Employee Appraiser (http://www.employeeappraiser.com/) presents a menu of more than a dozen evaluation dimensions, including dependability, initiative, and planning and productivity. Within each dimension are various performance factors, again presented in menu form. For example, under "Communication" are separate factors for writing, verbal communication, receptivity to feedback and criticism, and openness.

When the user clicks on a performance factor, he or she is presented with a version of a graphic rating scale. However, instead of numbers, Employee Appraiser uses behaviorally anchored examples. For example, for verbal communication there are six choices, ranging from "presents ideas clearly" to "lacks structure." After the manager picks the phrase that most accurately describes the worker, Employee Appraiser generates an appraisal with sample text. The eAppraisal system from Halogen Software is another example.[29] Employees using it can access the system year round, track their progress against goals in real time, and enter significant accomplishments.[30] PerformancePro.net from the HRN Management Group is an Internet-based appraisal system. It helps the manager and his or her subordinates develop performance objectives for the latter and conduct the annual review.[31] Figure 6.6 presents an example of an online appraisal tool.

Electronic Performance Monitoring

Electronic performance monitoring (EPM) systems use computer technology to allow managers access to their employees' computers and telephones. They thus allow "managers to determine at any moment throughout the day the pace at which employees are working, their degree of accuracy, log-in and log-off times, and even the amount of time spent on bathroom breaks."[32]

Research indicates that EPM can improve productivity in certain circumstances. For example, for less complex jobs, skilled and monitored subjects keyed in more data entries than did skilled unmonitored participants.[33] However, EPM can also backfire. In this same study, low-skilled but monitored participants did more poorly than did low-skilled, unmonitored participants. Empirical studies also link EPM with increased stress.[34]

Performance Management

If you were to spend time in many progressive firms, the absence of "appraisal" would soon be apparent. Supervisors don't sit with individual employees to fill out forms and appraise them. Instead, teams of employees monitor their own results. They continuously align those results with the work team's standards and with the plant's overall quality and productivity needs, by continuously adjusting

Figure 6.6 Online Performance Appraisal Tool

(Continued)

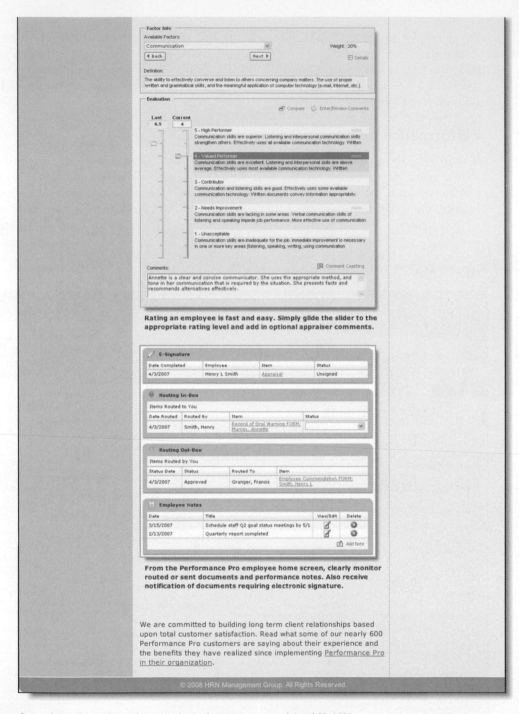

Rating an employee is fast and easy. Simply glide the slider to the appropriate rating level and add in optional appraiser comments.

From the Performance Pro employee home screen, clearly monitor routed or sent documents and performance notes. Also receive notification of documents requiring electronic signature.

We are committed to building long term client relationships based upon total customer satisfaction. Read what some of our nearly 600 Performance Pro customers are saying about their experience and the benefits they have realized since implementing Performance Pro in their organization.

Source: http://www.hrnonline.com/per_about.asp, accessed April 29, 2009.

how they and their team members do things. Team members who need coaching and training receive it, and procedures that need changing are changed. This is *performance management* in action. **Performance management** is the *continuous* process of identifying, measuring, and developing the performance of individuals and teams and *aligning* their performance with the organization's *goals*.[35] In comparing performance management and appraisal, "the distinction is the contrast between a year-end event—the completion of the appraisal form—and a process that starts the year with performance planning and is integral to the way people are managed throughout the year."[36] We can summarize performance management's basic elements as follows:[37]

- *Direction sharing* means communicating the company's goals throughout the company and then translating these into doable departmental, team, and individual goals.
- *Goal alignment* means having a method that enables managers to see the link between the employees' goals and those of their department and company.
- *Ongoing performance monitoring* usually includes using computerized systems that measure and then e-mail progress and exception reports based on the person's progress toward meeting his or her performance goals.
- *Ongoing feedback* includes both face-to-face and computerized feedback regarding progress toward goals.
- *Coaching and developmental support* should be an integral part of the feedback process.
- *Rewards, recognition, and compensation* provide the consequences needed to keep the employee's goal-directed performance on track.

Using Information Technology to Support Performance Management   Performance management needn't be high-tech. In many facilities, work teams simply meet daily to review their performance and to align with their performance with their standards. However, information technology does enable management to monitor and correct deviations in real time. We can sum up this IT-supported performance management process as follows:

- *Assign financial and nonfinancial goals* to each team's activities up the chain of command leading up to the company's overall strategic goals.
- *Inform all employees* of their goals.
- *Use IT-supported performance management software* to give employees and managers a real-time view of each team's performance, enabling it to,
- *Take corrective action* before things swing out of control.

Improving Productivity Through HRIS

Performance management, particularly for larger companies, usually does require Web-based performance management systems. For example, Seagate Technology uses "Enterprise Suite" for managing the performance of its 39,000 employees.[38] Early in Seagate's first fiscal quarter, employees enter the system and set goals and development plans for themselves that make sense in terms of Seagate's corporate objectives. Employees update their plans quarterly and then do self-evaluations at the end of the year, with follow-up reviews by their supervisors.

A Web-based system like this has several advantages. For one, it helps each employee see where his or her goals fit in the overall framework of what the company is trying to accomplish. Specifically, it enables individual employees to set their goals based on a "cascading goals" system: With Enterprise Suite, they can easily see the company's goals, their unit's goals, and their supervisor's goals. This makes it easier for employees to set goals that make sense in terms of Seagate's goals. And, of course, a system like this makes it easier for Seagate's widely disbursed employees to fill in and update their goals, plans, and appraisals whenever and wherever they need to.

SOME PRACTICAL SUGGESTIONS FOR MORE EFFECTIVE APPRAISALS

A few years ago, a long-term NASA employee smuggled a revolver into the space center and, after speaking with his former supervisor, said, "You're the one who's going to get me fired" and shot him. The supervisor had apparently given the shooter a poor job review.[39]

Such reactions certainly aren't the norm. However, as we said earlier, few supervisory tasks are fraught with more peril than appraising performance.[40] Managers therefore need to know the typical problems and how to deal with them.[41]

Ensure Fairness

Probably your first challenge is to make sure that your subordinate views the appraisal as fair. Studies confirm that, in practice, some managers ignore accuracy in performance appraisals. Instead, they use the process for political purposes (such as encouraging employees with whom they don't get along to leave the firm).[42] The employees' standards should be clear, employees should understand the basis on which you're going to appraise them, and the appraisals should be objective and fair.[43] Figure 6.7 summarizes some best practices for administering fair performance appraisals.

Figure 6.7 Selected Best Practices for Fair Performance Appraisals[44]

- Base the performance review on duties and standards from a job analysis.
- Base the performance review on objective performance data.
- Make it clear ahead of time what your performance expectations are.
- Use a standardized performance review procedure for all employees.
- Make sure the reviewers have frequent opportunities to observe the employee's performance.
- Either use multiple raters or have the rater's supervisor review the appraisal results.
- Include an appeals mechanism.
- Document the appraisal results.
- Discuss the appraisal results with the employee.
- Let the employee provide input regarding the assessment.
- Indicate what the employee needs to do to improve.

Deal with Common Appraisal Problems[45]

Several problems undermine appraisals and graphic rating scales in particular. Fortunately, there are ways to avoid or deal with these problems.

Unclear Standards   The unclear standards appraisal problem means the appraisal scale is too open to interpretation. As in Figure 6.8, the rating scale may seem objective but different supervisors would probably describe "good" performance differently. The same is true of traits such as "quality of work." The best way to rectify this problem is to include descriptive phrases that define each trait and degree of merit.[46]

Halo Effect   The **halo effect** means that the rating of a subordinate on one trait (such as "gets along with others") influences the way you rate the person on other traits (such as "quantity of work"). Thus a manager might rate an unfriendly employee unsatisfactory for all traits rather than just for the trait "gets along with others." Being aware of this problem is a major step toward avoiding it.

Central Tendency   The **central tendency** problem refers to a tendency to rate all employees about average. For example, if the rating scale ranges from 1 to 7, a supervisor may tend to rate most of his or her employees between 3 and 5. Such restriction can distort the evaluations, making them less useful for promotion, salary, and counseling purposes. Ranking employees instead of using a graphic rating scale can eliminate this problem.

Leniency or Strictness   Conversely, some supervisors tend to rate all their subordinates consistently high or low, a problem referred to as strictness/leniency. Again, one solution is to insist on ranking subordinates because that forces the supervisor to distinguish between high and low performers. One study focused on how personality influenced the peer evaluations that students gave their peers. Raters who scored higher on "conscientiousness" tended to give their peers lower ratings; those scoring higher on "agreeableness" gave higher ratings.[47]

Bias   Indeed, appraisees' (and appraisers') personal characteristics (such as age, race, and sex) can affect their ratings.[48] Studies suggest, "Rater idiosyncratic biases account for the largest percentage of the observed variances in performance ratings."[49]

For example, one study found that raters penalized successful women for their success.[50] Earlier studies had found that raters tend to demean women's performance,

Figure 6.8 A Graphic Rating Scale with Unclear Standards

	Excellent	Good	Fair	Poor
Quality of work				
Quantity of work				
Creativity				
Integrity				

Note: For example, what exactly is meant by "good," "quantity of work," and so forth?

particularly when they excel at what seems like male-typical tasks. The researchers found, "it is only women, not men, for whom a unique propensity toward dislike is created by success in a nontraditional work situation."[51]

The bottom line is that the appraisal often says more about the appraiser than about the appraisee.[52] This is a powerful reason for having the supervisor's boss review the rating or for using multiple raters.[53]

Table 6.1 summarizes the pros and cons of the most popular rating methods.

Table 6.1 Important Similarities and Differences, and Advantages and Disadvantages of Appraisal Tools

TOOL	SIMILARITIES/DIFFERENCES	ADVANTAGES	DISADVANTAGES
Graphic rating scale	These are both absolute scales aimed at measuring an employee's *absolute* performance based on objective criteria as listed on the scales.	Simple to use; provides a quantitative rating for each employee.	Standards may be unclear; halo effect, central tendency, leniency, bias can also be problems.
BARS		Provides behavioral "anchors." BARS is very accurate.	Difficult to develop.
Alternation ranking	These are both methods for judging the *relative* performance of employees relative to each other but still based on objective criteria.	Simple to use (but not as simple as graphic rating scales); avoids central tendency and other problems of rating scales.	Can cause disagreements among employees and may be unfair if all employees *are*, in fact, excellent.
Forced distribution method		Ends up with a predetermined number of people in each group.	Appraisal results depend on the adequacy of your original choice of cutoff points.
Critical incident method	These are both more subjective narrative methods for appraising performance, generally based, however, on the employee's absolute performance.	Helps specify what is "right" and "wrong" about the employee's performance; forces supervisor to evaluate subordinates on an ongoing basis.	Difficult to rate or rank employees relative to one another.
MBO		Tied to jointly agreed-upon performance objectives.	Time consuming.

In practice, employers choose appraisal tools based on several criteria. Accessibility and *ease of use* are probably first. That is why graphic rating scales are so popular, even within computerized appraisal packages. Ranking produces clearer results, but many employers (and supervisors) prefer to avoid the *pushback* that employees' rankings provoke. For those for whom *accuracy* is a great concern, BARS are superior but require much more time to develop and use. Critical incidents by themselves are seldom sufficient for making salary raise decisions.

Address Legal Issues in Performance Appraisal

Performance appraisals have legal implications, because they affect raises, promotions, training opportunities, and other HR actions. In one case, a 36-year-old supervisor ranked a 62-year-old subordinate at the bottom of the department's rankings and then terminated him. A U.S. Court of Appeals determined that the discriminatory motives of the younger boss might have influenced the termination decision.[54] You will find recommendations in the following *HR in Practice* box for ensuring an appraisal's legal defensibility.

Ace the Appraisal Feedback Interview

An appraisal usually culminates in an **appraisal interview,** in which the supervisor and subordinate review the appraisal and make plans to remedy deficiencies and reinforce strengths. Few people like to receive—or give—negative feedback.[55] Adequate preparation and effective implementation are therefore essential.

Preparing for the Appraisal Interview   Adequate preparation involves three steps. First, give the subordinate enough notice to review his or her work, and to compile questions and comments. Next, study his or her job description, compare the

---

HR in Practice: Making Sure Your Appraisals Are Legally Defensible

Steps to take to ensure your appraisals are legally defensible include:

1. Conduct a job analysis to establish performance criteria and standards.

2. Communicate performance standards to employees and to those rating them, in writing.

3. When using graphic rating scales, avoid undefined abstract trait names (such as "loyalty" or "honesty").

4. Use subjective narratives as only one component of the appraisal.

5. Train supervisors to use the rating instrument.

6. Allow appraisers substantial daily contact with the employees they're evaluating.

7. Remember that using a single overall rating of performance is usually not acceptable to the courts.[56]

8. Never let one appraiser have absolute authority to determine a personnel action.

9. Give employees the opportunity to review and make comments, and have a formal appeals process.

10. Document everything: "Without exception, courts condemn informal performance evaluation practices that eschew documentation."[57]

---

employee's performance to his or her standards, and review the files of the person's previous appraisals. Finally, find a mutually agreeable time for the interview and leave enough time—perhaps one-half-hour for lower-level personnel such as clerical workers and maintenance staff and an hour or so for management employees.

Conducting the Interview   Keep several things in mind when actually conducting appraisal interviews.

- First, conduct the interview in a private area without interruptions.
- Second, *talk in terms of objective work data*, using examples such as absences, quality records, inspection reports, and tardiness. Your main aim is to reinforce satisfactory performance or to diagnose and improve unsatisfactory performance.
- Third, *get agreement* before the subordinate leaves on how things will improve and by when. An action plan showing steps and expected results is advisable. If a formal written warning is required, it should make it clear that the employee was aware of the standard, specify any violation of the standard, and show that the employee had an opportunity to correct his or her behavior.
- Fourth, ensure that the process is *fair*. Letting the person express his or her opinions is therefore essential.[58]
- Fifth, know how to *deal with defensiveness*. For example, when a person is accused of poor performance, the first reaction is usually denial. By denying the fault, the employee avoids having to question his or her own competence. Such defensiveness is normal. It is prudent not to attack the person's defenses (for instance, by saying things like, "You know the real reason you're using that excuse is that you can't bear to be blamed for anything").

COACHING AND CAREER MANAGEMENT

After appraising performance, the manager typically faces several issues. The employee may require coaching, as well as career advice and mentoring. And, the manager and employer may want to review the employee's performance in the context of the company's overall talent management needs. The purpose of this section is to help you be more effective at coaching and mentoring employees and at supporting career planning and talent management needs.

Improving Your Coaching Skills

Great managers tend to be great coaches because they bring out the best in their employees. Coaching and the closely related *mentoring* are thus key managerial skills. **Coaching** means educating, instructing, and training subordinates. *Mentoring* means advising, counseling, and guiding. Coaching focuses on teaching shorter-term job-related skills, mentoring on helping employees navigate longer-term career hazards. Supervisors have coached and mentored employees from the dawn of management. But with more managers leading self-managing teams, supporting, coaching, and mentoring are fast replacing the manager's formal authority for getting things done.

The Basic Coaching Process

We can best think of coaching in terms of a four-step process: preparation, planning, active coaching, and follow-up.[59]

Preparing to Coach   *Preparation* means understanding the problem, the employee, and the employee's skills. Your aim here is to formulate a hypothesis about what the problem is. Preparation is partly an observational process. You'll watch the employee to see what he or she is doing and observe the workflow and how coworkers interact with the employee. In addition to observation, you may review objective data on things like productivity, absenteeism, and tardiness (as explained in Chapter 5, "Training and Developing Employees").

Planning   Perhaps the most powerful way to get someone to change is to obtain his or her enthusiastic agreement on what change is required. This requires reaching consensus on the problem and on what to change. In practice, you'll then lay out a change plan in the form, *Steps to Take, Measures of Success,* and *Date to Complete.*

Getting agreement on these items requires interpersonal communications skills. Figure 6.9 presents a short "course" in interpersonal communications.

Active Coaching   With agreement on a plan, you can start the actual "educating, instructing, and training"—namely, coaching. Here you are, in essence, in the role of teacher/trainer. Your toolkit will include what you learned about on-the-job training in Chapter 5. However, interpersonal communications skills are the heart of effective coaching. As one writer says, "[a]n effective coach offers ideas and advice in such a way that the subordinate can hear them, respond to them, and appreciate their value."[60]

Follow-Up   Bad habits sometimes reemerge. Reobserve the person's progress periodically.

Career Management Methods

Once you've appraised their performance, it's often necessary to address subordinates' career-related issues. We may define *career* as the "occupational positions a person has had over the years." **Career management** is a process for enabling

Figure 6.9 A Short Course in Improving Interpersonal Communications

- **Make yourself clear.** For example, if you mean immediately, say "immediately," not, "as soon as you can."
- **Be consistent.** Make sure your tone, expression, and words send a consistent meaning.
- **Confirm, "Message received."** Pilots and flight controllers know to confirm and reconfirm the message. You should do the same.
- **Do not attack the person's defenses.** Do not attack the other person's defenses (as in "You just can't stand being blamed for anything.").
- **Show that you are listening with an open mind.** Do not rush to interrupt the person.
- **Encourage the speaker to talk.** Ask open-ended questions, and confirm your understanding by summarizing what the employee said.[61]

employees to better understand and develop their career skills and interests and to use these skills and interests both within the company and even after they leave the firm. *Career development* is the lifelong series of activities (such as workshops) that contribute to a person's career exploration, establishment, success, and fulfillment. *Career planning* is the deliberate process through which someone becomes aware of personal skills, interests, knowledge, motivations, and other characteristics; acquires information about opportunities and choices; identifies career-related goals; and establishes action plans to attain specific goals.

Roles in Career Development

The employee, the manager, and the employer all play roles in guiding the employee's career. However, the employee must always accept full responsibility for his or her career development and career success. No employee should ever leave this task to a manager or employer. For the individual employee, the career-planning process means matching individual strengths and weaknesses with occupational opportunities and threats. The person wants to pursue occupations, jobs, and a career that capitalizes on his or her interests, aptitudes, values, and skills. He or she also wants to choose occupations, jobs, and a career that makes sense in terms of projected future demand for various types of occupations.

The Employee's Role

Making decisions like these is the employee's responsibility. For example, an employee unhappy with his or her job can do several things short of changing occupations. Ask yourself what you're looking for in a career and to what extent your current one is fulfilling your needs. Enhance your networks, for instance, by discussing your career goals with role models, conducting informational interviews with people whose jobs interest you, or becoming a board member for a nonprofit organization so you can interact with new people. If you are satisfied with your occupation and where you work, but not with your job as it is now, reconfigure your job. For example, consider alternative work arrangements such as flexible hours or telecommuting, delegate or eliminate the job functions that you least prefer, and seek out a "stretch assignment" that will let you work on something more challenging.[62]

Mentoring   Studies also suggest that having a mentor—a senior person who can be a sounding board for your career questions and concerns—can significantly enhance career satisfaction and success.[63] Suggestions for doing so include:

- Choose an appropriate mentor. For objectivity, someone who doesn't have direct supervisory responsibility of you may be best.
- Make it easier for a potential mentor to agree to your request by clarifying what you expect in terms of time and advice.
- Have an agenda. Bring an agenda to your first mentoring meeting that lays out key issues and topics for discussion.
- Respect the mentor's time. Be selective about the work-related issues that you bring to the table.

The Employer's Role in Career Management

The employer's career development roles depend on how long the employee has been with the firm.

Before hiring, *realistic job interviews* can help prospective employees gauge more accurately whether the job is indeed for them.

Especially for recent college graduates, the first job can be crucial for building confidence and a more realistic picture of strengths and weaknesses: Providing *challenging first jobs* and having an experienced mentor who can help the person learn the ropes are important. Some refer to this as preventing "reality shock," which occurs when a new employee's high expectations confront the reality of a boring, unchallenging job.

After the person has been on the job for a while, an employer can take steps to contribute in a positive way to the employee's career. *Career-oriented appraisals*—in which the manager is trained not just to appraise the employee but also to match the person's strengths and weaknesses with a feasible career path and required development work—is one important step. Similarly, providing periodic *job rotation* can help the person develop a more realistic picture of what he or she is (and is not) good at.

Innovative Corporate Career Development Initiatives

Employers' corporate career development initiatives may also include innovative programs like these:[64]

1. *Provide each employee with an individual career development budget.* He or she can use this budget for learning about career options and personal development.[65]
2. *Offer on-site or online career centers.* These might include an on- or offline library of career development materials, career workshops, and individual career coaches for career guidance.
3. *Encourage role reversal.* Have employees temporarily work in different positions to develop a better appreciation of their occupational strengths and weaknesses.
4. *Provide career coaches.* The coaches help individual employees identify their development needs and obtain the training, professional development, and networking opportunities that they need.[66]
5. *Provide career-planning workshops.* A career-planning workshop is a "planned learning event in which participants are expected to be actively involved, completing career planning exercises and inventories and participating in career skills practice sessions."[67]
6. *Computerized on- and offline programs are available for improving the organizational career-planning process.* For example, employees can use Self-Directed Search (www.self-directed-search.com) to identify career preferences.

Gender Issues in Career Development

Women and men face different challenges as they advance through their careers. In one study, promoted women had to receive higher performance ratings than promoted men to get promoted, "suggesting that women were held to stricter standards for promotion."[68] Women also report greater barriers (such as being excluded from informal networks) than do men, and more difficulty getting developmental assignments and geographic mobility opportunities. Because developmental experiences like these are so important, "organizations that are interested in helping female managers advance should focus on breaking down barriers that interfere with women's access to developmental experiences."[69]

Minority Women   In these matters, minority women seem particularly at risk. Women of color hold only a small percentage of professional and managerial private-sector positions.[70]

Adding to the problem is the fact that some corporate career development programs may be inconsistent with the needs of minority (and nonminority) women. For example, such programs may assume that career paths are continuous; yet the need to stop working for a time due to family issues punctuates the career paths of many women (and, often men).[71] One study concluded that fast-track development programs, individual career counseling, and career-planning workshops were less available to women than to men.[72] Many refer to this combination of subtle and not-so-subtle barriers to women's career progress as the *glass ceiling*.

Managing Employees' Promotions and Transfers

Promotions are, of course, one of the more significant HR decisions to result from the performance appraisal. In developing promotion policies, employers need to address several issues.

One issue concerns seniority versus competence. Competence is normally the basis for promotions, although in many organizations civil service or union requirements and similar constraints still give an edge to seniority.

Furthermore, if competence is to be the basis for promotion, how should we measure it? Defining past performance is usually straightforward. Managers use performance appraisals for this. However, sizing up how even a high-performing employee will do in a new job is not so easy. Innumerable great salespeople turn out to be awful managers, for instance. Many employers therefore use formal selection devices like tests and assessment centers to supplement the performance appraisals.

With more companies downsizing and flattening their organizations, "promotions" today often mean lateral moves or transfers. In such situations, the promotional aspect is not so much a higher-level job or more pay, but the opportunity to assume new, same-level responsibilities (such as a salesperson moving into HR) or increased decision-making responsibilities within the same job.

A *transfer* is a move from one job to another, usually with no salary or grade change. Employees may seek transfers not just for advancement but also for noncareer reasons, such as better hours, location of work, and so on.

Retirement

For most employees, years of appraisals and career development end with retirement. Retirement planning is now a significant issue for employers. In the United States, the number of 25- to 34-year-olds is growing relatively slowly, and the number of 35- to 44-year-olds is declining. With many older employees moving into the traditional 60-plus retirement age, employers will face a labor shortage. Many have wisely chosen to fill their staffing needs in part with current or soon-to-be retirees.

Therefore, "retirement planning" is no longer just for helping current employees slip into retirement.[73] It should also enable the employer to retain, in some capacity, the skills and brainpower of those who would normally leave the firm. Fortuitously, 78% of employees in one survey said they expect to continue working in some capacity after normal retirement age (64% said they want to do so part time). Only about a third said they plan to continue work for financial reasons; about 43% said they just wanted to remain active.[74]

Not surprisingly, studies show that employees who are more committed and loyal to the employer are more likely to stay beyond their normal retirement age.[75] Beyond that, specific suggestions include:

- **Create a culture that honors experience.** For example, the CVS pharmacy chain works through the National Council on Aging, city agencies, and community organizations to find such employees. They've also made it clear to retirees with their policies that they welcome older workers. As one dedicated older worker said, "I'm too young to retire. [CVS] is willing to hire older people. They don't look at your age but your experience."[76]
- **Modify selection procedures.** For example, one British bank stopped using psychometric tests, replacing them with role-playing exercises to gauge how candidates deal with customers.
- **Offer flexible work.** Companies "need to design jobs such that staying on is more attractive than leaving." One of the simplest ways to do this is through flexible work, in terms of hours and telecommuting.[77]
- **Phased retirement.** Phased retirement programs combine reduced work hours, job change, and reduced responsibilities, to extend the employee's participation in the company.

Employers should conduct the necessary numerical analyses for dealing with the prospect of retirements. This assessment should include such things as a demographic analysis of the company's employees and a determination of the average retirement age for the company's employees. The employer can then determine the extent of the "retirement problem" and take fact-based steps to address it.[78]

TALENT MANAGEMENT

Employees want to manage their careers so they take the right jobs at the right time. Talent management is career management from the employer's vantage point. Most simply, it involves getting the right talent to the right job at the right time.[79] To some extent, this just entails traditional staffing tools such as hiring, training, and appraising.[80] To HR managers, however, *talent management* means something more. First, talent management is *goal-directed*. The employer consciously adapts each underlying staffing process (such as recruiting and testing) so as to get the competencies the firm's strategy requires to the right job at the right time. Second, talent management is an *integrated* process: those same underlying processes need to work together in unison, towards the same aim. Third, talent management usually relies on *software* processes. As one expert says, **talent management** is "the automated end-to-end process of planning, recruiting, developing, managing, and compensating employees throughout the organization."[81]

Talent Management Systems

Several software providers offer specialized talent management suites. The suites include and integrate underlying talent management components such as e-recruiting, e-training, performance reviews, and rewards. Talent management software helps employers answer questions such as, Why are certain employees more successful than others? and Do I have the executive talent I need to lead this new project?[82] Talent management system components typically include workforce analytics and planning; recruitment and onboarding; recognition, rewards, and engagement; performance management; learning and development; career mapping; and succession planning.[83] Some talent management system examples follow.[84]

- The Talent Management Solutions (www.talentmanagement101.com) talent management suite includes e-recruiting software, employee performance management, a learning management system, and compensation management. Among other things, Talent Management Solutions' suite of programs "relieves the stress of writing employee performance reviews by automating the task," and ensures "that all levels of the organization are aligned—all working for the same goals."[85]
- Info HCM Talent Management "includes several upgrades including tracking and monitoring performance metrics, interactive online training via WebEx, support for e-commerce integration to enable training . . . , and full localization for additional countries including Spanish, French, and Chinese."[86]

REVIEW

Summary

1. Performance appraisal means evaluating an employee's current or past performance relative to his or her performance standards. Performance management is the continuous process through which companies ensure that employees are working toward organizational goals.
2. Managers appraise their subordinates' performance to obtain data on which promotion and salary raise decisions can be made, to develop plans for correcting performance deficiencies, and for career planning. Supervisory ratings are still the heart of most appraisal processes.
3. The appraisal is generally conducted using one or more popular appraisal methods or tools. These include graphic rating scales, alternation ranking, paired comparison, forced distribution, critical incidents, behaviorally anchored rating scales, management by objectives (MBO), computerized or Web-based appraisals, and electronic performance monitoring.
4. An appraisal typically culminates in an appraisal interview. Adequate preparation, including sufficient notice, reviewing his or her job description and past performance, choosing the right place for the interview, and leaving enough time are essential. In conducting the interview, the aim is to reinforce satisfactory performance or to diagnose and improve unsatisfactory performance. Employee defensiveness is normal and needs to be dealt with.
5. The appraisal process can be improved, first, by eliminating common problems such as unfairness, unclear standards, halo effect, central tendency, leniency or strictness, and bias.

6. Care should also be taken to ensure that the performance appraisal is legally defensible. For example, base appraisal criteria on documented job analyses. Employees should receive performance standards in writing, and multiple performance dimensions should be rated.

7. Career management is the process for enabling employees to better understand and develop their career skills and interests, and to use these most effectively, within the company and after they leave the firm.

8. *Talent management* is the automated end-to-end process of planning, recruiting, developing, managing, and compensating employees throughout the organization. Several software providers offer specialized talent management suites. The suites include and integrate underlying talent management components such as e-recruiting, e-training, performance reviews, and rewards.

KEY TERMS

- performance appraisal
- peer appraisal
- upward feedback
- graphic rating scale
- alternation ranking method
- paired comparison method
- forced distribution method
- critical incident method
- management by objectives (MBO)
- performance management
- halo effect
- central tendency
- appraisal interview
- coaching
- career management
- talent management

DISCUSSION QUESTIONS

1. Discuss the pros and cons of at least four performance appraisal tools.
2. Explain how you would use the alternation ranking method, the paired comparison method, and the forced distribution method.
3. Explain the problems to be avoided in appraising performance.
4. Discuss the pros and cons of using various potential raters to appraise an employee's performance.
5. Explain how to conduct an appraisal interview.

INDIVIDUAL AND GROUP ACTIVITIES

1. Working individually or in groups, develop a graphic rating scale for the following jobs: secretary, professor, directory assistance operator.
2. Working individually or in groups, describe the advantages and disadvantages of using the forced distribution appraisal method for college professors.
3. Working individually or in groups, develop, over the period of a week, a set of critical incidents covering the classroom performance of one of your instructors.
4. Working individually or in groups, evaluate the rating scale in Figure 6.1. Discuss ways to improve it.

APPLICATION EXERCISE

Case Incident   Appraising the Secretaries at Sweetwater U

Rob Winchester, newly appointed vice president for administrative affairs at Sweetwater State University, faced a tough problem shortly after his university career began. Three weeks after he came on board in September, Sweetwater's president, Rob's boss, told Rob that one of his first tasks was to improve the appraisal system used to evaluate secretarial and clerical performance at Sweetwater U. The main difficulty was that the performance appraisal was tied to salary increases given at the end of the year. Therefore, most administrators were less than accurate when they used the graphic rating forms that were the basis of the clerical staff evaluation. Each administrator simply rated his or her clerk or secretary as "excellent." This cleared the way for all support staff to receive a maximum pay increase every year.

But the current university budget simply did not include enough money to fund another "maximum" annual increase for every staffer. Furthermore, Sweetwater's president felt that the custom of providing invalid performance feedback to each secretary was not productive, so he had asked the new vice president to revise the system. In October, Rob sent a memo to all administrators telling them that in the future no more than half the secretaries reporting to any particular administrator could be appraised as "excellent." This move, in effect, forced each supervisor to begin ranking his or her secretaries for quality of performance. The vice president's memo met widespread resistance immediately— from administrators, who were afraid that many of their secretaries would leave for lucrative jobs; and from secretaries, who felt that the new system was unfair. A handful of secretaries had begun quietly picketing outside the president's home on the university campus. The picketing, caustic remarks by disgruntled administrators, and rumors of an impending slowdown by the secretaries (there were about 250 on campus) made Rob Winchester wonder whether he had made the right decision by setting up forced ranking. He knew, however, that there were a few performance appraisal experts in the School of Business, so he set up an appointment with them to discuss the matter.

He met with them the next morning. He explained the situation as he had found it: The present appraisal system had been set up when the university first opened 10 years earlier. A committee of secretaries had developed it. Under that system, Sweetwater's administrators filled out forms similar to the one in Figure 6.8. This once-a-year appraisal (in March) had run into problems almost immediately, since it was apparent from the start that administrators varied widely in their interpretations of job standards, as well as in how conscientiously they filled out the forms and supervised their secretaries. Moreover, at the end of the first year it became obvious to everyone that each secretary's salary increase was tied directly to the March appraisal. For example, those rated "excellent" received the maximum increases, those rated "good" received smaller increases, and those given neither rating received only across-the-board cost-of-living increases. Since universities in general—and Sweetwater in particular—have paid secretaries somewhat lower salaries than those in private industry, some secretaries left in a huff that first year. From that time on, most administrators simply rated all secretaries excellent in order to reduce staff turnover, thus ensuring each a maximum increase. In the process, they also avoided the hard feelings aroused by the significant performance differences otherwise highlighted by administrators.

Two Sweetwater experts agreed to consider the problem, and in 2 weeks they came back to the vice president with the following recommendations. First, the form used to rate the secretaries was grossly insufficient. It was unclear what "excellent" or "quality of work" meant, for example. They recommended instead a form like that in Figure 6.2. In addition, they recommended that the vice president rescind his earlier memo and no longer attempt to force university administrators to rate at least half their secretaries as less than excellent. The two consultants pointed out that this was, in fact, an unfair procedure since it was quite possible that any particular administrator might have staffers who were all excellent—or conceivably, although less likely, all below standard. The experts said that the way to get all the administrators to take the appraisal process more seriously was to stop tying it to salary increases. In other words, they recommended that every administrator fill out a form like that in Figure 6.2 for each secretary at least once a year and then use this form as the basis of a counseling session. Salary increases would be made on some basis other than the performance appraisal, so that administrators would no longer hesitate to fill out the rating forms honestly.

Rob thanked the two experts and went back to his office to ponder their recommendations. Some of the recommendations (such as substituting the new rating form for the old) seemed to make sense. Nevertheless, he still had serious doubts as to the efficacy of any graphic rating form, particularly if he were to decide in favor of his original forced ranking approach. The experts' second recommendation—to stop tying the appraisals to automatic salary increases—made sense but raised a practical problem: If salary increases were not to be based on performance appraisals, on what were they to be based? He began wondering whether the experts' recommendations weren't simply based on ivory-tower theorizing.

QUESTIONS

1. Do you think that the experts' recommendations will be sufficient to get most of the administrators to fill out the rating forms properly? Why? Why not? What additional actions (if any) do you think will be necessary?
2. Do you think that Vice President Winchester would be better off dropping graphic rating forms, substituting instead one of the other techniques we discussed in this chapter, such as a ranking method? Why?
3. What performance appraisal system would you develop for the secretaries if you were Rob Winchester? Defend your answer.

Continuing Case

LearnInMotion.com: The Performance Appraisal

Jennifer and Mel disagree over the importance of having performance appraisals. Mel says it's quite clear whether any particular LearnInMotion employee is doing his or her job. It's obvious, for instance, if the salespeople are selling, and if the Web designer is

designing. Mel's position, like that of many small-business managers, is that "we have 1,000 higher-priority things to attend to" such as boosting sales and creating the calendar. And in any case, he says, the employees already get plenty of day-to-day feedback from him or Jennifer regarding what they're doing right and what they're doing wrong.

This informal feedback notwithstanding, Jennifer believes that a more formal appraisal approach is required. For one thing, they're approaching the end of the 90-day introductory period for many of these employees, and the owners need to make decisions about whether they should go or stay. And from a practical point of view, Jennifer believes that sitting down and providing formal, written feedback is more likely to reinforce what employees are doing right, and to get them to modify what they may be doing wrong. "Maybe this is one reason we're not getting enough sales," she says. They've been debating this for about an hour. Now, they want you, their management consultants, to advise them on what to do. Here's what they want you to do for them. ■

QUESTIONS AND ASSIGNMENTS

1. Is Jennifer right about the need to evaluate the workers formally? Why or why not? If you think she's right, how do you counter Mel's arguments?
2. Develop a performance appraisal method for the salespeople, or Web designer, or Web surfer. Please make sure to include any form you want the owners to use.

Experiential Exercise

Appraising an Instructor

Purpose: The purpose of this exercise is to give you practice in developing and using a performance appraisal form.

Required Understanding: You are going to develop a performance appraisal form for an instructor and should therefore be thoroughly familiar with the discussion of performance appraisals in this chapter.

How to Set Up the Exercise/Instructions: Divide the class into groups of four or five students.

1. First, based on what you now know about performance appraisals, do you think Figure 6.1 is an effective scale for appraising instructors? Why or why not?

2. Next, your group should develop its own tool for appraising the performance of an instructor. Decide which of the appraisal tools (graphic rating scales, alternation ranking, and so on) you are going to use, and then design the instrument itself.
3. Next, have a spokesperson from each group put his or her group's appraisal tool on the board. How similar are the tools? Do they all measure about the same factors? Which factor appears most often? Which do you think is the most effective tool on the board? Can you think of any way of combining the best points of several of the tools into a new performance appraisal tool? ■

Chapter 7

Compensating Employees

- What Determines How Much You Pay?
- How Employers Establish Pay Rates
- Current Trends in Compensation
- Incentive Plans
- Employee Benefits

When you finish studying this chapter, you should be able to:

- Discuss *four basic factors determining pay rates.*
- Explain *each of the five basic steps in establishing pay rates.*
- Compare *and* contrast *piecework and team or group incentive plans.*
- List *and* describe *each of the basic benefits most employers might be expected to offer.*

INTRODUCTION

*W*hen you own about 14,000 stores around the world, you obviously can't be everywhere watching what's going on. Perhaps that's one reason why Starbucks' employee benefits are exceptional. Each employee gets a "Special Blend" of total pay and benefits that's unique to him or her. Benefits include (just for a start) health-care benefits, a retirement savings plan, life and disability coverage, adoption assistance, and of course, a pound of coffee each week.[1]

Employee compensation refers to all forms of pay or rewards going to employees and arising from their employment. It has two main components: *direct financial payments* (in the form of wages, salaries, incentives, commissions, and bonuses) and *indirect payments* (in the form of financial benefits like employer-paid insurance and vacations).

What Determines How Much You Pay?

Four basic factors determine what people are paid: legal, union, policy, and equity factors. We'll look at each, starting with legal.

Some Important Compensation Laws

Numerous laws stipulate what employers can or must pay in terms of minimum wages, overtime rates, and benefits. For example:[2]

1938 Fair Labor Standards Act   The **Fair Labor Standards Act (FLSA),** passed in 1938 and since amended many times, contains minimum wage, maximum hours, overtime pay, equal pay, recordkeeping, and child labor provisions covering most U.S. workers—virtually anyone engaged in producing or selling goods for interstate and foreign commerce.

One well-known provision governs overtime pay. It states that employers must pay overtime at a rate of at least one and a half times normal pay for any hours worked over 40 in a workweek.

The act also sets a minimum wage, which sets a floor for employees covered by the act (and usually bumps up wages for most workers when Congress raises the minimum). The minimum wage for the majority of those covered by the act was $7.25 per hour in 2010.[3] (Several states and about 80 municipalities have their own, higher, minimum wages. California's was $8.00 in 2010.)[4]

The act also contains child labor provisions. These prohibit employing minors between 16 and 18 years of age in hazardous occupations such as mining, and carefully restrict employment of those under 16.[5]

Exempt/Nonexempt   Specific categories of employees are *exempt* from the act or certain provisions of the act, and particularly from the act's overtime provisions—they are "exempt employees." A person's exemption depends on his or her responsibilities, duties, and salary. Bona fide executive, administrative (like office managers), and professional employees (like architects) are generally exempt from the act's minimum wage and overtime requirements.[6] A white-collar worker earning more than $100,000 and performing any one exempt administrative, executive, or professional duty is automatically ineligible for overtime pay. Other employees can generally earn up to $23,660 per year and still automatically get overtime pay (so most employees earning less than $455 per week are nonexempt and earn overtime).

Yet identifying exemptions is tricky.[7] Figure 7.1 presents a procedure for making this decision. Make sure, for instance, that the job currently does in fact require that the person perform an exempt-type supervisory duty.[8]

Figure 7.1 Who Is Exempt? Who Is Not Exempt?

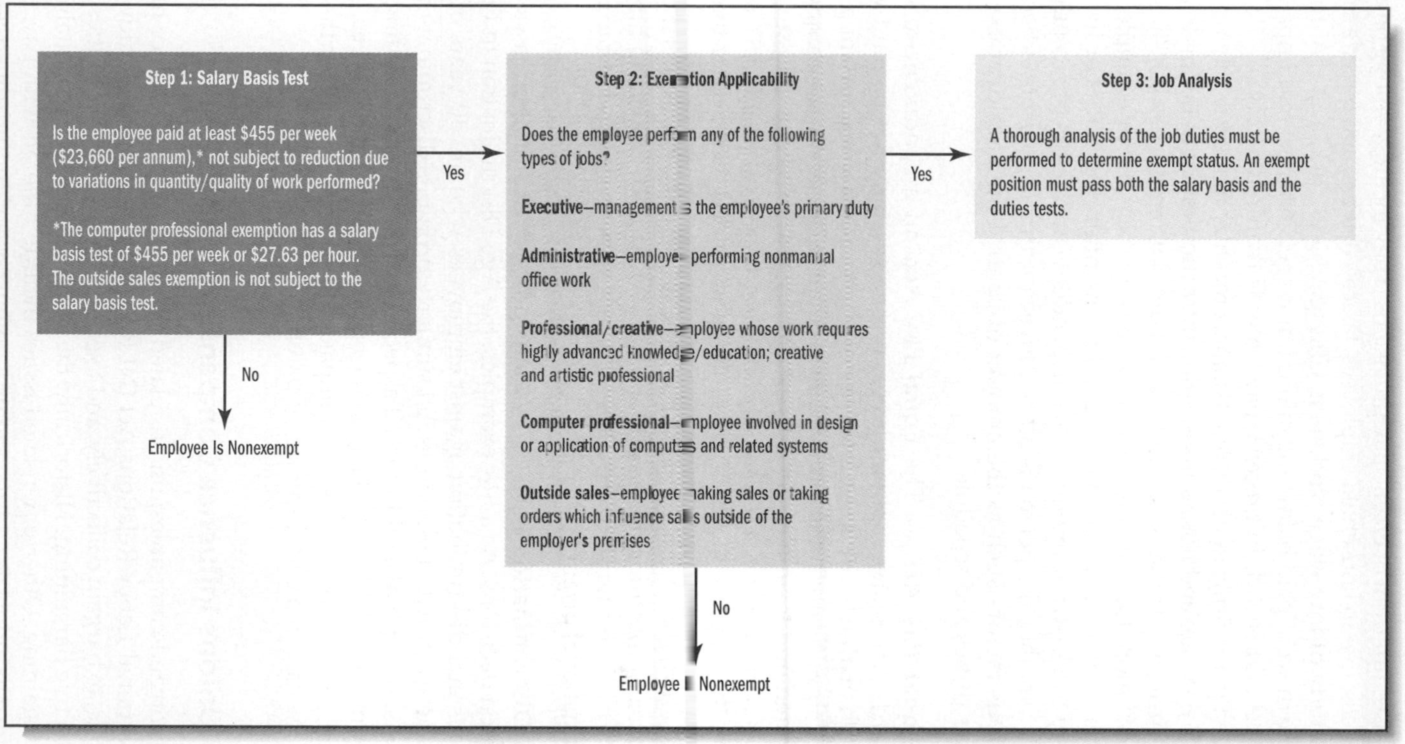

Step 1: Salary Basis Test

Is the employee paid at least $455 per week ($23,660 per annum),* not subject to reduction due to variations in quantity/quality of work performed?

*The computer professional exemption has a salary basis test of $455 per week or $27.63 per hour. The outside sales exemption is not subject to the salary basis test.

No → Employee Is Nonexempt

Yes →

Step 2: Exemption Applicability

Does the employee perform any of the following types of jobs?

Executive—management is the employee's primary duty

Administrative—employee performing nonmanual office work

Professional/creative—employee whose work requires highly advanced knowledge/education; creative and artistic professional

Computer professional—employee involved in design or application of computers and related systems

Outside sales—employee making sales or taking orders which influence sales outside of the employer's premises

No → Employee Is Nonexempt

Yes →

Step 3: Job Analysis

A thorough analysis of the job duties must be performed to determine exempt status. An exempt position must pass both the salary basis and the duties tests.

If an employee is exempt from the FLSA's minimum wage provisions, then he or she is also exempt from its overtime pay provisions. However, certain employees are always exempt from overtime pay provisions. They include, among others, agricultural employees, live-in household employees, taxicab drivers, and outside sales employees.[9]

A study of low-wage workers in Chicago, New York, and L.A. found that about one-fourth were paid below the minimum wage; 76% also had unpaid or underpaid overtime, and 56% didn't receive pay stubs as required by law.[10]

Even giant firms make errors. Walmart recently agreed to pay up to $640 million to settle 63 wage and hour suits alleging infractions such as failing to pay overtime.[11] Other firms assert that some individuals are not employees but "independent contractors," more like consultants not covered by the Act. For example, FedEx Ground is battling lawsuits to defend its right to maintain the status of its roughly 15,000 delivery truck owner-operators as independent contractors (it recently won one such case).[12] Whether the person is an employee or an *independent contractor* depends on numerous factors such as the amount of control the employer exercises over the person's duties and schedule.[13]

1963 Equal Pay Act The **Equal Pay Act,** an amendment to the Fair Labor Standards Act, states that employees of one sex may not be paid wages at a rate lower than that paid to employees of the opposite sex for roughly equivalent work.[14] Specifically, if the work requires equal skills, effort, and responsibility and is performed under similar working conditions, employees of both sexes must receive equal pay unless the differences in pay are based on a seniority system, a merit system, the quantity or quality of production, or any factor other than sex.[15]

1964 Civil Rights Act Title VII of the **Civil Rights Act** makes it unlawful for an employer to discriminate against any individual with respect to hiring, compensation, terms, conditions, or privileges of employment because of race, color, religion, sex, or national origin.

Other Discrimination Laws Various other discrimination laws influence compensation decisions. As a few examples, the Age Discrimination in Employment Act prohibits age discrimination against employees who are 40 years of age and older. The Americans with Disabilities Act similarly prohibits discrimination against qualified persons with disabilities in all aspects of employment, including compensation. The Family and Medical Leave Act entitles eligible employees, both men and women, to take up to 12 weeks of unpaid, job-protected leave for the birth of a child or for the care of a child, spouse, or parent.

How Unions Influence Compensation Decisions

For unionized companies, union-related issues of course influence pay plan design. The National Labor Relations Act (NLRA) of 1935 granted employees the right to organize, to bargain collectively, and to engage in concerted activities for the purpose of collective bargaining. Historically, the wage rate has been the main issue in collective bargaining. Other pay-related issues include time off with pay, income security (for those in industries with periodic layoffs), cost-of-living adjustments, and various benefits such as health care.[16]

Compensation Policies

As at Starbuck's, an employer's strategy and compensation policies significantly affect the wages and benefits it pays. For example, a hospital might have a policy of starting nurses at a wage 10% above the prevailing market wage. Other important policies include the basis for salary increases, foreign pay differentials, and overtime pay policy. Locality also plays a role. For example, the average base pay recently for an executive secretary would have ranged from $37,300 in Albuquerque, New Mexico, to $60,100 (San Francisco, California).[17]

Distinguishing between high and low performers is another important pay policy. For example, for many years Payless ShoeSource hardly distinguished in pay among high and low performers. After seeing its market share drop, management embarked on a turnaround plan. The plan included revising its compensation policies to differentiate more aggressively between top performers and others.[18]

The important point is that the compensation plan should support the employer's strategic aims—management should produce an *aligned reward strategy*. The basic aim is to create a total reward package, including wages, incentives, and benefits, that aims to elicit the employee behaviors the firm needs to support and achieve its competitive strategy.[19]

Equity and Its Impact on Pay Rates

The need for equity is a key factor in determining pay rates.[20] Externally, pay must compare favorably with rates in other companies, or an employer will find it hard to attract and retain qualified employees. Pay must also be equitable internally: Each employee should view his or her pay as equitable given other employees' pay in the organization.[21] It's not just paying too little that can reduce morale. Overpaying people relative to what they think they're worth can backfire too, perhaps "due to feelings of guilt or discomfort."[22] The challenging times feature shows how economic realities prompt employers to review what "equity" means.

When inequities do arise, conflicts ensue. To head off discussions that might prompt feelings of internal inequity, some firms maintain strict secrecy over pay

---

Managing HR in Challenging Times: Salary and Incentives in Tough Times

Not surprisingly, one way that employers deal with economically challenging times is by instituting policies to reduce salary increases and merit pay. Surveys by consulting companies such as Hewitt Associates and Mercer showed that as the recent recession deepened, at least half the employers in America (and more abroad) were planning to cut salary increases. On average, the survey suggested that salaried exempt employees' raises would drop from about 3.8% in 2008 to about 2.5% in 2009, while about 10% of U.S. employers surveyed were instituting pay freezes. Interestingly, though, the challenging times were also prompting employers to pay closer attention to their highest performing employees. For example, many were establishing special funds to reward high-performing employees with items like long-term equity grants and bonuses.[24]

rates, with mixed results. But for external equity, online pay sites like Salary.com of course make it easy for employees to see what they could earn elsewhere.[23]

HOW EMPLOYERS ESTABLISH PAY RATES

In practice, setting pay rates while ensuring external and internal equity usually entails five steps:

1. Conduct a salary survey of what other employers are paying comparable jobs (to price benchmark jobs and help ensure external equity).
2. Employee committee determines the worth of each job in your organization through job evaluation (to help ensure internal equity).
3. Group similarly paid jobs into pay grades.
4. Price each pay grade by using wage curves.
5. Develop rate ranges.

We explain each of these steps in this section, starting with salary surveys.

Step 1: Conduct the Salary Survey

Salary (or compensation) surveys—formal or informal surveys of what other employers are paying for similar jobs—play a central role in pricing jobs.

Employers use salary surveys in three ways. First, they use them to price *benchmark jobs*. These anchor the employer's pay scale. The manager slots other jobs around them, based on their relative worth to the firm. (*Job evaluation*, explained next, is the technique used to determine the relative worth of each job.) Second, employers usually price 20% or more of their positions directly in the marketplace (rather than relative to the firm's benchmark jobs), based on a formal or informal survey of what comparable firms are paying for comparable jobs. Finally, surveys also collect data on benefits such as insurance, sick leave, and vacations.[25]

Finding salary data is not as mysterious as it used to be, thanks to the Internet. Table 7.1 summarizes some popular salary Web sites. For example, the U.S. Department of Labor's Bureau of Labor Statistics' (BLS) *National Compensation Survey (NCS)* provides comprehensive reports of occupational earnings, compensation cost trends, and benefits (http://www.bls.gov/bls/wages.htm). Detailed occupational earnings are available from this survey for over 800 occupations in the United States, regions, states, and many metropolitan areas (http://stats.bls.gov/oes/current/ oes_nat.htm).

Step 2: Determine the Worth of Each Job: Job Evaluation

Purpose of Job Evaluation   **Job evaluation** is a formal and systematic comparison of jobs to determine the worth of one job relative to another. The basic job evaluation procedure is to compare the content of jobs in relation to one another, for example, in terms of their effort, responsibility, and skills. Suppose you know (based on your salary survey and compensation policies) how to price key benchmark jobs and can use job evaluation to determine the relative worth of all the other jobs in your firm

Table 7.1   Some Pay Data Web Sites

SPONSOR	INTERNET ADDRESS	WHAT IT PROVIDES	DOWNSIDE
Salary.com	http://salary.com	Salary by job and zip code, plus job and description, for hundreds of jobs	Adapts national averages by applying local cost-of-living differences
Wageweb	http://www.wageweb.com	Average salaries for more than 150 clerical, professional, and managerial jobs	Charges for breakdowns by industry, location, etc.
U.S. Office of Personnel Management	http://www.opm.gov/oca/09Tables/index.asp	Salaries and wages for U.S. government jobs, by location	Limited to U.S. government jobs
Job Smart	http://jobstar.org/tools/salary/index.php	Profession-specific salary surveys	Necessary to review numerous salary surveys for each profession
cnnmoney.com	http://money.cnn.com	Input your current salary and city, and this gives you comparable salary in destination city	Based on national averages adapted to cost-of-living differences

relative to these key jobs. Then you are well on your way to being able to price all the jobs in your organization equitably.

Compensable Factors   There are two basic approaches to comparing the worth of several jobs. First, you could take an intuitive approach. You might decide that one job is more important than another is and not dig any deeper into why, in terms of specific job-related factors.

As an alternative, you could compare the jobs based on certain basic factors they have in common. Compensation managers call these **compensable factors.** They are the factors that determine your definition of job content. And they establish how the jobs compare to each other, and set the compensation paid for each job. For example, the Equal Pay Act focuses on four compensable factors: skills, effort, responsibility, and working conditions. Walmart instituted a wage structure based on knowledge, problem-solving skills, and accountability requirements.

Job Evaluation Methods   The simplest job evaluation method ranks each job relative to all other jobs, usually based on some overall compensable factor such as job difficulty. There are several steps in this *job ranking* method, as the *HR in Practice* box summarizes. *Job classification* is another simple, widely used method. Here the manager categorizes jobs into groups based on their similarity in terms of compensable factors such as skill and responsibility categories. The groups are called *classes* if they contain similar jobs, or *grades*, if they contain jobs that are similar in difficulty but are otherwise different. Thus, in the federal government's pay grade system, a press secretary and a fire chief might both be graded GS-10 (GS stands for General Schedule). The *point method* is a quantitative job evaluation technique. It involves identifying several compensable factors, each having several degrees, and then assigning points based on the number of degrees, to come up with a total number of points for each job.

HR in Practice: Steps in Ranking Method of Job Evaluation

1. *Obtain job information.* Job analysis is the first step in the **ranking method.** Ranking involves ordering jobs from high to low, usually based on some overall measure such as job difficulty. You'll usually use the job description for each job to decide each job's rank, typically based on the whole job rather than separate compensable factors.

2. *Select raters and jobs to be rated.* The usual procedure is to rank jobs by department or in clusters (such as factory workers and clerical workers). This eliminates the need for having to compare directly, say, factory jobs and clerical jobs.

3. *Select compensable factors.* In the ranking method, it is common to use just one factor (such as job difficulty) and to rank jobs based on the whole job. Regardless of the number of factors you choose, explain the definition of the factor(s) to the evaluators so that they evaluate the jobs consistently.

4. *Rank jobs.* Next, rank the jobs. The simplest way is to give each rater a set of index cards, each of which contains a brief description of a job. These cards are then ranked from lowest to highest. Some managers use an alternation ranking method for making the procedure more accurate. Specifically, use the cards first to choose the highest and the lowest, and then the next highest and next lowest, and so forth, until all the cards are ranked. Because it is usually easier to choose extremes, this approach facilitates the ranking procedure. Table 7.2 illustrates a job ranking. Jobs in this small health facility rank from cleaner up to office manager. The corresponding pay scales are on the right.

5. *Combine ratings.* Usually several raters rank the jobs independently. Then the rating committee (or employer) can average the rankings. Online programs, as at http://www.hr-guide.com/data/G909.htm, can help rank your positions.

Table 7.2 Job Ranking by Jackson Hospital

RANKING ORDER	ANNUAL PAY SCALE
1. Office manager	$48,000
2. Chief nurse	47,500
3. Bookkeeper	39,000
4. Nurse	37,500
5. Cook	36,000
6. Nurse's aide	33,500
7. Cleaner	30,500

Note: After ranking, it becomes possible to slot additional jobs between those already ranked and to assign each an appropriate wage rate.

Step 3: Group Similar Jobs into Pay Grades

Once a job evaluation method has been used to determine the relative worth of each job, the evaluation committee can start assigning pay rates to each job; it usually first groups jobs into pay grades. A *pay grade* comprises jobs of approximately equal difficulty or importance as determined by job evaluation. If the point method were used, the pay grade would consist of jobs falling within a range of points. If the ranking plan were used, the grade would consist of all jobs that fall within two or three ranks. If the classification system were used, then the jobs are already categorized into classes or grades. Ten to 16 grades per job cluster (or logical grouping such as factory jobs, clerical jobs, etc.) are common.

Step 4: Price Each Pay Grade: Wage Curves

The next step is to assign average pay rates to each of the pay grades. (Of course, if you choose not to slot jobs into pay grades, you'll have to assign an individual pay rate to each individual job.) Assigning pay rates to each pay grade (or to each job) is usually accomplished with the help of a **wage curve,** which shows the average pay rates currently being paid for jobs in each pay grade, relative to the points or rankings assigned to each job or grade by the job evaluation.

   Figure 7.2 illustrates a wage curve. The purpose of a wage curve is to show the relationship between (1) the value of the job as determined by one of the job evaluation methods and (2) the current average pay rates for the grades. Basically, you create a wage curve as you would any graph: in this case, by showing pay rates on the "Y" vertical axis and job value or difficulty on the "X" horizontal axis, and then plotting the corresponding points based on what you are paying now for each job. The wage line then becomes the target for wages or salary rates for all the jobs in each pay grade. The result, including rate ranges, is a wage structure.

Figure 7.2
Wage Curve and
Wage Structure

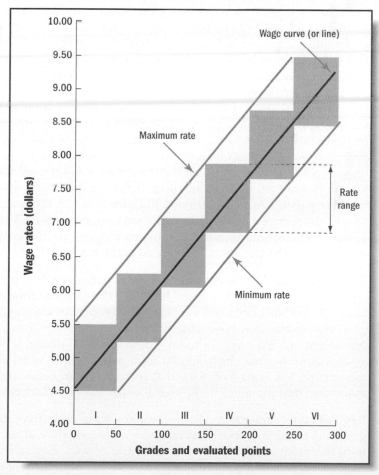

Step 5: Develop Rate Ranges

Finally, most employers do not just pay one rate for all jobs in a particular pay grade. Instead, they develop rate ranges for each grade. So, there might be 10 levels or steps and 10 corresponding pay rates within each pay grade. The employer may then fine-tune pay rates to account for any unique circumstances.

Pricing Managerial and Professional Jobs

For managerial and professional jobs, job evaluation provides only a partial answer to the question of pay. Managerial and professional jobs tend to emphasize nonquantifiable factors like judgment and problem solving more than do production and clerical jobs. There is also more of a tendency to pay managers and professionals based on their performance, on what competitors are paying, or on what they can do, rather than on intrinsic job demands such as working conditions. Studies provide some insights. One concluded that three main factors, *job complexity* (span of control, the number of divisions over which the executive has direct responsibility, and management level), the employer's *ability to pay* (total profit and rate of return), and the executive's *human capital* (educational level, field of study, work experience) accounted for most of executive compensation variance.[26] In another study, of large companies, labor market factors such as competitors' pay levels and whether the CEO was likely to be "raided" by other firms were as or more important than firm size and annual performance in determining CEO pay.[27]

However, the recent economic downturn exposed the enormous disconnect between what many executives were earning and their performance. President Obama appointed a "pay czar," to oversee executive compensation in the financial institutions in which the United States had taken an equity interest.[28] In general, this pay czar required them to deemphasize high salaries and big bonuses, substituting instead restricted stock (which the executives couldn't sell for at least two or three years). Now, even many nonbailout firms are moving toward such performance-based pay plans. At Ingersoll-Rand PLC, for instance, the company now grants stock to executives based on the company's performance over a 3-year period rather than 1 year.[29] There is no doubt that most employers, particularly large ones, are now linking executive pay more to financial performance.[30]

Research Note   The enormous risks apparently taken by some bonus-oriented employees in the past few years highlight the fact that incentives sometimes work too well. Evidence obtained via magnetic resonance imaging of people's brains suggests that money may have a bigger impact on behavior than previously thought. As one recent article notes, "in today's cash focused culture, where new research suggests that money may have similar influences on individual actions as drugs or sex, the unexpected impact of plans that reward certain behaviors with cash is perhaps more than first thought."[31] The global issues feature addresses a related issue.

Pay Package Elements   For a company's top executives, the compensation plan generally consists of four main components; base salary, short-term incentives, long-term incentives, and executive benefits and perks.[32] *Base salary* includes the obvious fixed compensation paid regularly as well as, often, guaranteed bonuses such as

"10% of pay at the end of the fourth fiscal quarter, regardless of whether the company makes a profit." *Short-term incentives* are usually paid in cash or stock for achieving short-term goals, such as year-to-year increases in sales revenue. Incentives equal 31% or more of a typical executive's base pay.[33] *Long-term incentives* include such things as stock options, which generally give the executive the right to purchase stock at a specific price for a specific period. They aim to encourage the executive to take actions that will drive up the price of the company's stock. Finally, special *executive benefits and perks* might include supplemental executive retirement plans, and health insurance without a deductible or coinsurance. Other popular executive perks include leased automobiles, automobile allowance, and free medical examinations.

Strategy and Executive Pay   As with any pay plans, those for professionals should make sense strategically. To accomplish this:

- Identify the company's strategic direction, and translate this into specific business goals.
- List the skills and competencies your professional employees should have and the behaviors they should exhibit to accomplish these goals.
- Evaluate the extent to which the existing pay plan produces these skills, competencies, and behaviors. (For example, ask, Does it motivate employees to achieve their goals?)[34]
- Finally, design and implement the new pay plan.[35]

CURRENT TRENDS IN COMPENSATION

How employers pay employees has been evolving.[36] This section looks at three important trends: competency-based pay, broadbanding, and board oversight of executive pay.[37]

Competency- and Skill-Based Pay

Some question whether job evaluation's tendency to slot jobs into narrow cubbyholes ("Machinist I," "Machinist II," and so on) might not actually be counterproductive in today's high-performance work systems. Systems like these depend on flexible, multiskilled job assignments, and on high-involvement techniques like teamwork and participative decision making. There's thus no place here for employees who say, "That's not my job." Competency-based pay (and broadbanding, explained later) aims to avoid that problem.[38]

With competency- or skill-based pay, you pay the employee for the skills and knowledge he or she is capable of using rather than for the responsibilities of the job currently held.[39] *Competencies* are demonstrable personal characteristics such as knowledge, skills, and behaviors.

Why pay employees based on the skill levels they achieve, rather than based on the jobs they're assigned to? The answer is, to encourage the person to become more multiskilled. With more companies organizing around project teams, you want employees to be able to rotate among jobs. Doing so requires having more skills.

Elements   Skill-based pay programs generally contain five elements. The employer *defines* specific required skills and chooses a *method* for tying the person's pay to his or her skill competencies. A *training* system lets employees seek and acquire skills. There is a formal competency *testing* system. And, the work is *designed* in such a way that employees can easily move among jobs of varying skill levels.

In practice, competency-based pay usually comes down to pay for knowledge or skill-based pay.[40] Pay-for-knowledge plans reward employees for learning organizationally relevant knowledge; for instance, you might pay a new server more once he or she memorizes the menu. With skill-based pay, the employee earns more after developing organizationally relevant skills—Microsoft pays programmers more as they master the skill of writing new programs.

Broadbanding

Most firms end up with pay plans that slot jobs into classes or grades, each with its own vertical pay rate range. For example, the U.S. government's pay plan consists of 18 main grades (GS-1 to GS-18), each with its own pay range. For an employee whose job falls in one of these grades, the pay range for that grade dictates his or her minimum and maximum salary.

The question is, how wide should the salary grades be, in terms of the number of job evaluation points they include? There is a downside to having narrow grades. For instance, if you want someone whose job is in grade 2 to fill in for a time in a job that happens to be in grade 1, it's difficult to reassign that person without lowering his or her salary. Similarly, if you want the person to learn about a job that happens to be in grade 3, the employee might object without a corresponding raise to grade 3 pay. Traditional grade pay plans thus breed inflexibility.

That is why some firms are broadbanding their pay plans. Broadbanding means collapsing salary grades and ranges into just a few wide ranges, or bands, each of which contains a relatively wide range of jobs and salary levels. Figure 7.3 illustrates this. It combines the company's previous six pay grades into two broadbands.

What to Broadband   The employer may create broadbands for all its jobs, or for specific groups such as managers or professionals. The pay rate range of each broadband is relatively large, since it ranges from the minimum pay of the lowest grade the firm merged into the broadband up to the maximum pay of the highest merged grade. For the jobs that fall in each broadband, there is therefore a much wider range of pay rates. You can move employees from job to job within the broadband more easily, without worrying about the employees moving outside the relatively narrow rate range associated with a traditional narrow pay grade. Broadbanding therefore breeds flexibility. The *Global Issues* box explains some issues in paying expatriate employees.

Board Oversight of Executive Pay

For 15 years, the board of directors of UnitedHealth Group Inc. supported its CEO with almost $2 billion in compensation. Then the board ousted him, allegedly

Figure 7.3
Broadbanded structure and how it relates to traditional pay grades and ranges

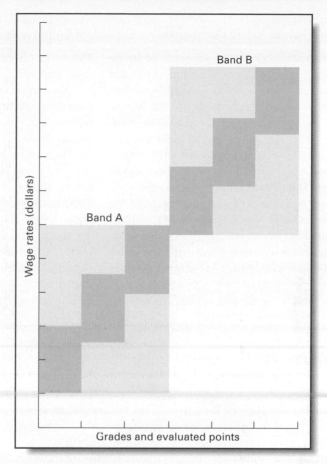

because, as the *Wall Street Journal* put it, "his explanation for a pattern of unusually well-timed stock option grants didn't add up."[41]

There are various reasons why boards are clamping down on executive pay. The Financial Accounting Standards Board now requires that most public companies recognize as an expense the fair value of the stock options they grant.[42] The Securities and Exchange Commission (SEC) now requires filing more compensation-related information. The Sarbanes-Oxley Act makes executives personally liable, under certain conditions, for corporate financial oversight lapses.[43] The net result is that lawyers specializing in executive pay suggest that boards of directors need to be fastidious about setting executive pay today. Among the questions they should ask:

- Is our compensation committee being appropriately advised?
- Do our procedures demonstrate diligence and independence? (This demands careful deliberations and records.)
- Is our committee appropriately communicating its decisions? How will shareholders react?[44]

With dramatically different costs of living among countries, compensating expatriate managers is never easy. Most North American companies use what experts call the *balance sheet method* to compute the expatriate manager's pay. The aim here is to make the person's compensation consistent with what it would have been if he or she had stayed home. The person's base salary reflects the salaries in his or her home country. Then, the employer adds supplements to cover things like housing costs, tax differences, and other living expenses (such as private schools for the person's children).[45] At the other extreme, some employers pay the manager based on what people are earning in the host country. This is the "host country–based" or "going-rate" approach.

Each approach has pros and cons. The balance sheet approach makes it easier to repatriate employees (who might object to having their salaries slashed just because they're moving from high-cost New York to low-cost Bangalore). On the other hand, paying the expatriate more can lead to tensions between the manager and his or her host-country peers. The host country–based approach has the advantage of integrating the expatriate better, since he or she is earning what his or her host country peers are earning. But it can mean reducing an employee's salary, hardly a practical option.

INCENTIVE PLANS

Many—perhaps most—employees don't just earn a salary or hourly wage. They also earn some type of incentive. This section addresses some popular **incentive plans.** *Individual incentive programs* give performance-based pay to individual employees. *Team-based incentives* of course aim to incentivize work teams. *Variable pay* refers to group pay plans that tie payments to productivity or to some other measure of the firm's profitability.[46]

Traditionally, all incentive plans are "pay-for-performance" plans. They pay all employees based on the employee's performance. Roughly 70% of employees feel that their firms' incentive plans are ineffective, so designing the plan right is paramount.[47] Several incentive plan examples follow.

Piecework Plans

Piecework is the oldest incentive plan and still the most common. The person is paid a "piece rate" for each unit he or she produces. Thus, if Tom Smith gets $0.40 apiece for finding addresses on the Web, then he would make $40 for finding 100 a day and $80 for 200.

Team or Group Incentive Plans

Companies often want to pay groups (rather than individuals) on an incentive basis, such as when they want to encourage teamwork. There are several ways to do so. Most firms pay all team members the same incentive, based on the team's overall performance. However, a group incentive plan's main drawback is that each worker's rewards don't necessarily reflect his or her own efforts. So if the person decides to relax and let others carry the load, the group plan may be less effective than an individual plan.[48] Therefore, some plans endeavor to pay team members somewhat different amounts, based on their individual efforts.

Incentives for Managers and Executives

Managers play a central role in influencing divisional and corporate profitability, and most firms therefore put considerable thought into how to reward them.[49] For CEOs, salary generally accounts for less than 25% of total direct compensation on average, with salary 18% of total compensation, bonus 24%, and long term incentives 58%.

Most managers get short-term bonuses and long-term incentives in addition to salary.[50] For firms offering short-term incentive plans, virtually all—96%—provide those incentives in cash. For those offering long-term incentive plans, about 48% offer stock options. These aim to motivate and reward management for long-term corporate growth in shareholder value. The size of the bonus (in terms of percentage of salary) is usually greater for top-level executives.

Stock Options The stock option is one incentive that companies use for managerial (and other) employees. A **stock option** is the right to purchase a specific number of shares of company stock at a specific price during a specific period. The executive hopes to profit by exercising his or her option to buy the shares in the future, but at today's price. The firm's profitability and growth affect its stock price, and because the executive can affect these factors, the stock option can be an incentive.

The chronic problem with stock options is that firms used them to reward managers for even lackluster performance. There is therefore a trend toward using new types of options, tied more explicitly to performance goals. For example, with *premium priced options*, the exercise price is higher than the stock's closing price on the date of the grant, so the executive can't profit from the options until the stock makes significant gains.[51]

The past few years have seen pressures both for and against awarding stock options. Until recently, most companies did not treat stock options as an expense. This could improve a company's reported financial performance by making expenses look less than they really were. Today, "The fact that this is now 'costing' them something will mean that they will have to do more of the cost/benefit analysis to see which design will give them the best return for their dollar."[52] Furthermore, many blame stock options for contributing to the exorbitant risks many companies took, and to corporate scandals, in which some executives manipulated the dates they received their options to maximize their returns. And the enormous paychecks some financial firms' professionals earned leading up to the economic turmoil of 2008–2009 prompted many government agencies and others to insist that these institutions deemphasize cash rewards and emphasize stock options.

In any case, when the market plummets, employers scramble to sweeten their stock option plans.[53] When stock markets dropped in 2008–2009, Google announced it would allow employees to exchange underwater options for stock, a decision that earned Googlers over $2 billion by year's end.[54]

Sarbanes-Oxley   The Sarbanes-Oxley Act of 2002 affects how employers formulate their executive incentive programs. Congress passed Sarbanes-Oxley to inject a higher level of responsibility into executives' and board members' decisions. It makes them personally liable for violating their fiduciary responsibilities to their shareholders. The act also requires that CEOs and CFOs of a public company repay any bonuses, incentives, or equity-based compensation received from the company during the 12-month period following the issuance of a financial statement that the company must restate due to material noncompliance with a financial reporting requirement as a result of misconduct.[55]

Incentives for Salespeople

Most companies pay their salespeople a combination of salary and commissions, usually with a sizable salary component. Typical is a 70% base salary/30% incentive mix. This cushions both the downside risk from the salesperson's point of view and limits the risk that the rewards would be too great from the firm's point of view.[56]

Setting effective quotas is an art.[57] Questions to ask include, Are quotas communicated to the sales force within 1 month of the start of the period? Does the sales force know how their quotas are set? Do you combine bottom–up information (like account forecasts) with top–down requirements (like the company business plan)? And, are quotas stable through the performance period?[58] One expert suggests the following as a rule of thumb as to whether the sales incentive plan is effective: 75% or more of the sales force achieving quota or better; 10% of the sales force achieving higher performance level (than previously); 5% to 10% of the sales force achieving below-quota performance and receiving development coaching.[59]

An Example: Auto Dealers   Commission rates vary by industry, but a look at how auto dealers set their salesperson's commission rates provides some insights. Compensation for car salespeople ranges from a high of 100% commission to a small base salary with commission accounting for most compensation. Commission is generally based on the net profit on the car delivered to the buyer. This promotes the desired behavior. For example, it encourages salespeople to hold firm on the retail price and to push "after-sale products" like floor mats. And, for helping sell slow-moving vehicles, the salesperson may get a "spiff"—an extra incentive.[60]

Non-tangible and Recognition-Based Awards

Studies show that recognition has a positive impact on performance, either alone or in conjunction with financial rewards.[61] It's therefore not surprising that in one survey, 78% of CEOs and 58% of HR vice presidents said their firms were using performance recognition programs.[62] At the financial planning firm American Skandia, customer service reps who exceed standards receive a plaque, a $500 check, their story on the internal Web site, and a dinner for them and their teams.[63] One survey of 235 managers found that the most-used rewards to motivate employees (down from most used to least) included:[64]

- Employee recognition
- Gift certificates

- Cash rewards
- Merchandise incentives
- Training programs
- Work/life benefits
- Individual travel
- Sweepstakes

Online Award Programs

If there's a downside to recognition programs, it's that they're expensive to administer. Many firms now therefore use online incentive firms to expedite the whole process. Management consultant Hewitt Associates uses www.bravanta.com to help its managers more easily recognize exceptional employee service with special awards. Other incentive/recognition sites include sales-driver.com and kudoz.com.

Merit Pay as an Incentive

Merit pay, or a **merit raise,** is any salary increase awarded to an employee based on his or her individual performance. Unlike a bonus, it usually becomes part of the employee's base salary, whereas a bonus is a one-time payment. Although the term *merit pay* can apply to the incentive raises given to any employee, the term is more often used with professional, office, and clerical employees.

Merit pay has advocates and detractors. Advocates argue that rewards tied directly to performance can motivate performance. Detractors say it can undermine teamwork, and that, since the merit pay typically depends on the performance appraisal, unfair appraisals lead employees to perceive pay as unfair, too.

The important thing is to differentiate between top and mediocre performers. As the consulting firm Mercer puts it, "in this less than robust economic environment . . . top-performing employees are an organization's best competitive weapon and [employers are] rewarding them accordingly."[65]

Profit-Sharing Plans

In a **profit-sharing plan,** most employees receive a share of the company's annual profits. Research on the effectiveness of such plans is sketchy. One study concludes that there is "ample" evidence that profit-sharing plans boost productivity, but that their effect on profits is insignificant, once you factor in their costs.[66] Although there are many such plans, cash plans are the most popular. Here, employees receive, say, 15% to 20% of profits as profit shares at regular intervals.

Employee Stock Ownership Plan

Employee stock ownership plans (ESOPs) are company-wide plans in which a corporation contributes shares of its own stock—or cash to purchase such stock—to a trust established to purchase shares of that stock for employees. The firm generally makes these contributions annually in proportion to total employee compensation, with a limit of 15% of compensation. The trust holds the stock in individual employee accounts. It then distributes it to employees upon retirement (or other separation), assuming the person has worked long enough to earn ownership of the stock. (Traditional stock options, as discussed elsewhere in this chapter, go directly to the employees individually.[67])

ESOPs have several advantages. The corporation receives a tax deduction equal to the fair market value of the shares that it transfers to the trustee. It can also claim an income tax deduction for dividends paid on stock the ESOP owns. Employees are not taxed until they receive a distribution from the trust, usually at retirement when they usually have a reduced tax rate. And the **Employee Retirement Income Security Act (ERISA)** allows a firm to borrow against employee stock held in trust. The employer can then repay the loan in pretax rather than in after-tax dollars, another ESOP tax incentive. ESOPs may also encourage employees to develop a sense of commitment to the firm.[68]

Broad-Based Stock Awards   For many years, employers have awarded stock options directly to all or most employees ("broad-based stock options") as part of the employers' profit-sharing incentive plans. Recently, a number of large companies including Microsoft and Charles Schwab announced they were discontinuing distributing stock options to most employees. Some, including Microsoft, are instead awarding stock. With companies now having to show the options as an expense when awarded, they apparently feel awarding stock instead of stock options is a more direct way to link pay to performance.[69]

Gainsharing Plans

There are many **gainsharing plans,** the aim of which is to encourage improved employee productivity by sharing resulting financial gains with employees. The oldest is the **Scanlon plan,** an incentive plan developed many years ago by Joseph Scanlon, a union official.[70] Other popular gainsharing plans include the Rucker and Improshare plans.

Features   Scanlon plans illustrate the five features that most gainsharing plans share.[71] The first is a *philosophy of cooperation.* This philosophy assumes that managers and workers should rid themselves of the "us" and "them" attitudes that normally inhibit employees from developing a sense of ownership. Instead, everyone cooperates because they all understand that economic rewards require cooperation.

A second feature is *identity.* This means that to focus employee efforts, management must articulate the company's mission, and employees must understand how the business operates in terms of customers, prices, and costs. *Competence* is a third basic feature. Employees must be trained and competent.[72]

The fourth feature is the *involvement system.*[73] Employees present productivity-improving suggestions to departmental committees, which transmit the valuable ones to the executive-level committee. The latter then decides whether to implement the suggestions.

The fifth feature of the plan is the *sharing of benefits formula*. For example, if a suggestion is implemented and successful, all employees might share in 75% of the savings.

Earnings-at-Risk Pay Plans

In an *earnings-at-risk* pay plan, employees agree to put a portion of their normal pay (say, 6%) at risk (they forego it) if they don't meet their goals, in return for the possibility of obtaining a much larger bonus (say, 12%), if they do exceed them. If they simply meet their goals, the employees get their full (100%) pay.

Incentives at Nucor Corporation

Nucor Corp. is the largest steel producer in the United States; it also has the highest productivity, highest wages, and lowest labor cost per ton in the American steel industry.[74]

Nucor employees can earn bonuses of 100% or more of base salary. All participate in one of four performance-based incentive plans. With the *production incentive plan*, plant operating and maintenance employees and supervisors get weekly bonuses based on their workgroup's productivity. The *department manager incentive* pays department managers annual incentive bonuses based mostly on the ratio of net income to dollars of assets employed for their division. With the *professional and clerical bonus plan*, employees who are not in one of the two previous plans get bonuses based on their division's net income return on assets. Finally, under the *senior officers' incentive plan*, Nucor senior managers (whose base salaries are lower than those in comparable firms) get bonuses based on Nucor's annual overall percentage of net income to stockholder's equity.[75]

HRIS and Productivity

Incentives are becoming more complicated. For one thing, as we've seen, more employees—not just salespeople—now get incentives. Furthermore, the range of behaviors for which employers pay incentives is now quite broad, from better service to cutting costs to answering more calls per hour.[76]

Tracking performance of dozens or hundreds of measures like these and then computing individual employees' incentives is time consuming. Several companies such as Incentive Systems Inc. therefore provide Enterprise Incentive Management (EIM) systems. As one expert says, "EIM software automates the planning, calculation, modeling, and management of incentive compensation plans, enabling companies to align their employees with corporate strategy and goals." [77]

Employers also increasingly use the Web to support their sales and other incentive programs. For example, SalesDriver, in Maynard, Massachusetts, runs Web-based sales performance–based incentive programs. Using the SalesDriver template, the sales manager can select from a catalog of 1,500 reward items, and award these to sales and marketing reps for meeting quotas for things like lead generation and total sales.[78]

EMPLOYEE BENEFITS

We can define **benefits** as indirect monetary and nonmonetary payments an employee receives for continuing to work for the company. Benefits include things like time off with pay, health insurance, and child care.

Most full-time employees in the United States receive benefits. Virtually all employers—99%—offer some health insurance coverage.[79] In one survey, 78% of employees cited health-care benefits as most crucial to retaining them; 75% cited compensation. But the survey found that only 34% are satisfied with their health-care benefits.[80]

Benefits are a major expense for most employers. Employee benefits account for about one-third of wages and salaries (or about 28% of total payrolls), with legally required benefits the biggest single benefit cost, followed by health insurance.[81]

There are many benefits and various ways to classify them. We'll classify benefits as pay for time not worked, insurance benefits, retirement benefits, and employee services benefits.

Pay for Time Not Worked

Supplemental pay benefits, or pay for time not worked, are typically one of an employer's most expensive benefits because of all the time off that employees receive. Common time-off-with-pay benefits include holidays, vacations, sick leave, maternity leave, and unemployment insurance payments.

Unemployment Insurance   All states have unemployment insurance or compensation acts. These provide for weekly benefits if a person is unable to work through some fault other than his or her own. The benefits derive from an unemployment tax on employers that can range from 0.1% to 5% of taxable payroll in most states.[82] States each have their own unemployment laws, which follow federal guidelines. An organization's unemployment tax reflects its experience with personnel terminations.

Strictly speaking, only employees, dismissed through no fault of their own are eligible for unemployment. Thus, strictly speaking, a worker fired for chronic lateness has no legitimate claim to benefits. But in practice, many managers are lackadaisical toward protecting their employers against unwarranted claims. Therefore, employers spend thousands of dollars more per year on unemployment taxes than would be necessary if they protected themselves—for instance, by keeping careful records of absences.[83]

Vacations and Holidays   On average, American workers get about 9 days of leave after one year's employment. Days off rises to about 11 after 3 years, 14 after 5 years, and 16 after 10 years. The average number of annual vacation days varies around the world. For example, vacation allowances vary from 6 days in Mexico to 10 days in Japan, and 25 in France. In the United States, the number of paid holidays similarly varies from employer to employer, from a minimum of about 5 to 13 or more.

Sick Leave   Sick leave provides pay to employees when they are out of work because of illness. Most sick leave policies grant full pay for a specified number of permissible sick days, usually up to about 12 per year. The sick days often accumulate at the rate of approximately 1 day per month of service.

The problem is that many employees (in the eyes of some employers) take advantage of sick leave by using it whether they are sick or not.[84] Tactics employers utilize to reduce this problem include:

- Using *pooled paid leave* (or paid time off, or "PTO") plans. These plans—which lump together sick leave, vacation, and holidays into a single leave pool—have grown in popularity.
- Buying back unused sick leave at the end of the year (although this can encourage sick employees to come to work despite illness).
- Holding lotteries in which only employees with perfect attendance can participate to win a cash prize.
- Aggressively investigating all unplanned absences, for instance, by calling the absent employees at their homes.

FMLA   Sick leave policy depends to some extent on the Family and Medical Leave Act of 1993 (FMLA). Among its provisions, the law stipulates that:

1. Private employers of 50 or more employees must provide eligible employees up to 12 weeks of unpaid leave for their own serious illness, the birth or adoption of a child, or the care of a seriously ill child, spouse, or parent.
2. Employers may require employees to take any unused paid sick leave or annual leave as part of the 12-week leave.
3. Employees taking leave are entitled to receive health benefits while they are on unpaid leave under the same terms as when they were on the job.
4. Employers must guarantee most employees the right to return to their previous or equivalent position with no loss of benefits at the end of the leave.[85]

Severance Pay   Many employers provide **severance pay**—a onetime separation payment—when terminating an employee. Others provide "bridge" severance pay by keeping employees (especially managers) on the payroll for several months. About half of employers surveyed give white-collar and exempt employees one week of severance pay per year of service, and about one-third do the same for blue-collar workers. It is common to award severance pay as part of a reduction in workforce. It is less common to award it when dismissing someone for poor performance. It is uncommon to pay severance when employees quit or are fired for cause.[86]

Severance payments are a humanitarian gesture and good public relations. In addition, most managers expect employees to give them at least 1 or 2 weeks' notice if they plan to quit; it is therefore appropriate (and in some states mandatory) to provide at least one pay period's severance pay if an employee is terminated. Such payments can also reduce the possibility that a terminated employee will litigate.

Things to keep in mind when designing the severance plan include:

- List the situations for which the firm will pay severance, such as layoffs resulting from reorganizations. Indicate that management will determine action regarding other situations, and reserve the right to terminate or alter the policy.
- Require signing of a waiver/general release prior to paying any severance, absolving the employer from employment-related liability. The signing of the release must be knowing and voluntary, and there are other legal requirements.
- Remember that the employer must make any severance payments equitably.[87]

The Worker Adjustment and Retraining ("plant closing") Act of 1989 requires covered employers to give employees 60 days' written notice of plant closures or mass layoffs (but not to necessarily award severance pay).

Insurance Benefits

Workers' Compensation   **Workers' compensation** laws aim to provide sure, prompt income, and medical benefits to work-related employee accident victims or their dependents, regardless of fault. Every state has its own workers' compensation law, with some offering their own insurance programs. However, most require employers purchase workers' compensation insurance through private state-approved insurance companies.

Workers' compensation benefits can be either monetary or medical. In the event of a worker's death or disablement, the person or his or her beneficiary receives a cash benefit based on prior earnings. Most states set a time limit—such as 500 weeks—for which an employee can receive benefits. In addition to these cash benefits, employers must furnish medical, surgical, and hospital services needed by the employee. For an injury or illness to be covered by workers' compensation, the employee need only prove that it arose while he or she was on the job. It does not matter that the employee may have been at fault or disregarded instructions.

Many, or most, workers' compensation claims are legitimate, but some are not. Supervisors should be aware of typical red flags of fraudulent claims, including vague accident details, minor accidents resulting in major injuries, and lack of witnesses.[88] Getting the employee back to work fast is essential.[89]

Hospitalization, Medical, and Disability Insurance

Health-care benefits top employees' desired benefits.[90] Most employers therefore offer their employees some type of hospitalization, medical, and disability insurance (see Table 7.3). Many offer membership in a health maintenance organization (HMO). The HMO is a medical organization consisting of specialists (surgeons, psychiatrists, etc.) operating out of a community-based health-care center. Preferred provider organizations (PPOs) let employees select providers (such as participating physicians) who agree to provide price discounts and submit to certain utilization controls, such as on the number of diagnostic tests that can be ordered.[91]

The Pregnancy Discrimination Act   The Pregnancy Discrimination Act (PDA) aims to prohibit sex discrimination based on "pregnancy, childbirth, or related medical conditions."

The act requires employers to treat women affected by pregnancy, childbirth, or related medical conditions the same as any employee not able to work, with respect to all benefits, including sick leave and health and medical insurance. For example, if an employer provides up to 26 weeks of temporary disability income to employees for all illnesses, it also must provide up to 26 weeks for pregnancy and childbirth.

COBRA Requirements   The ominously titled COBRA—Consolidated Omnibus Budget Reconciliation Act—requires most private employers to make available to terminated or retired employees and their families continued health benefits for a period of time, generally 18 months. A former employee who chooses to continue these benefits

Table 7.3 Percentage of Employers Offering Popular Health Benefits—Change Over Time

	Yes (%) 2005	Yes (%) 2009
Prescription drug program coverage	97	96
Dental insurance	95	96
Mail order prescription program	90	91
PPO (preferred provider organization)	87	81
Chiropractic coverage	56	80
Mental health insurance	72	80
Vision insurance	80	76
Employee assistance program	73	75
Medical spending account	80	71
Life insurance for dependants	67	58
HMO (health maintenance organization)	53	35

Source: Adapted from 2009 SHRM Employee Benefits Survey Report, p. 5.

during this period must pay for them, plus a small administrative fee.[92] In 2009, Congress passed legislation supporting unemployed workers' COBRA costs, temporarily.[93]

Take care with respect to informing employees of their COBRA rights. For example, you don't want a separated employee to be injured and come back and claim she didn't know she could have continued her insurance coverage. Therefore, when a new employee first becomes eligible for your company's insurance plan, he or she should receive and acknowledge an explanation of COBRA rights. More important, all employees separated from the company should sign a form acknowledging that they have received and understand their COBRA rights.[94]

Health-Care Insurance Cost Control   With health-care costs rising, containing those costs is a huge employer concern. As Figure 7.4 indicates, since 2004, health-care

Figure 7.4 U.S. Health-Care Cost Increases*

Total spending on health care	$1.9 trillion	$2.9 trillion	$4 trillion
% of GNP	16%	18%	20%
	2004	2009	2015

*Note: Figures for 2009 and 2015 estimated. Health-care costs rose 7.9% in 2004, about twice the rate of inflation, and are expected to rise at that rate through 2015.

Sources: Eric Perlmenter, "Controlling Health Care Costs," *Compensation & Benefits Review* (September/October 2002): 44; Victoria Colliver, "Health Care Costs Continue Double Digit Increase," *San Francisco Chronicle* (December 8, 2003); The National Coalition on Health Care, www.nchc.org/facts/cost.shtml, accessed March 21, 2007.

premiums have risen about 78% while inflation rose only 17%.[95] Cost control strategies include the following:[96]

- **Cost-Containment Specialists** Many use cost-containment specialists who help employers reduce their health-care costs. For example, they may use their contacts to help employers obtain the best PPO coverage for their needs.
- **Online Administration** Other big savings come from automating health-care plan administration, for instance, by requiring online enrollment by employees.[97]
- **Deductibles** Other firms are offering plans with high deductibles and copayments for individual coverage.[98] One study found that about 13% of surveyed employers had reduced subsidized health benefits for their future retirees.[99]
- **Outsourcing** For example, 84% of firms in one survey said they were outsourcing employee assistance and counseling, and 53% were outsourcing health-care benefits administration.[100]
- **Wellness Programs** Medical experts believe that controlling health risks can reduce illnesses and health-care costs.[101] Almost all large employers (and many small ones) therefore offer some preventive services as benefits. *Clinical prevention* programs include things like mammograms, immunizations, and routine checkups.[102] Top wellness programs include obesity management, stress management, senior health improvement, and tobacco cessation programs.[103] Incentives (even $50 to 100) can boost participation in wellness programs.[104]
- **Claims Audits** Many employers pay out thousands or millions of dollars in erroneous health claims. The industry standard for percentage of claims dollars paid in error is 1%; in two recent years the *actual* percentage of claims dollars paid in error were 3.5% and 3.3%. Setting standards for errors, and then aggressively auditing the claims paid, may be the most direct way to reduce employer health-care expenses.[105] One simple method is to ensure that any dependents enrolled are actually eligible for coverage.[106]
- **Medical Tourism** Here employers encourage employees to have some nonurgent medical procedures done overseas. Hospitals in Brazil or Malaysia may charge half what a U.S. hospital would for shoulder surgery, for instance. The key question is quality of care.[107]
- **Technology** Experts hope that the approximately $19 billion in health information technology funding in the federal government's 2009 stimulus package will also help employers reduce health-care benefit costs, by automating their paper-based systems.[108]
- **Mini Plans** Some employers are offering limited-benefit health-care insurance plans. Unlike typical health-care plans with lifetime coverage limits of $1 million or more, these new mini plans have annual caps of about $2,000 to 10,000 per year. The advantage is that the premiums are correspondingly lower as well.[109]

Long-Term Care

Today, there are many types of long-term care—care to support older persons in their old age—for which employers can provide insurance benefits. For example, adult day-care facilities offer social and recreational activities. Assisted-living facilities offer shared housing and supervision for those who can't function independently. Home care is care received at home from a nurse, an aide, or another specialist.

Retirement Benefits

Social Security   There are actually three types of Social Security benefits. First are the familiar *retirement benefits*, which provide an income if an employee insured under the Social Security Act retires at age 62 or thereafter. Second, survivor's or *death benefits* provide monthly payments to dependents regardless of the employee's age at death, again assuming the employee was insured under the Social Security Act. Finally, *disability payments* provide monthly payments to an employee and his or her dependents if the employee becomes disabled for work and meets specified work requirements.

"Full retirement age"—the usual age for receiving your full Social Security benefit—used to be 65. However, full retirement age to collect Social Security rose gradually over the years. It's now 67 for those born in 1960 or later. Social Security benefits are funded by a tax on earnings that the employer and employee share. As of 2010, the maximum amount of someone's earnings subject to Social Security tax was $106,800.[110] Employer and employee each paid 7.65%.[111]

Pension Plans   Pensions provide income to individuals in their retirement, and just over half of full-time workers participate in some type of pension plan at work.

We can classify pension plans in three ways: contributory versus noncontributory plans; qualified versus nonqualified plans; and defined contribution versus defined benefit plans.[112] The employee contributes to the contributory pension plan while the employer makes all contributions to the noncontributory pension plan. Employers derive certain tax benefits (such as tax deductions) for contributing to qualified pension plans (they are "qualified" for preferred tax treatment by the IRS); nonqualified pension plans get less favorable tax treatment.

With **defined benefit plans,** the employee's pension is specified or "defined" ahead of time. Here the person knows ahead of time the pension benefits he or she will receive. How is this possible? There is usually a formula that ties the person's pension to (1) a percentage of (2) the person's preretirement pay (for instance, to an average of his or her last 5 years of employment), multiplied by (3) the number of years he or she worked for the company. Due to tax law changes and other reasons, defined benefit plans now represent a minority of pension benefit plans.[113]

Defined contribution plans specify ("define") what contribution the employee and employer will make to the employee's retirement or savings fund. Here, the contribution is defined, not the pension. With a *defined benefit* plan, the employee can compute what his or her retirement benefits will be upon retirement. With a *defined contribution* plan, the person only knows for sure what he or she is contributing to the pension plan; the actual pension will depend on the amounts contributed to the fund *and* on the success of the retirement fund's investment earnings. Defined contribution plans are popular among employers because of their relative ease of administration, favorable tax treatment, and other factors. **Portability**—making it easier for employees who leave the firm prior to retirement to take their accumulated pension funds with them—is also easier with defined contribution plans.

401(k) Plans   The 401(k) plan is one defined contribution plan. Under the 401(k) plan (based on Section 401[k] of the Internal Revenue Code), employees have the employer place a portion of their compensation, which would otherwise be paid in cash, into a company profit-sharing or stock bonus plan, or into investments (such as mutual funds) the employee selects. This results in a pretax reduction in salary, so the employee isn't taxed on those set-aside dollars until after he or she retires (or removes the money from the pension fund). Some employers also match a portion of what the employee contributes to the 401(k) plan.

The employer has a fiduciary responsibility to its employees, and must monitor the pension fund and its administration.[114] Under the Pension Protection Act of 2006, employers who sponsor plans that facilitate both *automatic enrollment* and allocation to *default investments* (such as age-appropriate "lifestyle funds") reduce their compliance burdens.[115]

As the downturn intensified in 2008–2009, more employees began making "hardship withdrawals" from their 401(k) plans (on which no taxes are due, for a time).[116] Recent stories, like that of a 47-year-old engineer, suggest caution. His adviser told him that, "if we saved very aggressively, I might be able to retire in my early 70s." Such experiences underscore the need for employee education, or at least automatically directing funds into (relatively) prudent investments.[117]

Cash Balance Pension Plans   One problem with defined benefits plans is that to get your maximum pension, you generally must stay with your employer until you retire—the formula, recall, takes the number of years you work into consideration. With defined contribution plans, your pension is more portable—you can leave with it at any time, perhaps rolling it over into your next employer's pension plan. Without delving into all the details, *cash balance* plans are a hybrid; they have a defined benefit plan's more predictable benefits, but they have the portability advantages of defined contribution plans.[118]

ERISA   The Employee Retirement Income Security Act (ERISA) aims to protect the pensions of workers and to stimulate pension plan growth. Before enactment of ERISA, pension plans often failed to deliver expected benefits to employees. Various reasons, such as business failure and inadequate funding, could result in employees losing their expected pensions.

Vesting   Under ERISA, pension rights must be **vested**—guaranteed to the employee—under one of two minimum vesting schedules (employers can allow funds to vest faster if they wish). With *cliff vesting*, the period for acquiring a nonforfeitable right in employer matching contributions (if any) is 3 years. So, the employee must have nonforfeitable rights to these funds by the end of 3 years. With the second option (*graded vesting*) pension plan participants must receive nonforfeitable rights to the matching contributions as follows: 20% after 2 years, and then 20% for each succeeding year, with a 100% nonforfeitable right by the end of 6 years.

Among other things, the Pension Benefits Guarantee Corporation (PBGC) was established under ERISA to ensure that pensions meet their obligations should a plan fail.[119] However, the PBGC guarantees only defined benefit, not defined contribution plans. Furthermore, it will only pay an individual a pension of up to a maximum of about $54,000 per year for someone 65 years of age with a plan terminating in 2010.[120] So high-income workers may still end up with reduced pensions if their plan fails.

Employee Services and Family-Friendly/Work-Life Benefits

Although an employer's time off, insurance, and retirement benefits account for the main part of its benefits costs, many employers also provide a range of services. These include personal services (such as legal and personal counseling), job-related services (such as subsidized child care), educational subsidies, and executive perquisites ("perks" such as company cars and planes for executives).

For example, **Employee Assistance Programs (EAPs)** provide counseling and advisory services, such as personal legal and financial services, child- and elder-care referrals, adoption assistance, and mental health counseling.[121] EAPs are increasingly popular, with more than 60% of larger firms offering them. Most employers contract for the necessary services with vendors such as Magellan Health Services and CIGNA Behavioral Health.[122]

Some employers offer employees full or partial *college tuition* reimbursement. These may help employers attract applicants, retain employees who might otherwise leave, and provide promotable employees with the educations they need to move up. However, that same enhanced mobility makes it easier for employees to leave. Two researchers studied the U.S. Navy's tuition assistance program. Tuition assistance usage significantly decreased the probability of staying in the Navy.[123]

Family-Friendly Benefits   Companies today also offer *"family-friendly"* (or "work-life") benefits. For example, software giant SAS Institute offers preschool child-care centers, a gym, a full-time eldercare consultant, 3 weeks' paid vacation, a flexible ("flextime") work schedule, and a standard 35-hour workweek.[124] At least until the recent recession, surveys reported that workers felt they were working too much and putting too little time into "other things in life that really matter." In response, employers such as Hartford Financial Services Group were handing out *time off* as a performance reward; giving new hires more vacation; and offering employees more long weekends.[125]

More employers, such as Canadian financial services company CIBC, are also offering *emergency child-care benefits*, for instance, for when a young child's regular babysitter is a no-show.[126] Similarly, with the average age rising, about 120 million Americans now care for (or have cared for) an adult relative or friend. Employers therefore increasingly offer *adult-care support*, including counseling and adult day-care centers.[127] Some employers enrich their *parental leave plans* to make it more attractive for mothers to return from maternity leave, for instance, offering meaningful jobs with reduced travel and hours.[128]

Why Work-Life Benefits?   For the employer, programs like these produce advantages, not just costs. For example, sick family members and health problems such as depression account for much of the sick leave employees take. Employers can reduce these absences with programs that provide advice on issues like eldercare referrals, and personal counseling.[129] Work-life benefits may improve a firm's bottom line in some less-obvious ways. One study found that when employees experienced work–family conflict, they were more likely to exhibit hostility at work.[130]

Workplace Flexibility   As anyone who has flown next to someone tapping away on their laptop knows, employees are increasingly conducting business from nontraditional settings, using technology like BlackBerry-type devices.[131] **Workplace flexibility** means arming employees with the information technology tools they need to get their jobs done wherever they are. For example, Capital One Financial Corp. has its Future of Work program. Some Capital One employees received mobile technology tools such as wireless access laptops and BlackBerry-type cell phone devices. The program seems to have led to about a 41% increase in overall workplace satisfaction, a 31% reduction in time needed to get input from peers, and a 53% increase in those who say their workplace enhances group productivity.[132]

Flexible Benefits

Employees tend to differ in what benefits they want and need. Flexible benefits plans are thus popular.

Flexible benefits plans (also called cafeteria plans) enable employees to spend their benefits allowances on a choice of benefits options. The idea is to let the employee design his or her own benefit package, subject to two constraints. First, the employer must limit total cost for each person's package. Second, each benefit plan must include certain nonoptional items, including, for example, Social Security and unemployment insurance.

Benefits and Employee Leasing

Employee leasing firms (also known in various versions as *professional employer organizations*, or *human resource outsourcers*) arrange to have the employer's employees transferred to the employee leasing firm's payroll. The leasing firm becomes the legal employer and handles the employer's employee-related paperwork. This usually includes recruiting, hiring, paying tax liabilities (such as Social Security payments), and day-to-day details such as performance appraisals (with the onsite supervisor's assistance). However, it is with respect to benefits management that employee leasing is often most advantageous.

Getting insurance is often the biggest personnel problem smaller employers face. Even group rates can be high when only 20 or 30 employees are involved. This is where employee leasing comes in. The leasing firm is the legal employer of the client company's employees. Therefore, those employees are absorbed into a much larger insurable group (along with other clients' former employees). The employee leasing company can therefore often offer benefits smaller companies can't obtain at such a low cost.

Employee leasing is sometimes too good to be true. Some apparently successful employee leasing firms have gone out of business, in which case the original employer has to hire back all its employees and find new insurance for them. And when the employer views employees as strategic to its success, it may be reluctant to hand over hiring and training to others.

Benefits Web Sites

To reduce the costs of administering benefits, many employers enable employees to manage much of their own benefits changes (dependents, 401[k], and so on) themselves, via the employer's (or an outside vendor's) Web site.

Employers are adding new services to their benefits Web sites. In addition to offering things like self-enrollment, the insurance company USAA's Web site helps employees achieve better work–life balance. For example, click on the "today, I'm feeling . . ." menu. Here employees can respond to a list of words (such as "stressed"), and from there see suggestions for dealing with (in this case) stress.[133]

Strategy and HR   Employers should ask, what skills and performance does achieving our strategic goals require? And, do our compensation plans make sense in terms of the specific performances we expect from our employees?[134]

For example, cutting pay rates doesn't always make sense. For instance, despite competition from Walmart and other chains, supermarket chain Wegmans Food's pays above-average wages and provides all employees with free health coverage. Management's assumption is that "if we take care of our employees, they will take care of our customers."[135] Wegman's management decided that its competitive strategy was to compete with other grocery chains based on productivity and service. Its compensation strategy supports that competitive strategy, and it seems to be working. Their larger stores each average about $950,000 a week in sales, compared to the national average of about $361,564 for grocery stores. And Wegman's employee retention figures are well above national averages.

REVIEW

Summary

1. Establishing pay rates involves five steps: conduct salary survey, evaluate jobs, develop pay grades, use wage curves, and develop pay ranges.

2. Job evaluation aims to determine the relative worth of a job. It compares jobs to one another based on their content, usually defined in terms of compensable factors such as skills, effort, responsibility, and working conditions.

3. Most managers group similar jobs into wage or pay grades for pay purposes. These grades are composed of jobs of approximately equal difficulty or importance as determined by job evaluation.

4. For executive, managerial, and professional personnel, factors like performance and creativity take precedence over static factors such as working conditions. Market rates, performance, and incentives and benefits thus play a much greater role than does job evaluation here.

5. Broadbanding means collapsing salary grades and ranges into just a few wide levels or bands, each of which then contains a relatively wide range of jobs and salary levels.

6. Piecework is the oldest type of incentive plan; a worker is paid a piece rate for each unit he or she produces.

7. Profit sharing and the Scanlon plan are examples of organization-wide incentive plans. Here just about all employees can share in part of the company's profits.

8. Supplemental pay benefits provide pay for time not worked. They include unemployment insurance, vacation and holiday pay, and severance pay.

9. Insurance benefits are another type of employee benefit. Workers' compensation, for example, aims to ensure prompt income and medical benefits to work accident victims or their dependents, regardless of fault. Most employers also provide group life insurance and group hospitalization, accident, and disability insurance.

10. Social Security covers not only retirement benefits but also survivors and disability benefits. One of the critical issues in pension planning is vesting the money that employer and employee have placed in the latter's pension fund, which cannot be forfeited for any reason. ERISA ensures that pension rights become vested and protected after a reasonable amount of time.

KEY TERMS

- employee compensation
- Fair Labor Standards Act
- Equal Pay Act
- Civil Rights Act
- salary (or compensation) surveys
- job evaluation
- compensable factors
- ranking method
- wage curve
- incentive plan

- piecework
- stock option
- merit pay (merit raise)
- profit-sharing plan
- employee stock ownership plan (ESOP)
- Employee Retirement Income Security Act (ERISA)
- gainsharing plan
- Scanlon plan

- benefits
- severance pay
- workers' compensation
- defined benefit plan
- defined contribution plan
- portability
- vested
- Employee Assistance Program (EAP)
- workplace flexibility
- flexible benefits plan

DISCUSSION QUESTIONS

1. What is the difference between exempt and nonexempt jobs?

2. What is the relationship between compensable factors and job specifications?

3. What is merit pay? Do you think it's a good idea to award employees merit raises? Why or why not?

INDIVIDUAL AND GROUP ACTIVITIES

1. Working individually or in groups, conduct salary surveys for an entry-level accountant and an entry-level chemical engineer. What sources did you use, and what conclusions did you reach? If you were the HR manager for a local engineering firm, what would you recommend that you pay for each job?

2. Working individually or in groups, develop compensation policies for the teller position at a local bank. Assume that there are four tellers: two were hired in May and the other two were hired in December. The compensation policies should address the following: appraisals, raises, holidays, vacation

pay, overtime pay, method of pay, garnishments, and time cards.

3. Working individually or in groups, access relevant Web sites to determine what equitable pay ranges are for these jobs, chemical engineer, marketing manager, and HR manager, all with a bachelor's degree and 5 years of experience. Do so for the following cities: New York; San Francisco; Miami; and Washington, D.C. For each position in each city, what are the pay ranges and the average pay? Does geographical location affect the salaries of the different positions? How?

4. Working individually or in groups, use published (Internet or other) wage surveys to determine local area earnings for the following positions: file clerk I, accounting clerk II, and secretary V. How do the published figures compare with comparable jobs listed in your Sunday newspaper? What do you think accounts for any discrepancy?

5. Working individually or in groups, use the ranking method to evaluate the relative worth of the jobs listed in question 4.

6. Working individually or in groups, develop an incentive plan for the following positions: chemical engineer, plant manager, and used-car salesperson. What factors did you have to consider in reaching your conclusions?

7. A state university system in the Southeast instituted a Teacher Incentive Program for its faculty. Faculty committees within each of the university's colleges were told to award $5,000 raises (not bonuses) to about 40% of their faculty members based on how good a job they did teaching undergraduates and how many they taught per year. What are the potential advantages and pitfalls of such an incentive program? How well do you think it was accepted by the faculty? Do you think it had the desired effect?

8. Working individually or in groups, research and compile a list of the perks available to the following individuals: the head of your local airport, the president of your college or university, and the president of a large company in your area. Do they all have certain perks in common? What do you think accounts for any differences?

9. You are the HR consultant to a small business with about 40 employees. Now, the business offers 5 days of vacation, five paid holidays, and legally mandated benefits such as unemployment insurance payments. Develop a list of other benefits you believe the firm should offer, along with your reasons for suggesting them.

Case Incident

Salary Inequities at Acme Manufacturing

Joe Black was trying to figure out what to do about a salary problem he had in his plant. Black recently took over as president of Acme Manufacturing. The founder, Bill George, had been president for 35 years. The company was family owned and located in a small eastern Arkansas town. It had approximately 250 employees and was the largest employer in the community. Black was a member of the family that owned Acme, but he had never worked for the company prior to becoming president. He had an MBA and a law degree, plus 15 years of management experience with a large manufacturing organization, where he was senior vice president for human resources when he moved to Acme.

A short time after joining Acme, Black started to notice that there was considerable inequity in the pay structure for salaried employees. A discussion with the human resources director led him to believe that salaried employees' pay was very much a matter of individual bargaining with the past president. Hourly paid factory employees were not part of the problem because they were unionized with wages set by collective bargaining. An examination of the salaried payroll showed that there were 25 employees, ranging in pay from that of the president to that of the receptionist. A closer examination showed that 14 of the salaried employees were female. Three of these were frontline factory supervisors and one was the HR director. The other 10 were nonmanagement.

This examination also showed that the human resources director seemed underpaid, and that the three female supervisors were paid somewhat less than were any of the male supervisors. However, there were no similar supervisory jobs with both male and female job incumbents. When asked, the HR director said she thought the female supervisors may have been paid at a lower rate mainly because they were women, and perhaps Bill George did not think that women needed as much money because they had working husbands. However, she added that they may have been paid less because they supervised less-skilled employees than did male supervisors. Black was not sure that this was true.

The company from which Black had moved had a job evaluation system. Although he was thoroughly familiar and capable with this compensation tool, Black did not have time to do a job evaluation at Acme. Therefore, he decided to hire a compensation consultant from a nearby university to help him. Together they decided that all 25 salaried jobs should be in the job evaluation cluster, that they should use a ranking method, and that the job descriptions recently completed by the HR director were current and usable.

The job evaluation showed that there was no evidence of serious inequities or discrimination in the nonmanagement jobs. However, the HR director and the three female supervisors were underpaid relative to comparable male salaried employees.

Black was not sure what to do. He knew that if the underpaid female supervisors took the case to the local EEOC office, the company could be found guilty of sex discrimination and then have to pay back wages. He was afraid that if he gave these women an immediate salary increase large enough to bring them up to where they should be, the male supervisors would be upset, and the female supervisors might also want back pay. The HR director told Black that the female supervisors had never complained about pay differences, and they probably did not know the law to any extent.

The HR director agreed to take a sizable salary increase with no back pay, solving this part of the problem. Black believed he had four choices relative to the female supervisors:

1. To do nothing
2. To gradually increase the female supervisors' salaries
3. To increase their salaries immediately

4. To call the three supervisors into his office, discuss the situation with them, and jointly decide what to do ■

QUESTIONS

1. What would you do if you were Black? Why?
2. How do you think the company got into this situation in the first place?
3. Why would you suggest Black pursue the alternative you suggested?

Source: This case was prepared by Professor James C. Hodgetts of the Fogelman College of Business and Economics of the University of Memphis. All names are disguised. Used with permission.

Continuing Case

LearnInMotion.com: The Incentive Plan

Of all its HR programs, those relating to pay for performance and incentives are LearnInMotion. com's most fully developed. For one thing, the venture capital firm that funded it was very explicit about reserving at least 10% of the company's stock for employee incentives.

The agreement with the venture capital firm also included terms and conditions regarding LearnInMotion's stock option plan. The venture fund agreement included among its 500 or so pages a specific written agreement that LearnInMotion.com would have to send to each of its employees, laying out the details of the company's stock option plan. While there was some flexibility, the stock option plan details came down to this: (1) Employees would get stock options (the right to buy shares of LearnInMotion.com stock) at a price equal to 15% less than the venture capital fund paid for those shares when it funded LearnInMotion. com; (2) the shares will have a vesting schedule of 36 months, with one-third of the shares vesting

once the employee has completed 12 full months of employment with the company, and one third vesting upon successful completion of each of the following two full 12 months of employment; (3) if an employee leaves the company for any reason prior to his or her first full 12 months with the firm, the person is not eligible for no stock options; (4) if the person has stock options and leaves the firm for any reason, he or she must exercise the options within 90 days of the date of leaving the firm, or lose the right to exercise them.

The actual number of options an employee gets depends on the person's bargaining power and on how much Jennifer and Mel think the person brings to the company: The options granted generally range from options to buy 10,000 shares for some employees up to 50,000 shares for other employees, but this has not raised any questions to date. When a new employee signs on, he or she receives a letter of offer. This provides minimal details regarding the option plan; after the person has completed the 90-day introductory period, he or she receives the five-page document describing the stock option plan, which Jennifer or Mel, as well as the employee, signs.

Beyond that, the only company incentive plan is the one for the two salespeople. In addition to their respective salaries, both salespeople receive about 20% of any sales they bring in, whether those sales are from advertising banners or course listing fees. It's not clear to Jennifer and Mel whether this incentive is effective. Each salesperson gets a base salary regardless of what he or she sells (one gets about $50,000; the other, about $35,000). However, sales have simply not come up to the levels anticipated. Jennifer and Mel are not sure why. It could be that Internet advertising dried up in the recession. It could be that their own business model is no good, and there's not enough demand for their company's services. They may be charging too much or too little. It could be that the salespeople can't do the job due to inadequate skills or inadequate training. Or, of course, it could be the incentive plan. ("Or it could be all of the above," as Mel dejectedly said late one Friday evening.) They want to try to figure out what the problem is. They want you, their management consultants, to help them figure out what to do. Here's what they want you to do for them. ■

QUESTIONS AND ASSIGNMENTS

1. Up to this point, we've awarded only a tiny fraction of the total stock options available for distribution. Should we give anyone or everyone additional options? Why or why not?
2. Should we put other employees on a pay-for-performance plan that somehow links their monthly or yearly pay to company sales? Why or why not? If so, how should we do it?
3. Is there another incentive plan you think would work better for the salespeople? What is it?
4. On the whole, what do you think the sales problem is?

Experiential Exercise
Ranking the College's Administrators

Purpose: The purpose of this exercise is to give you experience in performing a job evaluation using the ranking method.

Required Understanding: You should be thoroughly familiar with the ranking method of job evaluation and obtain job descriptions for your college's dean, department chairperson, and your professor.

How to Set Up the Exercise/Instructions: Divide the class into groups of four or five students. The groups will perform a job evaluation

of the positions of dean, department chairperson, and professor using the ranking method.

1. Perform a job evaluation by ranking the jobs. You may use one or more compensable factors.
2. If time permits, a spokesperson from each group can put his or her group's rankings on the board. Did the groups end up with about the same results? How did they differ? Why do you think they differed? ■

Chapter 8

Ethics and Fair Treatment in Human Resource Management

- Ethics and Fair Treatment at Work
- What Shapes Ethical Behavior at Work?
- Ethics, Fair Treatment, and the Role of HR Management
- Employee Discipline and Privacy
- Managing Dismissals

When you finish studying this chapter, you should be able to:

■ Explain *what is meant by ethical behavior.*

■ Discuss *important factors that shape ethical behavior at work.*

■ Discuss *at least four specific ways in which HR management can influence ethical behavior at work.*

■ Exercise *fair disciplinary practices.*

■ Discuss *at least four important factors in managing dismissals effectively.*

INTRODUCTION

Shortly after the U.S. government spent $170 billion bailing out AIG a while ago, news spread that AIG was paying $165 million in bonuses to employees in the same department that had allegedly helped to contribute to AIG's huge losses. The disclosure enraged Congress, which threatened to get the bonuses back. One thing not in doubt was that the payments were legal; AIG was paying them to comply with the employees' employment contracts. But was it ethical for employees in that department to get bonuses? Could paying them be legal but not ethical? The ethics blogs had a field day.

ETHICS AND FAIR TREATMENT AT WORK

People face ethical choices every day. For example, is it wrong to use company supplies for personal reasons? Is a sick day really just another vacaton day? The quiz in Figure 8.1 provides some insights.

Most everyone reading this book rightfully views himself or herself as an ethical person, so we should start by asking, "Why include ethics in a human resource management book?" For two reasons. First, ethics is not theoretical. Instead, it greases the wheels that make businesses work. Managers who promise raises but don't deliver; salespeople who say, "The order's coming" when it's not; production managers who take kickbacks from suppliers—they all corrode the trust that day-to-day business transactions depend on, and eventually run the businesses (or at least the managers) into the ground. According to one recent lawsuit, marketers for Pfizer Inc. influenced the company to suppress unfavorable studies about one of its drugs.[1] Plaintiffs are suing for billions.

Second, managers' human resource–type decisions are usually replete with ethical consequences.[2] For example, one survey found that 6 of the 10 most serious ethical work issues—workplace safety, employee records security, employee theft, affirmative action, comparable work, and employee privacy—were HR related.[3] Another survey of human resource professionals found that 54% had observed misconduct, such as violations of the Occupational Safety and Health Act.[4]

Of course, the manager's human resource–related decisions need not be a hotbed of ethical misdeeds. Instead, HR activities can play a central role in the company's ethics efforts. Let's look first at what *ethics* means.

The Meaning of Ethics

Ethics refers to "the principles of conduct governing an individual or a group,"[5] and specifically to the standards that you use to decide what your conduct should be. Two things always characterize ethical decisions. First, ethical decisions always involve normative judgments.[6] A *normative judgment* implies that "something is good or bad, right or wrong, better or worse."[7] "You are wearing a skirt and blouse" is a nonnormative statement; "That's a great outfit!" is a normative one.

Ethical decisions—principles of conduct—are also always rooted in *morality*, which is society's accepted standards of behavior.[8] Moral standards address matters of serious consequence to society's well-being, such as murder, lying, and slander. And authoritative bodies like legislatures can't establish or change moral standards.[9] Many people believe that moral judgments are never situational. They say that something morally wrong in one situation would also be wrong in another situation. Violating moral standards may make you feel ashamed or remorseful.[10]

Figure 8.1 How Do My Ethics Rate?

Instrument

Indicate your level of agreement with these 15 statements using the following scale:

    1 = Strongly disagree
    2 = Disagree
    3 = Neither agree nor disagree
    4 = Agree
    5 = Strongly agree

1. The only moral of business is making money.	1	2	3	4	5
2. A person who is doing well in business does not have to worry about moral problems.	1	2	3	4	5
3. Act according to the law, and you can't go wrong morally.	1	2	3	4	5
4. Ethics in business is basically an adjustment between expectations and the ways people behave.	1	2	3	4	5
5. Business decisions involve a realistic economic attitude and not a moral philosophy.	1	2	3	4	5
6. "Business ethics" is a concept for public relations only.	1	2	3	4	5
7. Competitiveness and profitability are important values.	1	2	3	4	5
8. Conditions of a free economy will best serve the needs of society. Limiting competition can only hurt society and actually violates basic natural laws.	1	2	3	4	5
9. As a consumer, when making an auto insurance claim, I try to get as much as possible regardless of the extent of the damage.	1	2	3	4	5
10. While shopping at the supermarket, it is appropriate to switch price tags on packages.	1	2	3	4	5
11. As an employee, I can take home office supplies; it doesn't hurt anyone.	1	2	3	4	5
12. I view sick days as vacation days that I deserve.	1	2	3	4	5
13. Employees' wages should be determined according to the laws of supply and demand.	1	2	3	4	5
14. The business world has its own rules.	1	2	3	4	5
15. A good businessperson is a successful businessperson.	1	2	3	4	5

ANALYSIS AND INTERPRETATION

Rather than specify "right" answers, this instrument works best when you compare your answer to those of others. With that in mind, here are mean responses from a group of 243 management students. How did your responses compare?

1. 3.09	6. 2.88	11. 1.58
2. 1.88	7. 3.62	12. 2.31
3. 2.54	8. 3.79	13. 3.36
4. 3.41	9. 3.44	14. 3.79
5. 3.88	10. 1.33	15. 3.38

Source: Adapted from A. Reichel and Y. Neumann, *Journal of Instructional Psychology* (March 1988): 25–53. With permission of the authors.

Ethics and the Law

Perhaps surprisingly, laws aren't the best guide about what is ethical because something may be legal but not right, and something may be right but not legal. Firing a 38-year-old employee with 20 years' tenure without notice may be unethical, but still legal, for instance. Sometimes behavior is illegal and unethical. For example, a meat processor faced a federal indictment charging it with smuggling illegal immigrants from Mexico to cut costs.[11] The vice president for business practices at United Technologies Corp. put it this way: "Don't lie, don't cheat, don't steal. We were all raised with essentially the same values. *Ethics* means making decisions that represent what you stand for, not just what the laws are."[12]

The law may not be a foolproof guide to what's ethical, but some managers use it as if it is. Profits tend to be the initial screen when managers make decisions. "Is it legal" may then come next, because of the consequences of breaking laws, and because some managers do use legality as a surrogate for ethics. Unfortunately, "is it ethical" may then arise just as an afterthought, if at all.

Ethics, Fair Treatment, and Justice

Fair and just companies also tend to be ethical ones. One study concluded that, "to the extent that survey respondents believed that employees were treated fairly . . . [they] reported less unethical behavior in their organizations."[13] In practice, fair treatment reflects concrete actions such as "employees are trusted," "employees are treated with respect," and "employees are treated fairly" (see Figure 8.2).[14]

Workplace Unfairness   Some workplace unfairness is blatant. For example, some supervisors are bullies, yelling at subordinates. Not surprisingly, employees of abusive supervisors are more likely to quit their jobs, and to report lower job and life satisfaction and higher stress if they remain in those jobs.[15]

The employer should of course always prohibit such behavior. The policy at the Oregon Department of Transportation, is that "it is the policy of the department that all employees, customers, contractors and visitors to the work site are entitled to a positive, respectful and productive work environment, free from behavior, actions, [and] language constituting workplace harassment."[16]

Why Treat Employees Fairly?

There are many reasons that managers should be fair, some more obvious than others. The *golden rule* is one obvious reason: As management guru Peter Drucker has said, "[t]hey're not employees, they're people," and the manager should treat people with dignity and respect.

What may not be quite so obvious is that employees' perceptions of fairness also have important organizational ramifications. For example, perceptions of fairness relate to enhanced employee commitment, and enhanced satisfaction with the organization, jobs, and leaders.[17]

Example   A study provides a vivid illustration. College instructors completed surveys regarding the extent to which they saw their colleges as treating them with

Figure 8.2 Perceptions of Fair Interpersonal Treatment Scale

What is your organization like most of the time? Circle YES if the item describes your organization, NO if it does not describe your organization, and ? if you cannot decide.

IN THIS ORGANIZATION . . .

1. Employees are praised for good work	Yes	?	No
2. Supervisors yell at employees (R)	Yes	?	No
3. Supervisors play favorites (R)	Yes	?	No
4. Employees are trusted	Yes	?	No
5. Employees' complaints are dealt with effectively	Yes	?	No
6. Employees are treated like children (R)	Yes	?	No
7. Employees are treated with respect	Yes	?	No
8. Employees' questions and problems are responded to quickly	Yes	?	No
9. Employees are lied to (R)	Yes	?	No
10. Employees' suggestions are ignored (R)	Yes	?	No
11. Supervisors swear at employees (R)	Yes	?	No
12. Employees' hard work is appreciated	Yes	?	No
13. Supervisors threaten to fire or lay off employees (R)	Yes	?	No
14. Employees are treated fairly	Yes	?	No
15. Coworkers help each other out	Yes	?	No
16. Coworkers argue with each other (R)	Yes	?	No
17. Coworkers put each other down (R)	Yes	?	No
18. Coworkers treat each other with respect	Yes	?	No

Note: R = the item is reverse scored.

procedural and *distributive justice.* The former refers to fair processes, while the latter refers to fair outcomes. The procedural justice questions included, for example, "In general, the department/college's procedures allow for requests for clarification for additional information about a decision." The distributive justice questions included, "I am fairly rewarded considering the responsibilities I have." These instructors also completed organizational commitment questionnaires. These included questions such as "I am proud to tell others that I am part of this department/college." Their students then completed surveys. These contained items such as "the instructor put a lot of effort into planning the content of this course," and "the instructor treated me fairly."

The results were telling. Instructors who perceived high distributive and procedural justice reported higher organizational commitment. Furthermore, their students reported higher levels of instructor effort, prosocial behaviors, and fairness and had more positive reactions to their instructors.[18]

Rights and Fairness An increasingly *litigious workforce* is another reason to be fair. Realistically, few societies rely solely on managers' ethics or sense of fairness to ensure that they do what's right by their employees. They also establish various laws. Laws like Title VII give employees (or prospective employees, and sometimes past employees) numerous *rights*. The manager wants to institute disciplinary and

Figure 8.3
Some Areas under
Which Workers Have
Legal Rights

- Leave of absence and vacation rights
- Injuries and illnesses rights
- Noncompete agreement rights
- Employees rights on employer policies
- Discipline rights
- Rights on personnel files
- Employee pension rights
- Employee benefits rights
- References rights
- Rights on criminal records
- Employee distress rights
- Defamation rights
- Employees rights on fraud
- Rights on assault and battery
- Employee negligence rights
- Right on political activity
- Union/group activity rights
- Whistle-blower rights
- Workers' compensation rights

discharge procedures that will survive the scrutiny of arbitrators and the courts.[19] Figure 8.3 lists some other legislated areas under which workers have rights.[20]

Aside from legislation, employees also have certain rights under common law.[21] For example, an employee may have the right to sue an employer whose supervisor published embarrassing private and personal information about the employee.[22]

WHAT SHAPES ETHICAL BEHAVIOR AT WORK?

Whether a person acts ethically at work is usually not a consequence of any one thing. For example, could it be that everyone running some of the banks that triggered the subprime mess a few years ago was simply unethical? Not likely. There must be more to it.

Research Findings: What Do We Know about Ethical Behavior at Work?

Several experts reviewed the research concerning things that influence ethical behavior in organizations. Here's what they found:[23]

- Ethical behavior starts with *moral awareness*. In other words, does the person even recognize that a moral issue exists in the situation?
- *Managers* can do a lot to influence employee ethics by carefully cultivating the right norms, leadership, reward systems, and culture.

- Ethics slide when people undergo *"moral disengagement."* Doing so frees them from the guilt that would normally go with violating one's ethical standards. For example, you're more likely to harm others when you view the victims as "outsiders."
- The most powerful morality comes from *within*. In effect, when the moral person asks, "Why be moral?" the answer is, "because that is who I am." Then, failure to act morally creates emotional discomfort.[24]
- Beware the seductive power of an *unmet goal*. Unmet goals pursued blindly can contribute to unethical behavior.[25]
- Offering *rewards* for ethical behavior can backfire. Doing so may actually undermine the intrinsic value of ethical behavior.
- Don't inadvertently reward someone for *bad behavior*. For example, don't promote someone who got a big sale through devious means.[26]
- Employers should *punish unethical behavior*. Employees who observe unethical behavior expect you to discipline the perpetrators.
- The degree to which employees *openly talk about ethics* is a good predictor of ethical conduct. Conversely, organizations characterized by "moral muteness" suffer more ethically problematic behavior.
- People tend to alter their *moral compasses* when they join organizations. They uncritically equate "what's best for this organization (or team, or department)" with "what's the right thing to do?"

Based on this evidence, we'll look at several of the things that influence ethical behavior at work.[27]

The Person

Because people bring to their jobs their own ideas of what is morally right, the individual must shoulder much of the credit (or blame) for the ethical choices he or she makes. Researchers conducted a survey of CEOs to explain the CEOs' intentions to engage in two questionable business practices: soliciting a competitor's technological secrets and making payments to foreign government officials. The researchers concluded that the CEOs' personal predispositions more strongly affected their decisions than did outside pressures or organizational characteristics.[28]

Traits   It's hard to generalize about the characteristics of ethical or unethical people, but age is a factor. One study surveyed 421 employees to measure the degree to which things like age, gender, marital status, education, and years in business influenced responses to ethical decisions. (Decisions included "doing personal business on company time" and "calling in sick to take a day off for personal use.") Older workers in general made more ethical decisions than did younger employees.

In any case, honesty testing (as discussed in Chapter 4) shows that some people are more inclined toward making the wrong ethical choice. How would you rate your own ethics? Figure 8.1 (page 235) presented a short self-assessment survey for helping you answer that question.

Organizational Factors

If people did unethical things at work solely for personal gain, it perhaps would be understandable (although inexcusable). The scary thing about unethical behavior at work is that often personal interests do not drive it. Table 8.1 illustrates this. It summarizes the results of one survey of the principal causes of ethical compromises, as reported by six levels of employees and managers.

As you can see, "being under the gun to meet scheduling pressures" was the number-one factor in causing ethical lapses. For most of these employees, "meeting overly aggressive financial or business objectives" and "helping the company survive" were the two other top causes. "Advancing my own career or financial interests" ranked toward the bottom of the list. Thus (at least in this case), most ethical lapses occurred because employees were under the gun to do what they thought was best to help their companies.

Examples Several years ago, a judge sentenced a major company's former CFO to 5 years in jail, allegedly for helping the firm's former CEO mask the firm's deteriorating financial situation. Among other things, the government accused the CFO of instructing underlings to make fraudulent accounting entries and of filing false statements. Why, as someone trained to protect the interests of his shareholders, would the CFO do such a thing? "I took these actions, knowing they were wrong, in a misguided attempt to preserve the company to allow it to withstand what I believed were temporary financial difficulties."[29]

Having rules forbidding this sort of thing does not seem to work by itself. For example, several years ago, New York's attorney general filed charges against a big

Table 8.1 Principal Causes of Ethical Compromises

	SENIOR MGMT.	MIDDLE MGMT.	FRONT LINE SUPERVISOR	PROF. NONMGMT.	ADMIN. SALARIED	HOURLY
Meeting schedule pressure	1	1	1	1	1	1
Meeting overly aggressive financial or business objectives	3	2	2	2	2	2
Helping the company survive	2	3	4	4	3	4
Advancing the career interests of my boss	5	4	3	3	4	5
Feeling peer pressure	7	7	5	6	5	3
Resisting competitive threats	4	5	6	5	6	7
Saving jobs	9	6	7	7	7	6
Advancing my own career or financial interests	8	9	9	8	9	8
Other	6	8	8	9	8	9

Note: 1 is high; 9 is low.

Source: O. C. Ferrell and John Fraedrich, *Business Ethics*, 3rd ed. (New York: Houghton Mifflin, 1997), p. 28. Adapted from Rebecca Goodell, *Ethics in American Business: Policies, Programs, and Perceptions* (1994), p. 54. Permission provided courtesy of the Ethics Resource Center, 1120 6th Street, NW, Washington, DC, 20005.

brokerage firm, alleging that several of its analysts had issued optimistic ratings on stocks, while privately expressing concerns about those same stocks. The attorney general alleged that they did this to support the broker's investment banking relationships with these companies. In making his case, the attorney general released numerous e-mails and other documents written by the analysts. One, for instance, reportedly read:

> Some of the communication with the go-to people and the bankers prior to the initiation may have been a technical violation of the firm's written policies and procedures (which, I have now learned, say the company's bankers should not be told what the proposed rating is or will be, even if the company isn't currently under coverage), so my guess is the lawyers will want to offer this in detail. From what they've told me, however, even if there was a violation, this is not a big deal.[30]

The Boss's Influence

Another crucial element is the extent to which employees can model their ethical behavior on the ethical behavior of their supervisors. According to one report, for instance, "the level of misconduct at work dropped dramatically when employees said their supervisors exhibited ethical behavior."[31] Yet, in another poll, only about 27% of employees strongly agreed that their organizations' leadership is ethical.[32]

Examples of how supervisors knowingly (or unknowingly) lead subordinates astray ethically include:

- Tell staffers to do whatever is necessary to achieve results.
- Overload top performers to ensure that work gets done.
- Look the other way when wrongdoing occurs.
- Take credit for others' work or shift blame.[33]

The Organization's Culture

These examples illustrate an important feature of the boss's influence, which is often subliminal. He or she sends signals about the appropriate way to behave. Those signals then create the culture to which employees respond. We can define **organizational culture** as the "characteristic values, traditions, and behaviors a company's employees share." A *value* is a basic belief about what is right or wrong, or about what you should or shouldn't do. ("Honesty is the best policy" would be a value.) Values are important because they guide and channel behavior. Managing people and shaping their behavior therefore depends on shaping the values they use as behavioral guides. The firm's culture should therefore send clean signals about what is and isn't acceptable behavior. For example, if management really believes "honesty is the best policy," the written rules they follow and the things they do should reflect this value.

To an outside observer, a company's culture would reflect itself in several ways. You could sense it from the employees' *patterns of behavior*. For example, managers and employees may engage in behaviors such as hiding information or expressing honest concern when a colleague requires assistance. You could also sense it from *physical manifestations* or symbols of the company's behavior, such as written rules, office layouts, organizational structure, and dress codes.[34]

These cultural symbols and behaviors tend to reflect the firm's shared values, such as "the customer is always right." If management and employees really believe "honesty is the best policy," the written rules they follow and the things they do should reflect this value. To encourage ethical behavior, the manager therefore has to ask, how can I send the signal that we believe in ethical values?

Culture and the Manager   They do so in the following ways:

Clarify Expectations   First, make it clear what your expectations are with respect to the values you want subordinates to follow. Publishing a corporate ethics code is one way to do this. For example, Johnson & Johnson's ethical code says, "We believe our first responsibility is to the doctors, nurses and patients, to mothers and fathers and all others who use our products and services."[35]

Use Signs and Symbols   "Walk the talk." *Symbolism*—what the manager actually does and thus the signals he or she sends—ultimately does the most to create and sustain the company's culture. For example, don't take home office supplies while telling subordinates, "Always be honest."

Provide Physical Support   The physical manifestations of the manager's values—the firm's incentive plan, appraisal system, and disciplinary procedures, for instance—send strong signals regarding what employees should and should not do. Do we punish unethical behavior or condone it?

Ethics Policies and Codes

An ethics policy and code is another way to signal that the firm is serious about ethics. For example, IBM's code of ethics says this about tips, gifts, and entertainment:

> No IBM employee, or any member of his or her immediate family, can accept gratuities or gifts of money from a supplier, customer, or anyone in a business relationship. Nor can they accept a gift or consideration that could be perceived as having been offered because of the business relationship. "Perceived" simply means this: if you read about it in the local newspaper, would you wonder whether the gift just might have had something to do with a business relationship? No IBM employee can give money or a gift of significant value to a customer, supplier, or any one if it could reasonably be viewed as being done to gain a business advantage.[36]

Sometimes ethics codes work, and sometimes they don't. Several years ago, Enron Corp. was the target of various ethics and legal accusations. Yet Enron's ethical principles were widely available on the company's Web site. They included, "respect, integrity, communication and excellence."[37]

Quick Test   Some firms urge employees to apply a quick "ethics test" to evaluate whether what they're about to do fits the company's code of conduct. For example, the Raytheon Co. asks employees who face ethical dilemmas to ask:

Is the action legal?
Is it right?
Who will your actions affect?

Does it fit Raytheon's values?
How will it "feel" afterward?
How will it look in the newspaper?
Will it reflect poorly on the company?[38]

Enforcement   However, don't underestimate the importance of enforcement. As one ethics study concludes, "strong statements by managers may reduce the risk of legal and ethical violations by their work forces, but enforcement of standards has the greatest impact."[39] *Ethics audits* typically address topics like conflicts of interest, giving and receiving gifts, employee discrimination, and access to company information. An increasing number of firms, such as Lockheed Martin Corp., appoint chief ethics officers.[40]

ETHICS, FAIR TREATMENT, AND THE ROLE OF HR MANAGEMENT

Ethical dilemmas are a familiar part of human resource management. For example, you know that your team shouldn't work on the new machine until its safety measures are checked, but your boss wants you to get started. What should you do? You dismissed an employee, and now she has applied for unemployment insurance, saying you never warned her. Should you now place in her file a note of warning, to protect your employer from paying higher unemployment taxes? You have an incompetent employee who you want to get rid of, and someone just called you to get a job reference. How honest should you be? The point is, there's much HR managers can do to influence ethics. Let's consider specific examples.

Staffing and Selection

One writer says, "The simplest way to tune up an organization, ethically speaking, is to hire more ethical people."[41]

Dissuading ethically undesirable applicants starts before the applicant even applies. For example, the human resource department can create recruitment materials explicitly referencing the company's integrity and ethics. Employers can then use honesty tests and meticulous background checks (discussed in Chapter 4) to screen out those who may not fit their ethical standards.[42]

The selection process also sends signals about what the company's values really are. For example, "if prospective employees perceive that the hiring process does not treat people fairly, they may assume that ethical behavior is not important in the company."[43]

Managers don't necessarily need paper-and-pencil honesty tests to screen out ethically undesirable applicants. Background checks and having interviewers ask behavioral questions such as "Have you ever observed someone stretching the rules at work? What did you do about it?" are useful.[44]

Training

For all practical purposes, ethics training is mandatory. Since 1991, federal sentencing guidelines have prescribed reduced penalties for employers accused of misconduct who implement codes of conduct and ethics training.[45] And the Sarbanes-Oxley Act of 2002 (see the "Improving Productivity through HRIS" section) makes ethics training even more important.

Ethics training usually includes showing employees how to recognize ethical dilemmas, how to use codes of conduct to resolve problems, and how to use HR functions (such as interviews and disciplinary practices) in ethical ways.[46] However, emphasizing the mechanics of ethics compliance is not enough. Instead, the training should also emphasize the moral underpinnings of the ethical choice and the company's commitment to integrity.[47]

Improving Productivity through HRIS: Web-Based Training for Sarbanes-Oxley

Particularly in large companies, designing and managing ethics programs isn't easy or cheap. Doing so requires the almost continuous attention of the company's top managers, as well as a considerable investment in setting up and monitoring ethics codes and training employees.

Passage of the Sarbanes-Oxley Act of 2002 made ethics compliance even more expensive. Among other things, the act requires that the CEO and the CFO of publicly traded companies personally attest to the accuracy of their companies' financial statements and to the fact that its internal controls are adequate.[48] As one lawyer puts it, "Sarbanes-Oxley has added a wide range of new issues to the traditional compliance function."[49]

With their personal credibility on the line, the new law focused top management's attention on ensuring that all the firm's employees take ethics seriously. The problem is, training and following up on programs like this can be very expensive. Larger firms need a cost-effective way to make such training available. That's why when DTE Energy, with 14,000 employees, needed an ethics training system, it turned to a Web-based program from Integrity Interactive Corp. of Waltham, Massachusetts. Now, all the company's employees have easy access to a standardized ethics-training program through their PCs, and DTE can easily track who has taken the training and who has not. The employees can take the training when they want to, and the company can monitor their progress.

Figure 8.4 shows how other employers use training tools in their ethics programs. Other online training tools to help employers promote ethics at work include Business Ethics, an online course from skillsoft.com; and two online courses, Ethical Decision-Making and Managerial Business Ethics, both from NETg.com.[50]

Performance Appraisal

Some managers ignore accuracy and honesty in performance appraisals. Instead, they use the process for political purposes (such as encouraging employees with whom they don't get along to leave the firm).[51] To send the signal that fairness and ethics are supreme requires three things. The employees' standards should be clear, employees should understand the basis on which you're going to appraise them, and the appraisals should be conducted objectively and fairly.[52]

Figure 8.4 The Role of Training in Ethics

Company ethics officials use these actual training tools to convey ethics training to employees:

Copies of company policies — 78%

Ethics handbooks — 76%

Videotaped ethics programs — 59%

Online assistance — 39%

Ethics newsletters — 30%

Source: Susan Wells, "Turn Employees into Saints," *HR Magazine* (December 1999): p. 52. Copyright © 1999 by Society for Human Resource Management (SHRM). Reproduced with permission of Society for Human Resource Management (SHRM) in the format Textbook via Copyright Clearance Center.

Reward and Disciplinary Systems

To the extent that behavior is a function of its consequences, the company must ensure that the firm rewards ethical behavior and penalizes unethical behavior. In fact, "research suggests that employees expect the organization to dole out relatively harsh punishment for unethical conduct."[53] Where the company does not do so, the ethical employees (not the unethical ones) feel punished. This of course also means disciplining executives who misbehave.[54]

Building Two-Way Communication

The opportunity for two-way communication affects our perceptions of how fairly we're being treated. Studies support this commonsense observation. One study concluded that three actions contributed to perceived fairness in business settings:

- *Engagement* (involving individuals in the decisions that affect them by asking for their input and allowing them to refute the merits of one another's ideas and assumptions),
- *Explanation* (ensuring that everyone involved and affected understands why final decisions are made as they are, and the thinking that underlies the decisions), and
- *Expectation clarity* (making sure everyone knows up front by what standards they will be judged and the penalties).[55]

Steps to Take   Many employers therefore take steps to facilitate two-way communication. For example, some, like FedEx, administer periodic **opinion surveys.** For example, the FedEx Survey Feedback Action (SFA) program lets employees express feelings about the company, managers, and to some extent about service, pay, and benefits. Each manager then has an opportunity to discuss the anonymous department results with his or her subordinates and create an action plan for improving work group commitment. Sample questions include:

"I can tell my manager what I think."
"My manager tells me what is expected."
"My manager listens to my concerns."
"My manager keeps me informed."

Other Illustrative HR Ethics Activities

Human resource management supports the employer's ethics programs in other ways. For example, one study of Fortune 500 companies concluded that a human resources officer was responsible for the program in 28% of responding firms. The rest of the firms spread the responsibility among other departments.[56]

Strategy and HR   Some years ago, critics accused Walmart of unfairness after it instituted a new policy basically requiring employees to stand ready to come to work at a moment's notice, depending on their stores' needs. To Walmart, the change made strategic sense. Their competitive advantage is low costs (and thus "low prices—every day"). The new employee scheduling policy enabled Walmart to minimize labor costs when stores were slow. Would you consider Walmart's new store staffing policy unethical? Why? If it is, how do you think that might affect Walmart's performance going forward?

EMPLOYEE DISCIPLINE AND PRIVACY

The purpose of **discipline** is to encourage employees to behave sensibly at work (where *sensible* means adhering to rules and regulations). Rules and regulations are basically the company's laws. Discipline is called for when someone violates one of these rules or regulations.[57] A fair and just discipline process has three pillars: rules and regulations, a system of progressive penalties, and an appeals process.

Three Pillars

Rules   A set of clear rules and regulations is the first pillar. These rules address issues such as theft, destruction of company property, drinking on the job, and insubordination. Examples of rules include:

Poor performance is not acceptable. Each employee is expected to perform his or her work properly and efficiently and to meet established standards of quality.

Alcohol and drugs do not mix with work. The use of either during working
hours and reporting for work under the influence of either are both
strictly prohibited.
Gambling in any form is forbidden.

The purpose of these rules is to inform employees ahead of time what is and is
not acceptable behavior. Employees must be told, preferably in writing, what isn't
permitted. This usually occurs during the employee's orientation. The employee
handbook usually contains the rules and regulations.

Penalties   A system of progressive penalties is a second pillar of effective discipline. Penalties may range from oral warnings to written warnings to suspension
from the job to discharge. The severity of the penalty is usually a function of the type
of offense and the number of times the offense occurred. For example, most companies issue warnings for the first unexcused lateness. However, for a fourth offense,
discharge is the usual disciplinary action.

Appeals Process   Finally, an appeals process should be part of the disciplinary process; this helps to ensure that supervisors mete out discipline fairly and
equitably.

Consider FedEx's **guaranteed fair treatment** multistep program. In *step 1,
management review,* the complainant submits a written complaint to a member of
management (manager, senior manager, or managing director). Then the manager,
senior manager, and managing director of the employee's group review the information and make a decision to uphold, modify, or overturn management's action.

If not satisfied, then in *step 2, officer complaint,* the complainant submits a written
appeal to the vice president or senior vice president of the division within 7 calendar
days of the step 1 decision.

Finally, in *step 3, executive appeals review,* the complainant may submit a written
complaint within 7 calendar days of the step 2 decision to the employee relations
department. The appeals board—the CEO, the COO, the chief HR officer, and three
senior vice presidents—then reviews all relevant information and makes a decision
to uphold, overturn, or initiate a board of review or to take other appropriate
action.

Some supervisory behavior is difficult or impossible to overcome. For example,
the employer can sometimes mitigate the effects of unfair disciplinary procedures by
establishing disciplinary procedures that contain appeals processes. However,
behaviors that attack the employee's personal and/or social identity are difficult to
remedy.[58] The *HR in Practice* box summarizes discipline guidelines.

Discipline without Punishment

Traditional discipline has two potential flaws. It often leaves a residue of ill will.
And, forcing your rules on employees may gain their short-term compliance, but not
their cooperation when you're not around to enforce the rules.

Discipline without punishment (or nonpunitive discipline) aims to avoid
these disciplinary problems. It does this by gaining the employees' acceptance of

HR in Practice: Fair Discipline Guidelines

- *Make sure the evidence supports the charge of employee wrongdoing.*[59]
- *Ensure that the employees' due process rights are protected.*[60] Arbitrators normally reverse discharges and suspensions that employers impose in a manner that violates basic notions of fairness or due process procedures.[61]
- *The discipline should be in line with the way management usually responds to similar incidents.*[62]
- *Adequately warn the employee of the disciplinary consequences of his or her alleged misconduct.*
- *The rule that allegedly was violated should be "reasonably related" to the efficient and safe operation of the particular work environment.*
- *Management must fairly and adequately investigate the matter before administering discipline.*
- *The investigation should reveal substantial evidence of misconduct.*
- *Applicable rules, orders, or penalties should be applied evenhandedly and without discrimination.*
- *The penalty should be reasonably related to the misconduct and to the employee's past work history.*
- *Maintain the employee's right to counsel.* For example, all union employees generally have the right to bring help when they are called for an interview that they reasonably believe might lead to discipline.
- *Don't rob your subordinate of his or her dignity.* For example, discipline your subordinate in private.
- *Remember that the burden of proof is on you.* In U.S. society, a person is considered innocent until proven guilty.
- *Get the facts.* Don't base your decision on hearsay evidence or on your general impression.
- *Don't act while angry.* Very few people can be objective and sensible when they are angry.
- *Use ombudsmen.* Some companies establish independent ombudsmen, neutral counselors outside the normal chain of command to whom employees who believe they were treated unfairly can turn for confidential advice.[63]

your rules and by reducing the punitive nature of the discipline itself. Typical steps include:

1. *Issue an oral reminder.* Here, your goal is to get the employee to agree to solve the disciplinary problem.
2. *Should another incident arise within 6 weeks, issue the employee a formal written reminder, and place a copy in the personnel file.* In addition, privately hold a second discussion with the employee, again without any threats.
3. *Give a paid 1-day "decision-making leave."* If another incident occurs after the written warning in the next 6 weeks or so, the employee is told to take a 1-day leave with pay to stay home and consider whether the job is right for him or her and whether he or she wants to abide by the company's rules.
4. *If no further incidents occur in the next year or so, the 1-day paid suspension is purged from the person's file.* If the behavior reoccurs, dismissal (see later discussion) is required.[64]

The process would not apply to exceptional circumstances. Criminal behavior or in-plant fighting might be grounds for immediate **dismissal,** for instance.

And if several incidents occurred at very close intervals, the supervisor might skip step 2—the written warning.

Electronic Employee Privacy

A New Jersey court recently found an employer liable when one of its employees used his company computer at work to distribute child pornography. (Someone had previously alerted the employer to the suspicious activity, and the employer had not taken action.[65])

Managing and monitoring company e-mail is an urgent problem.[66] About one-third of U.S. companies recently investigated suspected leaks, via e-mail, of confidential or proprietary information. One hospital found that, to facilitate working at home, many medical staff were e-mailing patients' confidential health-care records to themselves, in violation of federal privacy statutes.

Extent   It's therefore not surprising that in one recent survey, over half of employers said they were monitoring their employees' incoming and outgoing e-mail; 27% monitor internal e-mail as well.[67] One survey found that 41% of employers with more than 20,000 employees have someone reading employee e-mails.[68] Ninety-six percent block access to adult Web sites, and 61% to game sites.[69] Employers ranging from UPS to the City of Oakland, California, use GPS units to monitor their truckers' and street sweepers' whereabouts.[70] And, many more employers, like Bronx Lebanon Hospital in New York, use biometric scanners, for instance, to ensure that the employee that clocks in is really who he or she says they are.[71] Some employers check employees' personal blogs or Facebook sites, to see if they're publicizing work-related matters.[72] Such monitoring raises privacy issues.[73]

Legal Issues   Electronic eavesdropping is legal—up to a point. For example, federal law and most states' laws allow employers to monitor their employees' phone calls "in the ordinary course of business," says one legal expert. However, they must stop listening once they see the conversation is personal, not business related.[74] E-mail service may be intercepted under federal law when it is to protect the property rights of the provider.[75] However, one recent U.S. Court of Appeals case suggests employers may have fewer rights to monitor e-mail than previously assumed.[76]

More employers are therefore issuing e-mail and online usage policies, and having employees sign e-mail and telephone monitoring acknowledgment statements.[77] One reason for explicit policy statements is the risk that employers may be liable for illegal acts committed by their employees via e-mail or blogging.[78] For example, messages sent by supervisors that contain sexual innuendo could cause problems for an employer who hasn't taken steps to prohibit such e-mail misuse. An attorney should review the e-mail policy. At a minimum, it must make it clear that employees should have no expectation of privacy in their e-mail and Internet usage, and that all messages sent and received on the employer's e-mail system are company property and not confidential.[79]

Videotaping in the workplace calls for more legal caution. In one case, one U.S. Court of Appeals ruled that an employer's continuous video surveillance of employees in an office setting did not constitute an unconstitutional invasion of privacy.[80] Yet, a Boston employer had to pay over $200,000 to five workers it secretly videotaped in an employee locker room, after they sued in state court.[81]

MANAGING DISMISSALS

Because dismissal is the strongest disciplinary step, the manager should ensure that the dismissal is fair, warranted, and just. On those occasions that require immediate dismissal, the manager still needs to ensure that the action is humane.

The best way to "handle" a dismissal is to avoid it in the first place, when possible. Many dismissals start with bad hiring decisions. Using good selection practices including tests, reference and background checks, drug testing, and clearly defined jobs can reduce the need for dismissals.[82]

Termination at Will   For more than 100 years, the prevailing rule in the United States has been that without an employment contract, either the employer or the employee can **terminate at will** the employment relationship. In other words, the employee could resign for any reason, at will, and the employer could similarly dismiss an employee for any reason, at will.

Termination at Will Exceptions   Today, however, three main protections against wrongful discharge have eroded the termination-at-will doctrine—statutory exceptions, common law exceptions, and public policy exceptions.

First, in terms of *statutory exceptions*, federal and state equal employment and workplace laws prohibit specific types of dismissals. For example, Title VII of the Civil Rights Act of 1964 prohibits discharging employees based on race, color, religion, sex, or national origin.[83]

Second, numerous *common law exceptions* exist. For example, a court may decide that an employee handbook promising termination only "for just cause" may create an exception to the at-will rule.[84]

Finally, under the *public policy exception*, courts have held a discharge to be wrongful when it was against an explicit, well-established public policy (for instance, the employer fired the employee for refusing to break the law).

Grounds for Dismissal

There are four bases for dismissal: unsatisfactory performance, misconduct, lack of qualifications for the job, and changed requirements of (or elimination of) the job. We can define *unsatisfactory performance* as a persistent failure to perform assigned duties or to meet prescribed standards on the job.[85] Specific reasons include excessive absenteeism; tardiness; a persistent failure to meet normal job requirements; or an adverse attitude toward the company, supervisor, or fellow employees. *Misconduct* is deliberate and willful violation of the employer's rules and may include stealing, rowdy behavior, and insubordination. *Lack of qualifications for the job* is an employee's inability to do the assigned work, although he or she is diligent. Because in this case the employee may be trying, it is reasonable for the employer to try to salvage him or her—perhaps by assigning the employee to another job. *Changed requirements of the job* involve an employee's incapability of doing the work assigned, after the nature of the job has changed. Similarly, you may have to dismiss an employee when his or her job is eliminated. Again, the employee may be industrious, so it is reasonable to retrain or transfer this person, if possible.

Insubordination, a form of misconduct, is sometimes the grounds for dismissal. Some acts should be deemed insubordinate whenever they occur. These include, for instance, direct disregard of the boss's authority, and disobedience of, or refusal to obey, the boss's orders—particularly in front of others.

Dismissing employees is never easy, but at least the employer can try to ensure that the employee views the process as fair and just. Communication is important. One study found that "individuals who reported that they were given full explanations of why and how termination decisions were made were more likely to (1) perceive their layoff as fair, (2) endorse the terminating organization, and (3) indicate that they did not wish to take the past employer to court."[86]

Avoiding Wrongful Discharge Suits

In what it referred to as "fear of the firing," *BusinessWeek* magazine described several examples of how some employers were reluctant to terminate disruptive employees for fear of lawsuits. In practice, plaintiffs only win a tiny fraction of such suits. However, the cost of defending the suits is still huge.[87]

Wrongful discharge occurs when an employee's dismissal does not comply with the law or with the contractual arrangement stated or implied by the firm via its employment application, employee manuals, or other promises. (In a *constructive discharge* claim, the plaintiff argues that he or she quit, but had no choice because the employer made the situation so intolerable at work.[88])

Procedural Steps Avoiding wrongful discharge suits requires a two-prong strategy. First is to lay the groundwork that will help avoid such suits. Steps to take here include

- Have applicants sign the employment application. It should contain a statement that employment is for no fixed term and that the employer can terminate at any time.
- Review your employee manual and delete statements that could prejudice your defense, such as, "employees can be terminated only for just cause."
- Have written rules listing infractions that may require discipline and discharge.
- If a rule is broken, get the worker's side of the story in front of witnesses, and preferably get it signed.
- Be sure that employees get a written appraisal at least annually. If an employee shows evidence of incompetence, give that person a warning and an opportunity to improve.
- Keep careful confidential records of all actions such as employee appraisals, warnings or notices, and so on.
- Consider his or her legal rights. For example, ask: Is the employee covered by any type of written agreement, including a collective bargaining agreement?[89]

Fairness Safeguards Second, use practices (such as those in this chapter) that help ensure fairness.[90] People who are fired and who walk away feeling that they've been embarrassed or treated unfairly financially are more likely to seek retribution in the courts. To some extent, employers can use severance pay to blunt a dismissal's sting.

The reason for the dismissal affects whether the employee gets severance pay. About 95% of employees dismissed due to downsizings got severance pay, while only about a third of employers offer severance when terminating for poor performance. It is uncommon to pay when employees quit. The average maximum severance is 39 weeks for executives and about 30 weeks for other downsized employees.[91] About half of employers surveyed give white-collar and exempt employees one week of severance pay per year of service, and about one-third do the same for blue-collar workers.[92] As the economy worsened in 2008–2009 and layoffs rose, more employers were reducing what they awarded for severance pay, for instance awarding lump-sum payments rather than payments tied to years with the company.[93]

Personal Supervisory Liability

Courts sometimes hold managers personally liable for their supervisory actions, particularly with respect to actions covered by the Fair Labor Standards Act and the Family and Medical Leave Act.[94] The Fair Labor Standards Act defines *employer* to include "any person acting directly or indirectly in the interest of an employer in relation to any employee," and this can mean the individual supervisor.

Steps to Take   There are several ways to avoid creating situations in which personal liability becomes an issue.

- *Follow company policies and procedures.* An employee may initiate a claim against a supervisor who he or she alleges did not follow company policies and procedures.
- Administer the discipline in a manner that does not add to the *emotional hardship* on the employee (as would dismissing the person in public, and making him or her publicly collect belongings and leave the office). Let the employee present "their side of the story."
- *Do not act in anger*, since doing so personalizes the situation and undermines any appearance of objectivity.
- Finally, *utilize the HR department* for advice regarding how to handle difficult disciplinary matters.

If humanitarianism and wrongful discharge suits aren't enough to encourage you to be fair in dismissing, consider this. Managers run double their usual risk of suffering a heart attack during the week after they fire an employee.[95] During one 5-year period, physicians interviewed 791 working people who had just undergone heart attacks to find out what might have triggered them. The researchers concluded that the stress associated with firing someone doubled the usual risk of a heart attack for the person doing the firing, during the week following the dismissal.

The Termination Interview

Dismissing an employee is one of the most difficult tasks you can face at work.[96] The dismissed employee, even if warned many times in the past, may still react with disbelief or even violence. Guidelines for the **termination interview** itself are as follows:

1. *Plan the interview carefully.* According to experts at Hay Associates, this includes:
   - Make sure the employee keeps the appointment time.
   - Allow 10 minutes as sufficient time for the interview.
   - Use a neutral site, not your own office.
   - Have employee agreements and a release announcement (internal and external) prepared in advance.
   - Be available at a time after the interview in case questions or problems arise.
   - Have phone numbers ready for medical or security emergencies.
2. *Get to the point.* As soon as the employee enters your office, give the person a moment to get comfortable and then inform him or her of your decision.
3. *Describe the situation.* Briefly, in three or four sentences, explain why the person is being let go. For instance, "Production in your area is down 4%, and we are continuing to have quality problems. We have to make a change."[97] Describe the situation rather than say things like, "Your production is just not up to par." Also, emphasize that the decision is final and irrevocable.
4. *Listen.* Continue the interview until the person appears to be talking freely and reasonably calmly.
5. *Review the severance package.* Describe severance payments, benefits, access to office support people, and the way references will be handled. However, do not make or imply any promises or benefits beyond those already in the support package.
6. *Identify the next step.* The terminated employee may be disoriented and unsure what to do next. Explain where the employee should go upon leaving the interview.

Outplacement Counseling   With **outplacement counseling**, the employer arranges to provide terminated employees with career planning and job search skills. Outplacement firms such as Right Associates, Inc., usually provide the actual outplacement services. Managers who are let go typically have office space and secretarial services they can use at local offices of such firms, in addition to the counseling services. The outplacement counseling is part of the terminated employee's support or severance package.

Exit Interviews   Many employers conduct final **exit interviews** with employees who are leaving the firm. The HR department usually conducts them. The aim is to elicit information that might give the employer a better insight into what is right—or wrong—about the company. Exit interview questions to ask include, Why did you join the company? Was the job presented correctly? And, Why did you decide to leave?[98] Women and minorities are more likely to quit early in their employment, so this is one issue for which to watch.[99]

The assumption, of course, is that because the employee is leaving, he or she will be candid. Based on one older survey, though, this is doubtful. The researchers found that at the time of separation, 38% of those leaving blamed salary and benefits, and only 4% blamed supervision. Followed up 18 months later, 24% blamed supervision and only 12% blamed salary and benefits.[100]

Layoffs and the Plant Closing Law

Nondisciplinary separations are a fact of life and may be initiated by either employer or employee. For the *employer*, reduced sales or profits or recession or the desire for more productivity may require large-scale layoffs.[101] *Employees* may leave to retire or to seek better jobs. The Worker Adjustment and Retraining Notification Act (WARN Act, or the plant closing law) requires employers of 100 or more employees to give 60 days' notice before closing a facility or starting a layoff of 50 or more people.[102]

A **layoff,** in which the employer sends workers home for a time for lack of work, is usually not a permanent dismissal (although it may turn out to be). Rather it's a temporary one, which the employer expects will be short term. However, some employers use the term *layoff* as a euphemism for discharge or termination. In the recession years of 2008 and 2009 combined, employers carried out a total of about 51,000 mass layoffs, idling over 5 million workers in total.[103]

Layoffs are often subject to additional constraints abroad, as the *Global Issues* box illustrates. (The challenging times feature provides an additional perspective)

The Layoff Process   A study illustrates one firm's layoff process. In this company, senior management first met to make strategic decisions about the size and timing of the layoffs. These managers also debated the relative importance of the skill sets they thought the firm needed going forward. Frontline supervisors assessed their subordinates, rating their nonunion employees either A, B, or C (union employees were laid off based on seniority). The frontline supervisors then informed each of their

Managing HR in Challenging Times: Preparing for Layoffs

As the United States slipped into recession, large layoffs climbed ominously, up by about 9.4% in mid-2009. How do managers prepare for the layoffs that result from such challenging times?

Interestingly, the initial focus isn't on the layoffs, but on the employer's appraisal systems. One expert says that in preparing for large-scale layoffs, management needs to make sure appraisals are up to date, and identify top performers and get them working on the company's future.[104]

Another HR consultant says companies that "don't closely manage their performance appraisal systems suddenly learn during a reduction in force that everyone has been ranked a 'four' out of 'five'; that information is meaningless."[105]

So the essential point about layoffs is to prepare in advance by making sure you have an effective performance appraisal system. If you don't, then when the time comes to lay off significant numbers of employers, you may find yourself with no rational basis on which to decide who stays or leaves.

subordinates about his or her A, B, or C rating and told them that those with C grades were most likely to be laid off.[106]

Layoff's Effects Layoffs "tend to result in deleterious psychological and physical health outcomes for employees who lose their jobs" as well as for the survivors who, witnessing the layoffs of their coworkers and friends, face uncertainty and discomfort.[107] Given this, many employers try to avoid or minimize layoffs during downturns. Reducing everyone's work hours and mandating short vacations are two options. Others reduce layoffs by offering financial bonuses for improved productivity.[108]

Adjusting to Downsizings and Mergers

Downsizing—reducing, usually dramatically, the number of people employed by a firm—is occurring more often.[109] The basic idea is to cut costs and raise profitability.

Downsizings (some call them "productivity transformation programs")[110] require careful consideration of several matters. One is to make sure you let go *the right people:* this requires having an effective appraisal system in place. Second is *compliance with all applicable laws*, including WARN. Third is ensuring that the employer executes the dismissals in a manner that is *just and fair.* Fourth is the practical consideration of *security,* for instance, with respect to retrieving keys and ensuring that those leaving don't take any prohibited items with them.

Fifth is to take steps to reduce the remaining *employees' uncertainty* and to address their concerns. This typically involves a post-downsizing announcement and meetings where senior managers deal with questions from the remaining employees. However, it's neither wise nor fair to make any assertions about "no more layoffs" unless they are true.

REVIEW

Summary

1. Ethics refers to the principles of conduct governing an individual or a group and specifically to the standards you use to decide what your conduct should be.
2. Two things characterize ethical decisions. Ethical decisions always involve normative judgments, and ethical decisions always involve morality, which we defined as society's accepted standards of behavior.
3. Numerous factors shape ethical behavior at work. These include individual factors, organizational factors, the boss's influence, ethics policies and codes, and the organization's culture.
4. HR management can influence ethics and fair treatment at work in numerous ways. For example, having a fair and open selection process that emphasizes integrity and ethics, establishing special ethics training programs, measuring employees' adherence to high ethical standards during performance appraisals, and rewarding (or disciplining) ethical (or unethical) work-related behavior are some examples.
5. Firms give employees avenues through which to express opinions and concerns. Firms such as FedEx engage in periodic anonymous opinion surveys.
6. Guaranteed fair treatment programs, such as the one at FedEx, help to ensure that grievances are handled fairly and openly. Steps include management review, officer complaint, and executive appeals review.
7. A fair and just discipline process is based on rules and regulations, a system of progressive penalties, and an appeals process. A number of guidelines are important, including that discipline should be in line with the way management usually responds to similar incidents; that management must adequately investigate the matter before administering discipline; and that managers should not rob a subordinate of his or her dignity.
8. The basic aim of discipline without punishment is to gain an employee's acceptance of the rules by reducing the punitive nature of the discipline itself. The employee is given a paid day off to consider his or her infraction before more punitive disciplinary steps are taken.
9. Among the reasons for dismissal are unsatisfactory performance, misconduct, lack of qualifications, changed job requirements, and insubordination. In dismissing one or more employees, however, remember that exceptions in many states have weakened the termination at will policy. Furthermore, take care to avoid wrongful discharge suits.
10. Dismissing an employee is always difficult, and the termination interview should be handled properly. Specifically, plan the interview carefully and then get to the point. Then discuss the severance package and identify the next step.
11. Nondisciplinary separations such as layoffs and retirement occur all the time. The plant closing law (the Worker Adjustment and Retraining Notification Act) outlines requirements to follow with regard to official notice before operations with 50 or more people are to be closed down.
12. Disciplinary actions are a big source of grievances. Discipline should be based on rules and adhere to a system of progressive penalties, and it should permit an appeals process.

KEY TERMS

- ethics
- organizational culture
- opinion surveys
- discipline
- guaranteed fair treatment
- dismissal
- terminate at will
- insubordination
- wrongful discharge
- termination interview
- outplacement counseling
- exit interviews
- layoff
- downsizing

DISCUSSION QUESTIONS

1. Describe the similarities and differences between programs such as FedEx's guaranteed fair treatment program and your college or university's student grievance process.
2. Explain how you would ensure fairness in disciplining, discussing particularly the prerequisites to disciplining, disciplining guidelines, and the discipline without punishment approach.
3. Why is it important to manage dismissals properly?

INDIVIDUAL AND GROUP ACTIVITIES

1. Working individually or in groups, interview managers or administrators at your college in order to identify the employee discipline process. Do they think it is effective? What do the employees (or faculty members) think of the programs in use?
2. Working individually or in groups, obtain copies of the student handbook for your college and determine to what extent there is a formal process through which students can air grievances. Based on your contacts with other students, has it been an effective grievance process? Why or why not?
3. Working individually or in groups, determine the nature of the academic discipline process in your college. Do you think it is effective? Based on what you read in this chapter, would you recommend any modifications?
4. What techniques would you use as alternatives to traditional discipline? What do such alternatives have to do with "organizational justice"? Why do you think alternatives like these are important, given industry's current need for highly committed employees?

APPLICATION EXERCISES

Case Incident

Enron, Ethics, and Organizational Culture

For many people, a company called Enron Corp. still ranks as one of history's classic examples of ethics run amok. During the 1990s and early 2000s, Enron was in the business of wholesaling natural gas and electricity. Rather than actually owning the gas or electric, Enron made its money as the intermediary (wholesaler) between suppliers and customers. Without getting into all the details, the nature of Enron's business, and the fact that Enron didn't actually own the assets, meant that its accounting procedures were unusual. For example, the profit statements and balance sheets listing the firm's assets and liabilities were unusually difficult to understand.

It turned out that the lack of accounting transparency enabled the company's managers to make Enron's financial performance look much better than it actually was. Outside experts began questioning Enron's financial statements in 2001. In fairly short order, Enron's house of cards collapsed, and courts convicted several of its top executives of things like manipulating Enron's reported assets and profitability. Many investors (including former Enron employees) lost all or most of their investments in Enron.

It's probably always easier to understand ethical breakdowns like this in retrospect, rather than to predict they are going to happen. However, in Enron's case the breakdown is perhaps more perplexing than usual. As one writer said, "Enron had all the elements usually found in comprehensive ethics and compliance programs: a code of ethics, a reporting system, as well as a training video on vision and values led by [the company's top executives]."[111]

Experts subsequently put forth many explanations for how a company that was apparently so ethical on its face could actually have been making

so many bad ethical decisions without other managers (and the board of directors) noticing. The explanations ranged from a "deliberate concealment of information by officers" to more psychological explanations (such as employees not wanting to contradict their bosses), and the "surprising role of irrationality in decision-making."[112]

But perhaps the most persuasive explanation of how an apparently ethical company could go so wrong concerns organizational culture. The reasoning here is that it's not the rules but what employees feel they should do that determines ethical behavior. For example, (speaking in general, not specifically about Enron) the executive director of the Ethics Officer Association put it this way:

> [W]e're a legalistic society, and we've created a lot of laws. We assume that if you just knew what those laws meant that you would behave properly. Well, guess what? You can't write enough laws to tell us what to do at all times every day of the week in every part of the world. We've got to develop the critical thinking and critical reasoning skills of our people because most of the ethical issues that we deal with are in the ethical gray areas. Virtually every regulatory body in the last year has come out with language that has said in addition to law compliance, businesses are also going to be accountable to ethics standards and a corporate culture that embraces them.[113]

How can one tell or measure when a company has an "ethical culture"? Key attributes of a healthy ethical culture include:

- Employees feel a sense of responsibility and accountability for their actions and for the actions of others.[114]

- Employees freely raise issues and concerns without fear of retaliation.
- Managers model the behaviors they demand of others.
- Managers communicate the importance of integrity when making difficult decisions. ∎

QUESTIONS

1. Based on what you read in this chapter, summarize in one page or less how you would explain Enron's ethical meltdown.

2. It is said that when one securities analyst tried to confront Enron's CEO about the firm's unusual accounting statements, the CEO publicly used vulgar language to describe the analyst, and that Enron employees subsequently thought doing so was humorous. If true, what does that say about Enron's ethical culture?

3. This case and chapter both had something to say about how organizational culture influences ethical behavior. What role do you think culture played at Enron? Give five specific examples of things Enron's CEO could have done to create a healthy ethical culture.

Continuing Case

LearnInMotion.com: Are Our Ethics Out of Control?

It's probably safe to say that in creating LearnInMotion.com, Jennifer and Mel gave absolutely no thought to ethical behavior in their company. They did of course put endless hours into developing their business plan, raising money, installing computers, and trying to generate sales. But as far as taking specific concrete steps toward ensuring that everything that they and their employees did was aboveboard and ethical, they were batting zero, not because they were unethical people, but simply because the matter never entered their minds.

However, several ethics-related issues have recently come up, and they're causing concern for both Jennifer and Mel. Yesterday they received word from one of the main Internet service providers that someone in their company was using spamming techniques to send unsolicited LearnInMotion.com advertising information to tens of thousands of its subscribers, and the provider was threatening legal action if the spamming did not cease. A customer called last week to complain that they'd recently learned that LearnInMotion.com was not reaching even half the number of potential users that LearnInMotion's sales brochures said it did, and the customer therefore wanted a rebate. The CEO of LearnInMotion's largest competitor called Mel to say that their own internal tracking systems had noticed that someone at LearnInMotion.com had been methodically downloading its customers' names and files, and that if the electronic monitoring did not cease, his company would file a lawsuit. All this, and more, led Jennifer and Mel to believe that they have to do something to ratchet up the ethical level in their company. Now, they want you, their management consultants, to help them actually do it. Here's what they want you to do for them. ∎

QUESTIONS AND ASSIGNMENTS

1. Are the sorts of issues raised in the case ethical ones? Why or why not?
2. Tell us: What are the sorts of factors that shape ethical behavior in a company like LearnInMotion.com?

3. In terms of human resource management, list at least six concrete staffing and selection, training, performance appraisal, and reward/disciplinary actions we can take right now to institute a greater appreciation for the high ethical standards we think our company should have.

Experiential Exercise
To Discipline or Not?

Purpose: The purpose of this exercise is to provide you with some experience in analyzing and handling an actual disciplinary action.

Required Understanding: Students should be thoroughly familiar with the following case, titled "Botched Batch." However, *do not read the "Award" or "Discussion" sections until after the groups have completed their deliberations.*

How to Set Up the Exercise/Instructions: Divide the class into groups of four or five students. Each group should take the arbitrator's point of view and assume that they are to analyze the case and make the arbitrator's decision. Review the case again at this point, but please do not read the award and discussion.

Each group should answer the following questions:

1. What would your decision be if you were the arbitrator? Why?
2. Do you think that following their experience in this arbitration the parties will be more or less inclined to settle grievances by themselves without resorting to arbitration?

Botched Batch

Facts: A computer department employee made an entry error that botched an entire run of computer reports. Efforts to rectify the situation produced a second set of improperly run reports. As a result of the series of errors, the employer incurred extra costs of $2,400, plus a weekend of overtime work by other computer department staffers. Management suspended the employee for 3 days for negligence, and also revoked a promotion for which the employee had previously been approved.

Protesting the discipline, the employee stressed that she had attempted to correct her error in the early stages of the run by notifying the manager of computer operations of her mistake. Maintaining that the resulting string of errors could have been avoided if the manager had followed up on her report and stopped the initial run, the employee argued that she had been treated unfairly because the manager had not been disciplined even though he compounded the problem, whereas she was severely punished. Moreover, citing her "impeccable" work record and management's acknowledgment that she had always been a "model employee," the employee insisted that the denial of her previously approved promotion was "unconscionable."

(Please do not read beyond this point until after you have completed the Experiential Exercise.)

Award: The arbitrator upholds the 3-day suspension, but decides that the promotion should be restored.

Discussion: "There is no question," the arbitrator notes, that the employee's negligent act "set in motion the train of events that resulted in running two complete sets of reports reflecting improper information." Stressing that the employer incurred substantial cost because of the error, the arbitrator cites "unchallenged" testimony that management had commonly issued 3-day suspensions for similar infractions in the past. Thus, the arbitrator decides, the employer acted with just cause in meting out an "evenhanded" punishment for the negligence.

Turning to the denial of the already approved promotion, the arbitrator says to view this action "in the same light as a demotion for disciplinary reasons." In such cases, the arbitrator notes, management's decision normally is based on a pattern of unsatisfactory behavior, an employee's inability to perform, or similar grounds. Observing that management had never before reversed a promotion as part of a disciplinary action, the arbitrator says that by tacking on the denial of the promotion in this case, the employer substantially varied its disciplinary policy from its past practice. Because this action on management's part was not "evenhanded," the arbitrator rules, the promotion should be restored.[115] ∎

Chapter 9

Managing Labor Relations and Collective Bargaining

- The Labor Movement
- Unions and the Law
- The Union Drive and Election
- The Collective Bargaining Process
- What's Next for Unions?

When you finish studying this chapter, you should be able to:

- Discuss *the nature of the major federal labor relations laws.*
- Describe *the process of a union drive and election.*
- Discuss *the main steps in the collective bargaining process.*

INTRODUCTION

The U.S. Department of Labor accused Starbucks of breaking the law in trying to prevent workers in some of its shops from unionizing. Among other things, it accused managers in those stores of retaliating against workers who wanted to unionize, by interrogating them about their union inclinations. A Starbucks spokesperson said the company believes the allegations are baseless and that the firm will vigorously defend itself.[1]

THE LABOR MOVEMENT

The labor union movement is important. Just over 17.7 million U.S. workers belong to unions—around 12.4% of everyone working in this country.[2] Many are still blue-collar workers. But workers including doctors, psychologists, graduate teaching assistants, and even fashion models are joining unions.[3] About 40% of America's 20 million federal, state, and municipal public employees belong to unions.[4] And in some industries—including transportation and public utilities, where over 26% of employees are union members—it's hard to get a job without joining a union.[5] Union membership in other countries is declining, but still very high (over 35% of employed workers in Canada, Mexico, Brazil, and Italy, for instance). And for the first time in many years, union membership in America actually rose a bit in 2008–2009.[6]

Furthermore, don't assume that unions only negatively affect employers. For example, perhaps by systematizing company practices, unionization may also improve performance. Thus in one study, researchers concluded that heart attack mortality among patients in hospitals with unionized registered nurses was 5% to 9% lower than in nonunion hospitals.[7] Another study found a significant negative relationship between union membership and employees' intent to leave their jobs.[8]

Why Do Workers Organize?

There's no simple answer to the question why workers unionize. It's clear that workers don't unionize just to get more pay, although the pay issue is important. For example, recent median weekly wages for union workers was $781, while that for nonunion workers was $612.[9]

But pay isn't always the issue. Often, the urge to unionize seems to boil down to the workers' belief that it is only through unity that they can protect themselves from managerial whims. For example, a butcher hired by Walmart said he was told he would possibly move up to supervisor. He started work and bought a new car. However, he said his supervisor never mentioned the promotion again after the employee hurt his back and was out for 5 weeks. Feeling cheated, the butcher went to the Grocery Workers Union, which sent an organizer to speak with the employee. The store's meat cutters eventually voted to unionize. A week later Walmart announced it would switch to prepackaged meat. Henceforth, the meat suppliers would do all the cutting at their factories, and the stores wouldn't need meat cutters.[10]

Research Findings   Studies suggest that two things—employer unfairness and the availability of a union that the employees believed had clout—explain why employees unionize.

In one study, of an Australia-based banking firm, researchers found that employer unfairness played a big role: "Individuals who believe that the company rules or policies were administered unfairly or to their detriment were more likely to turn to unions as a source of assistance."[11]

However, unfairness itself was not enough to prompt a vote to unionize; the union also needed clout. Employees were more likely to join in those situations where they "perceived that the union was effective in the area of wages and benefits and protection against unfair dismissals."[12] One labor relations lawyer put it this way, "the one major thing unions offer is making you a 'for cause' instead of an 'at will' employee, which guarantees a hearing and arbitration if you're fired."[13]

When a Kaiser Permanente medical center cut back on vacation and sick leave, its pharmacists' union won back the lost vacation days. Said one pharmacist, "Kaiser is a pretty benevolent employer, but there's always the pressure to squeeze a little."[14]

What Do Unions Want? What Are Their Aims?

We can generalize by saying that unions have two sets of aims, one for union security and one for improved wages, hours, working conditions, and benefits for their members.

Union Security   First and probably foremost, unions seek to establish security for themselves. They fight hard for the right to represent a firm's workers and to be the *exclusive* bargaining agent for all employees in the unit. (As such, they negotiate contracts for all employees, including nonunion members.) Five types of union security are possible:

1. *Closed shop*.[15]   The company can hire only union members. Outlawed in 1947, this still exists in some industries (such as printing).
2. *Union shop*.   The company can hire nonunion people, but they must join the union after a prescribed period and pay dues. (If not, they can be fired.)
3. *Agency shop*.   Employees who do not belong to the union still must pay union dues on the assumption that the union's efforts benefit *all* the workers.
4. *Preferential shop*.   Union members get preference in hiring, but the employer can still hire nonunion members.
5. *Maintenance of membership arrangement*.   Employees do not have to belong to the union. However, union members employed by the firm must maintain membership in the union for the contract period.

Not all states give unions the right to require union membership as a condition of employment. **Right to work** "is a term used to describe state statutory or constitutional provisions banning the requirement of union membership as a condition of employment."[16] Labor relations law permits states to forbid the negotiation of compulsory union membership provisions. Right-to-work laws don't outlaw unions. They do outlaw (within those states) any form of union security. This understandably inhibits union formation in those states. Several years ago, Oklahoma became the 22nd state to pass Right-to-Work legislation. Some believe that this helps explain why Oklahoma's union membership dropped dramatically in the next 3 years.[17] Recently there were 23 right-to-work states.[18]

Improved Wages, Hours, Working Conditions, and Benefits for Members   Once their security is assured, unions fight to improve their members' wages, hours, and working conditions. The typical labor agreement also gives the union a role in other HR activities, including recruiting, selecting, compensating, promoting, training, and discharging employees.

The AFL-CIO

The American Federation of Labor and Congress of Industrial Organizations (AFL-CIO) is a voluntary federation of about 56 national and international labor unions in the United States. It resulted from the merger of the AFL and CIO in 1955. For many people, it is synonymous with the word *union* in the United States.

Actually, though, union federation membership is in flux. Several years ago, six big unions—the Service Employees' International Union (SEIU), the International Brotherhood of Teamsters, the United Food and Commercial Workers, the United Farm Workers, the Laborers International Union, and UNITE HERE (which represents garment and service workers)—left the AFL-CIO and established their own federation, called the Change to Win Coalition. Together, the departing unions represented over one-fourth of the AFL-CIO's membership and budget. Change to Win plans to be more aggressive about organizing workers than they say the AFL-CIO was. Then in 2009, UNITE HERE rejoined the AFL-CIO, possibly slowing Change to Win's momentum.[19]

UNIONS AND THE LAW

Until about 1930, there were no special labor laws. Employers didn't have to engage in collective bargaining with employees and were virtually unrestrained in their behavior toward unions: The use of spies, blacklists, and the firing of agitators was widespread. "Yellow dog" contracts, whereby management could require nonunion membership as a condition for employment, were widely enforced. Most union weapons—even strikes—were illegal.

This one-sided situation lasted in the United States from the Revolution to the Great Depression (around 1930). Since then, in response to changing public attitudes, values, and economic conditions, labor law has gone through three stages, from "strong encouragement" of unions, to "modified encouragement coupled with regulation," to "detailed regulation of internal union affairs."[20]

Period of Strong Encouragement: The Norris-LaGuardia Act (1932) and the National Labor Relations Act (1935)

The **Norris-LaGuardia Act** set the stage for an era in which government encouraged union activity. The act guaranteed to each employee the right to bargain collectively "free from interference, restraint, or coercion." It declared yellow dog contracts unenforceable. It limited the courts' abilities to issue injunctions for activities such as peaceful picketing.[21]

Yet this act did little to restrain employers from fighting labor organizations. Therefore, Congress passed the National Labor Relations Act (or **Wagner Act**) in 1935 to add teeth to the Norris-LaGuardia Act. It did this by banning certain unfair labor practices, providing for secret-ballot elections and majority rule for determining whether a firm's employees were to unionize, and creating the **National Labor Relations Board (NLRB)** for overseeing and enforcing these two provisions.[22]

Unfair Employer Labor Practices   The Wagner Act deemed as "statutory wrongs" (but not crimes) five unfair employer labor practices:

1. It is unfair for employers to "interfere with, restrain, or coerce employees" in exercising their legal right of self-organization.
2. It is an unfair practice for company representatives to dominate or interfere with either the formation or the administration of labor unions. Among other management actions found to be unfair under practices 1 and 2 are bribing employees, using company spy systems, and moving a business to avoid unionization.
3. Employers are prohibited from discriminating in any way against employees for their legal union activities.
4. Employers are forbidden to discharge or discriminate against employees simply because the latter file unfair practice charges against the company.
5. Finally, it is an unfair labor practice for employers to refuse to bargain collectively with their employees' duly chosen representatives.

The union files the unfair labor practice charge (see Figure 9.1) with the NLRB. The board then investigates the charge and determines whether it should take formal action. Possible actions include dismissal of the complaint, request for an injunction against the employer, and an order that the employer cease and desist.

From 1935 to 1947   Union membership increased quickly after passage of the Wagner Act in 1935. Other factors such as an improving economy and aggressive union leadership contributed to this as well. But by the mid-1940s, the tide had begun to turn. Largely because of a series of massive postwar strikes, public policy began to shift against what many viewed as union excesses. The stage was set for passage of the Taft-Hartley Act of 1947.

Period of Modified Encouragement Coupled with Regulation: The Taft-Hartley Act (1947)

The **Taft-Hartley** (or Labor Management Relations) **Act** reflected the public's less enthusiastic attitudes toward unions. It amended the Wagner Act in four ways: by prohibiting unfair union labor practices, by enumerating the rights of union members, by enumerating the rights of employers, and by allowing the president of the United States to bar national emergency strikes temporarily.

Unfair Union Labor Practices   First, the Taft-Hartley Act enumerated certain prohibited labor practices:

1. Unions were banned from restraining or coercing employees from exercising their guaranteed bargaining rights.
2. It is an unfair labor practice for a union to cause an employer to discriminate in any way against an employee in order to encourage or discourage his or her membership in a union.
3. It is an unfair labor practice for a union to refuse to bargain in good faith with the employer about wages, hours, and other employment conditions.

Figure 9.1 NLRB Form 501: Filing an Unfair Labor Practice Charge

FORM EXEMPT UNDER 44 U.S.C 3512

INTERNET
FORM NLRB-501
(2-08)

UNITED STATES OF AMERICA
NATIONAL LABOR RELATIONS BOARD
CHARGE AGAINST EMPLOYER

DO NOT WRITE IN THIS SPACE

Case	Date Filed

INSTRUCTIONS:
File an original with NLRB Regional Director for the region in which the alleged unfair labor practice occurred or is occurring.

1. EMPLOYER AGAINST WHOM CHARGE IS BROUGHT

a. Name d Employer	b. Tel. No.
	c. Cell No.
	f. Fax No.
d. Address *(Street, city, state, and ZIP code)* e. Employer Representative	g. e-Mail
	h. Number of workers employed
i. Type of Establishment *(factory, mine, wholesaler, etc.)* j. Identify principalproduct or service	

k. The above-named employer has engaged in and is engaging in unfair labor practices within the meaning of section 8(a), subsections (1) and *(list subsections)* _____ of the National Labor Relations Act, and these unfair labor practices are practices affecting commerce within the meaning of the Act, or these unfair labor practices are unfair practices affecting commerce within the meaning of the Act and the Postal Reorganization Act.

2. Basis of the Charge *(set forth a clear and concise statement of the facts constituting the alleged unfair laborpractices)*

3. Full name of party filing charge *(if labor organization, give full name, including local name and number)*

4a. Address *(Street and number, city, state, and ZIP code)*	4b. Tel. No.
	4c. Cell No.
	4d. Fax No.
	4e. e-Mail

5. Full name of national or international labor organization of which it is an affiliate or constituent unit *(to be filled in when charge is filed by a labor organization)*

6. DECLARATION I declare that I have read the above charge and that the statements are true to the best of my knowledge and belief. By _____ _____ *(signature of representative or person making charge)* *(Print/typenameandtitleoroffice,ifany)*	Tel. No.
	Office, if any, Cell No.
	Fax No.
	e-Mail

Address _____   *(date)*

WILLFUL FALSE STATEMENTS ON THIS CHARGE CAN BE PUNISHED BY FINE AND IMPRISONMENT (U.S. CODE, TITLE 18, SECTION 1001)

PRIVACY ACT STATEMENT

Solicitation of the information on this form is authorized by the National Labor Relations Act (NLRA), 29 U.S.C. § 151 *et seq.* The principal use of the information is to assist the National Labor Relations Board (NLRB) in processing unfair labor practice and related proceedings or litigation. The routine uses for the inform ation are fully set forth in the Federal Register, 71 Fed. Reg. 74942-43 (Dec. 13, 2006). The NLRB will further explain these uses upon request. Disclosure of this information to the NLRB is voluntary; however, failure to supply the information will cause the NLRB to decline to invoke its processes.

Rights of Employees   The Taft-Hartley Act also protected the rights of employees against their unions. For example, many people felt that compulsory unionism violated the basic U.S. right of freedom of association. The new *right-to-work laws* sprang up in 19 states (mainly in the South and Southwest), outlawing labor contracts that made union membership a condition for keeping one's job.

In general, the National Labor Relations Act does not restrain unions from unfair labor practices to the extent that it does employers. Unions may not restrain or coerce employees. However, "violent or otherwise threatening behavior or clearly coercive or intimidating union activities are necessary before the NLRB will find an unfair labor practice."[23] Examples here would include physical assaults or threats of violence and mass picketing that restrains the lawful entry or leaving of a work site. In one typical case, *Pattern Makers* v. *National Labor Relations Board,* the U.S. Supreme Court found the union guilty of an unfair labor practice when it tried to fine some members for resigning from the union and returning to work during a strike.[24]

Rights of Employers   The Taft-Hartley Act also gave employers certain rights. For example, it gave them full freedom to express their views concerning union organization. Thus, a manager can tell his or her employees that in his or her opinion unions are worthless, dangerous to the economy, and immoral. A manager can even hint, generally speaking, that unionization and subsequent high-wage demands might result in the permanent closing of the plant (but not in its relocation). Employers can set forth the union's record concerning violence and corruption, if appropriate, and can play on the racial prejudices of workers by describing the union's philosophy toward integration. In fact, the only major restraint is that there can be no threat of reprisal or force or promise of benefit.[25]

The employer also cannot meet with employees on company time within 24 hours of an election or suggest to employees that they vote against the union while they are at home or in the employer's office. However, he or she can do so while in their work area or in the place where they normally gather.

National Emergency Strikes   The Taft-Hartley Act also allows the U.S. president to intervene in **national emergency strikes,** which are strikes (for example, on the part of steel firm employees) that might imperil national health and safety. The president may appoint a board of inquiry and, based on its report, apply for an injunction restraining the strike for 60 days. If no settlement is reached during that time, the injunction can be extended for another 20 days. During this period, employees are polled in a secret ballot to ascertain their willingness to accept the employer's last offer.

Period of Detailed Regulation of Internal Union Affairs: The Landrum-Griffin Act (1959)

In the 1950s, Senate investigations revealed unsavory practices by some unions, and the result was the **Landrum-Griffin Act** (officially, the Labor Management Reporting and Disclosure Act). Its aim was to protect union members from possible wrongdoing on the part of their unions.

The Landrum-Griffin Act contains a bill of rights for union members. Among other things, this provides for certain rights in the nomination of candidates for union office. It also affirms a member's right to sue his or her union. And it ensures that no member can be fined or suspended without due process (such as a list of specific charges and a fair hearing).

The act also laid out rules regarding union elections. For example, national and international unions must elect officers at least once every 5 years, using a secret-ballot mechanism.

The Senate investigators also discovered flagrant examples of employer wrongdoing. The Landrum-Griffin Act therefore also greatly expanded the list of unlawful employer actions. For example, companies can no longer pay their own employees to entice them not to join the union.

THE UNION DRIVE AND ELECTION

It is through the union drive and election that a union tries to be recognized to represent employees. This process has five basic steps: initial contact, authorization cards, hearing, campaign, and the election.

Step 1: Initial Contact

During the initial contact stage, the union determines the employees' interest in organizing and establishes an organizing committee.

The initiative for the first contact between the employees and the union may come from the employees, from a union already representing other employees of the firm, or from a union representing workers elsewhere. Sometimes, a union effort starts with a disgruntled employee's contacting the local union to learn how to organize his or her place of work. Sometimes, though, the campaign starts when a union decides it wants to expand to representing other employees in the firm, or when the company looks easy to organize, or when it already represents competitors' employees. (Thus the Teamsters Union—already in place at UPS—began organizing FedEx.) In any case, there is an initial contact between a union representative and a few employees.

The Union Rep When an employer becomes a target, a union official usually assigns a representative to assess employee interest. The representative visits the firm to determine whether enough employees are interested to make a campaign worthwhile. He or she also identifies employees who would make good leaders in the organizing campaign and calls them together to create an organizing committee. The objective is to "educate the committee about the benefits of forming a union, the law and procedures involved in forming a local union, and the issues management is likely to raise during a campaign."[26]

Contact Guidelines The union must follow certain guidelines when it starts contacting employees. The law allows union organizers to solicit employees for membership as long as it doesn't endanger the performance or safety of the employees. Therefore, much of the contact takes place off the job, perhaps at home or at places near work. Organizers can also safely contact employees on company grounds during off hours (such as lunch or break time). Under some conditions, union representatives may solicit employees at their workstations, but this is rare. In practice, there will be much informal organizing and debate going on at the workplace. In any case, this initial contact stage may be deceptively quiet. In some instances the first inkling management has of a union campaign is the distribution or posting of a handbill soliciting union membership.

Labor Relations Consultants   Labor relations consultants are increasingly influencing the unionization process, with both management and unions using outside advisors. The use by management of consultants (who unions often refer to as *union busters*) has grown considerably. One study found management consultants involved in 75% of the elections they surveyed.[27]

One expert says an employer's main goal shouldn't be to win representation elections but to avoid them altogether. He says doing so means taking fast action when the first signs of union activity appear. His advice in a nutshell: Don't just ignore the union's efforts while it spreads pro-union rumors, such as "If we had a union, we wouldn't have to work so much overtime." Retain an attorney and react at once.[28]

Union Salting   **Union salting** refers to a union-organizing tactic by which undercover union organizers who are employed full time by a union are hired by unwitting employers. The National Labor Relations Board defines "salting" as "placing of union members on nonunion job sites for the purpose of organizing."[29] A U.S. Supreme Court decision, *NLRB* v. *Town and Country Electric*, held the tactic to be legal.

The Web   The Web is a potent union contact tool. Unions can mass e-mail announcements to collective bargaining unit members, and use mass e-mail to reach supporters and government officials for their corporate campaigns. For example, the group trying to organize Starbucks workers (the Starbucks Workers Union) has their own Web site (www.starbucksunion.org). It includes notes like, "Starbucks managers monitored Internet chat rooms and eavesdropped on party conversations in a covert campaign to identify employees agitating for union representation."[30]

Step 2: Authorization Cards

For the union to petition the NLRB for the right to hold an election, it must show that a sizable number of employees may be interested in being organized. The next step is thus for union organizers to try to get the employees to sign **authorization cards** (see Figure 9.2). Before they can petition an election, 30% of the eligible employees in an appropriate bargaining unit must sign.

During this stage, both union and management typically use various forms of propaganda. The union claims it can improve working conditions, raise wages, increase benefits, and generally get the workers better deals. Management need not be silent; it can attack the union on ethical and moral grounds and cite the cost of union membership, for example. Management can also explain its record, express facts and opinions, and explain to its employees the law applicable to organizing campaigns and the meaning of the duty to bargain in good faith (if the union should win the election). However, neither side can threaten, bribe, or coerce employees. Further, an employer may not make promises of benefit to

Figure 9.2 Sample Authorization Card

Yes! I believe that by joining together with my co-workers to form a union, we can create a more democratic and fair workplace. I therefore authorize SEIU Local 503, OPEU to be my exclusive representative for the purposes of collective bargaining with my employer. I understand that my signature on this card may be used to obtain certification of SEIU Local 503, OPEU as our exclusive bargaining representative without an election.

Employer_____ Worksite_____

Signature_____ Date:_____

Printed Name:_____

Street Address:_____ City:_____ Zip:_____

Home Phone:_____ Cell Phone:_____ Home E-mail:_____

Department:_____ Job Title/Classification_____

- -

Signing a card means that you support forming a union with SEIU Local 503, OPEU.
When a majority of OJD employees sign union authorization cards, our decision to form a union will be recognized. We can then begin bargaining before the drastic cuts being considered for the next biennium are enacted. Under new rules, the state Employment Relations Board will verify whether a majority of OJD employees have signed union authorization cards. When a majority have signed up, OJD will recognize SEIU Local 503, OPEU as our union. There is no need for a union election.

You must print and mail in this authorization card for it to be recognized. Only original cards are valid and can be submitted to ERB.

Fill out all parts of the card to make sure you stay informed. To be valid, the card must be signed and dated.

If you have already signed a card, you do not need to send this one in. Instead, please pass it along to someone who hasn't had the opportunity to sign a card yet.

Send card to:
SEIU, Local 503
6401 SE Foster Rd
Portland, OR 97206

Questions? Contact **Mike Pageler**
pagelerm@opeuseiu.org
1.800.527.9374, x408

Source: http://seiu100.org/OLDSITE/membershipapp.htm, accessed August 9, 2007.

employees or make unilateral changes in terms and conditions of employment that were not planned to be implemented prior to the onset of union-organizing activity. Managers also should not look through signed authorization cards if confronted with them by union representatives. Doing so could be construed as an unfair labor practice by the NLRB, which could view it as spying on those who signed.

During this stage, unions can picket the company, subject to three constraints: The union must file a petition for an election within 30 days after the start of picketing, the firm cannot already be lawfully recognizing another union, and there cannot already have been a valid NLRB election during the past 12 months.

Step 3: The Hearing

After the authorization cards have been collected, one of three things can occur. The employer may choose not to contest union recognition, in which case no hearing is needed and a *consent election* is held immediately. The employer may choose not to contest the union's *right to an election* (and/or the scope of the bargaining unit, or which employees are eligible to vote in the election), in which case no hearing is needed and the parties can stipulate an election. Or the employer may contest the union's right, in which case it can insist on a *hearing* to determine those issues. An employer's decision about whether to insist on a hearing is a strategic one based on the facts of each case, and on whether it feels it needs additional time to develop a campaign to try to persuade its employees not to elect a union.

Most companies contest the union's right to represent their employees, and thus decline to recognize the union voluntarily: They claim that a significant number of their employees do not really want the union. It is at this point that the U.S. Labor Department's NLRB gets involved. The NLRB is usually contacted by the union, which requests a hearing. Based on this, the regional director of the NLRB sends a hearing officer to investigate. (For example, did 30% or more of the employees in an appropriate bargaining unit sign the authorization cards?) The examiner sends both management and the union a notice of representation hearing that states the time and place of the hearing.

The **bargaining unit** is one decision to come out of the hearing; it is the group of employees that the union will be authorized to represent and bargain for collectively.

Finally, if the results of the hearing are favorable for the union, the NLRB directs that an election be held. It issues a Decision and Direction of Election notice to that effect and has the employer post NLRB Form 666, Notice to Employees, announcing that an election may be held and informing employees of their rights (to organize, for instance) and of examples of unfair employer conduct (such as threatening loss of jobs or promising raises to influence the vote).

Step 4: The Campaign

During the campaign that precedes the election, the union and employer appeal to employees for their votes. The union emphasizes that it will prevent unfairness, set up a grievance/seniority system, and will improve unsatisfactory wages. Union strength, they'll say, will give employees a voice in determining wages and working conditions. Management emphasizes that improvements such as those don't require unionization, and that wages are equal to or better than they would be with a union contract. Management also emphasizes the financial cost of union dues; the fact that the union is an "outsider"; and that if the union wins, a strike may follow.[31] It can even attack the union on ethical and moral grounds, while insisting that employees will not be as well off and may lose freedom. But neither side can threaten, bribe, or coerce employees.

The Supervisor's Role Supervisors must be knowledgeable about what they can and can't do to hamper organizing activities legally, lest they commit unfair labor practices. Such practices could cause a new election to be held after the company has won a previous election or cause the company to forfeit the second election and go directly to contract negotiation. In one case, a plant superintendent reacted to a union's initial organizing attempt by prohibiting distribution of union literature in the plant's lunchroom. Because solicitation of off-duty workers in nonwork areas is generally legal, the company subsequently allowed the union to post union literature on the company's bulletin board and to distribute union literature in nonworking areas inside the plant. However, the NLRB still ruled that the initial act of prohibiting distribution of the literature was an unfair labor practice, one that was not "made right" by the company's subsequent efforts. The NLRB used the superintendent's action as one reason for invalidating an election that the company won.[32]

Strategy and HR Starbucks bases its strategy, in part, on owning its stores. Given the difficulties monitoring what employees are doing in its far-flung stores, Starbucks managers can't just rely on traditional control tools like budgets to control what's happening in each store. The company therefore works hard to encourage employees to control themselves—by making them "partners" and by providing excellent benefits. As a company that provides excellent benefits and working conditions, Starbucks executives were surprised that some employees expressed a desire to unionize. Nevertheless, the allegations that some local managers may have tried to retaliate against employees who favored the union were a wake-up call. They underscore why all employers must carefully train supervisors in how to react when the union comes to call.

To avoid such problems, employers should have rules governing distribution of literature and solicitation of workers and train supervisors in how to apply them.

Rules Regarding Literature and Solicitation An employer can take a number of steps to restrict union-organizing activity legally.[33] For example:

- Nonemployees can always be barred from soliciting employees when the employees are on duty and not on a break.
- Employers can usually stop employees from soliciting other employees for any purpose if one or both employees are on paid-duty time and not on a break.
- Most employers (not including retail stores, shopping centers, and certain other employers) can bar nonemployees from the building's interiors and work areas as a right of private property owners.

Such restrictions are valid only if the employer does not impose them in a discriminatory manner. For example, if it permits employees to collect money for a wedding shower, to sell Avon-type products, or to engage in other solicitation during their working time, the employer will not be able lawfully to prohibit them from union soliciting during work time.

Finally, remember that there are many more ways to commit unfair labor practices than just keeping union organizers off your private property. For example, one employer decided to have a cookout and paid day off 2 days before a union representation election. The NLRB said that was too much of a coincidence and represented coercive conduct. The union had lost the first vote but won the second vote as a result.[34]

Step 5: The Election

Finally, the election can be held within 30 to 60 days after the NLRB issues its Decision and Direction of Election. The election is by secret ballot. The NLRB provides the ballots (see Figure 9.3), as well as the voting booth and ballot box. It also counts the votes and certifies the results. Historically, the more workers that vote, the less likely is a union victory. This is probably because more workers

Figure 9.3 Sample NLRB Ballot

UNITED STATES OF AMERICA

National Labor Relations Board

OFFICIAL SECRET BALLOT

FOR CERTAIN EMPLOYEES OF

Do you wish to be represented for purposes of collective bargaining by —

MARK AN "S" IN THE SQUARE OF YOUR CHOICE

YES

NO

DO NOT SIGN THIS BALLOT. Fold and drop in ballot box.
If you spoil this ballot return it to the Board Agent for a new one.

who are not strong union supporters end up voting. The union is important, too: The Teamsters union is less likely than other unions to win a representation election.[35]

The union becomes the employees' representative if it wins the election, and winning means getting a majority of the votes cast, not a majority of the workers in the bargaining unit. (Also remember that if an employer commits an unfair labor practice, a "no union" election may be reversed. Supervisors must therefore be very careful not to commit such unfair practices.) In one recent year, the union win rate rose to 66.8%, higher than it had been for decades.[36]

Decertification Elections: When Employees Want to Oust Their Union

Winning an election and signing an agreement do not necessarily mean that the union is in the company to stay—quite the opposite. The same law that grants employees the right to unionize also gives them a legal way to terminate the union's right to represent them. The process is *decertification*. There are around 450 to 500 decertification elections each year, of which unions usually win around 30%.[37] That's actually a more favorable rate for management than the rate for the original representation elections.

Decertification campaigns don't differ much from certification campaigns.[38] The union organizes membership meetings and house-to-house visits, mails literature to homes, and uses phone calls, NLRB appeals, and (sometimes) threats and harassment to win the election. Managers use meetings—including one-on-one meetings, small-group meetings, and meetings with entire units—as well as legal or labor expert assistance, letters, improved working conditions, and subtle or not-so-subtle threats in its attempts to win a decertification vote.

THE COLLECTIVE BARGAINING PROCESS

What Is Collective Bargaining?

When and if the union is recognized as a company's employees' representative, a day is set for meeting at the bargaining table. Representatives of management and the union meet to negotiate a labor contract that contains agreements on specific provisions covering wages, hours, and working conditions.

What exactly is **collective bargaining?** According to the National Labor Relations Act:

> For the purpose of (this act) to bargain collectively is the performance of the mutual obligation of the employer and the representative of the employees to meet at reasonable times and confer in good faith with respect to wages, hours, and terms and conditions of employment, or the negotiation of an

agreement, or any question arising thereunder, and the execution of a
written contract incorporating any agreement reached if requested by
either party, but such obligation does not compel either party to agree to
a proposal or require the making of a concession.

In plain language, this means that both management and labor are required by law
to negotiate wages, hours, and terms and conditions of employment "in good faith."

What Is Good-Faith Bargaining?

Good-faith bargaining means that proposals are matched with counterproposals
and that both parties make every reasonable effort to arrive at an agreement. It does
not mean that either party is compelled to agree to a proposal. Nor does it require
that either party make any specific concessions (although as a practical matter, some
may be necessary).

When Is Bargaining Not in Good Faith?   In assessing whether a party violated
its good-faith obligations, the totality of each party's conduct is of prime importance.[39] However, as interpreted by the NLRB and the courts, examples of a violation
of the requirements for good-faith bargaining may include:

1. *Proposals and demands.* The NLRB considers the advancement of proposals as a
   positive factor in determining overall good faith.
2. *Withholding information.* The NLRB and courts expect management to furnish
   usable information on matters such as wages, hours, and other terms of employment that union negotiators request and legitimately require. Failing to do so
   may reflect bad-faith bargaining.[40]
3. *Dilatory tactics.* The law requires that the parties meet and "confer at reasonable
   times and intervals." It does not require management to meet at the time
   and place dictated just by the union. It may be that employers try to delay the
   meeting to "disrupt a union's bargaining momentum."[41] However, inor-
   dinately delaying the meeting or refusing to meet with the other party may
   reflect bad-faith bargaining.
4. *Unilateral changes in conditions.* This is viewed as a strong indication that the
   employer is not bargaining with the required intent of reaching an agreement.

The Negotiating Team

Both union and management send a negotiating team to the bargaining table, and
both teams usually go into the bargaining sessions having done their research. Union
representatives have sounded out union members on their desires and conferred
with union representatives of related unions.

Similarly, management compiles pay and benefit data, including comparisons to
local pay rates and rates paid for similar jobs in the industry. Management also carefully "costs" the current labor contract and determines the increased cost—total, per
employee, and per hour—of the union's demands. It also tries to identify probable
union demands and to size up which demands are more important to the union.

It uses information from grievances, and feedback from supervisors, to determine ahead of time what the union's demands might be and thus prepare counteroffers and arguments.[42]

Bargaining Items

"Wages, hours, and conditions of employment" is too broad to be useful in negotiations, so labor law and court decisions have set out categories of items that are subject to bargaining: These are *mandatory, voluntary,* and *illegal items.*

Voluntary (or permissible) **bargaining items** are neither mandatory nor illegal; they become a part of negotiations only through the joint agreement of both management and union. Neither party can be compelled against its wishes to negotiate over voluntary items. An employee cannot hold up signing a contract because the other party refuses to bargain on a voluntary item.

Illegal bargaining items are forbidden by law. The clause agreeing to hire "union members exclusively" would be illegal in a right-to-work state, for example.

About 70 **mandatory bargaining items** exist, some of which are in Figure 9.4. They include wages, hours, rest periods, layoffs, transfers, benefits, and severance pay. Others are added as the law evolves. For instance, drug testing evolved into a mandatory item as a result of NLRB decisions.

Figure 9.4 Bargaining Items

Mandatory	Permissible	Illegal
Rates of pay	Indemnity bonds	Closed shop
Wages	Management rights as	Separation of employees
Hours of employment	to union affairs	based on race
Overtime pay	Pension benefits of	Discriminatory treatment
Shift differentials	retired employees	
Holidays	Scope of the bargaining unit	
Vacations	Including supervisors in the	
Severance pay	contract	
Pensions	Additional parties to the	
Insurance benefits	contract such as the	
Profit-sharing plans	international union	
Christmas bonuses	Use of union label	
Company housing, meals,	Settlement of unfair labor	
and discounts	charges	
Employee security	Prices in cafeteria	
Job performance	Continuance of past	
Union security	contract	
Management–union	Membership of bargaining	
relationship	team	
Drug testing of employees	Employment of strikebreaker	

Source: Michael R. Carrell and Christina Heavrin, *Labor Relations and Collective Bargaining: Cases, Practice, and Law,* 4th, © 1995. Electronically reproduced by permission of Pearson Education, Inc., Upper Saddle River, New Jersey.

Bargaining Stages[43]

Bargaining typically goes through several stages.[44] First, each side presents its demands. At this stage, both parties are usually quite far apart on some issues. Indeed, labor negotiators use the term *blue sky* to refer to demands (such as swimming pools and 17 paid holidays, including Valentine's Day) that some negotiators have brought to the table.

Second, there is a reduction of demands. At this stage, each side trades off some of its demands to gain others, a process called *trading points*. Third are the subcommittee studies: The parties form joint subcommittees or study groups to try to work out reasonable alternatives. Fourth, the parties reach an informal settlement, and each group goes back to its sponsor. Union representatives check informally with their superiors and the union members; management representatives check with top management. Finally, when everything is in order, the parties fine-tune, proofread, and sign a formal agreement. The *HR in Practice* box summarizes negotiating guidelines.

Impasses, Mediation, and Strikes

Impasses Signing the agreement assumes everything is in order, and that there are no insurmountable disagreements. If there are, the parties may declare an impasse. For example, a few years ago, the National Hockey League informed the

HR in Practice: Negotiating Guidelines

1. *Set clear objectives* for every bargaining item.
2. *Do not hurry.*
3. When in doubt, *caucus* with your associates.
4. Be *well prepared* with firm data supporting your position.
5. Always strive to keep some *flexibility* in your position.
6. Don't just concern yourself with what the other party says and does; *find out why.*
7. Respect the importance of *face saving* for the other party.
8. Constantly be alert to the *real intentions* of the other party with respect not only to goals but also to priorities.
9. Be a good *listener.*
10. Build a reputation for *being fair but firm.*
11. Learn to *control your emotions;* don't panic.
12. Be sure as you make each bargaining move that you know its *relationship* to all other moves.
13. Measure each move against your *objectives.*
14. Pay close attention to the *wording* of every clause renegotiated; words and phrases are often sources of grievances.
15. Remember that collective bargaining negotiations are, by nature, part of a *compromise* process.
16. Consider the impact of present negotiations on those in *future years.*
17. Don't be so open and straightforward that you start making excessive concessions.[45]

NLRB that it had reached an impasse in its negotiations with the National Hockey League Players Association.[46] The parties must get past the impasse for the contract to be finalized and signed.

An impasse usually occurs because one party demands more than the other offers. Sometimes an impasse can be resolved through a third party, a disinterested person such as a mediator or arbitrator. If the impasse is not resolved in this way, the union may call a work stoppage, or *strike,* to pressure management.

Third-Party Involvement   Three types of third-party interventions are used to overcome an impasse: mediation, fact-finding, and arbitration. With **mediation,** a neutral third party tries to assist the principals in reaching agreement. The mediator usually holds meetings with each party to determine where each stands regarding its position. He or she then uses this information to find common ground for further bargaining. For example, in 2009, the union representing U.S. Airways pilots, which had been seeking a new contract since U.S. Air merged with America West Holdings Corp., in 2005, applied for federal mediation.[47] The mediator is always a go-between. As such, he or she communicates assessments of the likelihood of a strike, the possible settlement packages available, and the like. The mediator does not have the authority to insist on a position or make a concession. However, he or she may—and probably will—provide leadership by making his or her position on some issue clear.

In certain situations (as in a national emergency dispute in which the president of the United States determines that it would be a national emergency for a strike to occur), a fact-finder may be appointed. A **fact-finder** is a neutral party. He or she studies the issues and makes a public recommendation of what a reasonable settlement ought to be. For example, presidential emergency fact-finding boards have successfully resolved impasses in certain critical transportation disputes.

Arbitration is the most definitive type of third-party intervention because the arbitrator may have the power to decide and dictate settlement terms. Unlike mediation and fact-finding, arbitration can guarantee a solution to an impasse. With *binding arbitration,* both parties commit to accepting the arbitrator's award. With *nonbinding arbitration,* they do not. Arbitration may also be voluntary or compulsory (in other words, imposed by a government agency). In the United States, voluntary binding arbitration is the most prevalent.

Arbitration may not always be as impartial as it's thought to be. Researchers studied 391 arbitrated cases in baseball over about 20 years. They expected decisions to split about evenly between players and teams. In fact, arbitrator awards favored teams 61% of the time. They concluded that (at least in baseball) "self-interested behavior by arbitrators" may lead to bias against players, and particularly against players of African American and Latin ancestry.[48]

Sources of Third-Party Assistance   Various public and professional agencies make arbitrators and mediators available. For example, the American Arbitration Association (AAA) represents and provides the services of thousands of arbitrators and mediators to employers and unions requesting their services. The U.S. Office of Arbitration Services, part of the U.S. Office of Mediation & Conciliation Service (http://www.fmcs.gov/internet/), maintains a roster of arbitrators qualified to hear and decide disputes.

Strikes   A strike is a withdrawal of labor. There are four main types of strikes. An **economic strike** results from a failure to agree on the terms of a contract—from an impasse, in other words. **Unfair labor practice strikes** protest illegal conduct by the employer. A **wildcat strike** is an unauthorized strike occurring during the term of a contract. A **sympathy strike** occurs when one union strikes in support of the strike of another.

Strikes needn't be an inevitable result of the bargaining process. Instead, studies show that they are often avoidable, but occur because of mistakes made during the bargaining process. Mistakes include discrepancies between union leaders' and rank-and-file members' expectations and misperceptions regarding each side's bargaining goals.[49]

*Picketing i*s one of the first activities occurring during a strike. The purpose of picketing is to inform the public about the existence of the labor dispute and often to encourage others to refrain from doing business with the employer against whom the employees are striking.

Dealing with a Strike   Employers can make several responses when they become the object of a strike. One is to shut down the affected area and thus halt their operations until the strike is over. A second alternative is to contract out work during the duration of the strike in order to blunt the effects of the strike on the employer. A third alternative is for the employer to continue operations, perhaps using supervisors and other nonstriking workers. A fourth alternative is the hiring of replacements for the strikers. In an economic strike, such replacements can be deemed permanent and would not have to be let go to make room for strikers who decided to return to work. If the strike were an unfair labor practice strike, the strikers would be entitled to return to their jobs if the employer makes an unconditional offer for them to do so.

When the former Northwest Airlines began giving permanent jobs to 1,500 substitute workers it hired to replace striking mechanics, the strike by the Aircraft Mechanics Fraternal Association basically fell apart.[50]

Other Responses   Management and labor both use other methods to try to break an impasse. The union, for example, may resort to a *corporate campaign*. This is an organized effort by the union that exerts pressure on the corporation by pressuring the company's other unions, shareholders, directors, customers, creditors, and government agencies, often directly. Thus, the union might picket the homes of members of the board of directors, and organize a **boycott**—a removal of patronage—of the company's banks.[51]

Unions continue to use corporate campaigns to good effect. Sometimes also called *advocacy* or *comprehensive campaigns*, they helped unions organize several health-care firms, including Sutter Health in California.[52]

Inside games are union efforts to encourage employees to impede or to disrupt production. They might do this, for example, by slowing the work pace, refusing to work overtime, filing mass charges with governmental agencies, or refusing to do work without detailed instructions from supervisors. Other inside games include scolding management and holding sick-outs.[53] In one inside game at Caterpillar's Aurora, Illinois, plant, United Auto Workers' grievances in the final stage before arbitration rose from 22 to 336. The effect, of course, was to clog the grievance procedure and tie up workers and management.[54]

Lockouts   Employers can try to break an impasse with lockouts. A **lockout** is a refusal by the employer to provide opportunities to work. The company (often literally) locks out employees and prohibits them from doing their jobs (and thus from being paid).

The NLRB generally does not view a lockout as an unfair labor practice. For example, if the employer's product is perishable (such as vegetables), then it might legitimately use lockout to neutralize the union's power. The NLRB views a lockout as an unfair labor practice only when the employer acts for a prohibited purpose. It is not a prohibited purpose to try to bring about a settlement of negotiations on terms favorable to the employer.[55]

Injunctions   During the impasse, both employers and unions can seek injunctive relief if they believe the other side is taking actions that could irreparably harm the other party. To obtain such relief, the NLRB must show the district court that an unfair labor practice—such as interfering with the union-organizing campaign—if left unremedied, will irreparably harm the other party's statutory rights. (For example, if the employer is unfairly interfering with the union's organization campaign, or if the union is retaliating against employees for trying to gain access to the NLRB, the other side might press the NLRB for "10[j] injunctive relief.") Such relief is requested after the NLRB issues an unfair labor practices complaint. The *injunctive relief* is a court order compelling a party or parties either to resume or to desist from a certain action.[56]

The Contract Agreement

The contract agreement itself may be 20 or 30 pages long or longer. It may contain just general declarations of policy or a detailed specification of rules and procedures. However, the tendency today is toward the longer, more detailed contract. This is largely because of the increased number of items the agreements cover. The main sections of a typical contract cover subjects such as:

1. Management rights
2. Union security and automatic payroll dues deduction
3. Grievance procedures
4. Arbitration of grievances
5. Disciplinary procedures
6. Compensation rates
7. Hours of work and overtime
8. Benefits such as vacation, holidays, insurance, and pension
9. Health and safety provisions
10. Employee security seniority provisions
11. Contract expiration date

Handling Grievances   Signing the labor agreement is not the end of the process, because questions will always arise about what various clauses really mean. The *grievance process* addresses these issues. It is the process or steps that the employer and union have agreed to follow to ascertain whether some action violated the agreement. The grievance process is not supposed to renegotiate contract points. Instead, the aim is to clarify what those points really mean, in the context of addressing grievances regarding things like time off or disciplinary action.

The potential for grievances and discontent is always present at work. Employees will use just about any issue involving wages, hours, or conditions of employment as the basis of a grievance. Discipline cases and seniority problems (including promotions, transfers, and layoffs) probably top the list. Others include grievances growing out of job evaluations and work assignments, overtime, vacations, and incentive plans. Recently, the Cleveland Browns' head coach fined one of his players $1,701 for not paying the hotel's bill for a $3 bottle of water. Some of the other players quickly filed grievance with the NFL.[57]

Sometimes the grievance process gets out of hand. For example, members of American Postal Workers Union, Local 482, filed 1,800 grievances at the Postal Service's Roanoke, Virginia, mail-processing facility (the usual rate is about 800 grievances per year). The employees apparently were responding to job changes, including transfers triggered by the Postal Service's automation efforts.[58]

Whatever the source of the grievances, many firms today (and virtually all unionized ones) do (or should) give employees some means through which to air and settle their grievances. Grievance procedures are invariably a part of the labor agreement. But, even in nonunion firms, such procedures can help ensure that labor–management peace prevails.

The Grievance Procedure Grievance procedures are typically multistep processes. For example, step one might require the grievant to try to work out an agreement with his or her supervisor, perhaps with a union officer or colleague present. Appeals may then be taken successively to the supervisor's boss, then that person's boss, and perhaps finally to a special arbitrator.

Contract Administration In unionized companies, grievance handling is often called *contract administration,* because no labor contract can ever be so complete that it covers all contingencies. For example, suppose the contract says you can discharge an employee only for "just cause." You subsequently discharge someone for speaking back to you in harsh terms. Was it within your rights to discharge this person? Was speaking back to you harshly "just cause"?

Guidelines for Handling Grievances It is generally best, but not always possible, to develop a work environment in which grievances don't occur in the first place. Doing so depends on being able to recognize, diagnose, and correct the causes of potential employee dissatisfaction before they become formal grievances. Typical causes include unfair appraisals, inequitable wages, or poor communications. Yet, in practice, grievances might be minimized, but never eradicated. There will probably always be a need to interpret what some clause or clauses in the agreement mean. The *HR in Practice* box presents some guidelines for handling a grievance should one arise.

HR in Practice: How to Handle a Grievance[59]

DO:

- Investigate and handle every case as though it may eventually result in an arbitration hearing.
- Talk with the employee about his or her grievance.
- Require the union to identify specific contractual provisions allegedly violated.
- Comply with the contractual time limits for handling the grievance.
- Visit the work area of the grievance.
- Determine whether there were any witnesses.
- Examine the personnel record of the grievant.
- Treat the union representative as your equal.
- Hold your grievance discussion privately.
- Fully inform your own supervisor of grievance matters.

DON'T:

- Discuss the case with the union steward alone—the grievant should be there.
- Make arrangements with individual employees that are inconsistent with the labor agreement.
- Hold back the remedy if the company is wrong.
- Admit to the binding effect of a past practice.
- Relinquish to the union your rights as a manager.
- Settle grievances based on what is "fair." Instead, stick to the labor agreement.
- Bargain over items not covered by the contract.
- Treat as subject to arbitration claims demanding the discipline or discharge of managers.
- Give long written grievance answers.
- Trade a grievance settlement for a grievance withdrawal (or try to make up for a bad decision in one grievance by bending over backward in another).
- Deny grievances on the premise that your "hands have been tied by management."
- Agree to informal amendments in the contract.

WHAT'S NEXT FOR UNIONS?

For years, construction trade unions in western New York State placed a huge inflatable rat balloon in front of construction sites that they were protesting. However, they recently gave up the rat and are now taking a more "business-friendly approach." As the business manager for the local plumbers and steamfitters union put it, "our philosophy for the past 15 years hasn't created any more market share for us. We have been viewed as troublemakers. . . . Now we are going to use [public relations] to dispel those perceptions."[60]

Why the Union Decline?

Several factors contributed to the decline in union membership over the past 40 or so years. Unions traditionally appealed mostly to blue-collar workers, and the proportion of blue-collar jobs has been decreasing as service-sector and white-collar service jobs increased. Globalization increases competition, and competition increases pressures on employers to cut costs and boost productivity. This in turn puts unions in a squeeze (as in the American auto industry, where workers recently had to accept salary reductions). Other factors pressuring employers and unions include the deregulation of trucking, airlines, and communications (which also made competition more intense), outdated equipment and factories, mismanagement, and government regulations (such as Title VII).

The effect of all this has been the permanent layoff of hundreds of thousands of union members, the permanent closing of company plants, the relocation of companies to nonunion settings (either in the United States or overseas), and mergers and acquisitions that have eliminated union jobs and affected collective bargaining agreements.

How Unions Are Changing

Of course, unions are not sitting idly by.[61] For example, Change to Win says it will be very aggressive about trying to organize workers, will focus on organizing women and minority workers, will focus more on organizing temporary or contingent workers, and will target specific multinational companies for international campaigns.

The steps UNITE took against Cintas Corp. illustrate some of unions' new tactics. In their effort against Cintas, UNITE (which later merged with another union to form UNITE HERE) didn't petition for an NLRB election. Instead, UNITE proposed using the "card check process" (more on this later). They also filed a $100 million class action suit against the company. Then Cintas workers in California filed a lawsuit claiming that the company was violating a nearby municipality's "living wage" law. UNITE then joined forces with the Teamsters union, which in turn began targeting Cintas' delivery people.[62]

Employee Free Choice Act Unions are pushing Congress to pass the Employee Free Choice Act. Among other things, this would make it more difficult for employers to inhibit workers from trying to form a union. Unions are also pushing for a new means of obtaining union recognition. Instead of secret-ballot elections, unions are pushing for a *"card check"* system. Here the union would win recognition when a majority of workers signed authorization cards saying they want to unionize. Several large companies, including Cingular Wireless, agreed to the card check process.[63]

Class Action Lawsuits Unions are also using class action lawsuits to support employees in nonunionized companies, to pressure employers. For example, unions recently used class action lawsuits to support workers' claims under the Fair Labor Standards Act and the Equal Pay Act.[64]

Coordination Unions are becoming more proactive in terms of coordinating their efforts.[65] For example, UNITE used their "Voice at Work" campaign to coordinate 800 workers at one employer's distribution center with others at the employer's New York City headquarters and with local activists and international unions throughout Europe. This forced the employer's parent company, a French conglomerate, to cease resisting the union's organizing efforts. In its "Union Cities" campaigns, AFL-CIO planners work with local labor councils and individual unions to gain the support of a target city's elected officials. In Los Angeles, this helped the service workers' union organize janitors in that city.

Cooperative Arrangements Another, somewhat more risky (for the unions) approach is to agree to enter into more cooperative pacts with employers—for instance, working with them in developing team-based employee participation programs. About half of all collective bargaining agreements encourage cooperative labor–management relationships. *Cooperative clauses* cover things like joint committees to review drug problems, health care, and safety issues.[66]

A recent review of union research and literature provides an additional insight. The author says that unions "that have a cooperative relationship with management can play an important role in overcoming barriers to the effective adoption of practices that have been linked to organizational competitiveness."[67] However, she concludes that employers who want to capitalize on that potential must change their way of thinking, avoiding adversarial industrial relations and emphasizing a cooperative partnership with their unions.

Global Campaigns Unions are also forcefully extending their reach overseas, as the *Global Issues* feature explains.

Global Issues in HR: Unions Go Global

Any company that thinks it can avoid unions by sending manufacturing and jobs abroad is mistaken. Today, as we've seen, most businesses are "going global," and regional trade treaties like the North American Free Trade Agreement (NAFTA) are further boosting the business done by firms abroad. This fact is not lost on unions, some of which are already expanding their influence abroad.

The unions' new global campaigns reflect the belief, as the Service Employees International Union puts it, that "Huge global service sector companies routinely cross national borders and industry lines as they search for places where they can shift operations to exploit workers with the lowest possible pay and benefits."

The Service Employees International Union, for instance, is therefore strengthening its alliances with unions in other nations, with the goal of uniting workers in particular multinational companies and industries, around the globe.[68] For example, the former

head of the SEIU recently worked with China's All China Federation of Trade Unions (ACFTU) to help the latter organize China's Walmart stores.[69] Similarly, U.S. unions are helping Mexican unions to organize, especially in U.S.-owned factories. Thus, the United Electrical Workers is subsidizing organizers at Mexican plants of the General Electric Company. And recently, the United Steelworkers merged with the largest labor union in Britain to create "Workers Uniting" to better help the new union deal with multinational employers.[70]

U.S. unions gain several things by forming alliances with unions abroad. By helping workers in other countries unionize, they help raise the wage and living standards of local workers. That may in turn discourage corporate flight from the United States in search of low wages. Unions also help their own positions in the United States with the added leverage they get from having unions abroad that can help them fight their corporate campaigns back in the United States.

REVIEW

Summary

1. In addition to improved wages and working conditions, unions seek security when organizing. In addition to a completely open shop, there are five possible arrangements, including the closed shop, the union shop, the agency shop, the preferential shop, and maintenance of membership.

2. The AFL-CIO is a national federation comprising about 56 national and international unions.

3. During the period of strong encouragement of unions, the Norris-LaGuardia Act and the NLRA were passed; these marked a shift in labor law from repression to strong encouragement of union activity. They did this by banning certain types of unfair labor practices, providing for secret-ballot elections, and creating the NLRB.

4. The Taft-Hartley Act reflected the period of modified encouragement coupled with regulation. It enumerated the rights of employees with respect to their unions, enumerated the rights of employers, and allowed the U.S. president to bar temporarily national emergency strikes. Among other things, it also enumerated certain union unfair labor practices. For example, it banned unions from restraining or coercing employees from exercising their bargaining rights. And employers were explicitly given the right to express their views concerning union organization.

5. The Landrum-Griffin Act reflected the period of detailed regulation of internal union affairs. It grew out of discoveries of wrongdoing on the part of both management and union leadership and contained a bill of rights for union members. (For example, it affirms a member's right to sue his or her union.)

6. There are five steps in a union drive and election: the initial contact, obtaining authorization cards, holding a hearing with the NLRB, the campaign, and the election itself. Remember that the union need only win a majority of the votes cast, *not* a majority of the workers in the bargaining unit.

7. Bargaining collectively in good faith is the next step if the union wins the election. Good faith means that both parties communicate and negotiate, and that proposals are matched with counterproposals. Some hints on bargaining include do not hurry, be prepared, find out why, and be a good listener.

8. An impasse occurs when the parties aren't able to move further toward settlement. Third-party involvement—namely, arbitration, fact-finding, or mediation—is one alternative. Sometimes, though, a strike occurs. Responding to the strike involves such steps as shutting the facility, contracting out work, or possibly replacing the workers. Boycotts and lockouts are two other anti-impasse weapons sometimes used by labor and management.

KEY TERMS

- right to work
- Norris-LaGuardia Act
- Wagner Act
- National Labor Relations Board (NLRB)
- Taft-Hartley Act
- national emergency strikes
- Landrum-Griffin Act
- union salting
- authorization cards
- bargaining unit
- collective bargaining
- good-faith bargaining
- voluntary bargaining items
- illegal bargaining items

- mandatory bargaining items
- mediation
- fact-finder
- arbitration
- economic strike
- unfair labor practice strike
- wildcat strike
- sympathy strike
- boycott
- lockout

DISCUSSION QUESTIONS

1. Discuss the steps in an NLRB election.
2. Describe important tactics you would expect the union to use during the union drive and election.
3. Briefly explain why labor law has gone through a cycle of repression and encouragement.
4. What is good-faith bargaining? When is bargaining not in good faith?
5. Define *impasse, mediation,* and *strike,* and explain the techniques used to overcome an impasse.
6. In teams of five to six students, choose an organization (such as this university or a company in which one student works), and list the areas in which the union has had an impact.

INDIVIDUAL AND GROUP ACTIVITIES

1. You are the manager of a small manufacturing plant. The union contract covering most of your employees is about to expire. Working individually or in groups, discuss how to prepare for union contract negotiations.
2. Working individually or in groups, use Internet resources to find situations where company management and the union reached an impasse at some point during their negotiation process, but eventually resolved the impasse. Describe the issues on both sides that led to the impasse. How did they move past the impasse? What were the final outcomes?
3. Several years ago, 8,000 Amtrak workers agreed not to disrupt service by walking out, at least not until a court hearing was held. Amtrak had asked the courts for a temporary restraining order, and the Transport Workers Union of America was actually pleased to postpone its walkout. The workers were apparently not upset at Amtrak, but at Congress, for failing to provide enough funding for Amtrak. What, if anything, can an employer do when employees threaten to go on strike, not because of what the employer did, but what a third party—in this case, Congress—has done or not done? What laws would prevent the union from going on strike in this case?

APPLICATION EXERCISES

Case Incident

Negotiating with the Writers Guild of America

The talks between the Writers Guild of America (WGA) and the Alliance of Motion Picture & Television Producers (producers) began tense in 2007, and then got tenser. In their first meeting, the two sides got nothing done. As *Law & Order* producer Dick Wolf said, "Everyone in the room is concerned about this."[71]

The two sides were far apart on just about all the issues. However, the biggest issue was how to split revenue from new media, such as when television shows move on to DVDs or the Internet. The producers said they wanted a profit-splitting system rather than the current residual system. Under the residual system, writers continue to receive "residuals," or income from shows they write, every time they're shown (such as when the Jerry Seinfeld show appears in reruns, years after they shot the last original show). Writers Guild executives did their homework. They argued, for instance, that the projections showed producers' revenues from advertising and subscription fees jumped by about 40% between 2002 and 2006.[72]

The situation grew tenser. After the first few meetings, one producers' representative said, "we can see after the dogfight whose position will win out. The open question there, of course, is whether each of us takes several lumps at the table, reaches an agreement then licks their wounds later—none the worse for wear—or whether we inflict more lasting damage through work stoppages that benefit no one before we come to an agreement."[73] Even after meeting six times, it seemed that, "the parties' only apparent area of agreement is that no real bargaining has yet to occur."[74]

In October 2007, the Writers Guild asked its members for strike authorization, and the producers were claiming that the guild was just trying to delay negotiations until the current contract expired (at the end of October). As the president of the television producers association said, "We have had six across the table sessions and there was only silence and stonewalling from the WGA leadership. . . . The WGA leadership apparently has no intention to bargain in good faith."[75] As evidence, the producers claimed that the WGA negotiating committee left one meeting after less than an hour at the bargaining table.

Both sides knew timing in these negotiations was crucial. During the fall and spring, television series production is in full swing. So a strike now by the writers would have a bigger impact than waiting until, say, the summer to strike. Perhaps not surprisingly, by January 2008, some movement was discernible. In a separate set of negotiations, the Directors Guild of America reached an agreement with the producers that addressed many of the issues that the writers were focusing on, such as how to divide the new media income.[76] In February 2008, the WGA and producers finally reached agreement. The new contract was "the direct result of renewed negotiations between the two sides, which culminated Friday with a marathon session including top WGA officials and the heads of the Walt Disney Co. and News Corp."[77]

QUESTIONS

1. The producers said the WGA was not bargaining in good faith. What did they mean by that, and do you think the evidence is sufficient to support the claim?
2. The WGA did eventually strike. What tactics could the producers have used to fight back once the strike began? What tactics do you think the WGA used?
3. This was a conflict between professional and creative people (the WGA) and TV and movie producers. Do you think the conflict was therefore different in any way than are the conflicts between, say, the auto workers or Teamsters unions against auto and trucking companies? Why?
4. What role (with examples, please) did negotiating skills seem to play in the WGA-producers negotiations?

Continuing Case

LearnInMotion.com: Keeping a Watchful Eye Out for the Union

The employees at firms like LearnInMotion.com are young, well paid, and technologically sophisticated, and they're doing interesting, creative work with flexible hours. They are, in other words, exactly the sort of employees you might assume would have no interest in joining a union.

Jennifer, however, was surprised to find that unions are actively attempting to organize several dot-coms. For example, one article she happened to come across read, "Union activity at U.S. Internet companies is on the increase and is illustrated by the Washington alliance of technology workers attempting to unionize Amazon. com. [The union] claims to be receiving inquiries on a daily basis regarding union membership [from] workers at Amazon."[78] "That's all we'd need is to have some disgruntled current or former employee call a union in on us," said Mel.

The fact that LearnInMotion.com is in New York (which has a relatively high proportion of union workers) and that several employees have left under less-than-pleasant circumstances suggest to Jennifer that perhaps she should be vigilant, and take steps now to prevent a problem later. The question is, what should she and Mel do? Now, they want you, their management consultants, to help them decide what to do. Here's what they want you to do for them.

QUESTIONS AND ASSIGNMENTS

1. Use the Internet to determine if the union mentioned (or any other union) organized or tried to organize a dot-com in the New York area in the past 2 years.
2. Produce a one-page position paper for us explaining concrete steps we can take today to avoid being unionized tomorrow.
3. How can we tell we're in the first, early stages of an organizing campaign? How can we find out for sure?

Experiential Exercise

The Union-Organizing Campaign at Pierce U

Purpose: The purpose of this exercise is to give you practice in dealing with some of the elements of a union-organizing campaign.[79]

Required Understanding: You should be familiar with the material covered in this chapter, as well as the following incident, "An Organizing Question on Campus."

INCIDENT: An Organizing Question on Campus: Art Tipton is HR director of Pierce University, a private university located in a large urban city. Ruth Zimmer, a supervisor in the maintenance and housekeeping services division of the university, has just come into Tipton's office to discuss her situation. Zimmer's division is responsible for maintaining and cleaning physical facilities of the university. Zimmer is one of the department supervisors who supervise employees who maintain and clean on-campus dormitories.

In the next several minutes, Zimmer proceeds to express her concerns about a union-organizing campaign that has begun among her employees. According to Zimmer, a representative of the Service Workers Union has met with several of her employees, urging them to sign union authorization cards. She has observed several of her employees "cornering" other employees to talk to them about joining the union and to urge them to sign union authorization (or representation) cards. Zimmer even observed this during working hours as employees were going about their normal duties in the dormitories. Zimmer reports that a number of her employees have come to her asking for her opinions about the union. They told her that several other supervisors in the department had told their employees not to sign any union authorization cards and not to talk about the union at any time while they were on campus. Zimmer also reports that one of her fellow supervisors told his employees that anyone caught talking about the union or signing a union authorization card would be disciplined and perhaps dismissed.

Zimmer says that her employees are very dissatisfied with their wages and with the conditions that they have endured from students, supervisors, and other staff people. She says that several employees told her that they had signed union cards because they believed that the only way university administration would pay attention to their concerns was if the employees had a union. Zimmer says that she made a list of employees whom she felt had joined or were interested in the union, and she could share these with Tipton if he wanted. Zimmer closed her presentation with the comment that she and other department supervisors need to know what they should do in order to stomp out the threat of unionization in their department.

How to Set Up the Exercise/Instructions: Divide the class into groups of four or five students. Assume that you are labor relations consultants the university retained to identify the problems and issues involved and to advise Tipton on the university's rights and what to do next. Each group will spend about 45 minutes discussing the issues. Then, outline those issues, as well as an action plan for Tipton. What should he do next?

If time permits, a spokesperson from each group should list on the board the issues involved and the group's recommendations. What should Tipton do?

Chapter 10

Protecting Safety and Health

- Employee Safety and Health: An Introduction
- What Causes Accidents?
- How to Prevent Accidents
- Workplace Health Hazards: Problems and Remedies

When you finish studying this chapter, you should be able to:

- Discuss *OSHA and how it operates.*
- Describe *the supervisor's role in safety.*
- Explain *in detail three basic causes of accidents.*
- Explain *how to prevent accidents at work.*
- Discuss *major health problems at work and how employers remedy them.*

INTRODUCTION

It was a frightening way to die. The worker, 30 years old, "suffocated when the tumbling dirt and debris rose to his chest, creating pressure so great that he could not breathe, even though his head remained uncovered." Other workers had warned the owner of the Brooklyn construction site that the trench was an accident waiting to happen. He allegedly did nothing. The prosecutor subsequently charged the owner with manslaughter.[1]

EMPLOYEE SAFETY AND HEALTH: AN INTRODUCTION

Why Employee Safety and Health Are Important

Providing a safe work environment is important for several reasons, one of which is the staggering number of work-related accidents.[2] For example, in one recent year, about 5,600 U.S. workers died in workplace incidents. There were also over 3.8 million occupational injuries and illnesses at work—roughly 4.4 cases per 100 full-time U.S workers, per year.[3] And these official figures may underestimate the real number of injuries and illnesses by several times.[4] Accidents are also expensive. For example, the direct injury costs of a forklift accident might be $4,500, but the indirect costs for things like forklift damage, lost production time, maintenance, and emergency supplies could reach $18,000 or more.[5]

Dangerous workplaces aren't limited to manufacturing plants. For example, in restaurants, slips and falls account for about a third of all worker injury cases. Employers could eliminate most of these falls by requiring slip-resistant shoes.[6]

A Manager's Briefing on Occupational Law

Congress passed the **Occupational Safety and Health Act** in 1970 "to assure so far as possible every working man and woman in the nation safe and healthful working conditions and to preserve our human resources."[7] The main employers not covered by the act are self-employed persons, farms in which only immediate members of the employer's family work, and certain workplaces covered by other federal agencies or statutes. Federal agencies are covered by the act, although provisions of the act usually don't apply to state and local governments in their role as employers.

The act created the **Occupational Safety and Health Administration (OSHA)** within the Department of Labor. OSHA's basic purpose is to administer the act and to set and enforce the safety and health standards that apply to almost all workers in the United States. OSHA has inspectors working out of branch offices throughout the United States.

OSHA Standards   OSHA operates under the "general duty clause" that each employer "shall furnish to each of his [or her] employees employment and a place of employment which are free from recognized hazards that are causing or are likely to cause death or serious physical harm to his [or her] employees."

To carry out this basic mission, OSHA is responsible for promulgating legally enforceable standards. The standards are very complete and cover just about every conceivable hazard, in detail. Figure 10.1 shows a small part of the standard governing handrails for scaffolds.

OSHA Record-Keeping Procedures   Under OSHA, employers with 11 or more employees must maintain a record of, and report, occupational injuries and occupational illnesses. An *occupational illness* is any abnormal condition or disorder caused by exposure to environmental factors associated with employment. This includes acute and chronic illnesses caused by inhalation, absorption, ingestion, or direct contact with toxic substances or harmful agents.

Figure 10.1 OSHA Standards Example

Guardrails not less than 2" × 4" or the equivalent and not less than 36" or more than 42" high, with a midrail, when required, of a 1" × 4" lumber or equivalent, and toeboards, shall be installed at all open sides on all scaffolds more than 10 feet above the ground or floor. Toeboards shall be a minimum of 4" in height. Wire mesh shall be installed in accordance with paragraph [a] (17) of this section.

Source: www.osha.gov/pls/oshaweb/owadisp.show_document?p_id=9720&p_table=STANDARDS, accessed May 25, 2007.

As summarized in Figure 10.2, employers must report all occupational illnesses.[8] They must also report most occupational injuries, specifically those that result in medical treatment (other than first aid), loss of consciousness, restriction of work (1 or more lost workdays), restriction of motion, or transfer to another job.[9]

Figure 10.2 What Accidents Must Be Reported under the Occupational Safety and Health Act?

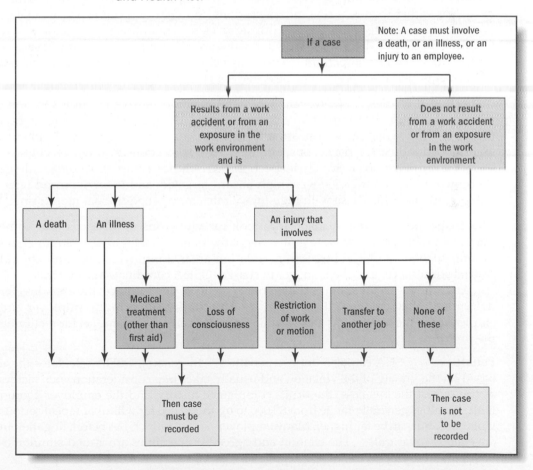

If an on-the-job accident results in the death of an employee or in the hospitalization of five or more employees, all employers, regardless of size, must report the accident to the nearest OSHA office. OSHA's latest record-keeping rules streamline the reporting. The rules continue to presume that an injury or work illness that resulted from an event in or exposure to the work environment is work related. However, it allows the employer to conclude that the event was not job related (and needn't be reported) if the fact so warrants—such as if a worker breaks his leg on his car's bumper when parked on the company lot.

Inspections and Citations   OSHA enforces its standards through inspections and (if necessary) citations. The inspection is usually unannounced. OSHA may not conduct warrantless inspections without an employer's consent. However, it may inspect after acquiring a search warrant or its equivalent.[10] With a limited number of inspectors, OSHA recently has focused on "fair and effective enforcement," combined with outreach, education and compliance assistance, and various OSHA–employer cooperative programs (such as its "Voluntary Protection Programs").[11]

Voluntary Consultation   OSHA has tried to encourage cooperative safety programs rather than rely only on inspections and citations. For example, OSHA provides free on-site safety and health services for small businesses, using state government safety experts. As the owner of one small business who used this service said, "Our workers' compensation costs have decreased significantly, we have had no accidents, and there is an awareness that we take safety seriously."[12]

Inspection Priorities   However, OSHA still makes extensive use of inspections, taking a "worst-first" approach to setting priorities. Priorities include, from highest to lowest, imminent dangers, catastrophes and fatal accidents, employee complaints, high-hazard industries inspections, and follow-up inspections.[13] In one recent year, OSHA conducted over 39,000 inspections. Of these, complaints or accidents prompted 9,176, about 21,500 were high-hazard targeted, and follow-ups and referrals prompted 8,415. Those with high injury rates may get additional monitoring.[14]

The Inspection   OSHA inspectors look for violations of all types, but some potential problem areas seem to grab more of their attention. Figure 10.3 summarizes the most frequent OSHA inspection violation areas. Employers may and should restrict admittance until the manager in charge/OSHA coordinator is on site.[15]

After the inspector submits the report to the local OSHA office, the area director determines what citations, if any, to issue. The **citations** inform the employer and employees of the regulations and standards violated and of the time set for rectifying the problem.

Penalties   OSHA can also impose penalties.[16] In general, OSHA calculates these based on the gravity of the violation and usually takes into consideration such factors as the size of the business, the firm's compliance history, and the employer's good faith. Penalties generally range from $5,000 to up to $70,000 for willful or repeat serious violations, but can be far higher. Many employers settle with OSHA before litigation in *pre-citation settlements*.[17] The citation and agreed-on penalties are issued simultaneously, after the employers initiate negotiation settlements with OSHA.[18]

Figure 10.3 Most Frequently Cited Hazards

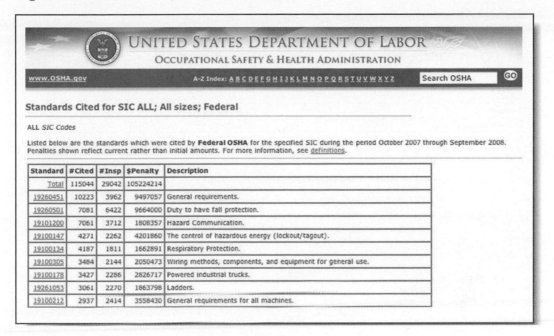

UNITED STATES DEPARTMENT OF LABOR
OCCUPATIONAL SAFETY & HEALTH ADMINISTRATION

www.OSHA.gov   A-Z Index: A B C D E F G H I J K L M N O P Q R S T U V W X Y Z   Search OSHA   GO

Standards Cited for SIC ALL; All sizes; Federal

ALL *SIC Codes*

Listed below are the standards which were cited by **Federal OSHA** for the specified SIC during the period October 2007 through September 2008. Penalties shown reflect current rather than initial amounts. For more information, see definitions.

Standard	#Cited	#Insp	$Penalty	Description
Total	115044	29042	105224214	
19260451	10223	3962	9497057	General requirements.
19260501	7081	6422	9664000	Duty to have fall protection.
19101200	7061	3712	1808357	Hazard Communication.
19100147	4271	2262	4201860	The control of hazardous energy (lockout/tagout).
19100134	4187	1811	1662891	Respiratory Protection.
19100305	3484	2144	2050473	Wiring methods, components, and equipment for general use.
19100178	3427	2286	2826717	Powered industrial trucks.
19261053	3061	2270	1863798	Ladders.
19100212	2937	2414	3558430	General requirements for all machines.

Inspectors and their superiors don't look just at specific hazards but also for evidence of a comprehensive safety approach. For example, factors contributing to a firm's OSHA liability include lack of a systematic safety approach, not following up on employee safety complaints, and failure to inspect the workplace regularly.[19]

While some employers understandably view OSHA inspections with some trepidation, the inspection checklist in Figure 10.4 can help the manager reduce problems ahead of time.[20]

Responsibilities and Rights of Employers and Employees   Both employers and employees have responsibilities and rights under the Occupational Safety and Health Act. For example, employers are responsible for providing "a workplace free from recognized hazards," for being familiar with OSHA standards, and for ensuring that workplace conditions conform with applicable standards.

Employees also have rights and responsibilities, but OSHA can't cite them for violations of their responsibilities. They are responsible, for example, for complying with all applicable OSHA standards, for following all employer safety and health rules and regulations, and for reporting hazardous conditions to the supervisor. Employees have a right to demand safety and health on the job without fear of punishment. Employers may not punish or discriminate against workers who complain to OSHA about safety and health hazards. But the Occupational Safety and Health Review Commission (which reviews OSHA decisions) says employers must make "a diligent effort to discourage, by discipline if necessary, violations of safety rules by employees."[21]

Figure 10.4 Manager's Safety Checklist

FORM **CD-574**
(2/03)

U.S. Department of Commerce
Office Safety Inspection Checklist for
Supervisors and Program Managers

Name:	Division:
Location:	Date:
Signature:	

This checklist is intended as a guide to assist supervisors and program managers in conducting safety and health inspections of their work areas. It includes questions relating to general office safety, ergonomics, fire prevention, and electrical safety. Questions which receive a "NO" answer require corrective action. If you have questions or need assistance with resolving any problems, please contact your safety office. More information on office safety is available through the Department of Commerce Safety Office website at **http://ohrm.doc.gov/safetyprogram/safety.htm**

Work Environment

Yes	No	N/A	
O	O	O	Are all work areas clean, sanitary, and orderly?
O	O	O	Is there adequate lighting?
O	O	O	Is the noise level within an acceptable range?
O	O	O	Is ventilation adequate?

Walking / Working Surfaces

Yes	No	N/A	
O	O	O	Are aisles and passages free of stored material that may present trip hazards?
O	O	O	Are tile floors in places like kitchens and bathrooms free of water and slippery substances?
O	O	O	Are carpet and throw rugs free of tears or trip hazards?
O	O	O	Are hand rails provided on all fixed stairways?
O	O	O	Are treads provided with anti-slip surfaces?
O	O	O	Are step ladders provided for reaching overhead storage areas and are materials stored safely?
O	O	O	Are file drawers kept closed when not in use?
O	O	O	Are passenger and freight elevators inspected annually and are the inspection certificates available for review on-site?
O	O	O	Are pits and floor openings covered or otherwise guarded?
O	O	O	Are standard guardrails provided wherever aisle or walkway surfaces are elevated more than 48 inches above any adjacent floor or the ground?
O	O	O	Is furniture free of any unsafe defects?
O	O	O	Are heating and air conditioning vents clear of obstructions?

Ergonomics

Yes	No	N/A	
O	O	O	Are employees advised of proper lifting techniques?
O	O	O	Are workstations configured to prevent common ergonomic problems? (Chair height allows employees' feet to rest flat on the ground with thighs parallel to the floor, top of computer screen is at or slightly below eye level, keyboard is at elbow height. Additional information on proper configuration of workstations is available through the Commerce Safety website at http://ohrm.doc.gov/safetyprogram/safety.htm)
O	O	O	Are mechanical aids and equipment, such as; lifting devices, carts, or dollies provided where needed?
O	O	O	Are employees surveyed annually on their ergonomic concerns?

Emergency Information (Postings)

Yes	No	N/A	
O	O	O	Are established emergency phone numbers posted where they can be readily found in case of an emergency?
O	O	O	Are employees trained on emergency procedures?
O	O	O	Are fire evacuation procedures/diagrams posted?
O	O	O	Is emergency information posted in every area where you store hazardous waste?
O	O	O	Is established facility emergency information posted near a telephone?
O	O	O	Are the OSHA poster, and other required posters displayed conspicuously?
O	O	O	Are adequate first aid supplies available and properly maintained?
O	O	O	Are an adequate number of first aid trained personnel available to respond to injuries and illnesses until medical assistance arrives?
O	O	O	Is a copy of the facility fire prevention and emergency action plan available on site?
O	O	O	Are safety hazard warning signs/caution signs provided to warn employees of pertinent hazards?

(Continued)

FORM **CD-574**
(2/03)

Fire Prevention

Yes	No	N/A	
O	O	O	Are flammable liquids, such as gasoline, kept in approved safety cans and stored in flammable cabinets?
O	O	O	Are portable fire extinguishers distributed properly (less than 75 feet travel distance for combustibles and 50 feet for flammables)?
O	O	O	Are employees trained on the use of portable fire extinguishers?
O	O	O	Are portable fire extinguishers visually inspected monthly and serviced annually?
O	O	O	Are areas around portable fire extinguishers free of obstructions and properly labeled ?
O	O	O	Is heat-producing equipment used in a well ventilated area?
O	O	O	Are fire alarm pull stations clearly marked and unobstructed?
O	O	O	Are proper clearances maintained below sprinkler heads (i.e., 18" clear)?

Emergency Exits

Yes	No	N/A	
O	O	O	Are doors, passageways or stairways that are neither exits nor access to exits and which could be mistaken for exits, appropriately marked "NOT AN EXIT," "TO BASEMENT," "STOREROOM," etc.?
O	O	O	Are a sufficient number of exits provided?
O	O	O	Are exits kept free of obstructions or locking devices which could impede immediate escape?
O	O	O	Are exits properly marked and illuminated?
O	O	O	Are the directions to exits, when not immediately apparent, marked with visible signs?
O	O	O	Can emergency exit doors be opened from the direction of exit travel without the use of a key or other significant effort when the building is occupied?
O	O	O	Are exits arranged such that it is not possible to travel toward a fire hazard when exiting the facility?

Electrical Systems

(Please have your facility maintenance person or electrician accompany you during this part of the inspection)

Yes	No	N/A	
O	O	O	Are all cord and cable connections intact and secure?
O	O	O	Are electrical outlets free of overloads?
O	O	O	Is fixed wiring used instead of flexible (…) conduit?
O	O	O	Is the area around electrical panels and breakers free of obstructions?
O	O	O	Are high-voltage electrical service rooms kept locked?
O	O	O	Are electrical cords routed such that they are free of sharp objects and clearly visible?
O	O	O	Are all electrical cords grounded?
O	O	O	Are electrical cords in good condition (free of splices, frays, etc.)?
O	O	O	Are electrical appliances approved (Underwriters Laboratory, Inc. (UL), etc)?
O	O	O	Are electric fans provided with guards of not over one-half inch, preventing finger exposures?
O	O	O	Are space heaters UL listed and equipped with shutoffs that activate if the heater tips over?
O	O	O	Are space heaters located away from combustibles and properly ventilated?
O	O	O	In your electrical rooms are all electrical raceways and enclosures securely fastened in place?
O	O	O	Are clamps or other securing means provided on flexible cords or cables at plugs, receptacles, tools, equipment, etc., and is the cord jacket securely held in place?
O	O	O	Is sufficient access and working space provided and maintained about all electrical equipment to permit ready and safe operations and maintenance? (This space is 3 feet for less than 600 volts, 4 feet for more than 600 volts)

Material Storage

Yes	No	N/A	
O	O	O	Are storage racks and shelves capable of supporting the intended load and materials stored safely?
O	O	O	Are storage racks secured from falling?
O	O	O	Are office equipment stored in a stable manner, not capable of falling?

Source: www.sefsc.noaa.gov/PDFdocs/CD-574OfficeInspectionChecklistSupervisors.pdf, accessed May 26, 2007.

WHAT CAUSES ACCIDENTS?

Following an accident in which four workers lost their lives, management at the Golden Eagle refinery east of San Francisco Bay shut down the facility for 4 months, retrained all employees in safety methods, and created six new safety management positions.[22]

Accidents occur for three main reasons: chance occurrences, unsafe working conditions, and unsafe acts by employees. Chance occurrences (such as getting hit by a car) contribute to accidents but are more or less beyond management's control; we will therefore focus on unsafe conditions and unsafe acts.

Unsafe Conditions

Unsafe conditions are one main cause of accidents. These include such obvious factors as:

- Improperly guarded equipment
- Defective equipment
- Unsafe storage, such as overloading
- Improper illumination, such as insufficient light
- Improper ventilation, such as insufficient air change[23]

The basic remedy here is to eliminate or minimize the unsafe conditions. OSHA standards address the mechanical and physical working conditions that cause accidents. The manager can use a checklist of unsafe conditions for spotting problems as in Figure 10.4; another checklist is in the *HR in Practice* box. The *EHS Today* Web site for environment, health, and safety officers (http://ehstoday.com/) is a good source for safety and health information.

HR in Practice: Checklist of Accident-Causing Conditions

I. GENERAL HOUSEKEEPING

Adequate and wide aisles—no materials protruding into aisles	Material piled in safe manner—not too high or too close to sprinkler heads
Parts and tools stored safely after use—not left in hazardous positions that could cause them to fall	All work areas clean and dry
	All exit doors and aisles clean of obstructions
Even and solid flooring—no defective floors or ramps that could cause falling or tripping accidents	Aisles kept clear and properly marked; no air lines or electric cords across aisles
Waste and trash cans—safely located and not overfilled	

II. MATERIAL-HANDLING EQUIPMENT AND CONVEYANCES

On all conveyances, electric or hand, check to see that the following items are all in sound working condition:

Brakes—properly adjusted	No loose parts
Not too much play in steering wheel	Cables, hooks, or chains—not worn or otherwise defective
Warning device—in place and working	
Wheels—securely in place; properly inflated	Suspended chains or hooks
	Safety loaded
Fuel and oil—enough and right kind	Properly stored

(Continued)

III. LADDERS, SCAFFOLD, BENCHES, STAIRWAYS, ETC.

The following items of major interest to be checked:

Safety feet on straight ladders

Guardrails or handrails

Treads, not slippery

No splintered, cracked, or rickety stairs

Ladders properly stored

Extension ladder ropes in good
condition

Toeboards

IV. POWER TOOLS (STATIONARY)

Point of operation guarded

Guards in proper adjustment

Gears, belts, shafting, counterweights
guarded

Foot pedals guarded

Brushes provided for cleaning
machines

Adequate lighting

Properly grounded

Tool or material rests properly adjusted

Adequate work space around machines

Control switch easily accessible

Safety glasses worn

Gloves worn by persons handling rough
or sharp materials

No gloves or loose clothing worn by
persons operating machines

V. HAND TOOLS AND MISCELLANEOUS

In good condition—not cracked, worn,
or otherwise defective

Properly stored

Correct for job

Goggles, respirators, and other personal
protective equipment worn where
necessary

VI. SPRAY PAINTING

Explosion-proof electrical equipment

Proper storage of paints and thinners
in approved metal cabinets

Fire extinguishers adequate and suitable;
readily accessible

Minimum storage in work area

VII. FIRE EXTINGUISHERS

Properly serviced and tagged

Readily accessible

Adequate and suitable for operations
involved

Source: Courtesy of the Insurance Services Office, Inc., from "A Safety Committee Man's Guide" (1977): 1–64.
Includes copyrighted material of ISO Properties, Inc. with its permission.

Although accidents can occur anywhere, there are high-danger zones. About one-third of industrial accidents occur around forklift trucks, wheelbarrows, and other handling and lifting areas. The most serious accidents usually occur near metal and woodworking machines and saws, or around gears, pulleys, and flywheels.

Other Working-Condition–Related Causes of Accidents   Some working-condition–related causes of accidents involve the psychology or "safety climate" of the workplace. One early study focused on the official hearings of fatal accidents suffered by British oil workers in the North Sea.[24] It found that some of the less obvious working conditions that set the stage for accidents included a strong pressure to complete the work quickly and employees who were under stress. Another study involved 1,127 nurses working in 42 large hospitals in the United States. The researchers measured safety climate using items like, "job duties on this unit often prevent nurses from acting as safely as they would like." Here "the results revealed that safety climate predicted medication errors, nurse back injuries, urinary tract infections, [and] patient satisfaction."[25]

Similarly, accident rates usually don't increase noticeably during the first 5 or 6 hours of the workday, but after 6 hours, the accident rate accelerates. This is due partly to fatigue and partly to the fact that accidents occur more often during night shifts.

Accidents also occur more frequently in plants with a high seasonal layoff rate, hostility among employees, garnished wages, and blighted living conditions. Temporary stress factors such as high workplace temperature and a congested workplace also relate to accident rates.

Unsafe Acts

In practice, you can't eliminate accidents just by reducing unsafe conditions. People cause accidents, and there's no surefire way to eliminate **unsafe acts** such as:

- Throwing materials
- Operating or working at unsafe speeds—either too fast or too slow
- Lifting improperly[26]

There is no one explanation for why an employee behaves unsafely. Sometimes (as noted earlier) working conditions such as stress may set the stage. Sometimes, employers don't provide employees with the correct safe procedures, and employees then simply develop their own (often bad) work habits. However, the employee's attitudes, personality, or skills often explain the bad behavior.

What Traits Characterize "Accident-Prone" People?

It may seem intuitively obvious that some people are simply accident prone, but the research isn't clear. On closer inspection it turns out some "accident repeaters" were just unlucky, or may have been more meticulous about reporting their accidents.[27] However, there is growing evidence that people with specific traits may indeed be accident prone. For example, people who are impulsive, sensation seeking, extremely extroverted, and less conscientious (in terms of being less fastidious and dependable) are more likely to have accidents.[28]

Furthermore, the person who is accident prone on one job may not be so on a different job. Driving is one example. Personality traits that correlate with filing vehicular insurance claims include *entitlement* ("bad drivers think there's no reason they should not speed or run lights"), *impatience* ("drivers with high claim frequency were 'always in a hurry'"), and *aggressiveness* ("always the first to want to move when the red light turns green"). A study in Thailand similarly found that drivers who are naturally competitive and prone to anger are particularly risky drivers.[29]

HOW TO PREVENT ACCIDENTS

The thing to remember about accidents is that it's not always the employee's fault. Certainly, screening out or firing impulsive employees may reduce unsafe behaviors. However, so will mopping up oil spills and placing guardrails around machines; psychological factors such as stress and pressure are important, too.[30] In practice, accident causes tend to be multifaceted, so the manager has to take a multifaceted approach to preventing them.[31]

Reduce Unsafe Conditions

Imagine that you decide to repair a lamp that you think is unplugged and then discover, with a shock, that you left it plugged in. At work, *lockout/tagout* is a procedure to disable equipment to avoid an unexpected release of electrical or other energy. It includes affixing a lockout/tagout tag to the equipment, to show it's disabled.[32]

Reducing unsafe conditions is an employer's first line of safety defense. Sometimes (as with the lamp) the solution is obvious. For example, debris or a slippery floor often causes slips and falls. For machinery, employees can use emergency stop devices, such as oversized buttons, to override other machine controls and instantly cut power.[33]

Next, management can provide personal protective equipment (PPE). For example, Prevent Blindness America estimates that each year, more than 700,000 Americans injure their eyes at work, and that employers could avoid 90% of these injuries with safety eyewear.[34]

Getting employees to wear personal protective equipment is famously difficult. Wearability is important.[35] In addition to providing reliable protection, protective gear should fit properly; be easy to care for and maintain; be flexible and lightweight; provide comfort and reduce heat stress; have rugged construction; be relatively easy to put on and take off; and be easy to clean, dispose of, and recycle.[36]

Note, though, that reducing unsafe conditions (such as enclosing noisy equipment) should always come first. Then use administrative controls (such as job rotation to reduce long-term exposure to the hazard). Only then, turn to PPE.[37] The accompanying *Managing the New Workforce* feature expands on this.

Reducing Unsafe Acts

While guardrails and personal protective equipment are indispensable, human misbehavior will short-circuit the best safety efforts. Misbehavior needn't be intentional. For example, distractions—whether from cell phones or glancing back to check on a child—contribute to at least half of all car accidents. At work, not noticing moving or stationary objects or that a floor is wet are frequent accident causers.[38] Furthermore (and ironically), "making a job safer with machine guards or PPE lowers people's risk perceptions and thus can lead to an increase in at-risk behavior."[39]

Unfortunately, just telling workers to "pay attention" is usually not enough. Instead, it requires a process. First, identify and try to eliminate potential risks, such

Employers should pay special attention to vulnerable workers, those "unprepared to deal with hazards in the workplace," either due to lack of education, ill-fitting personal protective equipment, physical limitations, or cultural reasons. Among others, these may include young, immigrant, aging, or women workers.[40]

For example, although about half of all workers are women, most machinery and PPE (like gloves) are designed for men.[41] (Hand injuries account for about one million emergency department visits annually by U.S. workers.[42]) Women may thus have to use makeshift platforms or stools to reach machinery controls, or safety goggles that don't really fit. The solution is to make sure the equipment and machines women use are appropriate for their size.[43]

Similarly, with more workers postponing retirement, older workers are doing more manufacturing jobs.[44] They can do these jobs very effectively. However, there are potential physical changes associated with aging, including loss of strength, loss of muscular flexibility, and reduced reaction time.[45] This means that employers should make special provisions, such as designing jobs to reduce heavy lifting.[46] The fatality rate for older workers is about three times that of younger workers.[47]

as slippery floors. Next, reduce potential distractions, such as noise, heat, and stress. (Thus, in 2009, President Obama signed an executive order prohibiting most federal employees from text messaging while driving on official business.[48]) Then, carefully screen and train employees, as we explain next.

Use Screening to Reduce Unsafe Acts

Accidents are similar to other types of poor performance, and psychologists have had success in screening out people who might be accident prone for specific jobs. The basic technique is to identify the human trait (such as visual skill) that might relate to accidents on the specific job. Thus, screening prospective delivery drivers for impatience and aggressiveness might be sensible.[49]

Use Posters and Other Propaganda

Propaganda such as safety posters can also help reduce unsafe acts. In one older study, their use apparently increased safe behavior by more than 20%.[50] However, posters should be combined with other techniques like screening and training to reduce unsafe conditions and acts.

Provide Safety Training

Safety training can also reduce accidents, especially with new employees.[51] You should instruct them in safe practices and procedures, warn them of potential hazards, and work on developing their predisposition toward safety. Delta Airlines encourages supervisors to use personal anecdotes to motivate employees to wear hearing protection. For example, "a lot of the old-timers have terrible stories and terrible hearing, because whatever they did in their past jobs . . . they didn't wear hearing protection."[52]

Employers also use the Web to support their safety training programs.[53] For example, PureSafety (www.puresafety.com) enables firms to create their own training Web sites, complete with a "message from the safety director." Once an employer installs the PureSafety Web site on its intranet, it can populate the site with courses from companies that supply safety courses via PureSafety.com. The courses are available in various formats, including digital and PowerPoint presentations.[54] OSHA, the National Institute for Occupational Safety and Health (NIOSH), and numerous private vendors also provide online safety training solutions.[55]

Use Incentives and Positive Reinforcement

Some firms award incentives (such as bonuses) for meeting safety goals. However, OSHA has argued that such plans don't actually cut down on injuries or illnesses but only on injury and illness *reporting*. One option is to emphasize nontraditional reinforcement, for instance, by providing recognition awards for attending safety meetings, or for identifying hazards.[56]

Safety incentives needn't be complicated. One employer uses a suggestion box. Employees make suggestions for improvements regarding unsafe acts or conditions. The employer follows up on all suggestions, the best of which result in gift certificates for their authors.[57] At the Golden Eagle refinery in California, employees earn "WINGS" points for engaging in one or more of 28 safety activities, such as taking emergency response training. Employees can earn up to $20 per month per person by accumulating points.[58]

Three Caveats With respect to safety incentives, keep three things in mind. First, such programs are *not substitutes for* but just parts of comprehensive safety programs.[59]

Second, make sure that your incentives program doesn't simply produce *false accident reporting*, by encouraging workers to underreport their accidents to obtain rewards.[60]

Third, such programs can have *unforeseen consequences*. Their basic aim is to produce, through reinforcement, safe habits. However, safety experts warn against relying on habitual behavior. Habitual behavior takes place without thinking. But when it comes to safety, it's usually better to have employees thinking about what they're doing.[61]

Emphasize Top-Management Commitment

Safety programs require a strong and observable management commitment to safety. For example:

> One of the best examples I know of in setting the highest possible priority for safety takes place at a DuPont Plant in Germany. Each morning at the DuPont Polyester and Nylon Plant, the director and his assistants meet at 8:45 to review the past 24 hours. The first matter they discuss is not

production, but safety. Only after they have examined reports of accidents and near misses and satisfied themselves that corrective action has been taken do they move on to look at output, quality, and cost matters.[62]

Similarly, Louisiana-Pacific Corp. starts all meetings with a brief safety message.[63] Weyerhaeuser discharged the plant manager and safety manager at its West Virginia facility, allegedly because they failed to report 38 injuries and illnesses.[64]

The Supervisor's Role in Safety

After inspecting a work site where workers were installing pipes in a trench, an OSHA inspector cited an employer for violating the rule requiring employers to have a "stairway, ladder, ramp, or other safe means of egress" in deep trenches.[65] Workers needed a quick way out. As in most such cases, the employer had the primary responsibility for safety; the local supervisor was responsible for day-to-day inspections. Here, the supervisor did not properly do his inspection. The trench collapsed, and several employees were severely injured. The point is that for a supervisor, "a daily [safety] walk-through of your workplace—whether you are working in outdoor construction, indoor manufacturing, or any place that poses safety challenges—is an essential part of your work."[66]

Foster a Culture of Safety

When it comes to creating a safety-oriented workplace, what supervisors do is usually more important than what they say. It's the signals you send that shapes the safety culture that guides your subordinates.[67]

According to one safety expert, five characteristics of a culture of safety include:

1. An *obvious management commitment* to and employee involvement in safety;
2. *Safety communications* and collaboration are visible and interactive;
3. A *shared vision* that all accidents are preventable;
4. *Assignment of critical safety functions* to specific individuals or teams; and,
5. A *continuous process of identifying* and correcting workplace hazards.[68]

Establish a Safety Policy

The firm's safety policy should emphasize that the firm will do everything practical to reduce accidents and injuries, and that accident and injury prevention is paramount.

Set Specific Loss Control Goals

Analyze the number of accidents and safety incidents, and then set specific safety goals to achieve, for example, in terms of "frequency of lost-time injuries per number of full-time employees."

Conduct Safety and Health Inspections Regularly

Inspection is important. Safety-conscious employers routinely inspect their premises for possible safety and health problems, using checklists as in the *HR in Practice* box (on pp. 298–299). Similarly, they investigate all accidents and "near misses," and have a system for letting employees notify management about hazardous conditions. *Safety audits* measure injury and illness statistics, workers' compensation costs, and vehicle accident statistics.[69] Typical *safety committee* activities include evaluating safety adequacy, monitoring safety audit findings, and suggesting strategies for improving safety performance. Metrics might include, for instance, percent conformance to safety critical behaviors and processes, level of exposure present in the workplace as measured through valid samples, and rate of adverse outcomes, such as injury rates.[70]

Beyond Zero Accidents

The trend is away from making safety something "employees are supposed to do," to making safety part of how each person lives. To paraphrase the safety director of one company, "we made the transition to the belief that safety is each employee's moral obligation. It is now something that is integral to how everyone thinks and lives." This company calls its safety program "Zero 4 life." "Zero" means zero injuries. The "4" means the program's four principles of accountability, behavior, communication, and dedication. "Life," means living safely all the time and sharing this value with family and friends.[71]

Figure 10.5 summarizes these and other safety steps.

Strategy and HR   Safety is a problem in a large, complex utility like New York's Con Ed, many of whose facilities go back 70 years or more. Back then, people didn't understand the risks of products like asbestos, so today Con Ed employees often must work with hazardous materials on a daily basis. That notwithstanding, Con Ed's policy was always, "get the lights back on fast." An explosion near New York's Grand Central Station a few years ago forced management to reconsider that policy. Today, "get the lights back on fast—but, do it safely" sums up the firm's basic policy.

Injecting a "safety first" mentality into all the firm's operations involved many HR activities. For example, Con Ed recruited and trained new people for its environmental health and safety staff. Con Ed also created thousands of pages of new policies and procedures. Con Ed's experience shows how top management can use human resources strategies and practices to support its strategy. The accompanying *Managing HR in Challenging Times* feature expands on this.

Figure 10.5 Steps to Take to Reduce Workplace Accidents

- Reduce unsafe conditions.
- Reduce unsafe acts.
- Use posters and other propaganda.
- Provide safety training.
- Use positive reinforcement.
- Emphasize top-management commitment.
- Emphasize safety.
- Establish a safety policy.
- Set specific loss control goals.
- Conduct safety and health inspections regularly.
- Monitor work overload and stress.

WORKPLACE HEALTH HAZARDS: PROBLEMS AND REMEDIES

Most workplace hazards aren't obvious like unguarded equipment or slippery floors. Many are unseen hazards (like chemicals) that the company produces as part of its production processes. Other problems, like drug abuse, the employees may create for themselves. In either case, these hazards are often more dangerous to workers' health and safety than are obvious hazards like slippery floors. Typical workplace exposure hazards include chemicals and other hazardous materials such as asbestos, as well as alcohol abuse, stressful jobs, ergonomic hazards (such as uncomfortable equipment), infectious diseases, smoking, and biohazards (such as mold and anthrax).[73] We'll look at several of these.

Chemicals and Industrial Hygiene

OSHA standards list exposure limits for about 600 chemicals. Hazardous substances like these require air sampling and other precautionary measures. They are also more widespread than most managers realize. For example, manufacturers use ethyl alcohol as a solvent in industrial processes.

Managing such exposure hazards comes under the area of *industrial hygiene* and involves recognition, evaluation, and control. First, the facility's health and safety officers must *recognize* possible exposure hazards. This typically involves activities like facility walk-around surveys.

Having identified a possible hazard, the *evaluation* phase involves determining how severe the hazard is. This requires measuring the exposure and comparing the measured exposure to some benchmark.[74]

Finally, the hazard *control* phase involves eliminating or reducing the hazard. Personal protective gear (such as face masks) is generally the last option. Before relying on these, the employer must install engineering controls (such as ventilation) and administrative controls (including training); this is mandatory under OSHA.

Asbestos Exposure at Work   OSHA standards regarding asbestos are representative of what employers can expect here. The standards require that companies monitor the air whenever an employer expects the level of asbestos to rise to half the allowable limit (0.1 fibers per cubic centimeter). Engineering controls—walls, special filters, and so forth—are required to maintain an asbestos level that complies with OSHA standards. If and only if additional efforts are required to achieve compliance can respirators be used.

Alcoholism and Substance Abuse

Workplace substance abuse is a serious problem at work. About two-thirds of people with alcohol disorders work full time.[75] One study concluded that about 15% of the U.S. workforce (about 19 million workers) "has either been hung over at work, been drinking shortly before showing up for work, or been drinking or impaired while on the job at least once during the previous year."[76]

Recognizing the alcoholic on the job isn't easy. Early symptoms such as tardiness can be difficult to classify. The supervisor is not a psychiatrist, and without specialized training, identifying and dealing with the alcoholic is difficult. For many employers, dealing with alcohol abuse begins with testing.[77]

Tools   The most widely used self-reporting screening instruments for alcoholism are the 4-item CAGE and the 25-item MAST.[78] The former asks questions such as: Have you ever (1) attempted to cut back on alcohol, (2) been annoyed by comments about your drinking, (3) felt guilty about drinking, (4) had an eye-opener first thing in the morning to steady your nerves.[79]

Table 10.1 shows observable behavior patterns that indicate alcohol-related problems. As you can see, alcohol problems range from tardiness in the earliest stages of alcohol abuse to prolonged absences in its later stages.[80] Whether the alcohol abuse reflects a "disability" under the ADA depends on several things including whether the person is alcohol dependant.[81] In general, employers can hold alcohol-dependent employees to the same performance standards as they hold nonalcoholics. Employers often make available employee assistance programs (EAPs) to provide counseling to support employees with alcohol or drug abuse problems.

Dealing with Substance Abuse

Ideally, a drug-free workplace program includes five components: a drug-free workplace policy, supervisor training, employee education, employee assistance, and drug testing. The policy should state, at a minimum, "The use, possession, transfer or sale of illegal drugs by employees is prohibited." And it should lay out the employer's rationale for the policy, and an explanation of the consequences for violating it (up to and including termination). Supervisors should be trained to

Table 10.1   Observable Behavior Patterns Indicating Possible
Alcohol-Related Problems

ALCOHOLISM STAGE	SOME POSSIBLE SIGNS OF ALCOHOLISM PROBLEMS	SOME POSSIBLE ALCOHOLISM PERFORMANCE ISSUES
Early	Arrives at work late Untrue statements Leaves work early	Reduced job efficiency Misses deadlines
Middle	Frequent absences, especially Mondays Colleagues mentioning erratic behavior Mood swings Anxiety Late returning from lunch Frequent multi-day absences	Accidents Warnings from boss Noticeably reduced performance
Advanced	Personal neglect Unsteady gait Violent outbursts Blackouts and frequent forgetfulness Possible drinking on job	Frequent falls, accidents Strong disciplinary actions Basically incompetent performance

Sources: Gopal Patel and John Adkins Jr., "The Employer's Role in Alcoholism Assistance," *Personnel Journal* 62, no. 7 (July 1983), p. 570; Mary-Anne Enoch and David Goldman, "Problem Drinking and Alcoholism: Diagnosis and Treatment," *American Family Physician*, February 1, 2002, www.aafp.org/afp/20020201/441.html, accessed July 20, 2008; and Ken Pidd et al., "Alcohol and Work: Patterns of Use, Workplace Culture, and Safety," www.nisu.flinders.edu.au/pubs/reports/2006/injcat82.pdf, accessed July 20, 2008.

monitor employees' performance and to be alert for drug-related performance problems.

For many employers, dealing with substance abuse then involves drug testing. In fact, many states require mandatory random drug testing of high-hazard workers. For example, New Jersey now requires random drug testing of electrical workers.[82]

Preemployment drug testing discourages drug users from both applying for and working for employers who test.[83] Some applicants or employees may try to evade the test, for instance, by purchasing "clean" specimens to use. Several states, including New Jersey, North Carolina, Virginia, Oregon, and Nebraska, have laws making drug-test fraud a crime. An oral fluid test is more reliable.[84]

Unfortunately, drug testing may not reduce workplace accidents. One study, conducted in three hotels, concluded that preemployment drug testing seemed to have little or no effect on workplace accidents. However, a combination of preemployment and random ongoing testing was associated with a significant reduction in workplace accidents.[85]

Increasingly, by the way, it's not intoxicated drivers but "intexicated" ones that are causing the problem. Studies indicate that cell phone activity probably contributes to over 636,000 motor vehicle crashes per year. Many businesses are therefore banning cell phone use and texting activities among their drivers.[86]

The Problems of Job Stress and Burnout

Problems such as alcoholism and drug abuse sometimes stem from stress, especially *job stress*.[87] One survey found that one-fourth of all employees surveyed viewed their jobs as the number-one stressor in their lives.[88] Yet only 5% of surveyed U.S. employers say they're addressing workplace stress.[89]

Various external factors can trigger stress. These include work schedule, pace of work, job security, route to and from work, workplace noise, and the number and nature of customers.[90] However, no two people react the same way to stressors because personal factors also influence stress. For example, people who are **workaholics** and who feel driven to always meet deadlines normally put themselves under more stress than do others.

Consequences   Job stress has serious consequences for the employee and the organization. The human consequences of job stress include anxiety, depression, anger, and physical consequences such as cardiovascular disease and headaches. Stress also has serious consequences for the employer. These include diminished performance, and increased absenteeism, turnover, and grievances.[91] A study of 46,000 employees concluded that health-care costs of high-stress workers were 46% higher than were those of their less-stressed coworkers.[92] Yet not all stress is dysfunctional. Some people, for example, find that they are more productive as a deadline approaches.

Reducing Your Own Job Stress   A person can do several things to alleviate stress. These include commonsense remedies like getting more sleep and eating better.[93] Finding a more suitable job, getting counseling, and planning each day's activities are other sensible responses.[94] In his book *Stress and the Manager*, Dr. Karl Albrecht suggests the following to reduce job stress:[95]

- Build rewarding, pleasant, cooperative relationships with as many of your colleagues and employees as you can.
- Don't bite off more than you can chew.
- Build an especially effective and supportive relationship with your boss.
- Understand the boss's problems and help him or her to understand yours.
- Negotiate with your boss for realistic deadlines on important projects.
- Find time every day for detachment and relaxation.
- Get away from your office from time to time for a change of scene and a change of mind.
- Don't put off dealing with distasteful problems.
- Write down the problems that concern you, and beside each write down what you're going to do about it.

Meditation is another possibility. Choose a quiet place with soft light and sit comfortably. Then meditate by focusing your thoughts (for instance, by counting breaths, or by visualizing a calming location such as a beach). When your mind wanders, just bring it back to focusing on your breathing, or the beach.[96] Several years ago, World Bank employees were apparently experiencing high stress levels. Several times a week trainers from a Washington, DC–based Buddhist meditation instruction group ran meditation classes at the bank. Employees generally felt the classes were useful in reducing stress.[97]

What the Employer Can Do The employer can help reduce job stress. One British firm follows a three-tiered approach to managing workplace stress.[98] First is *primary prevention*, which focuses on ensuring that things like job designs and workflows are correct. Second involves *intervention*, including individual employee assessment, attitude surveys to find sources of stress at work, and supervisory intervention. Third is *rehabilitation* through employee assistance programs and counseling.[99]

Burnout Burnout is a phenomenon closely associated with job stress. Experts define *burnout* as the total depletion of physical and mental resources caused by excessive striving to reach an unrealistic work-related goal. Burnout builds gradually, manifesting itself in symptoms such as irritability, discouragement, entrapment, and resentment.[100] Employers can head off burnout, for instance, by monitoring employees in potentially high-pressure jobs.[101]

What can a burnout candidate do? Here are some suggestions:

- *Break your patterns.* Are you doing a variety of things or the same one repeatedly? The more well rounded your life is, the better protected you are against burnout.
- *Get away from it all periodically.* Schedule occasional periods of introspection during which you can get away from your usual routine, perhaps alone.
- *Reassess your goals in terms of their intrinsic worth.* Are the goals you've set for yourself attainable? Are they really worth the sacrifice?
- *Think about your work.* Could you do as good a job without being so intense?

Depression Stress and burnout aren't the only psychological problems at work.[102] For example, employers need to work harder to ensure that depressed employees utilize support services. One survey found that while about two-thirds of large firms offered employee assistance programs covering depression, only about 14% of employees with depression said they used one.[103] Training managers to recognize signs of depression—persistent sad moods, sleeping too little, reduced appetite, difficulty in concentrating, and loss of interest in activities once enjoyed, for instance—and then making assistance more readily available can help. Depression is a disease. It does no more good to tell a depressed person to "snap out of it" than it would to tell someone with a heart condition to stop acting tired. Women (and men) should have access to domestic crisis hotlines, such as HYPERLINK "http://www.ndvh.org" www.ndvh.org, and to the employer's employee assistance programs.

Infectious Diseases

With many employees traveling to and from international destinations, monitoring and controlling infectious diseases is an important safety issue.[104]

Employers can take steps to prevent the entry or spread of infectious diseases. These steps include:

1. Closely monitor Centers for Disease Control and Prevention (CDC) travel alerts. Access this information at www.cdc.gov
2. Provide daily medical screenings for employees returning from infected areas.
3. Deny access for 10 days to employees or visitors who have had contact with suspected infected individuals.

4. Tell employees to stay home if they have a fever or respiratory system symptoms.
5. Clean work areas and surfaces regularly. Make sanitizers easily available.
6. Stagger breaks. Offer several lunch periods to reduce overcrowding.

Special situations prompt special requirements. For example, in 2009 the CDC advised employers that health-care workers working with H1N1 patients should use special respirators to reduce virus inhalation risks.[105]

Workplace Smoking

To some extent, the problem of workplace smoking is becoming moot. For example, a series of states including Delaware, Connecticut, California, and New York have barred smoking in most workplaces.[106] Yet smoking continues to be a problem for employees and employers. Costs derive from higher health and fire insurance, as well as increased absenteeism and reduced productivity (which occurs, for instance, when a smoker takes a 10-minute cigarette break down the hall).[107]

What You Can and Cannot Do   In general, you can deny a job to a smoker. The EEOC says that a policy of not hiring smokers is legal as long as the rules apply to all applicants and employees.[108] A "no-smokers hired" policy does not, according to one expert, violate the ADA. Smoking is not considered a disability, and, in general, "employers' adoption of a 'no-smokers-hired' policy is not illegal under federal law."[109] Therefore, you can probably institute a policy against hiring people who smoke.

Some firms take a hard-line approach. For example, WEYCO Inc., a benefits services company in Michigan, first gave employees 15 months warning and offered smoking cessation assistance. Then they began firing or forcing out all its workers who smoke, including those who do so just in their homes.[110]

Computer Monitor Health Problems and How to Avoid Them

Even with flat-panel screens, there's still a risk of monitor-related health problems at work. Problems include short-term eye burning, itching, and tearing, as well as eyestrain. Backaches and neck aches are also widespread. These often occur because employees try to compensate for monitor problems (such as glare) by maneuvering into awkward body positions. There may also be a tendency for computer users to suffer from carpal tunnel syndrome, caused by repetitive use of the hands at uncomfortable angles.[111] OSHA has no specific standards for computer workstations.[112]

NIOSH provides general recommendations regarding computer monitors. These include:[113]

1. *Give employees rest breaks.* NIOSH recommends a 15-minute rest break after 2 hours of continuous work.
2. *Design the maximum flexibility into the workstation so that it can be adapted to the individual operator.* For example, use movable keyboards and adjustable chairs.
3. *Reduce glare with devices such as shades over windows, antiglare screen filters, and recessed or indirect lighting.*
4. *Give workers a complete preplacement vision exam to ensure properly corrected vision.*

Other suggestions include:

5. The height of the table or chair should allow positioning of wrists at the same level as the elbow.
6. The wrists should be able to rest lightly on a pad for support.
7. The feet should be flat on the floor, or on a footrest.

Dealing with Violence at Work

A disgruntled long-term employee walked into Chrysler's Ohio Jeep assembly plant and fatally shot one worker, after reportedly being involved in an argument with a supervisor.[114]

Violence against employees is a big problem at work. As at the Jeep plant, a coworker or personal associate commits roughly one of seven workplace homicides (although robbery was the main motive for workplace homicide).[115] One report called bullying the "silent epidemic" of the workplace, "where abusive behavior, threats, and intimidation often go unreported."[116] And, workplace violence can also manifest itself in sabotaging the firm's property, software, or information databases.[117]

Most workplace violence is predictable and avoidable. *Risk Management Magazine* estimates that about 86% of past workplace violence incidents were anticipated by coworkers, who had brought them to management's attention prior to the incidents actually occurring. Yet, in most cases, management did little or nothing.[118] HR managers can take several steps to reduce the incidence of workplace violence. They include the following.

Adopt a Workplace Violence Policy   Start with adopting a workplace violence policy that outlines unacceptable employee behavior and a zero-tolerance policy toward workplace violence.[119]

Heighten Security Measures   Heightened security measures are an employer's next line of defense against workplace violence. According to OSHA, these measures include:[120]

- Improve external lighting;
- Use drop safes and post signs noting that only a limited amount of cash is on hand;
- Install silent alarms and surveillance cameras; increase the number of staff on duty;
- Issue a weapons policy that states, for instance, that regardless of their legality, firearms or other dangerous or deadly weapons cannot be brought onto the facility, either openly or concealed.[121]

Improve Employee Screening   With about 30% of workplace attacks committed by coworkers, screening out potentially explosive applicants is the employer's next line of defense.

Personal and situational factors both influence workplace aggression. In general, individuals scoring higher on "trait anger" (the predisposition to respond to situations with hostility) are more likely to exhibit workplace aggression. In terms of the situation, interpersonal injustice and poor leadership predict aggression against supervisors.[122]

Steps to Take   Obtain a detailed employment application and solicit an applicant's employment history, educational background, and references. Interview questions to ask might include, for instance, "What frustrates you?" and "Who was your worst supervisor and why?" Certain background circumstances, such as the following, may provide red flags indicating the need for a more in-depth background investigation:

- An unexplained gap in employment
- Incomplete or false information on the résumé or application
- A negative, unfavorable, or false reference
- Prior insubordinate or violent behavior on the job
- A criminal history involving harassing or violent behavior
- A prior termination for cause with a suspicious (or no) explanation
- History of drug or alcohol abuse
- Strong indications of instability in the individual's work or personal life as indicated, for example, by frequent job changes or geographic moves
- Lost licenses or accreditations

Use Workplace Violence Training   Supervisors can be trained to identify the clues that typify potentially violent employees. Common clues include:[123]

- An act of violence on or off the job
- Erratic behavior evidencing a loss of perception or awareness of actions
- Overly confrontational or antisocial behavior
- Sexually aggressive behavior
- Isolationist or loner tendencies
- Insubordinate behavior with a threat of violence[124]
- Tendency to overreact to criticism
- Exaggerated interest in war, guns, violence, mass murders, catastrophes, and so on
- Commission of a serious breach of security
- Possession of weapons, guns, knives, or like items in the workplace
- Violation of privacy rights of others, such as searching desks or stalking
- Chronic complaining and the raising of frequent, unreasonable grievances
- A retributory or get-even attitude

The U.S. Postal Service took steps to reduce workplace threats and assaults. The steps include more background checks, drug testing, a 90-day probationary period for new hires, more stringent security (including a hotline that allows employees to report threatening situations), a zero-tolerance policy for reporting and recording potentially violent incidents, and training managers to create a healthier workplace culture.[125]

The *HR in Practice* box presents some other suggestions.

Violence toward Women at Work   While men have more fatal occupational injuries than do women, the proportion of women who are victims of assault is much higher. The Gender-Motivated Violence Act, part of the Violence against Women Act passed by Congress in 1994 (and expanded in 2006), imposes significant liabilities on employers whose women employees become violence victims.[126]

When firing a high-risk employee:

- Plan all aspects of the meeting, including its time, location, the people to be present, and agenda;
- Involve security enforcement personnel;
- Advise the employee that he or she is no longer permitted onto the employer's property;
- Conduct the meeting in a room with a door leading to the outside of the building;
- Keep the termination brief and to the point;

- Make sure he or she returns all company-owned property at the meeting;
- Don't let the person return to his or her workstation; conduct the meeting early in the week and early in the morning so he or she has time to meet with employment counselors or support groups;
- Offer as generous a severance package as possible, and protect the employee's dignity by not publicizing the event.[127]

Fatal workplace violence against women has several sources. Of all females murdered at work, more than three-fourths are victims of random criminal violence carried out by an assailant unknown to the victim, as during a robbery. Coworkers, family members, or previous friends or acquaintances carry out the remaining criminal acts.[128] Tangible security improvements including better lighting, cash-drop boxes, and similar steps are especially pertinent in reducing such violent acts against women.

Terrorism

The employer can take several steps to protect its employees and physical assets from terrorist attack. Steps to take *institute policies* to check mail carefully; identify ahead of time a lean *crisis organization* that can run the company on an interim basis; identify in advance under what conditions you will *close the company* down, what the shutdown process will be, and who can order it; institute a process to put the *crisis management team* together; prepare *evacuation plans* and make sure exits are well marked and unblocked; designate an employee who will *communicate with families* and off-site employees; identify an off-site location near your facility to use as a *staging area* for evacuated personnel; and designate in advance several employees who will do *headcounts* at the evacuation staging area.[129] Employers also use text messaging to communicate hazardous conditions quickly.[130]

Enterprise Risk Management

Many of these actions stem from employers' heightened focus on risk management. Identifying security and other corporate risks falls within the domain of *enterprise risk management*, which means identifying risks, and planning to and actually mitigating these risks. Thus, as part of its risk management, Walmart asks questions such as, "What are the risks? And what are we going to do about these risks?"[131] Eliminating crime and enhancing facility security are two important issues here.

Setting Up a Basic Security Program   In simplest terms, instituting a basic security program[132] requires analyzing the current level of risk and then installing mechanical, natural, and organizational security systems.

Security programs often start with an analysis of the facility's current level of risk, preferably with security experts. Here, start with the obvious. For example, what is the neighborhood like? Is your facility close to major highways or railroad tracks (where, for instance, toxic fumes from the trains could present a problem)?

Having assessed the potential current level of risk, the employer then turns to assessing and improving three basic sources of facility security: natural security, mechanical security, and organizational security.[133]

Natural security means taking advantage of the facility's natural or architectural features to minimize security problems. For example, do stacks of boxes in front of your windows prevent police officers from observing what's happening in your facility? Are there unlit spots in your parking lot?

Mechanical security is the utilization of security systems such as locks, intrusion alarms, access control systems, and surveillance systems that will reduce the need for continuous human surveillance.[134] Here, technological advances are making it easier for employers. Thus, for access security, biometric scanners that read thumb or palm prints or retina or vocal patterns make it easier to enforce plant security.

Finally, *organizational security* means using good management to improve security. For example, it means making sure that security staff have written orders that clearly define their duties, especially in situations such as fire, elevator entrapment, or suspicious packages.[135]

The *Global Issues in HR* box provides a global perspective on safety abroad.

Global Issues in HR: Crime and Punishment Abroad

Particularly when traveling abroad where medical facilities may not meet developed-country standards, sudden illnesses or serious accidents can be very serious. Language difficulties, cultural misunderstandings, and lack of normal support systems combine to make an accident or illness a disaster. Legally, employers have a duty of care for protecting international assignees and their dependents and international business travelers.[136]

Cultural differences can cause surprises. In one hospital abroad, for instance, the doctor would not perform a heart surgery until receiving $40,000 in cash. As a result, many multinationals brief their business travelers and expatriates about what to expect and how to react when confronted with a health or safety problem abroad. Many employers contract with international security firms. For example, International SOS has over 1,300 medical professionals staffing its regional centers and clinics.[137]

One security expert says that the terrorist attacks on a Mumbai, India, hotel in 2008 show why employers need a way to track global employees, as well as methods for assessing overseas risks, and a response plan should a crisis occur.[138]

REVIEW

Summary

1. The area of safety and accident prevention is of concern because of the staggering number of deaths and accidents occurring at work.

2. The purpose of the Occupational Safety and Health Act is to ensure every working person a safe and healthful workplace. OSHA standards are complete and detailed, and are enforced through a system of workplace inspections. OSHA inspectors can issue citations and recommend penalties.

3. There are three basic causes of accidents: chance occurrences, unsafe conditions, and unsafe acts on the part of employees. In addition, three other work-related factors—the job itself, the work schedule, and the psychological climate—contribute to accidents.

4. Unsafe acts on the part of employees are a main cause of accidents. Such acts are to some extent the result of certain personal characteristics.

5. Experts differ on whether there are accident-prone people who have accidents regardless of the job. The consensus seems to be that the person who is accident prone in one job may not be on a different job. For example, vision is related to accident frequency for drivers, but not for other workers, such as accountants.

6. There are several approaches to preventing accidents. One is to reduce unsafe conditions. The other is to reduce unsafe acts—for example, through selection and placement, training, positive reinforcement, propaganda, and top-management commitment.

7. Alcoholism, drug addiction, stress, and emotional illness are four important health problems among employees. Alcoholism is a particularly serious problem that can drastically lower the effectiveness of your organization. Techniques including disciplining, discharge, in-house counseling, and referrals to an outside agency help deal with these problems.

8. Stress and burnout are other potential health problems at work. An employee can reduce job stress, for instance, by getting away from work for a while each day.

9. Violence against employees is an enormous problem at work. Steps that can reduce workplace violence include improved security arrangements, better employee screening, and violence-reduction training.

10. Basic facility security relies on natural security, mechanical security, and organizational security.

KEY TERMS

- Occupational Safety and Health Act
- Occupational Safety and Health Administration (OSHA)
- citations
- unsafe conditions
- unsafe acts
- workaholic
- burnout

DISCUSSION QUESTIONS

1. How would you go about providing a safer workplace for your employees?
2. Discuss how you would go about minimizing the occurrence of unsafe acts on the part of your employees.
3. Discuss the basic facts about the Occupational Safety and Health Act—its purpose, standards, inspection, and rights and responsibilities.
4. Explain the supervisor's role in safety.
5. Explain what causes unsafe acts.
6. Based on what you read here, is there such a thing as an accident-prone person?
7. Describe at least five techniques for reducing accidents.
8. Explain how an employee could reduce stress at work.

INDIVIDUAL AND GROUP ACTIVITIES

1. Working individually or in groups, answer the question, "Is there such a thing as an accident-prone person?" Develop your answer using examples of actual people you know who seemed to be accident prone on some endeavor.
2. Working individually or in groups, compile a list of the factors at work or in school that create dysfunctional stress for you. What methods do you use for dealing with the stress?
3. An issue of the journal *EHS* presented information about what happens when OSHA refers criminal complaints about willful violations of its standards to the U.S. Department of Justice (DOJ). Between 1982 and 2002, OSHA referred 119 fatal cases allegedly involving willful violations of OSHA to DOJ for criminal prosecution. The DOJ declined to pursue 57% of them, and some were dropped for other reasons. Of the remaining 51 cases, the DOJ settled 63% with pretrial settlements involving no prison time. So, counting acquittals, of the 119 cases OSHA referred to the DOJ, only 9 resulted in prison time for at least one of the defendants. "The Department of Justice is a disgrace," charged the founder of an organization for family members of workers killed on the job. One possible explanation for this low conviction rate is that the crime in cases like these is generally a misdemeanor, not a felony, and the DOJ generally tries to focus its attention on felony cases. Given this information, what implications do you think this has for how employers and their managers should manage their safety programs, and why do you take that position?
5. A few years ago, a 315-foot-tall, 2-million-pound crane collapsed on a construction site in East Toledo, Ohio, killing four iron-workers. Do you think catastrophic failures like this are avoidable? If so, what steps would you suggest the general contractor to take to avoid a disaster like this?
6. In groups of three or four students, spend 15 minutes walking around the building in which your class is held or where you are now, listing possible natural, mechanical, and organizational security measures you'd suggest to the building's owner.

APPLICATION EXERCISES

Case Incident   The New Safety Program

Employees' safety and health are very important matters in the laundry and cleaning business. Each dry-cleaning store is a small production plant in which machines, powered by high-pressure steam and compressed air, work at high temperatures washing, cleaning, and pressing garments often under very hot, slippery conditions. Chemical vapors are continually produced, and caustic chemicals are used in the cleaning process. High-temperature stills are almost continually "cooking down" cleaning solvents in order to remove impurities so that the solvents can be reused. If a mistake is made in this process—such as injecting too much steam into the still—a boilover occurs, in which boiling chemical solvent erupts out of the still, onto the floor, and onto anyone who happens to be standing in its way.

As a result of these hazards and the fact that chemically hazardous waste is continually produced in these stores, several government agencies (including OSHA and the Environmental Protection Agency) have strict guidelines regarding the management of these plants. For example, posters have to be placed in each store, notifying employees of their right to be told what hazardous chemicals they are dealing with, and what the proper method is for handling each chemical. Special waste-management firms must be used to pick up and properly dispose of the hazardous waste.

A chronic problem the owners have is the unwillingness on the part of the cleaning-spotting workers to wear safety goggles. Not all the chemicals they use require safety goggles, but some—like the hydrofluorous acid used to remove rust stains from garments—are very dangerous. The latter is kept in special plastic containers because it dissolves glass. Some of the employees feel that wearing safety goggles can be troublesome; they are somewhat uncomfortable, and they also become smudged easily and thus cut down on visibility. As a result, it is sometimes almost impossible to get employees to wear their goggles. ■

QUESTIONS

1. How should a dry cleaner go about identifying hazardous conditions that should be rectified? Name four probable hazardous conditions or areas in such a store, based on dry-cleaning stores that you have seen.
2. Would it be advisable for such a firm to set up a procedure for screening out accident-prone individuals?
3. How would you suggest that owners get all employees to behave more safely at work? Also, how would you advise them to get those who should be wearing goggles to do so?

Continuing Case

LearnInMotion.com: The New Safety and Health Program

At first glance, a dot-com is one of the last places you'd expect to find potential safety and health hazards—or so Jennifer and Mel thought. There's no danger of moving machinery, no high-pressure lines, no cutting or heavy lifting, and certainly no forklift trucks. However, there are safety and health problems.

In terms of accident-causing conditions, for instance, the one thing dot-com companies have is lots of cables and wires. There are cables connecting the computers to each other and to the servers, and in many cases separate cables running from some computers to separate printers. There are 10 telephones in the office, many with 15-foot phone lines that always seem to be snaking around chairs and tables. There is, in fact, an astonishing amount of cable considering this is an office with less than 10 employees.

When the installation specialists wired the office (for electricity, high speed cable, phone lines, burglar alarms, and computers), they estimated they used well over 5 miles of cables of one sort or another. Most of these are in the walls or ceilings, but many of them snake their way from desk to desk and under and over doorways. Several employees have tried to reduce the nuisance of having to trip over wires whenever they get up by putting their plastic chair pads over the wires closest to them. However, that still leaves many wires unprotected. In other cases, they brought in their own packing tape and tried to tape down the wires in those spaces where they're particularly troublesome, such as across doorways.

The cables and wires are only one of the more obvious potential accident-causing conditions. The firm's programmer, before he left the firm, had tried to repair the main server while the unit was still electrically alive. To this day, they're not sure exactly where he stuck the screwdriver, but the result was that he was "blown across the room," as Mel puts it. He was all right, but it was still a scare. And while they haven't yet received any claims, every employee spends hours at his or her computer, so carpal tunnel syndrome is a risk, as are a variety of other problems such as eyestrain and strained backs.

One recent accident particularly scared them. The firm uses independent contractors to deliver the firm's book- and DVD-based courses in New York and two other cities. A delivery person was riding his bike at the intersection of Second Avenue and East 64th Street in New York when he was struck by a car. Luckily he was not hurt, but the bike's front wheel was wrecked, and the close call got Mel and Jennifer thinking about their lack of a safety program.

It's not just the physical conditions that concern the company's two owners. They also have some concerns about potential health problems such as job stress and burnout. While the business may be (relatively) safe with respect to physical conditions, it is also relatively stressful in terms of the demands it makes in hours and deadlines. It's not unusual for employees to get to work by 7:30 or 8:00 in the morning and to work through until 11:00 or 12:00 at night, at least 5 and sometimes 6 or 7 days per week. Just getting the company's new calendar fine-tuned and operational required five of LearnInMotion.com's employees to work 70-hour workweeks for 3 weeks.

The bottom line is that both Jennifer and Mel feel that they need to do something about implementing a health and safety plan. Now, they want you, their management consultants, to help them actually to do it. Here's what they want you to do for them. ∎

QUESTIONS AND ASSIGNMENTS

1. Based on your knowledge of health and safety matters and your actual observations of operations that are similar to ours, make a list of the potential hazardous conditions employees and others face at LearnInMotion.com. What should we do to reduce the potential severity of the top five hazards?

2. Would it be advisable for us to set up a procedure for screening out stress-prone or accident-prone individuals? Why or why not? If so, how should we screen them?

3. Write a short position paper on what we should do to get all our employees to behave more safely at work.

4. Based on what you know and on what other dot-coms are doing, write a short position paper on what we can do to reduce the potential problems of stress and burnout in our company.

Experiential Exercise
Checking for Unsafe Conditions

Purpose: The purpose of this exercise is to give you practice in identifying unsafe conditions.

Required Understanding: You should be familiar with material covered in this chapter, particularly that on unsafe conditions and the checklist in the *HR in Practice* box (pages 298–299), and Figure 10.4.

How to Set Up the Exercise/Instructions: Divide the class into groups of four or five students.

Assume that you are a safety committee retained by your school to identify and report on any possible unsafe conditions in and around the school building.

Each group will spend about 45 minutes in and around the building you are now in for the purpose of identifying and listing possible unsafe conditions. (*Hint:* Make use of the *HR in Practice* checklist.)

Return to the class in about 45 minutes, and a spokesperson for each group should list on the board the unsafe conditions you think you have identified. How many were there? Do you think these also violate OSHA standards? How would you go about checking? ∎

Module  A

Managing HR Globally

- HR and the Internationalization of Business
- Improving International Assignments Through Selection
- Training and Maintaining International Employees
- How to Implement a Global HR System

HR AND THE INTERNATIONALIZATION OF BUSINESS

Walmart, a company famously resistant to unions in America, recently had a surprise. Opening stores in China at a fast clip, it attempted to dissuade local unions there from organizing Walmart's employees. However, the powerful All-China Federation of Trade Unions (ACFTU) quickly established itself in several Walmart stores. At first, it seemed likely that the union would succeed. But Walmart was vigorously resisting.[1]

Firms like IBM and Sony have long done business abroad. But with the rapid growth of demand in Asia and other parts of the world, even small firms' success depends on marketing and managing overseas.[2]

This confronts employers with some management challenges. For one thing, managers now need to formulate and execute their market and production plans on a worldwide basis. For another, they must therefore also address international human resource management issues. For example, "Should we staff the local offices with local or U.S. managers?"

In fact, employers are finding that even employees who never leave the home office need to be "internationalized." As one article said, "cultural diversity isn't just for expatriates or frequent flying executives. Cube dwellers increasingly need to work, often virtually, across borders with people . . . who don't approach business in the same way that Americans do."[3] We'll address these topics in this module.

The Human Resource Challenges of International Business

Dealing with global HR issues is complex. The employer faces numerous political, social, legal, and cultural differences among countries. In the face of these differences, the employer with operations abroad needs to create effective methods for candidate selection, cultural and language orientation and training, compensation administration, career planning and development, and handling of spouse and dependent matters.[4] So the challenge of conducting human resource activities abroad doesn't just stem from the distances involved but also from the cultural, political, legal, and economic differences among countries and their peoples.[5] Let's look at this.

How Intercountry Differences Affect Human Resource Management

Companies operating only within the United States deal with a relatively limited set of economic, cultural, and legal variables. The United States is a capitalist, competitive society. And while the U.S. workforce reflects many cultural and ethnic backgrounds, shared values (such as an appreciation for democracy) help to blur sharp cultural differences. Different states and municipalities certainly have their own laws affecting HR. However, a basic federal framework supplies a predictable set of legal guidelines regarding matters such as employment discrimination, labor relations, and safety and health.

A company operating abroad isn't blessed with such homogeneity. For example, even with the European Union's increasing standardization, minimum legally mandated holidays range from none in the United Kingdom to 5 weeks per year in Luxembourg. And while Italy has no formal requirements for employee representatives on boards of directors, they're required in Denmark.[6] The point is that the need to adapt personnel practices to differences among countries complicates HR management in multinational companies. For example, consider the following.

Cultural Factors   Countries differ widely in their cultures—in other words, in the basic values their citizens share, and in the ways these values manifest themselves in the nation's arts, social programs, politics, and ways of doing things. For example, in a study of about 330 managers from Hong Kong, the People's Republic of China, and the United States, the U.S. managers tended to be most concerned with getting the job done. Chinese managers were most concerned with maintaining harmony. Hong Kong managers fell between these extremes.[7]

A classic study by Professor Geert Hofstede identified other international cultural differences. For example, Hofstede says societies differ in *power distance*—in other words, the extent to which the less powerful members of institutions accept and expect an unequal distribution of power.[8] He concluded that acceptance of such inequality was higher in some countries (such as Mexico) than in others (such as Sweden).

Cultural differences influence human resource policies and practices.[9] For example, some argue that Americans' emphasis on "standing on one's own feet" helps to explain why European HR managers are more constrained than America's with respect to the notice they must give workers before firing them, and the complexity involved in laying off workers. Similarly, both union membership and union influences are much higher in Europe than in the United States.[10]

Legal and Political Factors   Legal differences blindside even sophisticated companies. After spending billions expanding into Germany, Walmart discovered that Germany's commercial laws discourage ads based on price comparisons. They soon left Germany.

As other examples, the U.S. practice of employment at will doesn't exist in Europe, where firing or laying off workers is usually expensive. And in many European countries, *work councils* are required, wherein formal, employee-elected groups of worker representatives meet monthly with managers to discuss topics ranging from no-smoking policies to layoffs.[11]

Co-determination is the rule in Germany and several other countries. **Co-determination** means employees have the legal right to a voice in setting company policies. Workers elect their own representatives to the supervisory board of the employer.[12] In the United States, by comparison, HR policies on most matters (such as wages and benefits) are set by the employer, or in negotiations with its labor unions.

Managing globally also requires monitoring political risks. *Political risks* "are any governmental actions or politically motivated events that could adversely affect the long run profitability or value of the firm."[13] For example, the president of Venezuela moved to nationalize his country's oil industries.

Economic Systems   Differences in economic systems also translate into differences in HR practices. For one thing, differences in labor costs are also substantial. Labor costs also vary widely. For example, hourly compensation costs in U.S. dollars for production workers recently ranged from $2.92 in Mexico to $6.58 in Taiwan, $24.59 in the United States, $29.73 in the United Kingdom, and $37.66 in Germany.[14]

Example 1: Legal and Industrial Relations Factors Abroad: The European Union
Over the past three decades, the separate countries of the former European Community (EC) were unified into a common market for goods, services, capital, and even labor called the European Union (EU). Tariffs for goods moving across borders from one EU country to another generally disappeared. Employees (with some exceptions) now find it easy to move freely between jobs in the EU countries. The introduction of a single currency—the euro—further blurred many of these differences.

Employers doing business in Europe must adjust their human resource practices to both EU directives and to country-specific employment laws. The directives are, basically, EU laws (although each member country can implement the directives as they choose). For example, the EU directive on confirmation of employment requires employers to provide employees with written terms and conditions of their employment, but these terms vary from country to country.[15] In England, a detailed written statement is required. Germany doesn't require a written contract, but it's still customary to have one.

The interplay of directives and country laws means that human resource practices must vary from country to country. For example:[16]

- **Minimum EU wages.**   Most EU countries have minimum wage systems in place. Some set national limits. Others allow employers and unions to work out their own.
- **Working hours.**   The EU sets the workweek at 48 hours, but most countries set it at 40 hours.

- **Employee representation.** Europe has many levels of employee representation. In France, for instance, employers with 50 or more employees must consult with their employees' representatives on matters including working conditions, profit-sharing plans, and layoffs. In Italy, all employers with 15 or more employees must consult with their works councils on internal work rules. Most EU companies must "inform and consult" employees about employee-related actions.[17]

Example 2: Legal and Industrial Relations Factors Abroad: China For many years, Walmart and other employers inside and outside China relied on that country's huge workforce to provide products and services at very low cost. Part of the reason for the low labor cost was the relative lack of labor laws governing things like severance pay, minimum wages, and benefits.

Now that's changing. Several years ago, the People's Republic of China implemented its new labor contract law. This law adds numerous new employment protections for employees. For example, multinational companies doing business in China said the new law would reduce employment flexibility, raise labor costs, and make it difficult to lay off employees by instituting new large severance package requirements.[18] In June, 2010, Honda about doubled wages at one China plant after worker protests.

IMPROVING INTERNATIONAL ASSIGNMENTS THROUGH SELECTION

Given differences like these, selecting, training, and maintaining employees in an international company requires some special practices and skills. We'll start with selecting employees for assignments abroad.

Why Do International Assignments Fail?

Discovering why such assignments fail is an important research task, and experts have made considerable progress.

Personality Personality is one factor. For example, in a study of 143 expatriate employees, extroverted, agreeable, and emotionally stable individuals were less likely to want to leave their posts abroad early.[19] And, the person's intentions are important: For example, people who want expatriate careers try harder to adjust to such a life.[20] Similarly, expatriates who are more satisfied with their jobs are more likely to adapt to the foreign assignment.[21] Studies also suggest that it's not how different culturally the host country is from the person's home country, it's the person's ability to adapt. Some do fine anywhere; others fail anywhere.[22]

Family Pressures Nonwork factors like family pressures usually loom large in expatriate failures. In one early study, U.S. managers listed, in descending order of importance for leaving early, inability of spouse to adjust, managers' inability to adjust, other family problems, managers' personal or emotional immaturity, and inability to cope with larger overseas responsibility.[23] Other studies similarly emphasize dissatisfied spouses' effects on the international assignment.[24]

The Problem   These findings underscore a truism regarding international assignee selection: It's usually not technical incompetence, but family and personal problems that torpedo the international assignee. Yet employers still tend to select expatriates based on technical competence rather than interpersonal skills or family situations.[25] As one expert puts it:

> The selection process is fundamentally flawed. . . . Expatriate assignments rarely fail because the person cannot accommodate to the technical demands. . . . They fail because of family and personal issues and lack of cultural skills that haven't been part of the process.[26]

Some Solutions   There are ways to improve the success rate of international assignments. Providing realistic previews of what to expect, careful screening, improved orientation, and improved benefits packages are some obvious solutions. One way to reduce assignment problems is simply to *shorten the length* of the assignment.[27] Some companies form *"global buddy"* programs. Here local managers assist new expatriates with advice on matters such as norms of behavior and on getting emergency medical assistance.[28] Many employers use "short-term," *"commuter,"* or "frequent-flier" assignments. These usually involve much travel but no formal relocation.[29] Other firms use Internet-based *video technologies* and group decision-making software to enable global virtual teams to do business without travel or relocation.[30]

International Staffing: Home or Local?

Multinational corporations (MNCs) employ several types of international managers. **Locals** are citizens of the countries where they are working. **Expatriates** are noncitizens of the countries in which they are working.[31] **Home-country nationals** are citizens of the country in which the multinational company has its headquarters.[32] **Third-country nationals** are citizens of a country other than the parent or the host country—for example, a British executive working in the Tokyo branch of a U.S. multinational.[33]

Expatriates represent a minority of multinationals' managers. "Most managerial positions are filled by locals rather than expatriates in both headquarters or foreign subsidiary operations."[34]

Why Local?   There are several reasons to rely on local managers to fill your foreign subsidiary's management ranks. Many people don't want to work in a foreign country, and the cost of using expatriates is usually far greater.[35] Locals may view the multinational as a "better citizen" if it uses local management talent. Some governments even press for the "nativization" of local management.[36] Others fear that expatriates, knowing they're posted to the foreign subsidiary for just a few years, may overemphasize short-term results.[37]

In the United States, it's not easy bringing workers in from abroad, so using U.S. "locals" may be a necessity. Under rules that went into effect in 2005, U.S. employers must try to recruit U.S. workers before filing foreign labor certification requests with the Department of Labor.[38]

Some companies don't realize what it actually costs to send an expatriate abroad. Agilent Technologies estimated that it cost about three times the expatriate's annual salary to keep the person abroad for 1 year. When Agilent outsourced its expatriate program, it discovered that the costs were much higher. The firm then dramatically reduced the number of expats, from about 1,000 to 300 per year.[39]

Why Expats?   Yet there are also reasons for using expatriates for staffing subsidiaries. The major reason is technical competence: In other words, employers often can't find local candidates with the required technical qualifications.[40] Multinationals also view a successful stint abroad as a required step in developing top managers. (For instance, after a term abroad, General Electric's Asia-Pacific head transferred back to a top executive position at GE.) Control is another important reason to use expatriates. The assumption is that home-office managers are already steeped in the firm's policies and culture and are thus more likely to implement headquarters' instructions and ways of doing things.

However, for the past 10 years or so, the trend has been toward using locals or other solutions. Posting expatriates abroad is very expensive, security problems increasingly give potential expatriates' pause, returning expatriates often soon leave for other employers, colleges are turning out top-quality candidates abroad, and the recent recession made the cost of posting employees abroad even more unattractive. One recent survey found that about 47% of US multinationals are maintaining the size of their ex-pat workforces; 18% were increasing it, and 35% were decreasing the number of expatriates.[41]

Hybrid Solutions   The choice is not just between expatriate versus local; there's a hybrid solution. One survey found that about 78% of employers had some form of "localization" policy. This policy makes particular sense when the transferee goes back to the country from which he or she originally emigrated. The assumption here is that the employee would not be treated as an expatriate but instead as a local hire.[42] For example, U.S. IBM employees originally from India eventually filled many of the 5,000 jobs that IBM recently shifted from the United States to India. These employees elected to move back to India, albeit at local, India pay rates.

Offshoring   *Offshoring*—having local employees abroad do jobs that the firm's domestic employees previously did in-house—is growing rapidly. Forrester Research estimated that about 588,000 U.S. jobs moved offshore between 2000 and 2005, and that that total will grow to over 3 million jobs by 2015.[43]

Offshoring is controversial. In the 1990s, it involved mostly manufacturing jobs. Between 2000 and 2015, experts estimate that about 288,000 management jobs will go offshore, 472,000 computer jobs, almost 75,000 legal jobs, and about 1.7 million office jobs. IBM recently announced that it was shifting about 5,000 U.S. software and sales jobs to India.[44]

Offshoring opponents naturally worry that this job drain will mean millions fewer white-collar jobs for American workers. Proponents contend that employers must offshore jobs to remain globally competitive. They say the money that U.S. employers save boosts research and development and, eventually, creates more domestic jobs for U.S. workers.

Values and International Staffing Policy

We've seen that things like technical competence determine whether firms use, say, locals or expatriates abroad. But it's not just facts that influence such decisions. In addition, the top executives' values also play a role. Some executives are just more "expat-oriented."

Experts sometimes classify people's values as **ethnocentric, polycentric,** or **geocentric,** and these values translate into corresponding corporate behaviors and policies.[45] In a firm whose top managers tend to be *ethnocentric,* "the prevailing attitude is that home country attitudes, management style, knowledge, evaluation criteria, and managers are superior to anything the host country might have to offer."[46] In the *polycentric* corporation, "there is a conscious belief that only host country managers can ever really understand the culture and behavior of the host country market; therefore, the foreign subsidiary should be managed by local people."[47] *Geocentric* executives believe they must scour the firm's whole management staff on a global basis, on the assumption that the best manager of a specific position anywhere may be in any country in which the firm operates.

Staffing Policies   These values translate into three broad international staffing policies. With an *ethnocentric* staffing policy, the firm fills key management jobs with parent-country nationals.[48] At Royal Dutch Shell, for instance, many financial officers around the world are Dutch nationals. Reasons given for ethnocentric staffing policies include lack of qualified host-country senior-management talent, a desire to maintain a unified corporate culture and tighter control, and the desire to transfer the parent firm's core competencies (for instance, a specialized manufacturing skill) to a foreign subsidiary more expeditiously.[49]

A *polycentric*-oriented firm would staff its foreign subsidiaries with host-country nationals and its home office with parent-country nationals. This may reduce the local cultural misunderstandings that might occur if it used expatriate managers. It will also usually be less expensive.

A *geocentric* staffing policy "seeks the best people for key jobs throughout the organization, regardless of nationality"—similar to what Ford Motor Company does. This lets Ford transfer the best person to the open job, wherever he or she (or the job) may be.

Ethics and Codes of Conduct   With operations in several countries, employers also need to ensure that their employees abroad are adhering to their firm's ethics codes.

Doing so is not easy. Exporting a firm's ethics rules requires more than having employees abroad use versions of its U.S. employee handbook. Relying on such handbooks can cause problems. For one thing, few countries adhere to "employment at will" as does the United States, so even handbooks with at-will disclaimers "can become binding contracts."[50] Similarly, employees in many countries have extensive rights under their labor laws, so U.S.-style handbooks may "breach an employer's information, consultation, and participation duty."[51]

One international lawyer recommends instituting, instead, a global code of conduct. Sometimes, the main concern may be establishing global standards for adhering to U.S. laws that have cross-border impacts. These employers should set broad policies on things like discrimination, harassment, bribery, and Sarbanes-Oxley Act. For other firms, such as some apparel manufacturers, the main concern may be with codes of conduct for avoiding sweatshop conditions.

Selecting International Managers

Selecting managers for domestic and foreign operations obviously have many similarities. Both candidates need the technical knowledge and skills to do the job, and the required intelligence and people skills.[52]

However, we've seen that foreign assignments are different. There is the need to cope with colleagues whose culture may be drastically different from one's own and the stress that being alone abroad can put on the manager and his or her family.

Testing   Selecting managers for expat assignments therefore sometimes means testing them for traits that predict success in adapting to new environments. One study asked 338 international assignees from various countries and organizations to specify which traits were important for success. The researchers identified five factors that contribute to success in such assignments: job knowledge and motivation, relational skills, flexibility/adaptability, extracultural openness, and family situation (spouse's positive opinion, willingness of spouse to live abroad, and so on; Figure M.1 shows some of the specific items that make up each of the five factors).[53] "Family situation was generally the most important factor."[54] Many firms also use tests such as the Overseas Assignment Inventory. This identifies the characteristics and attitudes international assignment candidates should have. Its publisher establishes local norms and conducts ongoing validation studies.[55]

Best Practices   Based on the research, best practices in international assignee selection include providing *realistic previews* to prospective international assignees, facilitating *self-selection* (to help expatriate candidates decide if the assignments are right for them), and *traditional selection procedures* focusing on traits such as openness.[56]

Realistic Previews   Realistic previews about the problems to expect (such as mandatory private schooling for the children) as well as about the cultural benefits, problems, and idiosyncrasies of the country are important. The rule should always be to "spell it all out" ahead of time.[57] Make sure the candidate and his or her family all have the information required to make a sound decision.

Adaptability Screening   With flexibility and adaptability appearing high in studies of what makes expats succeed, *adaptability screening* should be part of expat screening. Often conducted by a psychologist or psychiatrist, adaptability screening aims to assess the assignee's (and spouse's) probable success in handling the foreign transfer and to alert them to issues (such as the impact on children) the move may involve.[58]

Here, experience is often the best predictor of success. Companies look for overseas candidates whose work and nonwork experience, education, and language skills already demonstrate a facility for living and working with different cultures. Even several summers spent traveling overseas or participating in foreign student

Figure M.1 Five Factors and Specific Items Important to International Assignees' Success

I) Job Knowledge and Motivation
Managerial ability
Organizational ability
Imagination
Creativity
Administrative skills
Alertness
Responsibility
Industriousness
Initiative and energy
High motivation
Frankness
Belief in mission and job
Perseverance

II) Relational Skills
Respect
Courtesy and tact
Display of respect
Kindness
Empathy
Nonjudgmentalness
Integrity
Confidence

III) Flexibility/Adaptability
Resourcefulness
Ability to deal with stress
Flexibility
Emotional stability
Willingness to change
Tolerance for ambiguity
Adaptability
Independence
Dependability
Political sensitivity
Positive self-image

IV) Extracultural Openness
Variety of outside interests
Interest in foreign cultures
Openness
Knowledge of local language(s)
Outgoingness and extroversion
Overseas experience

V) Family Situation
Adaptability of spouse and family
Spouse's positive opinion
Willingness of spouse to live abroad
Stable marriage

Source: Adapted from Arthur Winfred Jr., and Winston Bennett Jr., "The International Assignee: The Relative Importance of Factors Perceived to Contribute to Success," *Personnel Psychology* 48 (1995): 106–107.

programs might provide some basis to believe the potential transferee can adjust when he or she arrives overseas.

Unfortunately, theory doesn't always translate into practice. The importance of adaptability screening notwithstanding, one study several years ago found that selection for positions abroad is so informal that the researchers called it "the coffee machine system": Two colleagues meet at the office coffee machine, strike up a conversation about a position abroad, and, based on that and little more, a selection decision is made.[59]

Things seem to be improving today. First, over the past two decades *there's been an increase in the number of selection criteria* companies in Germany, Japan, the United States, and the United Kingdom use to select expatriates. Employers now regularly use selection criteria such as technical/professional skills, expatriates' willingness to go, experience in the country, personality factors (including flexibility), leadership skills, the ability to work with teams, and previous performance appraisals in the selection process. Second, there's been a *big decline in U.S. companies' premature return rates*. This suggests that U.S. employers are becoming more successful at sending expatriates abroad.[60] The accompanying *Managing the New Workforce* feature expands on this.

Managing the New Workforce: Sending Women Managers Abroad

Recently, 56% of the overseas workforce was under 40, single (43%), and female (21%). So while women represent about 50% of the middle managers in U.S. companies, they represent only 21% of those sent abroad. That's up from about 15% in 2005, but still low.[61] What accounts for this?

Actually, many of the misperceptions that impeded women's progress over the years still exist.[62] Line managers make these assignments, and many assume that women don't want to work abroad, are reluctant to move their families abroad, or can't get their spouses to move.[63] In fact, one survey found, women do want international assignments, they are not less inclined to move their families, and their male spouses are not necessarily reluctant.

Safety is another issue. Employers tend to assume that women abroad are more likely to become crime victims. However, most surveyed women expats said that safety was no more an issue with women than it was with men. As one said, "It doesn't matter if you're a man or woman. If it's a dangerous city, it's dangerous for whomever."[64]

Fear of cultural prejudices against women is another common issue. In some cultures, women do have different rules, for instance, in terms of attire. But as one expat said, "Even in the more harsh cultures, once they recognize that the women can do the job, once your competence has been demonstrated, it becomes less of a problem."[65]

Employers take several steps to short-circuit misperceptions like these. For example, *formalize a process* for identifying employees who are willing to take assignments abroad. (At Gillette, for instance, supervisors use the performance review to identify such things.) *Train managers* to understand how employees really feel about going abroad, and what the real safety and cultural issues are. Let successful female expats *help recruit* prospective female expats, and discuss with them the pros and cons. Provide the expat's spouse with employment assistance.[66]

TRAINING AND MAINTAINING INTERNATIONAL EMPLOYEES

After deciding whom you'll send abroad, attention turns to providing the person with the training, pay, and other support he or she needs to be successful.

Orienting and Training Employees on International Assignment

When it comes to supplying the orientation and training required for success overseas, the practices of most U.S. firms reflect more talk than substance. Surveys show that many employers send employees abroad with little more than minimal training. In one survey, 56% of employers admitted that the people they sent abroad weren't sufficiently knowledgeable about the host country, but only 20% of them offered the necessary country training.[67]

What Training?   What sort of special training do overseas candidates need? One firm specializing in such programs prescribes a four-step approach.[68]

- Level 1 training focuses on the impact of cultural differences, and on raising trainees' awareness of such differences and their impact on business outcomes.
- Level 2 aims at getting participants to understand how attitudes are formed and how they influence behavior. (For example, unfavorable stereotypes may subconsciously influence how a new manager treats his or her new foreign subordinates.)
- Level 3 training provides factual knowledge about the target country.
- Level 4 provides skill building in areas like language and adjustment and adaptation skills.

Beyond these special training needs, managers abroad continue to need traditional training and development. IBM and other firms have management development centers around the world where executives can hone their skills. And classroom programs (such as those at the London Business School, or at INSEAD in France) provide the sorts of educational opportunities that similar stateside programs do for their U.S.-based colleagues.

Trends   There are several trends in expatriate training and development. First, rather than providing only predeparture cross-cultural training, more firms are providing continuing, in-country cross-cultural training during the early stages of an overseas assignment. Second, employers are using returning managers as resources. For example, automotive equipment producer Bosch holds regular seminars in which newly arrived returnees pass on their knowledge to relocating managers and their families.

There's also increased use of software and the Internet for cross-cultural training. For example, *Bridging Cultures* is a self-training multimedia package for people who will be traveling and/or living overseas. It uses short videos to introduce intercultural problems and then guides users to selecting the strategy for handling the situation. Cross-cultural training firms' Web sites include www.bennettinc.com/indexie.htm, www.livingabroad.com, www.worldwise-inc.com, and www.globaldynamics.com.[69]

Performance Appraisal of International Managers

Several things complicate appraising an expatriate's performance. Obviously, local management must have some input, but cultural differences here may distort the appraisals. Thus, host-country bosses might evaluate a U.S. expatriate manager in Peru somewhat negatively if they find his or her use of participative decision making culturally inappropriate. On the other hand, home-office managers often can't provide valid appraisals, since they're not fully aware of the situation the manager faces locally.

In fact, when it comes to appraising expatriates abroad, managers don't always do what they know they should. In one study, managers recognized that having a balanced set of appraisers from both the host and home countries and more frequent appraisals produced the best appraisals. But, in practice, most did not do this. Instead, they conducted appraisals less frequently, and used raters from the host or the home country, but not both.[70]

Suggestions for improving the expatriate appraisal process include:

1. Adapt the performance criteria to the situation.
2. Weigh the evaluation more toward the onsite manager's appraisal than the home-site manager's.
3. If the home-office manager does the actual written appraisal, have him or her use a former expatriate from the same overseas location for advice.

International Compensation

The whole area of international compensation presents some tricky problems. For example, how does the employer account for large differences in cost of living among countries?

The Balance Sheet Approach   The most common approach to formulating expatriate pay is to equalize purchasing power across countries, a technique known as the *balance sheet* approach.[71]

The basic idea is that each expatriate should enjoy the same standard of living he or she would have at home. The balance sheet approach focuses on four main home-country groups of expenses—*income taxes, housing, goods and services, and discretionary expenses* (child support, car payments, and the like). The employer estimates what each of these four expenses is in the expatriate's home country, and what each will be in the host country. The employer then pays any differences—such as additional income taxes or housing expenses.

In practice, this usually boils down to building the expatriate's total compensation around five or six separate components. For example, base salary will normally be in the same range as the manager's home-country salary. In addition, however, there might be an overseas or foreign service premium. The executive receives this as a percentage of his or her base salary, in part to compensate for the cultural and physical adjustments he or she will have to make.[72] There may also be several allowances, including a housing allowance and an education allowance for the expatriate's children. Income taxes represent another area of concern. A U.S. manager posted abroad must often pay not just U.S. taxes but also income taxes in the host country.

Table M.1 illustrates the balance sheet approach. In this case, assume the employee's annual earnings are $80,000, and she faces a U.S. income tax rate of 28% and a Belgium income tax rate of 70%. (The other costs are based on the index of living costs abroad published in the "U.S. Department of State Indexes of Living Costs Abroad, Quarters Allowances, and Hardship Differentials," available at http://aoprals.state.gov/content.asp?content_id=186&menu_id=81.) The employer would have to supplement the person's pay by $69,700.

To help the expatriate manage his or her home and foreign financial obligations, most employers use a *split pay* approach; they pay, say, half a person's actual pay in home-country currency and half in the local currency.[73]

Incentive Pay Abroad

With more business being done by huge multinationals such as IBM and banker HSBC, executive compensation systems around the world are becoming more

Table M.1 The Balance Sheet Approach (Assumes Base Salary of $80,000)

ANNUAL EXPENSE	CHICAGO, UNITED STATES	BRUSSELS, BELGIUM (US$ EQUIVALENT)	REQUIRED ALLOWANCE
Housing & utilities	$35,000	$ 67,600	$32,600
Goods & services	6,000	9,500	3,500
Taxes	22,400	56,000	33,600
Discretionary income	10,000	10,000	0
Total	$73,400	$143,100	$69,700

Source: Joseph J. Martocchio, *Strategic Compensation: A Human Resource Management Approach,* 2nd Edition, © 2001. Electronically reproduced by permission of Pearson Education, Inc., Upper Saddle River, NJ.

Note: For the latest figures, see http://aoprals.state.gov/content.asp?content_id=186&menu_id=81, accessed April 17, 2010.

similar,[74] but performance-based incentives still tend to be less important as a percent of compensation abroad. In Europe, for instance, compensation directors do want to see more performance-based pay. However, the public relations aspects of such a move still tend to inhibit them.

What U.S. companies do offer are various incentives to get expatriates to accept and stay on international assignment. Foreign service premiums are financial payments over and above regular base pay, and typically range between 10% and 30% of base pay. Hardship allowances compensate expatriates for exceptionally hard living and working conditions at certain foreign locations. (U.S. diplomats posted to Iraq receive about a 70% boost in base salary, among other incentives.)[75] Mobility premiums are typically lump-sum payments to reward employees for moving from one assignment to another.[76]

Managing HR in Challenging Times: Getting a Handle on Global Compensation

A recent report on global pay from Hewitt Associates highlights the challenge facing many managers with operations abroad. As the report says, "[W]ith exponential growth in the past years, many U.S. multinational organizations have not given prudent consideration to their compensation cost structures outside the U.S." Therefore, economic challenges now are forcing many employers to refocus on the effectiveness of their global compensation pay practices. For one thing, they're looking more carefully at who is making the global compensation pay decisions, and how they're making them. Are managers abroad involved? Is it the home-office human resources team? Is it clear that the people making these decisions are doing so within the framework of the company's overall pay practices? Employers are also focusing more diligently on the details of their overseas pay decisions. For example, is how we're paying our employees abroad competitive? And are we basing our overseas pay decisions by referencing (as the report says) "credible and defendable market data"?[77] Good pay practices abroad are always important, but particularly so in economically changing times.

International Labor Relations

As explained earlier, firms opening subsidiaries abroad will find substantial differences in labor relations practices among the world's countries and regions. For one thing, unions tend to be stronger abroad than in the United States Furthermore, as also explained earlier, *works councils* and *co-determination* are pivotal labor relations mechanisms in Europe. In the United States, HR policies on matters such as wages and benefits are set by the employer, or by the employer in negotiations with its labor unions. The co-determination laws, including the Works Constitution Act, largely determine the nature of HR policies in many German firms.

Safety and Fair Treatment Abroad

From drug wars on the U.S.-Mexico border to pirates capturing ships off Somalia, it's clear that ensuring employee safety and fair treatment can't stop at a country's borders. Furthermore, while the United States has often taken the lead in occupational safety, other countries are also quickly adopting such laws. In any event, it's hard to make a legitimate case for being less safety conscious with workers abroad than you are with those at home. High-profile companies including Nike, Inc. have bad publicity for—and taken steps to improve—the working conditions, long hours, and low pay rates for factory workers in countries such as Indonesia.

Employers are also facing more safety-related resistance from prospective expats. More are reluctant to accept foreign postings and take their families abroad. And for their employees and facilities abroad, employers have had to institute more comprehensive safety plans, including, for instance, evacuation plans to get employees to safety, if that becomes necessary. Even stationing employees in assumedly safe countries is no guarantee there won't be problems. In 2009, for instance, workers in the French factories of Sony Corp., Caterpillar Inc., and 3M Co. took their managers hostage in order to negotiate better benefits for laid-off employees.[78] Developments like these had already prompted employers to take steps to protect their expat employees better. Many employers purchase intelligence services for monitoring potential terrorist threats abroad.[79]

Keeping business travelers out of crime and terror's way is a specialty all its own, but suggestions here include:[80]

- Provide expatriates with training about traveling, living abroad, and the place they're going to, so they're more oriented when they get there.
- Tell them not to draw attention to the fact they're Americans—by wearing T-shirts with American names, for instance.
- Have travelers arrive at airports as close to departure time as possible and wait in areas away from the main flow of traffic.
- Equip the expatriate's car and home with adequate security systems.
- Tell employees to vary their departure and arrival times and take different routes.
- Keep employees current on crime and other problems by regularly checking, for example, the State Department's travel advisory service and consular information sheets (http://travel.state.gov/travelwarnings.html).
- Advise employees to remain confident at all times: Body language can attract perpetrators, and those who look like victims often become victimized.[81]

Repatriation: Problems and Solutions

One of the most confounding facts about sending employees abroad is that about half of them will probably quit within 3 years of returning home. One study suggests that a 3-year assignment abroad for one employee with a base salary of about $100,000 costs the employer $1 million, once extra living costs, transportation, and family benefits are included.[82] Given the investment, it obviously makes sense to do everything possible to make sure they stay with the firm.[83]

For this, formal repatriation programs can be quite useful. One study found that about 5% of returning employees resigned if their firms had formal repatriation programs, while about 22% of those left if their firms had no such programs.[84]

Steps in Repatriation   The heart and guiding principle of any repatriation program is this: Make sure that the expatriate and his or her family don't feel that the company has left them adrift. For example, one firm has a three-part repatriation program, one that starts before the employee leaves for abroad.[85]

First, the firm matches the expat and his or her family with a psychologist trained in repatriation issues. The psychologist meets with the family before they go abroad. The psychologist discusses the challenges they will face abroad, assesses with them how well he or she thinks they will adapt to their new culture, and stays in touch with them throughout their assignment.

Second, the program makes sure that the employee always feels that he or she is still "in the loop" with what's happening back at the home office. For example, the expat gets a mentor and periodically returns to the home office to meet with colleagues.

Third, once it's time for the expat employee and his or her family to return home, there's a formal repatriation service. About 6 months before the overseas assignment ends, the psychologist and an HR representative meet with the expat and the family to start preparing them for return. For example, they help plan the employee's next career move, help the person update his or her résumé, and begin putting the person in contact with supervisors back home.[86]

Probably the simplest thing the employer can do to improve repatriates' retention rates is to value their experience more highly. One study found that the skills expats acquired abroad were often unrelated or negatively related to their career advancement once they returned. As one returnee put it: "My company was, in my view, somewhat indifferent to my experience in China as evidenced by a lack of monetary reward, positive increase, or leverage to my career in any way." Such feelings then prompt the expat to look elsewhere for opportunities.[87]

HOW TO IMPLEMENT A GLOBAL HR SYSTEM

With employers increasingly relying on local rather than expatriate employees, transferring one's selection, training, appraisal, pay, and other human resource practices abroad is a top priority. But, given the cross-cultural differences in human resource management practices, one could reasonably ask, "Is it realistic for a company to try to institute a standardized human resource management system in its facilities around the world?"

A study suggests that the answer is "yes." In brief, the study's results show that employers may have to defer to local managers on some specific human resource management policy issues. However, the findings also suggest that big intercountry HR practice differences are often not necessary or even advisable. The important thing is how you implement the global human resource management system.

In this study, the researchers interviewed human resource personnel from six global companies—Agilent, Dow, IBM, Motorola, Procter & Gamble (P & G), and Shell Oil Co.—as well as international human resources consultants.[88] The study's overall conclusion was that employers who successfully implement global HR systems do so by applying several best practices. The basic idea is to *develop* systems that are *acceptable* to employees in units around the world, and ones that the employers can *implement* more effectively. We'll look at each of these three requirements' best practices.

Developing a More Effective Global HR System

First, these employers engage in two best practices in *developing* their worldwide human resource policies and practices.

Form Global HR Networks   To head off resistance, human resource managers around the world should feel that they're part of the firm's global human resource management team. Treat the local human resource managers as equal partners. The researchers found that in developing global HR systems, the most critical factor is "creating an infrastructure of partners around the world that you use for support, for buy-in, for organization of local activities, and to help you better understand their own systems and their own challenges."[89] For instance, they formed global teams to help develop the new human resources systems.

Remember that It's More Important to Standardize Ends and Competencies than Specific Methods   For example, IBM uses a more or less standardized recruitment and selection process worldwide. However, "details such as who conducts the interview (hiring manager vs. recruiter) or whether the prescreen is by phone or in person differ by country."[90]

Making the Global HR System More *Acceptable*

Next, employers engage in three best practices so that the global human resource systems they develop will be *acceptable* to local managers around the world. These practices include:

Remember that Truly Global Organizations Find it Easier to Install Global Systems   For example, truly global companies require their managers to work on global teams, and identify and recruit and place the employees they hire globally. As one Shell manager put it, "If you're truly global, then you are hiring here [the United States] people who are going to immediately go and work in the Hague, and vice versa."[91] This global mind-set makes it easier for managers everywhere to accept the wisdom of having a standardized human resource management system.

Investigate Pressures to Differentiate and Determine Their Legitimacy   Local managers will insist, "You can't do that here, because we are different culturally." These researchers found that these "differences" are usually not persuasive. For example, when Dow wanted to implement an online recruitment and selection tool abroad, the hiring managers there said that their managers would not use it. After investigating the supposed cultural roadblocks, Dow successfully implemented the new system.[92]

The operative word here is "investigate." Carefully assess whether the local culture or other differences might in fact undermine the new system. Be knowledgeable about local legal issues, and be willing to differentiate where necessary.

Try to Work within the Context of a Strong Corporate Culture   Companies that create a strong corporate culture find it easier to obtain agreement among far-flung employees. For example, because of how P&G recruits, selects, trains, and rewards them, its managers have a strong sense of shared values. For instance, new recruits quickly learn to think in terms of "we" instead of "I." They learn to value thoroughness, consistency, self-discipline, and a methodical approach. Because all P&G managers worldwide tend to share these values, they are in a sense more similar to each other than they are geographically different. Having such global unanimity in values makes it easier to implement standardized human resource practices worldwide.

Implementing the Global HR System

Finally, two best practices helped ensure success in actually *implementing* the globally consistent human resource policies and practices.

"You Can't Communicate Enough"   "There's a need for constant contact with the decision makers in each country, as well as the people who will be implementing and using the system."[93]

Dedicate Adequate Resources   For example, don't require the local human resource management offices to implement new job analysis procedures unless the head office provides adequate resources for these additional activities.

REVIEW

Summary

1. International business is important to almost every business today. This confronts managers with many new challenges, including coordinating production, sales, and financial operations on a worldwide basis. As a result, companies today have pressing international HR needs with respect to selecting, training, paying, and repatriating global employees.

2. Intercountry differences affect a company's HR management processes. Cultural factors such as individualism

suggest differences in values, attitudes, and therefore behaviors and reactions of people from country to country. Economic and labor cost factors help influence pay and other policies.

3. A large percentage of expatriate assignments fail, but the results can be improved through careful selection.

4. Selecting managers for expatriate assignments means screening them for traits that predict success in adapting to new environments. Such traits include adaptability and flexibility, cultural toughness, self-orientation, job knowledge and motivation, relational skills, and family situation. Adaptability screening focusing on the family's probable success in handling the foreign assignment can be an especially important step in the selection process.

5. Training for overseas managers typically focuses on cultural differences, on how attitudes influence behavior, on factual knowledge about the target country. The most common approach to formulating expatriate pay is to equalize purchasing power across countries, or the balance sheet approach. The employer estimates expenses for income taxes, housing, goods and services, and discretionary costs, and pays supplements to the expatriate in such a way as to maintain the same standard of living he or she would have had at home.

6. The expatriate appraisal process is complicated by the need to have both local and home-office supervisors provide input into the performance review. Suggestions for improving the process include weighing the on-site manager's appraisal more heavily, and having the home-site manager get background advice from managers familiar with the location abroad.

7. Repatriation problems are common, but you can minimize them. They include the often well-founded fear that the expatriate is "out of sight, out of mind" and difficulties in reassimilating the expatriate's family. Suggestions for avoiding these problems include using repatriation agreements, assigning a mentor, and keeping the expatriate plugged in to home-office business.

KEY TERMS

- co-determination
- locals
- expatriates

- home-country nationals
- third-country nationals
- ethnocentric

- polycentric
- geocentric

DISCUSSION QUESTIONS

1. What intercountry differences affect HR managers? Give several specific examples of how each may affect an HR manager.

2. You are the HR manager of a firm that is about to send its first employees overseas to staff a new subsidiary. Your boss, the president, asks you why such assignments often fail, and what you plan to do to avoid such failures. How do you respond?

3. What special training do overseas candidates need? In what ways is such training similar to and different from traditional diversity training?

4. How does appraising an expatriate's performance differ from appraising that of a home-office manager? How would you avoid some of the unique problems of appraising the expatriate's performance?

5. Working individually or in groups, write a one-page summary of what items your university, which is sending your professor to Bulgaria to teach HR for the next 3 years, should address to make his or her stay successful.

6. Give three specific examples of multinational corporations in your area. Check in the library or Internet or with each firm to determine in what countries these firms have operations. Then describe their operations, and explain what you can discern about their international HR policies.

7. Choose three traits useful for selecting international assignees, and create a straightforward test to screen candidates for these traits.

8. Use an Internet source to determine the relative cost of living in five countries as of this year, and explain the implications of such differences for drafting a pay plan for managers being sent to each country.

APPLICATION EXERCISES

Case Incident   *"Boss, I Think We Have a Problem"*

Central Steel Door Corp. has been in business for 20 years, successfully selling a line of steel industrial-grade doors, as well as the hardware and fittings for them. Focusing mostly in the United States and Canada, the company had gradually increased its presence from the New York City area, first into New England and then down the Atlantic Coast, then through the Midwest and West, and finally into Canada. The company's basic expansion strategy was always the same: Choose an area, open a distribution center, hire a regional sales manager, and then let that regional sales manager help staff the distribution center and hire local sales reps.

Unfortunately, the company's traditional success in finding sales help has not extended to its overseas operations. With the introduction of the new European currency, Mel Fisher, Central Steel Door's president, decided to expand his company abroad, into Europe. However, the expansion has not gone smoothly. He tried for 3 weeks to find a sales manager by advertising in the *International Herald Tribune*, which is read by businesspeople in Europe and by American expatriates living and working in Europe. Although the ads placed in the *Tribune* also run for about a month in the *Tribune's* Internet Web site, Mr. Fisher so far has received only five applications. One came from a possibly viable candidate, whereas four came from candidates whom Mr. Fisher refers to as "lost souls"— people who seem to have spent most of their time traveling aimlessly from country to country, sipping espresso in sidewalk cafés. When asked what he had done for the last 3 years, one told Mr. Fisher he'd been on a "walkabout."

Other aspects of his international HR activities have been equally problematic. Fisher alienated two of his U.S. sales managers by sending them to Europe to run the Europe operations temporarily, but neglected to work out a compensation package that would cover their relatively high living expenses in Germany and Belgium. One ended up staying the better part of the year, and Mr. Fisher was rudely surprised to be informed by the Belgian government that his sales manager owed thousands of dollars in local taxes. The managers had hired about 10 local people to staff each of the two distribution centers. However, without full-time local European sales managers, the level of sales was disappointing, so Fisher decided to fire about half the distribution center employees. That's when he got an emergency phone call from his temporary sales manager in Germany: "I've just been told that all these employees should have had written employment agreements and that in any case we can't fire anyone without at least 1 year's notice, and the local authorities here are really up in arms. Boss, I think we have a problem." ■

QUESTIONS

1. Based on the chapter and the case incident, compile a list of 10 international HR mistakes Mr. Fisher has made so far.
2. How would you have gone about hiring a European sales manager? Why?
3. What would you do now if you were Mr. Fisher?

APPENDIX

Comprehensive Cases

Bandag Automotive*

Jim Bandag took over his family's auto supply business in 2005, after helping his father, who founded the business, run it for about 10 years. Based in Illinois, Bandag employs about 300 people and distributes auto supplies (replacement mufflers, bulbs, engine parts, and so on) through two divisions, one that supplies service stations and repair shops, and a second that sells retail auto supplies through five "Bandag Automotive" auto supply stores.

Jim's father, and now Jim, have always endeavored to keep Bandag's organization chart simple. The company has a full-time controller, managers for each of the five stores, a manager that oversees the distribution division, and Jim Bandag's executive assistant. Jim (and his father, working part time) handles marketing and sales.

Jim's executive assistant administers the firm's day-to-day human resource management tasks, but they outsource most HR activities to others, including an employment agency that does their recruiting and screening, a benefits firm that administers their 401(k) plan, and a payroll service that handles their paychecks. Bandag's human resource management systems consist almost entirely of standardized HR forms they purchase from an HR supplies company. It supplies HR tools including forms such as application forms, performance appraisal forms, and an "honesty" test Bandag uses to screen the staff that works in the five stores.

Bandag performs informal salary surveys to see what other companies in the area are paying for similar positions, and uses these results for awarding annual merit increases (which in fact are more accurately cost-of-living adjustments).

Jim's father took a paternal approach to the business. He often walked around speaking with his employees, finding out what their problems were, and even helping them out with an occasional loan—for instance, when he discovered that one of their children was sick, or for part of a new home down payment. Jim, on the other hand, tends to be more abrupt, and does not enjoy the same warm relationship with the employees, as did his father. Jim is not unfair or dictatorial. He's just very focused on improving Bandag's financial performance, and so all his decisions, including his HR-related decisions, generally come down to cutting costs. For example, his knee-jerk reaction is usually to offer fewer days off rather than more, fewer benefits rather than more, and to be less flexible when an employee needs, for instance, a few extra days off because a child is sick.

It's therefore perhaps not surprising that over the past few years Bandag's sales and profits have increased markedly, but that the firm has found itself increasingly enmeshed in HR/equal employment–type issues. Indeed, Jim now finds himself spending a day or two a week addressing HR problems. For example, Henry Jaques, an employee of one of their stores, came to Jim's executive assistant and told her he was "irate" about his recent firing and was probably going to sue. On Henry's last performance appraisal, his store manager had said Henry did the technical aspects of his job well, but that he had "serious problems interacting with his coworkers."

He was continually arguing with them and complaining to the store manager about working conditions. The store manager had told Jim that he had to fire Henry because he was making "the whole place poisonous," and that (although he felt sorry because he'd heard rumors that Henry suffered from some mental illness) he felt he had to go. Jim approved the dismissal.

Gavin was another problem. Gavin had worked for Bandag for 10 years, the last two as manager of one of the company's five stores. Right after Jim Bandag took over, Gavin told him he had to take a Family and Medical Leave Act (FMLA) medical leave to have hip surgery, and Jim approved the leave. So far so good, but when Gavin returned from leave, Jim told him that his position had been eliminated. They had decided to close his store and open a new, larger store across from a shopping center about a mile away, and appointed a new manager in Gavin's absence.

However, the company did give Gavin a (nonmanagerial) position in the new store as a counter salesperson, at the same salary and with the same benefits as he had before. Even so, "This job is not similar to my old one," Gavin insisted. "It doesn't have nearly as much prestige." His contention is that FMLA requires that the company bring him back in the same or equivalent position, and that this means a supervisory position, similar to what he had before he went on leave. Jim said no, and they seem to be heading toward litigation.

In another sign of the times at Bandag, the company's controller, Miriam, who had been with the company for about 6 years, went on pregnancy leave for 12 weeks in 2005 (also under the FMLA), and then received an additional 3 weeks' leave under Bandag's extended illness days program. Four weeks after she came back, she asked Jim Bandag if she could arrange to work fewer hours per week, and spend about a day per week working out of her home. He refused, and about 2 months later fired her. Jim Bandag said, "I'm sorry, it's not anything to do with your pregnancy-related requests, but we've got ample reasons to discharge you—your monthly budgets have been several days late, and we've got proof you may have forged documents." She replied, "I don't care what you say your reasons are, you're really firing me because of my pregnancy, and that's illegal."

Jim felt he was on safe ground as far as defending the company for these actions, although he didn't look forward to spending the time and money that he knew it would take to fight each. However, what Jim learned over lunch from a colleague undermined his confidence about another case that he had been sure would be a "slam dunk" for his company. Jim was explaining to his friend that one of Bandag's truck maintenance people had applied for a job driving one of Bandag's distribution department trucks, and that Jim had turned him down because the worker was deaf. Jim (whose wife has occasionally said of him, "No one has ever accused Jim of being politically correct") was mentioning to his friend the apparent absurdity of a deaf person asking to be a truck delivery person. His friend, who happens to work for UPS, pointed out that the U.S. Court of Appeals for the Ninth Circuit had recently decided that UPS had violated the Americans with Disabilities Act by refusing to consider deaf workers for jobs driving the company's smaller vehicles.

Although Jim's father is semiretired, the sudden uptick in the frequency of such EEO-type issues troubles him, particularly after so many years of labor peace. However, he's not sure what to do about it. Having handed over the reins of the company to his son Jim, he's loath to inject himself back into its operational decision making. On the other hand, he is afraid that in the short run, these issues are going to drain a great deal of Jim's time and resources, and that in the long run they might be a sign of things to come, with problems like these eventually overwhelming Bandag Auto. He comes to you, who he knows consults in human resource management, and asks you the following questions.

QUESTIONS

1. Given Bandag Auto's size, and anything else you know about it, should we reorganize the human resource management function, and if so why and how?

2. What, if anything, would you do to change and/or improve upon the current HR systems, forms, and practices that we now use?

3. Do you think the employee that Jim fired for creating what the manager called a poisonous relationship has a legitimate claim against us, and if so why and what should we do about it?

4. Is it true that we really had to put Gavin back into an equivalent position, or was it adequate just to bring him back into a job at the same salary, bonuses, and benefits as he had before his leave?

5. Miriam, the controller, is basically claiming that the company is retaliating against her for being pregnant, and that the fact that we raised performance issues was just a smokescreen. Do you think the EEOC and/or courts would agree with her, and, in any case, what should we do now?

6. An employee who is deaf has asked us to be one of our delivery people and we turned him down. He's now threatening to sue. What should we do, and why?

7. In the previous 10 years, we've had only one equal employment complaint, and now in the last few years we've had four or five. What should we do about it? Why?

Sources: Based generally on actual facts, but Bandag is a fictitious company. Bandag source notes: "The Problem Employee: Discipline or Accommodation?" *Monday Business Briefing* (March 8, 2005); "Employee Says Change in Duties after Leave Violates FMLA," *BNA Bulletin to Management* (January 16, 2007): 24; "Manager Fired Days after Announcing Pregnancy," *BNA Bulletin to Management* (January 2, 2007): 8; "Ninth Circuit Rules UPS Violated ADA by Barring Deaf Workers from Driving Jobs," *BNA Bulletin to Management* (October 17, 2006): 329. Copyright Gary Dessler, PhD.

Angelo's Pizza*

Angelo Camero was brought up in the Bronx, New York, and basically always wanted to be in the pizza store business. As a youngster, he would spend hours at the local pizza store, watching the owner knead the pizza dough, flatten it into a large circular crust, fling it up, and then spread on tomato sauce in larger and larger loops.

After graduating from college as a marketing major, he made a beeline back to the Bronx, where he opened his first Angelo's Pizza store, emphasizing its clean, bright interior; its crisp green, red, and white sign; and his all-natural, fresh ingredients.

Within 5 years, Angelo's store was a success, and he had opened three other stores and was considering franchising his concept. Eager as he was to expand, his 4 years in business school had taught him the difference between being an entrepreneur and being a manager. As an entrepreneur/small-business owner, he knew he had the distinct advantage of being able to run the whole operation himself. With just one store and a handful of employees, he could make every decision and watch the cash register, check in the new supplies, oversee the takeout, and personally supervise the service.

When he expanded to three stores, things started getting challenging. He hired managers for the two new stores (both of whom had worked for him at his first store for several years) and gave them only minimal "how to run a store"–type training, on the assumption that, having worked with him for several years, they already knew pretty much everything they needed to know about running a store.

However, he was already experiencing human resource management problems. He knew there was no way he could expand the number of stores he owned, or (certainly) contemplate franchising his idea, unless he had a system in place that he could clone in each new store, to provide the manager (or the franchisee) with the necessary management knowledge and expertise to run their stores. Angelo had no training program in place for teaching his store managers how to run their stores. He simply (erroneously, as it turned out) assumed that by working with him they would learn how to do things on the job. Since Angelo himself really had no system in place, the new managers were, in a way, starting off below zero—there was no system to learn.

There are several issues that particularly concern Angelo. Finding and hiring good employees was number one. He'd read the new National Small Business Poll from the National Federation of Independent Business Education Foundation. It found that 71% of small-business owners believed that finding qualified employees was "hard." Furthermore, "the search for qualified employees will grow more difficult as demographic and education factors" continue to make it more difficult to find employees. Similarly, reading *The Kiplinger Letter* one day, he noticed that just about every type of business couldn't find enough good employees to hire. Small firms were particularly in jeopardy; the *Letter* said: giant firms can outsource many (particularly entry-level) jobs abroad, and can afford to pay better benefits and to train their employees. Small firms rarely have the resources or the economies of scale to allow outsourcing or to install the big training programs that would enable them to take untrained new employees and turn them into skilled ones.

Although finding enough employees was his biggest problem, finding enough honest ones scared him even more. Angelo recalled from one of his business school courses that companies in the United States are losing a total of well over $400 billion a year in employee theft. As a rough approximation, that works out to about $9 per employee per day and about $12,000 lost annually for a typical company. Furthermore, small companies like Angelo's were particularly in the crosshairs, because they are particularly prone to employee theft. Why are small firms particularly vulnerable? Perhaps they lack experience dealing with the problem. More importantly, small firms are more likely to have a single person doing several jobs, such as ordering supplies and paying the delivery person. This undercuts the checks and balances managers often strive for to control theft. Furthermore, the risk of stealing goes up dramatically when the business is largely based on cash. In a pizza store, many people come in and just buy one or two slices and a cola for lunch, and almost all pay with cash, not credit cards.

And Angelo was not just worried about someone stealing cash. They can steal your whole business idea, something he learned from painful experience. He had been planning to open a store in what he thought would be a particularly good location, and was thinking of having one of his current employees manage the store.

Instead, it turned out that this employee was, in a manner of speaking, stealing Angelo's brain—what Angelo knew about customers and suppliers, where to buy pizza dough, where to buy tomato sauce, how much everything should cost, how to furnish the store, where to buy ovens, store layout—everything. This employee soon quit and opened up his own pizza store, not far from where Angelo had planned to open his new store.

That he was having trouble hiring good employees, there was no doubt. The restaurant business is particularly brutal when it comes to turnover. Many restaurants turn over their employees at a rate of 200% to 300% per year—so every year, each position might have a series of two to three employees filling it. As Angelo said, "I was losing two to three employees a month." As he said, "We're a high-volume store, and while we should have about six employees per store, we were down to only three or four, so my managers and I were really under the gun."

The problem was bad at the hourly employee level: "Applicants would come in, my managers or I would hire them and not spend much time training them, and the good ones would leave in frustration after a few weeks, while often it was the bad ones who'd stay behind."

But in the last 2 years, Angelo's three company-owned stores also went through a total of three store managers—"They were just blowing through the door," as Angelo put it, in part because, without good employees, their workday was brutal. As a rule, when a small-business owner or manager can't find enough employees, about 80% of the time the owner or manager does the job himself or herself. So, these managers often ended up working 7 days a week, 10 to 12 hours a day, and many just burned out. One night, working three jobs himself with customers leaving in anger, Angelo decided he'd never just hire someone because he was desperate again, but would start doing his hiring more rationally.

Angelo knew he should have a more formal screening process. As he said, "If there's been a lesson learned, it's much better to spend time up-front screening out candidates that don't fit than to hire them and have to put up with their ineffectiveness."

He also knew that he could identify many of the traits that his employees needed. For example, he knew that not everyone has the temperament to be a server (he has a small pizza/Italian restaurant in the back of his main store). As Angelo said, "I've seen personalities that were off the charts in assertiveness or overly introverted, traits that obviously don't make a good fit for a waiter or a waitress."

As a local business, Angelo recruits by placing help wanted ads in two local newspapers, and he's been "shocked" at some of the responses and experiences he's had in response to his help wanted ads. Many of the applicants left voice mail messages (Angelo or the other workers in the store were too busy to answer), and some applicants Angelo "just axed" on the assumption that people without good telephone manners wouldn't have very good manners in the store either. He also quickly learned that he had to throw out a very wide net, even if only hiring one or two people. Many people, as noted, he just deleted because of the messages they left, and about half of the people he scheduled for interviews didn't show up.

He'd taken courses in human resource management, so (as he said) "I should know better," but he hired people based almost exclusively on a single interview (he occasionally made a feeble attempt to check references). In total, his HR approach was obviously not working. It wasn't producing enough good recruits, and the people he did hire were often problematical.

What was he looking for? Service-oriented, courteous people, for one. For example, he'd hired one employee who used profanity several times, including once in front of a customer. On that employee's third day, Angelo had to tell her, "I think Angelo's isn't the right place for you," and he fired her. As Angelo said, "I felt bad," but also knew that "everything I have is on the line for this business, so I wasn't going to let anyone run this business down." Angelo wants reliable people (who'll show up on time), honest people, and people who are flexible about switching jobs and hours as required.

Angelo's Pizza business has only the most rudimentary human resource management system. Angelo bought several application forms at a local Office Depot, and he rarely uses other forms of any sort. He uses his personal accountant for reviewing the company's books, and Angelo himself computes each employee's paycheck at the end of the week and writes the checks. Training is entirely on the job. Angelo personally trained each of his employees. For those employees who go on to be store managers, he assumes that they are training their own employees the way that Angelo trained them (for better or worse, as it turns out). Angelo pays "a bit above" prevailing wage rates (judging by other help wanted ads) but probably not enough to make a significant difference in the quality of employees that he attracts. If you asked Angelo what his reputation is as an employer, Angelo, being a candid and forthright person, would probably tell you that he is a supportive but hard-nosed employer who treats people fairly, but whose business reputation may suffer from disorganization stemming from inadequate organization and training. He approaches you to ask you several questions.

QUESTIONS

1. My strategy is to (hopefully) expand the number of stores and eventually franchise while focusing on serving only high-quality fresh ingredients. What are three specific human resource management implications of my strategy (including specific policies and practices)?
2. Identify and briefly discuss five specific human resource management errors that I'm currently making.
3. Develop a structured interview form that we can use for hiring (a) store managers, (b) waiters and waitresses, and (c) counter people/pizza makers.
4. Based on what you know about Angelo's, and what you know from having visited pizza restaurants, write a one-page outline showing specifically how you think Angelo's should go about selecting employees.

Sources: Based generally on actual facts, but Angelo's Pizza is a fictitious company. Angelo's Pizza source notes: Dino Berta, "People Problems: Keep Hiring from Becoming a Crying Game," *Nation's Business News* 36, no. 20 (May 20, 2002): 72–74; Ellen Lyon, "Hiring, Personnel Problems Can Challenge Entrepreneurs," *Patriot-News* (October 12, 2004); Rose Robin Pedone, "Businesses' $400 Billion Theft Problem," *Long Island Business News* 27 (July 6, 1998): 1B–2B; "Survey Shows Small-Business Problems with Hiring, Internet," *Providence Business News* 16 (September 10, 2001): 1B; "Finding Good Workers Is Posing a Big Problem as Hiring Picks Up," *The Kiplinger Letter* 81 (February 13, 2004). Copyright Gary Dessler, PhD.

Google*

Fortune magazine named Google the best of the 100 best companies to work for, and there is little doubt why. Among the benefits they offer are free employee shuttles equipped with Wi-Fi from San Francisco Bay area locations, unlimited sick days, annual all-expense-paid ski trips, free gourmet meals, five on-site free doctors, $2,000 bonuses for referring a new hire, free flu shots, a giant lap pool, on-site oil changes, on-site car washes, volleyball courts, TGIF parties, free on-site washers and dryers (with free detergent), Ping-Pong and foosball tables, and free famous people lectures. For many people, it's the gourmet meals and snacks that make Google stand out. For example, human resources director Stacey Sullivan loves the Irish oatmeal with fresh berries at the company's Plymouth Rock Cafe, near Google's "people operations" group. Engineer Jan Fitzpatrick loves the raw bar at Google's Tapas restaurant, down the road on the Google campus. Then, of course, there are the stock options—each new employee gets about 1,200 options to buy Google shares (recently worth about $550 per share). In fact, dozens of early Google employees ("Googlers") are already multimillionaires thanks to Google stock. The recession that began around 2008 did prompt Google and other firms to cut back on some of these benefits (cafeteria hours are shorter today, for instance), but Google still pretty much leads the benefits pack.

For their part, Googlers share certain traits. They tend to be brilliant, team oriented (teamwork is the norm, especially for big projects), and driven. *Fortune* describes them as people who "almost universally" see themselves as the most interesting people on the planet, and who are happy-go-lucky on the outside, but type A—highly intense and goal directed—on the inside. They're also superhardworking (which makes sense, since it's usual for engineers to be in the hallways at 3 A.M. debating some new solution to a Google search problem). They're so team oriented that when working on projects, it's not unusual for a Google team to give up its larger, more spacious offices and to crowd into a small conference room, where they can "get things done." Historically, Googlers generally graduate with great grades from the best universities, including Stanford, Harvard, and MIT. For many years, Google wouldn't even consider hiring someone with less than a 3.7 average—while also probing deeply into the why behind any B grades. Google also doesn't hire lone wolves but wants people who work together and people who also have diverse interests. Google also wants people with growth potential. The company is expanding so fast that they need to hire people who are capable of being promoted five or six times—it's only, they say, by hiring such overqualified people that they can be sure that the employees will be able to keep up as Google expands. The starting salaries are highly competitive. Experienced engineers start at about $130,000 a year, and new MBAs can expect between $80,000 and $120,000 per year. Most recently, Google had about 10,000 staff members, up from its start a few years ago with just three employees in a rented garage.

Of course, in a company that's grown from three employees to 10,000 and from zero value to hundreds of billions of dollars in about 9 years, it may be quibbling to talk about "problems," but there's no doubt that such rapid growth does confront Google's management, and particularly its "people operations" group, with some big challenges. Let's look at these.

For one, Google, as noted earlier, is a 24-hour operation, and with engineers and others frequently pulling all-nighters to complete their projects, the company needs to provide a package of services and financial benefits that helps its employees maintain an acceptable work–life balance.

As another challenge, Google's enormous financial success is a two-edged sword. While Google usually wins the recruitment race when it comes to competing for new employees against competitors like Microsoft or Yahoo!, Google does need some way to stem a rising tide of retirements. Most Googlers are still in their late twenties and early thirties, but many have become so wealthy from their Google stock options that they can afford to retire. Thus, a former engineering vice president retired (with his Google stock profits) to pursue his love of astronomy. The engineer who dreamed up Gmail recently retired (at the age of 30).

Another challenge is that the work not only involves long hours but can also be very tense. Google is a very numbers-oriented environment. For example, consider a typical weekly Google user interface design meeting. Marisa Meyer, the company's vice president of search products and user experience, runs the meeting, where her employees work out the look and feel of Google's products. Seated around a conference table are about a dozen Googlers, tapping on laptops. During the 2-hour meeting, Meyer needs to evaluate various design proposals, ranging from minor tweaks to a new product's entire layout. She's previously given each presentation an allotted amount of time, and a large digital clock on the wall ticks off the seconds. The presenters must quickly present their ideas, but also handle questions such as "What do users do if the tab is moved from the side of the page to the top?"

Furthermore, it's all about the numbers—no one at Google would ever say, for instance, "The tab looks better in red"—you need to prove your point. Presenters must come armed with usability experiment results, showing, for instance, that a certain percent preferred red or some other color, for instance. While the presenters are answering these questions as quickly as possible, the digital clock is ticking, and when it hits the allotted time, the presentation must end, and the next team steps up to present. It is a tough and tense environment, and Googlers must have done their homework.

Growth can also undermine the "outlaw band that's changing the world" culture that fostered the services that made Google famous. Even cofounder Sergi Brin agrees that Google risks becoming less "zany" as it grows. To paraphrase one of its top managers, the hard part of any business is keeping that original innovative, small-business feel. Creating the right culture is especially challenging now that Google is truly global. For example, Google works hard to provide the same financial and service benefits every place it does business around the world, but it can't exactly match its benefits in every country because of international laws and international taxation issues. Offering the same benefits everywhere is more important than it might initially appear. All those benefits make life easier for Google staff. On the one hand, Google does expect all of its employees to work superhard; on the other hand, it needs to help them maintain some sort of balance. As one manager says, Google acknowledges "that we work hard but that work is not everything."

Recruitment is another challenge. While Google certainly doesn't lack applicants, attracting the right applicants is crucial if Google is to continue to grow successfully. Working at Google requires a special set of traits, and screening employees is easier if they recruit the right people to begin with. For instance, they need to attract people who are superbright, love to work, have fun, can handle the stress, and who also have outside interests and flexibility.

As the company grows internationally, it also faces the considerable challenge of recruiting and building staff overseas. For example, Google now is introducing a new vertical market–based structure across Europe, to attract more business advertisers to its search engine. (By vertical market–based structure, Google means focusing on key vertical industry sectors such as travel, retail, automotive, and technology.) To build these industry groupings abroad from scratch, Google promoted its former head of its U.S. financial services group to be the vertical markets director for Europe; he

moved there recently. Google is thus looking for heads for each of its vertical industry groups for all of its key European territories.

Each of these vertical market heads will have to educate their market sector customers (in retailing, travel, and so on) so Google can attract new advertisers. Google already has about 12 offices across Europe, and its London office had tripled in size to 100 staff in just 2 years.

However, probably the biggest challenge Google faces is gearing up its employee selection system, now that the company must hire thousands of people per year. When Google started in business, job candidates typically suffered through a dozen or more in-person interviews, and the standards were so high that even applicants with years of great work experience often were turned down if they had just average college grades. But recently, even Google's cofounders have acknowledged that setting such an extraordinarily high bar for hiring was holding back Google's expansion. For Google's first few years, one of the company's cofounders interviewed nearly every job candidate before he or she was hired, and even today one of them still reviews the qualifications of everyone before he or she gets a final offer.

The experience of one candidate illustrates what Google is up against. They interviewed a 24-year-old for a corporate communications job at Google. Google first made contact with the candidate in May, and then, after two phone interviews, invited him to headquarters. There he had separate interviews with about six people and was treated to lunch in a Google cafeteria. They also had him turn in several "homework" assignments, including a personal statement and a marketing plan. In August, Google invited the candidate back for a second round, which they said would involve another four or five interviews. In the meantime, he decided he'd rather work at a start-up, and accepted another job at a new Web-based instant messaging provider.

Google's new head of human resources, a former GE executive, says that Google is trying to strike the right balance between letting

Google and the candidate get to know each other, while also moving quickly. To that end, Google recently administered a survey to all its current employees, in an effort to identify the traits that correlate with success at Google. In the survey, employees had to respond to questions relating to about 300 variables, including their performance on standardized tests, how old they were when they first used a computer, and how many foreign languages they speak. The Google survey team then went back and compared the answers against the 30 or 40 job performance factors they keep for each employee. They thereby identified clusters of traits that Google might better focus on during the hiring process. Google is also trying to move from the free-form interviews they've had in the past to a more structured process.

QUESTIONS

1. What do you think of the idea of Google correlating personal traits from the employee's answers on the survey to their performance, and then using that as the basis for screening job candidates? In other words, is it or is it not a good idea? Please explain your answer.
2. The benefits that Google pays obviously represent an enormous expense. Based on what you know about Google and on what you read in this book, how would you defend all these benefits if you're making a presentation to the security analysts who were analyzing Google's performance?
3. If you wanted to hire the brightest people around, how would you go about recruiting and selecting them?
4. To support its growth and expansion strategy, Google wants (among other traits) people who are superbright and who work hard, often round-the-clock, and who are flexible and maintain a decent work–life balance. List five specific HR policies or practices that you think Google has implemented or should implement to support its strategy, and explain your answer.

5. What sorts of factors do you think Google will have to take into consideration as it tries transferring its culture and reward systems and way of doing business to its operations abroad?
6. Given the sorts of values and culture Google cherishes, briefly describe four specific activities you suggest they pursue during new-employee orientation.

Sources: Notes for Google: "Google Brings Vertical Structure to Europe," *New Media Age* (August 4, 2005): 2; Debbie Lovewell, "Employer Profile—Google: Searching for Talent," *Employee Benefits* (October 10, 2005): 66; "Google Looking for Gourmet Chefs," *Internet Week* (August 4, 2005); Douglas Merrill, "Google's 'Googley' Culture Kept Alive by Tech," *eWeek* (April 11, 2006); Robert Hof, "Google Gives Employees another Option," *BusinessWeek Online* (December 13, 2005); Kevin Delaney, "Google Adjusts Hiring Process as Needs Grow," *Wall Street Journal* (October 23, 2006): B1, B8; Adam Lishinsky, "Search and Enjoy," *Fortune* (January 22, 2007): 70–82; www.nypost.com/seven/10302008/business/frugal_google_cuts_perks_136011.htm, accessed July 12, 2009. Copyright Gary Dessler, PhD.

Muffler Magic*

Muffler Magic is a fast-growing chain of 25 automobile service centers in Nevada. Originally started 20 years ago as a muffler repair shop by Ronald Brown, the chain expanded rapidly to new locations, and as it did so, it also expanded the services it provided, from muffler replacement to oil changes, brake jobs, and engine repair. Today, one can bring an automobile to a Muffler Magic shop for basically any type of service, from tires to mufflers to engine repair.

Auto service is a tough business. The shop owner is basically dependent upon the quality of the service people he or she hires and retains, and the most qualified mechanics find it easy to pick up and leave for a job paying a bit more at a competitor down the road. It's also a business where productivity is very important. The single largest expense is usually the cost of labor. Auto service dealers generally don't just make up the prices that they charge customers for various repairs; instead, they charge based on standardized industry rates for jobs like changing spark plugs or repairing a leaky radiator. Therefore, if, for instance, someone brings a car in for a new alternator, and the standard number of hours for changing the alternator is an hour, but it takes the mechanic 2 hours, the service center's owner may end up making less profit on the transaction.

Quality is a persistent problem as well. For example, "rework" has recently been a problem at Muffler Magic. A customer recently brought her car to a Muffler Magic to have the car's brake pads replaced, which the store did for her. Unfortunately, when she drove off, she only got about two blocks before she discovered that she had no brake power at all. It was simply fortuitous that she was going so slowly she was able to stop her car by slowly rolling up against a parking bumper. It turned out that the mechanic who replaced the brake pads had failed to properly tighten a fitting on the hydraulic brake tubes and the brake fluid had run out, leaving the car with no braking power. In a similar problem the month before that, a (different) mechanic replaced a fan belt, but forgot to refill the radiator with fluid; that customer's car overheated before he got four blocks away, and Muffler Magic had to replace the whole engine. Of course, problems like these not only diminish the profitability of the company's profits, but also, repeated many times over, have the potential for ruining Muffler Magic's word-of-mouth reputation.

Muffler Magic employs about 300 people total, and Ron runs his company with eight managers, including Mr. Brown as president, a controller, a purchasing director, a marketing director, and the human resource manager. He also has three regional managers to whom the eight or nine service center managers in each area of Nevada report. Over the past 2 years, as the company has opened new service centers, company-wide profits have actually diminished,

rather than gone up. In part, these diminishing profits probably reflect the fact that Ron Brown has found it increasingly difficult to manage his growing operation. ("Your reach is exceeding your grasp" is how Ron's wife puts it.)

The company has only the most basic HR systems in place. They use an application form that the human resource manager modified from one that she downloaded from the Web, and they use standard employee status change request forms, sign-on forms, I-9 forms, and so on that they purchased from a human resource management supply house. Training is entirely on the job. They expect the experienced technicians that they hire to come to the job fully trained; to that end, the service center managers generally ask candidates for these jobs basic behavioral questions that hopefully provide a window into these applicants' skills.

However, most of the other technicians they hire to do jobs like rotating tires, fixing brake pads, and replacing mufflers are untrained and inexperienced. They are to be trained, either by the service center manager or by more experienced technicians, on the job.

Ron Brown faces several HR-type problems. One, as he says, is that he faces the "tyranny of the immediate" when it comes to hiring employees. Although it's fine to say that he should be carefully screening each employee and checking their references, from a practical point of view, with 25 centers to run, the centers' managers usually just hire anyone who seems to be breathing, as long as they can answer some basic interview questions about auto repair, such as, "What do you think the problem is if a 2004 Camry is overheating, and what would you do about it?"

Employee safety is also a problem. An automobile service center is potentially dangerous. Employees are dealing with sharp tools, greasy floors, greasy tools, extremely hot temperatures (for instance, on mufflers and engines), and fast-moving engine parts including fan blades. There are some basic things that a service manager can do to ensure more safety, such as insisting that all oil spills be cleaned up immediately. But some work is inherently dangerous, such as when the technician must check out an engine while it is running.

With Muffler Magic's profits going down, Brown's HR manager says that the main problem is financial. As he says, "You get what you pay for" when it comes to employees; if you compensate technicians better than your competitors do, then you get better technicians, and then profits will rise. So the HR manager scheduled a meeting between himself, Ron Brown, and a professor of business who teaches compensation management at a local university. The HR manager has asked this professor to spend about a week looking at each of the service centers, analyzing the situation and coming up with a compensation plan to address Muffler Magic's quality and productivity problems. At this meeting, the professor makes three basic recommendations for changing the company's compensation policies.

Number one, she says she has found that Muffler Magic suffers from what she calls "presenteeism," in other words employees drag themselves into work even when they're sick, because the company does not pay them at all if they are out—there are no sick days. In just a few days, the professor couldn't quantify how much Muffler Magic is losing to presenteeism. However, from what she could see at each shop, there are typically one or two technicians working with various maladies like the cold or flu, and it seemed to her that each of these people was probably only working about half of the time (although they were getting paid for the whole day). So, for 25 service centers per week, Muffler Magic could well be losing 125 or 130 personnel days per week of work. The professor suggests that Muffler Magic start allowing everyone to take three paid sick days per year, a reasonable suggestion. However, as Ron Brown points out, "Right now, we're only losing about half a day's pay for each employee who comes in and who works unproductively; with your suggestion, won't we lose the whole day?" The professor says she'll ponder that one.

Second, the professor also recommends putting the technicians on a skill-for-pay plan. Basically, here's what she suggests. Give each technician a letter grade (A through E) based upon that technician's particular skill level and abilities. An "A" technician is a team leader and needs to show that he or she has excellent diagnostic troubleshooting skills, and the ability to supervise and direct other technicians. At the other extreme, an "E" technician would typically be a new apprentice with little technical training. The other technicians fall in between those two levels, based on their individual skills and abilities.

In the professor's system, the "A" technician or team leader would assign and supervise all work done within his or her area but generally not do any mechanical repairs himself or herself. The team leader does the diagnostic troubleshooting, supervises and trains the other technicians, and test-drives the car before it goes back to the customer. Under this plan, every technician receives a guaranteed hourly wage within a certain range, for instance:

A tech = $25–$30 an hour
B tech = $20–$25 an hour
C tech = $15–$20 an hour
D tech = $10–$15 an hour
E tech = $8–$10 an hour

Third, to directly address the productivity issue, the professor recommends that at the end of each day, each service manager calculate each technician team's productivity for the day and then at the end of each week. She suggests posting the running productivity total conspicuously for daily viewing. Then, the technicians as a group get weekly cash bonuses based upon their productivity. To calculate productivity, the professor recommends dividing the total labor hours billed by the total labor hours paid to technicians, in other words: total labor hours billed, divided by total hours paid to technicians.

Having done some homework, the professor says that the national average for labor productivity is currently about 60%, and that only the best-run service centers achieve 85% or greater. By her rough calculations, Muffler Magic was attaining about industry average (about 60%—in other words, they were billing for, as an example, only about 60 hours for each 100 hours that they actually had to pay technicians to do the jobs). (Of course, this was not entirely the technicians' fault. Technicians get time off for breaks, and for lunch, and if a particular service center simply didn't have enough business on a particular day, then several technicians may well sit around idly waiting for the next car to come in.) The professor recommends setting a labor efficiency goal of 80% and posting each team's daily productivity results in the workplace to provide them with additional feedback. She recommends that if at the end of a week the team is able to boost its productivity ratio from the current 60% to 80%, then that team would get an additional 10% weekly pay bonus. After that, for every 5% boost of increased productivity above 80%, technicians would receive an additional 5% weekly bonus.

(So, if a technician's normal weekly pay is $400, that employee got an extra $40 at the end of the week when his team moved from 60% productivity to 80% productivity.)

After the meeting, Ron Brown thanked the professor for her recommendations and told her he would think about them and get back to her. After the meeting, on the drive home, Ron was pondering what to do. He had to decide whether to institute the professor's sick leave policy, and whether to implement her incentive and compensation plan. Before implementing anything, however, he wanted to make sure he understood the context in which he was making his decision. For example, did Muffler Magic really have an incentive pay problem, or were the problems more broad? Furthermore, how, if at all, would the professor's incentive plan affect the quality of the work that the teams were doing? And should they really start paying for sick days? Ron Brown had a lot to think about.

QUESTIONS

1. Write out a one-page summary outline listing three or four recommendations you would make with respect to each HR function (recruiting, selection, training, and so on) that you think Ron Brown should be addressing with his HR manager now.
2. Develop a 10-question structured interview form Ron Brown's service center managers can use to interview experienced technicians.
3. If you were Ron Brown, would you implement the professor's recommendation addressing the presenteeism problem—in other words, start paying for sick days? Why or why not?
4. If you were advising Ron Brown, would you recommend that he implement the professor's skill-based pay and incentive pay plans as is? Why? Would you implement it with modifications? If you would modify it, please be specific about what you think those modifications should be, and why.

Sources: Based generally on actual facts, but Muffler Magic is a fictitious company. This case is based largely on information in Drew Paras, "The Pay Factor: Technicians' Salaries Can Be the Largest Expense in a Server Shop, as well as the Biggest Headache. Here's How One Shop Owner Tackled the Problem," *Motor Age* (November 2003): 76–79; see also Jennifer Pellet, "Health Care Crisis," *Chief Executive* (June 2004): 56–61; "Firms Press to Quantify, Control Presenteeism," *Employee Benefits* (December 1, 2002). Copyright Gary Dessler, PhD.

BP Texas City*

In March 2005, an explosion and fire at British Petroleum's (BP) Texas City, Texas, refinery killed 15 people and injured 500 people in the worst U.S. industrial accident in more than 10 years. The disaster triggered three investigations: one internal investigation by BP, one by the U.S. Chemical Safety Board (CSB), and another, independent investigation chaired by former U.S. secretary of state James Baker and an 11-member panel organized at BP's request.

To put the results of these three investigations into context, it's useful to understand that under its current management, BP had pursued, for the previous 10 or so years, a strategy emphasizing cost-cutting and profitability. The basic conclusion of the investigations was that cost-cutting helped compromise safety at the Texas City refinery. It's useful to consider each investigation's findings.

The CSB's investigation, according to Carol Merritt, the board's chairwoman, showed that "BP's global management was aware of problems with maintenance, spending, and infrastructure well before March 2005."

Apparently, faced with numerous earlier accidents, BP did make some safety improvements. However, it focused primarily on emphasizing personal employee safety behaviors and procedural compliance, and on thereby reducing safety accident rates. The problem (according to the CSB) was that "catastrophic safety risks remained." For example, according to the CSB, "unsafe and antiquated equipment designs were left in place, and unacceptable deficiencies in preventive maintenance were tolerated." Basically, the CSB found that BP's budget cuts led to a progressive deterioration of safety at the Texas City refinery. Said Ms. Merritt, "In an aging facility like Texas City, it is not responsible to cut budgets related to safety and maintenance without thoroughly examining the impact on the risk of a catastrophic accident."

Looking at specifics, the CSB said that a 2004 internal audit of 35 BP business units, including Texas City (BP's largest refinery), found significant safety gaps they all had in common. These included "systemic underlying issues" such as a widespread tolerance of noncompliance with basic safety rules and poor monitoring of safety management systems and processes. Ironically, the CSB found that BP's accident prevention effort at Texas City had achieved a 70% reduction in worker injuries in the year before the explosion. Unfortunately, this simply meant that individual employees were having fewer accidents. The larger, more fundamental problem was that the potentially explosive situation inherent in the depreciating machinery remained.

The CSB found that the Texas City explosion followed a pattern of years of major accidents at the facility. In fact, there had apparently been an average of one employee death every 16 months at the plant for the last 30 years. The CSB found that the equipment directly involved in the most recent explosion was an obsolete design already phased out in most refineries and chemical plants, and that key pieces of its instrumentation were not working. There had also been previous instances where flammable vapors were released from the same unit in the 10 years prior to the explosion. In 2003, an external audit had referred to the Texas City refinery's infrastructure and assets as "poor" and found what it referred to as a "checkbook mentality." In particular, the CSB found that BP had implemented a 25% cut on fixed costs between 1998 and 2000 and that this adversely impacted maintenance expenditures. Going on, the CSB found that in 2004, three major accidents at the refinery killed three workers.

BP's own internal report concluded that the problems at Texas City were not of recent origin, and instead were years in the making. It said BP was taking steps to address them. Its investigation found "no evidence of anyone consciously or intentionally taking actions or making decisions that put others at risk." Said BP's report, "The underlying reasons for the behaviors and actions displayed during the incident are complex. . . . it is evident that they were many years in the making and will require concerted and committed actions to address." BP's report concluded that there were five underlying causes for the massive explosion:

- A working environment that had eroded to one characterized by resistance to change, and a lack of trust
- Safety, performance, and risk reduction priorities had not been set and consistently reinforced by management

- Changes in the "complex organization" led to a lack of clear accountabilities and poor communication
- A poor level of hazard awareness and understanding of safety resulted in workers accepting levels of risk that were considerably higher than at comparable installations
- A lack of adequate early warning systems for problems, and no independent means of understanding the deteriorating standards at the plant.

The report from the BP-initiated but independent 11-member panel chaired by former U.S. secretary of state James Baker contained specific conclusions and recommendations. Basically, the Baker panel concluded that BP had not provided effective safety process leadership and had not established safety as a core value at the five refineries it looked at (including Texas City).

Like the CSB, the Baker panel found that BP had in fact improved personal safety performance in recent years. However, it had not emphasized the overall safety process. In fact, the Baker panel went on, by focusing on the improving personal injury rates, BP created a false sense of confidence that it was properly addressing process safety risks. It also found that the safety culture at Texas City did not have the positive, trusting, open environment that a safety culture required. The Baker panel's other findings included:

- BP did not always ensure that adequate resources were allocated effectively to support a high level of process safety performance.
- BP's refinery personnel are "overloaded" by corporate initiatives.
- Operators and maintenance personnel work high rates of overtime.
- BP tended to have a short-term focus and its decentralized management system delegated substantial discretion to refinery managers "without clearly defining process safety expectations, responsibilities, or accountabilities."

- The company's corporate safety management system did not make sure there was timely compliance with internal process safety standards and programs.
- BP's executive management either did not receive refinery specific information that showed safety deficiencies existed or did not effectively respond to any information it did receive.[1]

The Baker panel made several safety recommendations for BP, including these:

1. The company's corporate management must provide leadership on process safety.
2. The company should establish a process safety management system that identifies, reduces, and manages the process safety risks of the refineries.
3. The company should make sure its employees have an appropriate level of process safety knowledge and expertise.
4. BP should clearly define expectations and strengthen accountability for process safety performance.
5. BP should develop an integrated set of performance indicators for effectively monitoring process safety performance.
6. BP should establish and implement an effective system to audit process safety performance.
7. The company's board should monitor the implementation of the panel's recommendations and the ongoing process safety performance of the refineries.

Overall, the Baker panel found that BP's top management had not provided "effective leadership" on safety. It found that the failings went to the very top of the organization. The Baker panel emphasized the importance of top management commitment, saying, for instance that "it is imperative that BP leadership set the process safety tone at the top of the organization and establish appropriate expectations regarding process safety performance."

Lord Browne, the chief executive, stepped down about a year after the explosion. About the same time, some BP shareholders were calling for the company's executives and board directors to have their bonuses more closely tied to the company's safety and environmental performance in the wake of Texas City. In 2010 (and before BP's Gulf of Mexico rig explosion) OSHA fined BP over $87 million, for not taking the steps required to rectify the problems that had led to the 2005 explosion.

QUESTIONS

1. The textbook defines ethics as "the principles of conduct governing an individual or a group," and specifically as the standards one uses to decide what his or her conduct should be. To what extent do you believe that what happened at BP is as much a breakdown in the company's ethical systems as it is in its safety systems, and how would you defend your conclusion?

2. Are OSHA's standards, policies, and rules aimed at addressing problems like the ones that apparently existed at the Texas City plant? If so, how would you explain the fact that problems like these could have continued for so many years?

3. Since there were apparently at least three deaths in the year prior to the major explosion, and an average of about one employee death per 16 months for the previous 10 years, how would you account for the fact that mandatory OSHA inspections missed these glaring sources of potential catastrophic events?

4. The textbook lists numerous suggestions for "how to prevent accidents." Based on what you know about the Texas City explosion, what do you say Texas City tells you about the most important three steps an employer can take to prevent accidents?

5. Based on what you learned in Chapter 16, would you make any additional recommendations to BP over and above those

recommendations made by the Baker panel and the CSB? If so, what would those recommendations be?

6. Explain specifically how strategic human resource management at BP seems to have supported the company's broader strategic aims. What does this say about the advisability of always linking human resource strategy to a company's strategic aims?

Sources: Notes for BP Texas City: Sheila McNulty, "BP Knew of Safety Problems, Says Report," *The Financial Times* (October 31, 2006): 1; "CBS: Documents Show BP Was Aware of Texas City Safety Problems," *World Refining & Fuels Today* (October 30, 2006); "BP Safety Report Finds Company's Process Safety Culture Ineffective," *Global Refining & Fuels Report* (January 17, 2007); "BP Safety Record under Attack," *Europe Intelligence Wire* (January 17, 2007); Mark Hofmann, "BP Slammed for Poor Leadership on Safety, Oil Firm Agrees to Act on Review Panel's Recommendations," *Business Intelligence* (January 22, 2007): 3; "Call for Bonuses to Include Link with Safety Performance," *The Guardian* (January 18, 2007): 24; www.bp.com/generic article.do?categoryId=9005029&contentId=7015905, accessed July 12, 2009; Steven Greenhouse, "BP Faces Record Fine For '05 Blast," *New York Times* (October 30, 2009): 1, 6; "OSHA $100,000 Club of Safety Citations," *EHS Today* (February 2010): 34. Copyright Gary Dessler, PhD.

GLOSSARY

action learning A training technique by which management trainees are allowed to work full time analyzing and solving problems in other departments.

adverse impact The overall impact of employer practices that result in significantly higher percentages of members of minorities and other protected groups being rejected for employment, placement, or promotion.

affirmative action Steps that are taken for the purpose of eliminating the present effects of past discrimination.

Age Discrimination in Employment Act of 1967 The act prohibiting age discrimination and specifically protecting individuals over 40 years old.

agency shop A form of union security in which employees who do not belong to the union must still pay union dues on the assumption that union efforts benefit all workers.

Albemarle Paper Company* v. *Moody Supreme Court case in which it was ruled that the validity of job tests must be documented and that employee performance standards must be job related.

alternation ranking method An appraisal process in which the employee who is highest on a trait being measured and also the one who is lowest is identified, alternating between highest and lowest until all employees to be rated have been addressed.

Americans with Disabilities Act (ADA) The act requiring employers to make reasonable accommodations for disabled employees; it prohibits discrimination against disabled persons.

application form The form that provides information on education, prior work record, and skills.

appraisal interview The culmination of an appraisal, in which the supervisor and subordinate review the appraisal and make plans to remedy deficiencies and reinforce strengths.

arbitration The most definitive type of third-party intervention, in which the arbitrator often has the power to determine and dictate the settlement terms.

authority The right to make decisions, direct others' work, and give orders.

authorization cards In order to petition for a union election, the union must show that at least 30% of employees may be interested in being unionized. Employees indicate this interest by signing authorization cards.

bargaining unit The group of employees the union will be authorized to represent.

behavior modeling A training technique in which trainees are first shown good management techniques in a film, are then asked to play roles in a simulated situation, and are then given feedback and praise by their supervisor.

benefits Indirect financial payments given to employees. They may include health and life insurance, vacation, pension, education plans, and discounts on company products, for instance.

bona fide occupational qualification (BFOQ) Requirement that an employee be of a certain religion, sex, or national origin where that is reasonably necessary to the organization's normal operation. Specified by the 1964 Civil Rights Act.

boycott The combined refusal by employees and other interested parties to buy or use the employer's products.

burnout The total depletion of physical and mental resources caused by excessive striving to reach an unrealistic work-related goal.

business necessity Justification for an otherwise discriminatory employment practice, provided there is an overriding legitimate business purpose.

career management A process for enabling the employees to better understand and develop their career skills and interests, and to use the skills and interests most effectively both within the company and, if necessary, after they leave the firm.

case study method A development method in which the manager is presented with a written description of an organizational problem to diagnose and solve.

central tendency The tendency to rate all employees about average.

citations Summons informing employers and employees of the regulations and standards that have been violated in the workplace.

Civil Rights Act of 1991 (CRA 1991) This act places burden of proof back on employers and permits compensatory and punitive damages.

closed shop A form of union security in which the company can hire only union members. This was outlawed in 1947 but still exists in some industries (such as printing).

co-determination The right to a voice in setting company policies; workers generally elect representatives to the superadvisory board.

collective bargaining The process through which representatives of management and the union meet to negotiate a labor agreement.

compensable factors Fundamental, compensable elements of a job, such as skills, effort, responsibility, and working conditions.

competitive advantage The basis for differentiation over competitors and thus for hoping to claim certain customers.

content validity A test that is *content valid* is one in which the test contains a fair sample of the tasks and skills actually needed for the job in question.

controlled experimentation Formal methods for testing the effectiveness of a training program, preferably with before-and-after tests and a control group.

criterion validity A type of validity based on showing that scores on the test (*predictors*) are related to job performance (*criterion*).

critical incident method Keeping a record of uncommonly good or undesirable examples of an employee's work-related behavior and reviewing it with the employee at predetermined times.

defined benefit plan A plan that contains a formula for specifying retirement benefits.

defined contribution plan A plan in which the employer's contribution to employees' retirement or savings funds is specified.

discipline A procedure that corrects or punishes a subordinate for violating a rule or procedure.

dismissal Involuntary termination of an employee's employment with the firm.

disparate impact An unintentional disparity between the proportion of a protected group applying for a position and the proportion getting the job.

disparate treatment An intentional disparity between the proportion of a protected group and the proportion getting the job.

downsizing Refers to the process of reducing, usually dramatically, the number of people employed by the firm.

economic strike Strike that results from a failure to agree on the terms of a contract.

employee compensation Refers to all forms of pay or rewards going to employees and arising from their employment.

employee orientation A procedure for providing new employees with basic background information about the firm.

Employee Retirement Income Security Act (ERISA) Signed into law by President Ford in 1974 to require that pension rights be vested and protected by a government agency, the Pension Benefits Guarantee Corporation.

employee stock ownership plan (ESOP) A corporation contributes shares of its own stock to a trust to purchase company stock for employees. The trust distributes the stock to employees upon retirement or separation from service.

Equal Employment Opportunity Commission (EEOC) The commission, created by Title VII, empowered to investigate job discrimination complaints and sue on behalf of complainants.

Equal Pay Act of 1963 An amendment to the Fair Labor Standards Act designed to require equal pay for women doing the same work as men.

ethics The study of standards of conduct and moral judgment; also the standards of right conduct.

ethnocentric A management philosophy that leads to the creation of home market-oriented staffing decisions.

exit interviews Interviews conducted by the employer immediately prior to the employee leaving the firm with the aim of better understanding what the employee thinks about the company.

expatriates Noncitizens of the country in which they are working.

fact finder In labor relations, a neutral party who studies the issues in a dispute and makes a public recommendation for a reasonable settlement.

Fair Labor Standards Act Congress passed this act in 1936 to provide for minimum wages, maximum hours, overtime pay, and child labor protection. The law has been amended many times and covers most employees.

federal agency guidelines Guidelines issued by federal agencies explaining recommended employer equal employment federal legislation procedures in detail.

Federal Violence Against Women Act of 1994 Provides that a person "who commits a crime of violence motivated by gender and thus deprives another of her rights shall be liable to the party injured."

flexible benefits plan Individualized plans allowed by employers to accommodate employee preferences for benefits.

forced distribution method An appraisal method by which the manager places predetermined percentages of subordinate in performance categories.

gain-sharing plan An incentive plan that engages employees in a common effort to achieve productivity objectives and share the gains.

geocentric A staffing policy that seeks the best people for key jobs throughout the organization, regardless of nationality.

good-faith bargaining A term that means both parties are communicating and negotiating and that proposals are being matched with counterproposals, with both parties making every reasonable effort to arrive at agreements. It does not mean that either party is compelled to agree to a proposal.

graphic rating scale A scale that lists a number of traits and a range of performance for each. The employee is then rated by identifying the score that best describes his or her level of performance for each trait.

***Griggs* v. *Duke Power Company* Case** Supreme Court case in which the plaintiff argued that his employer's requirement that coal handlers be high school graduates was unfairly discriminatory. In finding for the plaintiff, the Court ruled that discrimination need not be overt to be illegal, that employment practices must be related to job performance, and that the burden of proof is on the employer to show that hiring standards are job related.

guaranteed fair treatment Employer programs aimed at ensuring that all employees are treated fairly, generally by providing formalized, well-documented, and highly publicized vehicles through which employees can appeal any eligible issues.

halo effect A common appraisal problem in which the rating of a subordinate on one trait influences the way the person is rated on other traits.

high-performance work system A set of human resource management policies and practices that together produce superior employee performance.

home-country nationals Citizens of the country in which the multinational company has its headquarters.

human resource management The policies and practices one needs to carry out the "people" or human resource aspects of a management position, including recruiting, screening, training, rewarding, and appraising.

illegal bargaining items Items in collective bargaining that are forbidden by law; for example, the clause agreeing to hire "union members exclusively" would be illegal in a right-to-work state.

incentive plan A compensation plan that ties pay to performance.

in-house development centers A company-based facility for exposing current or prospective managers to exercises to develop improved management skills.

insubordination Willful disregard or disobedience of the boss's authority or legitimate orders.

interview A procedure designed to solicit information from a person's oral responses to oral inquiries.

job analysis The procedure for determining the duties and skill requirements of a job and the kind of person who should be hired for it.

job description A list of a job's duties, responsibilities, reporting relationships, working conditions, and supervisory responsibilities—one product of a job analysis.

job evaluation A formal and systematic comparison of jobs to determine the worth of one job relative to another.

job posting Posting notices of job openings on company bulletin boards as a recruiting method.

job rotation A management training technique that involves moving a trainee from department to department to broaden his or her experience and identify strengths and weaknesses.

job specification A list of a job's "human requirements," that is, the requisite education, skills, personality, and so on—a product of a job analysis.

Landrum-Griffin Act A law aimed at protecting union members from possible wrongdoing on the part of their unions.

layoff A situation in which employees are told there is no work for them but that management intends to recall them when work is again available.

learning organization An organization "skilled at creating, acquiring, and transferring knowledge and at modifying its behavior to reflect new knowledge and insights."

line manager A manager who is authorized to direct the work of subordinates and responsible for accomplishing the organization's goals.

lockout A refusal by the employer to provide opportunities to work.

management assessment centers A facility in which management candidates are asked to make decisions in hypothetical situations and are scored on their performance.

management by objectives (MBO) A performance management method through which the manager sets organizationally relevant goals with each employee and then periodically discusses progress toward these goals, in an organization-wide effort.

management development Any attempt to improve current or future management performance by imparting knowledge, changing attitudes, or increasing skills.

mandatory bargaining items Items in collective bargaining that a party must bargain over if they are introduced by the other party—for example, pay.

mediation Labor relations intervention in which a neutral third party tries to assist the principals in reaching agreement.

merit pay (merit raise) Any salary increase awarded to an employee based on his or her individual performance.

national emergency strikes Strikes that might "imperil the national health and safety."

National Labor Relations Board (NLRB) The agency created by the Wagner Act to investigate unfair labor practice charges and to provide for secret-ballot elections and majority rule in determining whether or not a firm's employees want a union.

Norris-LaGuardia Act This law marked the beginning of the era of strong encouragement of unions and guaranteed to each employee the right to bargain collectively "free from interference, restraint, or coercion."

Occupational Safety and Health Act The law passed by Congress in 1970 "to assure so far as possible every working man and woman in the nation safe and healthful working conditions and to preserve our human resources."

Occupational Safety and Health Administration (OSHA) The agency created within the Department of Labor to set safety and health standards for almost all workers in the United States.

Office of Federal Contract Compliance Programs (OFCCP) The office responsible for implementing executive orders and ensuring compliance of federal contractors.

on-the-job training (OJT) Training a person to learn a job while working at it.

open shop Type of union security in which the workers decide whether or not to join the union, and those who join must pay dues.

opinion surveys Questionnaires that regularly ask employees their opinions about the company, management, and work life.

organizational development (OD) A development method aimed at changing the attitudes, values, and beliefs of employees so that employees can improve the organization.

outplacement counseling A systematic process by which a terminated person is trained and counseled in the techniques of self-appraisal and securing a new position.

paired comparison method An appraisal method in which every subordinate to be rated is paired with and compared to every other subordinate on each trait.

peer appraisal   Appraisal of an employee by his or her peers.

performance analysis   Verifying that there is a performance deficiency and determining whether that deficiency should be rectified through training or through some other means (such as transferring the employee).

performance appraisal Evaluating an employee's current and/or past performance relative to his or her performance standards.

performance management The process through which companies ensure that employees are working toward organizational goals. It includes practices through which the manager defines the employee's goals and work, develops the employee's skills and capabilities, evaluates the person's goal-directed behavior, and then rewards him or her in a fashion consistent with the company's and the person's needs.

personnel replacement charts Company records showing present performance and promotability of inside candidates for the firm's most important positions.

piecework   A system of incentive pay tying pay to the number of items processed by each individual worker.

polycentric   A management philosophy oriented toward staffing positions with local talent.

portability   Making it easier for employees who leave the firm prior to retirement to take their accumulated pension funds with them.

Pregnancy Discrimination Act (PDA) An amendment to Title VII of the Civil Rights Act that prohibits sex discrimination based on "pregnancy, childbirth, or related medical conditions."

profit-sharing plan   A plan whereby most employees share in the company's profits.

protected class   Persons such as older workers and women protected by equal opportunity laws including Title VII.

qualifications inventories   Manual or computerized records listing employees' education, career and development interests, languages, special skills, and so on, to be used in identifying inside candidates for promotion.

ranking method   The simplest method of job evaluation that involves ranking each job relative to all other jobs, usually based on a job's overall difficulty.

ratio analysis   A forecasting technique that involves analyzing and extrapolating the ratio of a dependent variable, such as salespersons required, with an independent variable, such as sales.

reliability   The characteristic that refers to the consistency of scores obtained by the same person when retested with the identical or equivalent tests.

right-to-work   A term used to describe state statutory or constitutional provisions banning the requirement of union membership as a condition of employment.

Scanlon plan   An incentive plan developed in 1937 by Joseph Scanlon and designed to encourage cooperation, involvement, and sharing of benefits.

sensitivity training   A method for increasing employees' insights into their own behavior through candid discussions in groups led by special trainers.

severance pay   A onetime payment that employers provide when terminating an employee.

sexual harassment   Harassment on the basis of sex that has the purpose or effect of substantially interfering with a person's work performance or creating an intimidating, hostile, or offensive work environment.

staff manager   A manager who assists and advises line managers.

stock option   The right to purchase a stated number of shares of company stock at a set price at some time in the future.

strategy   The company's plan for how it will match its internal strengths and weaknesses with external opportunities and threats in order to maintain a competitive advantage.

strategic human resource management Linking HRM policies and practices with strategic goals and objectives in order to improve business performance.

survey feedback   A method that involves surveying employees' attitudes and providing feedback to facilitate problems being solved by the managers and employees.

sympathy strike   A strike that takes place when one union strikes in support of another's strike.

Taft-Hartley Act (Labor Management Relations Act) A law prohibiting union unfair labor practices and enumerating the rights of employees as union members. It also enumerates the rights of employers.

task analysis A detailed study of a job to identify the skills required so that an appropriate training program may be instituted.

team building Improving the effectiveness of teams through the use of consultants and team-building meetings.

terminate at will The idea, based in law, that the employment relationship can be terminated at will by either the employer or the employee for any reason.

termination interview The interview in which an employee is informed of the fact that he or she has been dismissed.

test validity The degree to which a test, interview, and so on, measures what it purports to measure or fulfills the function it was designed to fill.

third-country nationals Citizens of a country other than the parent or host country.

Title VII of the 1964 Civil Rights Act The section of the act that says an employer may not discriminate on the basis of race, color, religion, sex, or national origin with respect to employment.

training The process of teaching new employees the basic skills they need to perform their jobs.

trend analysis Study of a firm's past employment needs over a period of years to predict future needs.

unfair labor practice strike Strike to protest illegal conduct by the employer.

union salting A union organizing tactic by which workers who are employed by a union as undercover union organizers are hired by unwitting employers.

union shop A form of union security in which the company can hire nonunion people but they must join the union after a prescribed

period of time and pay dues. (If they do not, they can be fired.)

unsafe acts Behaviors that potentially cause accidents.

unsafe conditions The mechanical and physical conditions that cause accidents.

upward feedback Having subordinates evaluate their supervisors' performance.

vested Point at which accumulated pension rights are guaranteed to the employee.

vestibule training A technique in which trainees learn on the actual or simulated equipment they will use on the job but receive their training off the job.

Vocational Rehabilitation Act of 1973 The act requiring certain federal contractors to take affirmative action for disabled persons.

voluntary bargaining items Items in collective bargaining for which bargaining is neither illegal nor mandatory—neither party can be compelled to negotiate over those items.

wage curve Shows the relationship between the relative value of the job and the average wage paid for this job.

Wagner Act A law that banned certain types of unfair labor practices and provided for secret-ballot elections and majority rule for determining whether or not a firm's employees want to unionize.

wildcat strike An unauthorized strike occurring during the term of a contract.

workers' compensation Provides income and medical benefits to work-related accident victims or their dependents regardless of fault.

works councils Formal employee-elected groups of worker representatives that meet with managers to discuss topics ranging, for instance, from no-smoking policies to layoffs.

wrongful discharge An employee dismissal that does not comply with the law or does not comply with the contractual arrangement stated or implied by the firm via its employment application forms, employee manuals, or other promises.

NOTES

Chapter 1

1. http://llbeancareers.com/culture.htm, accessed February 28, 2010.
2. http://llbeancareers.com/benefits.htm, accessed February 28, 2010.
3. Michael Arndt, "L.L.Bean Follows Its Shoppers to the Web," *BusinessWeek*, (March 1, 2010).
4. Quoted in Fred K. Foulkes, "The Expanding Role of the Personnel Function," *Harvard Business Review* (March/April 1975): 71–84. See also Warren Wilhelm, "HR Can Make the U.S. a Global Leader," *Personnel Journal* (May 1993): 280.
5. These data come from "Small Business: A Report of the President" (1998), www.SBA.gov/ADV/stats; see also "Statistics of US Businesses and Non-Employer Status," www.SBA.gov/ADV oh/research/data.html, accessed March 9, 2006.
6. Steve Bates, "No Experience Necessary? Many Companies Are Putting Non-HR Executives in Charge of HR with Mixed Results," *HR Magazine* 46, no. 11 (November 2001): 34–41. See also Fay Hansen, "Top of the Class," *Workforce Management* (June 23, 2008): 1, 25–30. After General Motors emerged from Chapter 11 bankruptcy recently, it replaced its long-term human resource director with Mary Barra, GM's vice president for Global Manufacturing Engineering, an executive with no human resource management experience. Jeremy Smerd, "Outsider Thinking for GM HR," *Workforce Management*, (August 17), 2009: 1–3.
7. "Human Resource Activities, Budgets & Staffs, 1999–2000," *BNA Bulletin to Management* 51, no. 25 (June 29, 2000): S1–S6. In fact, one study found that delegating somewhat more of the HR activities to line managers "had a positive effect on HR managers' perceptions of their units' reputation among line managers." Carol Kulik and Elissa Perry, "When Less Is More: The Effect of Devolution on HR as a Strategic Role and Construed Image," *Human Resource Management* 47, no. 3 (Fall 2008): 541–58.
8. Some employers, like Google, are adding "chief sustainability officers" within human resource management, responsible for fostering the company's environmental sustainability efforts. Nancy Woodward, "New Breed of Human Resource Leader," *HR Magazine* (June 2008): 53–57.
9. Susan Mayson and Rowena Barrett, "The 'Science' and 'Practice' of HR in Small Firms," *Human Resource Management Review* 16 (December 2006): 447–55.
10. See Dave Ulrich, "The New HR Organization," *Workforce Management* (December 10, 2007): 40–44; and Dave Ulrich, "The 21st-Century HR Organization," *Human Resource Management* 47, no. 4 (Winter 2008): 829–50. Some writers

11. distinguish among three basic human resource management subfields: micro HRM (which covers the HR subfunctions such as recruitment and selection), strategic HRM, and international HRM. Mark Lengnick Hall et al., "Strategic Human Resource Management: The Evolution of the Field," *Human Resource Management Review* 19 (2009): 64–85.
11. Robert Grossman, "IBM's HR Takes a Risk," *HR Management* (April 2007): 54–59.
12. "Immigrants in the Workforce," *BNA Bulletin to Management Datagraph* (August 15, 1996): 260–61. See also Shari Caudron et al., "80 People, Events and Trends that Shaped HR," *Workforce* (January 2002): 26–56.
13. See, for example, "HR 2018: Top Predictions," *Workforce Management* 87, no. 20 (December 15, 2008): 20–21.
14. For discussions of some other important trends, see, for example, "Workplace Trends: An Overview of the Findings of the Latest SHRM Workplace Forecast," *Society for Human Resource Management, Workplace Visions* 3 (2008): 1–8; and Ed Frauenheim, "Future View," *Workforce Management* (December 15, 2008): 18–23.
15. http://www.census.gov/foreign-trade/statistics/historical/gands.pdf, accessed April 23, 2009.
16. Kerry Capell, "Zara Thrives by Breaking All the Rules," *BusinessWeek* (October 20, 2008): 66.
17. Timothy Appel, "Better Off a Blue-Collar," *Wall Street Journal* (July 1, 2003): B-1.
18. "Workforce Readiness and the New Essential Skills," *Society for Human Resource Management, Workplace Visions* 2 (2008): 5.
19. See "Charting the Projections: 2004–2014," *Occupational Outlook Quarterly* (Winter 2005–2006).
20. Richard Crawford, *In the Era of Human Capital* (New York: Harper Business, 1991), p. 26.
21. Peter Drucker, "The Coming of the New Organization," *Harvard Business Review* (January–February 1988): 45. See also James Combs et al., "How Much Do High-Performance Work Practices Matter? A Meta-Analysis of Their Effects on Organizational Performance," *Personal Psychology* 59 (2006): 501–28.
22. www.knowledge.wharton.upe.edu, "Human Resources Wharton," accessed January 8, 2006.
23. See, for example, Anthea Zacharatos et al., "High-Performance Work Systems and Occupational Safety," *Journal of Applied Psychology* 90, no. 1 (2005): 77–93.
24. Michael Schroeder, "States Fight Exodus of Jobs," *Wall Street Journal* (June 3, 2003): 84. See also Monica Belcourt, "Outsourcing—The Benefits and the Risks," *Human Resource Management Review* 16 (2006): 69–279; and Roger J. Moncarz, Michael G. Wolf, and Benjamin Wright, "Service-Providing

Occupations, Offshoring, and the Labor Market," *Monthly Labor Review* (December 2008): 71–86.

25. "Charting the Projections: 2004–2014," *Occupational Outlook Quarterly* (Winter 2005–2006): 48–50; and www.bls.gov/emp/emplabor01.pdf, accessed October 20, 2008.

26. As one example, see "Changing Makeup of Workforce Translates into Need for Multilingual Approach by HR," *BNA Bulletin to Management* (January 20, 2008): 25.

27. Tony Carnevale, "The Coming Labor and Skills Shortage," *Training & Development* (January 2005): 39.

28. "Talent Management Leads in Top HR Concerns," *Compensation & Benefits Review* (May/June 2007): 12. Similarly, in terms of what they expect from HR, top executives tend to emphasize ensuring an adequate supply of management talent. For example, about 76% of global senior executives said their main people-management issue is "leadership development and ensuring an adequate number of capable candidates in the pipeline." Seventy two percent listed "talent management," 72% "creating a high performance culture," and 65% "training and development." The accompanying figure helps to illustrate this Fay Hansen, "Chief Concern: Leaders," *Workforce Management* (July 20, 2009): 18.

29. For example, see Kathryn Tyler, "Generation Gaps," *HR Magazine* (January 2008): 69–72.

30. Eva Kaplan-Leiserson, "The Changing Workforce," *Training and Development* (February 2005): 10–11. See also C. A. Hewlett et al., "How Gen Y & Boomers Will Reshape Your Agenda," *Harvard Business Review* 87, no. 7/8 (July/August 2009): 71–76.

31. By one report, the economic downturn of 2008 made it more difficult for dissatisfied Generation Y employees to change jobs and is contributing to a buildup of "griping" among some of them. "Generation Y, Goes to Work," *The Economist* (January 3, 2009): 47.

32. Nadira Hira, "You Raised Them, Now Manage Them," *Fortune* (May 20, 2007): 38–46; Katheryn Tyler, "The Tethered Generation," *HR Magazine* (May 2007): 41–46; Jeffrey Zaslow, "The Most Praised Generation Goes to Work," *Wall Street Journal* (April 20, 2007): W1, W7; Rebecca Hastings, "Millennials Expect a Lot from Leaders," *HR Magazine* (January 2008): 30.

33. To capitalize on this, more employers are using social networking tools to promote employee interaction and collaboration, particularly among Generation Y employees. "Social Networking Tools Aimed at Engaging Newest Employees," *BNA Bulletin to Management* (September 18, 2007): 303.

34. "Talent Management Leads in Top HR Concerns," *Compensation & Benefits Review* (May/June 2007): 12.

35. Jennifer Schramm, "Exploring the Future of Work: Workplace Visions," *Society for Human Resource Management* 2 (2005): 6; Rainer Strack, Jens Baier, and Anders Fahlander, "Managing Demographic Risk," *Harvard Business Review* (February 2008): 119–28.

36. Rita Zeidner, "Does the United States Need Foreign Workers?" *HR Magazine* (June 2009): 42–44.

37. http://www.census.gov/foreign-trade/Press-Release/current_press_release/ft900.pdf, accessed April 4, 2010.

38. http://www.bls.gov/opub/ted/2006/may/wk2/art01.htm, accessed April 18, 2009.

39. Sydney Robertson and Vic Dayal, "When Less Is More: Managing Human Resources with Reduced Staff," *Compensation & Benefits Review* (March/April 2009): 21–26.

40. Ben Nagler, "Recasting Employees into Teams," *Workforce* (January 1998): 101–6.

41. A recent survey found that HR managers referred to "strategic/critical thinking skills" as the top "most important factor in attaining next HR job." See "Career Development for HR Professionals," *Society for Human Resource Management Research Quarterly* (Second Quarter 2008): 3.

42. John W. Boudreau and Peter M. Ramstad, *Beyond HR: The New Science of Human Capital* (Boston: Business School Press, 2007), p. 9.

43. For example, see Sandra Fisher et al., "Human Resource Issues in Outsourcing: Integrating Research and Practice," *Human Resource Management* 47, no. 3 (Fall 2008): 501–23; and "Sizing up the HR Outsourcing Market," *HR Magazine* (November 2008): 78.

44. Studies suggest that IT usage does support human resource managers' need to participate more in strategic planning. See Victor Haines III and Genevieve LaFleur, "Information Technology Usage and Human Resource Roles and Effectiveness," *Human Resource Management* 47, no. 3 (Fall 2008): 525, 540.

45. Connie Winkler, "Quality Check," *HR Magazine* (May 2007): 93–98.

46. Stefan Strohmeier, "Research in e-HRM: Review and Implications," *Human Resource Management Review* 17 (2007): 19–37.

47. Kevin Wooten, "Ethical Dilemmas in Human Resource Management," *Human Resource Management Review* 11 (2001). 161.

48. Chad van Iddekinge et al., "Effects of Selection and Training on Unit Level Performance over Time: A Latent Growth Modeling Approach," *Journal of Applied Psychology* 94, no. 4 (2009): 829–43.

49. Olivier Herrbach et al., "Perceived HRM Practices, Organizational Commitment, and Voluntary Early Retirement among Late Career Managers," *Human Resource Management* 48, no. 6 (November/December 2009): 895–916.

50. "Super Human Resources Practices Result in Better Overall Performance, Report Says," *BNA Bulletin to Management* (August 26, 2004): 273–74. See also Wendy Boswell, "Aligning Employees with the Organization's Strategic Objectives: Out of Line of Sight, Out of Mind," *International Journal of Human Resource Management* 17, no. 9 (September 2006): 1014–41. Another study suggests that it's not always necessary to implement the full range of high-performance HR practices to achieve improved results. Even implementing smaller "bundles" of HR related practices (such as empowerment, motivation, and improving skills) can improve business outcomes if the activities themselves are synergistic. Mahesh Subramony, "A Meta-Analytic Investigation of the

Relationship between HRM Bundles and Firm Performance," *Human Resource Management* 48, no. 5 (September–October 2009): 745–58.

51. As one expert puts it, "A great deal of what passes as 'best practice' in HRM most likely is not. In some cases, there is simply no evidence that validates what are thought to be best practices, while in other cases there is evidence to suggest that what are thought to be best practices are inferior practices." Edward Lawler III, "Why HR Practices Are not Evidence-Based," *Academy of Management Journal* 50, no. 5 (2007): 1033.

52. See, for example, http://www.personneltoday.com/blogs/hcglobal-human-capital-management/2009/02/theres-no-such-thing-as-eviden. html, accessed April 18, 2009.

53. Ibid.

54. The evidence-based movement began in medicine. In 1996, in an editorial published by the *British Medical Journal*, David Sackett, M.D., defined "evidence based medicine" as "use of the best-available evidence in making decisions about patient care," and urged his colleagues to adopt its tenets. "Evidence-Based Training™: Turning Research Into Results for Pharmaceutical Sales Training," An AXIOM White Paper © 2006 AXIOM Professional Health Learning LLC. All rights reserved.

55. Chris Brewster et al., "What Determines the Size of the HR Function? A Cross National Analysis," *Human Resource Management* 45, no. 1 (Spring 2006): 3–21. See also "SHRM Survey Report, 2006 Strategic HR Management," *Society for Human Resource Management*, pp. 18–19.

56. Bill Roberts, "How to Put Analytics on Your Side," *HR Magazine* (October 2009): 43–46.

57. Robert Grossman, "IBM's HR Takes a Risk," *HR Management* (April 2007): 54–59. See also Robert Grossman, "Close the Gap between Research and Practice," *HR Magazine* (November 2009): 31–37.

58. Chris Brewster et al., "What Determines the Size of the HR Function? A Cross National Analysis," *Human Resource Management* 45, no. 1 (Spring 2006): 3–21.

59. Contact the Society for Human Resource Management, (703) 535-6366.

60. Except as noted, most of this section is based on Richard Vosburgh, "The Evolution of HR: Developing HR as an Internal Consulting Organization," *Human Resource Planning* 30, no. 3 (September 2007): 11–24.

61. See, for example, "Employers Seek HR Executives with Global Experience, SOX Knowledge, Business Sense," *BNA Bulletin to Management* (September 19, 2006): 297–98; and Robert Rodriguez, "HR's New Breed," *HR Magazine* (January 2006): 67–71.

62. Susan Wells, "From HR to the Top," *HR Magazine* (June 2003): 49. SHRM's 2008 Managing Your HR Career Survey Report concluded that HR professionals need several key skills "to get to the top," including interpersonal communication, drive/ambition, reputation in the organization, and strategic/critical thinking skills. Kathy Gurchiek, "Survey: 'Key' Skills Advance HR Career," *HR Magazine* (April 2008): 38.

63. See also James Hayton et al., "Conversations on What the Market Wants from HR Graduates, and How Can We Institutionalize Innovation in Teaching," *Human Resource Management Review* 15 (2005): 38–45. For a contrary view, see for example, P. J. Kiger, "Survey: HR Still Battling for Leaders' Respect," *Workforce Management* 87, no. 20 (December 15, 2008): 8.

64. Jessica Marquez, "As the Economy Goes," *Workforce Management* (August 17, 2009): 27–33.

65. "The Human Resource Certification Institute (HRCI) Announces the California Certification," www.hrci.org/HRCI_Files/_Items/HRCI-MR-TAB2-951/Docs/At_A_Glance.pdf, accessed December 28, 2007.

66. "Automation Improves Retailer's Hiring Efficiency and Quality," *HR Focus* 82, no. 2 (February 2005): 3.

67. Patrick Gunnigle and Sara Moore, "Linking Business Strategy and Human Resource Management: Issues and Implications," *Personnel Review* 23, no. 1 (1994): 63–84; Gary Dessler, *Human Resource Management* (Upper Saddle River, NJ: Prentice Hall, 2008), pp. 77–97.

68. Gunnigle and Moore, "Linking Business Strategy," 64.

69. Michael Porter, *Competitive Strategy* (New York: The Free Press, 1980), p. 14.

70. Gary Dessler, *Human Resource Management* (Upper Saddle River, NJ: Prentice Hall, 2008), p. 86.

71. Jeffrey Schmidt, "The Correct Spelling of M&A Begins with HR," *HR Magazine* 46, no. 6 (June 2001): 102–8. See also Wendy Boswell, "Aligning Employees with the Organization's Strategic Objectives: Out of Line of Sight, Out of Mind," *International Journal of Human Resource Management* 17, no. 9 (September 2006): 1014–41. In practice, the extent to which top executives rely on their HR managers to support their strategic planning efforts is a matter of some debate. Clearly many employers still view HR managers mostly as strategy executors, rather than as managers who can influence the strategy development process. However, a recent study of larger employers (with more than 50,000 employees each) found that 71% of the management teams do see HR as a "strategic player." See Patrick Kiger, "Survey: HR Still Battling for Leaders' Respect," *Workforce Management* (December 15, 2008): 8.

Chapter 2

1. Betsy Morris, "How Corporate America Is Betraying Women," *Fortune* (January 10, 2005): 64–70.

2. Plaintiffs still bring equal employment claims under the Civil Rights Act of 1866. For example, in 2008, the U.S. Supreme Court held that the act prohibits retaliation against someone who complains of discrimination against others when contract rights (in this case an employment agreement) are at stake. Charles Louderback, "US Supreme Court Decisions Expand Employees' Ability to Bring Retaliation Claims," *Compensation & Benefits Review* (September/October 2008): 52.

3. Note that private employers are not bound by the U.S. Constitution.

4. Based on or quoted from Principles of Employment Discrimination Law (Washington, DC: International Association of Official Human Rights Agencies). See also Bruce Feldacker, Labor Guide to Labor Law (Upper Saddle River, NJ: Prentice Hall, 2000); "EEOC Attorneys Highlight How Employers Can Better Their Nondiscrimination Practices," BNA Bulletin to Management (July 20, 2008): 233; and www.eeoc.gov. Employment discrimination law is a changing field, and the appropriateness of the rules, guidelines, and conclusions in this chapter and book may also be affected by factors unique to the employer's operation. They should be reviewed by the employer's attorney before implementation.

5. James Higgins, "A Manager's Guide to the Equal Employment Opportunity Laws," Personnel Journal 55, no. 8 (August 1976): 406.

6. The Equal Employment Opportunity Act of 1972, Subcommittee on Labor or the Committee of Labor and Public Welfare, United States Senate, March 1972, p. 3. In general, it is not discrimination, but unfair discrimination against a person merely because of that person's race, age, sex, national origin, or religion that is forbidden by federal statutes. In the federal government's Uniform Employee Selection Guidelines, unfair discrimination is defined as follows: "unfairness is demonstrated through a showing that members of a particular interest group perform better or poorer on the job than their scores on the selection procedure (test, etc.) would indicate through comparison with how members of the other groups performed." For a discussion of the meaning of fairness, see James Ledvinka, "The Statistical Definition of Fairness in the Federal Selection Guidelines and Its Implications for Minority Employment," Personnel Psychology 32 (August 1979): 551–62. In summary, it's not necessarily unfair for a selection device (such as a test) to discriminate—for example, between low performers and high performers. However, unfair discrimination—discrimination that is based solely on the person's race, age, sex, national origin, or religion—is illegal.

7. "The Employer Should Validate Hiring Tests to Withstand EEOC Scrutiny, Officials Advise," BNA Bulletin to Management (April 1, 2008): 107.

8. "Restructured, Beefed Up OFCCP May Shift Policy Emphasis, Attorney Says," BNA Bulletin to Management (August 18, 2009): 257.

9. Note that the U.S. Supreme Court (in General Dynamics Land Systems Inc. v. Cline, 2004) held that the ADEA does not protect younger workers from being treated worse than older ones. "High Court: ADEA Does Not Protect Younger Workers Treated Worse than Their Elders," BNA Bulletin to Management 55, no. 10 (March 4, 2004): 73–80. The U.S. Supreme Court also recently held that, unlike the 1964 Civil Rights Act title VII, the age discrimination in employment act does not permit an employee to prove discrimination just by showing that age was a motivating factor. Instead, he or she might show that age was the determining factor in the personnel action. See "Justices, 5–4, Reject Burden Shifting," BNA Bulletin to Management (June 20, 2009): 199.

10. Pregnancy claims to the EEOC rose about 39% in the early 2000s; plaintiff victories rose 66%. John Kohl, Milton Mayfield, and Jacqueline Mayfield, "Recent Trends in Pregnancy Discrimination Law," Business Horizons 48, no. 5 (September 2005): 442–29.

11. Nancy Woodward, "Pregnancy Discrimination Grows," HR Magazine (July 2005): 79.

12. Thomas Dhanens, "Implications of the New EEOC Guidelines," Personnel 56 (September/October): 32–39.

13. See, for example, www.uniformguidelines.com/uniformguidelines.html, accessed November 23, 2007.

14. Griggs v. Duke Power Company, 3FEP cases 175.

15. IOFEP cases 1181.

16. Bruce Feldacker, Labor Guide to Labor Law (Upper Saddle River, NJ: Prentice Hall, 2000), p. 513.

17. "The Eleventh Circuit Explains Disparate Impact, Disparate Treatment," BNA Fair Employment Practices (August 17, 2000): 102. See also Kenneth York, "Disparate Results in Adverse Impact Tests: The 4/5ths Rule and the Chi Square Test," Public Personnel Management 31, no. 2 (Summer 2002): 253–62. A recent analysis based on mathematical simulations concluded that employee selection effectiveness, in general, and the potential weaknesses of applying the 4/5 rule, in particular, can be ameliorated by formulating and using a multistage selection strategy, for instance, basing the initial screen, say for conscientiousness, on paper-and-pencil tests, and then one or two subsequent screens on other selection procedures including interviews. See David Finch et al., "Multistage Selection Strategies: Simulating the Effects on Adverse Impact and Expected Performance for Various Predictor Combinations," Journal of Applied Psychology 94, no. 2 (2009): 318–40.

18. Commerce Clearing House, "House and Senate Pass Civil Rights Compromise by Wide Margin," Ideas and Trends in Personnel (November 13, 1991): 182.

19. Ibid., p. 265. See also Miller Brownstein, "Inquiry Free, but Money for Me: Whether the Civil Rights Act of 1991 Permits Punitive Damages in the Absence of Compensatory Damages," Boston University Law Review 84, no. 4 (October 2004): 1049–76.

20. "Expansion of Employment Laws Abroad Impacts U.S. Employers," BNA Bulletin to Management (April 11, 2006): 119; Richard Posthuma, Mark Roehling, and Michael Campion, "Applying U.S. Employment Discrimination Laws to International Employers: Advice for Scientists and Practitioners," Personnel Psychology 59 (2006): 2705–39; "We're a Multinational Corporation with US Citizens Working in Several Countries. Do Laws Such as the Fair Labor Standards Act or the Family and Medical Leave Act Apply to Them?" HR Magazine (February 2008): 333.

21. Larry Drake and Rachel Moskowitz, "Your Rights in the Workplace," Occupational Outlook Quarterly (Summer 1997): 19–20.

22. Richard Wiener et al., "The Fit and Implementation of Sexual Harassment Law to Workplace Evaluations," Journal of Applied Psychology 87, no. 4 (2002): 747–64.

23. http://www.eeoc.gov/types/sexual_harassment.html, accessed April 24, 2009. The Federal Violence against Women Act of 1994 provides another

avenue that women can use to seek relief for violent sexual harassment. It provides that a person "who commits a crime of violence motivated by gender and thus deprives another of her rights shall be liable to the party injured."

24. Edward Felsenthal, "Justice's Ruling Further Defines Sexual Harassment," *Wall Street Journal* (March 5, 1998): B1, B5. Similarly, a series of compliments and "requests for a hug" were not sufficient to rise to the level of sexual harassment in one case involving a female supervisor and her female subordinate. ("Compliments, Request for Hug Were Not Harassment by Female Supervisor, Court Says," *BNA Human Resources Report* [November 20, 2003]: 1193).

25. Hilary Gettman and Michele Gelfand, "When the Customer Shouldn't Be King: Antecedents and Consequences of Sexual Harassment by Clients and Customers," *Journal of Applied Psychology* 92, no. 3 (2007): 757–70.

26. For example, a server/bartender recently filed a sexual harassment claim against Chili's Bar & Grill. She claimed that her former boyfriend, also a restaurant employee, had harassed her. The court ruled that the restaurant's prompt response warranted ruling in favor of it. "Ex-Boyfriend Harassed, but Employer Acted Promptly," *BNA Bulletin to Management* (January 8, 2008): 14.

27. See Mindy D. Bergman et al., "The (Un)reasonableness of Reporting: Antecedents and Consequences of Reporting Sexual Harassment," *Journal of Applied Psychology* 87, no. 2 (2002): 230–42; see also W. Kirk Turner and Christopher Thrutchley, "Employment Law and Practices Training: No Longer the Exception—It's the Rule," *Society for Human Resource Management Legal Report* (July–August 2002): 1–2.

28. Chelsea Willness et al., "A Meta-Analysis of the Antecedents and Consequences of Workplace Sexual Harassment," *Personnel Psychology* 60, no. 60 (2007): 127–62.

29. Jennifer Berdahl and Celia Moore, "Workplace Harassment: Double Jeopardy for Minority Women," *Journal of Applied Psychology* 91, no. 2 (2006): 426–36.

30. Jennifer Berdahl and Karl Aquino, "Sexual Behavior at Work: Fun or Folly?" *Journal of Applied Psychology* 94, no. 1 (2009): 34–47.

31. Maria Rotundo et al., "A Meta-Analytic Review of Gender Differences in Perceptions of Sexual Harassment," *Journal of Applied Psychology* 86, no. 5 (2001): 914–22. See also Nathan Bowling and Terry Beehr, "Workplace Harassment from the Victim's Perspective: A Theoretical Model and Meta Analysis," *Journal of Applied Psychology* 91, no. 5 (2006): 998–1012.

32. Jennifer Berdahl, "The Sexual Harassment of Uppity Women," *Journal of Applied Psychology* 92, no. 2 (2007): 425–37.

33. Lilia Cortina and S. Arzu Wasti, "Profile to Coping: Response to Sexual Harassment across Persons, Organizations, and Cultures," *Journal of Applied Psychology* 90, no. 1 (2005): 182–92.

34. In fact, this apparently is common. Alleged harassers often say "yes, I did it, but. . . ," and then explain they meant no harm. However, intent is usually not the issue to the court. The issues are whether the conduct was unwelcome and objectively offensive to a reasonable person. Jonathan Segal, "I Did It, But. . . : Employees May Be as Innocent as They Say, but Still Guilty of Harassment," *HR Magazine* (March 2008): 91.

35. See the discussion in "Examining Unwelcome Conduct in Sexual Harassment Claims," *BNA Fair Employment Practices* (October 19, 1995): 124. See also Molly Bowers et al., "Just Cause in the Arbitration of Sexual Harassment Cases," *Dispute Resolution Journal* 55, no. 4 (November 2000): 40–55.

36. "New EEOC Guidance Explains Standards of Liability for Harassment by Supervisors," *BNA Fair Employment Practices* (June 24, 1999): 75.

37. "Adequate Response Bars Liability," BNA Fair Employment Practices (June 26, 1997): 74.

38. Shereen Bingham and Lisa Scherer, "The Unexpected Effects of a Sexual Education Program," *Journal of Applied Behavioral Science* 37, no. 2 (June 2001): 125–53.

39. Federick L. Sullivan, "Sexual Harassment: The Supreme Court Ruling," *Personnel* 65, no. 12 (December 1986): 42–44. See also Gillian Flynn, "A Pioneer Program Nurtures a Harassment Free Workplace," *Workforce* (October 1997): 38–43; and for the EEOC's statement, see www.eeoc.gov, accessed November 11, 2007.

40. Bergman et al., "The (Un)reasonableness of Reporting," 237.

41. Elliot H. Shaller and Dean Rosen, "A Guide to the EEOC's Final Regulations on the Americans with Disabilities Act," *Employee Relations* 17, no. 3 (Winter 1991–1992): 405–20. See also Brenda Sunoo, "Accommodating Workers with Disabilities," *Workforce* 80, no. 2 (February 2001): 86–93.

42. Shaller and Rosen, "A Guide to the EEOC's Final Regulations on the Americans with Disabilities Act," 408. The ADEA does not just protect against intentional discrimination (disparate treatment). Under the Supreme Court's *Smith* v. *Jackson, Miss* decision, it also covers employer practices that seem neutral but actually bear more heavily on older workers (disparate impact). "Employees Need Not Show Intentional Bias to Bring Claims under ADEA, High Court Says," *BNA Bulletin to Management* 56, no. 14 (April 5, 2005): 105.

43. Ibid., p. 409.

44. See, for example, Paul Starkman, "The ADA's 'Essential Job Function' Requirements: Just How Essential Does an Essential Job Function Have to Be?" *Employee Relations Law Journal* 26, no. 4 (Spring 2001): 43–102.

45. http://www.ada.gov/reg3a.html#Anchor-Appendix-52467, accessed January 23, 2009.

46. "No Sitting for Store Greeter," *BNA Fair Employment Practices* (December 14, 1995): 150.

47. M. P. McQueen, "Workplace Disabilities Are on the Rise," *Wall Street Journal* (May 1, 2007): A1.

48. "Odds against Getting Even Longer in ADA Cases," *BNA Bulletin to Management* (August 20, 2000): 229; "Determining Employers' Responsibilities Under ADA," *BNA Fair Employment Practices* (May 16, 1996): 57.

49. "Supreme Court Says Manual Task Limitation Needs Both Daily Living, Workplace Impact," *BNA Fair Employment Practices* (January 17, 2002): 8.

50. For example, a U.S. circuit court recently found that a depressed former kidney dialysis technician could not claim ADA discrimination after the employer fired him for attendance problems. The court said he could not meet the essential job function of predictably coming to work. "Depressed Worker Lacks ADA Claim, Court Decides," *BNA Bulletin to Management* (December 18, 2007): 406. See also, http://www.eeoc.gov/press/5-10-01-b.html, accessed January 8, 2008.

51. "Home Depot Did Not Violate ADA by Barring Deaf Worker from a Forklift Training Program," *BNA Human Resources Report* (November 10, 2003): 1192.

52. "Differing Views: Punctuality as Essential Job Function," *BNA Fair Employment Practices* (April 27, 2000): 56.

53. James McDonald Jr., "The Americans with Difficult Personalities Act," *Employee Relations Law Journal* 25, no. 4 (Spring 2000): 93–107.

54. "EEOC Guidance on Dealing with Intellectual Disabilities," *Workforce Management* (March 2005): 16.

55. *Palmer v. Circuit Court of Cook County*, Illinois, c7#95–3659–6/26/97; reviewed in "No Accommodation for Violent Employee," *BNA Fair Employment Practices* (July 10, 1997): 79. This general rule may not apply under all circumstances. For example, a recent EEOC update suggests that employers may have to accommodate a disruptive employee who has a military-connected posttraumatic stress disorder. "EEOC Letter Addresses ADA Implications of PTSD, Medical Exams," *BNA Bulletin to Management* (June 3, 2008). 183.

56. Lawrence Postol, "ADAAA Will Result in Renewed Emphasis on Reasonable Accommodations," *Society for Human Resource Management Legal Report* (January 2009): 1–3. The EEOC's recent implementing rules add sitting, reaching, and interacting with others to the number of major life activities. "EEOC OKs Proposed Rule to Implement ADA Amendments Act," *BNA Bulletin to Management* (September 20, 2009): 303.

57. "Airline Erred in Giving Test before Making Formal Offer," *BNA Bulletin to Management* (March 15, 2005): 86.

58. Lee, "Implications of ADA Litigation for Employers," 35–50.

59. "Determining Employers' Responsibilities Under ADA," 57.

60. Lee, "Implications of ADA Litigation for Employers," 35–50.

61. Ibid.

62. Timothy Bland, "The Supreme Court Focuses on the ADA," *HR Magazine* (September 1999): 42–46. See also James Hall and Diane Hatch, "Supreme Court Decisions Require ADA Revision," *Workforce* (August 1999): 60–66.

63. Mark Lengnick-Hall et al., "Overlooked and Underutilized: People with Disabilities Are an Untapped Human Resource," *Human Resource Management* 47, no. 2 (Summer 2008): 255–73.

64. Susan Wells, "Counting on Workers with Disabilities," *HR Magazine* (April 2008): 45. Similarly, Verizon Wireless has a formal program aimed at assisting current employees to better manage a transition from healthy to disabled. For example, they train supervisors to identify potentially disability-related deterioration in their employees' performance and to speak with these employees to try to identify what the issues are. If it becomes necessary for an employee to take a disability leave, the program encourages the employee to remain in contact with Verizon's HR professionals and to work with them to set realistic return dates. J. Adam Shoemaker, "A Welcome Back for Workers with Disabilities," *HR Magazine* (October 2009): 30–32.

65. Martha Frase, "An Underestimated Talent Pool," *HR Magazine* (April 2009): 55–58.

66. IOFEP cases 1181. See also Joe Mullich, "Hiring Without Limits," *Workforce Management* (June 2004): 52–58.

67. http://www.eeoc.gov/press/2-25-09.html, accessed April 3, 2009.

68. Bill Leonard, "Bill to Ban Sexual Orientation Bias Introduced," *HR Magazine* 54, no. 8 (August 2009): 18.

69. http://employment.findlaw.com/employment/employment-employee-discrimination-harassment/employment-employee-gay-lesbian-discrimination.html

70. http://www.leg.state.fl.us/Statutes/index.cfm?App_mode=Display_Statute&Search_String=&URL=Ch0448/SEC07.HTM&Title=-%3E2009-%3ECh0448-%3ESection%2007#0448.07, accessed April 3, 2010.

71. John Klinefelter and James Thompkins, "Adverse Impact in Employment Selection," *Public Personnel Management* (May/June 1976): 199–204.

72. John Moran, *Employment Law* (Upper Saddle River, NJ: Prentice Hall, 1997), p. 168. A study found that using the 4/5ths rule often resulted in false-positive ratings of adverse impact, and that incorporating tests of statistical significance could improve the accuracy of applying the 4/5ths rule. See Philip Roth, Philip Bobko, and Fred Switzer, "Modeling the Behavior of the 4/5ths Rule for Determining Adverse Impact: Reasons for Caution," *Journal of Applied Psychology* 91, no. 3 (2006): 507–22.

73. Don't be lulled into thinking that such cases are ancient history. For example, a U.S. Appeals Court recently upheld a $3.4 million jury verdict against Dial Corp. Dial allegedly rejected 52 women for entry-level jobs at a meat processing plant because they failed strength tests, although strength was not a job requirement. "Eighth Circuit OKs $3.4 Million EEOC Verdict Relating to Pre-Hire Strength Testing Rules," *BNA Bulletin to Management* (November 28, 2006): 377.

74. "Eleventh Circuit Explains Disparate Impact, Disparate Treatment," p. 102.

75. The Fair Treatment for Experienced Pilots Act raised commercial pilots' mandatory retirement age from 60 to 65 in 2008. Allen Smith, "Congress Gives Older Pilots a Reprieve," *HR Magazine* (February 2008): 24.

76. http://www.foxnews.com/story/0,2933,517334,00.html, accessed January 7, 2010.

77. *U.S. v. Bethlehem Steel Company,* 3FEP cases 589.
78. *Spurlock v. United Airlines,* 5FEP cases 17.
79. Ledvinka and Gatewood, "EEO Issues with Preemployment Inquiries," 22–26.
80. Anderson and Levin-Epstein, *Primer of Equal Opportunity,* 28.
81. "Many Well-Intentioned HR Policies Hold Legal Headaches, Consultant Says," *BNA Bulletin to Management* (February 17, 2000): 47.
82. Jenessa Shapiro et al., "Expectations of Obese Trainees: How Stigmatized Trainee Characteristics Influence Training Effectiveness," *Journal of Applied Psychology* 92, no. 1 (2007): 239–49. See also Svetlana Shkolnikova, "Weight Discrimination Could Be as Common as Racial Bias," http://www.usatoday.com/news/health/weightloss/2008-05-20-overweight-bias_N.htm, accessed January 21, 2009.
83. "American Airlines, Worldwide Flight Sued by EEOC over Questioning of Applicants," *BNA Fair Employment Practices* (October 12, 2000): 125.
84. "EEOC Weighs Guidance on Use of Criminal Records in Hiring," *BNA Bulletin to Management* (November 20, 2008): 383.
85. Richard Connors, "Law at Work," lawatwork.com/news/applicat.html.
86. This is based on Anderson and Levin-Epstein, *Primer of Equal Opportunity,* 93–97.
87. "EEOC Issues New Enforcement Guidance on Discrimination in Employee Benefits," *BNA Fair Employment Practices* (October 12, 2000): 123.
88. Matthew Miklave, "Sorting Out a Claim of Bias," *Workforce* 80, no. 6 (June 2001): 102–3. Dress codes are a different matter. For example, the U.S. Court of Appeals for the Third Circuit recently upheld the city of Philadelphia's decision to refuse to relax its dress code to permit a female Muslim police officer to wear a headscarf while in uniform. "City Can Bar Muslim Police Woman from Wearing Scarf," *BNA Bulletin to Management* (April 20, 2009): 126.
89. Prudent employers often purchase employment practices liability insurance to insure against some or all of the expenses involved with defending against discrimination, sexual harassment, and wrongful termination type claims. Antone Melton-Meaux, "Maximizing Employment Practices Liability Insurance Coverage," *Compensation & Benefits Review* (May/June 2008): 55–59.
90. In 2007, the U.S. Supreme Court, in *Ledbetter* v. *Goodyear Tire & Rubber Company* held that employees claiming Title VII pay discrimination must file their claims within 180 days of when they first receive the allegedly discriminatory pay. In 2009, Congress formulated and the president signed new legislation enabling employees to file claims anytime, as long as the person is still receiving a paycheck.
91. "High Charging Rate, Record Monetary Results at EEOC," *BNA Bulletin to Management* (November 24, 2009): 375.
92. Timothy Bland, "Sealed Without a Kiss," *HR Magazine* (October 2000): 85–92.
93. "EEOC Has 18 Nationwide, 300 Local Accords with Employers to Mediate Job Bias Claims Charges," *BNA Human Resources Report* (October 13, 2003): H-081.
94. Bland, "Sealed Without a Kiss," 85–92.
95. "Conducting Effective Investigations of Employee Bias Complaints," *BNA Fair Employment Practices* (July 13, 1995): 81.
96. Jonathan Zeigert and Paul Hanges, "Employment Discrimination: The Role of Implicit Attitudes, Motivation, and a Climate for Racial Bias," *Journal of Applied Psychology* 90, no. 3 (2005): 553–62.
97. "Charting the Projections: 2004–2014," *Occupational Outlook Quarterly* (Winter 2005–2006): 48–50; and www.bls.gov/emp/emplabor01.pdf, accessed October 20, 2008.
98. James Coil III and Charles Rice, "Managing Work-Force Diversity in the 90s: The Impact of the Civil Rights Act of 1991," *Employee Relations Law Journal* 18, no. 4 (Spring 1993): 547–65. See also Stephanie Mehta, "What Minority Employees Really Want," *Fortune* (July 10, 2000): 81–88, and "Diversity Is Used as Business Advantage by Three Fourths of Companies, Survey Says," *BNA Bulletin to Management* (November 7, 2006): 355. Writers list race and ethnicity diversity, gender diversity, age diversity, disability diversity, sexual orientation diversity, and cultural and national origin diversity as examples of diversity. Lynn Shore et al., "Diversity in Organizations: Where Are We Now and Where Are We Going?" *Human Resource Management Review* 19 (2009): 117–33.
99. See, for example, Michael Carrell and Everett Mann, "Defining Work-Force Diversity in Public Sector Organizations," *Public Personnel Management* 24, no. 1 (Spring 1995): 99–111; Richard Koonce, "Redefining Diversity," *Training and Development Journal* (December 2001): 22–33; Kathryn Canas and Harris Sondak, *Opportunities and Challenges of Workplace Diversity* (Upper Saddle River, NJ: Pearson, 2008), pp. 3–27.
100. Taylor Cox Jr., *Cultural Diversity in Organizations* (San Francisco: Berrett Kohler, 1993), p. 88.
101. Ibid., p. 64.
102. Ibid., pp. 179–80.
103. J. H. Greenhaus and S. Parasuraman, "Job Performance Attributions and Career Advancement Prospects: An Examination of Gender and Race Affects," *Organizational Behavior and Human Decision Processes* 55 (July 1993): 273–98.
104. Madeleine Heilmann and Lewis Saruwatari, "When Beauty Is Beastly: The Effects of Appearance and Sex on Evaluation of Job Applicants for Managerial and Nonmanagerial Jobs," *Organizational Behavior and Human Performance* (June 1979): 360–72. See also Tracy McDonald and Milton Hakel, "Effects of Applicant Race, Sex, Suitability, and Answers on Interviewer's Questioning Strategy and Ratings," *Personnel Psychology* (Summer 1985): 321–34.
105. Patrick McKay et al., "A Tale of Two Climates: Diversity Climate from Subordinates and Managers Perspectives and Their Role in Store Unit Sales Performance," *Personnel Psychology* 62 (2009): 767–91.
106. David Thomas, "Diversity as Strategy," *Harvard Business Review* (September 2004): 98–104. See also J. T. Childs Jr., "Managing Global Diversity at IBM: A Global HR Topic that Has Arrived," *Human Resource Management* 44, no. 1 (Spring 2005): 73–77.
107. Ibid., p. 99.

108. As another example, leaders who facilitated high levels of power sharing within their groups helped to reduce the frequently observed positive relationship between increased diversity and increase turnover. But leaders who were inclusive of only a select few followers "may actually exacerbate the relationship between diversity and turnover" (p. 1422). Lisa Nishii and David Mayer, "Do Inclusive Leaders Help to Reduce Turnover in Diverse Groups? The Moderating Role of a Leader-Member Exchange in the Diversity to Turn Over Relationship," *Journal of Applied Psychology* 94, no. 6 (2009): 1412–26.

109. Patricia Digh, "Creating a New Balance Sheet: The Need for Better Diversity Metrics," *Mosaics, Society for Human Resource Management* (September/October 1999): 1. For diversity management steps, see Taylor Cox Jr., *Cultural Diversity in Organizations: Theory, Research and Practice* (San Francisco: Berrett-Koehler, 1993), p. 236; see also Richard Bucher, *Diversity Consciousness: Opening Our Minds to People, Cultures, and Opportunities* (Upper Saddle River, NJ: Pearson Prentice Hall, 2004), pp. 109–37.

110. Ibid., pp. 132–33.

111. Ibid., p. 133.

112. Frank Jossi, "Reporting Race," *HR Magazine* (September 2000): 87–94.

113. U.S. Equal Employment Opportunity Commission, *Affirmative Action and Equal Employment* (Washington, DC: Author, January 1974). See also David Kravitz and Steven Klineberg, "Reactions to Two Versions of Affirmative-Action among Whites, Blacks, and Hispanics," *Journal of Applied Psychology* 85, no. 4 (2000): 597–611.

114. Coil and Rice, "Managing Work-Force Diversity in the 90s," 548.

115. Ibid., pp. 562–63.

116. David Harrison et al., "Understanding Attitudes Toward Affirmative Action Programs in Employment: Summary and Meta-Analysis of 35 Years of Research," *Journal of Applied Psychology* 91, no. 5 (2006): 1031–36.

117. http://newsfeedresearcher.com/data/articles_n17/tests-city-court.html, accessed April 24, 2009.

Chapter 3

1. "Help Wanted—And Found," *Fortune* (October 2, 2006): 40; http://www.cakecareers.com/, accessed March 25, 2009.

2. Frederick Morgenson and Michael Campion, "Accuracy in Job Analysis: Toward an Inference Based Model," *Journal of Organizational Behavior* 21, no. 7 (November 2000): 819–27. See also Frederick Morgenson and Stephen Humphrey, "The Work Design Questionnaire (WDQ): Developing and Validating a Comprehensive Measure for Assessing Job Design and the Nature of Work," *Journal of Applied Psychology* 91, no. 6 (2006): 1321–39; and "Job Analysis," http://www.paq.com/index.cfm?Fuse Action=bulletins.job-analysis, accessed February 3, 2009.

3. One writer recently called job analysis "the hub of virtually all human resource management activities necessary for the successful functioning organizations." See Parbudyal Singh, "Job Analysis for a Changing Workplace," *Human Resource Management Review* 18 (2008): 87.

4. See also T. A. Stetz et al., "New Tricks for an Old Dog: Visualizing Job Analysis Results," *Public Personnel Management* 38, no. 1 (Spring 2009): 91–100.

5. Erik Dirdorff and Mark Wilson, "A Meta Analysis of Job Analysis Reliability," *Journal of Applied Psychology* 88, no. 4 (2003): 635–46.

6. Darin Hartley, "Job Analysis at the Speed of Reality," *Training and Development* (September 2004): 20–22.

7. Arthur Martinez et al., "Job Title Inflation," *Human Resource Management Review* 18 (2008): 19–27.

8. Frederick Morgeson et al., "Self Presentation Processes in Job Analysis: A Field Experiment Investigating Inflation in Abilities, Tasks, and Competencies," *Journal of Applied Psychology* 89, no. 4 (November 2004): 674–86.

9. Ibid., p. 674.

10. Roni Reiter-Palmon et al., "Development of an O*Net Web Based Job Analysis and Its Implementation in the U.S. Navy: Lessons Learned," *Human Resource Management Review* 16 (2006): 294–309.

11. Ibid., p. 294.

12. Matthew Mariani, "Replaced with a Data-Base: O*NET Replaces the *Dictionary of Occupational Titles*," *Occupational Outlook Quarterly* (Spring 1999): 3–9.

13. See, for example, Christelle Lapolice et al., "Linking O'Net Descriptors to Occupational Literacy Requirements Using Job Component Validation," *Personnel Psychology* 61 (2008): 405–41.

14. "OMB, Federal Agencies Set to Update Job Descriptions for All Workers in 2010," *BNA Bulletin to Management* (March 10, 2009): 73.

15. Ibid., p. 18.

16. Gary Dessler, *Human Resource Management*, 9th ed. (Upper Saddle River, NJ: Prentice Hall, 2002), pp. 64–76.

17. Michael Esposito, "There's More to Writing Job Descriptions than Complying with the ADA," *Employee Relations Today* (Autumn 1992): 279.

18. Deborah Kearney, *Reasonable Accommodations: Job Descriptions in the Age of ADA, OSHA, and Workers Comp* (New York: Van Nostrand Reinhold, 1994), p. 9.

19. Steven Hunt, "Generic Work Behavior: An Investigation into the Dimensions of Entry-Level, Hourly Job Performance," *Personnel Psychology* 49 (1996): 51–83.

20. Jeffrey Shippmann et al., "The Practice of Competency Modeling," *Personnel Psychology* 53, no. 3 (2000): 703.

21. Ibid. For a good comparison of competency modeling and job analysis, see Juan Sanchez and Edward Levine, "What Is (or Should Be) the Difference between Competency Modeling and Traditional Job Analysis?" *Human Resource Management Review* 19 (2009): 53–63.

22. See, for example, Carol Spicer, "Building a Competency Model," *HR Magazine* (April 2009): 34–36.

23. Carolyn Hirschman, "Putting Forecasting in Focus," HR Magazine (March 2007): 44–49.
24. Michael Laff, "Talent Management: From Hire to Retire," *Training & Development* (November 2006): 42–48.
25. "More Companies Turn to Workforce Planning to Boost Productivity and Efficiency," the Conference Board, press release/news, August 7, 2006; Carolyn Hirschman, "Putting Forecasting in Focus," *HR Magazine* (March 2007): 44–49.
26. See, for example, Fay Hansen, "The Long View," *Workforce Management* (April 20, 2008): 1, 14.
27. Chaman Jain and Mark Covas, "Thinking about Tomorrow: Seven Tips for Making Forecasting More Effective," *Wall Street Journal* (July 7, 2008): R10.
28. Based on an idea in Elmer H. Burack and Robert D. Smith, *Personnel Management: A Human Resource Systems Approach* (St. Paul, MN: West, 1997), pp. 134–35.
29. For a recent discussion, see, for example, "Pitfalls Abound for Employers Lacking Electronic Information Retention Policies," *BNA Bulletin to Management* (January 1, 2008): 1–2.
30. "Traditional Security Insufficient to Halt File-Sharing Threat," *BNA Bulletin to Management* (January 29, 2008): 39.
31. This is a modification of a definition found in Peter Wallum, "A Broader View of Succession Planning," *Personnel Management* (September 1993): 45. See also Michelle Harrison et al., "Effective Succession Planning," *Training & Development* (October 2006): 22–23.
32. Ibid., pp. 43–44. See also "Succession Planning: A Never-Ending Process that Must Mesh with Talent Management," *HR Focus* 84, no. 5 (May 2007): 8.
33. Bill Roberts, "Matching Talent with Tasks," *HR Magazine* (November 2002): 91–96.
34. Ibid.
35. See, for example, "HR's Insight into the Economy," *Society for Human Resource Management Workplace Visions* 4 (2008): 5. See also D. Mattioli, "Only the Employed Need Apply," *Wall Street Journal* (Eastern Edition) (June 30, 2009): D1.
36. Benjamin Wright, "Employment, Trends, and Training in Information Technology," *Occupational Outlook Quarterly* (Spring 2009): 34–36.
37. Tony Carnevale, "The Coming Labor and Skills Shortage," *Training and Development* (January 2005): 36–41. "Report Says More Companies Focus on Workforce Planning to Heighten Productivity," *Training & Development* (October 2006): 10–12.
38. Tom Porter, "Effective Techniques to Attract, Hire, and Retain 'Top Notch' Employees for Your Company," *San Diego Business Journal* 21, no. 13 (March 27, 2000): B36.
39. Greet van Hoye and Filip Lievens, "Tapping the Grapevine: A Closer Look at Word-of-Mouth as a Recruitment Source," *Journal of Applied Psychology* 94, no. 2 (2009): 341–52.
40. Jonathan Segal, "Land Executives, Not Lawsuits," *HR Magazine* (October 2006): 123–30.
41. Susan Ladika, "Unwelcome Changes," *HR Magazine* (February 2005): 83–90.
42. Kevin Carlson et al., "Recruitment Evaluation: The Case for Assessing the Quality of Applicants Attracted," *Personnel Psychology* 55 (2002): 461–90.

For a recent survey of recruiting source effectiveness, see "The 2007 Recruiting Metrics and Performance Benchmark Report, 2nd ed.," Staffing.org, Inc., 2007.
43. Ibid., p. 120.
44. Arthur R. Pell, *Recruiting and Selecting Personnel* (New York: Regents, 1969), pp. 10–12.
45. Jonathan Segal, "Strings Attached," *HR Magazine* (February 2005): 119–23.
46. See, for example, C. Fernandez-Araoz et al., "The Definitive Guide to Recruiting in Good Times and Bad," *Harvard Business Review*, 87 no. 5 (May 2009): 74–84.
47. J. De Avila, "Beyond Job Boards: Targeting the Source," *Wall Street Journal* (Eastern Edition) (July 2, 2009): D1, D5.
48. "Help Wanted—And Found," *Fortune* (October 2, 2006): 40.
49. James Breaugh, "Employee Recruitment: Current Knowledge and Important Areas for Future Research," *Human Resource Management Review* 18 (2008): 114.
50. Ibid., p. 111.
51. H. Jack Walker et al., "Displaying Employee Testimonials on Recruitment Websites: Effects of Communication Media, Employee Race, and Jobseeker Race on Organizational Attraction and Information Credibility," *Journal of Applied Psychology* 94, no. 5 (2009): 1354–64.
52. Jessica Marquez, "A Global Recruiting Site Helps Far-Flung Managers at the Professional Services Company Acquire the Talent They Need—And Saves One Half-Million Dollars a Year," *Workforce Management* (March 13, 2006): 22.
53. See, for example, Rita Zeigner, "Strategies for Saving in a Down Economy," *HR Magazine* (February 2009): 31.
54. Jennifer Taylor Arnold, "Recruiting on the Run," *HR Magazine* (February 2010): 65–67.
55. Jennifer Berkshire, "Social Network Recruiting," *HR Magazine* (April 2005): 95–98. See also S. DeKay, "Are Business-Oriented Social Networking Web Sites Useful Resources for Locating Passive Jobseekers? Results of a Recent Study," *Business Communication Quarterly* 72, no. 1 (March 2009): 101–5.
56. James Breaugh, "Employee Recruitment: Current Knowledge and Important Areas for Future Research," *Human Resource Management Review* 18 (2008): 114.
57. Ed Frauenheim, "Logging off of Job Boards," *Workforce Management* (June 20, 2009): 25–27.
58. Jennifer Arnold, "Twittering at Face Booking While They Were," *HR Magazine* (December 2009): 54.
59. "ResumePal: Recruiter's Friend?" *Workforce Management* (June 20, 2009): 28.
60. Dawn Onley, "Improving Your Online Application Process," *HR Magazine* 50, no. 10 (October 2005): 109.
61. Martha Frase-Blunt, "Make a Good First Impression," *HR Magazine* (April 2004): 81–86. See also "Corporate Recruiting Web Sites Luring Workers, but Could Be Improved, Experts Say," *BNA Bulletin to Management* (March 14, 2006): 81–82.
62. Laura Romei, "Human Resource Management Systems Keep Computers Humming," *Managing Office Technology* (November 1994): 45.

63. Furthermore, strictly speaking, employers are supposed to track applicants' race, sex, and ethnic group. But many Internet applicants don't aim at specific jobs. Are these "applicants" under EEOC rules? Probably not. The EEOC says that an "applicant" must apply for a specific advertised job, and follow the employer's standard application procedure. "EEOC Issues Much Delayed Definition of 'Applicant,'" *HR Magazine* (April 2004): 29; Valerie Hoffman and Greg Davis, "OFCCP's Internet Applicant Definition Requires Overhaul of Recruitment and Hiring Policies," *Legal Report, the Society for Human Resource Management* (January/February 2006): 2.

64. Jim Meade, "Where Did They Go?" *HR Magazine* (September 2000): 81–84.

65. Note that the U.S. Department of Labor's office of federal contract compliance programs recently announced it would review federal contractors' online application tracking systems to ensure they're providing equal opportunity to qualify prospective applicants with disabilities. "Feds Want a Look at Online Job Sites," *HR Magazine* (November 2008): 12.

66. "E-recruiting Software Providers," *Workforce Management* (June 22, 2009): 14.

67. Robert Bogner Jr. and Elizabeth Salasko, "Beware the Legal Risks of Hiring Temps," *Workforce* (October 2002): 50–57.

68. Fay Hansen, "A Permanent Strategy for Temporary Hires," *Workforce Management* (February 26, 2007): 27.

69. Carolyn Hirschman, "Are Your Contractors Legal?" *HR Magazine* (March 2004): 59–63.

70. See, for example, Stephenie Overman, "Searching for the Top," *HR Magazine* (January 2008): 49.

71. Stephen Miller, "Collaboration Is Key to Effective Outsourcing," *HR Magazine* (December 2007): 58, 60–61.

72. See G. Anders, "Secrets of the Talent Scouts," *New York Times* (Late New York Edition) (March 15, 2009): 1, 7 (Sec 3).

73. "In Negotiating Game, Most Recruiters Hold Back, Knowing Few Candidates Hold Out for Better Offer," *BNA Bulletin to Management* (2000): 291.

74. See, for example, James Breaugh, "Employee Recruitment: Current Knowledge and Important Areas for Future Research," *Human Resource Management Review* 18 (2008): 111.

75. "Internships Growing in Popularity among Companies Seeking Fresh Talent and Ideas," *BNA Bulletin to Management* (March 20, 2007): 89–90; Gerard Beenen and Denise Rousseau, "Getting the Most from MBA Internships: Promoting Intern Learning and Job Acceptance," *Human Resource Management* 49, no. 1 (January/February 2010): 19.

76. Lisa Munniksma, "Career Matchmakers," *HR Magazine* (February 2005): 93–96.

77. Joel Mullich, "Finding the Schools that Yield the Best Job Applicant ROI," *Workforce Management* (March 2004): 67–68.

78. Donna Owens, "College Recruiting in a Downturn," *HR Magazine* (April 2009): 52.

79. See for example, "Economics of Offshoring Shifting, as Some Reconsider Ventures," *BNA Bulletin to Management* (September 23, 2008): 311.

80. Breaugh, "Employee Recruitment," 109.

81. Recruitment source has a significant effect on reducing turnover. Studies suggest that individuals recruited through personal recruitment sources such as employee referral programs are less likely to terminate their employment early. As a researcher says: "On the basis of the findings of this study, organizations suffering from high levels of premature turnover will likely benefit most from implementing and institutionalizing referral in rehiring practices" (p. 1157). Ingo Weller et al., "Level and Time Effects of Recruitment Sources on Early Voluntary Turnover," *Journal of Applied Psychology* 94, no. 5 (2009): 1146–62

82. Michelle Martinez, "The Headhunter Within," *HR Magazine* (August 2001): 48–56.

83. Bill Roberts, "Manage Candidates Right from the Start," *HR Magazine* (October 2008): 73–76.

84. Michael Zottoli and John Wanous, "Recruitment Source Research: Current Status and Future Directions," *Human Resource Management Review* 10 (November 4, 2000): 353–82.

85. Jennifer Taylor Arnold, "Customers as Employees," *HR Magazine* (April 2007): 77–82.

86. Martha Frase-Blunt, "Call Centers Come Home," *HR Magazine* (January 2007): 85–90.

87. "Help Wanted—And Found," *Fortune* (October 2, 2006): 40.

88. Theresa Minton-Eversole, "Mission: Recruitment," *HR Magazine* (January 2009): 43–45.

89. Derek Avery and Patrick McKay, "Target Practice: An Organizational Impression Management Approach to Attracting Minority and Female Job Applicants," *Personnel Psychology* 59 (2006): 157–89, 177.

90. Daniel Newman and Julia Lyon, "Recruitment Efforts to Reduce Adverse Impact: Targeted Recruiting for Personality, Cognitive Ability, and Diversity," *Journal of Applied Psychology* 94, no. 2 (2009): 298–317.

91. Phaedra Brotherton, "Tapping into an Older Workforce," *Mosaics, Society for Human Resource Management* (March/April 2000). See also Thomas Ng and Daniel Feldman, "The Relationship of Age to Ten Dimensions of Job Performance," *Journal of Applied Psychology* 93, no. 2 (2008): 392–423.

92. "Older Workers Valued but Hard to Find, Employers Say," *BNA Bulletin to Management* (April 30, 1998): 129–34.

93. Gary Adams and Barbara Rau, "Attracting Retirees to Apply: Desired Organizational Characteristics of Bridge Employment," *Journal of Organizational Behavior* 26, no. 6 (September 2005): 649–60.

94. Sue Shellenbarger, "Firms Try Harder, but Often Fail to Help Workers Cope with Elder Care Problems," *Wall Street Journal* (June 23, 1993): B1. See also Robert Grossman, "Keep Pace with Older Workers," *HR Magazine* (May 2008): 39–46.

95. Judith Casey and Marci Pitt-Catsouphes, "Employed Single Mothers: Balancing Job and Home Life," *Employee Assistance Quarterly* 9, no. 3/4 (1994): 37–53.

96. Ibid., p. 48.

97. Jessica Marquez, "Tailor Made Careers," *Workforce Management* (January 2010): 16–18.

98. Ibid.

99. Scott Graham, "Hospitals Recruiting Overseas," *Baltimore Business Journal* (June 1, 2001): 1.

100. Jennifer Laabs, "Recruiting in the Global Village," *Workforce* (Spring 1998): 30–33.

101. Ibid. See also Helen Deresky, *International Management* (Upper Saddle River, NJ: Pearson Prentice Hall, 2008), pp. 354–55.

102. Rong Ma and David Allen, "Recruiting across Cultures: A Value-Based Model of Recruitment," *Human Resource Management Review* 19 (2009): 334–46.

103. Allison Wellner, "Welcoming Back Mom," *HR Magazine* (June 2004): 77–78.

104. Herbert Greenberg, "A Hidden Source of Talent," *HR Magazine* (March 1997): 88–91.

105. "Welfare-to-Work: No Easy Chore," *BNA Bulletin to Management* (February 13, 1997): 56.

106. Linda Moore, "Firms Need to Improve Recruitment, Hiring of Disabled Workers, EEO Chief Says," *Knight Ridder/Business News* (November 2003): Item 03309094. See also "Recruiting Disabled More than Good Deed, Experts Say," *BNA Bulletin to Management* (February 27, 2007): 71.

107. Murray Barrick and Ryan Zimmerman, "Hiring for Retention and Performance," *Human Resource Management* 48, no. 2 (March/April 2009): 183–206.

108. J. Craig Wallace et al., "Applying for Jobs Online: Examining the Legality of Internet-Based Application Forms," *Public Personnel Management* 20, no. 4 (Winter 2000): 497–504.

109. *Ryan's Family Steakhouse Inc.* v. *Floss*, "Supreme Court Let Stand Decision Finding Prehire Arbitration Agreements Unenforceable," *BNA Bulletin to Management* (January 11, 2001): 11.

110. Douglas Mahoney et al., "The Effects of Mandatory Employment Arbitration Systems on Applicants' Attraction to Organizations," *Human Resource Management* 44, no. 4 (Winter 2005): 449–70.

111. Kathy Gurchiek, "Video Resumes Spark Curiosity, Questions," *HR Magazine* (May 2007): 28–30; and "Video Resumes Can Illuminate Applicants Abilities, but Pose Discrimination Concerns," *BNA Bulletin to Management* (May 29, 2007): 169–70.

112. Scott Erker, "What Does Your Hiring Process Say about You?" *Training & Development* (May 2007): 67–70.

Appendix

1. Note that the PAQ (and other quantitative techniques) can also be used for job evaluation, which is explained in Chapter 7, http://www.paq.com/index.cfm?FuseAction=bulletins.job-analysis, accessed February 3, 2009.

2. Organization chart software vendors include Nakisa, Aquire, and HumanConcepts. See "Advanced Org Charting," *Workforce Management* (May 19, 2008): 34.

3. David Shair, "Wizardry Makes Charts Relevant," *HR Magazine* (April 2000): 127.

Chapter 4

1. Kevin Delaney, "Google Adjusts Hiring Process as Needs Grow," *Wall Street Journal* (October 23, 2006): B1, B8; http://googleblog.blogspot.com/2009/01/changes-to-recruiting.html, accessed March 25, 2009.

2. See Rebecca Bennett and Sandra Robinson, "Development of a Measure of Workplace Deviance," *Journal of Applied Psychology* 85, no. 3 (2000): 349.

3. For an example, see C. Tuna et al., "Job-Test Ruling Cheers Employers," *Wall Street Journal* (July 1, 2009): B1–2.

4. "Wal-Mart to Scrutinize Job Applicants," *CNN Money* (August 12, 2004), http://money.cnn.com/2004/08/12/News/fortune500/walmart_jobs/index.htm, accessed August 8, 2005.

5. Fay Hansen, "Taking 'Reasonable' Action to Avoid Negligent Hiring Claims," *Workforce Management* (September 11, 2006): 31.

6. Anne Anastasi, *Psychological Patterns* (New York: Macmillan, 1968). See also Kevin Murphy and Charles David Shafer, *Psychological Testing* (Upper Saddle River, NJ: Prentice Hall, 2001), pp. 108–24.

7. Robert M. Guion, "Changing Views for Personnel Selection Research," *Personnel Psychology* 40, no. 2 (Summer 1987): 199–213. The Standards for Educational and Psychological Testing define validity as "the degree to which accumulated evidence and theories support specific interpretations of test scores entailed by proposed uses of a test." Deborah Whetzel and Michael McDaniel, "Situational Judgment Tests: An Overview of Current Research," *Human Resource Management Review* 19 (2009): 191.

8. http://www.siop.org/workplace/employment%20testing/information_to_consider_when_cre.aspx, accessed March 22, 2009.

9. "Hiring Based on Strength Test Discriminates against Women," *BNA Bulletin to Management* (February 22, 2005): 62.

10. Brad Bushman and Gary Wells, "Trait Aggressiveness and Hockey Penalties: Predicting Hot Tempers on the Ice," *Journal of Applied Psychology* 83, no. 6 (1998): 969–74.

11. "One-Third of Job Applicants Flunked Basic Literacy and Math Tests Last Year, American Management Association Survey Finds," American Management Association, www.amanet.org/press/amanews/bjp2001.htm, accessed January 11, 2008.

12. Scott Hayes, "Kinko's Dials into Automated Applicants Screening," *Workforce* 78, no. 11 (November 1999): 71–73; Note that the U.S. Department of Labor recently reminded federal contractors that even if they use a third party to prepare an employment test, the contractors themselves are "ultimately responsible" for ensuring the tests' job relatedness and EEO compliance. "DOL Officials Discuss Contractors' Duties on Validating Tests," *BNA Bulletin to Management* (September 4, 2007): 287. Furthermore, the EEOC and federal contract compliance office are increasing their scrutiny of employers who rely on tests and screening. See "Litigation Increasing with Employer Reliance on Tests, Screening," *BNA Bulletin to Management* (April 8, 2008): 119.

13. For some other examples, see William Shepherd, "Increasing Profits by Assessing Employee Work Styles," *Employment Relations Today* 32, no. 1 (Spring 2005): 19–23; and Eric Krell, "Personality Counts," *HR Magazine* (November 2005): 47–52.

14. Kevin Hart, "Not Wanted: Thieves," *HR Magazine* (April 2008): 119.
15. Sarah Needleman, "Businesses Say Theft by Their Workers Is Up," *Wall Street Journal* (December 11, 2008): B8.
16. Sarah Gale, "Three Companies Cut Turnover with Tests," *Workforce* (April 2002): 66–69.
17. William Wagner, "All Skill, No Finesse," *Workforce* (June 2000): 108–16. See also, for example, James Diefendorff and Kajal Mehta, "The Relations of Motivational Traits with Workplace Deviance," *Journal of Applied Psychology* 92, no. 4 (2007): 967–77.
18. Toddi Gutner, "Applicants' Personalities Put to the Test," *Wall Street Journal* (August 20, 2008): D4.
19. See, for example, Douglas Cellar et al., "Comparison of Factor Structures and Criterion-Related Validity Coefficients for Two Measures of Personality Based on the Five Factor Model," *Journal of Applied Psychology* 81, no. 6 (1996): 694–704; Joyce Hogan et al., "Personality Measurement, Faking, and Employee Selection," *Journal of Applied Psychology* 92, no. 5 (2007): 1270–85.
20. Murray Barrick and Michael Mount, "The Big Five Personality Dimensions and Job Performance: A Meta Analysis," *Personnel Psychology* 44, no. 1 (Spring 1991): 1–26. See also Robert Schneider, Leatta Hough, and Marvin Dunnette, "Broad-Sided by Broad Traits: How to Sink Science in Five Dimensions or Less," *Journal of Organizational Behavior* 17, no. 6 (November 1996): 639–55. See also Paula Caligiuri, "The Big Five Personality Characteristics as Predictors of Expatriate's Desire to Terminate the Assignment and Supervisor Rated Performance," *Personnel Psychology* 53 (2000): 67–68; Timothy Judge and Amir Erez, "Interaction and Intersection: The Constellation of Emotional Stability and Extroversion in Predicting Performance," *Personnel Psychology* 60 (2007): 573–96; and Ryan Zimmerman, "Understanding the Impact of Personality Traits on Individuals' Turnover Decisions: A Meta-Analytic Path Model," *Personnel Psychology* 60, no. 1 (2008): 309–48. A review of personality testing reached several conclusions. Employers are increasingly using personality tests. The weight of evidence is that personality measures (particularly the big five) contribute to predicting job performance. And employers can reduce personality test faking by warning applicants that faking may reduce the chances of being hired. Mitchell Rothstein and Richard Goffin, "The Use of Personality Measures in Personnel Selection: What Does Current Research Support?" *Human Resource Management Review* 16 (2006): 155–80.
21. Frederick Morgeson et al., "Reconsidering the Use of Personality Tests in Personnel Selection Contexts," *Personnel Psychology* 60 (2007): 683.
22. Frederick Morgeson et al., "Are We Getting Fooled Again? Coming to Terms with Limitations in the Use of Personality Tests for Personnel Selection," *Personnel Psychology* 60 (2007): 1046.
23. Robert Tett and Neil Christiansen, "Personality Tests at the Crossroads: A Response to Morgeson, Campion, Dipboye, Hollenbeck, Murphy, and Schmitt (2007)," *Personnel Psychology* 60 (2007): 967.

See also Deniz Ones et al., "In Support of Personality Assessment in Organizational Settings," *Personnel Psychology* 60 (2007): 995–1027.
24. See, for example, W. A. Scroggins et al., "Psychological Testing in Personnel Selection, Part III: The Resurgence of Personality Testing," *Public Personnel Management* 38, no. 1 (Spring 2009): 67–77. Part of the problem with self-report personality tests is that some applicants will see through to the aim of the test and provide answers they think the employer is looking for (they "fake" the test). The problem here, of course, is that less-worthy candidates may actually succeed in earning higher test scores than more-worthy candidates. In one study, researchers extensively studied this question. They concluded that one way to minimize the effects of faking was to compute "pass fail" cut points by having nonapplicants such as supervisors and existing employees take the test (rather than applicants). It remains a tricky problem, however. Christopher Berry and Paul Sackett, "Faking in Personnel Selection: Trade-Offs in Performance versus Fairness Resulting from Two Cut Score Strategies," *Personnel Psychology* 62 (2009): 835–63.
25. Paula Caliguri, "The Big Five Personality Characteristics as Predictors of Expatriates' Desire to Terminate the Assignment and Supervisor-Rated Performance," *Personnel Psychology* 53, no. 1 (Spring 2000): 67–88.
26. Gretchen Spreitzer, Morgan McCall, Jr., and Joan Mahoney, "Early Identification of International Executive Potential," *Journal of Applied Psychology* 82, no. 1 (February 1997).
27. Jan Selmer, "Expatriation: Corporate Policy, Personal Intentions and International Adjustment," *International Journal of Human Resource Management* 9, no. 6 (December 1998): 997–1007.
28. Winfred Arthur Jr. and Winston Bennett Jr., "The International Assignee: The Relative Importance of Factors Perceived to Contribute to Success," *Personnel Psychology* 48 (1995): 110; see also, Gretchen Spreitzer, Morgan McCall Jr., and Joan Mahoney, "Early Identification of International Executive Potential," *Journal of Applied Psychology* 82, no. 1 (1997): 62–69; Handan Kepir Sinangil and Deniz Ones, "Expatriate Management," in Neil Anderson, Deniz Ones,; Handan Kepir Sinangil, and Chockalingam Viswesvaran (eds.), *Handbook of Industrial, Work and Organizational Psychology*, vol. 1: *Personnel Psychology* (Thousand Oaks, CA: Sage Publications Ltd, 2002), pp. 424–443; Regina Hechanova, Terry Beehr, and Neil Christiansen, "Antecedents and Consequences of Employees' Adjustment to Overseas Assignment: A Meta-Analytic Review," *Applied Psychology: An International Review* 52, no. 2 (April 2003): 213–236; and Raymond Edward Branton, "A Multifaceted Assessment Protocol for Successful International Assignees," *Dissertation Abstracts International: Section B: The Sciences and Engineering* 64(8B) (2004): 4024.
29. Discussed in Charles Hill, *International Business*, pp. 511–515.
30. Kathryn Tyler, "Put Applicants' Skills to the Test," *HR Magazine* (January 2000): 75–79.
31. Gilbert Nicholson, "Automated Assessments," 102–7.

32. Ibid.

33. Robert Plyhart et al., "Web-Based and Paper-and-Pencil Testing of Applicants in a Proctored Setting: Are Personality, Biodata and Situational Judgment Tests Comparable?" *Personnel Psychology* 56 (2003): 733–52.

34. Denise Potosky and Philip Bob Bobko, "Selection Testing Via the Internet: Practical Considerations and Exploratory Empirical Findings," *Personnel Psychology* 57 (2004): 1025.

35. Laurence Siegel and Irving Lane, *Personnel and Organizational Psychology* (Burr Ridge, IL: McGraw-Hill, 1982), pp. 182–83.

36. However, studies suggest that blacks may be somewhat less likely to do well on work sample tests than whites. See, for example, Philip Roth, Philip Bobko, and Lynn McFarland, "A Meta-Analysis of Work Sample Test Validity: Updating and Integrating Some Classic Literature," *Personnel Psychology* 58, no. 4 (Winter 2005): 1009–37; and Philip Roth et al., "Work Sample Tests in Personnel Selection: A Meta-Analysis of Black-White Differences in Overall and Exercise Scores," *Personnel Psychology* 60, no. 1 (2008): 637–62.

37. See, for example, George Thornton III and Alyssa Gibbons, "Validity of Assessment Centers for Personnel Selection," *Human Resource Management Review* 19 (2009): 169–87.

38. Annette Spychalski, Miguel Quinones, Barbara Gaugler, and Katja Pohley, "A Survey of Assessment Center Practices in Organizations in the United States," *Personnel Management* 50, no. 10 (Spring 1997): 71–90. See also Winfred Arthur Jr. et al., "A Meta Analysis of the Criterion Related Validity of Assessment Center Data Dimensions," *Personnel Psychology* 56 (2003): 124–54.

39. Kobi Dayan et al., "Entry-Level Police Candidate Assessment Center: An Efficient Tool or a Hammer to Kill a Fly?" *Personnel Psychology* 55 (2002): 827–48. See also, for example, John Meriac et al., "Further Evidence for the Validity of Assessment Center Dimensions: A Meta-Analysis of the Incremental Criterion-Related Validity of Dimension Ratings," *Journal of Applied Psychology* 93, no. 5 (2008): 1042–52.

40. Quoted from Deborah Whetzel and Michael McDaniel, "Situational Judgment Tests: An Overview of Current Research," *Human Resource Management Review* 19 (2009): 188–202.

41. Ibid.

42. Michael McDaniel et al., "The Validity of Employment Interviews: A Comprehensive Review and Meta-Analysis," *Journal of Applied Psychology* 79, no. 4 (1994): 599. See also Richard Posthuma et al., "Beyond Employment Interview Validity: A Comprehensive Narrative Review of Recent Research and Trends over Time," *Personnel Psychology* 55 (2002): 1–81. For an argument against holding selection interviews, see D. Heath et al., "Hold the Interview," *Fast Company* no. 136 (June 2009): 51–52.

43. Therese Macan, "The Employment Interview: A Review of Current Studies and Directions for Future Research," *Human Resource Management Review* 19 (2009): 203–18.

44. Ibid., p. 601. See also Allen Huffcutt et al., "Comparison of Situational and Behavior Description Interview Questions for Higher Level Positions," *Personnel Psychology* 54 (Autumn 2001): 619–44; Stephen Maurer, "A Practitioner Based Analysis of Interviewer Job Expertise and Scale Format as Contextual Factors in Situational Interviews," *Personnel Psychology* 55 (2002): 307–27.

45. Bill Stoneman, "Matching Personalities with Jobs Made Easier with Behavioral Interviews," *American Banker* 165, no. 229 (November 30, 2000): 8a.

46. Aparna Nancheria, "Anticipated Growth in Behavioral Interviewing," *Training & Development* (April 2008): 20.

47. "Phone Interviews Might Be the Most Telling, Study Finds," *BNA Bulletin to Management* (September 1998): 273.

48. Susan Strauss et al., "The Effects of Videoconference, Telephone, and Face-to-Face Media on Interviewer and Applicant Judgments in Employment Interviews," *Journal of Management* 27, no. 3 (2001): 363–81. If the employer records a video interview with the intention of sharing it with hiring managers who don't participate in the interview, it's advisable to first obtain the candidates written permission. Matt Bolch, "Lights, Camera . . . Interview!" *HR Magazine* (March 2007): 99–102.

49. Emily Maltby, "To Find the Best Hires, Firms Become Creative," *Wall Street Journal* (November 17, 2009): B6.

50. See, for example, M. M. Harris, "Reconsidering the Employment Interview: A Review of Recent Literature and Suggestions for Future Research," *Personnel Psychology* 42 (1989): 691–726; Richard Posthuma et al., "Beyond Employment Interview Validity: A Comprehensive Narrative Review of Recent Research and Trends over Time," *Personnel Psychology* 55, no. 1 (Spring 2002): 1–81.

51. Timothy Judge et al., "The Employment Interview: A Review of Recent Research and Recommendations for Future Research," *Human Resource Management* 10, no. 4 (2000): 392. There is disagreement regarding the relative superiority of individual versus panel interviews. See, for example, Marlene Dixon et al., "The Panel Interview: A Review of Empirical Research and Guidelines for Practice," *Public Personnel Management* (Fall 2002): 397–428.

52. Frank Schmidt and Ryan Zimmerman, "A Counter-intuitive Hypothesis about Employment Interview Validity and Some Supporting Evidence," *Journal of Applied Psychology* 89, no. 3 (2004): 553–61.

53. The validity discussion and these findings are based on McDaniel et al., "Validity of Employment Interviews," 607–10. See also Robert Dipboye et al., "The Validity of Unstructured Panel Interviews," *Journal of Business & Strategy* 16, no. 1 (Fall 2001): 35–49; Marlene Dixon et al., "The Panel Interview: A Review of Empirical Research and Guidance," *Public Personnel Management* 3, no. 3 (Fall 2002): 397–428; and Todd Maurer and Jerry Solamon, "The Science and Practice of a Structured Employment Interview Coaching Program," *Personnel Psychology* 59 (2006): 433–56.

54. McDaniel et al., "Validity of Employment Interviews," 608.

55. Anita Chaudhuri, "Beat the Clock: Applying for a Job? A New Study Shows that Interviewers Will

Make up Their Minds about You Within a Minute," *The Guardian* (June 14, 2000): 2–6.

56. Don Langdale and Joseph Weitz, "Estimating the Influence of Job Information on Interviewer Agreement," *Journal of Applied Psychology* 57 (1973): 23–27.

57. R. E. Carlson, "Selection Interview Decisions: The Effects of Interviewer Experience, Relative Quota Situation, and Applicant Sample on Interview Decisions," *Personnel Psychology* 20 (1967): 259–80.

58. R. E. Carlson, "Effects of Applicant Sample on Ratings of Valid Information in an Employment Setting," *Journal of Applied Psychology* 54 (1970): 217–22.

59. See, for example, Scott Fleischmann, "The Messages of Body Language in Job Interviews," *Employee Relations* 18, no. 2 (Summer 1991): 161–76. See also James Westpall and Ithai Stern, "Flattery Will Get You Everywhere (Especially if You're a Male Caucasian): How Ingratiation, Board Room Behavior, and a Demographic Minority Status Affect Additional Board Appointments at U.S. Companies," *Academy of Management Journal* 50, no. 2 (2007): 267–88.

60. Tim DeGroot and Stephen Motowidlo, "Why Visual and Vocal Interview Cues Can Affect Interviewer's Judgments and Predicted Job Performance," *Journal of Applied Psychology* (December 1999): 968–84.

61. David Caldwell and Jerry Burger, "Personality Characteristics of Job Applicants and Success in Screening Interviews," *Personnel Psychology* 51 (1998): 119–36.

62. Amy Kristof-Brown et al., "Applicant Impression Management: Dispositional Influences and Consequences for Recruiter Perceptions of Fit and Similarity," *Journal of Management* 28, no. 1 (2002): 27–46. See also Linda McFarland et al., "Impression Management Use and Effectiveness Across Assessment Methods," *Journal of Management* 29, no. 5 (2003): 641–61.

63. See, for example, Cynthia Marlowe, Sondra Schneider, and Carnot Nelson, "Gender and Attractiveness Biases in Hiring Decisions: Are More Experienced Managers Less Biased?" *Journal of Applied Psychology* 81, no. 1 (1996): 11–21; see also Shari Caudron, "Why Job Applicants Hate HR," *Workforce* (June 2002): 36.

64. Marlowe et al., "Gender and Attractiveness Biases in Hiring Decisions," 11.

65. Ibid., p. 18. See also Timothy Judge, Charlice Hurst, and Lauren Simon, "Does It Pay to Be Smart, Attractive, or Confident (or All Three)? Relationships among General Mental Ability, Physical Attractiveness, Core Self-Evaluations, and Income," *Journal of Applied Psychology* 94, no. 3 (2009): 742–55.

66. Emily Duehr and Joyce Bono, "Men, Women, and Managers: Are Stereotypes Finally Changing?" *Personnel Psychology* 59 (2006): 837.

67. Amelia J. Prewett-Livingston et al., "Effects of Race on Interview Ratings in a Situational Panel Interview," *Journal of Applied Psychology* 81, no. 2 (1996): 178–86; see also Richard White Jr., "Ask Me No Questions, Tell Me No Lies: Examining the Uses

and Misuses of the Polygraph," *Public Personnel Management* 30, no. 4 (Winter 2001): 483–93.

68. Chad Higgins and Timothy Judge, "The Effect of Applicant Influence Tactics on Recruiter Perceptions of Fit and Hiring Recommendations: A Field Study," *Journal of Applied Psychology* 89, no. 4 (2004): 622–32.

69. Andrea Rodriguez and Fran Prezant, "Better Interviews for People with Disabilities," *Workforce*, accessed from workforce.com, November 14, 2003.

70. Madeline Heilman and Tyler Okimoto, "Motherhood: A Potential Source of Bias in Employment Decisions," *Journal of Applied Psychology* 93, no. 1 (2008): 189–98.

71. Ibid., p. 196.

72. Williamson et al., "Employment Interview on Trial," 901; Michael Campion, David Palmer, and James Campion, "A Review of Structure in the Selection Interview," *Personnel Psychology* 50 (1997): 655–702.

73. Unless otherwise specified, the following are based on Williamson et al., "Employment Interview on Trial," 901–2.

74. Todd Maurer and Jerry Solamon, "The Science and Practice of a Structured Employment Interview Coaching Program," *Personnel Psychology* 59 (2006): 433–56.

75. Carlson, "Selection Interview Decisions," 259–80.

76. Catherine Middendorf and Therese Macan, "Note Taking in the Employment Interview: Effects on Recall and Judgment," *Journal of Applied Psychology* 87, no. 2 (2002): 293–303.

77. "Looking to Hire the Very Best? Ask the Right Questions. Lots of Them," *Fortune* (June 21, 1999): 192–94.

78. Panel Kaul, "Interviewing Is Your Business," *Association Management* (November 1992): 29. See also Nancy Woodward, "Asking for Salary Histories," *HR Magazine* (February 2000): 109–12. Gathering information about specific interview dimensions such as social ability, responsibility, and independence (as is often done with structured interviews) can improve interview accuracy, at least for more complicated jobs. See also Andrea Poe, "Graduate Work: Behavioral Interviewing Can Tell You if an Applicant Just out of College Has Traits Needed for the Job," *HR Magazine* 48, no. 10 (October 2003): 95–96.

79. These are from Alan M. Saks and Julie M. McCarthy, "Effects of Discriminatory Interview Questions and Gender on Applicant Reactions," *Journal of Business and Psychology* 21, no. 2 (Winter 2006): 175–91.

80. Kristen Weirick, "The Perfect Interview," *HR Magazine* (April 2008): 85.

81. These are quoted or adapted from www.careerfaqs.com.au/getthatjob_video_interview.asp, accessed March 2, 2009.

82. "Are Your Background Checks Balanced? Experts Identify Concerns over Verifications," *BNA Bulletin to Management* (May 13, 2004): 153.

83. Matthew Heller, "Special Report: Background Checking," *Workforce Management* (March 3, 2008): 35.

84. Based on Samuel Greengard, "Have Gangs Invaded Your Workplace?" *Personnel Journal* (February 1996): 47–57; Carroll Lachnit, "Protecting People and Profits with Background Checks," *Workforce* (February 2002): 52.

85. Lachnit, "Protecting People and Profits with Background Checks," 52. See also Robert Howie

and Lawrence Shapero, "Preemployment Criminal Background Checks: Why Employers Should Look Before They Leap," *Employee Relations Law Journal* (Summer 2002): 63–77.

86. Bill Leonard, "Fraud Factories," *HR Magazine* (September 2008): 54–58.

87. See for example, A. M. Forsberg et al., "Perceived Fairness of a Background Information Form and a Job Knowledge Test," *Public Personnel Management* 38, no. 1 (Spring 2009): 33–46.

88. Matthew Heller, "Special Report: Background Checking," *Workforce Management* (March 3, 2008): 35–54.

89. Alan Finder, "When a Risqué Online Persona Undermines a Chance for a Job," *New York Times* (June 11, 2006): 1.

90. "Vetting Via Internet Is Free, Generally Legal, but Not Necessarily Smart Hiring Strategy," *BNA Bulletin to Management* (February 20, 2007): 57–58.

91. Rita Zeidner, "How Deep Can You Probe?" *HR Magazine* (October 1, 2007): 57–62.

92. "Web Searches on Applicants Are Potentially Perilous for Employers," *BNA Bulletin to Management* (October 14, 2008): 335.

93. Ibid., pp. 50 ff.

94. "Employment Related Screening Providers," *Workforce Management* (February 16, 2009): 14.

95. Lachnit, "Protecting People, and Profits with Background Checks," 52.

96. For example, see Lawrence Dube Jr., "Employment References and the Law," *Personnel Journal* 65, no. 2 (February 1986): 87–91. See also Mickey Veich, "Uncover the Resume Ruse," *Security Management* (October 1994): 75–76; Anjali Athavaley, "Job References You Can't Control," *Wall Street Journal* (September 27, 2007): B1.

97. "Undercover Callers Tipoff Job Seekers to Former Employers' Negative References," *BNA Bulletin to Management* (May 27, 1999): 161. See also Diane Cadrain, "Job Detectives Dig Deep for Defamation," *HR Magazine* 49, no. 10 (October 2004): 34 ff.

98. Lachnit, "Protecting People and Profits with Background Checks," 54; Shari Caudron, "Who Are You Really Hiring?" *Workforce* (November 2002): 31.

99. Polygraphs are still widely used in law enforcement and reportedly quite useful. See, for example, Laurie Cohen, "The Polygraph Paradox," *Wall Street Journal* (March 22, 2008): A1.

100. These are based on "Divining Integrity Through Interviews," *BNA Bulletin to Management* (June 4, 1987): 184; and Commerce Clearing House, Ideas and Trends (December 29, 1998): 222–23.

101. John Bernardin and Donna Cooke, "Validity of an Honesty Test in Predicting Theft among Convenience Store Employees," *Academy of Management Journal* 36, no. 5 (1993): 1097–108, and Commerce Clearing House, Ideas and Trends (December 29, 1998): 222–23. Note that some suggest that by possibly signaling mental illness, integrity tests may conflict with the Americans with Disabilities Act, but one review concludes that such tests pose little legal risk to employers. Christopher Berry et al., "A Review of Recent Developments in Integrity Test Research," *Personnel Psychology* 60 (2007): 271–301.

102. Steven Thomas and Steve Vaught, "The Write Stuff: What the Evidence Says about Using Handwriting Analysis in Hiring," *Advanced Management Journal* 66, no. 4 (Autumn 2001): 31–35.

103. Mick Haus, "Pre-Employment Physicals and the ADA," *Safety and Health* (February 1992): 64–65. See also Bridget A. Styers and Kenneth S. Shultz, "Perceived Reasonableness of Employment Testing Accommodations for Persons with Disabilities," *Public Personnel Management* 38, no. 3 (Fall 2009): 71–91.

104. MacDonald et al., "The Limitations of Drug Screening in the Workplace," *International Labor Review* 132, no. 1 (1993): 98. See also Diane Cadrain, "Are Your Employees' Drug Tests Accurate?" *HR Magazine* (January 2003): 40–45.

105. MacDonald et al., "The Limitations of Drug Screening."

106. Ibid.

107. Diane Cadrain, "Are Your Employees' Drug Tests Accurate?" *HR Magazine* (January 2003): 40–45.

108. MacDonald et al., "The Limitations of Drug Screening," 105–6.

109. Lewis Maltby, "Drug Testing: A Bad Investment," *Business Ethics* 15, no. 2 (March 2001): 7.

110. Frank Lockwood et al., "Drug Testing Programs and Their Impact on Workplace Accidents: A Time Series Analysis," *Journal of Individual Employment Rights* 8, no. 4 (2000): 295–306.

111. O'Neill, "Legal Issues Presented by Hair Follicle Testing," 411.

112. Richard Lisko, "A Manager's Guide to Drug Testing," *Security Management* 38, no. 8 (August 1994): 92.

113. *Exxon Corp. v. Esso Workers Union, Inc.*, CA1#96–2241, July 8, 1997; discussed in *BNA Bulletin to Management* (August 7, 1997): 249.

114. Coleman Peterson, "Employee Retention, the Secrets behind Wal-Mart's Successful Hiring Policies," *Human Resource Management* 44, no. 1 (Spring 2005): 85–88. See also Murray Barrick and Ryan Zimmerman, "Reducing Voluntary, Avoidable Turnover Through Selection," *Journal of Applied Psychology* 90, no. 1 (2005): 159–66.

115. James Breaugh, "Employee Recruitment: Current Knowledge and Important Areas for Future Research," *Human Resource Management Review* 18 (2008): 106–7.

116. Lawrence Kellner, "Corner Office," *New York Times* (September 26, 2009), http://projects.nytimes.com/corner-office, accessed April 8, 2010.

117. Note that the acceptable documents on page 3 of the current (as of 2009) I-9 form do not reflect the current list of acceptable documents. For this, refer to the Website of the U.S. Department of Homeland Security. Margaret Fiester et al., "Affirmative Action, Stock Options, I-9 Documents," *HR Magazine* (November 2007): 32.

118. "Conflicting State E-Verify Laws Troubling for Employers," *BNA Bulletin to Management* (November 4, 2008): 359.

119. "President Bush Signs Executive Order: Federal Contractors Must Use E-Verify," *BNA Bulletin to Management* (June 17, 2008): 193. "DHS to Implement E-verify Mandate, Will Strengthen Eligibility Verification, Secretary Says," *BNA Bulletin to Management* (July 14, 2009): 217.

120. Russell Gerbman, "License to Work," *HR Magazine* (June 2000): 151–60. Recently the Department of Homeland Security announced it was inspecting about 652 businesses nationwide as part of its new I-9 audit program. "I-9 Used to Conduct High Nine Audits at 652 Businesses as Focus of Enforcement Ships to Employers," *BNA Bulletin to Management* (July 7, 2009): 211. The employment and training administration agency of the US Department of Labor installed a new system called ICERT to make it easier for employers to receive labor condition applications for the H1B program. "EPA Announces Electronic Portal to Receive Applications for H1B, Perm Certifications," *BNA Bulletin to Management* (April 20, 2009): 123.

121. "As E-Verify, No Match Rules, I-9 Evolve, Employers Need to Stay on Top of Issues," *BNA Bulletin to Management* (April 15, 2008): 121.

122. Actually, there may be other complications too. For example, you may want to decide which of several possible potential jobs is best for your candidate.

123. This is based on Robert Gatewood and Hubert Feild, *Human Resource Selection* (Fort Worth, TX: The Dryden Press, 1994), pp. 278–79.

Chapter 5

1. David Raths, "Virtual Reality in the OR," *Training and Development* (August 2006).

2. For a slide show of a similar training process, see http://www.slideshare.net/magistra12/a-second-life-virtual-clinic-for-medical-student-training-presentation, accessed October 4, 2009.

3. Marjorie Derven, "Management on Boarding," *Training & Development* (April 2008): 49–52.

4. For a good discussion of socialization, see, for example, George Chao et al., "Organizational Socialization: Its Content and Consequences," *Journal of Applied Psychology* 79, no. 5 (1994): 730–43; see also Talya Bauer et al., "Newcomer Adjustment During Organizational Socialization: A Meta-Analytic Review of Antecedents, Outcomes, and Methods," *Journal of Applied Psychology* 92, no. 3 (2007): 707–21.

5. Charlotte Garvey, "The Whirlwind of a New Job," *HR Magazine* (June 2001): 111. See also Talya Bauer et al., "Newcomer Adjustment during Organizational Socialization: A Meta-Analytic Review of Antecedents, Outcomes, and Methods," *Journal of Applied Psychology* 92, no. 3 (2007): 707–21.

6. Sheila Hicks et al., "Orientation Redesign," *Training and Development* (July 2006): 43–46.

7. John Kammeyer-Mueller and Connie Wanberg, "Unwrapping the Organizational Entry Process: Disentangling Multiple Antecedents and Their Pathways to Adjustments," *Journal of Applied Psychology* 88, no. 5 (2003): 779–94.

8. Sabrina Hicks, "Successful Orientation Programs," *Training & Development* (April 2000): 59. See also Howard Klein and Natasha Weaver, "The Effectiveness of an Organizational Level Orientation Program in the Socialization of New Hires," *Personnel Psychology* 53 (2000): 47–66; and Laurie Friedman, "Are You Losing Potential New Hires at Hello?" *Training & Development* (November 2006): 25–27.

9. This section is based on Darin Hartley, "Technology Kicks Up Leadership Development," *Training and Development* (March 2004): 22–24.

10. Ed Frauenheim, "IBM Learning Programs Get a 'Second Life,'" *Workforce Management* (December 11, 2006): 6. See also J. T. Arnold, "Gaming Technology Used to Orient New Hires," *HR Magazine* (2009 HR Trendbook suppl): 36, 38.

11. Brenda Sugrue et al., "What in the World Is WLP?" *Training and Development* (January 2005): 51–54.

12. "Companies Invested More in Training Despite Economic Setbacks, Survey Says," *BNA Bulletin to Management* (March 7, 2002): 73. See also Andrew Paradise, "The 2008 ASTD State of the Industry Report Shows Sustained Support for Corporate Learning," *Training & Development* (November 2008): 45–51.

13. Winfred Alfred Jr. et al., "Effectiveness of Training in Organizations: A Meta Analysis of Design and Evaluation Features," *Journal of Applied Psychology* 88, no. 2 (2003): 242.

14. Christine Ellis and Sarah Gale, "A Seat at the Table," *Training* (March 2001): 90–96.

15. Nancy DeViney and Brenda Sugrue, "Learning Outsourcing: A Reality Check," *Training and Development* (December 2004): 41. See also Rita Smith, "Aligning Learning with Business Strategy," *Training & Development* (November 2008): 41–43; and "How Are Organizations Training Today?" *HR Focus* 86, no. 7 (July 2009): S2–3.

16. Employers increasingly utilize learning content management systems (LCMS) to compile and author training content. See, for example, Bill Perry, "Customized Content at Your Fingertips," *Training & Development* (June 2009): 29–30.

17. Jay Bahlis, "Blueprint for Planning Learning," *Training & Development* (March 2008): 64–67.

18. Marcia Jones, "Use Your Head when Identifying Skills Gaps," *Workforce* (March 2000): 118.

19. P. Nick Blanchard and James Thacker, *Effective Training: Systems, Strategies, and Practices* (Upper Saddle River, NJ: Prentice Hall, 1999), pp. 154–56.

20. Richard Montier et al., "Competency Models Develop Top Performance," *Training and Development* (July 2006): 47–50. See also Jennifer Salopek, "The Power of the Pyramid," *Training & Development* (May 2009): 70–73.

21. Richard Camp et al., *Toward a More Organizationally Effective Training Strategy and Practice* (Upper Saddle River, NJ: Prentice Hall, 1986), p. 100.

22. Kenneth Wexley and Gary Latham, *Development and Training Human Resources in Organizations* (Upper Saddle River, NJ: Prentice Hall, 2002), p. 107.

23. Ibid., p. 82.

24. Ibid., p. 87.

25. Ibid., p. 90.

26. The American Society for Training and Development (ASTD) offers thousands of packaged training programs, such as "Be a Better Manager," "Strategic Planning 101," "12 Habits of Successful Trainers," "Mentoring," and "Using Job Aids." American Society for Training and Development, Spring and Fall Line Catalog 2007; American Society for Training and Development 2007 Buyers Guide, American Society for Training and Development, 1640 King St., Box 1443, Alexandria, VA 22313.

27. See, for example, the HRDQ Winter 2008 catalog, www.HRDQ.com.

28. Donna Goldwaser, "Me a Trainer?" *Training* (April 2001): 60–66.

29. Robert Weintraub and Jennifer Martineau, "The Just in Time Imperative," *Training and Development* (June 2002): 52; and Andrew Paradise, "Informal Learning: Overlooked or Overhyped?" *Training & Development* (July 2008): 52–53.

30. Aparna Nancherla, "Knowledge Delivered in Any Other Form Is . . . Perhaps Sweeter," *Training & Development* (May 2009): 54–60.

31. Harley Frazis et al., "Results from the 1995 Survey of Employer-Provided Training," http://www.bls.gov/mlr/1998/06/art1full.pdf, accessed April 11, 2010.

32. The recession that began around 2008 prompted a downturn in training expenditures. For example, one study estimates that total training spending in U.S. firms dropped from about $56 billion in 2008 to $48 billion in 2009. Garry Kranz, "Study: Training More Targeted Amid Downturn," *Workforce Management* (November 16, 2009): 6.

33. Rita Zeidner, "Strategies for Saving in a Down Economy," *HR Magazine* (February 2009): 33. See also Katharine Giacalone, "Making New Employees Successful in Any Economy," *Training & Development* (June 2009): 37–39.

34. Kathryn Tyler, "Mining for Training Treasure," *HR Magazine* (September 2009): 99–102.

35. Cindy Waxer, "Steelmaker Revives Apprentice Program to Address Graying Workforce, Forge Next Leaders," *Workforce Management* (January 30, 2006): 40.

36. Kermit Kaleba, "New Changes to Apprenticeship Program Could Be Forthcoming," *Training & Development* (February 2008): 14.

37. Paula Ketter, "What Can Training Do for Brown?" *Training & Development* (May 2008): 30–36.

38. Michael Blotzer, "Distance Learning," *Occupational Hazards* (March 2000): 53–54.

39. Michael Emery and Margaret Schubert, "A Trainer's Guide to Videoconferencing," *Training* (June 1993): 60. See also Mark Van Buren, "Learning Technologies: Can They or Can't They?" *Training & Development* (April 2000): 62.

40. For a slide show of a similar training process, see http://www.slideshare.net/magistra12/a-second-life-virtual-clinic-for-medical-student-training-presentation, accessed October 4, 2009.

41. See, for example, Kim Kleps, "Virtual Sales Training Scores a Hit," *Training & Development* (December 2006): 63–64.

42. Dina Berta, "Computer-Based Training Clicks with Both Franchisees and Their Employees," *Nation's Restaurant News* (July 9, 2001): 1, 18; see also "What Do Simulations Cost?" *Training & Development* (June 2007): 88.

43. Michael Laff, "Simulations: Slowly Proving Their Worth," *Training & Development* (June 2007): 30–34.

44. Jenni Jarventaus, "Virtual Threat, Real Sweat," *Training & Development* (May 2007): 72–78.

45. Pat Galagan, "Second That," *Training & Development* (February 2008): 34–37. See also David Wilkins, "Learning 2.0 and Workplace Communities," *Training & Development* (April 2009): 28–31.

46. Traci Sitzmann et al., "The Comparative Effectiveness of Web-Based and Classroom Instruction: A Meta-Analysis," *Personnel Psychology* 59 (2006): 623–64.

47. For a list of guidelines for using e-learning, see, for example, Mark Simon, "E-learning No How," *Training & Development* (January 2009): 34–39.

48. Tom Barron, "A Portrait of Learning Portals," www.learningcircuits.com/may2000/barron.html, accessed 2000. See also Paul Giguere and Jennifer Minotti, "Rethinking Web-Based E-Learning," *Training and Development* (January 2005): 15–16.

49. John Zonneveld, "GM Dealer Training Goes Global," *Training & Development* (December 2006): 47–51.

50. "The Next Generation of Corporate Learning," *Training and Development* (June 2004): 47; and Jennifer Hofmann and Nanatte Miner, "Real Blended Learning Stands Up," *Training & Development* (September 2008): 28–31.

51. Jennifer Taylor Arnold, "Learning on-the-Fly," *HR Magazine* (September 2007): 137. A new Microsoft Word add-on enables someone to convert instantly any Word document into multimedia content that one can play on a portable MP3 player. Paul Harris, "A New Era for Accessibility," *Training & Development* (April 2009): 58–61.

52. http://www.dominknow.com/, accessed March 23, 2009.

53. Elizabeth Agnvall, "Just-In-Time Training," *HR Magazine* (May 2006): 67–78.

54. Ibid.

55. For a similar program, and Accenture, see Don Vanthournout and Dana Koch, "Training at Your Fingertips," *Training & Development* (September 2008): 52–57.

56. Marcia Conner, "Twitter 101: Are You Reading?" *Training & Development* (August 2009): 24–26.

57. Traci Sitzmann et al., "The Comparative Effectiveness of Web-Based and Classroom Instruction: A Meta-Analysis," *Personnel Psychology* 59 (2006): 623–64.

58. Paula Ketter, "The Hidden Disability," *Training and Development* (June 2006): 34–40.

59. Jeremy Smerd, "New Workers Sorely Lacking Literacy Skills," *Workforce Management* (December 10, 2008): 6.

60. Valerie Frazee, "Workers Learn to Walk so They Can Run," *Personnel Journal* (May 1996): 115–20. See also Kathryn Tyler, "I Say Potato, You Say Patata: As Workforce and Customer Diversity Grow, Employers Offer Foreign Language Training to Staff," *HR Magazine* 49, no. 1 (January 2004): 85–87.

61. Jennifer Salopek, "The Growth of Succession Management," *Training & Development* (June 2007): 22–24; and Kermit Kalleba, "Businesses Continue to Push for Lifelong Learning," *Training & Development* (June 2007): 14.

62. "Adams Mark Hotel & Resorts Launches Diversity Training Program," *Hotel and Motel Management* 216, no. 6 (April 2001): 15.

63. Sara Rynes and Benson Rosen, "What Makes Diversity Programs Work?" *HR Magazine* (October 1994): 64. See also Thomas Diamante and Leo

Giglio, "Managing a Diverse Workforce: Training as a Cultural Intervention Strategy," *Leadership & Organization Development Journal* 15, no. 2 (1994): 13–17.

64. Douglas Shuit, "Sound of the Retreat," *Workforce Management* (September 2003): 40.

65. Susan Ladika, "When Learning Lasts a Lifetime," *HR Magazine* (May 2008): 57.

66. "For Gap, Management Training Doesn't Stop at the Border," *BNA Bulletin to Management* (February 2005): 63.

67. See, for example, Jeff Kristick, "Filling the Leadership Pipeline," *Training & Development* (June 2009): 49–51.

68. Christopher Glynn, "Building a Learning Infrastructure," *Training & Development* (January 2008): 38–43.

69. Jack Zenger, Dave Ulrich, and Norm Smallwood, "The New Leadership Development," *Training & Development* (March 2000): 22–27. See also W. David Patton and Connie Pratt, "Assessing the Training Needs of High Potential Managers," *Public Personnel Management* 31, no. 4 (Winter 2002): 465–74; and Ann Locke and Arlene Tarantino, "Strategic Leadership Development," *Training & Development* (December 2006): 53–55.

70. Mike Czarnowsky, "Executive Development," *Training & Development* (September 2008): 44–45.

71. Wexley and Latham, *Developing and Training Human Resources in Organizations*, 193.

72. See, for example, Michael Laff, "Serious Gaming: The Trainer's New Best Friend," *Training & Development* (January 2007): 52–56.

73. Jean Thilmany, "Acting Out," *HR Magazine* (January 2007): 95–100.

74. "AMA Seminars," October 2009–2010, the American Management Association, www.AMA seminars.org.

75. Thus for a list of Harvard programs, see, for example, their intensive two-day conferences in the 2008 brochure from their Center for Management Research, "Programs on Leadership for Senior Executives," www.execseminars.com, 2008.

76. Chris Musselwhite, "University Executive Education Gets Real," *Training & Development* (May 2006): 57.

77. Jeanne Meister, "Universities Put to the Test," *Workforce Management* (December 11, 2006): 27–30.

78. Ann Pomeroy, "Head of the Class," *HR Magazine* (January 2005): 57.

79. Russell Gerbman, "Corporate Universities 101," *HR Magazine* (February 2000): 101–6. Before creating an in-house university, the employer needs to ensure that the corporate university's vision, mission, and programs support the company's strategic goals. See also Michael Laff, "Centralized Training Leads to Nontraditional Universities," *Training & Development* (January 2007): 27–29.

80. See, for example, Joyce Bono et al., "A Survey of Executive Coaching Practices," *Personnel Psychology* 62 (2009): 361–64.

81. Joseph Toto, "Untapped World of Peer Coaching," *Training and Development* (April 2006): 69–72.

82. James Smither et al., "Can Working with an Executive Coach Improve Multiscore Feedback Ratings over Time?" *Personnel Psychology* 56, no. 1 (Spring 2003): 23–44.

83. "As Corporate Coaching Goes Mainstream, Keyed Prerequisite Overlooked: Assessment," *BNA Bulletin to Management* (May 16, 2006): 153.

84. For an example of a successful organizational change see, for example, Jordan Mora et al., "Recipe for Change," *Training & Development* (March 2008): 42–46.

85. The 10 steps are based on Michael Beer et al., "Why Change Programs Don't Produce Change," *Harvard Business Review* (November/December 1990): 158–66; John Kotter, *Leading Change* (Boston: Harvard Business School Press, 1996). See also David Herold et al., "Beyond Change Management: A Multilevel Investigation of Contextual and Personal Influences on Employee's Commitment to Change," *Journal of Applied Psychology* 92, no. 4 (2007): 949. See also Remco Schimmel and Dennis Muntslag, "Learning Barriers: A Framework for the Examination of Structural Impediments to Organizational Change," *Human Resource Management* 48, no. 3 (May–June 2009): 399–416; and John Austin, "Mapping Out a Game Plan for Change," *HR Magazine* (April 2009): 39–42.

86. Stacie Furst and Daniel Cable, "Employee Resistance to Organizational Change: Managerial Influence Tactics and Leader Member Exchange," *Journal of Applied Psychology* 3, no. 2 (2008): 453.

87. Wendell French and Cecil Bell Jr., *Organization Development* (Upper Saddle River, NJ: Prentice Hall, 1999). See also D. Dick Blanchard and James Thacker, *Effective Training* (Upper Saddle River, NJ: Pearson, 2007), pp. 38–46.

88. Darin Hartley, "OD Wired," *Training and Development* (August 2004): 20–24.

89. David A. Garvin, "Building a Learning Organization," *Harvard Business Review* (July/August 1993): 80.

90. See, for example, Charlie Morrow, M. Quintin Jarrett, and Melvin Rupinski, "An Investigation of the Effect and Economic Utility of Corporate-Wide Training," *Personnel Psychology* 50 (1997): 91–119. See also Antonio Aragon-Sanchez et al., "Effects of Training on Business Results," *International Journal of Human Resource Management* 14, no. 6 (September 2003): 956–80.

91. See, for example, Jack Phillips and Patti Phillips, "Measuring What Matters: How CEOS View Learning Success," *Training & Development* (August 2009): 45–49.

92. Jeffrey Berk, "Training Evaluations," *Training and Development* (September 2004): 39–45.

93. Tony Bingaman and Pat Galagan, "Training: They're Lovin' It," *Training & Development* (November 2006): 30.

94. Todd Raphel, "What Learning Management Reports Do for You," *Workforce* 80, no. 6 (June 2001): 56–58.

95. Alan Saks and Monica Belcourt, "An Investigation of Training Activities and Transfer of Training in Organizations," *Human Resource Management* 45, no. 4 (Winter 2006): 629–48. See also George Vellios, "On the Level," *Training & Development* (December 2008): 26–29; and K. Lee, "Implement

Training Successfully," *Training* [Minneapolis, MN] 46, no. 5 (June 2009): 16.

96. Elaine Biech, "Learning Eye to Eye: Aligning Training to Business Objectives," *Training & Development* (April 2009): 50–53.

Chapter 6

1. Drew Robb, "Building a Better Workforce," *HR Magazine* (October 2004): 87–94.

2. For a good recent discussion of this, see, for example, Samuel Culbert, "Get Rid of the Performance Review!" *Wall Street Journal* (October 20, 2008): R4.

3. Experts debate the pros and cons of tying appraisals to pay decisions. One side argues that doing so distorts the appraisals. A recent study concludes the opposite. Based on an analysis of surveys from over 24,000 employees in more than 6,000 workplaces in Canada, the researchers concluded that (1) linking the employees' pay to their performance appraisals contributed to improved pay satisfaction; (2) even when appraisals are not directly linked to pay, they apparently contributed to pay satisfaction, "probably through mechanisms related to perceived organizational justice"; and (3) whether or not the employees received performance pay, "individuals who do not receive performance appraisals are significantly less satisfied with their pay." Mary Jo Ducharme et al., "Exploring the Links between Performance Appraisals and Pay Satisfaction," *Compensation & Benefits Review* (September/October 2005): 46–52. See also Robert Morgan, "Making the Most of Performance Management Systems," *Compensation & Benefits Review* (September/October 2006): 22–27.

4. Vesa Suutari and Marja Tahbanainen, "The Antecedents of Performance Management among Finnish Expatriates," *Journal of Human Resource Management* 13, no. 1 (February 2002): 53–75.

5. See, for example, Doug Cederblom and Dan Pemerl, "From Performance Appraisal to Performance Management: One Agency's Experience," *Personnel Management* 31, no. 2 (Summer 2002): 131–40.

6. See, for example, Robert Renn, "Further Examination of the Measurement of Properties of Leifer & McGannon's 1996 Goal Acceptance and Goal Commitment Scales," *Journal of Occupational and Organizational Psychology* (March 1999): 107–14.

7. Vanessa Druskat and Steven Wolf, "Effects and Timing of Developmental Peer Appraisals in Self-Managing Work-Groups," *Journal of Applied Psychology* 84, no. 1 (1999): 58–74.

8. See, for example, Brian Hoffman and David Woehr, "Disentangling the Meaning of Multisource Performance Rating Source and Dimension Factors," *Personnel Psychology* 62 (2009): 735–65.

9. As one study recently concluded, "far from being a source of nonmeaningful error variance, the discrepancies among ratings from multiple perspectives can in fact capture meaningful variance in multilevel managerial performance." In Sue Oh and Christopher Berry, "The Five Factor Model of Personality and Managerial Performance: Validity Gains Through the Use of 360°

Performance Ratings," *Journal of Applied Psychology* 94, no. 6 (2009): 1510.

10. Such findings may be culturally related. One study compared self and supervisor ratings in "other-oriented" cultures (as in Asia, where values tend to emphasize teams). It found that self and supervisor ratings were related. M. Audrey Korsgaard et al., "The Effect of Other Orientation on Self: Supervisor Rating Agreement," *Journal of Organizational Behavior* 25, no. 7 (November 2004): 873–91.

11. Forest Jourden and Chip Heath, "The Evaluation Gap in Performance Perceptions: Illusory Perceptions of Groups and Individuals," *Journal of Applied Psychology* 81, no. 4 (August 1996): 369–79. See also Sheri Ostroff, "Understanding Self-Other Agreement: A Look at Rater and Ratee Characteristics, Context, and Outcomes," *Personnel Psychology* 57, no. 2 (Summer 2004): 333–75.

12. Paul Atkins and Robert Wood, "Self versus Others Ratings as Predictors of Assessment Center Ratings: Validation Evidence for 360 Degree Feedback Programs," *Personnel Psychology* 55, no. 4 (Winter 2002): 871–904.

13. Manuel London and Arthur Wohlers, "Agreement between Subordinate and Self-Ratings in Upward Feedback," *Personnel Psychology* 44 (1991): 375–90; see also Todd Maurer et al., "Peer and Subordinate Performance Appraisal Measurement Equivalents," *Journal of Applied Psychology* 83, no. 5 (1998): 693–702; and Herman Aguinis, *Performance Management* (Upper Saddle River, NJ: Pearson, 2007), p. 130.

14. David Antonioni, "The Effects of Feedback Accountability on Upward Appraisal Ratings," *Personnel Psychology* 47 (1994): 349–55.

15. Alan Walker and James Smither, "A Five-Year Study of Upward Feedback: What Managers Do with Their Results Matters," *Personnel Psychology* 52 (1999): 393–423.

16. Kenneth Nowack, "360-Degree Feedback: The Whole Story," *Training and Development* (January 1993): 69; Matthew Budman, "The Rating Game," *Across the Board* 31, no. 2 (February 1994): 35–38. See also "360-Degree Feedback on the Rise Survey Finds," *BNA Bulletin to Management* (January 23, 1997): 31. See also Leanne Atwater et al., "Multisource Feedback: Lessons Learned and Implications for Practice," *Human Resource Management* 46, no. 2 (Summer 2007): 285.

17. However, a small number of employers are beginning to use 360-degree feedback for performance appraisals, rather than just development. See, for example, Tracy Maylett, "360° Feedback Revisited: The Transition from Development to Appraisal," *Compensation & Benefits Review* (September/October 2009): 52–59.

18. James Smither et al., "Does Performance Improve Following Multi-Source Feedback? A Theoretical Model, Meta Analysis, and Review of Empirical Findings," *Personnel Psychology* 58 (2005): 33–36. See also Fred Luthans and Suzanne Peterson, "360 Degree Feedback with Systematic Coaching: Empirical Analysis Suggests a Winning Combination," *Human Resource Management* 42, no. 3 (Fall 2003): 243–55.

19. Herman Aguinis, *Performance Management* (Upper Saddle River, NJ: Pearson, 2007), p. 179.

20. Christine Hagan et al., "Predicting Assessment Center Performance with 360 Degree, Top-Down, and Customer-Based Competency Assessments," *Human Resource Management* 45, no. 3 (Fall 2006): 357–90.

21. http://www.echospan.com/echositenew/solutions/360_Feedback/default.asp accessed June 2010.

22. Jeffrey Facteau and S. Bartholomew Craig, "Performance Appraisal Ratings from Different Rating Scores," *Journal of Applied Psychology* 86, no. 2 (2001): 215–27.

23. See also Kevin Murphy et al., "Raters Who Pursue Different Goals Give Different Ratings," *Journal of Applied Psychology* 89, no. 1 (2004): 158–64.

24. Steven Scullen et al., "Forced Distribution Rating Systems and the Improvement of Workforce Potential: A Baseline Simulation," *Personnel Psychology* 58 (2005): 1; and Jena McGregor, "The Struggle to Measure Performance," *BusinessWeek* (January 9, 2006): 26.

25. Del Jones, "More Firms Cut Workers Ranked at Bottom to Make Way for Talent," *USA Today* (May 30, 2001): B1; "Straight Talk about Grading on a Curve," *BNA Bulletin to Management* (November 1, 2001): 351; Steve Bates, "Forced Ranking," *HR Magazine* (June 2003): 63–68. See also D. J. Schleicher et al., "Rater Reactions to Forced Distribution Rating Systems," *Journal of Management* 35, no. 4 (August 2009): 899–927.

26. "Survey Says Problems with Forced Ranking Include Lower Morale and Costly Turnover," *BNA Bulletin to Management* (September 16, 2004): 297.

27. Steve Bates, "Forced Ranking: Why Grading Employees on a Scale Relative to Each Other Forces a Hard Look at Finding Keepers, Losers May Become Weepers," *HR Magazine* 48, no. 6 (June 2003): 62.

28. "Straight Talk about Grading Employees on a Curve," *BNA Bulletin to Management* (November 1, 2001): 351.

29. www.halogensoftware.com/products/halogen-eappraisal/, accessed January 10, 2008.

30. Drew Robb, "Appraising Appraisal Software," *HR Magazine* (October 2008): 68.

31. Gary Meyer, "Performance Reviews Made Easy, Paperless," *HR Magazine* (October 2000): 181–84. See also www.employeeappraiser.com/index.php, accessed January 10, 2008.

32. John Aiello and Kathryn Kolb, "Electronic Performance Monitoring and Social Context: Impact on Productivity and Stress," *Journal of Applied Psychology* 80, no. 3 (1995): 339. See also Stoney Alder and Maureen Ambrose, "Towards Understanding Fairness Judgments Associated with Computer Performance Monitoring: An Integration of the Feedback, Justice, and Monitoring Research," *Human Resource Management Review* 15, no. 1 (March 2005): 43–67.

33. Aiello and Kolb, "Electronic Performance Monitoring and Social Context," 339–53.

34. See, for example, John Aiello and Y. Shao, "Computerized Performance Monitoring," Paper presented at the Seventh Conference of the Society for Industrial and Organizational Psychology, Montreal, Quebec, Canada, May 1992.

35. Peter Glendinning, "Performance Management: Pariah or Messiah," *Public Personnel Management* 31, no. 2 (Summer 2002): 161–78. See also Herman Aguinis, *Performance Management* (Upper Saddle River, NJ, 2007), p. 2.

36. Howard Risher, "Getting Serious about Performance Management," *Compensation & Benefits Review* (November/December 2005): 19.

37. These are quoted or paraphrased from Howard Risher, "Getting Serious about Performance Management," *Compensation & Benefits Review* (November/December 2005): 19.

38. Drew Robb, "Building a Better Workforce," *HR Magazine* (October 2004): 87–94.

39. Rasha Madkour, "NASA Shooting Suspect Received Poor Job Review. Feared Being Fired," *Associated Press News* (April 21, 2007), http://www.denverpost.com/ci_5722419?source=pkg, accessed April 12, 2010.

40. See, for example, "Communicating Beyond the Ratings Can Be Difficult," *Workforce, Workforce Management* (April 24, 2006): 35.

41. See for example, A. Fox, "Curing What Ails Performance Reviews," *HR Magazine* 54, no. 1 (January 2009): 52–56.

42. M. Ronald Buckley et al., "Ethical Issues in Human Resources Systems," *Human Resource Management Review* 11 (2001): 11, 29. See also Ann Pomeroy, "The Ethics Squeeze," *HR Magazine* (March 2006): 48–55.

43. Weaver and Trevino, "Role of Human Resources," 113–34. Researchers recently conducted studies of 490 police officers undergoing standardized promotional exams. Among their conclusions was that "Organizations should strive to ensure that candidates perceived justice both in the content of personnel assessments and in the way they are treated during the assessment process. Julie McCarthy et al., "Progression Through the Ranks: Assessing Employee Reactions to High Stakes Employment Testing," *Personnel Psychology* 62 (2009): 826.

44. See, for example, Manuel London, Edward Mone and John C. Scott, "The Contributions of Psychological Research to HRM: Performance Management and Assessment—Methods for Improved Rater Accuracy and Employee Goal Setting," *Human Resource Management* 43, no. 4 (Winter 2004): 319–36.

45. Richard Posthuma, "Twenty Best Practices for Just Employee Performance Reviews," *Compensation & Benefits Review* (January/February 2008): 47–54.

46. See, for example, Adrienne Fox, "Curing What Ails Performance Reviews," *HR Magazine* (January 2009): 52–55; and "How to . . . Improve Appraisals," *People Management* 15, no. 3 (January 29, 2009): 57.

47. H. John Bernardin et al., "Conscientiousness and Agreeableness as Predictors of Rating Leniency," *Journal of Applied Psychology* 85, no. 2 (2000): 232–34.

48. Clinton Wingrove, "Developing a New Blend of Process and Technology in the New Era of Performance Management," *Compensation & Benefits Review* (January/February 2003): 25–30.

49. Gary Gregures et al., "A Field Study of the Effects of Rating Purpose on the Quality of Multiscore Ratings," *Personnel Psychology* 56 (2003): 1–21.

50. Madeleine Heilman et al., "Penalties for Success: Reactions to Women Who Succeed at Male Gender Type Tasks," *Journal of Applied Psychology* 89, no. 3 (2004): 416–27.

51. Ibid., p. 426. Another study found that successful female managers didn't usually suffer such a fate when those rating them saw them as supportive, caring, and sensitive to their needs. Madeleine Heilmann and Tyler Okimoto, "Why Are Women Penalized for Success at Male Tasks?: The Implied Communality Deficit," *Journal of Applied Psychology* 92, no. 1 (2007): 81–92.

52. Wingrove, "Developing a New Blend of Process and Technology," 25–30.

53. Joanne Sammer, "Calibrating Consistency," *HR Magazine* (January 2008): 73–74.

54. "Flawed Ranking System Revives Workers Bias Claim," *BNA Bulletin to Management* (June 28, 2005): 206.

55. Donald Fedor and Charles Parsons, "What Is Effective Performance Feedback?" in Gerald Ferris and M. Ronald Buckley (eds.), *Human Resources Management*, 3rd ed. (Upper Saddle River, NJ: Prentice Hall, 1996), pp. 265–70. See also Herman Aguinis, *Performance Management* (Upper Saddle River, NJ: Pearson 2007), pp. 196–219.

56. James Austin, Peter Villanova, and Hugh Hindman, "Legal Requirements and Technical Guidelines Involved in Implementing Performance Appraisal Systems," in Gerald Ferris and M. Ronald Buckley (eds.), *Human Resources Management*, 3rd ed. (Upper Saddle River, NJ: Prentice Hall, 1996), pp. 271–88.

57. Ibid., p. 282.

58. Brian Cawley et al., "Participation in the Performance Appraisal Process and Employee Reactions: A Meta-Analytic Review of Field Investigations," *Journal of Applied Psychology* 83, no. 4 (1998): 615–33.

59. This is based on Richard Luecke, *Coaching and Mentoring* (Boston: Harvard Business School Press, 2004), pp. 8–9.

60. Source: Adapted from Paula J. Caprioni, *The Practical Coach: Management Skills for Everyday Life* (Upper Saddle River, NJ: Prentice Hall, 2001), p. 86.

61. Luecke, *Coaching and Mentoring*, p. 9.

62. Deb Koen, "Revitalize Your Career," *Training and Development* (January 2003): 59–60. See also P. Bronson, "What Should I Do with My Life Now?" *Fast Company* 134 (April 2009): 35–37; and R. Zeidner, "When It Doesn't Pay to Stay," *HR Magazine* 54, no. 1 (January 2009): 26.

63. Michael Doody, "A Mentor Is a Key to Career Success," *Health-Care Financial Management* 57, no. 2 (February 2003): 92–94.

64. See also Yehuda Baruch, "Career Development in Organizations and Beyond: Balancing Traditional and Contemporary Viewpoints," *Human Resource Management Review* 16 (2006): 131.

65. Barbara Greene and Liana Knudsen, "Competitive Employers Make Career Development Programs a Priority," *San Antonio Business Journal* 15, no. 6 (July 20, 2001): 27.

66. Julekha Dash, "Coaching to Aid IT Careers, Retention," *Computerworld* (March 20, 2000): 52.

67. Fred Otte and Peggy Hutcheson, *Helping Employees Manage Careers* (Upper Saddle River, NJ: Prentice Hall, 1992), p. 143.

68. Karen Lyness and Madeline Heilman, "When Fit Is Fundamental: Performance Evaluations and Promotions of Upper-Level Female and Male Managers," *Journal of Applied Psychology* 91, no. 4 (2006): 775–77.

69. Karen Lyness and Donna Thompson, "Climbing the Corporate Ladder: Do Female and Male Executives Follow the Same Route?" *Journal of Applied Psychology* 85, no. 1 (2000): 86–101.

70. "Minority Women Surveyed on Career Growth Factors," *Community Banker* 9, no. 3 (March 2000): 44.

71. In Ellen Cook et al., "Career Development of Women of Color and White Women: Assumptions, Conceptualization, and Interventions from an Ecological Perspective," *Career Development Quarterly* 50, no. 4 (June 2002): 291–306.

72. Jan Selmer and Alicia Leung, "Are Corporate Career Development Activities Less Available to Female than to Male Expatriates?" *Journal of Business Ethics* (March 2003): 125–37.

73. See for example, Matt Bolch, "Bidding Adieu," *HR Magazine* (June 2006): 123–27; and Claudia Deutsch, "A Longer Goodbye," *New York Times* (April 20, 2008): H1, H10.

74. "Employees Plan to Work Past Retirement, but Not Necessarily for Financial Reasons," *BNA Bulletin to Management* (February 19, 2004): 57–58. See also Mo Wang, "Profiling Retirees in the Retirement Transition and Adjustment Process: Examining the Longitudinal Change Patterns of Retirees' Psychological Well-Being," *Journal of Applied Psychology* 92, no. 2 (2007): 455–74.

75. Andrew Luchak et al., "When Do Committed Employees Retire? The Effects of Organizational Commitment on Retirement Plans under a Defined Benefit Pension Plan," *Human Resource Management* 47, no. 3 (Fall 2008): 581–99.

76. Ken Dychtwald et al., "It's Time to Retire Retirement," *Harvard Business Review* (March 2004): 52.

77. Ibid.

78. Luis Fleites and Lou Valentino, "The Case for Phased Retirement," *Compensation & Benefits Review* (March/April 2007): 42–46.

79. Reviewers have noted that there "isn't a single consistent or concise definition of talent management. David Collings and Kanel Mellahi, "Strategic Talent Management: A Review and Research Agenda," *Human Resource Management Review* 19 (2009): 304.

80. http://www.successfactors.com/info/en/talent-management/?source=Google_ppc&kw=Talent%20Management&gclid=CNzA-YmRgpkCFQS7sgodnkdLnw, accessed March 1, 2009.

81. www.talentmanagement101.com, accessed December 10, 2007. The American Society for Training and Development defines talent management as "a holistic approach to optimizing human capital, which enables an organization to drive short and long-term results by building culture, engagement, capability, and capacity

through integrated talent acquisition, development, and deployment processes federal line to business goals." Andrew Paradise, "Talent Management Defined," *Training & Development* (May 2009): 69.

82. Lois Webster, "Leaving Nothing to Chance," *Training & Development* (February 2009): 56–60.

83. Bill Leisy and Dina Pyron, "Talent Management Takes On New Urgency," *Compensation & Benefits Review* (July/August 2009): 58–63.

84. Other integrated talent management software providers include Authoria (www.authoria.com), HRsmart (www.HRsmart.com), Kenexa (www.kenexa.com), and Saba (www.Saba.com). "Integrated Talent Management Software Providers," *Workforce Management* (April 20, 2009): 11.

85. www.talentmanagement101.com, downloaded December 10, 2007.

86. "Software Facilitates Talent Management," *Product News Network* (May 18, 2007), downloaded December 9, 2007.

Chapter 7

1. http://www.starbucks.com/aboutus/jobcenter_thesbuxexperience.asp, accessed March 24, 2009.

2. Richard Henderson, *Compensation Management* (Reston, VA: Reston 1980); Joseph Martocchio, *Strategic Compensation* (Upper Saddle River, NJ: Prentice Hall, 2004), pp. 44–60.

3. "Senate Passes Minimum Wage Increase that Includes Small-Business Tax Provisions," *BNA Bulletin to Management* (February 6, 2007): 41; www.dol.gov/esa/whd/flsa/, accessed August 12, 2007.

4. John Kilgour, "Wage and Hour Law in California," *Compensation & Benefits Review* 42, no. 1 (January/February 2010): 17.

5. The recently approved genetic information nondiscrimination act amended the fair labor standards act to increase penalties for the death or serious injury of employees under age 18. Allen Smith, "Penalties for Child Labor Violations Increase," *HR Magazine* (July 2008): 19.

6. For a description of exemption requirements, see Jeffrey Friedman, "The Fair Labor Standards Act Today: A Primer," *Compensation* (January/February 2002): 51–54.

7. FLSA exemption lawsuits are on the rise. For example sales reps for a drug firm argue in one suit that the FLSA "outside salesperson" exemption doesn't cover them because they market and advise—not sell—drugs to doctors. More "administrative secretaries" are arguing that the administrative exemption does not apply because they don't make decisions that influence their firms' finances. "Supervisors" are saying they don't really themselves supervise two or more employees. So, again, it's not the title, it is what the employees actually do. See, "Drug Sales Reps Raise Questions about Outside Sales Exemption," *BNA Bulletin to Management* (April 1, 2008): 111; Diane Cadrain, "Guard against FLSA claims," *HR Magazine* (April 2008): 97–100; For another example, this one involving technical writers working for Sun Microsystems, see "Court Certifies Class of Technical Writers Working for Sun Microsystems, See Beyond," *BNA Bulletin to Management* (May 20, 2008): 161.

8. See, for example, Jeffrey Friedman, "The Fair Labor Standards Act Today: A Primer," *Compensation* (January/February 2002): 53; Andre Honoree, "The New Fair Labor Standards Act Regulations and the Sales Force: Who Is Entitled to Overtime Pay?" *Compensation and Benefits Review* (January/February 2006): 31; www.shrm.org/issues/FLSA, accessed August 12, 2007; www.dol.gov/esa/whd/flsa/, accessed August 12, 2007. Congress periodically changes the Fair Labor Standards Act's rules regarding who is covered. For example, it recently amended the act to bring drivers, helpers, and mechanics of smaller trucks under the Fair Labor Standards Act's overtime provisions. "Changes to FLSA Present Opportunities, Challenges," *BNA Bulletin to Management* (December 8, 2009): 391.

9. Because the overtime and minimum wage rules only changed in 2004, exactly how to apply these rules is still in a state of flux. If there's doubt about exemption eligibility, it's probably best to check with the local Department of Labor Wage and Hour office. See, for example, "Attorneys Say FLSA Draws a Fine Line between Exempt/Nonexempt Employees," *BNA Bulletin to Management* (July 5, 2005): 219; "DOL Releases Letters on Administrative Exemption, Overtime," *BNA Bulletin to Management* (October 18, 2005): 335.

10. "Study Finds Widespread Wage Theft," *Workforce Management* (November 16, 2009): 29.

11. "Wal-Mart to Settle 63 Wage and Hour Suits, Paying up to $640 Million to Resolve Claims," *BNA Bulletin to Management* (January 13, 2009): 11.

12. "FedEx Ground in Reverse on Driver Status," *Workforce Management* (April 21, 2008): 4. In April 2009, one jury in Seattle ruled in favor of FedEx, deeming the drivers to be independent contractors. Another jury in California ruled instead for the drivers in another case. Alex Roth, "Verdict Backs FedEx in Labor Case," *New York Times* (April 2, 2009): B4.

13. Recently, several state legislatures have moved to tighten regulations regarding misclassifying workers as independent contractors, some going so far as adding criminal penalties for violations. "Misclassification Cases Draw More Attention, Attorneys Say," *BNA Bulletin to Management* (December 15, 2009): 399.

14. Recently, women earned about 24% less than men overall. The gender gap was actually largest between men and women with advanced degrees (31%) and narrowest for those with high school degrees and some college (27%). "Women's Wage Gap Ranges from 25% to 31%, Census Bureau Report Finds," *BNA Bulletin to Management* (February 17, 2009): 51.

15. In January 2009, Congress passed the Lilly Ledbetter Fair Pay Act. This overturns the U.S. Supreme Court's Ledbetter decision, and basically says that each new paycheck triggers a new potential discrimination claim. See "Ledbetter Law Raises Open Legal Issues, Practical Issues for Covert Employees," *BNA Bulletin to Management* (November 17, 2009): 361.

16. Henderson, *Compensation Management*, pp. 101–27.

17. "Salaries for Similar Jobs Vary Significantly across the United States," *Compensation & Benefits Review* (January/February 2006): 9.

18. Jessica Marquez, "Raising the Performance Bar," *Workforce Management* (April 24, 2006): 31–32.

19. See, for example, Robert Heneman, "Implementing Total Rewards of Strategies," SHRM foundation, www.shrm.org/foundation, accessed March 2, 2009.

20. As one study recently put it, "Our research suggests that employees who perceived organization as providing competitive pay are likely to hold positive work attitudes and conceivably engage in behaviors leading to high levels of labor productivity and customer satisfaction." Mahdesh Subramony et al., "The Relationship between Human Resource Investments and Organizational Performance: A Firm Level Examination of Equilibrium Theory," *Journal of Applied Psychology* 93, no. 4 (2008): 786.

21. James DeConick and Dane Bachmann, "An Analysis of Turnover among Retail Buyers," *Journal of Business Research* 58, no. 7 (July 2005): 874–82.

22. Michael Harris et al., "Keeping Up with the Joneses: A Field Study of the Relationships among Upwards, Lateral, and the Downward Comparisons and a Level Satisfaction," *Journal of Applied Psychology* 93, no. 3 (2008): 665–673.

23. Millicent Nelson et al., "Pay Me More: What Companies Need to Know about Employee Pay Satisfaction," *Compensation & Benefits Review* (March/April 2008): 35–42.

24. http://markets.on.nytimes.com/research/stocks/news/press_release.asp?docKey=600-200902040900BIZWIRE_USPR____BW5153-7ENARVBIKO0QHDGGFHUTBKEMIS&provider=Businesswire&docDate=February%204%2C%202009&press_symbol=US%3BHEW, accessed March 21, 2009; www.shrm.org/hrdisciplines/benefits/Articles/Pages/AmericanstoSeeLowestPayRaisesinThreeDecades.aspx, accessed March 21, 2009.

25. See, for example, http://www.watsonwyatt.com/search/publications.asp?ArticleID=21432, accessed October 29, 2009.

26. Syed Tahir Hijazi, "Determinants of Executive Compensation and Its Impact on Organizational Performance," *Compensation & Benefits Review* (March/April 2007): 58–59. See also "Appraising and Rewarding Managerial Performance in Challenging Economic Times: Part 2," *Journal of Compensation & Benefits* 25, no. 4 (July/August 2009): 5–12.

27. Ingrid Fuller, "The Elephant in the Room: Labor Market Influences on CEO Compensation," *Personnel Psychology* 62 (2009): 659–95.

28. In 2008 and 2009, the U.S. government adopted executive compensation restrictions as part of its troubled asset relief program and American Recovery and Reinvestment Act of 2009 program. The programs themselves were aimed at supporting financial institutions that would otherwise have been in danger of failing in the financial crisis. The executive compensation restrictions were numerous. For example, other than long-term restricted stock, senior executives had a $500,000 annual on their compensation. Severance payments to senior executives were severely restricted. Boards of directors had to adopt company-wide policies on luxury expenditures such as office renovations and aviation services. Laura Thatcher, "Executive Compensation Restrictions under the American Recovery and Reinvestment Act of 2009," *Compensation & Benefits Review* (May/June 2009): 20–28.

29. "Range of Firms Alter Executive-Pay Policies," *Wall Street Journal* (October 24–25, 2009): 84.

30. "Executive Pay Remains Linked to Performance," *Compensation & Benefits Review* (March/April 2008): 10. See also K. Dillon, "The Coming Battle over Executive Pay," *Harvard Business Review* 87, no. 9 (September 2009): 96–103.

31. Christine Bevilacqua and Parbudyal Singh, "Pay for Performance—Panacea or Pandora's Box? Revisiting an Old Debate in the Current Economic Environment," *Compensation & Benefits Review* (September/October 2009): 21–26.

32. Mark Meltzer and Howard Goldsmith, "Executive Compensation for Growth Companies," *Compensation & Benefits Review* (November/December 1997): 41–50. See also Bruce Ellig, "Executive Pay: A Primer," *Compensation & Benefits Review* (January/February 2003): 44–50.

33. "Executive Pay," *Wall Street Journal* (April 11, 1996): R16, R170; and Fay Hansen, "Current Trends in Compensation and Benefits," *Compensation & Benefits Review* 36, no. 2 (March/April 2004): 7–8.

34. Patricia Zingheim and Jay Schuster, "Designing Pay and Rewards in Professional Services Companies," *Compensation & Benefits Review* (January/February 2007): 55–62.

35. A recent analysis of how companies arrive at executive compensation decisions revealed six potential problem areas: Often, the human resource department hires in the executive compensation consultant, who may in turn feel obligated to formulate CEO incentives that favor the CEO; if the board is going to identify a peer group of firms for executive compensation comparison purposes, those firms should be ones that compete for talent and for business; boards of directors and senior executive should have a "clear understanding of the measures that drive shareholder value if they are going to be used for reward or compensation purposes"; using stock options and executive compensation is potentially risky, given the possibility that an executive can indirectly manipulate share prices through misleading disclosure; don't simply adapt another employer's incentive plan, instead, develop one with the companies' business strategy and compensation plan objectives in mind; the board should make sure that it fully understands the cost of long-term implications of the executive compensation decisions. Michel Magnan and Imen Tebourbi, "A Critical Analysis of Six Practices underlying Executive Compensation Practices," *Compensation & Benefits Review* (May/June 2009): 42–54.

36. See, for example, Patricia Zingheim and Jay Schuster, "The Next Decade for Pay and Rewards," *Compensation & Benefits Review* (January/February 2005): 29; Patricia Zingheim and Jay Schuster, "What Are Key Pay Issues Right Now?" *Compensation & Benefits Review* (May/June 2007): 51–55; and "A Framework for Understanding New Concepts in Compensation Management,"

Benefits & Compensation Digest 46, no. 9 (September 2009): front cover, 13–16.

37. Another dubious trend is that U.S. wage disparities are rising. Those with high salaries have seen their pay rise much faster in the past 20 or so years than have those at the bottom. Increased demand for the skills that come through education (for instance, for more skilled workers as manufacturing facilities became computerized) explains much of this. The wage gap has not grown as much in Europe, in part because "unions in Europe were and are still more powerful and able to keep up [workers'] wages." Thomas Atchison, "Salary Trends in the United States and Europe," *Compensation & Benefits Review* (January/February 2007): 36.

38. See for example, Hai-Ming Chen et al., "Key Trends of the Total Reward System in the 21st Century," *Compensation & Benefits Review* (November/December 2006): 64–70.

39. See, for example, Robert Henneman and Peter LeBlanc, "Development of an Approach for Valuing Knowledge Work," *Compensation & Benefits Review* (July/August 2002): 47.

40. Martocchio, *Strategic Compensation*, p. 168. See also B. Lokshin et al., "Crafting Firm Competencies to Improve Innovative Performance," *European Management Journal* 27, no. 3 (June 2009): 187–96.

41. Jamison Bandler and Charles Forelle, "How a Giant Insurer Decided to Oust Hugely Successful CEO," *Wall Street Journal* (December 7, 2006): A1.

42. Mark Poerio and Eric Keller, "Executive Compensation 2005: Many Forces, One Direction," *Compensation & Benefits Review* (May/June 2005): 34–40.

43. The federal government also recently introduced new compensation disclosure rules, and these are affecting executive compensation. For example, corporations must now list a single dollar figure to represent an executive's total pay, including salary, bonus, perquisites, long-term incentives, and retirement benefits. They must also be more diligent in listing all executive perquisites. The net effect of this greater transparency will probably be to pressure employers to increasingly link their executives' pay with the company's performance. See Brent Longnecker and James Krueger, "The Next Wave of Compensation Disclosure," *Compensation & Benefits Review* (January/February 2007): 50–54.

44. Ibid.

45. Bobby Watson Jr. and Gangaram Singh, "Global Pay Systems: Compensation in Support of Multinational Strategy," *Compensation & Benefits Review* (January/February 2005): 33–36.

46. Note that the employer needs to beware of instituting so many incentive plans (cash bonuses, stock options, recognition programs, and so on) tied to so many different behaviors that employees don't have a clear picture of the employer's priorities. Stephen Rubenfeld and Jennifer David, "Multiple Employee Incentive Plans: Too Much of a Good Thing?" *Compensation & Benefits Review* (March/April 2006): 35–43.

47. Peter Kurlander, "Building Incentive Compensation Management Systems: What Can Go Wrong?" *Compensation and Benefits Review,* (July/August 2001): 52–56. Employers may be moving to emphasize merit increases and deemphasize performance pay.

The average percentage of payroll employers spent on broad-based performance pay plans pay rose until 2005, and then fell for the past few years. "Companies Pull Back from Performance Pay," *Workforce Management* (October 23, 2006): 26. For one of many good discussions of why pay for performance tends to be ineffectual, see, for example, Fay Hansen, "Merit-Pay Payoff?" *Workforce Management* (November 3, 2008): 33–39.

48. See, for example, Kimberly Merriman, "On the Folly of Rewarding Team Performance, While Hoping for Teamwork," *Compensation & Benefits Review* (January/February 2009): 61–66.

49. See, for example, Bruce Ellig, "Executive Pay Financial Measurements," *Compensation & Benefits Review* (September/October 2008): 42–49.

50. Mark Meltzer and Howard Goldsmith, "Executive Compensation for Growth Companies," *Compensation and Benefits Review* (November/December 1997): 41–50; and Barbara Kiviat, "Everyone into the Bonus Pool," *Time* (December 15, 2003): A5.

51. Meltzer and Goldsmith, "Executive Compensation," 47–48. See also Steven Balsam and Setiyono Miharjo, "The Effect of Equity Compensation on Voluntary Executive Turnover," *The Journal of Accounting and Economics* 43, no. 1 (March 2007): 95.

52. Elaine Denby, "Weighing Your Options," *HR Magazine* (November 2002): 46.

53. Benjamin Dunford et al., "Underwater Stock Options and Voluntary Executive Turnover: A Multidisciplinary Perspective Integrating Behavioral and Economic Theories," *Personnel Psychology* 61 (2008): 687–726.

54. "Google Announces It Will Allow Employees to Exchange 'Underwater' Options for Stock," *BNA Bulletin to Management* (January 27, 2009): 27. See also Phred Dvorak, "Slump Yields Employee Rewards," *Wall Street Journal* (October 10, 2008): B2; Don Clark and Jerry DiColo, "Intel to Let Workers Exchange Options," *Wall Street Journal* (March 24, 2009): B3.

55. "Impact of Sarbanes-Oxley on Executive Compensation," downloaded December 11, 2003, from www.thelenreid.com, Thelen, Reid, and Priest, L.L.P. See also Brent Longnecker and James Krueger, "The Next Wave of Compensation Disclosure," *Compensation & Benefits Review* (January/February 2007): 50–54.

56. See, for example, Leslie Stretch, "From Strategy to Profitability: How Sales Compensation Management Drives Business Performance," *Compensation & Benefits Review* (May/June 2008): 32–37; and Pankaj Madhani, "Sales Employees Compensation: An Optimal Balance between Fixed and Variable Pay," *Compensation & Benefits Review* (July/August 2009): 44–51.

57. See, for example, C. Albrech, "Moving to a Global Sales Incentive Compensation Plan," *Compensation and Benefits Review* 41, no. 4 (July/August 2009): 52.

58. S. Scott Sands, "Ineffective Quotas: The Hidden Threat to Sales Compensation Plans," *Compensation & Benefits Review* (March/April 2000): 35–42. "Driving Profitable Sales Growth: 2006/2007 Report on Sales Effectiveness," www.watsonwyatt.com/research/resrender.asp?id=2006-US-0060&page=1, accessed May 20, 2007.

59. Peter Gundy, "Sales Compensation Programs: Built to Last," *Compensation & Benefits Review* (September/October 2002): 21–28.

60. Peter Glendinning, "Kicking the Tires of Automotive Sales Compensation," *Compensation & Benefits Review* (September/October 2000): 47–53; and Michele Marchetti, "Why Sales Contests Don't Work," *Sales and Marketing Management* 156 (January 2004): 19.

61. See, for example, Suzanne Peterson and Fred Luthans, "The Impact of Financial and Nonfinancial Incentives on Business Unit Outcomes over Time," *Journal of Applied Psychology* 91, no. 1 (2006): 156–65.

62. "Employee Recognition," WorldatWork, April 2008, at http://www.worldatwork.org/waw/adimLink?id=25653, accessed November 3, 2009.

63. See, for example, Leslie Yerkes, *Fun Works: Creating Places Where People Love to Work* (San Francisco: Berrett-Koehler, 2007).

64. Charlotte Huff, "Recognition That Resonates," *Workforce Management* (September 11, 2006): 25–29. See also Scott Jeffrey and Victoria Schaffer, "The Motivational Properties of Tangible Incentives," *Compensation & Benefits Review* (May/June 2007): 44–50. Reward and recognition programs like these represent about 2.7% of the annual payroll for U.S. employers. Michelle Rafter, "Back in a Giving Mood," *Workforce Management* (September 14, 2009): 25.

65. "Base Pay Will Rise More Slowly in 2009," *Compensation & Benefits Review* (November/December 2008): 5.

66. Seongsu Kim, "Does Profit Sharing Increase Firms' Profits?" *Journal of Labor Research* (Spring 1998): 351–71. See also Jacqueline Coyle-Shapiro et al., "Using Profit-Sharing to Enhance Employee Attitudes: A Longitudinal Examination of the Effects on Trust and Commitment," *Human Resource Management* 41, no. 4 (Winter 2002): 423–49. One recent study, conducted in Spain, concluded that profit sharing plans can enhance employees' commitment toward the organization. Alberto Bayo-Moriones and Martin Larraza-Kintana, "Profit Sharing Plans and Effective Commitment: Does the Context Matter?" *Human Resource Management* 48, no. 2 (March–April 2009): 207–26.

67. See, for example, S. Coomes, "Employee Stock Plans Can Save Taxes, Attract Talent," *Nation's Restaurant News* 42, no. 36 (September 15, 2008): 12.

68. John Gamble, "ESOPs: Financial Performance and Federal Tax Incentives," *Journal of Labor Research* 9, no. 3 (Summer 1998): 529–42.

69. "Time Warner Stops Granting Stock Options to Most of Staff," *New York Times* (February 19, 2005): page NA.

70. Brian Moore and Timothy Ross, *The Scanlon Way to Improved Productivity: A Practical Guide* (New York: Wiley, 1978), p. 2. See also Woodruff Imberman, "Is Gainsharing the Wave of the Future?" *Management Accounting* (November 1995): 35–38.

71. Based in part on Steven Markham, K. Dow Scott, and Walter Cox Jr., "The Evolutionary Development of a Scanlon Plan," *Compensation & Benefits Review* (March/April 1992): 50–56.

72. Ibid., p. 51.

73. Moore and Ross, *Scanlon Way to Improved Productivity*, pp. 1–2.

74. Janet Wiscombe, "Can Pay for Performance Really Work?" *Workforce* (August 2001): 30.

75. Susan Marks, "Incentives That Really Reward and Motivate," *Workforce* (June 2001): 108–14. For other examples, see also "Delivering Incentive Compensation Plans That Work," *Financial Executive* 25, no. 7 (September 2009): 52–54.

76. William Bulkeley, "Incentives System Fine-Tunes Pay/Bonus Plans," *Wall Street Journal* (August 16, 2001): B4.

77. Nina McIntyre, "Using EIM Technology to Successfully Motivate Employees," *Compensation & Benefits Review* (July/August 2001): 57–60; see also Jeremy Wuittner, "Plenty of Incentives to Use E.I.M. Software Systems," *American Banker* 168, no. 129 (July 8, 2003): 680.

78. Kathleen Cholewka, "Tech Tools," *Sales and Marketing Management* 153, no. 7 (July 2001): 24. See also Andrew Perlmutter, "Taking Motivation and Recognition Online," *Compensation & Benefits Review* (March–April 2002): 70–74.

79. "Survey Finds 99 Percent of Employers Providing Health-Care Benefits," *Compensation & Benefits Review* (September/October 2002): 11. See also National Compensation Survey: Employee Benefits in Private Industry in the United States March 2006, U.S. Department of Labor, U.S. Bureau of Labor Statistics, August 2006.

80. "Trouble Ahead? Dissatisfaction with Benefits, Compensation," *HR Trendbook* (2008), p. 16.

81. "Employers Face Fifth Successive Year of Major Heath Cost Increases, Survey Finds," *BNA Human Resources Report* (October 6, 2003): 1050; and National Compensation Survey: Employee Benefits in Private Industry in the United States, March 2006, U.S. Department of Labor, U.S. Bureau of Labor Statistics, August 2006.

82. As unemployment rose dramatically the past few years, many states responded by increasing significantly the tax they levy on employers to support their state unemployment funds. About 14 states reportedly had to obtain federal unemployment trust fund loans, and the unemployment insurance trust funds in 18 states were reportedly "near insolvency." Susan Wells, "Unemployment Insurance: How Much More Will It Cost?" *HR Magazine* (July 2009): 35–38.

83. See, for example, Laurie Nacht, "Make an Appealing Case: How to Prepare for and Present an Unemployment Insurance Appeal," *Society for Human Resource Management Legal Report* (March/April 2004): 1–8.

84. "Unscheduled Employee Absences Cost Companies More than Ever," *Compensation and Benefits Review* (March/April 2003): 19.

85. The Department of Labor updated its revised regulations for administering the Family and Medical Leave Act in November 2008. See "DOL Issues Long-Awaited Rules; Address a Serious Health Condition, Many Other Issues," *BNA Bulletin to Management* (November 18, 2008): 369. In 2008, Congress also amended the Family and Medical Leave Act to include, among other things, leave rights particularly for military families.

See Sarah Martin, "FMLA Protection Recently Expanded to Military Families: Qualifying Exigency and Servicemember Family Leave," *Compensation & Benefits Review* (September/October 2009): 43–51.

86. Terry Baglieri, "Severance Pay," www.SHRM.org, accessed December 23, 2006.

87. Ibid.

88. "Workers Comp Claims Rise with Layoffs, but Employers Can Identify, Prevent Fraud," *BNA Bulletin to Management* (October 4, 2001): 313.

89. The involvement of an attorney and the duration of the claim both influence the workers' claim cost. "Workers' Comp Research Provides Insight into Curbing Health Care Costs," *EHS Today* (February 2010): 18.

90. "Healthcare Tops List of Value Benefits," *BNA Bulletin to Management* (April 24, 2007): 132.

91. As an example of the direction new federal health insurance may take post-2009, see A. Mathews, "Making Sense of the Debate on Health Care," *Wall Street Journal* (Eastern Edition) (September 30, 2009): D1, D5.

92. When unemployment began rising in 2008–2009, Congress passed, and President Obama signed on February 17, 2009, the American Recovery and Reinvestment Act of 2009. His new law had the immediate effect of making it easier for qualified employees who were involuntarily dismissed for any reason (other than gross misconduct) anytime after September 1, 2008 (the act was retroactive), to sign up for COBRA. It makes it easier to utilize COBRA because the new law requires that the employer pay 65% of the premium. (The employer then receives a credit for that full amount back from the U.S. government.) The former employee must pay the remaining 35%. See http://www.recovery.gov/, accessed March 21, 2009.

93. Patrick Muldowney, "Cobra and the Stimulus Act: A Sign of Things to Come?" *Compensation & Benefits Review* 42, no. 1 (January/February 2010): 24–49.

94. Note that the American Recovery and Reinvestment Act of 2009 includes changes to several benefits-related programs including COBRA, the Mental Health Parity Act, and the Americans with Disabilities Act Amendments Act. Susan Relland, "Compliance Requirements and What More to Expect for Health and Welfare Plan for Sponsors in 2009," *Compensation & Benefits Review* (May/June 2009): 29–41.

95. "Health Coverage Premiums: Upward Bound," HR Trendbook (2008), p. 8. However, in 2009, employee costs rose only 6.4% compared with an average 15% since 2002, largely because of the employer cost containment efforts we'll discuss shortly. "Health Benefit Costs Expected to Rise 7%," *BNA Bulletin to Management* (October 20, 2009): 332.

96. "Hewitt Says Employer Measures to Control Increases in Health Care Costs Are Working," *BNA Bulletin to Management* (October 7, 2008): 323. A survey concluded that employer medical benefit costs will rise 7% in 2010, equaling an annual average of $10,000 per employee for the first time. "Health Benefit Trends: Employer Medical Benefit Costs Will Rise 7% in 2010,"

Compensation & Benefits Review 42, no. 1 (January/February 2010): 9–10.

97. "As Workers Feel the Effect of Cost Hikes, Employers Turn to Health Remedies," *BNA Bulletin to Management* (April 18, 2002): 121.

98. "Hewitt Says Employer Measures," 323.

99. "One in Five Big Firms May Drop Coverage for Future Retirees, Health Survey Finds," *BNA Bulletin to Management* (December 12, 2002): 393. Reducing retiree benefits requires a preliminary legal review. See James McElligott Jr., "Retiree Medical Benefit Developments in the Courts, Congress, and EEOC," *Compensation and Benefits Review* (March/April 2005): 23–28, and Natalie Norfus, "Retiree Benefits: Does an Employer's Obligation to Pay Ever End?" *Compensation & Benefits Review* (January/February 2008): 42–45.

100. "HR Outsourcing: Managing Costs and Maximizing Provider Relations," *BNA, Inc.* 21, no. 11 (Washington, DC: November 2003): 10. Benefits management ranks high on any list of HR activities that employers outsource. For example, in one survey, 94% outsource flexible spending accounts, 89% outsource defined contribution plans, 72% outsource defined benefit plans, and 68% outsource the auditing of dependents. Bill Roberts, "Outsourcing in Turbulent Times," *HR Magazine* (November 2009): 45.

101. Ron Finch, "Preventive Services: Improving the Bottom Line for Employers and Employees," *Compensation & Benefits Review* (March/April 2005): 18.

102. Ibid. See also Josh Cable, "The Road to Wellness," *Occupational Hazards* (April 2007): 23–27.

103. George DeVries, "The Top 10 Wellness Trends for 2008 and Beyond," *Compensation & Benefits Review* (July/August 2008): 60–63.

104. Susan Wells, "Getting Paid for Staying Well," *HR Magazine* (February 2010): 59.

105. Vanessa Fuhrmanns, "Oops! As Health Plans Become More Complicated, They're Also Subject to a Lot More Costly Mistakes," *Wall Street Journal* (January 24, 2005): R4.

106. "Dependent Eligibility Audits Can Help Rein in Health Care Costs, Analysts Say," *BNA Bulletin to Management* (September 9, 2008): 289.

107. Betty Liddick, "Going the Distance for Health Savings," *HR Magazine* (March 2007): 51–55. J. Wojcik, "Employers Consider Short-Haul Medical Tourism," *Business Insurance* 43, no. 29 (August 24 2009): 1, 20.

108. Jeremy Smerd, "Digitally Driven," *Workforce Management* (April 6, 2010): 23–26.

109. Martha Frase, "Minimalist Health Coverage," *HR Magazine* (June 2009): 107–12.

110. http://www.ssa.gov/pressoffice/colafacts.htm, accessed March 6, 2009.

111. The 7.65% tax rate is the combined rate for Social Security and Medicare.

112. Martocchio, *Strategic Compensation*, pp. 245–248; and Lin Grensing-Pophal, "A Pension Formula That Pays Off," *HR Magazine* (February 2003): 58–62.

113. Many employers are considering terminating their plans, but most employers are considering instead either ceasing benefits accruals for all participants or just for future participants. Michael Cotter, "The Big

Freeze: The Next Phase in the Decline of Defined Benefit Plans," *Compensation & Benefits Review* (March/April 2009): 44–53.

114. Nancy Pridgen, "The Duty to Monitor Appointed Fiduciaries under ERISA," *Compensation & Benefits Review* (September/October 2007): 46–51; "Individual 401(k) Plan Participant Can Sue Plan Fiduciary for Losses, Justices Rule," *BNA Bulletin to Management* (February 20, 2008): 65.

115. Jack VanDerhei, "The Pension Protection Act and 401(k)s," *Wall Street Journal* (April 20, 2008): A12. The Bureau of Labor Statistics reports that about half of companies automatically enrolled employees into defined contribution benefit plans. "Nearly Half of Employers Automatically Enrolled Employees," *BNA Bulletin to Management* (October 6, 2009): 316.

116. Jessica Marquez, "More Workers Yanking Money Out of 401(k)s," *Workforce Management* (August 11, 2008): 4.

117. Jessica Marquez, "Retirement Out of Reach," *Workforce Management* (November 3, 2008): 1, 24.

118. "New Pension Law Plus a Recent Court Ruling Doom Age-Related Suits, Practitioners Say," *BNA Bulletin to Management* 57, no. 36 (September 5, 2006): 281–82; and http://www.dol.gov/ebsa/FAQs/faq_consumer_cashbalanceplans.html, accessed January 9, 2010.

119. James Benson and Barbara Suzaki, "After Tax Reform, Part III: Planning Executive Benefits," *Compensation and Benefits Review* 20, no. 2 (March/April 1988): 45–57; "Post-Retirement Benefits Impact of FASB New Accounting Rule" (February 23, 1989): 57.

120. www.pbgc.gov/workers-retirees/benefits-information/content/page789.html, accessed March 6, 2009.

121. Joseph O'Connell, "Using Employee Assistance Programs to Avoid Crises," *Long Island Business News* (April 19, 2002): 10. The Mental Health Parity Act of 1996 (as amended in 2008) sets minimum mental health-care benefits; it also prohibits employer group health plans from adopting mental health benefits limitations without comparable limitations on medical and surgical benefits. "Mental-Health Parity Measure Enacted as Part of Financial Rescue Signed by Bush," *BNA Bulletin to Management* (October 7, 2008): 321.

122. "EAP Providers," *Workforce Management* (July 14, 2008): 16.

123. Richard Buddin and Kanika Kapur, "The Effect of Employer-Sponsored Education on Job Mobility: Evidence from the U.S. Navy," *Industrial Relations* 44, no. 2 (April 2005): 341–63; see also Michael Laff, "US Employers Tighten Reins on Tuition Reimbursement," *Training and Development* (July 2006): 18.

124. See, for example, "Compressed Workweeks Gain Popularity, but Concerns Remain about Effectiveness," *BNA Bulletin to Management* (September 16, 2008): 297.

125. Sue Shellenbarger, "Companies Retool Time Off Policies to Prevent Burnout, Reward Performance," *Wall Street Journal* (January 5, 2006): D1.

126. http://www.SHRM.org/rewards/library Brian O'Connell, "No Baby Sitter? Emergency Child Care to the Rescue" (May 2005), www.SHRM.org/rewards/library, accessed December 23, 2006; Kathy Gurchiek, "Give Us Your Sick," *HR Magazine* (January 2007): 91–93.

127. "Employers Gain from Elder Care Programs by Boosting Workers Morale, Productivity," *BNA Bulletin to Management* 57, no. 10 (March 7, 2006): 73–74.

128. Sue Shellenbarger, "The Mommy Drain: Employers Beef Up Perks to Lure New Mothers Back to Work," *Wall Street Journal* (September 28, 2006): D1.

129. "Making Up for Lost Time: How Employers Can Curb Excessive Unscheduled Absences," *BNA Human Resources Report* (October 20, 2003): 1097. See also W. H. J. Hassink et al., "Do Financial Bonuses Reduce Employee Absenteeism? Evidence from a Lottery," *Industrial and Labor Relations Review* 62, no. 3 (April 2009): 327–42.

130. Timothy Judge et al., "Work Family Conflict and Emotions: Effects at Work and at Home," *Personnel Psychology* 50, no. 9 (2006): 779–814; also 807.

131. Farrokh Mamaghani, "Impact of Information Technology on the Workforce of the Future: An Analysis," *International Journal of Management* 23, no. 4 (2006): 845–50; Jessica Marquez, "Connecting a Virtual Workforce," *Workforce Management* (September 20, 2008): 1–3.

132. Ann Pomeroy, "The Future Is Now," *HR Magazine* (September 2007): 46–52.

133. Scott Harper, "Online Resources System Boosts Worker Awareness," *BNA Bulletin to Management* (April 10, 2007): 119.

134. See, for example, Jessica Marquez, "Retooling Pay: Premium on Productivity," *Workforce Management* 84, no. 12 (November 7, 2005): 1, 22–3, 25–6, 28, 30; http://www.scribd.com/doc/12824332/NUCOR-CORP-8K-Events-or-Changes-Between-Quarterly-Reports-20090224, accessed November 3, 2009; and http://www.nucor.com/careers/, accessed November 3, 2009.

135. Elayne Robertson Demby, "Two Stores Refused to Join the Race to the Bottom for Benefits and Wages," *Workforce Management* (February 2004): 57.

Chapter 8

1. Keith Winstein, "Suit Alleges Pfizer Spun Unfavorable Drug Studies," *Wall Street Journal* (October 8, 2008): B1.

2. "What Role Should HR Play in Corporate Ethics?" *HR Focus* 81, no. 1 (January 2004): 3. See also Dennis Moberg, "Ethics Blind Spots in Organizations: How Systematic Errors in Person Perception Undermine Moral Agency," *Organization Studies* 27, no. 3 (2006): 413–28.

3. Kevin Wooten, "Ethical Dilemmas in Human Resource Management: An Application of a Multidimensional Framework, A Unifying Taxonomy, and Applicable Codes," *Human Resource Management Review* 11 (2001): 161. See also Sean Valentine et al., "Employee Job Response as a Function of Ethical Context and Perceived Organization Support," *Journal of Business Research* 59, no. 5 (2006): 582–88.

4. Paul Schumann, "A Moral Principles Framework for Human Resource Management Ethics," *Human Resource Management Review* 11 (2004): 94.

5. Manuel Velasquez, *Business Ethics: Concepts and Cases* (Upper Saddle River, NJ: Prentice Hall, 1992), p. 9. See also Joel Lefkowitz, "The Constancy of Ethics amidst the Changing World of Work," *Human Resource Management Review* 16 (2006): 245–68.

6. The following discussion, except as noted, is based on Manuel Velasquez, *Business Ethics*, 9–12. See also O. C. Ferrell, John Fraedrich, and Linda Ferrell, *Business Ethics* (Boston: Houghton Mifflin, 2008).

7. Ibid., p. 9.

8. This discussion is based on ibid., pp. 12–14.

9. Ibid., p. 12. For further discussion, see Kurt Baier, *Moral Points of View,* abbr. ed. (New York: Random House, 1965), p. 88. See also Milton Bordwin, "The 3 R's of Ethics," *Management Review* (June 1998): 59–61.

10. For further discussion of ethics and morality, see Tom Beauchamp and Norman Bowie, *Ethical Theory and Business* (Upper Saddle River, NJ: Prentice Hall, 2001), pp. 1–19.

11. Carroll Lachnit, "Recruiting Trouble for Tyson," *Workforce, HR Trends and Tools for Business Results* 81, no. 2 (February 2002): 22.

12. Richard Osborne, "A Matter of Ethics," *Industry Week* 49, no. 14 (September 4, 2000): 41–42.

13. Gary Weaver and Linda Trevino, "The Role of Human Resources in Ethics/Compliance Management: A Fairness Perspective," *Human Resource Management Review* 11 (2001): 115.

14. Michelle Donovan et al., "The Perceptions of Fair Interpersonal Treatment Scale: Development and Validation of a Measure of Interpersonal Treatment in the Workplace," *Journal of Applied Psychology* 83, no. 5 (1998): 683–92.

15. Bennett Tepper, "Consequences of Abusive Supervision," *Academy of Management Journal* 43, no. 2 (2000): 178–90. See also Samuel Aryee et al., "Antecedents and Outcomes of Abusive Supervision: A Test of a Trickle-Down Model," *Journal of Applied Psychology* 92, no. 1 (2007): 191–201.

16. Rudy Yandrick, "Lurking in the Shadows," *HR Magazine* (October 1999): 61–68.

17. Weaver and Trevino, "Role of Human Resources," 117.

18. Suzanne Masterson, "A Trickle-Down Model of Organizational Justice: Relating Employees' and Customers' Perceptions of and Reactions to Fairness," *Journal of Applied Psychology* 86, no. 4 (2001): 594–601.

19. Kenneth Sovereign, *Personnel Law* (Upper Saddle River, NJ: Prentice Hall, 1999), p. 150.

20. This list is from www.legaltarget.com/employee_rights, accessed January 3, 2008.

21. Basically, common law refers to legal precedents. Judges' rulings set precedents that then generally guide future judicial decisions.

22. Sovereign, *Personnel Law*, p. 192.

23. This list based on Linda K. Treviño, Gary R. Weaver, Scott J. Reynolds, "Behavioral Ethics in Organizations: A Review," *Journal of Management* 32, no. 6 (2006): 951–90.

24. R. Bergman, "Identity as Motivation: Toward a Theory of the Moral Self," in D. K. Lapsley & D. Narvaez (Eds.), *Moral Development, Self and Identity* (Mahwah, NJ: Lawrence Erlbaum, 2004), pp. 21–46.

25. M. E. Schweitzer, L. Ordonez, and B. Douma, "Goal Setting as a Motivator of Unethical Behavior," *Academy of Management Journal* 47, no. 3 (2004): 422–32.

26. N. M. Ashkanasy, C. A. Windsor, and L. K. Treviño, "Bad Apples in Bad Barrels Revisited: Cognitive Moral Development, Just World Beliefs, Rewards, and Ethical Decision Making," *Business Ethics Quarterly* 16 (2006): 449–74.

27. For an excellent analysis of what produces unethical behavior, see Jennifer Kish-Gephart, David Harrison, and Linda Treviño, "Bad Apples, Bad Cases, and Bad Barrels: Meta-Analytic Evidence about Sources of Unethical Decisions That Work," *Journal of Applied Psychology* 95, no. 1 (2010): 1–31.

28. Sara Morris et al., "A Test of Environmental, Situational, and Personal Influences on the Ethical Intentions of CEOs," *Business and Society* (August 1995): 119–47. See also Dennis Moberg, "Ethics Blind Spots in Organizations: How Systematic Errors in Person's Perception Undermine Moral Agency," *Organization Studies* 27, no. 3 (2006): 413–28.

29. "Former CEO Joins WorldCom's Indicted," *Miami Herald* (March 3, 2004): 4C.

30. Gretchen Morgenson, "Requiem for an Honorable Profession," *New York Times* (May 5, 2002): Business 1.

31. "Ethics Policies Are Big with Employers, but Workers See Small Impact on the Workplace," *BNA Bulletin to Management* (June 29, 2000): 201.

32. Jennifer Schramm, "Perceptions on Ethics," *HR Magazine* (November 2004): 176.

33. From Guy Brumback, "Managing above the Bottom Line of Ethics," *Supervisory Management* (December 1993): 12. See also F. E. Umphress et al., "The Influence of Distributive Justice on Lying for and Stealing from a Supervisor," *Journal of Business Ethics* 86, no. 4 (June 2009): 507–18.

34. James G. Hunt, *Leadership* (Newbury Park, CA: Sage, 1991), pp. 220–24. One writer describes organizational culture as a sort of "organizational DNA," since "it's the stuff, mostly intangible, that determines the basic character of a business." See James Moore, "How Companies Have Sex," *Fast Company* (October–November 1997): 66–68.

35. Heather Won Tesoriero and Avery Johnson, "Suit Details How J&J Pushed Sales of Procrit," *Wall Street Journal* (April 10, 2007): B1(1).

36. Quoted in Beauchamp and Bowie, *Ethical Theory and Business,* p. 109.

37. James Kunen, "Enron Division (and Values) Thing," *New York Times* (January 19, 2002): A19. For another example, see Heather Tesoriero and Avery Johnson, "Suit Details How J&J Pushed Sales of Procrit," *Wall Street Journal* (April 10, 2007).

38. Dayton Fandray, "The Ethical Company," *Workforce* 79, no. 12 (December 2000): 74–77.

39. Richard Beatty et al., "HR's Role in Corporate Governance: Present and Prospective," *Human Resource Management* 42, no. 3 (Fall 2003): 268.

40. Dale Buss, "Corporate Compasses," *HR Magazine* (June 2004): 127–32. Eric Krell, "How to Conduct an Ethics Audit," HR Magazine (April 2010): pages 48–51.

41. J. Krohe Jr., "The Big Business of Business Ethics," *Across the Board* 34 (May 1997): 23–29, in Deborah Wells and Marshall Schminke (Eds.), Ethical Development and Human Resources Training: An Integrative Framework, 135–58. For an interesting explanation of how the U.S. Military Academy uses its student admission and socialization processes to promote character development, see Evan Offstein and Ronald Dufresne, "Building Strong Ethics and Promoting Positive Character Development: The Influence of HRM at the United States Military Academy at West Point," *Human Resource Management* 46, no. 1 (Spring 2007): 95–114.

42. Editorial, "Ethical Issues in the Management of Human Resources," *Human Resource Management Review* 11 (2001): 6.

43. Weaver and Trevino, "Role of Human Resources," 123. In a similar study, researchers conducted studies of 490 police officers undergoing standardized promotional exams. Among their conclusions was that "Organizations should strive to ensure that candidates perceived justice both in the content of personnel assessments and in the way they are treated during the assessment process." Julie McCarthy et al., "Progression Through the Ranks: Assessing Employee Reactions to High Stakes Employment Testing," *Personnel Psychology* 62 (2009): 793–832.

44. William Byham, "Can You Interview for Integrity?" *Across-The-Board* 41, no. 2 (March/April 2004): 34–38.

45. Kathryn Tyler, "Do the Right Thing: Ethics Training Programs Help Employees Deal with Ethical Dilemmas," *HR Magazine* (February 2005): 99–102.

46. Editorial, "Ethical Issues in the Management of Human Resources," 6.

47. Weaver and Trevino, "Role of Human Resources," 123.

48. Michael Burr, "Corporate Governance: Embracing Sarbanes-Oxley," *Public Utilities Fortnightly* (October 15, 2003): 20–22.

49. Ibid.

50. Tom Asacker, "Ethics in the Workplace," *Training and Development* (August 2004): 44.

51. M. Ronald Buckley et al., "Ethical Issues in Human Resources Systems," *Human Resource Management Review* 11 (2001): 11, 29. See also Ann Pomeroy, "The Ethics Squeeze," *HR Magazine* (March 2006): 48–55.

52. Weaver and Trevino, "Role of Human Resources," 113–34. See also McCarthy et al., "Progression Through the Ranks," 826.

53. Ibid., p. 125.

54. Robert Grossman, "Executive Discipline," *HR Magazine* 50, no. 8 (August 2005): 46–51.

55. Kim and Mauborgne, "Fair Process: Managing in the Knowledge Economy," 65–75.

56. Weaver and Trevino, "Role of Human Resources," 114.

57. Lester Bittel, *What Every Supervisor Should Know* (New York: McGraw-Hill, 1974), p. 308; see also Paul Falcone, "The Fundamentals of Progressive Discipline," *HR Magazine* (February 1997): 90–92; and Thomas Salvo, "Practical Tips for Successful Progressive Discipline," SHRM White Paper, July 2004, http://www.shrm.org/hrresources/whitepapers_published/CMS_009030.asp, accessed January 5, 2008.

58. David Mayer et al., "When Do Fair Procedures Not Matter? A Test of the Identity Violation Effect," *Journal of Applied Psychology* 94, no. 1 (2009): 142–61.

59. In one study, the most frequent reason arbitrators gave for reinstating discharged employees was, "the employer's evidence did not support the charge of employee wrongdoing."

60. George Bohlander, "Why Arbitrators Overturn Managers in Employee Suspension and Discharge Cases," *Journal of Collective Negotiations* 23, no. 1 (1994): 76–77.

61. For example, don't deny the employee an opportunity to tell his or her side of the story. Ibid., 82.

62. Ibid. See also Ahman Karim, "Arbitration Considerations in Modifying Discharge Decisions in the Public Sector," *Journal of Collective Negotiations* 22, no. 3 (1993): 245–51; Joseph Martocchio and Timothy Judge, "When We Don't See Eye to Eye: Discrepancies between Supervisors and Subordinates in Absence Disciplinary Decisions," *Journal of Management* 21, no. 2 (1995): 251–78.

63. "Employers Turn to Corporate Ombuds to Defuse Internal Ticking Time Bombs," *BNA Bulletin to Management* (August 9, 2005): 249.

64. Nonpunitive discipline discussions based on David Campbell et al., "Discipline Without Punishment—At Last," *Harvard Business Review* (July/August 1995): 162–78; "Positive Discipline Replaces Punishment," *BNA Bulletin to Management* (April 27, 1995): 136.

65. "After Employer Found Liable for Worker's Child Porn, Policies May Need to Be Revisited," *BNA Bulletin to Management* (March 21, 2006): 89. Rita Zeidner, "Keeping E-Mail in Check," *HR Magazine* (June 2007): 70–74.

66. See also "Twitter Is Latest Electronic Tool to Pose Challenges and Opportunities for Employers," *BNA Bulletin to Management* (June 16, 2009): 185. See also Sean Valentine, et al., "Exploring the Ethicality of Firing Employees Who Blog," *Human Resource Management* 49, no. 1 (January/February 2010): 87:108.

67. Zeidner, "Keeping E-Mail in Check."

68. Fredric Leffler and Lauren Palais, "Filter Out Perilous Company E-Mails," *Society for Human Resource Management Legal Report* (August 2008): 3. A recent survey of 220 large U.S firms suggests that about 38% of them have people reading or otherwise analyzing employees outgoing e-mail. Dionne Searcy, "Some Courts Raise the Bar on Reading Employee E-Mail," *Wall Street Journal* (November 19, 2009): 817.

69. Bill Roberts, "Stay Ahead of the Technology Use Curve," *HR Magazine* (October 2008): 57–61.

70. "Do You Know Where Your Workers Are? GPS Units Aid Efficiency, Raise Privacy Issues," *BNA Bulletin to Management* (July 22, 2004): 233.

71. "Time Clocks Go High Touch, High Tech to Keep Workers from Gaining the System," *BNA Bulletin to Management* (March 25, 2004): 97.

72. One attorney notes that problems can arise with the Federal Stored Communications Act if the employer uses illicit or coercive means to access

the employees' private social media accounts. *BNA Bulletin to Management* (July 20, 2009): 225.

73. Some employers, such as Eastman Kodak, are appointing chief privacy officers to ensure that the human resource management and other departments don't endanger the company by conducting inappropriate investigations of job applicants or employees. Rita Zeidner, "New Face in the C-Suite," *HR Magazine* (January 2010): 39.

74. "Surveillance of Employees," *BNA Bulletin to Management* (April 25, 1996): 136.

75. "Telephone and Electronic Monitoring: A Special Report on the Issues and the Law," *BNA Bulletin to Management* (April 3, 1997): 2.

76. *Quon v. Arch Wireless Operating Co.*, 529f.3d 892 (Ninth Circuit 2008), "Employers Should Re-examine Policies in Light of Ruling," *BNA Bulletin to Management* (August 12, 2008): 263.

77. Many employees probably assume that their communications using the corporate e-mail system are open to review, but that e-mails they send via the employer's system but using their personal e-mail accounts (such as Gmail) aren't subject to review. Recently, courts in New York and New Jersey have supported this assumption, although on a limited basis. It's still not entirely clear-cut situation, but at a minimum the employer should take steps to make it clear that no employee has a reasonable expectation that any e-mails he or she sends using the employer's systems are private. Dionne Searcey, "Some Courts Raise the Bar on Reading Employee E-Mail," *Wall Street Journal* (November 19, 2009): 817.

78. A recent U.S. Federal Trade Commission decision may even make employers liable for deceptive endorsements that employees post on their own blogs or on social media sites such as Facebook, even if the employers didn't authorize the statements. "FTC Rules May Make Employers Liable for Worker Web Conduct," *BNA Bulletin to Management* (January 19, 2010): 23.

79. "When Can an Employer Access Private E-Mail on Its System?" *BNA Bulletin to Management* (July 14, 2009): 224.

80. *Vega-Rodriguez v. Puerto Rico Telephone Company*, CAL 962061, April 8, 1997; discussed in "Video Surveillance Withstands Privacy Challenge," *BNA Bulletin to Management* (April 17, 1998): 121.

81. "Secret Videotaping Leads to $200,000 Settlement," *BNA Bulletin to Management* (January 22, 1998): 17.

82. Andrea Poe, "Make Foresight 20/20," *HR Magazine* (February 20, 2000): 74–80. See also Nancy Hatch Woodward, "Smoother Separations," *HR Magazine* (June 2007): 94–97.

83. Robert Lanza and Morton Warren, "United States: Employment at Will Prevails Despite Exceptions to the Rule," *Society for Human Resource Management Legal Report* (October–November 2005): 1–8.

84. Ibid.

85. Joseph Famularo, *Handbook of Modern Personnel Administration* (New York: McGraw-Hill, 1982), pp. 63–65. See also Carolyn Hirschman, "Off Duty, Out of Work," *HR Magazine*, www. shrm.org/ hrmagazine/articles/0203/0203hirschman.asp, accessed January 1, 2008.

86. Connie Wanderg et al., "Perceived Fairness of Layoffs among Individuals Who Have Been Laid Off: A Longitudinal Study," *Personnel Psychology* 52 (1999): 59–84. See also Nancy Hatch Woodward, "Smoother Separations," *HR Magazine* (June 2007): 94–97.

87. Michael Orey, "Fear of Firing," *BusinessWeek* (April 23, 2007): 52–54.

88. Paul Falcon, "Give Employees the (Gentle) Hook," *HR Magazine* (April 2001): 121–28.

89. Sovereign, *Personnel Law*, p. 185.

90. "Fairness to Employees Can Stave Off Litigation," *BNA Bulletin to Management* (November 27, 1997): 377.

91. Adrienne Fox, "Prune Employees Carefully," *HR Magazine* (April 1, 2008), http://findarticles.com/ p/articles/mi_m3495/is_4_53/ai_n25358109/? tag=content;col1, accessed April 14, 2010.

92. Ibid.

93. Ibid. Also "Severance/Retention Practices: 2002; Pension Benefits," October 2002, p. 11; "Severance Pay," July 2007; Culpepper Compensation & Benefits Surveys.

94. Terry Baglieri, "Severance Pay," www.SHRM.org, downloaded December 23, 2006.

95. "Severance Decisions Swayed by Cost, Legal, Morale Concerns," *BNA Bulletin to Management* (May 12, 2009): 151.

96. Edward Isler et al., "Personal Liability and Employee Discipline," *Society for Human Resource Management Legal Report* (September–October 2000); 1–4.

97. "One More Heart Risk: Firing Employees," *Miami Herald* (March 20, 1998): C1, C7.

98. Based on James Coil III and Charles Rice, "Three Steps to Creating Effective Employee Releases," *Employment Relations Today* (Spring 1994): 91–94. See also Martha Frase-Blunt, "Making Exit Interviews Work," *HR Magazine* (August 2004): 9–11. "Severance Pay: Not Always the Norm," *HR Magazine* (May 2008): 28.

99. William J. Morin and Lyle York, *Outplacement Techniques* (New York: AMACOM, 1982), pp. 101–31; F. Leigh Branham, "How to Evaluate Executive Outplacement Services," *Personnel Journal* 62 (April 1983): 323–26; Sylvia Milne, "The Termination Interview," *Canadian Manager* (Spring 1994): 15–16. There is debate regarding what is the "best day of the week" on which to terminate an employee. Some say Friday to give the employee a few days to "cool off"; others suggest midweek, in order to allow employees "who remain in the department or in the immediate work group some time to process the change and to talk with each other to sort it out." See Jeffrey Connor, "Disarming Terminated Employees," *HR Magazine* (January 2000): 113–14.

100. Paul Brada, "Before You Go. . . ," *HR Magazine* (December 1998): 89–102.

101. Peter Hom et al., "Challenging Conventional Wisdom about Who Quits: Revelations from Corporate America," *Journal of Applied Psychology* 93, no. 1 (2008): 1–34.

102. Joseph Zarandona and Michael Camuso, "A Study of Exit Interviews: Does the Last Word Count?" *Personnel* 62, no. 3 (March 1981): 47–48.

103. "Workers Hit by Mass Layoffs Rose to 143,977 in February," *BNA Bulletin to Management* (April 3, 2007), 109.

104. See also Rodney Sorensen and Stephen Robinson, "What Employers Can Do to Stay Out of Legal Trouble When Forced to Implement Layoffs," Compensation & Benefits Review (January/February 2009): 25–32.

105. "Mass Layoffs at Lowest Level Since July 2008, BLS Says," *BNA Bulletin to Management* (January 12, 2010): 13.

106. Leon Grunberg, Sarah Moore, and Edward Greenberg, "Managers' Reactions to Implementing Layoffs: Relationship to Health Problems and Withdrawal Behaviors," *Human Resource Management* 45, no. 2 (Summer 2006): 159–78.

107. Ibid.

108. "Adopting Laid-Off Alternatives Could Help Employers Survive, Even Thrive, Analysts Say," *BNA Bulletin to Management* (February 20, 2009): 57.

109. See, for example, "Cushioning the Blow of Layoffs," *BNA Bulletin to Management* (July 3, 1997): 216; "Levi Strauss Cushions Blow of Plant Closings," *BNA Bulletin to Management* (November 20, 1997): 370. In one recent year, U.S. employers implemented about 1,300 mass layoffs, involving a total of almost 133,000 workers. "Layoffs: 133,914 Workers Idled by Mass Layoffs in April, BLS Says," *BNA Bulletin to Management* (June 3, 2008): 181.

110. "Calling a Layoff a Layoff," *Workforce Management* (April 21, 2008): 41.

111. David Gebler, "Is Your Culture a Risk Factor"? *Business and Society Review* 111, no. 3 (Fall 2006): 337–62.

112. John Cohan, "'I Didn't Know'" and 'I Was Only Doing My Job': Has Corporate Governance Careened out of Control? A Case Study of Enron's Information Myopia," *Journal of Business Ethics* 40, no. 3 (October 2002): 275–99.

113. Gebler, "Is Your Culture a Risk Factor"?

114. Ibid.

115. Facts adapted from Bureau of National Affairs, *Bulletin to Management* (September 13, 1985): 3.

Chapter 9

1. Steven Greenhouse, "Board Accuses Starbucks of Trying to Block Union," *New York Times* (April 3, 2007): B2; http://www.starbucksunion.org/, accessed March 25, 2009.

2. http://www.bls.gov/news.release/union2.nr0. htm, accessed April 2, 2009.

3. Ibid. "Union Membership Rises," *Compensation & Benefits Review* (May/June 2008): 9.

4. Joseph Adler, "The Past as Prologue? A Brief History of the Labor Movement in the United States," *International Personnel Management Association for HR* 35, no. 4 (Winter 2006): 311–29. As of 2009, for the first time most of those union members (7.6%) are in the public sector, as opposed to the private sector (7.2%). Stephen Greenhouse, "Most US Union Members Are Working for the Government, New Data Shows," *New York Times* (January 23, 2010): B1–5.

5. Ibid.

6. http://www.bls.gov/news.release/union2.nr0. htm, accessed April 2, 2009.

7. Michael Ash and Jean Seago, "The Effect of Registered Nurses' Unions on Heart Attack Mortality," *Industrial and Labor Relations Review* 57, no. 3 (April 2004): 422–42.

8. Steven Abraham et al., "The Impact of Union Membership on Intent to Leave," *Employee Responsibilities and Rights* 17, no. 4 (2005): 21–23.

9. Paul Monies, "Unions Hit Hard by Job Losses, Right to Work," *Daily Oklahoman* (via Knight Ridder/Tribune Business News) (February 1, 2005), downloaded May 25, 2005.

10. Ann Zimmerman, "Pro-Union Butchers at Wal-Mart Win a Union Battle But Lose War," *Wall Street Journal* (April 11, 2000): A14. See also Steven Greenhouse, "Report Assails Wal-Mart over Unions," *New York Times* (May 1, 2007): C3.

11. Donna Buttigieg et al., "An Event History Analysis of Union Joining and Leaving," *Journal of Applied Psychology* 92, no. 3 (2007): 829–39.

12. Ibid., p. 836; see also Lois Tetrick et al., "A Model of Union Participation: The Impact of Perceived Union Support, Union Instrumentality, and Union Loyalty," *Journal of Applied Psychology* 92, no. 3 (2007): 820–28.

13. Robert Grossman, "Unions Follow Suit," *HR Magazine* (May 2005): 49.

14. Kris Maher, "The New Union Worker," *Wall Street Journal* (September 27, 2005): B1, B11.

15. Benjamin Taylor and Fred Witney, *Labor Relations Law* (Upper Saddle River, NJ: Prentice Hall, 1992), pp. 157–84. See also Arthur Sloane and Fred Whitney, *Labor Relations* (Upper Saddle River, NJ: Prentice Hall, 2007), pp. 335–36.

16. Taylor and Witney, *Labor Relations Law*, pp. 170–71.

17. "Unions Hit Hard by Job Losses, Right to Work," *Daily Oklahoman* (via Knight Ridder/Tribune Business News) (February 1, 2005), downloaded May 25, 2005; and www. dol. gov/esa/programs/ whd/state/righttowork.htm, accessed January 13, 2008.

18. http://www.dol.gov/esa/programs/whd/state/ righttowork.htm, accessed January 13, 2008.

19. Steven Greenhouse, "Union Rejoining AFL-CIO," *New York Times* (September 18, 2009): A18.

20. The following material is based on Arthur Sloane and Fred Witney, *Labor Relations* (Upper Saddle River, NJ: Prentice Hall, 2001), pp. 63–120. See also www.NLRB.gov/NRLB/, "The National Labor Relations Board and You: Unfair Labor Practices."

21. Ibid., p. 106.

22. Karen Robinson, "Temp Workers Gain Union Access," *HR News, Society for Human Resource Management* 19, no. 10 (October 2000): 1.

23. Michael Carrell and Christina Heavrin, *Labor Relations and Collective Bargaining* (Upper Saddle River, NJ: Pearson, 2004), p. 180.

24. Ibid., p. 179.

25. Sloane and Witney, *Labor Relations*, 102–6.

26. William Fulmer, "Step by Step Through a Union Election," *Harvard Business Review* 60 (July/August 1981): 94–102. For an interesting description of contract negotiations, see Peter Cramton and Joseph Tracy, "The Determinants of U.S. Labor

Disputes," *Journal of Labor Economics* 12, no. 2 (April 1994): 180–209. Sloane and Witney, *Labor Relations*, p. 29.

27. Sloane and Witney, *Labor Relations*, p. 29.

28. Jonathan Segal, "Expose the Union's Underbelly," *HR Magazine* (June 1999): 166–76.

29. "Some Say Salting Leaves Bitter Taste for Employers," *BNA Bulletin to Management* (March 4, 2004): 79. For a management lawyer's perspective, see www.fklaborlaw.com/union_salt-objectives. html, accessed May 25, 2007.

30. For more information on the Starbucks Workers Union, go to www.starbucksunion.org, accessed January 14, 2008.

31. Fulmer, "Step by Step Through a Union Election," 94.

32. Frederick Sullivan, "Limiting Union Organizing Activity Through Supervisors," *Personnel* 55 (July/August 1978): 55–65. Richard Peterson, Thomas Lee, and Barbara Finnegan, "Strategies and Tactics in Union Organizing Campaigns," *Industrial Relations* 31, no. 2 (Spring 1992): 370–81. See also Edward Young and William Levy, "Responding to a Union-Organizing Campaign: Do You and Your Supervisors Know the Legal Boundaries in a Union Campaign?" *Franchising World* 39, no. 3 (March 2007): 45–49. Some labor lawyers report an increase in the use by unions of corporate campaigns. Janet Walthall, "Unions Increasingly Using Corporate Campaigns," *BNA Bulletin to Management* (February 16, 2010): 55.

33. Sullivan, "Limiting Union Organizing Activity."

34. B&D Plastics, Inc. 302 NLRB No. 33, 1971, 137 LRRM 1039; discussed in "No Such Thing as a Free Lunch," *BNA Bulletin to Management* (May 23, 1991): 153–54.

35. Edwin Arnold et al., "Determinants of Certification Election Outcomes in the Service Sector," *Labor Studies Journal* 25, no. 3 (Fall 2000): 51.

36. "2008 Union Win Rate Rose to 66.8%; Number of Elections Increased, Data Show," *BNA Bulletin to Management* (May 12, 2009): 145–52.

37. "Union Decertifications Up in First Half of 1998," *BNA Bulletin to Management* (December 24, 1998): 406. See also www. nlrb.gov/nlrb/shared_files/ brochures/rpt_ september2002.pdf, accessed January 14, 2008.

38. Carrell and Heavrin, *Labor Relations and Collective Bargaining*, pp. 120–21.

39. Terry Leap, *Collective Bargaining and Labor Relations* (Upper Saddle River, NJ: Prentice Hall, 1995). See also www.nlrb.gov/nlrb/shared_files/brochures/ basicguide.pdf, accessed January 14, 2008.

40. Leap, *Collective Bargaining and Labor Relations*, pp. 307–9.

41. Ibid., p. 308.

42. Kathryn Tyler, "Good-Faith Bargaining," *HR Magazine* (January 2005): 52.

43. Bargaining items based on Reed Richardson, *Collective Bargaining by Objectives* (Upper Saddle River, NJ: Prentice Hall, 1997), pp. 113–15; see also Sloane and Witney, *Labor Relations*, pp. 180–217.

44. Sloane and Witney, *Labor Relations*, pp. 192–220.

45. D. Scott DeRue et al., "When Is Straightforwardness a Liability in Negotiations? The Role of Integrative Potential and Structural Power," *Journal of Applied Psychology* 94, no. 4 (2009): 1032–47.

46. "The Road to Impasse," *CBS Sports Online*, March 4, 2005, www.CDC.com/sports/.

47. http://www.thedeal.com/corporatedealmaker/ 2009/11/us_airways_pilots_seek_federal.php, accessed November 17, 2009.

48. John Burger and Steven Walters, "Arbitrator Bias and Self-Interest: Lessons from the Baseball Labor Market." *Journal of Labor Research* 26, no. 2 (Spring 2005): 267–80.

49. Jonathan Kramer and Thomas Hyclak, "Why Strikes Occur: Evidence from the Capital Markets," *Industrial Relations* 41, no. 1 (January 2002): 80–93.

50. Micheline Maynard and Jeremey Peters, "Northwest Airlines Threatens to Replace Strikers Permanently," *New York Times* (August 26, 2005): C3.

51. For a discussion, see Herbert Northrup, "Union Corporate Campaigns and Inside Games as a Strike Form," *Employee Relations Law Journal* 19, no. 4 (Spring 1994): 507–49.

52. Melanie Evans, "Labor Pains: As Membership Slides, Unions Have Turned to Provocative Corporate Campaigns," *Modern Health Care* 34, no. 26 (December 6, 2004): 26.

53. Northrup, "Union Corporate Campaigns and Inside Games as a Strike Form."

54. Ibid., p. 518.

55. The NLRB held in 1986 in Charter Equipment, Inc. 280 NLRB No. 71, that an employer could lawfully hire temporary replacements during the course of a lockout, in the absence of proof of specific antiunion motivation, in order to bring economic pressure to bear upon a union to support a legitimate bargaining position.

56. Clifford Koen Jr., Sondra Hartmen, and Dinah Payne, "The NLRB Wields a Rejuvenated Weapon," *Personnel Journal* (December 1996): 85–87; and (Sloane and Whitney, *Labor Relations* (2007), p. 84.

57. http://sports.espn.go.com/nfl/news/story?id= 4508545, accessed November 17, 2009.

58. Duncan Adams, "Worker Grievances Consume Roanoke, VA, Mail Distribution Center," *Knight Ridder/Tribune Business News* (March 27, 2001): Item 1086009.

59. Walter Baer, *Grievance Handling: 101 Guides for Supervisors* (New York: American Management Association, 1970).

60. Jessica Marquez, "N Y Unions Cage Inflatable Rat, Try Teamwork," *Workforce Management* (November 3, 2008): 10.

61. See, for example, Jo Blandon et al., "Have Unions Turned the Corner? New Evidence on Recent Trends in Union Recognition in UK Firms," *British Journal of Industrial Relations* 44, no. 2 (June 2006): 169–90; see also Mark Schoeff Jr., "Labor on the March," *Workforce Management* (February 2010): 1, 18–19.

62. "Unions Using Class Actions to Pressure Nonunion Companies," *BNA Bulletin to Management* (August 22, 2006): 271. Some believe that today, "long-term observers see more bark than bite in organized labor's efforts to revitalize." See, for example, Robert Grossman, "We Organized Labor and Code," *HR Magazine* (January 2008): 37–40.

63. "Chris Maher, "Specter Won't Support Union-Backed Bill," *Wall Street Journal* (March 20, 2009): A3.

64. "Unions Using Class Actions to Pressure Nonunion Companies," *BNA Bulletin to Management* (August 22, 2006): 271.

65. Dean Scott, "Unions Still a Potent Force," *Kiplinger Business Forecasts* (March 26, 2003).

66. "Contracts Call for Greater Labor Management Teamwork," *BNA Bulletin to Management* (April 29, 1999): 133.

67. Carol Gill, "Union Impact on the Effective Adoption of High Performance Work Practices," *Human Resource Management Review* 19 (2009): 39–50.

68. Jennifer Schramm, "The Future of Unions," *Workplace Visions, Society for Human Resource Management,* (2005): 6.

69. Mei Fong and Kris Maher, "US Labor Chief Moves into China," *Wall Street Journal Asia* (June 22–24, 2007): 1.

70. Steven Greenhouse, "Steelworkers Merge with British Union," *New York Times* (July 3, 2008): C4.

71. Chris Purcell, "Rhetoric Flying in WGA Talks," *Television Week* 26, no. 30 (July 20, 2007): 3, 35; Peter Sanders, "In Hollywood, a Tale of Two Union Leaderships," *Wall Street Journal* (January 7, 2008): B2.

72. Purcell, "Rhetoric Flying in WGA Talks."

73. Ibid.

74. James Hibberd, "Guild Talks Break with No Progress," *Television Week* 26, no. 38 (October 8–15, 2007): 1, 30.

75. Ibid.

76. "DGA Deal Sets the Stage for Writers," *Television Week* 27, no. 3 (2008): 3, 33.

77. "WGA, Studios Reach Tentative Agreement," *UPI News Track* (February 3, 2008).

78. "U.S.: Rise in Union Activity at Dot.Com Firms," *Guardian* (December 13, 2000): 18.

79. Raymond Hilgert and Cyril Ling, *Cases and Experiential Exercises in Management* (Upper Saddle River, NJ: Prentice Hall, 1996), pp. 201–3.

Chapter 10

1. Michael Wilson, "Manslaughter Charge in Trench Collapse," *New York Times* (June 12, 2008): B1.

2. For a discussion of specific strategies for reducing fatalities at work, see, for example, Laura Walter, "Facing the Unthinkable: Fatality Prevention in the Workplace," *Occupational Hazards* (January 2008): 32–39.

3. All data refer to 2006. See www.OSHA.gov http:// www.bls.gov/iif/oshwc/osh/os/ostb1757.txt, accessed January 19, 2008.

4. The U.S. government's government accounting office recently conducted a survey in which it concluded that OSHA overlooks certain worker injuries and illnesses. "OSHA: GAO Findings on Injury and Illness Reporting Are Alarming," *EHS Today* (December 2009): 12.

5. David Ayers, "Mapping Support for an E. H. S. Management System," *Occupational Hazards* (June 2006): 53–54.

6. Katherine Torres, "Stepping into the Kitchen: Food Protection for Food Workers," *Occupational Hazards* (January 2007): 29–30.

7. Based on *All About OSHA*, rev. ed. (Washington, DC: U.S. Department of Labor, 1980); www.OSHA. gov, accessed January 19, 2008.

8. "OSHA Hazard Communication Standard Enforcement," *BNA Bulletin to Management* (February 23, 1980): 13. See also William Kincaid, "OSHA vs. Excellence in Safety Management," *Occupational Hazards* (December 2002): 34–36.

9. "What Every Employer Needs to Know about OSHA Record Keeping," U.S. Department of Labor, Bureau of Labor Statistics (Washington, DC), report 412–13, p. 3.

10. "Supreme Court Says OSHA Inspectors Need Warrants," *Engineering News Record* (June 1, 1978): 9–10; W. Scott Railton, "OSHA Gets Tough on Business," *Management Review* 80, no. 12 (December 1991): 28–29. Steve Hollingsworth, "How to Survive an OSHA Inspection," *Occupational Hazards* (March 2004): 31–33.

11. http://osha.gov/as/opa/oshafacts.html, accessed January 19, 2008; Edwin Foulke Jr., "OSHA's Evolving Role in Promoting Occupational Safety and Health,"*EHS Today* (November 2008): 44–49. Some believe that under the new Democratic administration of President Obama, OSHA may move from voluntary programs back to increased attention on inspections. See, for example, Laura Walter, "Safety Roundtable: The View from the End of an Era,"*EHS Today* (December 2008): 30–31.

12. Lisa Finnegan, "Industry Partners with OSHA," *Occupational Hazards* (February 1999): 43–45. OSHA instituted a pilot Voluntary Protection Program (VPP) for companies with exemplary safety practices. On-site VPP evaluation teams evaluate such things as supervisory safety training and safety and health communications programs. VPP certification removes a facility from OSHA's routine inspection list. Sara Escborn and Mary Giddings, "The Ripple Effect of Fluor's Corporate VPP Status," *EHS Today* (February 2009): 44–45.

13. http://www.osha.gov/Publications/osha2098. pdf+OSHA+inspection+priorities&hl=en&ct= clnk&cd=1&gl=us, accessed January 19, 2008.

14. www.OSHA.gov, downloaded May 28, 2005, and http://osha.gov/pls/oshaweb/owadisp.show_doc ument?p_table=NEWS_RELEASES&p_id=14883, accessed January 19, 2008. "OSHA Sends 15,000 Letters to Employers with High Injury Rates and Offers Assistance," *BNA Bulletin to Management* (March 16, 2010): 83.

15. Patricia Poole, "When OSHA Knocks," *Occupational Hazards* (February 2008): 59–61.

16. For example, OSHA recently settled with Murphy Oil USA with Murphy paying just over $179,000 in OSHA fines for a variety of violations such as activated alarms, and OSHA recently proposed a penalty of $195,200 against a masonry contractor with a total of 21 violations. See "Enforcement Briefs," *Occupational Hazards* (March 2008): 13.

17. http://www.osha.gov/Publications/osha2098. pdf+OSHA+inspection+priorities&hl=en&ct= clnk&cd=1&gl=us, accessed January 19, 2008.

18. For a discussion of how to deal with citations and proposed penalties, see, for example, Michael Taylor, "OSHA Citations and Proposed Penalties: How to Beat the Rap," *EHS Today* (December 2008): 34–36.

19. Jim Lastowka, "Ten Keys to Avoiding OSHA Liability," *Occupational Hazards* (October 1999): 163–70; and www.osha.gov/Publications/osha2098.pdf+OSHA+ inspection+priorities&hl= en&ct=clnk&cd= 1&gl=us, accessed January 19, 2008.

20. Robert Grossman, "Handling Inspections: Tips from Insiders," *HR Magazine* (October 1999): 41–50.

21. Arthur Sapper, "The Oft-Missed Step: Documentation of Safety Discipline," *Occupational Hazards* (January 2006): 59.

22. Don Williamson and Jon Kauffman, "From Tragedy to Triumph: Safety Grows Wings at Golden Eagle," *Occupational Hazards* (February 2006): 17–25.

23. "A Safety Committee Man's Guide," *Aetna Life and Casualty Insurance Company,* Catalog 872684. See also Todd Nighswonger, "Get a Grip on Slips," *Occupational Hazards* (September 2000): 47–50.

24. For a discussion of this, see David Hofmann and Adam Stetzer, "A Cross-Level Investigation of Factors Influencing Unsafe Behaviors and Accidents," *Personnel Psychology* 49 (1996): 307–8.

25. David Hofman and Barbara Mark, "An Investigation of the Relationship between Safety Climate and Medication Errors as Well as Other Nurse and Patient Outcomes," *Personnel Psychology* 50, no. 9 (2006): 847–69.

26. List of unsafe acts from "A Safety Committee Man's Guide," *Aetna Life and Casualty Insurance Company.*

27. Robert Pater and Robert Russel, "Drop That Accident Prone Tag: Look for Causes beyond Personal Issues," *Industrial Safety and Hygiene News* 38, no. 1 (January 2004): 50.

28. Discussed in Douglas Haaland, "Who's the Safest Bet for the Job? Find Out Why the Fun Guy in the Next Cubicle May Be the Next Accident Waiting to Happen," *Security Management* 49, no. 2 (February 2005): 51–57.

29. "Thai Research Points to Role of Personality in Road Accidents," *Asia and Africa Intelligence Wire* (February 23, 2005); Donald Bashline et al., "Bad Behavior: Personality Tests Can Help Underwriters Identify High-Risk Drivers," *Best's Review* 105, no. 12 (April 2005): 63–64.

30. See, for example, Michael Christian et al., "Workplace Safety: A Meta-Analysis of the Roles of Person and Situation Factors," *Journal of Applied Psychology* 94, no. 5 (2009): 1103–27.

31. Michael Frone, "Predictors of Work Injuries among Employed Adolescents," *Journal of Applied Psychology* 83, no. 4 (1998): 565–76.

32. Benjamin Mangan, "Lockout/Tagout Prevents Workplace Injuries and Saves Lives," *Occupational Hazards* (March 2007): 59–60; Jimi Michalscheck, "The Basics of Lock Out/Tag Out Compliance: Creating an Effective Program," *EHS Today* (January 2010): 35–37.

33. Mike Carlson, "Machine Safety Solutions for Protecting Employees and Safeguarding against Machine Hazards," *EHS Today* (July 2009): 24.

34. James Nash, "Beware the Hidden Eye Hazards," *Occupational Hazards* (February 2005): 48–51. A combustible dust explosion at a sugar refinery recently killed 14 employees and injured dozens of others, many with serious burns. The employers subsequently required all employees and visitors to the manufacturing areas to wear fire-resistant clothing. But if that requirement had been in effect *before* the explosion, many burns might have been avoided. Laura Walter, "FR Clothing: Leaving Hazards in the Dust," *EHS Today* (January 2010): 20–22.

35. You can find videos about new personal protective products at "SafetyLive TV" at www.occupational hazards.com, accessed March 14, 2009.

36. James Zeigler, "Protective Clothing: Exploring the Wearability Issue," *Occupational Hazards,* (September 2000): 81–82; Sandy Smith, "Protective Clothing and the Quest for Improved Performance," *Occupational Hazards* (February 2008): 63–66.

37. "The Complete Guide to Personal Protective Equipment," *Occupational Hazards* (January 1999): 49–60. See also Edwin Zalewski, "Noise Control: It's More than Just Earplugs: OSHA Requires Employers to Evaluate Engineering and Administrative Controls before Using Personal Protective Equipment," *Occupational Hazards* 68, no. 9 (September 2006): 48. You can find videos about new personal protective products at "SafetyLive TV" at www.occupationalhazards. com, accessed March 14, 2009.

38. Robert Pater and Ron Bowles, "Directing Attention to Boost Safety Performance," *Occupational Hazards* (March 2007): 46–48.

39. E. Scott Geller, "The Thinking and Seeing Components of People-Based Safety," *Occupational Hazards* (December 2006): 38–40.

40. Sandy Smith, "Protecting Vulnerable Workers," *Occupational Hazards* (April 2004): 25–28. In addition to millions of women in factory jobs, about 10% of the construction industry workforce is female, and there are almost 200,000 women in the U.S. military. Women also represent almost 80% of health-care workers, where puncture- and chemical-resistant gloves are particularly important. David Shutt, "Protecting the Hands of Working Women," *EHS Today* (October 2009): 29–32.

41. See, for example, Laura Walter, "What's in a Glove?" *Occupational Hazards* (May 2008): 35–36.

42. Donald Groce, "Keep the Gloves On!" *Occupational Hazards* (June 2008): 45–47.

43. Linda Tapp, "We Can Do It: Protecting Women Workers," *Occupational Hazards* (October 2003): 26–28.

44. Katherine Torres, "Don't Lose Sight of the Older Workforce," *Occupational Hazards* (June 2008): 55–59.

45. Robert Pater, "Boosting Safety with an Aging Workforce," *Occupational Hazards* (March 2006): 24.

46. Michael Silverstein, M.D., "Designing the Age Friendly Workplace," *Occupational Hazards* (December 2007): 29–31.

47. Elizabeth Rogers and William Wiatrowski, "Injuries, Illnesses, and Fatalities among Older Workers," *Monthly Labor Review* 128, no. 10 (October 2005): 24–30.

48. "Feds Ordered, Contractors Urged, Not to Text While Driving," *BNA Bulletin to Management* (October 6, 2009): 314.

49. "Thai Research Points to Role of Personality in Road Accidents," *Asia and Africa Intelligence Wire* (February 23, 2005), accessed May 28, 2005; Donald Bashline et al., "Bad Behavior: Personality Tests Can

Help Underwriters Identify High-Risk Drivers," *Best's Review* 105, no. 12 (April 2005): 63–64.

50. S. Laner and R. J. Sell, "An Experiment on the Effect of Specially Designed Safety Posters," *Occupational Psychology* 34 (1960): 153–69; Ernest McCormick and Joseph Tiffin, *Industrial Psychology* (Upper Saddle River, NJ: Prentice Hall, 1974), p. 536.

51. See, for example, Laura Walter, "10 Tips for More Effective EHS Training," *EHS Today* (February 2009): 35–37.

52. See also Josh Cable, "Erring on the Side of Caution," *Occupational Hazards* (February 2007): 21–22; and Shel Siegel, "Incentives: Small Investments Equal Big Rewards," *Occupational Hazards* (August 2007): 42–44.

53. See, for example, Ron Bruce, "Online from Kazakhstan to California," *Occupational Hazards* (June 2008): 61–65.

54. Michael Blotzer, "PDA Software Offers Auditing Advances," *Occupational Hazards* 63, no. 12 (December 2001): 11. See also Eric Anderson, "Automating Health & Safety Processes Creates Value," *Occupational Hazards* (April 2008): 53–63.

55. Laura Walter, "Surfing for Safety," *Occupational Hazards* (July 2008): 23–29.

56. James Nash, "Rewarding the Safety Process," *Occupational Hazards* (March 2000): 29–34.

57. J. Nigel Ellis and Susan Warner, "Using Safety Awards to Promote Fall Prevention," *Occupational Hazards* (June 1999): 59–62. See also William Atkinson, "Safety Incentive Programs: What Works?" *Occupational Hazards* (August 2004): 35–39.

58. Don Williamson and Jon Kauffman, "From Tragedy to Triumph: Safety Grows Wings at Golden Eagle," *Occupational Hazards* (February 2006): 17–25.

59. Quoted in Josh Cable, "Seven Suggestions for a Successful Safety Incentives Program," *Occupational Hazards* 67, no. 3 (March 2005): 39–43. See also J. M. Saidler, "Gift Cards Make Safety Motivation Simple," *Occupational Health & Safety* 78, no. 1 (January 2009): 39–40.

60. John Dominic, "Improve Safety Performance and Avoid False Reporting," *HR Magazine* 49, no. 9 (September 2004): 110–19; see also Josh Cable, "Safety Incentives Strategies," *Occupational Hazards* 67, no. 4 (April 2005): 37.

61. See also Kelly Rowe, "OSHA and Small Businesses: A Winning Combination," *Occupational Hazards* (March 2007): 33–38.

62. Willie Hammer, *Occupational Safety Management and Engineering* (Upper Saddle River, NJ: Prentice Hall, 1985), pp. 62–63. See also "DuPont's 'STOP' Helps Prevent Workplace Injuries and Incidents," *Asia Africa Intelligence Wire* (May 17, 2004).

63. Sandy Smith, "Louisiana-Pacific Corp. Bills Safety into Everything It Does," *Occupational Hazards* (November 2007): 41–42.

64. James Nash, "Weyerhaeuser Fires Plant, Safety Managers for Record-Keeping Abuses," *Occupational Hazards* (November 2004): 27–28.

65. In a similar case, in 2008, the owner of a Brooklyn, New York, construction site was arrested for manslaughter when a worker died in a collapsed trench. Michael Wilson, "Manslaughter Charge

in Trench Collapse," *New York Times* (June 12, 2008): B1.

66. "A Safety Committee Man's Guide," 17–21.

67. Dov Zohar, "A Group Level Model of Safety Climate: Testing the Effect of a Group Climate on Students in Manufacturing Jobs," *Journal of Applied Psychology* 85, no. 4 (2000): 587–96. See also Steven Yule, Rhona Flin, and Andy Murdy, "The Role of Management and Safety Climate in Preventing Risk-Taking at Work," *International Journal of Risk Assessment and Management* 7, no. 2 (December 20, 2006): 137.

68. Quoted from Sandy Smith, "Breakthrough Safety Management," *Occupational Hazards* (June 2004): 43. For a discussion of developing a safety climate survey, see Sara Singer et al., "Workforce Perceptions of Hospital Safety Culture: Development and Validation of the Patient Safety Climate in Health-care Organizations Survey," *Health Services Research* 42, no. 5 (October 2007): 1999.

69. Howard Street, "Getting Full Value from Auditing and Metrics," *Occupational Hazards* (August 2000): 33–36.

70. Thomas Krause, "Steps in Safety Strategy: Executive Decision-Making & Metrics," *EHS Today* (September 2009): 24.

71. Sandy Smith, "Zero Isn't Good Enough at AMEC Earth & Environmental," *EHS Today* (November 2009): 26; Laura Walter, "Safety Evolves at the Concrete Pipe Division of Cemex US Operations," *EHS Today* (November 2009): 27.

72. www.zeraware.com, accessed March 22, 2009.

73. This is based on Paul Puncochar, "The Science and Art to Identifying Workplace Hazards," *Occupational Hazards* (September 2003): 50–54.

74. Ibid., p. 52.

75. Based on the report *Workplace Screening & Brief Intervention: What Employees Can and Should Do about Excessive Alcohol Use*, in "Report Says Employee Alcohol Abuse Closely to Companies," *BNA Bulletin to Management* (June 10, 2008): 101.

76. "15% of Workers Drinking, Drunk, or Hung Over While at Work, According to New University Study," *BNA Bulletin to Management* (January 24, 2006): 27. By some estimates, employee alcoholism costs U.S. employees about $226 billion per year. (Samuel Bacharach, et al. "Alcohol Consumption and Workplace Absenteeism: The Moderating Effect of Social Support," *Journal of Applied Psychology* 95, no. 2 (2010): 334–348.

77. See for example, L. Claussen, "Can You Spot the Meth Addict?" *Safety & Health* 179, no. 4 (April 2009): 48–52.

78. CAGE is an acronym for the first letters of four of its questions: Cut Down, Annoyed, Guilty, and Eye Opener. MAST is the Michigan Alcoholism Screening Test.

79. www.DOL.gov/ASP/programs/drugs/workingpartners, accessed May 28, 2005.

80. Gopal C. Pati and John I. Adkins Jr., with Glenn Morrison, *Managing and Employing the Handicapped: The Untapped Potential* (Lake Forest, IL: Brace-Park, Human Resource Press, 1981); See also Commerce Clearing House, "How Should Employers Respond to Indications an Employee May Have an Alcohol or Drug Problem?" *Ideas*

and *Trends* (April 6, 1989): 53–57; and "Employer's Role," 568–72. "The Employer's Role in Alcoholism Assistance," *Personnel Journal* 62, no. 7 (July 1983): 568–72.

81. Beth Andrus, "Accommodating the Alcoholic Executive," *Society for Human Resource Management Legal Report* (January 2008): 1, 4.

82. "New Jersey Union Takes on Mandatory Random Drug Tests," *Record* (Hackensack, NJ) (January 2, 2008): p. NA.

83. William Current, "Pre-Employment Drug Testing," *Occupational Hazards* (July 2002): 56. See also William Current, "Improving Your Drug Testing ROI," *Occupational Health & Safety* 73, no. 4 (April 2004): 40, 42, 44.

84. Diane Cadrain, "Are Your Employees' Drug Tests Accurate?" *HR Magazine* (January 2003): 41–45; and Sally Roberts, "Random Drug Testing Can Help Reduce Accidents for Construction Companies; Drug Abuse Blamed for Heightened Risk in the Workplace," *Business Insurance* 40 (October 23, 2006): 6.

85. Frank Lockwood et al., "Drug Testing Programs and Their Impact on Workplace Accidents: A Time Series Analysis," *Journal of Individual Employment Rights* 8, no. 4 (2000): 295–306.

86. Teresa Long, "Intoxicated Drivers and Employer Liability," *EHS Today* (September 2009): 22–23.

87. The research is quite clear that work-stress increases alcohol use among normal drinkers, and this has several implications for employers. Employers and supervisors should take steps to reduce stressful daily work experiences such as interpersonal conflicts at work, role ambiguity, and excessive workloads as way to reduce stress. Songqi Liu et al., "Daily Work Stress and Alcohol Use: Testing the Cross Level Moderation Effects of Neuroticism and Job Involvement," *Personnel Psychology* 60, no. 2 (2009): 575–97.

88. www.OSHA.gov, accessed May 28, 2005.

89. "Few Employers Addressing Workplace Stress, Watson Wyatt Surveys Find," *Compensation & Benefits Review* (May/June 2008): 12.

90. Eric Sundstrom et al., "Office Noise, Satisfaction, and Performance," *Environment and Behavior* 2 (March 1994): 195–222; and javascript:bkmUrl ('/purl=rc1_GBFM_0_A153706318&dyn=38!xrn_ 35_0_A153706318'), "Stress: How to Cope with Life's Challenges," *American Family Physician* 74 no. 8 (October 15, 2006).

91. Michael Manning, Conrad Jackson, and Marcelline Fusilier, "Occupational Stress, Social Support, and the Costs of Health Care," *Academy of Management Journal* 39, no. 3 (1996): 738–50; "Failing to Tackle Stress Could Cost You Dearly," *Personnel Today* (September 12, 2006); and http://www. sciencedaily.com/releases/2007/06/070604170722. htm, accessed November 3, 2009.

92. "Stress, Depression Cost Employers," *Occupational Hazards* (December 1998): 24. See also Patricia B. Gray, "Hidden Costs of Stress," *Money* 36, no. 12 (December 2007): 44.

93. Sabine Sonnentag et al., " 'Did You Have a Nice Evening?' A Day-Level Study on Recovery Experiences, Sleep, and Affect," *Journal of Applied Psychology* 93, no. 3 (2008): 674–84.

94. See, for example, Elizabeth Bernstein, "When a Coworker Is Stressed Out," *Wall Street Journal* (August 26, 2008): B1, B2.

95. Karl Albrecht, *Stress and the Manager* (Upper Saddle River, NJ: Prentice Hall, 1979), pp. 253–55. Reprinted by permission. See also "Stress: How to Cope with Life's Challenges," *American Family Physician* 74, no. 8 (October 15, 2006).

96. "Meditation Gives Your Mind Permanent Working Holiday; Relaxation Can Improve Your Business Decisions and Your Overall Health," discussed in *Investor's Business Daily* (March 24, 2004): 89. See also, "Workplace Yoga, Meditation Can Reduce Stress," *EHS Today* (September 2009): 21.

97. "Meditation Helps Employees Focus, Relieve Stress," *BNA Bulletin to Management* (February 20, 2007): 63.

98. "Going Head to Head With Stress," *Personnel Today* (April 26, 2005): 1.

99. Ibid.

100. See for example, Christina Maslach and Michael Leiter, "Early Predictors of Job Burnout and Engagement," *Journal of Applied Psychology* 93, no. 3 (2008): 498–512.

101. Ibid.

102. Andy Meisler, "Mind Field," *Workforce Management* (September 2003): 58.

103. "Employers Must Move from Awareness to Action in Dealing with Worker Depression," *BNA Bulletin to Management* (April 29, 2004): 137.

104. Sandy Smith, "SARS: What Employers Need to Know," *Occupational Hazards* (July 2003): 33–35.

105. "CDC Recommends N95 Respirators in Revised H1N1 Flu Guidance for Healthcare Workers," *BNA Bulletin to Management* (October 20, 2009): 329–36; Pamela Ferrante, "H1N1: Spreading the Message," *EHS Today* (January 2010): 25–27.

106. Diane Cadrain, "Smoking and Workplace Laws Ensnaring HR," *HR Magazine* 49, no. 6 (June 2004): 38–39.

107. "Smoking Succession Plans Aimed at Curbing Health Care Costs," *BNA Bulletin to Management* (October 20, 2009): 343.

108. Daniel Warner, "We Do Not Hire Smokers: May Employers Discriminate against Smokers?" *Employee Responsibilities and Rights* no. 2 (June 1994): 129–40.

109. Ibid., p. 138.

110. Stephen Bates, "Where There Is Smoke, There Are Terminations: Smokers Fired to Save Health Costs," *HR Magazine* 50, no. 3 (March 2005): 28–29.

111. J. A. Savage, "Are Computer Terminals Zapping Workers' Health?" *Business and Society Review* (1993) 41–43; http://www.ninds.nih.gov/ disorders/repetitive_motion/repetitive_motion. htm, accessed February 28, 2010.

112. www.OSHA.gov, accessed May 28, 2005. See also www.cdc.gov/od/ohs/Ergonomics/ compergo.htm, accessed May 26, 2007.

113. Anne Chambers, "Computer Vision Syndrome: Relief Is in Sight," *Occupational Hazards* (October 1999): 179–84; and www.OSHA.gov/ETOOLS/ computerworkstations/index.html, accessed May 28, 2005.

114. "Worker Opens Fire at Ohio Jeep Plant," *Occupational Hazards* (March 2005): 16.

115. Gus Toscano and Janice Windau, "The Changing Character of Fatal Work Injuries," *Monthly Labor Review* (October 1994): 17. See also Robert Grossman, "Bulletproof Practices," *HR Magazine* (November 2002): 34–42, Chuck Manilla, "How to Avoid Becoming a Workplace Violence Statistic," *Training & Development* (July 2008): 60–64.

116. "Bullies Trigger 'Silent Epidemic' at Work, but Legal Cures Remain Hard to Come By," *BNA Bulletin to Management* (February 24, 2000): 57.

117. Jennifer Laabs, "Employees Sabotage," *Workforce* (July 1999): 33–42; see also "Workplace Violence Takes a Deadly Toll," *EHS Today* (December 2009): 17.

118. Paul Viollis and Doug Kane, "At Risk Terminations: Protecting Employees, Preventing Disaster," *Risk Management Magazine* 52, no. 5 (May 2005): 28–33.

119. Jean Thilmany, "In Case of Emergency," *HR Magazine* (November 2007): 79–82; Chuck Manilla, "How to Avoid Becoming a Workplace Violence Statistic," *Training & Development* (July 2008): 60–64.

120. See also "Creating a Safer Workplace: Simple Steps Bring Results," *Safety Now* (September 2002): 1–2; see also L. Claussen, "Disgruntled and Dangerous," *Safety & Health* 180, no. 1 (July 2009): 44–47.

121. Florida recently passed a law giving employees the right to carry guns in cars parked at work. See "Right to Carry Guns in Cars Parked at Work Becomes Loaded Issue in Florida, Elsewhere," *BNA Bulletin to Management* (May 13, 2008): 153.

122. M. Sandy Hershcovis et al., "Predicting Workplace Aggression: A Meta-Analysis," *Journal of Applied Psychology* 92, no. 1 (2007): 228–38.

123. Felin, "Workplace Violence and the Duty of Care," 401–2.

124. See, for example, James Thelan, "Is That a Threat?" *HR Magazine* (December 2009): 61–63.

125. Paul Viollis and Doug Kane, "At Risk Terminations: Protecting Employees, Preventing Disaster," *Risk Management* 52, no. 15 (May 2005): 28–33.

126. Kenneth Diamond, "The Gender-Motivated Violence Act: What Employers Should Know," *Employee Relations Law Journal* 25, no. 4 (Spring 2000): 29–41; and "Bush Signs 'Violence against Women Act'; Funding Badly Needed Initiatives to Prevent Domestic & Sexual Violence, Help Victims," *America's Intelligence Wire* (January 5, 2006).

127. "Employers Battling Workplace Violence Might Consider Postal Service Plan," *BNA Bulletin to Management* (August 5, 1999): 241.

128. http://www.cdc.gov/ncipc/dvp/ipv_factsheet. pdf, accessed February 28, 2010.

129. Lloyd Newman, "Terrorism: Is Your Company Prepared?" *Business and Economic Review* 48, no. 2 (February 2002): 7–10.

130. Li Yuan et al., "Texting When There's Trouble," *Wall Street Journal* (April 18, 2007): B1.

131. Sources of *external* risk include legal/regulatory, political, and business environment (economy, e-business, etc.). *Internal* risks sources include financial, strategic, operational [including safety and security] and integrity (embezzlement, theft, fraud, etc.). William Atkinson, "Enterprise Risk Management at Wal-Mart," http://www.rmmag. com/MGTemplate.cfm?Section=RMMagazine&

NavMenuID=128&template=/Magazine/ DisplayMagazines.cfm&MGPreview=1&Volume= 50&IssueID=205&AID=2209&ShowArticle=1, accessed April 1, 2009.

132. Unless otherwise noted, the following is based on Richard Maurer, "Keeping Your Security Program Active," *Occupational Hazards* (March 2003): 49–52.

133. Ibid., p. 50.

134. Ibid.

135. Ibid., p. 52.

136. Lisbeth Claus, "International Assignees at Risk," *HR Magazine* (February 2010): 73. Employers should even probably take precautions to protect workers who might be at risk for developing blood clots, for instance in their legs, as a result of sitting sedentary or flying long distances. "Employees Who Are Sedentary or Take Long Trips May Be at Risk for Blood Clot Disorder," *BNA Bulletin to Management* (March 2, 2010): 65.

137. Cynthia Ross, "How to Protect the Aging Workforce," *Occupational Hazards* (January 2005): 38–42; and Cynthia Ross, "How to Protect the Aging Workforce," *Occupational Hazards* (February 2005): 52–54.

138. "Importance of Taking Precautions for Overseas Operations Underscored by Mumbai Attacks," *BNA Bulletin to Management* (January 6, 2009): 1–8.

Module A

1. http://talkingunion.wordpress.com/2008/09/27/ is-union-reform-possible-in-china/, accessed March 25, 2009.

2. See, for example, Kimberly Manion, "Venturing Abroad," *HR Magazine* (June 2008): 86–90.

3. Martha Frase, "Show All Employees a Wider World," *HR Magazine* (June 2007): 99–102.

4. Nancy Wong, "Mark Your Calendar! Important Task for International HR," *Workforce* (April 2000): 72–74.

5. "Fifteen Top Emerging Markets," *Global Workforce* (January 1998): 18–21. The living conditions in China's big cities are improving. See, for example, Kate Sarsfield, "Medical Assistance; Business Jet Prescription Peps up China Medevac; Increase in Corporate and Tourist Traffic Leads to Market Opening with Converted Hawker," *Flight International* (February 11, 2003): 24; and Justin Fox, "The New China Syndrome," *Time* 170, no. 7 (August 13, 2007): 52.

6. For companies with more than 30 employees.

7. David Ralston et al., "Eastern Values: A Comparison of Managers in the United States, Hong Kong, and the People's Republic of China," *Journal of Applied Psychology* 71, no. 5 (1992): 664–71. See also P. Christopher Earley and Elaine Mosakowski, "Cultural Intelligence," *Harvard Business Review* (October 2004): 139–46.

8. Geert Hofstede, "Cultural Dimensions in People Management," in Vladimir Pucik, Noel Tishy, and Carole Barnett (Eds.), *Globalizing Management* (New York: John Wiley & Sons, 1992), p. 143; and http://www.geert-hofstede.com/, accessed February 28, 2010.

9. Chris Brewster, "European Perspectives on Human Resource Management," *Human Resource Management Review* 14 (2004): 365–82.

10. Ibid.

11. See, for example, http://www.fedee.com/ewc1.html, accessed November 4, 2009.

12. This is discussed in Eduard Gaugler, "HR Management: An International Comparison," *Personnel* (1988): 28. See also E. Poutsma et al., "The Diffusion of Calculative and Collaborative HRM Practices in European Firms," *Industrial Relations* 45, no. 4 (October 2006): 513–46.

13. Helen Deresky, *International Management* (Upper Saddle River, NJ: Pearson: 2008), p. 17.

14. Annual 2007 figures, http://www.bls.gov/news.release/pdf/ichcc.pdf, accessed February 19, 2010.

15. Frances Taft and Cliff Powell, "The European Pensions and Benefits Environment: A Complex Ecology," *Compensation & Benefits Review* (January/February 2005): 37–50.

16. Ibid.

17. "Inform, Consult, Impose: Workers' Rights in the EU," *The Economist* (June 16, 2001): 3. See also J. Banyuls et al., "European Works Council at General Motors Europe: Bargaining Efficiency in Regime Competition?" *Industrial Relations Journal* 39, no. 6 (November 2008): 532–47.

18. Lisbeth Clause, "What You Need to Know about the New Labor Contract Law of China," *SHRM Global Law Special Report* (October–November 2008). As one employer said, "Migrant workers are a lot more fussy than before. They don't just talk of money; they talk about working environments, holidays and other fringe benefits we have not even heard of before. Workers have more say than us now because they have a wider choice." Qiu Quanlin and Gao Changxin, "Workers Call the Shots," *China Daily* (March 11, 2010): P1.

19. Paula Caligiuri, "The Big Five Personality Characteristics as Predictors of Expatriates' Desire to Terminate the Assignment and Supervisor-Rated Performance," *Personnel Psychology* 53, no. 1 (Spring 2000): 67–88.

20. Jan Selmer, "Expatriation: Corporate Policy, Personal Intentions and International Adjustment," *International Journal of Human Resource Management* 9, no. 6 (December 1998): 997–1007. See also Barbara Myers and Judith K. Pringle, "Self-Initiated Foreign Experience as Accelerated Development: Influences of Gender," *Journal of World Business* 40, no. 4 (November 2005): 421.

21. Hung-Wen Lee and Ching-Hsing, "Determinants of the Adjustment of Expatriate Managers to Foreign Countries: An Empirical Study," *International Journal of Management* 23, no. 2 (2006): 302–11.

22. Sunkyu Jun and James Gentry, "An Exploratory Investigation of the Relative Importance of Cultural Similarity and Personal Fit in the Selection and Performance of Expatriates," *Journal of World Business* 40, no. 1 (February 2005): 1–8. See also Jan Selmer, "Cultural Novelty and Adjustment: Western Business Expatriates in China," *International Journal of Human Resource Management* 17, no. 7 (2006): 1211–22.

23. Discussed in Charles Hill, *International Business* (Burr Ridge, IL: Irwin, 1994), pp. 511–15. See also Julia Richardson, "Self-Directed Expatriation: Family Matters," *Personnel Review* 35, no. 4 (July 2006): 469–86.

24. Charlene Solomon, "One Assignment, Two Lives," *Personnel Journal* (May 1996): 36–47; Michael Harvey, "Dual-Career Couples during International Relocation: The Trailing Spouse," *International Journal of Human Resource Management* 9, no. 2 (April 1998): 309–30.

25. Barbara Anderson, "Expatriate Selection: Good Management or Good Luck?" *International Journal of Human Resource Management* 16, no. 4 (April 2005): 567–83.

26. Michael Schell, quoted in Charlene Marmer Solomon, "Success Abroad Depends on More Than Job Skills," 52.

27. Carla Joinson, "Cutting Down the Days," *HR Magazine* (April 2000): 90–97; "Employers Shortened Assignments of Workers Abroad," *BNA Bulletin to Management* (January 4, 2001): 7.

28. Eric Krell, "Budding Relationships," *HR Magazine* 50, no. 6 (June 2005): 114–18.

29. Helene Mayerhofer et al., "Flexpatriate Assignments: A Neglected Issue in Global Staffing," *International Journal of Human Resource Management* 15, no. 8 (December 2004): 1371–89; Martha Frase, "International Commuters," *HR Magazine* (March 2007): 91–96.

30. Michael Harvey et al., "Global Virtual Teams: A Human Resource Capital Architecture," *International Journal of Human Resource Management* 16, no. 9 (September 2005):1583–99.

31. John Daniels and Lee Radebaugh, *International Business*, p. 767. See also Carlos Casillo, "Collective Labor Rights in Latin America and Mexico," *Relations Industrielles/Industrial Relations* 55, no. 1 (Winter 2000): 59.

32. Arvind Phatak, *International Dimensions of Management* (Boston: PWS Kent, 1989), pp. 106–7.

33. Ibid., p. 106.

34. Daniels and Radebaugh, *International Business*, p. 767.

35. Ibid., p. 769; Phatak, *International Dimensions of Management*, p. 106.

36. Phatak, *International Dimensions of Management*, p. 108.

37. Daniels and Radebaugh, *International Business*, p. 769.

38. "DOL Releases Final Rule Amending Filing, Processing of Foreign Labor Certifications," *BNA Bulletin to Management* (January 11, 2005): 11.

39. Leslie Klass, "Fed Up with High Costs, Companies Winnow the Ranks of Career Expats," *Workforce Management* (October 2004): 84–88.

40. Ibid., p. 769; Phatak, *International Dimensions of Management*, p. 106.

41. Michelle Rafter, "Return Trip for Ex-Pats," *Workforce Magazine* (March 16, 2009): 1, 3. "Workforce Trends: Companies Continue to Deploy Ex-pats," *Compensation & Benefits Review* 42, no. 1 (January/February 2010): 6.

42. Timothy Dwyer, "Localization's Hidden Costs," *HR Magazine* (June 2004): 135–44.

43. Based on Pamela Babcock, "America's Newest Export: White Collar Jobs," *HR Magazine* (April 2004): 50–57.

44. William Bulkeley, "IBM to Cut US jobs, Expand in India," *Wall Street Journal* (March 26, 2009): B1.

45. Howard Perlmutter, "The Tortuous Evolution of the Multinational Corporation," *Columbia Journal of World Business* 3, no. 1 (January–February 1969): 11–14, discussed in Phatak, *International Dimensions of Management*, p. 129. See also Helen Deresky, *International Management* (Upper Saddle River, NJ: Pearson, 2008), p. 343.

46. Phatak, *International Dimensions of Management*, p. 129.

47. Ibid.

48. Hill, *International Business*, p. 507.

49. Ibid., pp. 507–10.

50. Donald Dowling Jr., "Export Codes of Conduct, Not Employee Handbooks," *The Society for Human Resource Management Legal Report* (January/February 2007): 1–4.

51. Ibid.

52. Chuck Csizmar, "Does Your Expatriate Program Follow the Rules of the Road?" *Compensation & Benefits Review* (January/February 2008): 61–69.

53. Winfred Arthur Jr. and Winston Bennett Jr., "The International Assignee: The Relative Importance of Factors Perceived to Contribute to Success," *Personnel Psychology* 48 (1995): 99–114; table on 106–7. See also Raymond Edward Branton, "A Multifaceted Assessment Protocol for Successful International Assignees," *Dissertation Abstracts International: Section B: The Sciences and Engineering* 64, no. 8B (2004): 4024.

54. Arthur and Bennett, "The International Assignee," 110; Gretchen Spreitzer, Morgan McCall Jr., and Joan Mahoney, "Early Identification of International Executive Potential," *Journal of Applied Psychology* 82, no. 1 (1997): 6–29.

55. http://www.performanceprograms.com/ Surveys/Overseas.shtm, accessed January 31, 2008.

56. Paula Caligiuri et al., "Selection for International Assignments," *Human Resource Management Review* 19 (2009): 251–62.

57. P. Blocklyn, "Developing the International Executive," *Personnel* 66 (March 1989): 44–47. See also Paula M. Caligiuri and Jean M. Phillips, "An Application of Self-Assessment Realistic Job Previews to Expatriate Assignments," *International Journal of Human Resource Management* 14, no. 7 (November 2003): 1102–15.

58. Phatak, *International Dimensions of Management*, p. 119.

59. Hilary Harris and Chris Brewster, "The Coffee Machine System: How International Selection Really Works," *International Journal of Human Resource Management* 10, no. 3 (June 1999): 488–500.

60. Zsuzsanna Tungli and Maury Peiperl, "Expatriate Practices in German, Japanese, UK and US Multinational Companies: A Comparative Survey of Changes," *Human Resource Management* 48, no. 1 (January–February 2009): 153–71.

61. "More Women, Young Workers on the Move," *Workforce Management* (August 20, 2007): 9.

62. For a good discussion of this, see Yochanan Altman and Susan Shortland, "Women and International Assignments: Taking Stock—A 25 Year Review," *Human Resource Management* 47, no. 2 (Summer 2008): 199–216.

63. Kathryn Tyler, "Don't Fence Her In," *HR Magazine* 46, no. 3 (March 2001): 69–77.

64. Ibid.

65. Ibid.

66. See Nancy Napier and Sully Taylor, "Experiences of Women Professionals Abroad," *International Journal of Human Resource Management* 13, no. 5 (August 2002): 837–51; Iris Fischlmayr, "Female Self-Perception as a Barrier to International Careers?" *International Journal of Human Resource Management* 13, no. 5 (August 2002): 773–83; and Wolfgang Mayrhofer and Hugh Scullion, "Female Expatriates in International Business: Evidence from the German Clothing Industry," *International Journal of Human Resource Management* 13, no. 5 (August 2002): 815–36; Altman and Shortland, "Women and International Assignments."

67. Ann Pace, "Training for the League Overseas," *Training & Development* (August 2009): 18.

68. Valerie Frazee, "Expats Are Expected to Dive Tight In," *Personnel Journal* (December 1996): 31. See also Rita Bennett et al., "Cross-Cultural Training: A Critical Step in Ensuring the Success of National Assignments," *Human Resource Management* 39, no. 2–3 (Summer–Fall 2000): 239–50.

69. Mark Mendenhall and Gunther Stahl, "Expatriate Training and Development: Where Do We Go from Here?" *Human Resource Management* 39, no. 2–3 (Summer–Fall 2000): 251–65.

70. Hal Gregersen et al., "Expatriate Performance Appraisal in U.S. Multinational Firms," *Journal of International Business Studies* 27, no. 4 (Winter 1996): 711–39. See also Anne Francesco and Barry Gold, *International Organizational Behavior* (Upper Saddle River, NJ: Pearson, 2005), pp. 152–53.

71. Hill, *International Business*, pp. 519–20; Valerie Frazee, "Is the Balance Sheet Right for Your Expats?" *Global Workforce* (September 1998): 19–26; Stephanie Overman, "Focus on International HR," *HR Magazine* (March 2000): 87–92. See also Sheila Burns, "Flexible International Assignee Compensation Plans," *Compensation and Benefits Review* (May/June 2003): 35–44. Thomas Shelton, "Global Compensation Strategies: Managing and Administering Split Pay for an Expatriate Workforce," *Compensation and Benefits Review* (January/February 2008): 56–59.

72. Joseph J. Martocchio, *Strategic Compensation: A Human Resource Management Approach*, 2nd ed. (Upper Saddle River, NJ: Pearson, 2006), pp. 280–94. See also "China to Levy Income Tax on Expatriates," *Asia Africa Intelligence Wire* (August 3, 2004).

73. Shelton, "Global Compensation Strategies."

74. See, for example, "More Multinational Organizations Are Taking a Global Approach to Compensation," *Compensation & Benefits Review* (May/June 2008): 5.

75. Mark Schoeff Jr., "Danger and Duty," *Workforce Magazine* (November 19, 2007): 1, 3.

76. Ibid., pp. 23–40.
77. "Recommendations for Managing Global Compensation Clause in a Changing Economy," Hewitt Associates, M17_DESS9957_12_SE_C17.QXD 10/30/09 7:50 PM Page 658, www.hewittassociates.com/_MetaBasicCMAsset Cache_/Assets/Articles/2009/hewitt_pov_globalcomp_0109.pdf, accessed March 22, 2009.
78. Jessica Marquez, "Hostage-Taking in France Has US Observers on Their Guard," *Workforce Management* (April 20, 2009): 10.
79. Fay Hansen, "Skirting Danger," *Workforce Magazine* (January 19, 2009): 1, 3.
80. These are based on or quoted from Samuel Greengard, "Mission Possible: Protecting Employees Abroad," *Workforce* (August 1997): 30–32. See also Z. Phillips, "Global Firms Consider Additional Cover for Overseas Execs," *Business Insurance* 43, no. 23 (June 15–22, 2009): 4, 22.
81. Ibid., p. 32.
82. Carla Joinson, "Save Thousands Per Expatriate," *HR Magazine* (July 2002): 77.
83. For a discussion of some personality aspects of the issue, see, for example, Jeffrey Herman and Lois Tetrick, "Problem Focused versus Emotion Focused Coping Strategies and Repatriation Adjustment," *Human Resource Management* 48, no. 1 (January–February 2009): 69–88.
84. Quoted in Leslie Klaff, "The Right Way to Bring Expats Home," *Workforce* (July 2002): 43.
85. Ibid.
86. Ibid.
87. Maria Kraimer et al., "The Influence of Expatriate and Repatriate Experiences on Career Advancement and Repatriate Retention," *Human Resource Management* 48, no. 1 (January–February 2009): 27–47, 41.
88. Ann Marie Ryan et al., "Designing and Implementing Global Staffing Systems: Part 2—Best Practices," *Human Resource Management* 42, no. 1 (Spring 2003): 85–94.
89. Ibid., p. 89.
90. Ibid., p. 90.
91. Ibid., p. 86. See also M. Schoeff, "Adopting an HR Worldview," *Workforce Management* 87, no. 19 (November 17, 2008): 8.
92. Ibid., p. 87.
93. Ibid., p. 92.

Name Index

NETg.com, 244
Neumann, Y., 235
News Corp., 288
New York Times, The, 112
NFL, 282
Nike Inc., 82, 156–157, 334
Nissan, 20, 142
Northwest (hospital), 89
Northwest Airlines, 280
Nucor Corp., 217

O

Obama, Barack, 32, 53, 208, 302
Occupational Safety and Health
    Administration (OSHA),
    292–315
Office of Federal Contract
    Compliance Programs
    (OFCCP), 32
Oregon Department of
    Transportation, 236
OSHA (Occupational Safety and
    Health Administration),
    292–315
Outback Steakhouse, 112
Outward Bound, 154

P

Papa John's Pizza, 19
PAQ Services, Inc., 98, 99
Paras, Drew, 352
Patel, Gopal, 308
Patton, W. David, 155
Payless ShoeSource, 203
Pedone, Rose Robin, 346
Pellet, Jennifer, 352
Pension Benefits Guarantee
    Corporation (PBGC),
    224–225
PepsiCo, 18–19
Perlmenter, Eric, 221
Pfizer Inc., 75, 234
Pidd, Ken, 308
Pilat NAI, 75
Pizza Hut, 19
Portman Ritz-Carlton,
    21, 22
Posthuma, Richard, 35
Pratt, Connie, 155
Prevent Blindness America, 301
Procter & Gamble (P&G),
    336, 337
Pulakos, Elaine D., 176
PureSafety, 152, 303

Q

Quaker Oats, 18, 19

R

Raytheon Co., 242–243
Reichel, A., 235
Rhapsody restaurant, 154
Right Associates, Inc., 254
*Risk Management
    Magazine,* 312
Ritz-Carlton Hotel, 20, 21
Roberts, Bill, 15
Royal Dutch Shell, 327

S

Salary.com, 203, 205
SalesDriver, 217
sales-driver.com, 215
Sales Management, 81
SAS Institute, 225
Scalia, Antonin, 36
Scanlon, Joseph, 216
Seagate Technology, 169,
    183–184
Second City Communications,
    156–157
Securities and Exchange
    Commission (SEC), 211
Service Employees' International
    Union (SEIU), 265, 285
Sharp Electronics, 146
Shell Group, 84–85
Shell Oil Co., 336
Shroeder, Michael, 9
Siemens Power Transmission
    and Distribution, 148
Signicast Corp., 14, 143
Silkroad Technology, 80
Sinai hospital, 89
SkillSoft, 152, 244
Skype, 128
Small Business Administration, 149
Smallwood, Norm, 155
Social Security Administration, 134
Society for Human Resource
    Management (SHRM),
    17–18, 84–85, 87–88,
    131, 157
Sony Corp., 160, 321, 334
Sovereign, Kenneth, 49
Stanford University, 141–142,
    150–151
Starbucks, 199, 203, 262,
    270, 273
Sullivan, Stacey, 346
Sun Microsystems, 148
Supreme Court. *see* U.S.
    Supreme Court
surveymonkey.com, 161
Sutter Health, 280
Sweetwater State University,
    196–197

T

Tarantino, Arlene, 155
Tetra PAK, Inc., 89
Thacker, James, 145, 155
Thomas International
    USA, 116
3M Co., 334
Titus, 149
Toulouse, Chad, 8
Toyota, 40
Trilogy Enterprises Inc., 95
Trump, Donald, 28–29

U

Ulrich, Dave, 155
Unicru, 18
United Airlines, 45–46
United Auto Workers,
    280–281
United Electrical Workers, 285
United Farm Workers, 265
United Food and Commercial
    Workers, 265
UnitedHealth Group Inc.,
    210–211
United Parcel Service (UPS), 150,
    249, 269
U.S. Airways, 279
U.S. Army, 87
U.S. Bureau of Labor Statistics
    (BLS), 51, 76, 204
U.S. Chemical Safety Board (CSB),
    352–354
U.S. Circuit Court of Appeals, 40,
    187, 249
U.S. Civil Service Commission,
    33, 98
U.S. Congressional Budget Office
    (CBO), 76
U.S. Department of Labor, 32, 33,
    67, 76, 81, 98, 103, 149, 262,
    272, 292
U.S. Department of Transportation,
    133
U.S. Navy, 225
U.S. Office of Arbitration
    Services, 279
U.S. Office of Mediation &
    Conciliation Service, 279
U.S. Office of Personnel
    Management, 205
U.S. Postal Service, 313
U.S. Supreme Court, 33–37, 268
United Steelworkers, 285
United Technologies Corp., 236
UNITE HERE, 265, 284
UPS (United Parcel Service), 150,
    249, 269
USAA, 227

SUBJECT INDEX

Strategic human resource management (HRM), 20–22
  corporate strategies and, linking, 21
  defined, 20
  employee benefits, 227
  in ethics, 245–246
  executive pay rates, 209
  HR's role in executing strategy, 20
  HR's role in formulating, 20
  strategy and HR, 21
  testing potential employees, 117–118
  in training and development, 143, 151
  union drive and election, 273
Strategic planning in HRM, 18–20
  competitive advantage and, 19–20
  employee's role in executing, 21
  example of, 18
  levels of, 18–20
Strategy
  basic HR process and, 22
  business-level and competitive strategy, 19
  competitive strategy, 19
  corporate-level strategy, 18–19
  defined, 18
  differentiation competitive strategy, 19
  diversification strategy, 19
  diversity and, 52
  HR and, 21
  HR example and, 21
  vertical integration strategy, 19
Streaming PC video, 15
Stress and the Manager (Albrecht), 309
Strictness/leniency problem, 185–187
Strikes, 280–281
  advocacy or comprehensive campaigns, 280
  corporate campaign, 280
  dealing with, 280
  economic strike, 280
  injunctions, 281
  inside games, 280–281
  lockouts, 281
  national emergency strikes, 268
  picketing, 280
  sympathy strike, 280
  unfair labor practice strike, 280
  wildcat strike, 280
Stromberg Dexterity Test, 113
Subordinate appraisals, 173
Substance abuse, workplace, 307–308
Succession planning in forecasting personnel needs, 75–76

Sun Learning eXchange, 148
Supervisory training abroad, 154
Supplemental pay benefits, 218
Survey feedback, 160
Symbolism, 242
Sympathy strike, 280

T

Taft-Hartley Act of 1947, 266–268
  national emergency strikes, 268
  rights of employees, 268
  rights of employers, 268
  unfair union labor practices, 266
Talent management, defined, 193
Talent management systems, 194
Task analysis, 144
Team building, 161
Team or group incentive plans, 212–213
Teamwork, in training and development, 154
Technology
  advances in HRM, 8
  computerized information systems, 74–75
  computerized testing, 115–116
  employee orientation and, 142–143
  health information, 222
  manager's use of, 15
  in performance management, 183
  productivity improved through, 8–9
Telecommuters, 87
Temporary workers, 82
10-step process for organizational change, 160
Termination at will, 250
Termination at will exceptions, 250
Termination interview, 253–254
Terrorism as workplace health hazard, 314
Testing potential employees. See also Selecting employees
  achievement tests, 115
  cognitive ability tests, 112–113
  computerized testing, 115–116
  EEO aspects of, 110–111
  graphology, 132
  honesty testing, 130, 132
  interest inventories, 114, 115
  management assessment centers, 117
  motor or physical ability tests, 113
  personality tests, 114, 115
  quick ethics test, 242–243
  reliability of tests, 107–108
  sample selection test, 112

security of tests and rights of test takers, 111
situational judgment tests, 117
strategy and HR, 117–118
tests used as supplements, 111
types of tests used at work, 111–118
validity of tests, 108–110
Web-based testing, 116
work sampling techniques, 116
Test of Mechanical Comprehension, 113
Tests in selection standards, 47
Test validity, 108–109
Third-country nationals, 325
Third-party assistance, 279
Three pillars, 246–247
  appeals process, 247
  penalties, 247
  rules, 246–247
360-degree performance feedback, 158, 173–174
Title VII of the 1964 Civil Rights Act, 31–32, 43, 202, 250
Tokenism, 51
Top-down programs in diversity management, 52–53
Toyota Motor Manufacturing of Kentucky, Inc. v. Williams, 40
Trading points, 278
Traditional selection procedures, 328
Training and development. See also Organizational change programs, managing
  action learning, 156
  apprenticeship training, 148, 149
  audiovisual tools, 150
  behavior modeling, 150
  case study method, 156
  competency models, 146, 147
  computer-based training (CBT), 150–151
  defined, 143
  diversity training, 153–154
  DVD-based training, 151
  employee orientation, 142–143
  ethics, 243–244, 245
  evaluating, 161–163
  free training alternatives, 149
  guidelines, 155
  informal learning, 148
  in-house development centers, 158
  learning management systems (LMS), 152
  learning portals, 152
  lifelong learning, 154
  literacy training techniques, 153
  management games, 156–157
  managerial development and, 155–158